HIGHER
EDUCATION
IN
AMERICA

DEREK BOK

HIGHER EDUCATION IN AMERICA

REVISED EDITION

PRINCETON UNIVERSITY PRESS

PRINCETON AND OXFORD

Published by Princeton University Press, 41 William Street, Princeton,
New Jersey 08540
In the United Kingdom: Princeton University Press, 6 Oxford Street,
Woodstock, Oxfordshire OX20 1TW

press.princeton.edu

First revised edition printing, 2015

Paperback ISBN 978-0-691-16558-5

Library of Congress Control Number 2014952263

British Library Cataloging-in-Publication Data is available

This book has been composed in Minion Pro and Trajan Pro

Printed on acid-free paper. ∞

Printed in the United States of America

3 5 7 9 10 8 6 4 2

TO CAMERON AND NICHOLAS
AND
ERIK AND ANNIKA

||||||||||||||||||||||||||||||||||||||||||||||||||||||||||||||||||||||||||||||||||||||||||||||||||||||||||||||||||||||||||||||||||||||||||||||||||

CONTENTS

PREFACE TO THE REVISED EDITION

This edition is not simply a replica of the hard cover volume that appeared in the fall of 2013. Because the field of higher education is evolving rapidly, Princeton University Press agreed to let me make changes to ensure that the paperback edition was accurate and up to date.

I have made a number of alterations, a few of them substantial. In Chapter Three, I have revised the conclusion to reflect a more considered description of important, unresolved issues involving campus governance and state oversight of higher education. In Chapters Four and Five, I have tried to clarify the complicated and often confusing relationship between college enrollments, graduation rates, and educational attainment levels (the percentage of individuals within a given age cohort who have acheived a specified level of education, such as a BA degree). In Chapter Seven, I have supplied a more complete assessment of the impact of information technology on colleges and their methods of instruction. Finally, I have rewritten the last few pages of the book to provide greater clarity and emphasis to the conclusion. In addition to these more substantial improvements, I have made numerous small changes to note recent developments occuring since the hard cover version went to press in the spring of 2013.

ACKNOWLEDGMENTS

||||||||||||||||||||||||||||||||||||||||||||||||||||||||||||||||||||||||||||||||||||||||||||||||

Writing this book led me into many areas of higher education with which I had no direct experience. I might never have attempted such a task had I not been able to seek the counsel of a variety of friends and colleagues. A number of them kindly read particular chapters and offered valuable comments: Sandy Baum, Hilary Bok, Joe Bower, Bill Fitzsimmons, David Garvin, Elizabeth Huidekoper, Andy Kaufman, Rakesh Khurana, David Korn, Richard Light, Mike McPherson, Martha Minow, Vel Nair, David Nathan, John Simon, and Lloyd Weinreb.

Bob Atwell, a longtime comrade-in-arms from our days working together at the American Council on Education, read all of part I and offered many helpful comments. My close friend and colleague Henry Rosovsky read the entire manuscript and commented with rare insight, not only on what I wrote but on how I expressed my thoughts. To another old and dear friend, Bill Bowen, I owe a special debt for going far beyond the call of duty to assist me. Not only did he read the entire manuscript with meticulous care and share a number of valuable unpublished reports about online education. He even arranged for me to have the help of his assistant, Johanna Brownell, who lent her formidable editorial skills to the manuscript and supplied me with a host of useful articles and studies to fill various gaps in the text.

I am also indebted to the three outside readers enlisted by the Princeton University Press. Each of them clearly worked hard to provide me with detailed suggestions to improve what I had written. In making this assistance possible— and in much else as well—the Press has given me guidance and encouragement throughout. Lauren Lepow unerringly ferreted out my grammatical mistakes and improved my prose. My longtime editor, Peter Dougherty, helped in numerous ways, great and small. I could not ask for more of any publisher.

As always, I owe a great debt to my assistant, Connie Higgins, who has done everything from typing and retyping endless drafts to checking footnotes, finding innumerable books and articles, extracting little-known reports from distant offices and government agencies, and even supplying me with newspaper columns she discovered that she thought might be of use. It would have been quite impossible for me to complete this book without her help.

Finally, I am particularly grateful to Sissela, who has read the entire manuscript several times and offered candid comments on matters of tone and style that even good friends might hesitate to make. From start to finish, she has been a constant source of encouragement. For more than fifty years, she has helped to make writing a joy and not merely an occupation.

HIGHER
EDUCATION
IN
AMERICA

INTRODUCTION

||||||||||||||||||||||||||||||||||||||||||||||||||||||||||||||||||||||||||||||||||||||||||||||||||||||||

In the modern world, colleges and universities have assumed an importance far beyond their role in earlier times. They are now the country's chief supplier of three ingredients essential to national progress—new discoveries in science, technology, and other fields of inquiry; expert knowledge of the kind essential to the work of most important institutions; and well-trained adults with the skills required to practice the professions, manage a wide variety of organizations, and perform an increasing proportion of the more demanding jobs in an advanced, technologically sophisticated economy.* In addition, they help to strengthen our democracy by educating its future leaders, preparing students to be active, knowledgeable citizens, and offering informed critiques of government programs and policies. Not least, they supply the knowledge and ideas that create new industries, protect us from disease, preserve and enrich our culture, and inform us about our history, our environment, our society, and ourselves.

Because of the essential role that colleges and universities play, almost everyone has a stake in having them perform well. By several measures, they have succeeded handsomely. In a recent ranking compiled by a group of Chinese scholars, all but three of the twenty highest-rated universities in the world were located in the United States.† More than half of all Nobel laureates in science

---

*According to the National Governors Association, "the driving force behind the 21st century economy is knowledge, and developing human capital is the best way to ensure prosperity." National Governors Association (2001), Policy Position H-R44, Postsecondary Education Policy, http:/www.nga.org. Similarly, economists rank additional investment in education and research as a top priority among federal policies to increase long-term economic growth. See, e.g., Claudia Goldin and Lawrence F. Katz, *The Race between Education and Technology* (2008).

†Jonathan R. Cole, *The Great American University: Its Role to Preeminence, Its Indispensable National Role, Why It Must Be Protected* (2009), p. 515. Not all world rankings treat American universities quite so kindly, perhaps because they are not based as heavily on research as the Chinese compilation but attempt to give considerable weight to the quality of education. The 2011–12 Times Higher Education World University rankings, for example, published by the British magazine *Times Higher Education*, gives US universities only fourteen of the top twenty places. http://www.timeshighereducation.co.uk/world-university-rankings/2011-2012/top-400.html.

and economics since World War II did their most important work while serving on faculties in this country. Our colleges and graduate schools have long been the destination of choice for students around the world who have the chance to study outside their own country. Because of these achievements, more and more nations are adapting their systems of higher education to conform more closely to our model.

The worldwide respect accorded to American higher education should be a source of satisfaction to many people, not least to those who work in the academy. Ironically, however, this newfound prominence has brought many problems in its wake. No longer are colleges and universities left to function more or less as they please. As they have grown in size and importance, they have attracted closer scrutiny from each of the constituencies affected by their performance. State legislators want to know what taxpayers and parents are getting for all the money spent on public higher education. Politicians and media commentators pay attention to what colleges are teaching and to the ideas of professors on matters of public concern. Employers ask whether the students graduating from our colleges and professional schools are well enough trained for the jobs they are hired to do. Communities take an increasing interest in what universities are contributing to the local economy and wonder whether they should pay more taxes to the cities and towns in which they sit.

This added attention has produced a bumper crop of complaints. Whatever the world may think about the quality of American colleges and universities, the public here at home is far from satisfied. Parents feel that tuitions are too high and that too little is done to hold down costs. Their children struggle to repay the loans incurred to pay for their college education. Legislators complain of waste and inefficiency, of low graduation rates, of a reluctance to be held accountable for performance. Employers grumble that far too many graduates cannot write clearly, think analytically, work collaboratively, deal with other people effectively, or observe proper ethical standards. Conservatives charge that faculties display a marked liberal bias, while critics on the left insist that universities are too beholden to corporate interests. Meanwhile, editorial writers chastise college presidents for their bloated salaries, outsized administrative staffs, and half-hearted responses to a variety of problems.

It is tempting to make light of these criticisms and point to the unequaled global stature of American higher education as proof of the excellence of our colleges and universities. Yet it would be a mistake to make too much of this reputation. The impressive global rankings of American universities reflect the accomplishments of only a handful of institutions, and even the high regard in which the latter are held is largely due to the excellence of their research rather than the quality of education they provide.* No one yet has managed to measure how well our professors teach or how much our students learn, let alone compare the results with those of other nations.

It is also likely that our impressive standing in the world owes less to the success of our own system than it does to the weakness of foreign universities, which were long overregulated, underfinanced, and neglected by their governments until their importance to the economy was finally recognized late in the twentieth century. In recent years, however, member states in the European Union have agreed to invest more heavily in higher education and have resolved, collectively, to lead the world in scientific research by 2020.[1] Germany and France have recently appropriated special funds to develop universities of international distinction. China has been expanding its universities and enlarging their student population at astounding rates, while making remarkable strides in increasing the number of scientists and published research papers.[2]

To be sure, the ambitious plans of these nations may not be realized within the time frame set by their leaders. It takes much longer than most public officials think to bring about major academic reform, let alone build great universities and produce outstanding research, and far more than money is required. Still, it would be unwise to take the preeminence of our universities for granted. Like nations, academic institutions can start to decline at the very time their status in the world stands highest.

One can already detect warning signs that such a fate could eventually overtake American higher education. For generations, our colleges enrolled and graduated a much higher proportion of young people than any other nation in the world. In the past thirty years, however, as other parts of the globe have made the transition to mass higher education, a growing number of countries have surpassed us on both counts. Our attractiveness to students abroad may also be on the wane. Although America still attracts the largest number of overseas students, our share has dropped sharply in the last decade, and many nations now enroll much higher proportions of foreign students than the United States.[3]

In addition to the growing challenges from overseas, our colleges and universities are facing major changes that are transforming the environment in which they function. Technological advances have brought new methods of teaching and research. Improvements in communication, most notably the

---

*The so-called CQ World University Rankings do attempt to take the quality of education into account. Interestingly, these rankings (for 2011–12) place only thirteen American universities in the top twenty and even fewer—just seven of our universities—in the next thirty. http://www.top universities.com/university-rankings/world-university-rankings/2011.

Internet, have vastly expanded the potential student audience to include people of all ages in all areas of the world. New providers, notably for-profit universities and online organizations, have created alternative models for delivering instruction that are starting to make inroads on the work of traditional colleges and universities. Growing numbers of working adults, first-generation students, and graduates of troubled urban high schools are seeking college degrees, creating added problems for those who teach them. Meanwhile, young Americans attending college need a better education than ever before now that many jobs they are accustomed to holding in fields such as accounting, computer programming, and corporate research can be outsourced overseas to college graduates willing to work for much lower salaries.

The challenges facing American higher education give rise to several questions. How vigorously are our universities responding to their emerging problems and opportunities? Which of the many criticisms of their activities are truly valid and which are unfounded or highly exaggerated? What can our colleges do to improve their performance and how can such reforms be best brought about?

In addressing these questions, I will try to take a comprehensive view of American higher education and examine not merely undergraduate studies but graduate and professional training too; not education *or* research but both together; not simply PhD-granting universities but two- and four-year colleges along with for-profit providers as well. One caveat, however, is in order. Although I will discuss the role of government at various points, my principal aim in writing this study is to consider what colleges and universities can do to improve themselves, rather than to argue about what others should do to help them thrive.

By attempting such a comprehensive study, I hope to offer something of interest to all of the various audiences with a stake in the performance of higher education—policy-makers, academic leaders, faculty members, trustees, even students and parents. I have a special concern for readers who have chosen to enter that particular vineyard known as "academic administration." Like so many others who have ventured down this path, I had no opportunity to study higher education in detail before finding myself consumed by its demands. Only after my active service ended did I find the time to read deeply about the subject that had already filled my life for a quarter of a century. Having done so, I often look back with some chagrin, realizing how differently I might have acted had I understood then what I only came to appreciate much later. If I can offer something useful to those whose opportunity to serve still lies before them, this book will have been well worth writing.

PART I

THE CONTEXT

FOREWORD (I)

||||||||||||||||||||||||||||||||||||||||||||||||||||||||||||||||||||||||||||||||||||||||||||||||||||||

There is more than one way to organize a study of higher education. One can proceed, as this book does, by discussing each of the most important functions of colleges and universities—undergraduate education, professional training, and research. One can also follow the example of David Riesman and Christopher Jencks in their influential 1960s volume—*The Academic Revolution*—and arrange the material by types of institution: liberal arts colleges, research universities, religiously affiliated institutions, and the like.[1] There are doubtless other plausible ways to divide the pie.

Whatever method one chooses, it is helpful to begin with an overview of the system in which our colleges and universities function—the different kinds of institutions that exist, their purposes and goals, the influence that governments exert on their behavior, and the way they are organized and governed. Such information has a bearing on what one can reasonably expect universities to accomplish, the strengths and weaknesses they possess, and the prospects for bringing about any needed reforms.

Providing such an overview is the aim of the initial section of this book. The first chapter analyzes the nature of our higher education system—the principal types of institutions it contains, the extent to which they are controlled or influenced by government, the way in which they interact with one another, and how they are financed. In order to bring out key points about our system, its main features are compared with those of other advanced industrial nations. Not surprisingly, the characteristics that make our colleges and universities distinctive do much to explain why they have managed to achieve such an enviable reputation around the world. At the same time, these same characteristics harbor tensions and vulnerabilities that could lead to problems and limit what higher education can accomplish.

The second chapter in this sequence considers the purposes that shape the behavior of colleges and universities. Not all of these institutions share the same ends, although each is engaged in one way or another with teaching students.

Some colleges pursue a single goal; most universities have several. Where multiple goals exist, they may conflict with each other or complement one another. How wisely individual colleges and universities select their aims and what kinds of programs they create in order to achieve them have a lot to do with how effectively they perform, and how well the system as a whole meets the full range of needs that society expects it to serve.

Chapter 2 also considers the tendency for universities to grow continuously and eventually strain the capacity of academic leaders to oversee and guide the organization. Such a process may be inevitable for an institution with so many opportunities to serve and so many inventive individuals who perceive the possibilities and try to make the most of them. Yet some kinds of growth are needless and ill-advised. The discussion in this chapter tries to identify them and suggest the difference between prudent and unwise expansion.

The third and final chapter in this section describes how individual colleges and universities are typically governed—who within them exercises influence and authority and how this distribution of power affects the way in which they behave. Some critics have warned that defects in the current system of governance are weakening universities to a degree that seriously interferes with their ability to adapt to changing needs and opportunities. Such a charge warrants close attention. Whether or not it is correct, one must understand university governance in order to recognize who is responsible for any problems that occur and whose support will be needed to bring about desirable reform.

Rounding out this initial section is a brief afterword to introduce the values that affect how a college or university carries out its work. These values include various rights and privileges, such as academic freedom, that are widely considered essential to effective teaching and research. Also included are responsibilities long recognized by the academic profession, some of which belong to professors and others to those who occupy leadership positions in colleges and universities. These norms, sometimes codified but often not, define the shared ends and means that bring some order to what could otherwise become an inchoate collection of independent teachers and scholars.

Academic values also affect the efforts of campus leaders to maintain and improve their universities. Proposed reforms that offend these values often meet resistance from the faculty and ultimately fail. What is less understood is that academic values can also be a powerful force for constructive change, since faculties will usually experience discomfort and agree to reforms once they are persuaded that existing practices conflict with the principles and responsibilities that help define their professional identity and shape the aspirations that give meaning to their lives.

CHAPTER ONE

THE AMERICAN SYSTEM
OF HIGHER EDUCATION

||||||||||||||||||||||||||||||||||||||||||||||||||||||||||||||||||||||||||||||||||||||||||||||||||||||||||

AMERICA'S INITIAL VENTURE in the realm of higher learning gave no hint of future accomplishments. Nor could the handful of young men who arrived in Cambridge, Massachusetts, in 1638 to enter the nation's first college have had the faintest idea of what the future had in store for American universities. Before the year was out, the head of that tiny institution, Nathaniel Eaton, had been charged with assault for beating a tutor almost to death, while his wife stood accused of serving too little beer to the students and adulterating their food. Master Eaton was eventually dismissed and promptly fled, allegedly taking much of the endowment with him, whereupon the college shut down for an entire academic year.[1]

From these modest beginnings, higher education in the United States has grown to become a vast enterprise comprising some 4,500 different colleges and universities, more than 20 million students, 1.4 million faculty members, and aggregate annual expenditures exceeding 400 billion dollars. Within this system are schools ranging from tiny colleges numbering a few hundred students to huge universities with enrollments exceeding 50,000. For descriptive purposes, however, the system can be broken down into several kinds of institutions, each with its own distinctive aims and characteristics.

RESEARCH UNIVERSITIES

Within this category one finds renowned centers of learning such as Columbia, Yale, and Princeton that were founded before the American Revolution; a substantial number of flagship public universities dating back to the nineteenth century; a handful of private institutions, such as Chicago, Stanford, and Cornell, created through the generosity of wealthy industrialists following the Civil War; and a few newcomers like Brandeis and the University of California, San Diego, that were begun after World War II.

ere are only approximately two hundred research universities, r a large majority of the PhDs awarded, most of the degrees ind medicine, and more than a quarter of all the students in __ ᴗyꜱtem.[2] The most prominent—say the top sixty or so—dominate the national and international rankings, award at least half of the PhDs, and receive the greater part of the billions of dollars spent each year by the federal government on academic research. They have the largest budgets, the biggest endowments, the best professional schools, and the most extensive libraries. Most of their colleges accept less than half of the students who apply for admission. A few are extremely selective, turning away several applicants for every one they admit.

COMPREHENSIVE UNIVERSITIES

There are more than seven hundred so-called comprehensive universities offering a wide variety of professional master's and doctoral programs while also carrying on at least a modest amount of research.[3] Many are public and have large undergraduate enrollments. Their student bodies are diverse, with higher percentages of commuters, ethnic minorities, part-time students, and adults over thirty years of age than one would normally find attending a major research university. They are rarely very selective in their admissions policies. Instead, they typically accept most of those who apply, and their students tend to have significantly lower high school grade-point averages and college admission test scores than those enrolled in the research universities.

Many comprehensives evolved from technical colleges or from normal schools that trained teachers for the public schools. Now that they have grown in size and have mounted a wide variety of vocationally oriented degree programs, they have sometimes struggled to define their distinctive mission. A few have managed to become research universities. Many more that are located in cities have identified themselves as "metropolitan universities," with special responsibilities to serve the needs of their surrounding urban area. As such, they concentrate on offering programs to match the employment opportunities in their city and its environs. Much of their research is oriented toward the practical problems of local employers, government agencies, and community organizations. In addition, they frequently offer a variety of special services for local public schools, community colleges, small businesses, and other entities that can benefit from their expertise and technical assistance.

FOUR-YEAR COLLEGES

A very different group are the almost one thousand, mainly private, nonprofit colleges.[4] Some are more than two hundred years old and were begun under the sponsorship of a religious denomination. They tend to be much smaller than research or comprehensive universities, enrolling, in all, only two percent of undergraduates. A century ago, most of these colleges would have concentrated primarily or even exclusively on the liberal arts. As more and more young people have come to college to prepare for a career, private colleges have found it necessary to offer vocational programs in order to attract enough students to survive. Only a minority still award more than half of their undergraduate degrees to liberal arts majors, and no more than twenty-five are exclusively devoted to this form of education.

A few private colleges, such as Amherst and Williams, attract outstanding students and offer an education of the highest quality. With more applicants than they can accept and substantial endowments contributed by grateful alumni, they are highly successful and financially secure. Once one moves beyond these fortunate few, however, the situation changes dramatically. Most of the remaining private colleges are hard-pressed to compete for undergraduates with state-subsidized public universities that charge much lower tuitions. Many constantly struggle to balance the books, and scores of them over the past fifty years have had to give up the fight and close their doors.[5]

COMMUNITY COLLEGES

Beyond universities and private four-year colleges are more than one thousand two-year, nonprofit community colleges.[6] All but approximately eighty-five are public, supported by state and local funds. Together, they account for more than 40 percent of all undergraduate enrollments.

The community college movement began early in the twentieth century chiefly as a means to accommodate students who wanted a BA degree but needed a lower-cost school close to home that they could attend for two years before transferring to a four-year college. Although many community colleges had long offered job training as well as liberal arts programs, it was only after World War II that vocational education began to attract a majority of the students enrolled. By now, in addition to liberal arts courses, most community colleges offer a wide variety of vocational degree programs along with shorter courses, often developed in cooperation with nearby employers, that train students for specific jobs.

In contrast to the faculties of four-year institutions, only a small minority of those teaching in community colleges are PhDs. In earlier decades, most of their instructors came to them from high school teaching. Increasing numbers now come from industry, bringing practical skills they can teach to students in vocational programs. Most of these instructors are only part-time and either hold other jobs of a different kind or piece together several part-time teaching assignments at different educational institutions.

Community colleges have enjoyed a boom over the past several decades. From 1963 to 2006, their enrollments grew by 740 percent compared with approximately 200 percent growth for four-year colleges. Together, community colleges currently enroll over seven million students attending for credit. In keeping with the American ideal of opportunity for all, they offer a chance at a college education to many people who might not otherwise enroll. In doing so, they attract students who, if anything, are even more diverse in age, ethnicity, and ambition than those of the typical metropolitan university. Sixty percent of students who enroll attend part-time, and 80 percent have full- or part-time jobs. Forty-five percent are minorities and 42 percent are first-generation college students. Many arrive lacking basic skills in reading, writing, and mathematics and are required to take remedial courses and complete them successfully before they can begin taking regular classes for credit.

There is a continuing debate over whether community colleges increase or diminish the number of students who eventually earn a BA degree. For some, the chance to enroll in a nearby, inexpensive community college undoubtedly makes it possible to begin undergraduate studies and then move on to a four-year college and earn a BA degree. Yet graduation rates are low, even when one takes account of the academic background of those who enter. Many students who could have qualified for a four-year college but elected to start their postsecondary education in a community college never transfer, often because they receive inadequate counseling, or are turned off by indifferently taught courses, or are diverted into vocational classes that do not qualify for credit at a four-year college. In all, only some 20–25 percent of those who enroll in a community college eventually transfer to a four-year institution, many fewer than the two-thirds or more who claim an intention to do so when they enter.[7] Whether more students would have enrolled in a four-year college and earned a degree had community colleges not existed is a question hotly debated but still unresolved.[8]

FOR-PROFIT INSTITUTIONS

Beyond the several categories mentioned above lies a large and growing for-profit sector composed of more than thirteen hundred schools. Roughly half of these give college degrees; the rest are two-year colleges or institutions that

grant certificates signifying completion of a training program for a specific occupation such as cosmetology or the culinary arts.[9] For-profits chiefly offer vocational instruction, especially for older students seeking to prepare themselves
for higher-paying jobs. Collectively, they award approximately 10 percent of all
college degrees.

While most for-profits are small proprietary schools, a few are huge, with
tens of thousands, even hundreds of thousands of students. The largest fifteen
alone enroll almost 60 percent of all students in the entire for-profit sector. With
branches in a number of states and even overseas, these mega-universities have
constituted the fastest-growing segment in the entire higher education system,
both in traditional face-to-face classes and in online instruction.* Over the past
two years, however, enrollments at these institutions have leveled off or declined
following "a steady drumroll of negative publicity about the sector's recruiting
abuses, low graduation rates and high default rates [on student loans]."[10]

Unlike public universities and most private, nonprofit institutions, for-
profits rely almost entirely on tuition payments as a source of revenue. Since
the vast majority of their students have modest incomes, they are heavily subsidized by Pell Grants and educational loans from the federal government. In
2008–9, although for-profits accounted for less than 10 percent of total undergraduate enrollments, their students were awarded 24 percent of all Pell Grants
and 26 percent of federally guaranteed loans while incurring larger debts than
nonprofit students.[11]

For-profit universities rarely compete directly with liberal arts colleges or
research universities. Their typical student is older, part-time, often employed
and intent on acquiring the skills to qualify for a higher-paying job. By cutting costs, providing year-round education, renting space, and doing without
research, athletics, extracurricular activities, and other nonessential amenities

---

*The University of Phoenix is the largest and most highly publicized for-profit university. Its
total enrollment now exceeds 400,000 with branches in at least 38 states, the District of Columbia,
Puerto Rico and Canada, Mexico, the Netherlands, and the United Kingdom. In 2009, 86 percent of
its $3.77 billion in revenues came from Pell Grants and other federal financial aid programs. Only
a small fraction of its students seek a liberal arts degree. Most are enrolled part-time in vocational
programs with just enough liberal arts courses to meet accreditation requirements. The education
provided is of a no-frills variety with classes taught in rented space without student unions, massive
libraries, elaborate buildings, or extensive extracurricular activities. A small cadre of faculty are
hired on a full-time basis and have extensive oversight and administrative responsibilities in addition to a reduced teaching load. The rest of the instructors are mainly working professionals who
teach part-time and are typically required to have at least a master's degree along with five years
or more of practical experience. All must prepare for teaching by taking a variety of workshops on
subjects such as adult learning theory, online teaching, and methods of grading, assessment, and
feedback. The course materials they use are prepared at headquarters by a professional staff and
revised periodically to reflect changes in job requirements and student feedback.

and services, for-profits can charge a tuition well below that of most private nonprofit colleges and still earn a tidy surplus. The best of them offer convenient locations, schedule classes in the evenings and on weekends to accommodate working students, and devote much effort to placing their graduates and keeping their courses closely aligned with opportunities in the job market. They have aggressively pursued online instruction, providing added convenience for working adults who find it difficult to travel to classes. By concentrating on serving the needs of their older, vocationally oriented students as effectively and efficiently as possible, they offer a welcome alternative for many individuals who might otherwise attend a community college or not enroll at all.

Despite these accomplishments, the record of the for-profits is not unblemished. While some of them seem to perform well, others have high dropout rates and limited success in helping students find the jobs for which they have ostensibly been trained. They are extremely aggressive in recruiting students, sometimes spending more on expanding their enrollments than they do on instruction. A few have accepted applicants with very low prospects of graduating or finding a desirable job. A recent investigation by the General Accounting Office found that each of the fifteen for-profits it examined had engaged in deceptive practices or made misleading statements in its effort to enlist as many applicants as possible.[12]

Once enrolled in a for-profit college, many students drop out before completing their studies. Thereafter, they default on their educational loans at a much higher rate than their counterparts in any other type of college. Six years after entering a for-profit institution, students are more likely to be unemployed and out of school than students of similar qualifications who entered not-for-profit institutions. Their average earnings tend to be 8–9 percent lower.[13] For the federal government, therefore, whose student grants and guaranteed loans provide most of the revenue received by the larger for-profits, this segment of the higher education system represents a mixed blessing.

THE SPECIAL NATURE OF OUR
HIGHER EDUCATION SYSTEM

Throughout most of its history, American higher education has differed in several respects from the university systems of other advanced industrial democracies. While the differences have narrowed in recent years, they are still sufficiently important to give our system a special flavor. Much of what is most praiseworthy about higher education in this country (as well as much that is troubling) can be linked in one way or another to these distinctive characteristics.

DIVERSITY OF INSTITUTIONS

America's colleges and universities are unusually numerous and diverse. Most of them are private, although collectively they enroll only 20 percent of all students. Some institutions are tiny, numbering only a few hundred students, while others are very large, with enrollments of fifty thousand or more. Some have very limited resources while others have huge budgets and multibillion-dollar endowments. Many are stand-alone colleges, but others are much larger universities containing a wide variety of graduate and professional schools. A few colleges (about 10 percent) are truly selective in the sense that they attract a much larger number of applicants than they can admit. The rest accept at least a majority, and many take virtually all those who apply. Some private colleges and universities are connected to religious denominations but most are not. The vast majority are coeducational, but a handful enroll only women. Still others are almost exclusively attended by black students or Native Americans. More than one thousand specialize in a single field of study such as business, the arts, or allied health professions, while others offer scores of different programs. Within such a varied array, almost any student can find a college that caters to a particular special interest, such as the performing arts, or foreign languages, or conservative religious values.

Highly selective colleges, such as Princeton, Stanford, or Amherst, offer a more intense, all-encompassing experience for their students than one normally finds in other countries. Most undergraduates in these institutions live and eat their meals in residences on campus. They can participate in a bewildering variety of extracurricular activities sponsored by the college—athletic teams, orchestras, campus newspapers, political clubs, community service activities, and countless others. They can become active in campus government and play at least an advisory role in matters of curriculum and student life. Their residence halls and fraternities and sororities organize dances, parties, and other social activities. Student affairs offices arrange a wide array of public lectures, concerts, dramatic productions, and intramural athletics. In short, these colleges create a vast smorgasbord of activities, academic and extracurricular, with which to fill most of the waking hours of their students' lives. In doing so, they offer an experience very different from that provided in most other countries, where universities do little more than offer instruction, leaving students to organize their extracurricular lives as they see fit.

Although the residential college just described represents most people's image of undergraduate life in America, less than 20 percent of students actually share this experience today. The vast majority of colleges, including almost all community colleges, rarely house a substantial fraction of their undergraduates or play nearly as active a role as a residential campus in organizing undergraduates' social and extracurricular lives. Instead, students typically commute from home or live in apartments in the surrounding community. They tend to work longer hours at outside jobs, and many of them attend only part-time and take more than four years to complete their studies. A majority pursue vocational majors and go to work immediately after they graduate instead of spending additional years in a professional school.

More than most other countries, the United States is a nation of second (or third or fourth) chances. Students who do poorly in high school can still find colleges to enter and eventually earn a BA degree. Students who drop out of college can enter another institution at a later point in their lives on a full- or part-time basis. They can even pursue a degree online without quitting their job or changing their place of residence. At present, more than 40 percent of all undergraduates in this country are over the age of twenty-four, and close to 40 percent study part-time.

In contrast to the tradition in Europe, most Americans entering the so-called learned professions, notably law and medicine, do not begin their professional education until they have completed college. The same is true of students who hope to become professors, although most of these will have majored as undergraduates in the same discipline in which they eventually plan to receive their PhD. Even vocational majors must usually take at least one year of coursework designed to give them a broad foundation of learning. While the contrast with European practice is real, it is not quite as great as it might seem, since some of the breadth that American students receive in college is incorporated into professional studies in Europe, and some is provided by the secondary schools, which tend to keep students longer and cover more ground than most high schools in the United States.

THE ROLE OF GOVERNMENT

American colleges and universities have been subject to less government supervision and control than their counterparts in most other nations. In some countries, such as France and Germany, virtually all institutions of higher education are officially treated as agencies of the state. Their professors are formally classified as civil servants, and their budgets and administrative operations have been subject to detailed government oversight. Throughout Europe, universities continue to receive almost all of their funding from the government, although policy-makers in most of these nations are now taking steps to encourage institutions to seek other sources of support as well.

Because our higher education system has a large private sector along with a federal system in which much funding and oversight of universities is provided by the states, it is harder to create a coherent and effective national policy for higher education than is the case in most other countries. The federal government does have power to institute a national research policy, since state governments give little support of this kind to universities. Even here, however, the ability to effectuate a unitary policy is complicated by the fact that several federal departments and agencies distribute their own research money (not to mention the funds provided for research by industry and foundations). Whether the lack of a strong national policy is considered a help or a hindrance depends very much on one's attitude toward government.

Of course, American colleges and universities are hardly free from government influence. As in every country, they are subject to general legislation, such as laws forbidding the use of drugs or prohibiting discrimination on the basis of race, religion, age, gender, and sexual orientation. As universities have become more expensive and more important to the public, their activities have been subjected to increasing regulation. A few state legislatures have even passed laws requiring public universities to teach a particular course or prescribing minimum teaching loads for faculty. For the most part, however, state lawmakers have refrained from regulating matters of curriculum or teaching methods.

The federal government is the principal source of research funding and financial aid for students, and officials naturally have an interest in how the funds are used. But financial aid goes directly to students and is seldom accompanied by restrictions on institutional policy. Research support is subject to detailed regulations to provide accountability in the use of the funds and appropriate rules for safety and the protection of human subjects. Nevertheless, most research grants go directly to individual professors based on recommendations by study groups composed of established researchers who typically belong to university faculties. Thus, while the government sets priorities, professors exert much influence over how the funds are spent and which investigators receive support.

Because private colleges and universities rarely receive direct funding from their state legislature, they are usually free of any control by state officials over their budgets or tuitions. Public universities are in a far different position, since they have always received substantial sums from their state legislature or municipality. For several decades, however, these subsidies have been diminishing as a percentage of the operating budgets of state universities. In fact, several leading public universities now obtain a smaller fraction of their total budget from their state than they do from tuition payments or federal research grants. Paradoxically, however, while state funding has dwindled, the same is not necessarily true of state supervision. In response, public universities in several states have sought agreements to free themselves, at least partially, from government control in exchange for accepting less direct state support.[14]

SOURCES OF FUNDING

American colleges and universities, public as well as private, have traditionally been free to seek funds from any source. Public universities have long been allowed to charge students tuition, a practice only recently introduced in Europe on a more modest scale. As a result, households contribute more to the total expenditures of American colleges and universities than they do in any other country. By successfully drawing on multiple sources of support, our higher education system is one of the few that receives a majority of its financing (55 percent) from private sources. Through vigorous pursuit of their various sources of support, American colleges and universities enjoy the highest levels of funding of any system in the world.[15] Counting all forms of support, expenditures on higher education in this country amount to 2.4 percent of national income, roughly twice the average level for members of the European Union.*

The prominent role of America's private universities and the long tradition of seeking funds from nongovernmental sources have helped to create larger differences in size, wealth, and reputation than one would normally find in other countries. Thanks to generous donors, a small but growing fraction of American universities have managed to accumulate large endowments that yield a substantial annual income to help defray their operating expenses. At least eighty institutions have managed to amass funds totaling more than one billion dollars, an achievement matched by very few foreign universities. At the same time, however, most American colleges and universities make do with far less money and much lower salaries, smaller libraries, and less impressive facilities.

COMPETITION

A final distinguishing characteristic of our higher education system is the intensity with which its institutions compete with one another. Their rivalry

---

* It should be pointed out, however, that a significant amount of university support in this country goes to activities that are not strictly academic, such as athletic programs and the operation of university-owned hospitals.

extends to almost every area of university activity—attracting students, recruiting faculty, raising money, and, most visibly, engaging in intercollegiate sports. The more prominent colleges and universities constantly vie with one another for prestige, aware that the better their reputation, the easier it will be to raise money and attract able students and faculty. Community colleges and metropolitan universities are less inclined to strive for prestige. But they too face increasing pressure from the large for-profit colleges that are recruiting students aggressively. Many small private colleges, in particular, have to struggle constantly to attract enough students away from lower-cost public institutions.

Competition in higher education has long been encouraged in America by the presence of private colleges and universities that vie with one another and with public institutions. After World War II, the rivalry grew much keener as improved transportation enabled colleges to recruit students nationwide, and federal agencies began awarding growing amounts of research funding to university scientists on a competitive basis. The decision by Congress in the 1970s to give financial aid directly to students gave a further boost to competition by enabling more young people to consider distant colleges as well as ones close to home, thus encouraging universities to search more widely for promising applicants.

Competition has increased even further in recent decades because of the appearance of highly publicized rankings that compare the overall quality of hundreds of colleges and graduate and professional schools. These ratings have touched off an intense struggle among institutions to outdo one another in the research reputations of the faculty and the academic qualifications of students. Although the methods used to create the rankings are regularly (and justly) criticized, the results do seem to influence student choices and even private donations, causing colleges to try all the harder to reach a higher rung on the ladder.[16]

A GROWING CONVERGENCE

The discussion thus far has emphasized the qualities that have long distinguished America's universities from their counterparts abroad. In the last twenty-five years, however, higher education systems in most advanced nations have been gradually growing more alike. As research and education have come to be looked upon as vital ingredients of economic growth, countries with highly developed, knowledge-based economies are all being driven by a common desire to strengthen their universities. In doing so, most have been influenced by the success of the American system and have consciously attempted to adopt many of its features.

In an effort to harmonize the educational practices of its member countries and encourage the movement of students from one institution to another, the European Union has recently adopted a structure of degrees—undergraduate, master's, and doctoral—that roughly resembles our own.[17] To attract more students from other parts of the world, a number of departments and even a few entire universities in Europe and elsewhere are now teaching all or many of their courses in English. Holland has even begun building three-year liberal arts colleges taught in English and modeled on American institutions such as Amherst and Williams.

Many nations have also changed the way they train professors and researchers to resemble more closely the doctoral programs in this country. Funding for research has been increased to come closer to the prevailing levels in America. Several governments, including those of China, South Korea, France, Germany, and even Saudi Arabia, have set out to build "world-class" universities resembling those of the United States.[18]

Having made the transition to mass higher education, European governments, like our own, are struggling to pay the heavy costs of educating ever-larger numbers of students while building a first-rate research capability. In response, their officials have pressed universities to seek outside funding by restricting the amount of money directly appropriated by the state. As in this country, policy-makers have encouraged academic leaders to seek partnerships with industry, create spin-off companies built on university research, and engage in other profit-seeking ventures. Throughout Europe (save in Scandinavia), governments have begun to allow their universities to charge tuition, although the maximum amounts permitted have tended to be well below those commonly charged in the United States. Thus far, the efforts to create new sources of support have produced only limited results; government appropriations still account for 75–85 percent of university budgets throughout most of Europe. In time, however, outside funding is likely to assume a larger role in paying for the mounting costs of higher education.

In an attempt to stimulate improvement, lawmakers in most European countries have begun to introduce more competition into the system through national rankings of universities and competitive bidding for research funding. Many governments have also tried to encourage entrepreneurial vigor by relaxing some regulatory controls over the planning, budgeting, and day-to-day administration of their universities, and giving academic leaders and their professional staffs more authority within their institution. In return, policy-makers have sought greater accountability for results by creating elaborate systems to evaluate the research and educational effectiveness of universities. Several countries have begun to link government appropriations to various desired outcomes or measures of quality, an experiment that has been tried by a number of states in this country, thus far with only limited success.

To facilitate the changes just described, European governments have modified their systems of university governance. In order to encourage more responsiveness to national needs, officials in many countries have given a stronger voice to stakeholder groups, especially business, by creating boards of trustees or supervisory councils.[19] In the effort to strengthen academic leaders and their administrative staffs, faculty senates, which once exercised extensive control over internal affairs, have tended to lose some of their power over matters such as the selection of university rectors and deans, personnel, budgeting, and strategic planning. Internal governance bodies composed of representatives from the senior and junior faculty, employees, and even students, which several national governments mandated after the student protests of the late 1960s, have likewise lost much of their decision-making power and become largely consultative bodies.[20]

Interventions such as those just described have not proved necessary in the United States, since most of the changes introduced in Europe existed already in this country. American colleges and universities have traditionally had powerful presidents supported by professional staffs that enjoyed considerable autonomy from state control. Stakeholders, especially from business, have been well represented on boards of trustees. American universities have long relied on outside sources of funding, including tuition income, to balance their budgets, and are used to competing vigorously with one another.

THE STRENGTHS OF OUR SYSTEM

Despite the narrowing of differences just described, higher education in the United States remains distinctive in several important respects. It is still characterized by an unusually varied collection of colleges and universities. The differences between institutions in the abilities of students, the quality of faculty, and the level of available resources are much greater than one would normally find overseas. Because of the extensive role of private universities and the existence of our federal structure of government, American higher education is more decentralized than that of most other leading nations. It is also unusual in the amount of money spent on colleges and universities, the levels of financial support received from private sources, and the intensity with which institutions compete with one another for students, faculty, financial resources, and, in many cases, for recognition and prestige.

The special features of American higher education have brought many advantages. The existence of multiple funding sources has helped our higher education system to attract a higher level of financial support than in any other nation. The number and diversity of our colleges and universities allow prospective students to find a program to suit almost any special need or preference. The competition among institutions creates a constant pressure to respond to student needs, while also generating much effort to improve and excel. Mistakes are often made, but in a system composed of fifty states and several thousand institutions, the errors are almost always local and do not harm the entire system. The multitude of colleges and universities and the degree of autonomy they enjoy provide many centers of initiative and hence encourage innovation and experimentation. In recent decades, for example, this entrepreneurial spirit has led American universities to respond quickly to government encouragement by helping professors to work with business and launch companies to produce new products, sometimes fostering the economic development of entire regions, such as Silicon Valley in California and the greater Boston area.

To be sure, not all the successes of American higher education are attributable to the distinctive features of our system; fortuitous coincidences have helped as well. To cite the most important, much of the financial strength of American universities has been due to the exceptional wealth of the United States and its strong tradition of private philanthropy. The accidents of history spared the United States from the massive destruction of World War II while making this country a natural haven for outstanding scientists and scholars fleeing from Hitler in the 1930s. Not least, the emergence of English as the lingua franca of the scientific and scholarly world has enabled our universities to recruit talented professors from around the globe far more easily than institutions in countries such as France, Germany, or Japan.

With full recognition of the factors just mentioned, it remains true that the advantages of our system are impressive. They have served us well in the past and continue to contribute much to the achievements of our colleges and universities. The worldwide tendency to conform more closely to the American model gives eloquent testimony to the strengths of our approach.

VULNERABILITIES IN OUR SYSTEM

Helpful as they are, the distinctive features of our system do not remove all problems, let alone guarantee continued success. On the contrary, one can identify a number of risks that could seriously hamper the performance of our colleges and universities in the years to come.

Some of the threats are external to higher education itself and are common to every nation. For example, nothing in our system can forestall the damage resulting from a severe, protracted decline in government funding. The long tradition of support from philanthropy, tuition, and other sources of private funds may cushion the effects of government cutbacks but cannot possibly escape them entirely. Moreover, even if the government proves to be generous in the amount and constancy of its support, all sorts of political pressures and misguided ideas may cause lawmakers to distribute the funds in ways that do not serve universities well. In addition to the uncertainties of external funding, our system is also vulnerable to well-intentioned but misguided regulations that impatient legislatures may impose in an effort to improve the performance of colleges and universities. With higher education becoming ever more costly yet ever more important to the nation, the risk of such intervention is bound to grow. Finally, the work of our colleges and universities is inevitably affected by the quality of earlier levels of education. As the percentage of young Americans seeking an undergraduate education continues to rise, the widely recognized difficulties of our public schools promise to create increasing problems for colleges as well.*

Of greater relevance to this study are threats to the quality of our colleges and universities intrinsic to higher education itself, for these are problems that academic leaders and their faculties are likely to have at least some power to overcome. Despite the successes of our system and its many obvious advantages, there are various points of stress and vulnerability that could keep our colleges and universities from accomplishing everything society needs and expects. Among the potential sources of difficulty, the following seem especially significant.

The first of these possible weaknesses arises from the very nature of the academic enterprise. Colleges and universities are deeply engaged in endeavors that can be very hard to evaluate. In particular, changes in the quality and effectiveness of educational programs are difficult to perceive except over a period of years and may not be evident even then. Much better information is available about the quality of a university's research, since the results are published and usually evaluated by other experts in the field. Even so, it is hard to aggregate the

---

*Some might not consider the difficulties of the public schools to be a problem external to higher education, because they blame faculties of education and their methods of training teachers for the failings of K–12 education. There is doubtless more that universities could do to improve teacher education and work more closely with local schools. Still, teacher education is probably only a minor part of the problem. Much more important are the well-documented difficulties of families, child-rearing practices, and neighborhood pathologies, especially in low-income segments of the population, together with the inability of public schools to attract academically talented college graduates to careers in teaching. See, e.g., Richard Murnane and Greg Duncan (eds.), *Whither Opportunity? Rising Inequality, Schools, and Children's Life Chances* (2011); McKinsey and Company, *Closing the Talent Gap: Attracting and Retaining Top-Third Graduates to Careers in Teaching* (2010).

reputations of many different scientists and scholars, and the resulting impressions about the work of entire universities are often questionable and out of date.

The fuzzy and uneven knowledge about the performance of universities could easily lead academic leaders to make unwise decisions about the goals and priorities of the institution. If presidents and trustees cannot be sure how well a university is performing, they are more likely to become complacent or to ignore important problems that urgently need attention. Tangible goals may be emphasized too much, while objectives that are hard to evaluate count for too little. Lacking reliable measures of success, leaders may also begin to place excessive emphasis on the university's public image or on indicia of success that may appear to be valid but are in fact quite spurious.

The lack of reliable knowledge about the performance of colleges and universities also threatens to affect the decisions of government officials in troublesome ways. In seeking to hold universities accountable, officials may concentrate on measures of accomplishment that are concrete and precise at the expense of behaviors that are less tangible though equally important. Similarly, efforts to protect the public by imposing minimum standards of quality could either become excessively arbitrary or be allowed to grow lax through an unwillingness to impose harsh sanctions on the basis of crude and uncertain evidence. In a system such as ours, where there are very large numbers of separate colleges and universities, and new ones can be started relatively easily by states, individuals and groups, or even corporations, there is a particular danger that institutions of marginal quality will be allowed to continue operating indefinitely.

The absence of firm data about the quality of universities and the value of the services they provide could also affect how institutions compete in ways that diminish the value of the education they provide. Competition works well in commercial markets, because customers are the best arbiters to decide such things as which automobile offers the best value for the money or which perfume has the most appealing fragrance. In higher education, however, students have no way of knowing in advance where they will learn the most or what type of learning will prove to be most important to them in the long run. Instead, their judgment may be clouded by misguided priorities. They may exaggerate the importance of acquiring the skills to get their first job or succumb to the desire to attend an institution with an active party life or a big-time athletic program while underestimating the long-term benefits that a good undergraduate education can provide. Under these conditions, if competition causes colleges to become too responsive to student preferences in an effort to attract more and better applicants, they may adapt their curricula and their undergraduate programs in questionable ways.

In addition, unlike most goods and services, the quality of education provided by colleges and universities is a matter of concern not only to their students but to the entire society. It is important for the economy that undergraduates develop the skills employers need whether or not students care deeply about acquiring them. It also matters to the public that undergraduates become engaged and informed citizens and ethically responsible human beings even if students do not attach much importance to these goals. As a result, as colleges vie with one another to attract more and better applicants, their competition may fail to yield optimum results if it causes college authorities to shape their programs to conform too closely to the desires of students.

Competition could also lead universities to be overly attentive to the wishes of other groups besides students. Deans and presidents, in their zeal to enhance their university's reputation, might become reluctant to raise controversial issues that could provoke conflict or cause unfavorable publicity. They might shrink from initiating discussions about the quality of teaching. They might refrain from insisting on proper standards of faculty behavior for fear of antagonizing prominent scholars. Rules limiting outside consulting could be allowed to languish. Restrictions on financial conflicts of interest in carrying out research could become weak or inadequately enforced.

For similar reasons, the relentless competition to raise the money needed to keep up with rival institutions could lead universities to respond too readily to the wishes of alumni and other donors. In an effort to satisfy alumni "boosters," university officials might relax academic standards and tolerate shoddy admissions and recruitment practices to enroll athletes talented enough to win on the football field and basketball court. In order to gain corporate support, science professors might be tempted to emphasize research of an immediate, practical value at the expense of fundamental work of more enduring importance. Similarly, plans for the university's growth and development could be shaped too much by the interests and priorities of wealthy philanthropists. In their eagerness for added resources, academic leaders could even allow powerful donors to influence decisions about the nature of the curriculum or the research agenda of programs founded through their generous donations.

As universities grow larger and ever more costly to operate, the struggle to improve and excel could also lead to an all-consuming effort to raise more money—an effort that could gradually spread like a virus to affect every aspect of a university. Presidents could be appointed more for their fund-raising abilities than for their academic judgment and educational vision. Trustees might be selected because of their capacity to make large gifts rather than their wisdom and experience. Admissions policies could favor the children of wealthy parents over more accomplished applicants. New programs and activities might be initiated more for their moneymaking potential than for their intellectual promise. Even the appointment of professors could be influenced by the candidates' record in attracting government and corporate support. More worrisome still, the search for ever-larger sums of money could tempt academic leaders into questionable commercial ventures that might tarnish the university's reputation and undermine the values on which the success of the academic enterprise ultimately depends.

The gradual growth of universities and the increasing variety of their activities suggest a further hazard for higher education. As universities launch more and more new programs and new activities in response to emerging educational needs and research opportunities, they are bound to become increasingly complicated and difficult to manage. This trend creates a dilemma for those entrusted with selecting presidents, provosts, and deans. On the one hand, universities need leaders with the management ability and fund-raising skills to keep such a vast and variegated enterprise running smoothly. On the other, in order to appoint leaders who command the respect of the faculty and have the knowledge and experience to guide an academic institution, search committees need to select individuals with a solid record as a teacher and scholar. Yet candidates who possess both of these qualities may prove to be in short supply. Those who are skilled in management and fund-raising may not possess the needed academic credentials, while those with strong academic reputations may lack sufficient administrative experience to demonstrate the necessary management and fund-raising capabilities. In view of this problem, there is a danger that trustees will end up choosing candidates who are markedly deficient in one respect or the other, thus threatening to create serious problems for their institutions.

The very nature of higher education, together with the size and complexity of its universities, suggests a final potential weakness. Will it be possible to govern such institutions effectively? Unlike corporations, military organizations, and government agencies, universities cannot be guided and controlled hierarchically. No academic leader ever improved the quality of education by commanding the faculty to give better lectures, nor was a university's reputation for research ever enhanced by ordering professors to write better books. Improving the performance of the university necessarily demands the willing participation and cooperation of the faculty, while first-rate teaching and research require that individual professors have wide freedom and independence to proceed as they think best. As a result, universities, by the very nature of the work they do, are perforce rather anarchic institutions. Under these conditions, the risks of conflict, stalemate, and inertia are likely to be greater than they are in many other kinds of prominent organizations.

The difficulties and complications just described reveal how our system of higher education, despite its impressive strengths, harbors tensions and weaknesses that could keep it from becoming all that society needs and expects. These dangers may not materialize and result in any serious damage, but they do suggest the kinds of problems that are most likely to develop. Much of what follows in the remainder of this book will touch on one or another of these vulnerabilities and consider the effects they have had on the performance of our colleges and universities and the steps that can be taken to minimize any adverse consequences.

CHAPTER TWO

PURPOSES, GOALS, AND LIMITS TO GROWTH

||||||||||||||||||||||||||||||||||||||||||||||||||||||||||||||||||||||||||||||||||||||||||||||||||

IN 1996, A CANADIAN PROFESSOR, Bill Readings, published a book with the provocative title *The University in Ruins*.[1] The message of the book was that universities were in serious disarray because they no longer had a single unifying purpose to guide their activities. In earlier times, he explained, they had acted "as producer, protector, and inculcator of an idea of national culture." Now that globalization had spread and nation-states seemed less important, this role had lost much of its meaning. In its absence, he claimed, academic programs proliferated without any underlying goal save the pursuit of "excellence," which, of course, wasn't a goal at all but merely a standard, and so vague a standard that it gave no genuine guidance. Amid the ensuing confusion, Readings saw nothing to replace the earlier purpose. Instead, he suggested only that campuses become a forum for an ongoing debate about the mission of the university in a muddled, contested world.

THE PURPOSES OF THE UNIVERSITY

Whatever one might think about Professor Readings's book, he is surely correct in attaching such importance to the purposes of the university, for purposes help to focus effort and set priorities. His account is also accurate in at least one other respect. American colleges and universities do not have a single goal. In contradiction to his thesis, however, this is not a recent development. Our universities have not had a single, unifying purpose for well over one hundred years.

THE GROWTH OF MULTIPLE AIMS

Until the Civil War, most colleges in this country did have only one aim—to educate an elite group of young men for the learned professions and positions of leadership in society. Toward this end, they sought to discipline the mind and build the character of their students by means of a rigidly prescribed curriculum, a strict disciplinary code, and a concern for religion reinforced by compulsory attendance at chapel.[2] In the last half of the nineteenth century, however, this unity of purpose began to lose favor and give way to three separate movements, each with its own animating goal.

The first of the new movements was inspired by the need to prepare students for a useful occupation. The growth of the American economy and its rapid industrialization brought increasing demands for practical training. In the nineteenth century, the first public universities began providing courses of study in such fields as domestic science, engineering, business administration, physical education, teacher training, and sanitation and public health. In 1862, Congress passed the Morrill Act, promoting the development of land-grant universities that would give instruction in agriculture and the mechanical arts. Meanwhile, private universities in the East responded by strengthening their professional schools of law and medicine and adding programs in business and commerce, beginning with the Wharton School at the University of Pennsylvania.

The second movement featured an explicit emphasis on research. Johns Hopkins led the way in 1876 with the founding of a graduate school dedicated to research and training students for careers of scientific inquiry and scholarship. Other universities, such as Stanford and Chicago, Columbia and Harvard, soon created graduate schools of their own and began awarding research-oriented PhDs in addition to college and professional degrees. Before long, every major American university claimed research as part of its mission.

The third movement in American higher education grew out of the earlier effort to educate an elite. Its center lay in the humanities. Members of the faculty who shared this aim dedicated themselves to cultivating the minds of undergraduates through a well-rounded, liberal education while also producing scholarly works on literature, foreign languages, history, and philosophy.

Not every institution of higher learning embraced all three movements. For a long time, liberal arts colleges paid scant attention to research and shunned vocational programs of the kind emphasized by many of the land-grant universities. Teachers' colleges also placed little emphasis on research. After World War II, however, more and more liberal arts colleges felt compelled to add vocational majors in order to compete with public universities for students. Teachers' colleges evolved to become comprehensive universities offering professional master's programs together with vocational and liberal arts majors for undergraduates. Eventually, as more and more colleges and universities began to hire PhDs, one faculty after another made research a prerequisite for appointment or promotion.

By the 1970s, only a few institutions, such as arts academies and proprietary schools, could still claim to be organized around a single objective. All the others claimed at least two major aims. Community colleges, though not embracing research, emphasized vocational training, while also providing a liberal arts foundation for students hoping to transfer to a four-year college. Most private four-year colleges offered both liberal arts and vocational majors. Those few that still hewed closely to the liberal arts encouraged their faculties to publish serious research as well. Meanwhile, the leading American universities were the most eclectic of all. From Oxford and Cambridge, they took the concept of a residential, liberal education. From Germany, they added the role of pure research and doctoral training. From Scottish universities, they developed a commitment to practical instruction, and from the great medieval universities of Paris and Bologna, they inherited the building of strong professional schools.

In recent decades, two newer purposes have attracted wide support in addition to the three already mentioned. To begin with, as the society has grown more complex and ever more dependent on specialized knowledge, universities have increasingly engaged in a variety of service activities—offering technical advice and expertise to local businesses, government agencies, school systems, and other organizations; developing affordable housing in their neighborhoods; helping to build universities overseas; and releasing faculty members for periods of full-time public service. Although initiatives of this kind can be traced back over a century or more to the early extension programs of Midwest land-grant institutions, their scope and variety have now grown to such a point that most universities include "service" as an explicit part of their mission, along with teaching and research.

An even later addition to the purposes of research universities is the deliberate encouragement of local, regional, and even national economic development. Stanford's role in helping to foster Silicon Valley was an early, highly successful example. Many universities have now built technology transfer offices with professional staffs that scan the work of faculty scientists in search of discoveries that can be patented and licensed to interested companies. With government support, academic scientists and their counterparts in industry work together to create new products and technologies. Engineering faculties participate in outreach programs to advise local businesses on new methods to improve their products or increase their productivity. A growing number of universities employ specialists to counsel interested professors on how to start companies that will develop and market new products based on their discoveries. Some institutions have even created "incubators" to nurture fledgling enterprises until they can function profitably on their own. Others have founded their own venture capital funds to pay for the development of creative new ideas from campus laboratories to the point at which financial organizations will invest the money needed to launch a successful start-up company.

Adding an economic development program to the university's traditional functions remains a work in progress for most institutions. Academic leaders are still experimenting with different ways to play this role without unduly diverting their professors from teaching and research. Yet efforts to spur economic development are now so favored by industry and government that they seem destined to win a permanent place among the explicit aims of higher education.

In short, by the time Professor Readings published *The University in Ruins*, lamenting the loss of a single animating purpose, he was describing a state of affairs that had existed for more than a century in American higher education. The culmination of this process was the "multiversity," the creation described so memorably by Clark Kerr in his extended essay *The Uses of the University*, delivered first as a series of lectures in 1963 and subsequently printed and reprinted in several editions.[3] The institution Kerr described, far from floundering in confusion and falling into ruins as Readings claimed, has grown and prospered to become a model for other countries throughout the world.

THE ADVANTAGES AND DISADVANTAGES OF MULTIPLE AIMS

In many ways, pursuing several purposes at once has proved especially advantageous to universities because the different aims often complement one another to produce a whole greater than the sum of its parts. For example, having faculty members mentor graduate students who are active in research helps train the latter to become successful investigators and scholars, while giving professors added intellectual stimulation along with valuable assistance in their courses and their own scholarly work. Teaching undergraduates helps to keep a research-oriented faculty from growing excessively specialized while giving the students a chance to learn from scholars working at the frontiers of their field. At a more practical level, because the undergraduate experience inspires unusual loyalty among its alumni, the existence of a college makes possible much of the philanthropy to build the facilities, create the extensive libraries, and endow the professorships that allow the university to produce first-rate research.

Economic development and research also complement one another. A university is in the best position to know of discoveries in its laboratories that can be turned into useful products and processes. The willingness to work with professors to build new companies has allowed universities to retain the services of productive scientists who would otherwise have left academic life to pursue their commercial interests. At the same time, closer collaboration with industry has given many scientists access to valuable databases and other research materials while exposing them to new problems and ideas that have led to important discoveries.

Service activities can also be helpful not only to the beneficiaries but to those in the university who donate their time and knowledge. Professors who advise government agencies, assist nonprofit organizations, or work with local schools often gain insights that enrich their own teaching and research. Undergraduates who tutor underprivileged children or visit old age homes consistently report that they started volunteering to help others but quickly realized how much they learned themselves. Students in law school clinics who represent low-income clients develop basic professional skills in the process, as do medical students caring for Medicaid patients on the wards of teaching hospitals.

Finally, there are many reciprocal benefits from teaching the liberal arts and professional and vocational skills in the same university. The existence of strong liberal arts faculties can help to keep vocational programs from becoming excessively practical and neglecting the broader perspectives on society, ethics, and globalization that many employers consider important for success in higher-level jobs. The presence of established scholars in the basic disciplines also helps professional school faculty keep abreast of developments in fields of knowledge that bear upon their teaching and research. In turn, professional school faculty can contribute valuable teaching to a liberal arts curriculum through their knowledge of subjects such as applied ethics, constitutional law, and biomedical science. Moreover, professional school faculties have attracted more and more professors of international stature who are worthy colleagues and collaborators for their counterparts in arts and sciences departments.

While colleges and universities have benefited from the synergies derived from pursuing several goals at once, such a strategy is not without risks. For one thing, multiple goals sometimes conflict with one another. It is often alleged, for example, that research routinely causes professors to slight their teaching responsibilities. Although this charge has never been convincingly proved, at least *some* professors have undoubtedly neglected their teaching to spend more hours in the library or the laboratory. The coexistence of teaching and research can also impede efficiency and drive up costs, since successful research programs may require more faculty than are needed for teaching undergraduates, and hence give rise to many highly specialized courses with very limited enrollments.

Multiple goals can come into conflict in other ways as well. The strong student demand for practical training can marginalize the humanities and undermine efforts to offer a broad liberal arts foundation to undergraduates. The effort to promote economic development by encouraging professors to patent their discoveries and work more closely with business may eventually divert their energies from basic research and lure them into commercial relationships that threaten the objectivity of their published work. Maintaining a proper balance among the several goals of the institution has consequently become a necessary function for university leaders.

LIMITS TO GROWTH

Whatever its advantages and disadvantages, embracing multiple purposes surely increases the pressure for growth. Opportunities for new activities crop up continuously. Government agencies, corporations, foundations, and other donors perceive needs that academic institutions can help to meet. New industries spring up offering jobs that faculties must prepare their students to fill. The Internet and other emerging technologies bring new audiences within reach of the campus and create possibilities for research that professors are eager to exploit.

When universities undertake additional functions, the burden of providing adequate oversight becomes heavier. More and more time must be spent seeking capable people to manage the growing array of programs and oversee their performance. Some university activities may become so specialized that they are not well understood by the academic leaders who are ultimately responsible for their development. In an effort to cope, the central administration must continually hire more deputy provosts, vice presidents, budget officers, and other specialists. Administrative costs consume a larger share of the budget. The distance between the faculty and the administration increases as well, creating greater risks of distrust and misunderstanding.

When programs multiply, problems also arise more frequently in one endeavor or another that require the time and attention of top officials and distract them from the core responsibilities of the institution. As universities find more ways of responding to public needs, they acquire new constituencies that must be consulted and informed. The effort to obtain the resources required to keep the whole show going causes fund-raising to become an all-consuming preoccupation of campus leaders.

Signs of this process are apparent everywhere. In most universities, administrative staffs have been growing much faster for several decades than faculties or student bodies. Universities are involved with more and more regulatory agencies, laws, and oversight bodies. There are increasing numbers of committees to consult and reports to be filed. Presidents spend larger portions of their day on management, fund-raising, and public relations. Gradually, provosts, deans, and even heads of centers and programs find themselves diverted by administrative chores from attending to the core activities of education and research.

DEFINING GOALS

The burdens of growth make it more important for colleges and universities to be clear about their purposes and priorities so that they can concentrate on important activities and avoid taking on unnecessary responsibilities. An obvious first step is to prepare a mission statement. Such a task can provide a useful opportunity to engage the academic leadership, the board, and the faculty in a serious discussion to specify the basic purposes and goals of the institution and define its particular niche in the cavalcade of American higher education. Yet the opportunity is frequently missed.[4] More often than not, the product is a vacuous statement that seems designed primarily to appeal to potential applicants and donors rather than set a clear direction. It frequently does little more than recite the familiar mantra of teaching, research, and service, a formula too vague to have any practical value.

One might think that terms such as teaching and research could at least rule out such seemingly unrelated endeavors as providing mass entertainment, or operating a farm, or becoming a major supplier of health care. Yet universities are often engaged in all three of these activities. Their basketball and football teams play before huge paying audiences, both live and on television. Several land-grant institutions operate model farms for purposes of agricultural research and development. Many universities own large teaching hospitals, some of which offer the best care in the nation. A few have actually created prepaid managed care programs that deliver health services to tens of thousands of people.

In recent decades, academic leaders have ventured even further afield in an effort to earn profits they can use to support more traditional research and educational programs. Universities currently organize cruises for alumni to exotic places in the world, operate colleges and business schools abroad in exchange for handsome sums, and collect money worldwide in return for the use of their logo on sweatshirts and coffee mugs. Once academic leaders start to launch new ventures simply to make money to support education and research, the potential scope of their activities becomes virtually limitless.

In order to provide a clearer set of directions and priorities, almost every college or university will periodically create a strategic plan containing specific goals to achieve within a stated period of years. Strategic planning can easily go astray, however, because it is so hard to set meaningful goals or measure progress for the activities that matter most, education and research. With very few exceptions, no college really knows whether its students are learning more than they did a decade ago. Research may be a bit easier to evaluate in a general way, since the results are published so that individual faculty members acquire a reputation from their peers around the country and the world. Even so, unless unusually dramatic changes have occurred, it is impossible to judge whether the collective quality of science and scholarship for an entire university has risen or fallen over any limited period of years.

Notwithstanding these difficulties, those responsible for colleges and universities often insist on setting measurable goals, if only to provide some way of determining whether their institution is progressing. As two experienced academic leaders put it in a recent book, "How can an institution develop a meaningful strategic plan and set realistic goals without understanding how to measure and track the plan's outcomes?"[5] Trustees want to evaluate the performance of the president. Presidents and deans need some means to reassure themselves that all the time and effort they devote to their work has not been in vain. Alumni relish visible signs of improvement. In the competitive world of higher education, everyone wants some demonstrable way to determine who is succeeding and who is falling behind. If it is impossible to measure progress toward the ends that matter most, other goals will be found instead.

The more objective and measurable the goals, the more attractive they will seem to those in charge. As a result, presidents and trustees frequently look to such tangible signs of progress as growth in the size of the endowment, or gains in the average SAT or ACT scores of incoming freshmen, or new buildings built and new programs begun. Such achievements do not necessarily reflect genuine improvement in teaching, learning, and research. But in the absence of better measures, they seem to offer concrete evidence of forward movement and success.

Such calculations help to bring about an evolution on the part of many institutions from community colleges to comprehensive universities, and, eventually, in some cases, to research universities. From 1995 to 2006, dozens of community colleges changed into four-year institutions, while scores of comprehensives turned into research universities.[6] During the 1990s, 105 colleges changed their name to "university" and increased the number of their graduate students and graduate degree programs.[7]

In some cases, this evolution occurs in response to genuine educational needs. Population increases and industrial growth may generate legitimate demands for new degree programs and more advanced training. In other cases, universities decide to create new vocational master's programs to attract the additional students that the institution needs to remain financially viable. Very often, however, attempts to move to a higher level reflect a desire on the part of academic leaders for greater prestige and a chance to gain the larger state appropriations and research grants that often accompany a higher rank in the educational hierarchy.[8]*

Climbing to the next level—or "mission creep," as it is often called—tends to be expensive. It typically calls for building larger faculties, new degree programs, and more elaborate facilities. Above all, it requires an emphasis on research, with the PhD programs, new laboratories, larger libraries, higher faculty salaries, and lower teaching loads that such an effort usually entails. These changes are expensive and usually necessitate higher tuitions.

In addition to driving up costs, experience suggests that attempting to rise in the academic hierarchy, especially trying to become a successful research university, is a risky strategy that rarely brings much success. Despite the constant efforts to outdo rival institutions, the rankings of universities are remarkably stable, far more so than is true for corporations. Of the nine colleges founded before the American Revolution, six were still ranked in the top dozen in 2010, and all nine fit comfortably within the top one hundred. Similarly, while few of the leading corporations from a century ago continue to be successful, or even to exist, the top five universities in 1910 were still ranked among the top five in 2010, and at least two-thirds of the top twenty retained that distinction a century later.

Once a university has obtained a lofty position in the hierarchy, powerful forces help to keep it there. Outstanding scholars prefer to locate in leading universities where their colleagues will also be outstanding. Government agencies that distribute research funds give the bulk of the money to the same institutions, since that is where the best researchers work. Foundations and philanthropists seeking to support research on subjects that concern them typically do likewise. In much the same way, lacking better information to guide them, unusually talented students tend to apply to universities that have a strong reputation and are populated by other talented students. Because they are exceptionally able, more of these students are likely to make a lot of money after they graduate and to be generous to the institutions that educated them. In short, to

---

*One observer claims that fully half of American four-year colleges and universities seek prestige. William F. Massy, *Honoring the Trust: Quality and Cost Containment and Higher Education* (2003), p. 23. According to another observer, "institutions pursue graduate education and a higher Carnegie classification, not primarily to serve a present need but to adopt the practices and structures of universities perceived as having the most prestige and highest status." Christopher C. Morphew, "A Rose by Any Other Name," 25 *Review of Higher Education* (2002), pp. 207, 211.

those that have, more is given. This principle clearly works to the advantage of universities with established reputations and makes it difficult for institutions lower in the hierarchy to challenge them successfully.

Successful universities also benefit from the fact that failures of leadership and poor decisions rarely cause immediate or lasting harm to the institution. In business, a faulty strategy or a serious error of judgment can ruin a company. In the case of universities, such mistakes tend to have much milder effects, both because decision-making in matters that count the most—education and research—are much more highly decentralized and because declines in teaching and even research take longer to detect. As a result, trustees almost always have much more time than directors of a company to recognize weak leadership or poor decisions and take corrective action before any lasting damage occurs.

Apart from the low odds of success, trying to climb to a higher rung on the ladder of prestige is also unfortunate from a public interest standpoint. By and large, universities seek prestige not by developing innovative programs but by hiring more well-published professors, attracting abler students, and otherwise aping institutions that enjoy a higher reputation. Unlike improvements in education or discoveries from research, which benefit everyone, luring talented students and able faculty from one institution to another usually fails to improve higher education as a whole. Building newer and bigger PhD programs may not accomplish anything of value if there are already more than enough new PhDs to fill the available jobs. Increasing the research "output" of a faculty does not contribute much to society if the publications are never cited and rarely, if ever, read. The overall effect is often much like having more and more automobile manufacturers set their sights on moving from making low-cost compacts to producing midsize sedans, and ultimately luxury vehicles. The plainer, less expensive cars may not attract much attention from passersby, but they are often just as important as the luxury models, if not more so, whether or not they generate as much excitement.

In much the same way, the quest for greater prestige can lead to the neglect of more important needs that do not happen to rank high among the conventional measures of success. The most substantial contribution that community colleges can make is not to grow into four-year institutions but to become more effective in educating and graduating their existing students. By doing so, they can enroll a highly diverse set of young people, many of them with weak academic backgrounds, and help them to earn a degree, realize their ambitions, and do things for their communities they could never otherwise accomplish. Similarly, the public will often benefit more if four-year colleges concentrate on finding ways to lower dropout rates and improve the quality of the education they provide, instead of devoting their energies and resources to creating new master's and professional doctorate programs in an attempt to become comprehensive universities. A metropolitan university that excels in teaching students is likely to add more value than it would by becoming another medium-quality research institution. Even so, because the contributions from first-rate teaching are hard to evaluate and seldom win public acclaim or achieve much prestige, they tend to be overshadowed by more tangible, measurable gains, such as higher SAT scores, new programs, and successful fund drives.

The point is not that colleges and universities should stop competing with one another or give up striving to improve. Far from it. Much of the success achieved by American higher education has been due to the effort and energy fueled by the desire to be among the best. The problem lies in defining "best" by emphasizing the test scores students bring with them when they enter rather than how much they learn after they arrive, or thinking that research must necessarily matter more than teaching, or caring more about the number of articles professors publish than about the quality and originality of what they write.

The tendency to equate progress with prestige has intensified in recent decades with the advent of periodic rankings of colleges and universities in publications such as *U.S. News & World Report*.* These rankings are especially seductive since they purport to offer clear-cut evidence of an institution's quality and to reveal in precise terms whether its standing is improving or declining. A survey of presidents in America and Europe found that 72 percent aspired to be ranked within the top 10 percent of universities in the nation.[9] Even presidents who do not believe that success can be measured in this way will shrink from the prospect of falling to a lower rank and being thought of as a failure by trustees, alumni, and members of the faculty.

A cursory look at the way such ratings are compiled will reveal that they are not a reliable yardstick for measuring progress, especially progress in educating students.[10] What they mainly reflect is an institution's reputation in the eyes of other educators and the average SAT scores of its entering students. Neither of these factors gives an accurate measure of the value of the education provided by the faculty. Estimates of an institution's reputation are only the crude impressions of officials from other universities about the strengths of the faculty's

---

* *U.S. News* rankings are not the only form of prestige-driven goals. Some institutions will seek to create more graduate programs. For example, the University of Illinois, Chicago aspired to be ranked as a so-called Research I University and hence set a goal of adding one or two new PhD programs every year. Ohio State announced a goal of having ten departments in the top ten in the country according to the National Research Council's evaluations and twenty departments in the top twenty, all by 2020. Still other universities set their sights on gaining admission to the Association of American Universities, an elite group of the sixty or so leading research universities. See Frank Donoghue, *The Last Professors: The Corporate University and the Fate of the Humanities* (2008), p. 134.

research. They are often out of date and have no bearing at all on the quality of instruction, a matter on which outsiders are usually quite ignorant. Average SAT scores likewise tell little about the effectiveness of a college's teaching, or how much more a student will learn by enrolling in one school rather than another. Other factors used in the ratings, such as the proportion of the faculty with PhDs or the size of the college's endowment, have an equally tenuous relation to the quality of an institution's education or research.

In the absence of better measures of genuine progress and accomplishment, published rankings exert more influence than they should on the aims of universities.* They tend to impose a single definition of excellence ill-suited to the many different kinds of educational institutions and the variety of student needs. Since they seem objective and precise, and because they can have an effect on alumni donations and student recruitment, they reinforce the tendency of colleges and universities to shape their plans and priorities by a desire for conventional prestige instead of striving toward more worthwhile goals.[11] Some boards of trustees offer bonuses to their president if their university reaches a stipulated level in the rankings, and state governments have occasionally set a similar goal for their flagship institution.[12] The practical result, once again, is to intensify the effort to find the money to fund new programs, hire more faculty, build larger facilities, offer more merit scholarships, and launch other initiatives that are often wasteful and draw the energies of academic leaders away from reforms that would matter more.

THE PROBLEM OF NEEDLESS GROWTH

Robert Maynard Hutchins once declared that "it is a good principle of educational administration that a college or university should do nothing that any other agency can do as well."[13] Despite this admonition, universities frequently disregard the advice and undertake new activities that others could perform as well or better. Many of these ventures are costly and complicated, and consume much time and energy on the part of academic leaders.

---

*The influence of rankings is so great that many institutions resort to questionable tactics in an effort to improve their position. A number of colleges and professional schools spend substantial sums on glossy brochures, which they send to presidents and other officials of hundreds of institutions in the hope of creating a better impression in the minds of those who may be evaluating them as part of the ranking process. Other colleges and professional schools ask professors to take their sabbaticals in the spring in order not to increase their student-faculty ratios used by the rankings (which base their findings on the number of faculty in residence during the fall semester). In rare cases, institutions have even submitted false data to obtain a higher rating.

A particularly colorful example is big-time intercollegiate athletics, a form of mass entertainment reaching many millions of people, costing large sums of money, and often leading to petty scandals involving improprieties in recruiting players, cheating on exams, or under-the-table payments to members of a team.[14] Because of the visibility of college athletics, many university presidents spend much of their time dealing with various aspects of the program. More than a few have claimed that the largest single category of mail they receive consists of unsolicited comments on one sport or another, often involving the quality of the coaching staff. None of this, of course, is necessary to the operation of an academic institution. Other countries manage to provide abundant opportunities for athletes, from young children to world-class performers, without involving their universities in semiprofessional, high-visibility, mass audience competition. Even in the United States, a number of first-rate universities exist without engaging in anything like the high-powered programs mounted by colleges engaged in Division I competition. Nevertheless, hundreds of colleges and universities continue to devote the money and time required to keep these activities going.

Another case of undertaking functions that others could perform as well is the ownership of teaching hospitals. Some of these institutions have become billion-dollar enterprises serving many thousands of patients each year. It is not necessary, however, for universities to own hospitals. Several medical schools, including some of the best, function very well by simply developing a working relationship with one or more independently run hospitals in the vicinity. By so doing, they avoid the administrative burdens that come with managing such a large and complicated operation, burdens that can absorb much of the time and energy of university leaders when things go wrong and the wholly owned hospital runs large losses or encounters serious management problems.

A different form of unnecessary growth occurs when universities initiate programs not because of their intrinsic contribution to the core mission of the institution but for some other motive—to please a donor, attract a prestigious new professor, or keep an existing faculty member from leaving. Activities undertaken for such reasons often turn out to be disappointing and unnecessary. It is always tempting to accept a handsome donation, but doing so when the purpose does not fit existing plans and priorities often leads to trouble. The new initiative may not attract much faculty interest, or the activity involved may lack intellectual value, or the donation provided for the purpose may not cover all of the costs and thus may divert resources from more important uses. As for attracting or retaining valued faculty, few scientists or scholars are worth the creation of a new institute or program that does not fit the purposes of the institution or stand on its own intellectual merits. Professors who will not come or stay without such an added investment will usually be quick to depart when even better opportunities come along, leaving the university with additional costs and little to show in exchange.

The last familiar category of unnecessary activity consists of programs undertaken not because of their potential contribution to research or their educational value but primarily to generate revenue to help pay for other programs in the university. Early in the twentieth century, several major universities instituted correspondence courses for this purpose that were administered on a for-profit basis. More recently, universities have entered into moneymaking activities as varied as offering online education, starting branch operations overseas, conducting routine testing of new drugs, and investing in the commercial development of scientific discoveries by professors, all in the hope of earning a surplus to support other campus programs.

Profit-seeking activities carry a special risk because they tend to create a conflict between the desire to make money and the basic academic values of the university. Such conflicts can easily result in dubious compromises and petty scandals, such as those that have long plagued intercollegiate athletic programs. Other profitable services, such as testing drugs for pharmaceutical companies or giving instruction to entry-level management trainees for corporations, bear the added disadvantage of forcing instructors and investigators into routine teaching and research of little value to the university or its faculty aside from the generation of additional funds. Educational ventures, such as vocational programs that are created to make money, can easily lead to compromises in quality to increase profit margins. Investing in start-up companies based on discoveries by the faculty or "incubating" their development into commercially profitable products may present fewer ethical hazards. Even so, these activities call for skills other than those normally found in academic institutions, and hence make success more doubtful and proper oversight more difficult. Reviews of such efforts have found that they rarely improve upon the results of normal market processes.[15]

Because universities are chronically short of funds, campus officials have often elected to run these risks in the hope of earning money that can be used for academic purposes. Occasionally, they succeed. A look at the record, however, reveals that they often fail. Only a handful of institutions have consistently earned a surplus from big-time intercollegiate athletics if the costs involved are fully accounted for.[16] Several of the early, widely publicized, for-profit, online educational programs ended by losing money. Industrial research parks more often than not have had disappointing results. Venture capital investing in companies founded to exploit the discoveries of faculty members have seldom yielded a significant return or achieved anything that independent companies and investors could not have accomplished equally well.[17] What *is* clear is that all these profit-seeking activities have placed added burdens on the administration and have often led to scandals, embarrassing financial losses, or other problems that cast discredit on the institution.

THE NECESSITY OF GROWTH

While unwise ventures can cause needless problems, even the most prudent university will find it difficult, and probably impossible, to avoid becoming ever larger, more variegated, and harder to administer. Few institutions in our society are so filled with creative, intelligent, driven individuals or so surrounded by opportunities to expand the number and variety of worthwhile activities. Faced with this array of attractive possibilities, the wisest academic leaders may avoid unnecessary or inappropriate new ventures, but they can no more stop institutional growth entirely than King Canute could halt the incoming tides on the beaches of England. A university that ceased to launch new programs would soon begin to stagnate and lose its most creative and venturesome professors to other, bolder institutions.

It is sometimes said that universities grow too large and too complicated only because they are so quick to add new activities and so slow to do away with ones that have ceased to have much value. Such charges are easily exaggerated. In fact, colleges and universities do manage to eliminate entire programs and departments at an average rate of more than two every five years, according to one of the few surveys on the subject.[18] Critics may reply that many more should be terminated. Those who hold this view, however, often overestimate the number of plausible candidates for extinction. Professors engaged in activities that have outlived their original purpose are usually quite skillful at developing new aims that offer a reason for continuing to exist. It is also harder than one might think to decide which intellectual fields no longer have a future. For example, following World War II, Harvard decided to abandon its program in computer science on the ground that it was not a genuine academic subject. Although the decision must have seemed reasonable at the time, it hardly looks prescient in the light of subsequent history.

Closing a department or a research center can also prove more difficult and save less money than outsiders might suppose. Terminating faculty, especially if they are tenured, can be costly and difficult. Students already enrolled in soon-to-be abandoned programs must be taken care of in one way or another, and their tuitions, once they disappear, will leave with them. Facilities made available by the closing of a program often prove unsuitable for other purposes or require expensive renovations. Endowments are frequently restricted by the donor for a specific purpose and may be difficult to liberate and put to other uses. Moreover, a decision by a university to close a school or department will usually provoke a storm of protest from students, professors, and assorted allies in similar programs elsewhere, resulting in much unfavorable publicity and even lawsuits.

None of the problems just mentioned justifies perpetuating programs that have truly outlived their usefulness. Yet anyone who believes that the number of programs that ought to be closed comes anywhere near to equaling the opportunities for useful new activities has not had much experience administering a university. Despite its burdens, growth is virtually inevitable. All that campus leaders can do is to keep from aggravating the problem by falling prey to the familiar errors and temptations that often lead to ill-conceived and wasteful ventures that divert time and effort from more important purposes.

THE FUNDAMENTAL ISSUE

The preceding discussion has confirmed the existence of a problem identified as a risk in chapter 1. Some of the essential aspects of academic institutions—in particular, the quality of the education they provide—are largely intangible and their results are difficult to measure. Without reliable means of estimating progress, effort tends to flag and attention turns to other things. The result is that much of what is most important to the work of colleges and universities may be neglected, undervalued, or laid aside in the pursuit of more visible goals. These tendencies are not inevitable; some institutions have done much better than others in avoiding them. In the end, the record of a university will depend on how clearly the president and trustees appreciate what is truly important and how consistently they maintain this vision, instead of succumbing to the glitter of conventional goals that often matter less than is generally believed to the genuine success of the institution.

CHAPTER THREE

THE GOVERNANCE OF NONPROFIT UNIVERSITIES

||||||||||||||||||||||||||||||||||||||||||||||||||||||||||||||||||||||||||||||||||||||||||||||||||||||

FEW CRITICS WITHIN OR OUTSIDE the academic world are satisfied with the way universities are governed. Even seasoned observers seem discouraged over existing procedures. According to a commission assembled by the Association of Governing Boards, "the current practice of shared governance leads to gridlock. Whether the problem is with presidents who lack the courage to lead an agenda for change, trustees who ignore institutional goals in favor of the football team, or faculty members who are loath to surrender the status quo, the fact is that each is an obstacle to progress."[1] In 2000, a distinguished gathering of current and former university leaders sounded an even more apocalyptic note: "universities are . . . facing a dilemma: to make a greater effort in adapting their decision process according to the requirements of the epoch or to be condemned to become obsolete and replaced by other forms of academic institutions."[2]

These appraisals are somber indeed. But are they accurate? How could they be if American universities have achieved such success and acquired such a high standing in the world?

In order to answer these questions, one must have in mind some notion of what a proper system of university governance needs to achieve in order to be successful. To begin with, such a system should be appropriately responsive to the various constituencies that have valuable knowledge and views to contribute or legitimate interests in how the institution functions. For example, students have an obvious interest in receiving a good education and having their talents and accomplishments fairly evaluated. Faculty members have a clear personal stake in all decisions affecting the content of education and the conditions and facilities needed for effective teaching and research. Academic leaders and trustees have responsibilities for administering the university and maintaining its financial viability that justify a central role in supervising the goals, plans, budgets, and policies of the institution. Finally, the public has a legitimate concern for the accessibility of universities, the tuitions they charge, the amounts of money they receive from taxpayer funds, and the contributions they make to the prosperity and well-being of their community, state, and nation.

To function properly, therefore, the process of decision making in universities must first of all provide an opportunity for the principal interested groups—the public, the faculty, the administrative staff, and the students—to have their views heard and their needs considered without allowing any of them to dominate the others or block needed reform. In addition, the system should work efficiently enough that decisions can be made in a timely manner that encourages, or at least allows, continuing improvement to occur in the quality of teaching, research, and other appropriate services while still ensuring the long-term viability of the institution. The current methods of governance must be judged with these objectives in mind.

THE FORMAL STRUCTURE OF GOVERNANCE

At first glance, the form of campus governance typically found in American universities seems appropriate enough for these purposes. Ultimate authority resides in a board of trustees that is normally appointed by the governor in the case of public universities or chosen by the alumni or the board itself in private institutions. Trustees choose presidents and remove them if necessary. They approve the budget. They also participate in discussions about the university's future plans while exercising ultimate supervisory power over the affairs of the institution.

The board of trustees provides a way to keep universities accountable, ensure capable leadership, and represent the needs of society. At the same time, since trustees do not live and work on campus, they must perforce delegate most of their powers to others. Responsibility for managing the administrative operations of the institution is left to the president assisted by a provost, a team of vice presidents and deans, and a growing army of staff specialists. In most nonprofit colleges and universities, authority over academic affairs, including professorial appointments, curriculum, criteria for admitting students, and research, rests largely in the hands of the faculty under some degree of oversight by the academic leadership—the president, the provost, and the deans.

In addition to the system of governance just described, public universities and colleges have further layers of supervision established by their state government to watch over their use of money, the quality of education they provide, and their contributions to the economy and the community. The special problems that this extra supervision creates are the subject of a separate section later in this chapter.

Described in this summary fashion, the governance structure seems quite straightforward and logical. In practice, however, the role and the influence of each of the principal actors differ significantly from what the formal system might suggest. To understand how the system actually works, one must have a clearer understanding of the strengths and weaknesses of the principal actors on campus and the informal ways in which they participate in the decision-making process.

TRUSTEES

Trustees bring various talents to their role at the top of the university hierarchy. Because they usually include successful individuals from a variety of careers, they have the collective capacity to reflect the interests of society in helping to guide the institution. Many of them are also more experienced than the president in matters of finance, construction, personnel, and the management of large organizations, and hence can offer useful advice on the administration and financing of the university. Individual trustees often give valuable counsel to the president and take leadership positions in helping to raise money for the institution.

At the same time, trustees are handicapped because they typically lack much experience in academic life and meet too infrequently to learn a great deal through their membership on the board. While some long-serving trustees manage to acquire considerable knowledge of the university, they must normally act discreetly behind the scenes and take pains to work through and with the president. When they try to intervene openly in appointment decisions or curricular matters, they can provoke determined opposition from the faculty with unfortunate results for the university. If they try to have influence by dealing directly with deans and professors or meeting privately with representatives of the athletic department, they can cause a lot of mischief.

In public universities, the usefulness of the board is frequently impaired by the way in which trustees are selected. In most states, members are appointed by the governor, sometimes with the help of recommendations from a panel of advisers. Although many public boards have had some extremely capable members, especially in matters of finance and dealings with state governments and other outside groups, governors often appoint persons with limited knowledge of higher education, such as campaign contributors or individuals recommended by political allies, labor unions, business organizations, and other prominent interest groups.* As a result, presidents are sometimes frustrated by

---

* According to a survey in 2007, less than 15 percent of public university trustees felt "very well prepared" for their duties, while 40 percent felt "not at all" or only "slightly" prepared. Mary Beth Marklein, "College Trustees Feel Unprepared," *USA Today* (May 11, 2007), p. A13.

board members who take up time with impractical proposals or argue excessively for the special constituencies they represent. At times, trustees try to interfere heavy-handedly in academic affairs, often with disruptive results. More often, they simply do not add a great deal to the progress of the institution.

Trustees of private universities have provoked fewer complaints. Their members are almost all alumni who are usually proud of the institution and united in their concern for its welfare. Particular trustees often become close advisers of the president and act both as a sounding board for new ideas and as a source of good advice. Yet private boards suffer from their own peculiar disadvantages. Because the members are almost always loyal to their alma mater, they do a good job of promoting its interests but perform less well at urging its leaders to pay attention to legitimate needs and concerns of the larger society. In addition, since service on the board often inspires trustees to give more money to the university, most private boards are deliberately well stocked with wealthy individuals. As universities are chronically short of funds, they can never have too many donors. Hence, private boards are frequently allowed to grow in size to thirty, forty, or even fifty members. Under these conditions, meetings can subtly change from serious occasions for discussing important issues to celebratory events filled with upbeat presentations to impress trustees in the hope of eliciting gifts.

ACADEMIC LEADERS

A century or more ago, presidents were the principal moving figures in bringing about major reforms in higher education. Charles W. Eliot of Harvard persuaded his faculty to abandon almost all undergraduate course requirements and thereby do away with the heavily prescribed classical curriculum that had been a fixture in American colleges for two centuries. President Daniel Coit Gilman of Johns Hopkins introduced the graduate school with its PhD degree, which has shaped the preparation of future faculty members from that time forward. David Starr Jordan, Andrew White, William Rainey Harper, and others played major roles in helping to create entire universities, such as Stanford, Cornell, and the University of Chicago.

It is often said that the era of academic giants has passed, and that the work of university presidents has changed so profoundly that they no longer have the capacity to initiate fundamental reforms or bring about major changes. In a widely cited study of academic leadership, Michael Cohen and James March went so far as to claim that "the college president is an executive who does not know exactly what he should be doing and does not have much confidence that he can do anything important anyway."[3] A look at the record, however, suggests that such descriptions are overdrawn. Several of the public universities in the California system have made remarkable strides in the past fifty years. The University of California, San Diego did not even exist half a century ago and is now numbered among the leading universities of the world. Private institutions such as New York University and the University of Southern California have risen in stature dramatically in the past twenty-five years, just as Stanford and Notre Dame did a generation earlier. While progress of this kind is always the work of many people, it is hard to believe that it could occur without able leadership. Similarly, dozens of other institutions that are not as visible as research universities—Arizona's Maricopa District with its ten community colleges, Alverno College, Elon College (now Elon University), to name just a few—have also made remarkable strides under the direction of gifted, energetic presidents.

In most instances, however, these advances occur in pursuit of traditional goals—increased resources, successful faculty recruitment, a more academically talented student body. Much rarer today are presidentially inspired innovations in education or research comparable to Eliot's mainly elective undergraduate curriculum or Gilman's creation of a research university. Sister Joel Read is responsible for a thoroughly innovative curriculum at Alverno College, and Kim Clark has imaginatively reorganized the entire educational program at Brigham Young–Idaho, but their accomplishments are exceptional.

Although dramatic, transformative changes seem less common today, it would be wrong to attribute the difference to some pervasive deficiency in the current crop of academic leaders. University presidents now face difficulties of a kind unknown to the legendary figures of yesteryear. They have far less power than their predecessors, who had no unions to contend with, little interference from their state legislature, not even tenure to shield recalcitrant professors from their wrath. Save in small colleges, presidents today also preside over much larger, more complicated institutions than those of a century ago. The duties of presidents have expanded accordingly. They are often expected not only to develop a vision for the university and persuade the faculty to accept it, but to raise huge sums of money; organize and supervise a staff that often runs to thousands of people; represent the institution before alumni, legislators, government agencies, and local officials; preside and speak at numerous ceremonial events; and resolve a never-ending cycle of crises great and small that crop up every year.

For many presidents, these burdens are heavy enough to rule out any chance of initiating major improvements in the quality of education or research. A survey by the American Council on Education to determine how presidents spend their day found that academic affairs ranked last in a set of six familiar types of activity.[4] Except in small colleges, presidents usually lack the time to engage in the study and reflection required to provide truly informed and innovative educational leadership. For this reason, presidents today tend to delegate most of the responsibility over academic affairs to provosts and deans. The result is paradoxical. Presidents are chosen from the ranks of teachers and scholars in order to provide intellectual leadership and gain the confidence and respect of the faculty. In actual practice, however, they have less and less time to spend on matters of education and research but must devote almost all of their attention to financial, administrative, and ceremonial tasks for which their past academic experience has scarcely prepared them.

Trustees have responded to this problem in several ways when they search for a president. While boards sometimes look outside academe and appoint corporate executives or lawyers to lead their institution, less than 20 percent of college presidents have had no previous faculty position.[5] Occasionally, choosing such a leader works well, especially for community colleges or comprehensive universities that emphasize vocational programs and have modest research ambitions. Even in these settings, however, presidents who come from law practice or business will often encounter heavy weather. Their lack of familiarity with higher education can easily cause their administrative efforts to founder for lack of sufficient feel for the peculiarities of campus environments. Since their background often lies in more hierarchical institutions, they may have limited patience for consultation and fail to win the trust of the faculty. Having little knowledge of education, they are unlikely to possess sound ideas about improving teaching or reforming the curriculum, thus weakening their capacity for creative leadership. Their lack of academic experience can often undermine their self-confidence and cause them to be weak and indecisive in addressing issues involving education or research.

Because of these risks, most boards respond by choosing a president who began academic life as a professor but has had years of administrative experience as a president, provost, or dean. By hiring such a person, trustees hope to gain the best of both worlds—someone who not only has firsthand knowledge of teaching and research but is one of the rare academics with a proven talent for leadership and administration.

While seeking such a president is an understandable way to proceed, it can often result in competent management rather than distinguished leadership. The candidate whom trustees tend to choose is someone who left teaching and research long ago to become a professional administrator, moving from one institution to the next as better opportunities presented themselves. Such individuals can balance the budget and manage the institution reasonably well, but they often lack vision or imaginative ideas about improving the quality of teaching and research. Instead, as one former president has put it, they "keep their heads low, avoid making waves, and polish their resumes for their next career stop."[6] Most of them serve for six years or less, a period too brief for the long, patient effort needed to bring about important academic reforms. Their duties leave little time for reading and thinking deeply about issues of teaching and research. As a result, their ambition for the institution often consists of conventional short-term goals such as higher SAT scores and increased fund-raising to satisfy the faculty, and a modest improvement in the rankings of *U.S. News & World Report* to please the trustees and alumni.

Despite the burdens of their office, presidents continue to occupy the best position to influence the direction of the university because they have the most comprehensive knowledge of the institution, the largest staff, and the powers of the purse and the bully pulpit at their disposal. In matters of administration, budgeting, planning, and construction, their voice carries more weight than any other. Nevertheless, most presidents have little direct control over the quality of teaching or the conduct of research, which depend primarily on the talent, interest, and commitment of professors. The influence that presidents can exert in these domains is often determined by the trust and respect they inspire in their faculty, sentiments that vary greatly according to the character and skill of the leader. To be sure, in community colleges and comprehensive universities, where most of those who teach are on short-term contracts, presidents and deans have greater power over the faculty because of their ability to replace instructors. Yet even in these institutions, faculty are often represented by unions that can resist presidents who behave autocratically.

In many universities, the influence of presidents is further limited because of their reluctance to make statements on academic issues that might seem controversial or raise questions about their own institution. In part, they may be worried that such pronouncements will provoke unwelcome publicity or expressions of disapproval that could disturb alumni, donors, or trustees. In research universities, presidents may be even more concerned not to risk giving offense to the faculty. Thus, a former executive head of the Association of American Universities, Robert Rosenzweig, in a book based on the reflections of former heads of research universities, expressed surprise to hear several interviewees remark that they had been afraid of their professors, and hence reluctant to risk their opposition. In the words of one of the ex-presidents, "We are frightened of the faculty and with good reason, because they can discharge us [by votes of no confidence] more readily than our boards."[7] When presidents feel inhibited by such concerns, they will often relinquish one of their most important leadership functions by refraining from identifying weaknesses in their academic programs and trying to mobilize faculty support to bring about improvement.

PROFESSORS

The third major center of influence in nonprofit four-year colleges and universities is the faculty. The influence of the faculty tends to vary depending on the nature of the institution. As a practical matter, regardless of the formal organization, ultimate power resides with those who are most difficult to replace. In research universities, therefore, where the reputation and the quality of the institution depend on the distinction of its professors, the faculty hold the greatest power, at least when they are exercised enough about a policy or issue to act together. In comprehensive universities and community colleges, however, the faculty tend to have less power unless they are represented by a well-organized and effective union.

Collectively, professors possess the most intimate, up-to-date knowledge of education and research. In administering their departments, they generally work conscientiously and effectively in searching for new faculty recruits and deciding which younger colleagues should be promoted to tenure. At the faculty-wide level, however, though their support is essential to the adoption of a new curriculum or a change in instructional methods, their ability to formulate such changes is often limited. For one thing, they are generally too immersed in their separate disciplines and departments to appreciate the needs of the college as a whole or to pay attention to the growing body of research about teaching and learning. In addition, being heavily preoccupied with their research and classroom duties, they are often reluctant to support reforms that would disrupt familiar routines and take a lot of time to implement.

When asked to participate in university-wide planning, professors are further handicapped by insufficient knowledge of the administrative and financial limits that help to define what is possible. Moreover, although they are competent enough in dealing with the affairs of their department, they are much less capable of agreeing on priorities for the entire institution. When asked to do so, they often arrive at solutions that offer something to every department and interest group while avoiding controversial judgments about the relative merits of particular units and programs.

Professors everywhere report longer workweeks and added pressures on their schedule that further limit their capacity to participate actively in addressing governance issues beyond the affairs of their own department.[8] In response to this problem, most nonprofit universities have created institution-wide academic senates to attract professors who have the time and interest to familiarize themselves with the workings of the university and with issues broader than their own special field of expertise.

Unfortunately, while some senates do useful work and provide a faculty perspective on important academic problems, they are often a disappointment. Too much of their time tends to be taken up by issues such as parking, athletics, or the academic calendar rather than larger questions of institutional direction. As a result, they frequently fail to enlist many of the most admired, influential members of the faculty but attract professors who agree to serve because they have become less absorbed by their teaching and research. Those who answer to this description seldom command the highest respect among their colleagues and often lack the prestige to speak authoritatively for the faculty or to contribute effectively to the direction of the institution.

Students

Students are the fourth important body within colleges and universities capable of having an effect on policy. They are seldom able to exert much influence through the formal structure of governance, although they may have token representation on university committees or even boards of trustees. As a practical matter, however, they have informal ways of exerting a significant effect on decisions affecting their lives.

As undergraduates demonstrated so vividly in the 1960s, they can be a potent force for change when they become sufficiently aroused. Although their demonstrations and building occupations during that period were chiefly directed at external issues such as ending the war in Vietnam or boycotting goods of companies that mistreated their workers, they also brought pressure to bear to force universities to admit more minority applicants, hire more minority professors, and create programs and departments in subjects such as women's studies or Latino and African American studies. More recently, undergraduates in public universities have occasionally protested against policies such as large tuition increases, reductions in financial aid, or serious overcrowding. In most cases, however, their efforts have been aimed at legislators and public officials rather than university leaders.

The influence of students on academic affairs has its most substantial effect through the choices young people make about which colleges to attend and which undergraduate majors to pursue. As student preferences shifted markedly in favor of coeducation in the 1960s and early 1970s, the number of applications to single-sex colleges plummeted and ultimately forced many of these institutions to begin admitting both men and women. Growing student concern about finding good jobs produced a swing toward vocational majors in the 1970s and 1980s, while stiff competition for the brightest applicants led many selective colleges to spend heavily on improved student services, better dorms rooms, and other amenities in the 1990s.

Students can also exert a subtle influence once they begin their studies. Their resistance to campus rules and regulations effectively put an end to *in loco parentis* policies in the 1960s and led to less prescriptive curricula thereafter. College authorities abandoned parietal rules and agreed to previously unheard-of changes in living arrangements, such as coed dormitories and even unisex bathrooms. In subsequent decades, increasing numbers of undergraduates have taken part-time jobs to earn the money to stay in school while also devoting more time and attention to extracurricular activities, computer games, and other forms of entertainment. To accommodate these pursuits, they have exerted a quiet pressure for easier grading and less homework. Because of their extensive freedom to choose which courses to take and their power to pass judgment on their instructors through published course evaluations, they have had some success in realizing their desires. Over the past forty years, the time undergraduates spend on homework has markedly diminished while the grades they receive have gradually risen.[9]

The preceding discussion makes clear that all of the parties with an interest in the work of universities have at least some opportunity to make their feelings known and have a tangible impact. Yet each group has limitations and self-serving interests as well as valuable perspectives to contribute. Under such circumstances, the results of their interaction are uncertain. Depending on the issue involved, the positions of each interested group can complement or conflict with the views of others. Together, such an ensemble can produce either a symphony or a cacophony of clashing sounds and cadences. Where the results actually fall between these polar extremes is the subject of the following section.

THE SYSTEM IN PRACTICE

Observing the practice of governance, one can readily point to individual colleges and universities where the system is not working well according to the criteria mentioned at the beginning of the chapter. There are universities in which decision making is dominated by a forceful president who acts with scant regard for the views of faculty and students and sees to it that the board is stacked with like-minded, supportive trustees. There are other universities in which strong faculty unions and faculty senates block needed reforms and insist on self-serving employment policies. Yet failures of this kind occur in every system of governance. They do not prove that the system as a whole has flaws sufficient to justify major reform. To determine whether drastic change is needed, one must look more closely at the available evidence. Two aspects of governance, in particular, have been controversial enough to warrant such careful scrutiny: shared governance and the methods of state supervision.

SHARED GOVERNANCE

In colleges and universities with a large complement of full-time faculty and a substantial commitment to research, both faculty and administration need to play an important part in university governance. Each has vital interests in the conduct of university affairs, and each has valuable knowledge and perspectives to offer that can improve the quality of decisions. Presidents and provosts have a unique vantage point from which to see the institution whole and understand the needs, the dangers, and the opportunities that the outside world presents. They have a better grasp than the faculty of the resources available to pay for current operations and exploit new opportunities. With the aid of their staff, they have a greater capacity to analyze costs, identify inefficiencies and waste that require attention, and assess the possibilities for raising additional financial resources. Finally, because they do not belong to any department or faculty, presidents and provosts are in a better position than anyone else to weigh competing needs objectively and establish appropriate priorities.

Professors, on the other hand, understand far more than the central office does about their various fields of study. No president or provost is likely to know how best to teach string theory or comparative government or Elizabethan drama. The faculty also have a greater knowledge of the specific needs and opportunities within the different departments and a better sense of the effects that changes in staffing, library resources, support services, and the like can have on the quality of teaching and research. Moreover, although some presidents would disagree, experience suggests that professors frequently have a clearer appreciation of academic values than the top leadership and are less tempted to sacrifice these principles to raise more money or gain a competitive advantage.

For issues of genuine importance in which both faculty and academic leaders have significant competence, shared participation can improve university governance rather than impede it. It can also raise morale and help to mobilize support for the programs of the university. Leaders have to believe in the activities of the institution in order to explain them and defend them to donors, alumni, and other interested groups. Faculty members need to have confidence in what the university is doing if they are to implement its policies conscientiously. Both academic leaders and their faculties are more likely to support the institution's policies and practices if they have had a role in shaping them.*

My views about the value of shared governance were influenced by close observation of two separate efforts at Harvard University to reform the undergraduate curriculum. The first of these reviews took place in the 1970s when Dean Henry Rosovsky launched a wide-ranging study of undergraduate education, which had existed without substantial change for many years.[10] As is usual on such occasions, the focal point of the review was the general education portion of the curriculum and its course requirements that all students had to fulfill.

The process used would have struck outsiders as extremely cumbersome. Dean Rosovsky began by issuing a twenty-two-page letter to the faculty in October 1973, listing weaknesses in the undergraduate program that justified a review. Having considered dozens of responses to the letter, he devoted his annual report in 1976 to reflections on the characteristics of an educated person. After receiving more reactions and talking with individual faculty members, he appointed seven separate task forces, each with one or two student members, to review different aspects of the undergraduate program from admissions procedures and criteria to concentrations (or majors).

In January 1977, the task force on general education issued its first report suggesting a new approach built around eight intellectual goals. The report was then subjected to prolonged discussion with the faculty in a variety of settings— informal gatherings, department meetings, open sessions, and other groupings large and small. Gradually, the recommended structure was altered to reflect opinions and arguments expressed in the meetings. Thereafter, the amended report was debated by the full faculty, and the general approach was approved.

Eight subcommittees were then created to draft the detailed criteria that courses for each required group would have to satisfy. The general education committee as a whole then deliberated and set forth its criteria in a thirty-five-page report submitted to the faculty in January 1978. During the months

---

*Large for-profit universities admittedly do not practice much shared governance, yet they are the fastest-growing institutions in all higher education. But for-profits do work closely on academic matters with a small cadre of full-time faculty. Moreover, they differ from most nonprofits in ways that make shared governance much less necessary. Their courses are almost all vocational in nature and hence are easier for a central office to create by consulting closely with industry representatives. Their faculties are largely composed of part-time instructors whose principal job is in a company and who give a course in their spare time because they enjoy teaching or welcome the chance to earn some extra money. Such individuals do not have nearly the same personal stake in the institution or the same interest in shaping its educational program and course content as full-time professors in a four-year college. Nor do they possess the advanced knowledge acquired through years of specialized training that makes professors indispensable participants in the development and administration of most college courses.

that followed, the faculty discussed the report in a series of meetings where extended debates took place over such issues as whether the proposed requirements would discourage able students from applying to Harvard or whether anything of lasting value about science could be taught to nonscientists in two semester-long courses. Eventually, after many hours of discussion and various minor amendments and clarifications, a final vote was taken and the new curriculum passed by a vote of 182–65.

The procedure just described will strike some readers as byzantine. Nevertheless, the many discussions in gatherings large and small accomplished several things. The faculty gradually came to feel that the curriculum was *their* curriculum, which they had played a part in making, rather than the product of a small blue-ribbon committee to which they had dutifully given their assent. Individual members came to appreciate more clearly the common educational goals to which their individual courses could contribute. Along the way, they acquired a greater concern for undergraduate education, a crucial shift after several decades in which faculty interest and effort had swung perceptibly toward doctoral training and research.

The principal benefit of the process was a burst of faculty energy and participatory zeal in creating courses for the new core curriculum. A report compiled two years later revealed that over one hundred new or heavily revised courses had been prepared and approved. More than 80 percent of them were created and taught by tenured members of the faculty, many of whom had not been significantly engaged in teaching undergraduates during the years prior to the new curriculum. By 1981, the core courses were attracting 50 percent more enrollments than the required number, as many students chose to take additional offerings from the new curriculum as electives.

Over the next three decades, the initial energy slowly diminished, and the shared appreciation of common purposes gradually dimmed as more and more members of the founding faculty retired and were replaced by new scholars who had had no part in planning the curriculum. But for a generation, at least, undergraduate education received an infusion of energy and creativity from which it benefited greatly.

While the faculty had to decide ultimately whether to adopt the new curriculum, the administration made several contributions essential to the final result. It was Dean Rosovsky, first of all, who was willing to speak openly and frankly about the state of undergraduate education and persuade the faculty that a full-scale review was needed. He then played a critical role in organizing the highly participatory process that followed. In particular, he was responsible for choosing the faculty members for the key committees and persuading them to devote the necessary time to the task. Through his efforts, those who played the leading roles were among the most accomplished and respected scholars in the faculty. Their presence and dedication throughout the long sequence of meetings and debates lent a sense of importance and legitimacy to the process that helped not only to improve the result but to enlist the energy of the faculty in implementing the new curriculum.

Almost three decades later, I returned unexpectedly for fifteen months as interim president while the governing boards searched for a new leader to succeed Lawrence Summers. By coincidence, when I began this assignment, the faculty had just spent two years reviewing the general education curriculum in an effort to make improvements. On this occasion, however, the initial committee report and recommendations had elicited scant enthusiasm and more than a little frustration. Rather than let the process die, I decided to appoint another committee and try to produce a new curriculum by the end of the academic year, when a new president would take office.

In contrast to the first review, which came early in my initial term as president, I had now given considerable time and thought to undergraduate education and had even published a book on the subject shortly before being called back to office. Much of what I wrote was quite critical of the current state of college curricula. Among other weaknesses, I pointed to the questionable rationale for many familiar curricular requirements and the curious lack of attention paid by most college faculties to the large body of empirical research on teaching and learning. The initial curriculum report I had reviewed seemed to reflect both these weaknesses. Through several informal meetings and exchanges with the new curriculum committee, I was able to communicate my thoughts to the members, while respecting their independence in making recommendations for change.

After an exceptional effort on the part of the committee to draft a report and conduct informal meetings with numerous groups of professors, the full faculty debated the new proposals. At times, the discussions seemed endless. More than once, I was reminded of Morris Udall's remarks about congressional debates: "Everything has been said but not everyone has said it."[11] In the end, however, the faculty voted and passed the new curriculum by a large majority. Because of the limited time available, not all the important issues of undergraduate education could be considered. Just as before, however, the many informal discussions and lengthy faculty debates unleashed much energy on the part of scores of professors to produce new courses to fit the criteria they had just approved.

The second review convinced me of a further point about the practice of shared governance in matters of educational policy. The faculty, of course, had to approve and take ownership of any new curriculum, not merely because they were the acknowledged experts in the subjects to be taught but also because they had to feel that the curriculum was their creation in order to muster the effort and enthusiasm to make it a success. With very few exceptions, however, faculty members were not conversant with the growing body of literature on undergraduate education. Even the committee I appointed to make recommendations had more than enough to do without spending hours wading through the many published essays on the competing theories of general education.

This situation is likely to exist in almost every major review of the undergraduate curriculum. Yet some means is surely needed to ensure that review committees are made aware of the relevant empirical studies and other thoughtful writings so that the final product will not be entirely based on the personal views and experiences of individual professors. This task seems one that the administration is in the best position to perform while still leaving the outcome firmly in the hands of the faculty.

There are other issues in the university in which the ultimate decision should properly rest with the leadership rather than the faculty, either because the administration and trustees know more about the subject, or because they are more disinterested, or—in the case of important issues involving money— simply because the trustees are legally charged with ultimate responsibility for the financial health of the institution. Questions involving the final approval of budgets and the allocation of funds among different faculties are prominent examples. Even here, however, some form of consultation is often useful, both to build greater trust on the part of the faculty and to take advantage of particular kinds of faculty expertise.

Another example from my own experience illustrates the point. In deciding every year how much money from the endowment should be spent the following year for current activities, I asked each of the deans of Law, Business, and Arts and Sciences to nominate a professor with special knowledge of investments and finance to sit with myself, the treasurer, and the vice president for financial affairs to discuss an appropriate recommendation to forward to the governing boards. This procedure helped to maintain the confidence of the faculty, especially during the 1970s when rapid inflation and a sluggish stock market made it all but impossible either to sustain the real value of the endowment or to avoid a gradual erosion of faculty salaries. Even more important, the advice of the faculty experts proved to be very helpful in making complex judgments about endowment spending during those difficult and uncertain economic times.

In the end, final responsibility for deciding issues of importance must reside somewhere, either with the faculty or with the administration. Each side is capable of mistakes. University administrations are largely responsible for the scandals and excesses of big-time intercollegiate athletics. On the other hand, many faculties were pressured by students into unwise decisions during the heated protests of the late 1960s. Errors of judgment of this kind are bound to occur under any system. They are less likely to happen, however, when the decision-makers are willing at least to listen to the views of others who have an interest in the subject and the knowledge and experience to improve the outcome.

In practice, of course, there is no guarantee that the faculty and administration will cooperate effectively. In fact, there are differences in outlook that suggest they may frequently disagree. For example, members of the administration are acutely concerned with the financial health of the institution. When resources are strained, they are often inclined to initiate such cost-saving measures as hiring freezes and the closure of nonessential programs. They may also try to enhance the institution's visibility and improve its bottom line by strengthening its athletic programs, aggressively pursuing commercialization of research, and launching new ventures that could earn a surplus to ease budgetary pressures. Faculty members often take a dim view of these initiatives. They are more likely to support efforts to strengthen graduate programs and hire additional professors while preferring vigorous fund-raising and a smaller bureaucracy to cutbacks in academic programs. They may also be reluctant to support attempts by a forward-looking administration to expand online education or institute other reforms that threaten to change the way they teach or force them to offer courses outside their area of special expertise.

There is no reason to regret such disagreements; if none existed, there would be no need for shared governance. When the collaboration works well, the differences can be settled amicably, and the results will be improved as each side helps to counteract the errors and excesses of the other. At the same time, the divisions of opinion create abundant opportunities for controversy and stalemate, especially when relationships are clouded by suspicion and distrust.

If one listens to what commentators say about shared governance, one can easily gain the impression that disagreement is the rule and that the system is working very badly. Professors who write about the subject regularly insist that faculty views are frequently ignored and that greater participation is urgently needed.[12] On the other hand, former university presidents who comment on governance often assert that having to consult endlessly with faculty committees in search of a consensus delays important decisions and prevents the leadership from moving rapidly enough to respond to emerging opportunities and problems.[13] In short, as Jack Schuster and Martin Finkelstein observe in their massive study of the academic profession, "almost no one is pleased with the way campuses are governed: not the faculty, not administrators, not governing boards."[14]

Despite the grumbling, closer scrutiny suggests that shared governance has worked better than many of its critics would allow. To begin with, notwithstanding the complaints of some professors, large majorities of all of the various interested groups believe that faculties do exert *some* influence in the conduct of university affairs. Sixty-three percent of faculty members agree on this point, as do more than 80 percent of top administrators and faculty representatives who serve on governance bodies.[15]

These overall responses mask substantial differences depending on whom one asks and what kinds of decisions one is talking about. Well over two-thirds of all the interested parties agree that the faculty has either decisive power or joint decision-making responsibility over such matters as faculty appointments and promotions, curriculum, and the choice of which degrees the institution should offer.[16] At the same time, only about one-third and often many fewer of the faculty answer the same way about decisions involving appointing deans, setting faculty salaries, approving budgets, or authorizing construction projects.[17]

There is a logic to these differences. In view of their superior knowledge, it is only natural that professors have great influence in deciding on curricular requirements or evaluating the qualifications of prospective faculty members. It is also understandable that faculties tend to have much less say about matters on which they are not well informed, such as administering construction projects, or about subjects in which they have personal interests too strong to guarantee objective judgment, such as setting their own salaries or deciding how many faculty positions should be allocated to their department.

There are also persistent and substantial differences between the estimates of administrators and professors concerning the amount of influence exerted by the faculty. Although large majorities of both groups feel that the faculty has at least *some* influence in campus affairs, 65 percent of top administrators believe that the faculty has "a great deal of say" in institutional affairs, while only 17 percent of the faculty agree.[18] Looking further, however, one discovers much smaller differences on this point between top administrators and professors who actually participate in governance by serving on policy committees or as members of university senates.[19] Apparently, then, firsthand observation reveals a good deal more faculty influence than is apparent to more distant spectators. Such differences of opinion as remain between faculty representatives and top administrators probably reflect the fact that administrators are aware of the degree to which they take faculty views into account in formulating proposals for discussion, while faculty representatives see only the proposals themselves and gauge their influence by the extent to which the administration agrees to additional changes as a result of joint discussion.

Finally, professors in small institutions consistently have a more favorable view of faculty influence than those who teach in large universities. Thus, while

39 percent of professors in baccalaureate colleges (that grant only the BA degree) believe that their faculty has "a great deal of say" in the affairs of the institution, only 13 percent of their counterparts in research universities agree.[20] Much of this difference probably results from the fact that among baccalaureate colleges there are many small liberal arts institutions in which professors are much more likely to be personally involved in campus governance or to have close friends and colleagues who are active participants. As a result, their views lie closer to those of their faculty representatives who are directly engaged in the work of campus governance bodies.

Has faculty influence in the governance process increased or diminished over the past several decades? According to Schuster and Finkelstein, faculty surveys from 1969 to 1997 suggest some decline in the proportion of faculty members who believe that they personally have some influence over the affairs of their institution.[21] More informative, however, is a comparison of responses to national surveys of professors in 1970 and 2001 containing a common set of questions about the extent of faculty participation in campus governance. These surveys clearly suggest that the influence of faculty has *increased* substantially in most important decision-making areas. The 2001 survey also found that among both top administrators and faculty representatives, the percentages of those who felt that faculty influence had increased over the preceding twenty years far exceeded the percentages who felt it had declined.[22]

There is a plausible reason why professors have become less likely to feel involved in governance while still believing that faculty participation has increased. Most faculties have grown larger so that the fraction of professors actively participating in governance activities has presumably diminished. Quite naturally, then, smaller percentages of the faculty feel a sense of personal influence over campus affairs. The changes in the impressions of the faculty and their representatives from 1970 to 2001 probably convey a much more

Percentage of Professors Believing That Faculty Decide or Jointly Participate in Deciding Selected Issues

Issue	1970	2001
Appointment of full-time faculty	30.6%	72.8%
Promotions to tenure	35.1%	68.1%
Curriculum	83%	90.7%
Average teaching load	24%	38.6%
Appointing academic deans	13.3%	29.7%
Setting faculty salary scales	5.1%	19.1%
Size of faculty in different disciplines	9.0%	33.2%

Gabriel Kaplan, "How Academic Ships Actually Navigate," in Ronald G. Ehrenberg, *Governing Academia* (2004), pp. 165, 200.

accurate view of the changes that have actually occurred in their role in the university.

Perhaps most revealing for our purposes is how different groups regard the quality of relations between the faculty and the administration. Sixty-two percent of top administrators see relationships as "cooperative," while another 35 percent regard them as having some conflict but nevertheless collegial.[23] Only 2.9 percent of these administrators consider relations to be "suspicious and adversarial."[24] Faculty representatives are a bit less sanguine. Only 47 percent judge relationships to be "cooperative."[25] Still, only 9.3 percent would characterize them as "suspicious and adversarial," with the remainder describing them as sometimes conflictual but still collegial.[26] On the other hand, 19 percent of the entire faculty indicate that "the faculty [in their institution] is typically at odds with the administration."[27]

Once again, relations in baccalaureate colleges are viewed more positively by professors and their representatives than relationships in comprehensive and research universities. And, just as before, administrators have a more favorable impression than faculty representatives, although majorities of both groups seem to feel that relations are getting better.*

Administrators and faculty representatives would seem to have the most accurate sense of the condition of shared governance, since they are clearly the best informed and have the most detailed, firsthand perception of how the system actually works. Thus, it is encouraging that fewer than 10 percent of either group believe that relations have fallen into serious disrepair. More troubling is the finding that only a minority of all faculty members (42 percent) agree with the direction their institution is taking "all or most of the time."[28] It is also worrisome that rank-and-file professors are so much less inclined to feel that the faculty has significant influence in campus affairs. These findings suggest either that faculty representatives are not communicating effectively with the rest of their colleagues or that the rank-and-file professors are paying little attention to what their representatives tell them about campus governance.

In the end, it is difficult to accept the view of trustees and former presidents who claim that the system is dysfunctional and that faculty participation should diminish. Professors have such obvious interests in the internal affairs of universities, and their support for decisions affecting teaching and research is so essential to success, that there is no real alternative to shared governance. While faculty representatives can move slowly, it is hard to identify important developments affecting higher education today that are proceeding with such speed as to preclude meaningful consultation. Moreover, giving greater power

---

* The *Chronicle of Higher Education* (October 11, 2013), p. A25. See also, William K. Cummings and Martin J. Finkelstein, *Scholars in the Changing American Academy* (2012), p. 118.

to academic leaders to act unilaterally can also lead to mistakes that might be averted through prior discussion with the faculty. It is executive authority, after all, not shared governance, that was primarily responsible for such debacles as the well-known excesses of big-time college athletics and the costly failure of for-profit Internet ventures undertaken by several prominent universities around the beginning of this century.

However authority is divided, shared governance is unlikely to succeed where mutual trust is low and consultation tends to be contentious and frustrating to faculty members and academic leaders alike. On most campuses, fortunately, the process need not descend to this level if the parties involved try hard enough to make it succeed. When presidents and members of the faculty work together to ensure that governance bodies spend their time on substantive discussions of important issues, respected and responsible colleagues will usually participate. When they do, consultation will normally yield sensible decisions, provided the administration takes care to marshal adequate facts and arguments to support its recommendations.

Apparently, most universities do manage to make shared governance work. Otherwise, one would suppose that much larger percentages of the participants would regard the relations between administrators and faculties as hostile and at loggerheads. Instead, the available evidence suggests that neither the complaints of professor-critics about the lack of faculty influence nor the concerns about endless gridlock expressed by some trustees and former presidents are well founded. As Gabriel Kaplan puts it in concluding his comprehensive survey of governance:

> Despite much current concern among both faculty and observers of higher education about the state of shared governance, the data collected here depict an image neither as cumbersome and unloved as some critics seem to believe nor as threatened or supplanted as some advocates seem to fear. Faculty seem to have a significant role in governance in many institutions, and their participation appears to be valued. Few administrators suggested that faculty participation presented a significant obstacle to effective governance.[29]

STATE OVERSIGHT

Not all decision making takes place within the college or university. Government officials, especially at the state level, play an important role in guiding and supervising public institutions. No wonder. Public universities receive large amounts of taxpayer money from their state; they have an important impact on local economies; and they affect the educational opportunities provided to the state population through the tuitions they charge, the financial aid they supply, and the quality of instruction they offer.

Not surprisingly, the nature of government supervision has evolved as public universities have grown larger and their activities have come to matter more to more people. Until well into the nineteenth century, most states interfered very little in campus affairs. From then on, however, oversight gradually increased. Today, state governments set limits on tuitions and approve annual budgets, sometimes line by line. Most states have also established system-wide governing boards or coordinating bodies of some sort to review the plans of member universities and decide whether new programs are needed and which campuses should supply them.[30]

The extent of supervision varies widely from one state to another. Some universities, such as those in Michigan and California, have been granted autonomy by law to protect them from political meddling in routine management decisions. Other states supervise the administration of their universities more closely and require advance approval for all manner of expenditures, minor changes in the budget, and other management decisions.

During the past thirty years, most states have made a serious effort to make their universities more accountable for results. For a time, many legislatures experimented with performance-budgeting schemes in which a portion of annual appropriations would be allocated among campuses according to their success in fulfilling a variety of prescribed results.[31] Within a few years, however, these efforts faded as the recession of 2000–2001 left states without enough revenue to fund the program, and efforts to develop reliable outcome measures proved more difficult than lawmakers had anticipated.

In recent years, a number of states have shown renewed interest in the record of universities in matters such as access for state residents, graduation rates, and research grants received. In many cases efforts to improve performance have amounted to little more than requiring a detailed reporting of results, such as the number of students who enroll and graduate, the employment of recent graduates, and the patents obtained from campus research. Increasingly, however, states have begun once again to use appropriations to induce universities to achieve public goals, such as raising graduation rates.*

There are inherent differences in priorities and methods that often make state supervision contentious and irritating to the parties involved. The very

* For an excellent analysis of performance funding, see Kevin J. Dougherty and Vikash Reddy, "The Impacts of State Performing Systems on Higher Education Institutions," Community College Research Center, Working Paper No. 37 (December, 2011).

existence of another layer of supervision, on top of the oversight provided by the campus board of trustees and the consultations required by shared governance, can easily make the process of administering a public university very cumbersome. As Clark Kerr and Marian Gade described the situation in their book on boards of trustees:

> The increasing number of groups or power blocs, both inside and outside the institution, that can veto any important action has multiplied rapidly in recent years. . . . The results of all this are that fewer decisions can be made because of more veto power; that those decisions that can be made are made more slowly due to extensive consultation and confrontation; that there is less of a central vision for the institution and more of a congeries of competing visions.[32]

Relations between campus representatives and state officials can also be contentious because of persistent differences in the values and priorities of the two groups. State officials tend to be chiefly interested in broad access to universities for state residents, low tuitions, improvements in the quality of undergraduate education, and, more recently, stronger research and vocational programs that help to stimulate the local economy. University officials are likely to be more concerned with raising revenues by setting higher tuitions and admitting additional out-of-state students (who can be charged more), strengthening graduate education and research in all fields (not just those affecting economic growth), and attracting talented faculty and students who will enhance the reputation of their institution. The tensions inherent in these differing priorities can easily cause frustration, especially in states where campus representatives feel better educated and informed than the state employees who supervise them.

These strains have been exacerbated in recent years by the special nature of universities and their financing. Unlike public schools, prisons, and other programs that depend on state support, universities can raise funds from alternative sources, such as tuition, research grants, and private gifts. Since legislators are well aware of this fact, public universities tend to lose out when times are tough and they have to compete with other programs for shrinking government resources.

Since 1980, state officials have been hard-pressed by mounting demands on their treasuries from primary and secondary education and the burgeoning cost of Medicaid and prisons, to name just a few prominent examples. These competing demands have caused lawmakers to grant higher education a steadily diminishing share of state appropriations—from 9.8 percent in 1980 to 6.9 percent in 2000.[33] The recession of 2008 has led to even more drastic cuts in state appropriations. By 2009, the share of public university revenues coming from the state had declined from 32 percent in 1980 to just 18 percent. In the aftermath of the recession of 2008, the reductions have become serious enough to raise widespread concerns about the future of public higher education and the ability of its flagship universities to keep pace with the leading private research institutions.

There are also inherent differences between the kind of funding that academic institutions need and what a state government is able to deliver. Universities require a steady, reliable growth of support in order to plan and keep up with the mounting costs of their operations. State tax revenues, however, fluctuate with the economy, creating a boom-and-bust environment in which public universities move rapidly from periods of ample funding in good times to periods of retrenchment when the economy falters, tax revenues decline, and appropriations must be cut. Such fluctuations make it difficult for academic officials to plan, or even to maintain, their programs of education and research.

In recent years, the combination of rapidly declining state support and more intrusive government oversight has predictably been the source of great concern to many academic leaders and caused them to seek changes in the relationship between public universities and their state governments. A number of possibilities have emerged. The most extreme reform is essentially to get rid of state supervision altogether by privatizing all or parts of a state university. This idea has already been carried to fruition in Virginia through an agreement between state officials and the schools of business and law at the flagship university in Charlottesville.[34] Under the new arrangement, the two professional schools have agreed to forgo any state funding in return for freedom to set their own tuition, admit more nonresident students, and escape state supervision over their internal affairs.

While this solution has benefits for both sides, privatization is likely to work well only for schools and universities with a sufficient reputation to allow them to boost tuitions significantly, attract out-of-state students, and raise substantial sums from other sources, notably private gifts and federal and corporate research grants. Once freed from legislative control, these universities are likely to admit more students from outside the state and fewer from within. Some state residents may no longer be able to afford the higher tuitions that the newly independent institutions charge and may not be offered enough financial aid to allow them to enroll. More generally, once state universities are essentially privatized, they may not feel as much responsibility as they previously did do to render a variety of other services to the public.

James Garland, former president of Miami University of Ohio, has suggested a more radical plan to give all public colleges and universities greater power over their own affairs. He proposes that state governments phase out the direct subsidies they give to universities and relinquish all power to approve their budgets, supervise their operations, and limit their tuitions. Instead, states would maintain levels of support similar to those previously given to institutions but give the funds to students in the form of scholarships shaped to further the governments goals and priorities. Individual campuses would no longer receive money directly from the state but would be free to set their own tuitions, determine their own budgets, and carry on their chosen activities subject to the overall authority of their own separate boards of trustees.[35]

This sweeping reform offers several advantages. It would neither increase nor diminish state funding, which would continue to be determined by the legislature. But states would be able to spend their money more efficiently. No longer would they use it to subsidize rich and poor students alike by requiring that public tuitions be fixed at an unnaturally low level. Instead, colleges would set their own tuitions, and the legislature could tailor all of its scholarship funds to further its policy objectives, whether by granting generous financial aid to needy students to increase opportunity, by giving larger amounts to students entering programs that will promote economic growth, or by adjusting the terms of the scholarships to achieve some other government priority.

Meanwhile, colleges and universities would be freed from cumbersome, bureaucratic controls over their budgets and current operations. They would gain the power to chart their own course and set their own priorities while being held accountable for the results by market forces. Competition would keep campus officials from charging excessive tuitions or instituting unnecessary programs and force them to work at satisfying the needs of students and other constituency groups.[36] The threat of bankruptcy would be the ultimate discipline to prevent extravagance and waste.

The advantages of this proposal are real. The success achieved by many private colleges and universities suggests that campuses can operate with substantial freedom from government control and consistently provide high-quality education and research. Using the state's resources to fund scholarships rather than subsidizing universities directly to keep tuitions low would certainly allow a more efficient use of public money. The ability of state lawmakers to shape the scholarships to fit the government's priorities provides an additional means to induce colleges and universities to complete vigorously for in-state students while paying close and continuing attention to public needs.

Notwithstanding these attractive features, such a radical change in the funding of higher education is not without risk. Would states maintain traditional levels of funding if their role were restricted to providing scholarships? Is the threat of bankruptcy a realistic deterrent against unwise and profligate behavior? (Would a state ever allow one of its major universities to close its doors and cease operations?) If all state support took the form of scholarship aid, would community colleges be able to find the resources to provide a quality education for students who often come poorly prepared for college work? Could legislators count on campus authorities to expand to accommodate growing student populations and satisfy emerging needs such as a demand for a new medical school or a school of engineering?

Perhaps public colleges and universities, free of state control, would meet all these challenges successfully and do so more effectively than the system now in place. Still, it is difficult to be entirely sure. As a result, Garland's proposal may suffer the fate of many bold, imaginative schemes for social reform. On paper, the proposal may seem to hold much promise. In practice, however, such a drastic change carries the risk of unintended consequences that could be hard to remedy once they occur. That danger, coupled with the likely reluctance of state officials to give up power and the resistance of others who benefit from the status quo, seems great enough to dim the chances of instituting such a bold proposal any time soon.

A third possibility is to guarantee a fixed level of state support while freeing public colleges and universities from detailed state controls in exchange for a commitment to fulfill a series of minimum outcome requirements, such as graduating a certain number of students each year from colleges and professional schools and enrolling stipulated numbers of freshmen, including agreed-on percentages of lower-income applicants. Virginia adopted this approach in 2005 by granting several of its universities greater freedom from government controls on purchasing and construction in return for a pledge to hold down tuition for state residents and meet prescribed goals for student retention and graduation. Since this scheme was adopted, the agreed-on goals have been elaborated to include twelve performance targets covering everything from enrollment and graduation goals to external research funding and technology transfer efforts, the completion of articulation agreements with community colleges, and even specific campus measures to promote student safety.[37]

Such an arrangement can help to avoid excessively burdensome oversight. The problem is to reach agreement on a satisfactory set of university goals, which are often hard to specify given the intangible nature of many outcomes of potential interest to state officials. Politically, it may also be difficult to impose financial consequences on universities that fail to meet their performance goals, especially when state funding for all public colleges and universities is declining.

For state governments that are unwilling to introduce any of the innovative schemes just described, there is much to be said for at least simplifying decision making by devolving authority to the lowest level capable of making responsible decisions. Such a policy would involve strengthening campus boards and giving each university more power to manage its own affairs, subject to the right of higher levels of authority to monitor performance, approve tuition levels, and continue taking steps to prevent wasteful duplication of programs and determine how much money to appropriate to the various units in the system.

Modest changes of this kind would still subject public universities to the constant fluctuations of state finances and to government control over tuition and major expenditures. But public officials could at least remove some of the more onerous forms of state supervision, and refrain from meddling in matters such as curriculum and faculty workloads. Since analysts have found no evidence that the methods of state oversight have any significant effect on university performance, such a change might lessen the burden on university officials without much risk of adverse consequences.[38]

ARE MORE FUNDAMENTAL REFORMS NEEDED?

The evidence to date strongly suggests that the familiar complaints about the prevailing system of campus governance are exaggerated. Relations between faculty and administration do not appear to be nearly as subject to acrimonious breakdowns and protracted delays as critics often charge. Nor have most faculties lost their influence to an increasingly powerful administration, as a number of professors have complained. Thus, there is no compelling reason to suppose that our basic system of governance is in need of fundamental change of the kind that has recently occurred in much of Western Europe. Indeed, Americans can take satisfaction from the fact that most of the changes made in Europe have served to bring their systems closer to ours.

To be sure, not all issues of governance have yet been settled satisfactorily. For example, the role of faculty members who are not on the tenure track is far from being resolved on many campuses, leaving a vacuum that is increasingly troublesome now that part-time adjuncts and term-limited instructors constitute a large majority of the teaching staff of most colleges and universities. Still, important as they are, issues of this kind are likely to be dealt with in time through discussions between faculty representatives and the administration or, failing that, by unionization and collective bargaining.

There are other problems, however, that may not call the familiar structure of campus governance into question but do suggest that the system is not working as well as it should. One of these deficiencies, as the preceding chapter brought out, is that governing boards and academic leaders in many universities have been so preoccupied with tangible goals—such as raising more money, balancing the budget, starting new programs, and climbing higher in the media rankings—that they have neglected, at least until recently, the more important tasks of raising graduation rates and improving the quality of education.

Further problems that are apparent on many campuses result, not from too much shared governance, but from too little. On the one hand, university officials have allowed questions of teaching and learning to drift too far under the control of professors and their departments. On the other, decisions involving new programs, budgets, and other matters with heavy financial implications have been left too often to presidents and their administrative staff with little faculty input.

There are good reasons why the faculty should be ultimately responsible for educational policy and why the administration must have the last word on matters of major financial importance. Nevertheless, something important is often lost if academic leaders feel reluctant to initiate discussions with the faculty about the quality of education, or if professors are not consulted by the administration about such subjects as costly new programs, athletics, or major expenditure cuts. Because academic leaders have been slow to interfere in educational matters, faculty inertia has caused many colleges to respond very slowly to deficiencies in existing methods of instruction or to emerging needs to improve the curriculum. Conversely, the lack of serious discussion with the faculty must have helped to permit intercollegiate athletics to run roughshod over academic values and to allow the hiring and treatment of adjunct instructors to continue to be haphazard, unplanned, and quite possibly detrimental to the quality of education.

One final problem of governance tends to overshadow all others. Even if more consultation took place between faculty and administration, many universities would still fail to respond appropriately to legitimate needs of the larger society. In theory, trustees drawn from various sectors of life should keep universities properly attuned to societal needs. In practice, however, governing boards are ill-equipped to play this role effectively. Their members meet too infrequently to fully appreciate what universities can and cannot accomplish. Often, they are chosen to satisfy other purposes, and all too frequently, their meetings are organized by presidents to suit institutional purposes, not to examine the university's record in serving external needs.

As universities become more important to society, therefore, a variety of forces in the outside world have sought to influence their behavior. State legislatures have stepped up their supervisory role over public universities and are increasingly using performance budgeting to align campus priorities with social needs. The federal government has exerted a growing influence brought about by its role in funding scientific research and providing massive amounts of student aid. Accreditors are bringing pressure to bear through their periodic campus visits and their efforts not merely to disaccredit woefully weak institutions but to improve the performance of all universities they inspect. The media have an influence through their reporting on campus problems and their periodic rankings that purport to rate the comparative performance of hundreds of institutions. Meanwhile, foundations have frequently used the lure of financial grants to induce universities to make efforts to raise graduation rates or to start new programs to meet important needs.

A crucial question for the governance of higher education is whether this disparate group of actors acting largely independently of one another can keep universities suitably responsive to society's needs. Do these outside forces counter the inertia and the inward-looking tendencies of universities and help them play a socially responsive role, or do they produce a jumble of demands that work at cross-purposes to one another or ignore the proper limits on what academic institutions should be asked to accomplish? That is the ultimate question of governance in the largest sense of the term and one that will recur repeatedly in the chapters that follow.

AFTERWORD (I)

In a system as competitive, as decentralized, and as free from hierarchical control as that of American higher education, one may wonder why the entire enterprise does not sink into anarchy and confusion. In fact, as keen an observer of organizations as James March of Stanford University has described the inner workings of American universities in almost precisely these terms.[1] Yet such characterizations are belied by the fact that our academic institutions do manage to function and do so quite effectively. One is driven, therefore, to look for the glue that allows these autonomous institutions, with their legions of highly independent scientists and scholars and their practice of shared governance, to cohere and cooperate as successfully as they do.

An important part of the answer, surely, is the existence of common values and norms that are understood by professors and administrators alike as fundamental to the academic enterprise. These values define the responsibilities of the faculty and their academic leaders, establish the principles that guide their behavior, and mark the limits to their independence of action. As such, values provide a structure that helps create a set of mutual expectations and a framework for resolving differences of opinion. Although sometimes embodied in rules, academic values are often left unwritten, preserving an appearance of freedom and independence while actually guiding behavior in silent but predictable ways to bring order and cooperation out of a seeming jumble of individual ambitions and interests.

There is no definitive collection of academic values. Different people will compile somewhat different lists and define important items in slightly different ways. Yet most educators who have thought about the matter agree on certain values or norms that they consider essential to a flourishing college or university.

Some of these norms take the form of duties that academic leaders need to fulfill in order to create an environment conducive to good work. Thus, it is widely assumed that presidents, deans, and trustees should strive to maintain as much freedom of thought and expression as they can for their faculty and students. They should see to it that appropriate standards and procedures are developed and faithfully observed so that members of the faculty are appointed and rewarded because of the quality of their teaching and research, and not on the basis of their personal connections, political views, or other unrelated considerations. They should likewise make sure that each student is admitted in accordance with criteria designed to further the educational purposes of the institution rather than for extraneous reasons. They should invite faculty and students to participate in the planning and governance of the institution insofar (and only insofar) as they have the knowledge and experience to contribute significantly to discussions of the issues involved. As plans take shape, academic leaders should endeavor to the best of their ability to obtain and husband the resources required to meet the needs of the institution.

Since members of the faculty play an essential role in carrying out the central functions of the university, they too have an ample list of basic values to uphold. In particular, they should strive conscientiously to enhance the learning and development of their students through their teaching and advising. They should treat all students with respect, avoiding favoritism, indoctrination, and other abuses of their power. As members of an intellectual community, they should respect the views of colleagues and assist them, when asked, by discussing their research and critiquing their teaching. They should devote their fair share of time and effort to furthering the work of the institution by serving on committees, accepting positions of responsibility, such as chairing a committee or department when invited to do so, and participating in discussions of faculty appointments and other issues of common concern. In carrying out their research, they should observe the highest possible standards of honesty and refrain from appropriating the ideas of others without proper acknowledgment. They should avoid outside activities that interfere unreasonably with their academic duties, or create conflicts of interest, or threaten in other ways to compromise the impartiality and disinterestedness of their scholarship, and they should disclose any activities or associations that could reasonably cast doubt on their impartiality.

No informed observer would claim that either academic leaders or members of the faculty consistently honor all these responsibilities. Some university presidents have done too little to protect academic freedom in the face of outside pressures. Some professors on every campus spend too much time on outside activities, shirk their administrative responsibilities, and neglect their teaching or their research. Such lapses are bound to occur in any organization. The critical question that will recur at various points in succeeding chapters is whether important values are being so widely ignored or allowed to deteriorate to such a point as to threaten the ability of universities to function properly.

In an environment as competitive as the world of higher education, values are always at risk. As university leaders struggle to find the money to fulfill their ambitions and satisfy their faculties, and as their professors strive to win respect and recognition in their field of study, opportunities frequently arise to employ questionable means to achieve the hoped-for results. If a few succumb to these temptations, competitors will feel under pressure to follow suit. The danger is not so much a threat of outrageous behavior, which can be easily detected and punished. Rather, the risk is of a slow chipping away at existing norms through borderline behavior of debatable propriety, which is subsequently copied, first by a few and then by more until old values become weaker and standards of behavior are gradually relaxed and redefined.

The job of defending values properly and explaining their importance to faculty, students, and other audiences rests primarily with the leadership. It is not always easy. In striving to uphold traditional standards, presidents and deans can irritate donors and other interested groups to the point of provoking controversy and confrontation. By calling the faculty's attention to issues of personal responsibility and appropriate behavior, academic leaders can antagonize professors and invite unwelcome publicity. Such risks are real and immediate, while the costs of letting the status quo go on a while longer will often seem intangible and distant. Under these conditions, defending academic values can easily become a task forever left to another day.

If university presidents believe that they will be judged almost entirely by their success in "growing" the institution, increasing donations, and rising in the rankings, they are more likely to resort to dubious methods of raising money and to overlook nascent threats to academic values in order to avoid controversy. As a result, the role of the trustees is critical. If they make clear that the board appreciates the importance of academic values and will stand behind the leadership in defending them vigorously, presidents will feel freer to work with deans to discharge this vital responsibility. Deans in turn can work with members of their faculty to make sure that they understand and observe appropriate academic standards and responsibilities. In the end, therefore, preserving basic values is a collective enterprise. Trustees must work with presidents, presidents with deans, and both presidents and deans with members of the faculty. A failure at any point in this chain threatens the entire effort and strains the delicate web of professional responsibility on which the strength of the academic enterprise ultimately depends.

PART II

UNDERGRADUATE EDUCATION

FOREWORD (II)

||||||||||||||||||||||||||||||||||||||||||||||||||||||||||||||||||||||||||||||||||||||||||||||||||||||||||||

Much has changed in undergraduate education during the last half century. Students have increased in number—from roughly four million in 1960 to more than eighteen million in 2012—while growing far more diverse in age, race, and economic background. Nearly 80 percent of all high school graduates today will enter college at some point, although many fewer will finish. For most colleges, the struggle to attract students—either to raise the academic level of the entering class or simply to fill the seats—has grown more intense as increased financial aid and improvements in transportation have enabled admissions officers to appeal to more geographically distant audiences. For students hoping to enter a selective college, the competition has increased to the point that parents often spend large sums on tutoring and other special efforts to give their children an edge, while high school seniors worry about whether they will be able to attend the institution of their choice.

Going to college is no longer simply a private matter involving only colleges, applicants, and their parents. The supply of highly educated people has important effects on economic growth and the supply of skilled labor that employers need in order to expand and compete effectively in the global economy. In addition, the ability of all young people, including students of limited means, to enter and graduate from college has consequences for the distribution of income and the realization of the American Dream, not to mention its effects on the quality of out democracy, the physical health of the people, and even the incidence of crime, divorce, and unemployment. Now that these results are widely understood, the policies pursued in admitting and educating young people, setting their tuition, and offering them financial aid have come to be matters of concern to the entire nation.

The transition from elite to mass higher education has greatly expanded the opportunities for young people, but it has also created a growing problem of how to pay the bills. As universities have come to compete with a host of other programs needing taxpayer support, state and federal lawmakers have responded by gradually shifting more of the cost to students and their families.

This process has been particularly hard on low- and moderate-income students, causing many of them to attend less expensive community colleges while forcing others to work longer hours at part-time jobs or even to drop out of college entirely.

Financial burdens are not the only barrier inhibiting the pursuit of a college degree. On the one hand, highly qualified students from low-income families often fail to apply to institutions appropriate to their talents because they have exaggerated notions about the true costs of attending a selective college. On the other hand, the much-publicized deficiencies of our public schools cause many freshmen to arrive on campus poorly prepared for college work. Because of these and other problems, the percentage of young Americans earning college degrees has risen sluggishly over the past few decades, causing concern in many quarters over the consequences for the nation.

The difficulties just described have given rise to a series of questions regarding the role of undergraduate education. How many students possess the talent and the ambition to go to college? How much opportunity should they have to choose which college to attend, and who will pay the cost of their education? What can be done to ensure that as many students as possible enter a college commensurate with their ability and ambition and not be prevented from doing so by disadvantages of poverty, neighborhood, and upbringing? What can colleges do to keep students from dropping out before they earn a degree? Last but not least, how will the nation pay for educating the growing numbers of students needed to meet the needs of an ever more sophisticated economy?

Students with strong high school records and high SAT scores face a further set of problems. Now that the competition for good jobs is growing keener, these young people and their parents are chiefly concerned not with *whether* to go to college but with *which* college they can attend. As a result, controversy has arisen over the criteria used by the selective colleges that pick their students from large pools of applicants. Should everyone be judged solely by high school grades and SAT scores? Or are selective colleges justified in giving some preference to certain kinds of students, such as athletes, minorities, or children of alumni?

Young Americans are not the only ones who are interested in entering our colleges. In the last few decades, the desire of older age groups for further education has risen dramatically. More recently still, the Internet has expanded the reach of higher education to students anywhere in the world. How should educators respond to these vast new audiences? Which categories of students deserve priority? Should universities follow the lead of multinational corporations and build new campuses in other parts of the world? Should they invest time and money offering courses via the Internet to new and distant populations? If so, should they seek to serve these emerging audiences on a for-profit or a nonprofit basis?

Still other changes in society have raised new questions about what undergraduates need to learn. How can colleges prepare their students for a world in which their lives are likely to be linked increasingly with countries and cultures far different from their own? How can they be helped to live and work effectively in a society in which minorities seem destined to become a majority? What should colleges do to prepare their students to become engaged and knowledgeable citizens of a nation in which government policies have a more pervasive effect than ever before on people's lives, and the issues involved are harder than ever to understand? And how can all these educational needs be accommodated within the traditional curricular structure, with its tripartite division into majors, general education, and electives?

A final set of questions has to do not with *what* faculties should teach but how *well* they are teaching. The transition to mass education has transformed the makeup of the undergraduate population. Student bodies are now much more diverse. Large numbers are arriving on campuses without the basic preparation to succeed in college-level courses, creating difficult problems for those who must try to remedy their academic deficiencies. Half of all undergraduates are over twenty-four years of age and no longer depend on their parents for support. Eighty percent work during college; in fact, almost one-third hold down a full-time job and are enrolled only on a part-time basis. How should faculties adapt their teaching to serve the needs of these new audiences?

The growing corpus of research on student learning in college has also raised important questions about the way professors teach. Recent studies suggest that undergraduates today are not studying as hard as their parents did. A host of other activities compete for their time and attention—jobs, athletics, an ever-expanding variety of extracurricular pursuits, and an array of beguiling diversions from television and compact discs to the Internet, Facebook, and Twitter. Many undergraduates seem uninterested in a broad liberal education and care only about acquiring the skills and credentials that will qualify them for higher-paying jobs. In this challenging environment, what can be done to engage students sufficiently to teach them all they need to learn, and how can faculty know how well they are succeeding?

Most of the questions mentioned above are but different aspects of the two principal challenges facing undergraduate education today. The first is how to increase the *quantity* of education by raising the percentage of young people in the United States who earn a college degree. After thirty years of stagnant graduation rates, America has fallen behind many other advanced nations in the educational levels of its citizens under thirty. According to economists, the numbers of college-educated workers have become insufficient to meet the needs of employers. As a result, the earnings of college graduates have increased relative to those of Americans with only a high school diploma, causing greater income inequality and inhibiting economic growth.

The second major challenge is to improve the *quality* of education so that undergraduates learn more. Effective teaching is essential in order to motivate students, help them overcome deficiencies in their prior education, and enable them to compete successfully for jobs with other college graduates not only in America but around the world. Fortunately, more is becoming known about new ways to facilitate learning and elicit greater interest and effort on the part of undergraduates. To take but one example, computers can enable students to explore distant museums and historic places, tutor undergraduates using methods that adapt automatically to fit different cognitive styles, and engage audiences in elaborate games that can make learning more engrossing. The success or failure of American colleges in the coming generation will depend in no small measure on how well faculties succeed in adapting their teaching to make the most of these possibilities.

How successful will colleges be in meeting these two critical challenges? In the past, faculties have been notoriously sluggish in changing their curricula and the ways in which they teach. What can government agencies, foundations, and, most of all, colleges themselves do to improve upon this record? Finding answers to this question promises to be the most important task for higher education to fulfill over the course of the next generation.

CHAPTER FOUR

GOING TO COLLEGE
AND EARNING A DEGREE

||||||||||||||||||||||||||||||||||||||||||||||||||||||||||||||||||||||||||||||||||||||||||||||||||||||||

AMERICANS HAVE LONG DISPLAYED a high regard for education. Already in the nineteenth century, the United States was a leader in requiring young people to attend primary school and, later, high school. Churches of many denominations built affiliated colleges. In 1862, Congress passed the Morrill Act, giving away large tracts of land to encourage the growth of public (and some private) universities. By the end of the century, the United States contained no fewer than 977 institutions of higher learning. The number in Massachusetts alone was *several times* the figure for major European nations such as England or France.

The ranks of high school graduates attending college also grew steadily, albeit more slowly. Although no other country's universities educated even half as large a proportion of its young people as the United States, only one in seven young Americans went to college as late as 1940. After World War II, however, the rate of increase quickened. The share of high school graduates entering college the following fall grew steadily from 45 percent in 1960 to 50 percent in 1980, 63 percent in 2000, and 66 percent in 2013. Along the way, the United States became the first nation to make the transition from elite to mass and then to universal higher education.*

In the past thirty years, the earnings premium for completing college has greatly increased. By 2010, the median annual income for adults holding college degrees reached $54,000 compared with $32,600 for those with only a high school diploma.[1] This trend has not gone unnoticed. In 2005, 87 percent of American adults agreed that "a college education has become as important as a high school diploma used to be," while the percentage of respondents in Public Agenda surveys who considered a college education to be "necessary for

---

* According to a frequently used classification, countries with fewer than 15 percent of eighteen-to twenty-one-year-olds attending college have "elite" systems; countries with 15–40 percent have "mass systems," and countries with more than 40 percent have "universal" systems. See John A. Douglass, Judson King, and Irwin Feller (eds.), *Globalization's Muse: Universities and Higher Education Systems in a Changing World* (2009), p. 483.

a person to be successful in today's work world" jumped from 31 percent in 2000 to 55 percent in 2009.[2] Meanwhile, the share of ninth and tenth graders expressing an intent to go to college rose to almost 80 percent.[3]

Despite these high educational aspirations, a look at the figures for college enrollments and graduation rates shows all too clearly how far young people are from fulfilling their ambitions.[4] According to the Department of Education, of every 100 students who begin ninth grade, only 75 graduate from high school, only 51 enter college, and only 29 actually graduate.[*] These figures convey the essence of the problem that will occupy the next two chapters.

HOW MANY YOUNG PEOPLE SHOULD GO TO COLLEGE?

Although most people are in favor of increasing the percentage of Americans who enter college and earn degrees, not everyone agrees. A few observers have argued strenuously that more young people are already going to college than are truly required to meet the needs of the economy. If that is true, efforts to expand access will only increase the number of overeducated Americans, causing disappointment for many graduates and wasting resources on inflated college enrollments.

Andrew Hacker has recently sounded this theme in the *New York Review of Books*.[5] As he sees it, the occupational projections issued by the Labor Department do not anticipate enough growth in the kinds of jobs that require a college degree to warrant any further expansion in college enrollments. For example, he points out that the demand for engineers is estimated to increase no faster than the growth rate for the population as a whole, and argues that many of the jobs projected for technicians can be filled by workers with only a high school diploma. To illustrate his point, he cites the decision of carmakers such as Honda and Toyota to locate their American plants in areas with relatively few college graduates despite the sophistication of their products.

Hacker's conclusions are not widely shared. Considering the projections for all types of employment, the Bureau of Labor Statistics has estimated that the fastest-growing jobs will be those requiring at least an associate's degree. The number of these jobs is projected to rise at an average of 15–20 percent by 2018,

---

[*]US Department of Education, *College Completion Toolkit* (2011), p. 8. Some scholars have charged that the official high school graduation rate is greatly exaggerated. Thus, Paul Barton claims that over a span of 35 years the true graduation rate declined from 77 percent in 1969 to as low as 66 percent. *Rising Dropout Rates and Declining Opportunities* (2005).

while occupational groups requiring only a high school diploma or less will increase at rates averaging 10 percent or less.[6] In another study of job growth through 2018, Anthony Carnevale and his colleagues at Georgetown University report that 63 percent of all job openings will require *some* college education.[7]

Hacker's argument also assumes that one can readily distinguish between college and noncollege jobs. It is doubtful that such a clear line exists. Many jobs that previously called for only a high school education now require some college study. Either the nature of the work has been reorganized to make greater use of computer technology or jobs have been reconfigured into autonomous work groups that are asked to address such practical problems as increasing productivity, enhancing quality, or improving safety.

Even work that is still performed by employees with only a high school education may be done better or more efficiently by college graduates. Thus, a Labor Department study found that roughly 10 percent of college graduates were working at jobs typically held by employees with only a high school diploma but that those who had gone to college received higher wages.[8] Could it be, however, that employers who pay college graduates more for jobs that high school graduates can perform are simply exhibiting an irrational faith in credentials? Not likely. Why would firms employ thousands of BAs and pay them substantially more than necessary to get the work done? Companies are much too eager to cut costs by eliminating jobs and hiring temporary workers to waste money so needlessly. Instead, as Anthony Carnevale and Donna Desrochers point out, "studies of productivity have consistently found that people with postsecondary education, even those not working in their fields [of study], have acquired general skills that make them more productive than workers in the same job who have less education."[9] Among these general skills are an improved ability to solve problems, communicate clearly, work effectively in teams, and benefit from further training to master changes in specific skill requirements.

Further evidence of the economy's capacity to absorb more educated workers can be seen in the higher average earnings of employees with a BA degree.* The current earnings gap between college graduates and those with only a high school diploma is very large by historical standards. During the past thirty-five years, although the number of college-educated Americans has tripled, the average premium of an undergraduate degree over a high school diploma has climbed to levels not seen since 1915.[10] Such large differences suggest that

---

* As of November 2010, Americans with a BA degree or higher had a labor market participation rate of 76.6 percent and an unemployment rate of 4.4 percent compared with a participation rate of only 61.1 percent and an unemployment rate of 10 percent for those with only a high school diploma and no college. US Department of Education, *College Completion Toolkit* (2010), p. 20.

America does not have a glut but a shortage of suitably educated workers, so that boosting the numbers of college graduates will help the economy. That is the conclusion reached by Claudia Goldin and Lawrence Katz in their detailed study of the subject.[11] In their view, the supply of college graduates in America over the past few decades has not kept up with demand and thus has impeded economic growth and contributed to increased income inequality. An MIT economist, Paul Osterman, estimates that even a substantial rise in the number of college graduates would have a sufficiently positive effect on the economy to more than repay the added investment in education.*

Whatever one's opinion on this question, it would be a grave mistake to weigh the effects of encouraging more young people to go to college merely in economic terms, as if education had no other benefits. Studies show that college graduates have healthier lifestyles and live longer than those whose education did not extend beyond high school. They smoke less, are less likely to be obese, and suffer less from depression.[12]

A host of other studies have confirmed Jefferson's belief in the importance of education to our democracy. College graduates consistently vote at rates far above those with only a high school diploma. In fact, political scientist Robert Putnam has found education to be the single greatest factor in explaining differences in all forms of political and civic activity from running for office and working for a political party to merely attending a campaign rally or writing to a member of Congress.[13]

Still further studies have identified a number of other ways in which society gains from higher enrollment and graduation rates.[14] For example, those who continue their education beyond high school tend to have lower levels of crime and unemployment, a reduced likelihood of being on welfare, and greater racial tolerance. College-educated parents make more use of child-rearing methods that contribute to cognitive development. Their children are more inclined to attend college. Scholars have concluded that the various civic, health, and social benefits are at least equal in value to the added earnings associated with a college education.[15]

Notwithstanding these results, Charles Murray has suggested a different reason not to encourage more young people to go to college. In a recent book,

---

*Some writers point out that the high average earnings premium today is artificially inflated by the extremely high compensation received by the small minority of BAs who happen to be CEOs and investment bankers. Such figures, they add, do not prove that most young people will achieve anything like the current average premium simply by graduating from college. Nevertheless, the large premiums exist even if one looks at *median* earnings (which exclude the effects of the small minority of high-earners). Paul Osterman, "College for All? The Labor Market for College-Educated Workers," Center for American Progress (August 2008), p. 23.

he argues that many of the students currently enrolled are simply not capable of performing college-level work.[16] Murray derives a standard for "college-readiness" by estimating the grades and test scores needed to understand the kinds of readings widely used in introductory undergraduate courses. A similar calculation has been made by Jay Greene and Greg Forster of the Manhattan Institute.[17] These authors used a three-pronged test of college readiness—whether students graduated from high school; completed a core academic curriculum (i.e., four years of English, three years of math, and two years of science, social science, and a foreign language); and received a minimum score on a recognized test of reading comprehension. By this standard, only 32 percent of all students who enter high school and fewer than half of all high school graduates are capable of succeeding at a four-year college. As Greene and Forster point out, the total number of high school seniors who met the standard in 2000 was approximately 1,299,000, a figure slightly *lower* than the 1,341,000 high school graduates who actually enrolled that year as freshmen in four-year colleges.

It is possible that larger numbers of students are at least qualified to attend community colleges, which currently educate over 40 percent of all students entering postsecondary institutions.* Although an Associate's degree from a two-year college is not the equivalent of a BA degree, researchers have found that a year of study at either kind of institution increases subsequent earnings by nearly the same amount.[18] As a result, raising enrollments and graduation rates at community colleges would appear to contribute almost as much to the economy and to students' incomes as similar periods of study at four-year institutions.

At the same time, many high school counselors encourage students to attend college regardless of their ability to do college work.[19] As a result, an estimated 25 percent of the young people coming to four-year colleges and as many as 58 percent of those entering community colleges require remedial study before they can begin taking regular courses.[20] These figures alone might not constitute a problem if remediation were consistently successful in equipping participants for college work. At present, however, that is far from being the case.

Disturbingly large numbers of students currently assigned to remedial classes never complete the work successfully. While 68 percent of students enrolled in the basic writing courses manage to pass, as do 71 percent of those

---

*In theory, students admitted to degree programs in community colleges are qualified to do college-level work. It is not clear how often this standard is actually achieved in many community colleges. As one instructor wrote after teaching in two community colleges, "In no other age but our own—idealistic, inclusive, unwilling to limit anyone's possibilities for self-determination—would some of my students be considered ready for college." Professor X, *In the Basement of the Ivory Tower: Confessions of an Accidental Academic* (2011), p. 81.

in reading courses, only 30 percent succeed in remedial math.[21] Overall, fewer than half of all students requiring remediation complete the program success-fully. Many more who are assigned to such courses never enroll but simply give up and abandon college. Worse yet, though studies of different states come to different conclusions as to whether students completing remedial courses are more likely to graduate as a result, even the positive findings suggest that the benefits are modest.[22]

In short, while remediation offers a second chance to students who finish high school without the requisite academic skills, there does seem to be a limit on the number of current high school graduates who are capable of college-level work. That limit could be eased if high schools did a better job of prepar-ing students for college or if remedial classes were more effective in overcoming the deficiencies of the students they serve. Unfortunately, it is not at all clear that either result will occur in the near future.

What are the prospects, then, for increasing the number of academically qualified high school graduates who enter college? At first glance, the outlook is not encouraging. Over 70 percent of high school graduates currently enter a two- or four-year college at some point,[23] many more than the estimated num-ber truly qualified for college study. Under these conditions, is further progress even possible? Have we reached a saturation point at which no further increase of significant proportions is likely to occur?

Surprisingly, although many young people come to college without the nec-essary skills, a substantial number of high school graduates who are academi-cally qualified do not even apply. The percentage of qualified children from well-to-do homes who enter a four-year college may be high enough already that further increases are unlikely. Of all capable students from families with incomes over $75,000 who finished high school in 1991, 86 percent had begun their studies at a four-year college within two years and others presumably en-tered later or started at a two-year college.[24] However, the percentages of aca-demically qualified students from less affluent homes who attend a four-year college are much lower. One study issued by the US Department of Education found that among the high school graduates of 1992 who were college-qualified, only 52 percent of low-income students and 62 percent of middle-income stu-dents had entered a four-year college by 1994.[25]

Even among the most talented low-income students, enrollment figures are surprisingly modest. Of the high school seniors in the class of 1992 from fami-lies in the lowest income quartile, only 58 percent of those scoring in the top quartile of ability entered a four-year college within two years.[26] By the year 2000, only 29 percent of these highly talented low-income students had earned a BA degree, an additional 8 percent had received an associate's (two-year) degree, and another 3 percent had completed a vocational program and earned a certificate.[27]

Many capable students from families of limited means do not seek admission to a four-year institution but begin instead at a community college. According to a recent estimate, more than 20 percent of students from the bottom half of the socioeconomic scale who ranked in the top quartile of academic ability took this route.[28] Unfortunately, the odds that these students will eventually transfer and earn a BA degree are much lower than if they had entered a four-year institution initially.[29] Some of them undoubtedly choose a community college (or avoid further education altogether) either for financial reasons or for a variety of personal and family considerations. Yet studies of inner-city high school students suggest another explanation.[30] Most of these young people are very poorly informed about the tuitions charged by four-year colleges for which they are qualified or about the availability of financial aid. Still others are inhibited by the complex process of applying to such institutions or do not realize why they might improve their prospects by doing so. Often, they come from families in which no adult has ever attended college. Few of their high school friends may even contemplate further education. As a result, they receive little encouragement to go to college and little advice about how and where to apply apart from what their high school can give them.

Persuading high school seniors to go to a college commensurate with their abilities would require a major improvement in the number and quality of guidance counselors. At present, counselors are heavily burdened, with each responsible for advising an average of more than three hundred students.[31] Often, they have other duties to perform, and their information about selective colleges is limited. However, since increasing their numbers and giving them proper training would be a costly enterprise, it is far from clear that either state governments or Congress will be willing to launch such an undertaking in the current fiscal climate.

RAISING GRADUATION RATES

Entering college is one thing; earning a degree is quite another. In 2013, the National Student Clearinghouse reported that only 54 percent of students starting a four-year college in 2007 graduated in six years from the college they entered or some other institution.*[32] This overall figure masked large differences.

---

*Estimates of college graduation rates vary widely depending on whether or not one counts only full-time students, or only students entering four-year colleges, or only students graduating

While 78.1 percent of students attending college exclusively full-time earned a degree within six years, only 43 percent of those attending part-time for some period of their education and 21 percent of those attending exclusively part-time graduated during the same period. Differences between types of colleges were also substantial.[33] Whereas almost 70 percent of those enrolling in a private, non-profit four-year college and 57.3 percent of students entering a public four-year institution earned a BA within six years (either from the school they entered or from some other institution), only 41 percent of students attending a for-profit four-year college graduated during the same six-year period.[34]

The percentages of students entering community colleges who earn an Associate's degree or a job training certificate within six years are even lower. In 2012, the National Student Clearinghouse Research Center issued nationwide figures showing that only 23.9 percent of the students entering public community colleges in 2006 had graduated from the institution they entered by 2012, another 3 percent had graduated from a different community college, and an additional 9.3 percent had transferred without earning an Associate's degree and graduated from a four-year college.[35]

While both the numbers and percentages of young adults with degrees beyond high school have risen steadily for decades, America has been losing ground to other advanced nations in the level of education of its workforce. Because the United States was among the very first to move from an elite to a universal system of higher education, its workers were the most educated in the early decades following World War II. Since 1980, however, enrollments and graduation rates have surged in other industrialized countries with the result that several of them now surpass America in the percentage of younger workers with some sort of college degree. While there are various reasons for this turn of events, our low graduation rates, especially from community colleges, are widely considered to be among the most important.[*36]

Just as with enrollments, graduation rates vary markedly according to the income levels of the families involved. The problem is not simply one of

---

within six years rather than a longer period, or only students who graduate from the college they entered and not those who transfer and graduate from a different school. See Clifford Adelman, *The Toolbox Revisited: Paths to Degree Completion from High School through College*, U.S. Department of Education (2006).

* Although the United States now appears to rank below several other nations in educational attainment, two cautionary points should be kept in mind. First of all, international comparisons are often misleading, since different countries calculate graduation rates in different ways. See Clifford Adelman, *The Spaces between Numbers: Getting International Data on Higher Education Straight*, Institute for Higher Education Policy (2009). In addition, since our population has kept growing in recent decades, unlike that of many other developed nations, the number of young Americans with college degrees may have risen at a faster rate than in countries that have acheived higher percentages of college-educated young adults. Arthur M. Hauptman, "U.S. Attainment Rates, Demographics, and the Supply of College Graduates," *Change* (May-June 2013), p. 24.

differences in ability. Among students who are academically qualified to do college work, 81 percent of those from high-income families complete a bachelor's degree within eight years, while only 36 percent of qualified low-income students manage to do so.[37] The difference in achievement between rich and poor has been growing for several decades. Interestingly, however, the principal reason is not increasing income inequality but the growing tendency among young women from high-income families to go to college and pursue a career.

Because of the importance of education for economic growth and opportunity, America's relatively low graduation rates have caused consternation in high places. President Obama has repeatedly called attention to the problem, while urging the nation to regain its historic lead in educational attainment by raising the percentage of young Americans earning some sort of college degree to 60 percent by 2020.[38]

WHAT COLLEGES CAN DO

What can be done to raise the percentage of Americans who earn a college degree? While there are many reasons for dropping out, not all of them are subject to much influence by colleges and universities. For example, universities have only a limited ability to increase the supply of college-ready students by improving the quality of K–12 education or strengthening preschool programs. Several conditions that can cause attrition from college are also very difficult to remedy. For example, while research suggests that undergraduates who live off campus are more likely to drop out than classmates living in college residence halls, building dormitories is simply not feasible financially for many institutions. Similarly, dropout rates tend to be higher in colleges with large student bodies, but this too is not a condition that is easily changed. Family crises, illness, drugs, and many other personal problems that can cause students to leave college are also largely beyond the reach of campus officials.

Nevertheless, there are several steps that colleges *can* take to improve graduation rates. Two-thirds of all undergraduates in four-year colleges, according to one recent study, "strongly agreed" that they would have worked harder in high school and taken more demanding courses if they had known what college was like.[39] All too often, however, no one in their high school ever informed them that the courses they took were not sufficient to prepare them for college work. Once they enter college and find that they must first take noncredit remedial classes, many become discouraged and leave. Those who remain often fail to complete their remedial work successfully.

Unfortunately, many high school counselors regularly advise students to go to college even if they are plainly unprepared. Apparently, they do not like to discourage the young people who seek their advice. If they do mention the possibility of having to take remedial classes, they often fail to explain that these courses may not count toward graduation or give credits that are transferable to a four-year college.[40] Lacking proper information, as James Rosenbaum and colleagues point out, "many high school students believe that high school effort is not important because they can get into college without working."[41]

Another reason why many students do not prepare properly is that there is far less coordination of standards between American high schools and colleges than in any other industrial nation. In most states, school systems and higher education bodies are completely separate and seldom work closely together. When they do meet to achieve better coordination, community colleges are often left out of the discussion even though they are the point of entry for most of the students who are especially likely to experience academic problems and leave before earning a degree.

In principle, state officials should be able to persuade schools, universities, and community colleges to create a closer alignment between the courses taught in high school and the academic skills and knowledge required for college. Other countries have solved this problem. If America could do likewise, fewer students would presumably be forced to take remedial courses, states would save money as a result, and graduation rates from college would probably rise. However, the marked decentralization of education in the United States, with its tradition of local autonomy, makes the problem of coordination especially difficult. Universities resist having to accept a statewide definition of college readiness. Many high school authorities feel that they have enough problems graduating students with the standards already in place without raising the requirements to conform more closely to college demands. Whatever the reason, although a number of states are now working hard to create a better alignment, David Spence reported in 2009 that "no state has brought its entire public higher education system to agreement on specific college and career readiness standards that can be applied by all state two-year and four-year colleges and universities."[42]

Many colleges could act on their own to alleviate the problem of misalignment and reduce the number of students who arrive on their doorstep unprepared. If states cannot bring about closer coordination, colleges that draw most of their applicants from the surrounding area could presumably work with local high schools to let students know about the nature of college work so that they can prepare themselves accordingly. College personnel could organize summer or weekend sessions with local high school guidance counselors to inform them about academic requirements along with other useful information concerning costs and financial aid. They could allow high school students to enroll in selected courses, as some already do, in order to gain firsthand acquaintance with the demands of college work. Better yet, they could work with high schools to give sophomores and juniors early warning of what they need to do to prepare themselves properly. For example, community colleges in each state could agree on a common test for determining which students have to take remedial courses. The test could then be given to tenth grade students to alert them to the skills they need to develop in order to be ready to take college courses for credit.[43]

Colleges should be eager to take such initiatives in their own self-interest. After all, they bear the burden of having to try to remediate underprepared students, a task that is both expensive and unrewarding for many instructors. As a result, they have much to gain by working with local high schools to reduce the number of students who come to them lacking the skills to succeed academically.

Another way to increase graduation rates would be to improve remedial education. At present, only about one-third of high school graduates are prepared to do college work successfully. As a result, if the United States is to raise the share of younger Americans who earn college degrees, it will be essential to help more students achieve the proficiency in basic skills that will enable them to succeed in college.

Remediation has long been the unwanted stepchild of higher education. Taxpayers resist having to pay for such instruction, and at least ten states actually refuse to do so. Other states insist that all such courses be given by community colleges, thus directing many students into institutions where their chances of eventually earning a BA degree are sharply reduced. Almost everywhere, remediation is left to adjunct instructors, since the regular faculty tends to consider such teaching beneath its ability and status. Most classes are large and taught by "skill and drill" techniques that are considered ineffective. Fortunately, various efforts are now underway to try to improve such instruction.*

A third step that colleges could take is to adopt more engaging ways of teaching their regular courses. Recent research has discovered that certain classroom practices can lower dropout rates.[44] More active methods of pedagogy, such as having students work collaboratively at solving problems, seem to help. So do opportunities for undergraduates to do research under faculty supervision. Even as simple a matter as having clearer, better organized lectures may make a difference. Such methods can affect graduation rates by making classes more interesting and worthwhile, fostering closer ties among classmates, and providing encouragement and feedback to give students confidence that they are making progress.

A final way to raise graduation rates is to strengthen the various kinds of assistance and support that colleges give students to prevent them from leaving

---

*In one such effort, Carol Twigg reports significant success by reducing lecturing and substituting problem-solving exercises with interactive software. "Improving Learning and Reducing Costs," *Change* (July-August 2013) p. 6.

college. A number of helpful interventions seem to make a difference in keeping them enrolled.[45] Campus authorities can try to identify students at risk of dropping out at the earliest possible point in order to give them the counseling and tutoring that may keep them from leaving. Freshman seminars, summer bridge programs, and learning communities (in which groups of freshmen take a set of courses together) can all make a difference. So can initiatives of all kinds to integrate new students into the life of the college. Even on-campus work-study jobs seem to help. Other kinds of valuable support include mental health services, financial aid assistance, and better job counseling and job placement that can remind students of the value of graduating. A good first step might simply be to coordinate or consolidate these services in order to make them seem less bewildering to students. For eighteen-year-olds with multiple problems to resolve, especially those whose parents never went to college, seeking help from an array of different offices in different locations is often more than they can deal with successfully.

Vincent Tinto, who has studied dropouts more intensively than anyone else, ranks these preventive measures among the most promising ways to keep students enrolled.[46] Since graduation rates differ greatly among colleges with students of similar ability and background, many institutions appear to have ample room for improvement.* Like better remediation, of course, such reforms tend to be labor intensive and thus cost money, always a problem when the economy is weak, especially for colleges with limited resources. Still, Douglas Webber and Ronald Ehrenberg have found that colleges with dropout rates above 50 percent can raise the graduation rates of low-income students by a net of 1.3 percent without any additional cost simply by shifting five hundred dollars per student from educational budgets to improved student services.[47]

THE COST OF A COLLEGE EDUCATION

Among the many reasons for leaving college, financial problems are among the most obvious. Costs do not seem to deter many students from entering. Analysts agree that fewer than 10 percent of academically qualified high school

---

*For example, there are many hundreds of modestly selective colleges that admit 75–85 percent of their applicants and enroll students with SAT scores of 500–572 who finished in the top 50–65 percent of their high school class. The top third of these colleges have graduation rates of 62 percent while the bottom third graduate an average of only 35 percent of their entering students. College categories with different levels of selectivity and student ability have similarly large disparities in graduation rates. Frederick M. Hess, Mark Schneider, Kevin Carey, and Andrew P. Kelley, *Diplomas and Dropouts: Which Colleges Actually Graduate Their Students (and Which Don't)*, American Enterprise Institute (2009).

graduates fail to begin college for lack of funds.[48] Many who begin, however, find that college is costing them more than they anticipated. In fact, money is the most common reason undergraduates give for dropping out.[49] Older students who are no longer supported by their parents and younger high school graduates from families of limited means often conclude either that it is too difficult to continue working long hours and still keep up with their coursework, or that they simply cannot afford to go further in debt.

Are colleges responsible for these difficulties because their tuitions are so high? Many people believe so. "College May Be Unaffordable for Most in U.S." was the headline of a *New York Times* article in 2008.[50] In 2005, the *Economist* included among the potential signs of weakness in American higher education that universities were raising tuitions at such a rate that they were in danger of pricing themselves out of the market.[51]

The point most often made to support these charges is that tuitions have been rising at a much faster rate than the cost of living.[52] This tendency has existed for a century or more but has become more pronounced in recent decades. From 1982–84 to 2010, college tuition and fees (unadjusted for inflation) rose by 439 percent, health-care costs increased by 251 percent, m edian faculty incomes grew by only 147 percent, and the consumer price index climbed by a mere 106 percent.[53] Such trends provoke criticism, even alarm. On closer scrutiny, however, the figures do not tell us as much as one might think about the appropriateness of existing tuition levels or even about the rate at which the burden of paying for college has increased in the past few decades.

An initial problem with most generalizations about tuitions is that the amounts colleges charge vary widely—from an average of only $2,960 at public community colleges in 2011–12 to $28,500 at private four-year colleges.[54] Moreover, since tuitions are usually set well below the full cost of the education provided—not only in state colleges and universities but even in the most expensive private institutions—it is not self-evident that the amounts being charged are excessive. It is even less likely that universities are pricing themselves out of the market. On the contrary, many very expensive, selective colleges, far from losing applicants, have experienced continuing growth for decades in the numbers of students seeking admission. Some of these institutions now reject ten, twelve, or even fifteen students for every one they admit. Despite the cost, the competition to enter has become so intense that parents engage high-priced counselors to help their children apply and sometimes even make strenuous efforts to have their children accepted by particular kindergartens that are thought to give their little charges an edge in eventually gaining admission to an elite, Ivy League college.*

---

*The reasons for this seeming paradox are easily explained. While it is true that the prices charged by the most selective institutions have risen faster than the cost of living, the amounts per

Tuitions also give a misleading picture of college costs, since 70 percent of students receive scholarships, loans, or some other form of financial aid.* Impressive amounts of money are provided for these purposes. Colleges themselves spent $29.7 billion on scholarships during the academic year 2010–11.[55] The federal government provided $33.9 billion more in grants, while state governments added another $9.1 billion. The effects on the actual cost of college are substantial. If one subtracts all forms of grant aid (not loans) from tuition and fees, the average amount (including fees) that students pay to attend a private four-year college drops from $28,500 in 2011–12 to a net average of $12,970.[56] The average net cost at public four-year colleges falls from $8,240 to $2,490.[57] At public two-year (community) colleges, the average grant award actually exceeds the average tuition, leaving slightly more than $800.00 to help pay for room and board expenses.[58] For students from the lowest income quartile who claim the largest share of need-based aid, the average net cost (tuition and fees minus scholarship

---

student these colleges spend on the education of undergraduates have gone up even faster. As a result, according to economist Caroline Hoxby, the subsidy that the most selective colleges give their undergraduates over and above the full tuition has now grown to the point that tuitions cover only about one-fifth of the amount that these colleges devote to educating each student, and the subsidies students receive are almost *ten times* those provided by the least selective colleges, Caroline M. Hoxby, "The Changing Selectivity of American Colleges," 23 *Journal of Economic Perspectives* (2009), p. 95.

Hoxby finds that although the most selective private universities subsidize their students heavily by spending so much on their education, the average return that graduates receive over their working lives on the full cost of their education (tuition, room and board, *plus the subsidy*) has also risen at least to equal the average return on common stocks. Since most students get financial aid and hence do not pay the full tuition, and since no student is under any obligation to pay back the subsidy, it is understandable why more and more applicants try to attend these institutions and why their graduation rates are typically the highest in the nation.

* More generally, when one considers the significance of college costs for college students and their families, it is helpful to keep several figures in mind. The first figure is the "*sticker price*," or the amount derived by adding up the annual tuitions over the four years of attendance. The second is the *full cost of the education to the college*, which tends to be significantly greater than the tuition, often very much greater. The third, and perhaps most important, figure is the *actual cost to students and their families*, which is significantly less than the sticker price for the great majority of students because of the existence of financial aid. The final figure is the *value* of a college degree, which by most accounts provides at least a reasonable return on the sticker price.

Of these four figures, tuition is by far the least useful in considering the impact of college costs because only a minority of students actually pay the full sticker price and those who do are almost always the children of well-to-do parents whose incomes are far above those of the rest of the population. In contrast to the experience in middle-income homes where incomes rose only 15 percent from 1978 to 2008, families in the top 20 percent saw their incomes rise by 52 percent, while families in the top 5 percent enjoyed a 78 percent increase. College Board, *Trends in College Pricing* 2009 (2009), p. 16. For well-to-do parents, then, although they bore the brunt of tuition increases, the impact was cushioned by the substantial growth in their incomes. There is no evidence that rising costs affected them enough to lower the college enrollments or graduation rates of their children.

aid but not loans) for in-state students at a public four-year college was zero in 2013–14; the figure for the average private college was $2,186.[59]

Scholarships and grants also have a marked effect on the rate at which college costs are increasing. For example, from 2003–2004 to 2013–14, tuitions rose at private colleges from $24,070 to $30,090 in constant dollars, an increase of more than 25 percent. Because financial aid rose even faster, however, average net costs (tuition and fees minus grants and tax benefits) actually <u>declined</u> from $13,600 to $12,460.[60]

Today, 70 percent of all undergraduates receive some sort of financial aid. In addition to the more than $90 billion in scholarships from all sources in 2011–12 and another $13.4 billion in tax credits for parents, students obtained roughly $70 billion in federal student loans, bringing the total amount of financial support to well over $170 billion per year.[61] College enrollments and graduation rates would never have reached their present levels without this financial help.

Much has been written of late about the growing amount of educational debt, which now totals more than one trillion dollars. By 2011–12, seniors who graduated from non-profit colleges owed an average of $26,500.[62] Even so, only 7 percent of households with educational loans owe more than $50,000, and the share of the average borrower's income needed for repayment has not increased in 20 years.[63] At the same time, most low-income students do not receive enough aid to cover their expenses and hence must either incur credit card debt to make up the difference or work more hours per week than colleges recommend. Many drop out owing thousands of dollars with poor job prospects and no degree.

What accounts for the current financial situation, with its constant tuition increases and the resulting pressure on the resources of students and their families? The most common response today is to blame college officials. While this verdict is partly true, the reality is more complicated. Several factors have combined to create the current predicament.

First of all, the tendency for college costs to rise more rapidly than the cost of living is not confined to higher education. Most entities like colleges and universities that make extensive use of highly skilled labor raise their prices faster than the cost of living. The reason is that it is difficult to substitute machines for employees and achieve the productivity increases common to manufacturing, agriculture, and other sectors of the economy. Thus, college costs have not outpaced the cost of living only in the past few decades. They have been doing so since statistics on tuitions began to be collected in the early years of the twentieth century and probably before. The same has been true of prices for many labor-intensive services such as health care, legal services, insurance, and symphony orchestras.[64]

This historic tendency has been aggravated in recent decades by a more intense competition among colleges in many segments of higher education. Competition in most industries tends to lower prices. In higher education, however, what appeals to talented students, foundation officers, philanthropists, and other valued audiences is often not lower prices but higher quality, or what is commonly thought to be higher quality. And quality of this kind costs money, whether it be for more attractive dormitories and classrooms, bigger and better libraries and laboratories, or a faculty with larger numbers of highly esteemed scientists and scholars. As a result, the competition for students waged by many four-year colleges gives rise to constant pressure to increase tuitions.

Still further upward pressure has resulted from the gradual decline in the relative contribution of state subsidies to public higher education. As the share of public university revenues contributed by the states has dropped—from 32 percent in 1980 to 18 percent in 2009—campus officials have felt impelled to raise tuitions faster to avoid a deterioration in the quality of their programs.

A final factor contributing to the impact of higher college costs on students and their families has been the tendency for income growth to stagnate in recent decades for all but the top 20 percent of American households.[65] As a result, while rising tuitions in the 1950s and 1960s did not consume an increasing share of family income because they were offset by growing earnings, incomes stalled for middle- and low-income households toward the end of the 1970s. Since then, higher tuitions have tended to take a larger bite out of the pocketbooks of most families, making it ever more difficult for many students and their parents to find the resources to pay for college.[66]

The growing burden of college costs has been alleviated to a considerable extent by the programs of federal financial aid. Increasingly, however, as the cost to the government mounted, aid has shifted from a predominance of grants to a predominance of loans. Hence, while most undergraduates and their families can still find the resources to pay for college, more and more students have had to take on heavy debt loads or work increasing numbers of hours to continue in school. Many have dropped out as a result.

The trends in college costs just described, for both tuitions and financial aid, scarcely seem sustainable for very much longer. Over the past several decades, each of the parties involved in financing undergraduate education has been trying to shift the burden of increasing costs to some other party. States have been trying to hand it off to the federal government. Washington has relied increasingly on loans in order to place more of the cost in the hands of families. Families have allowed their children to go deeper into debt. Students are increasingly defaulting on their loans. Through it all, colleges have continued to raise their prices in hopes that someone else will find the money to pay the bills.

At some point, the process will have to stop. Colleges are already finding it hard to continue raising the costs to students. Government-backed student loans, which enable so many students to pay for rising college costs, have led to levels of debt that cannot rise much further without inhibiting access and graduation rates and creating intolerable financial burdens for many who do earn degrees.* In short, something will have to change before long if there is to be much hope of boosting the growth in educational attainment or even of sustaining the levels already achieved.

*The current system may be able to survive a while longer if federal officials manage to persuade students to take out loans under a contingent repayment plan, which requires borrowers to repay a fixed, affordable percentage of their disposable income each year for a stipulated period of years. See Nicholas W. Hillman, "Reforming Repayment: Using Income-Related Ways to Reduce Default," paper prepared for American Enterprise Institute Conference (June 24, 2013). Under such a scheme, which has now been adopted by Australia, borrowers can be reasonably confident of being able to repay their student loans even if they do not earn much money. The plan can remain financially viable because graduates who earn higher incomes subsidize those who earn much less. The net effect is to significantly reduce the risk involved in borrowing substantial amounts to finance one's education. Thus far, however, although an income contingent option has been available in the United States for several years, few students have chosen to take advantage of it.

CHAPTER FIVE

PAYING FOR COLLEGE: THE CHALLENGE FOR POLICY-MAKERS AND ACADEMIC LEADERS

||||||||||||||||||||||||||||||||||||||||||||||||||||||||||||||||||||||||||||||||||||||||||||||||||||||||

IN AN ERA OF UNIVERSAL higher education, the financial burdens that weigh so heavily on many students turn a spotlight on the troublesome question of how to pay for the cost of college. State governments, universities, and students are all struggling with this issue. The problem seems destined to grow larger. According to a recent study by McKinsey consultants, in order to reach President Obama's goal of regaining America's lead in educational attainment within the next decade, the number of two- and four-year degrees and certificates awarded from 2010 to 2020 would have to rise by roughly 3.5–4 percent per year.[1] If current methods of educating students continue as they are, the added annual cost would grow to exceed $50 billion.[2]

Most of the additional enrollments needed to raise attainment levels will have to come from low- and moderate-income families, since children from more affluent homes already graduate in high enough numbers to leave little room for further growth. Because needier students and their families usually lack the resources not only for tuition but for the cost of room and board as well, deciding how to make it financially possible for larger numbers of them to enroll and graduate will be a major problem for policy-makers. Unless some way can be found, it is likely that economic growth will be slowed, income inequality will rise even further, and millions of young Americans will be unable to fulfill their hopes and ambitions.

There are no one-size-fits-all solutions to this dilemma. The nature of the problem varies profoundly depending on the sector of higher education involved. To understand the challenge facing policy-makers, therefore, one must examine each sector individually. Only then can one appreciate the kinds of choices that government officials will need to make.

HIGHLY SELECTIVE PRIVATE COLLEGES

While colleges in this category charge the highest tuitions, they are likely to play only a minor part in achieving larger enrollments and higher completion rates at an affordable cost to the government. Students who pay the full "sticker price" at these elite colleges cost the government very little, since their parents foot the bills. Although the price tag seems formidable, they continue to apply in growing numbers, in part because they tend to come from well-to-do families whose incomes have steadily risen since the 1970s even as the earnings of other segments of the population have stagnated.[3] Once admitted, students in these colleges graduate at very high rates and rarely drop out for financial reasons.

Those who cannot pay the sticker price receive varying amounts of financial aid, both scholarships and loans. Some colleges in this category tend to provide enough scholarship money to those who need it that even the poorest students can graduate without having to incur huge debts or work excessive numbers of hours. In fact, a few of the most selective colleges now allow all students they admit from families earning less than $60,000 or $65,000 per year to finish their studies while hardly paying anything or even having to incur any debt.

Because of private scholarships, the federal government contributes very little of the financial aid received by students in these institutions. The number receiving Pell Grants is limited, since only a small percentage of the undergraduates involved come from families eligible for such assistance. Many more students receive federally guaranteed student loans, but graduates typically find good jobs, and their default rates are lower than those in any other sector of higher education. All in all, therefore, the cost to the taxpayer per graduating student is exceptionally low.*

If highly selective colleges have any further contribution to make in helping to pay for an expanded undergraduate population, it is by enrolling more students from low- and moderate-income families, a subject treated in detail in the next chapter. Under the best of circumstances, however, such an effort will not do much to solve the underlying problem. Although the highly selective colleges attract a lot of media attention, they enroll only a tiny percentage of the total undergraduate student population, and there is very little chance that they

---

*Of course, apart from financial aid, governments contribute indirectly to private colleges through revenues forgone because of tax credits and property tax exemptions. But even these amounts represent a good investment. Each federal tax dollar lost via the charitable exemption brings more than a dollar in private donations to help defray the cost of higher education, while state and local governments benefit from the new businesses, additional employment, and increased taxes resulting from the presence of a college or university.

will expand significantly in the future. Even if they could, many of them lack the resources to educate a lot more students needing large amounts of financial aid. The number of low- and moderate-income students with high enough grades and test scores to qualify academically for these colleges is also limited. For these reasons, the challenge of educating millions of additional students over the next decade or two will have to be met almost entirely by other sectors of the higher education system.

THE FLAGSHIP STATE UNIVERSITIES

The great public research universities educate many more undergraduates than the highly selective private institutions. Although they collectively enroll as many National Merit Scholars as the privates, their student bodies include higher proportions of children from low- and moderate-income families. In recent years, however, fewer of such students have attended these institutions. The principal reason is the shrinking support provided by state appropriations, which dropped by 20 percent per public college student from 1987 to 2011.[4] Many flagship institutions have responded by raising their tuitions at a rapid clip, capping their enrollments, and recruiting larger numbers of well-to-do students from other states and overseas who can be charged substantially more than the in-state rate.[5] As a result, lower-income students have gravitated in increasing numbers to the less expensive comprehensive universities and community colleges. From 1982 to 2006, the percentage of community college enrollments made up of students from the lowest income quartile rose from 21 to 28, while the percentage of students from the highest quartile dropped from 24 to 16.[6]

In the past twenty years, these trends have accelerated further, because state governments, often with the support of flagship universities, have allocated more money to merit scholarships in an effort to attract or retain highly talented students. From 1991 to 2008–9, merit awards rose three times faster than need-based grants.[7] Since the individuals who receive these awards tend to come disproportionately from well-to-do families, the effect has been to further limit the number of low-income students who can afford to enroll.

Because of this combination of events, many flagship universities are coming increasingly to resemble selective private colleges by catering to students of high ability from more affluent segments of the population. Already, according to William Bowen, Matthew Chingos, and Michael McPherson, barely 40 percent of students from the lowest income quartile who are academically qualified to enter a flagship university attend these institutions. The rest enroll in less selective colleges where their chances of earning a degree are reduced.[8]

While the increased use of merit scholarships seems unnecessary and unfortunate, it is only fair to reiterate that the principal reason for the higher cost of attending flagship universities has been the declining levels of support from state governments. It is unlikely that the flagships could have done much more to offset this lost revenue by trimming wasteful expenditures. Most of them have already had to engage in serious cost cutting during the past decade. If they knew how to cut a great deal further, they would presumably have done so already rather than see their faculty salaries fall, as they have, by some $25,000 per year below the levels earned by professors in the private universities with which they compete. As it was, they felt they had little choice but to raise their tuitions sharply, or else let the quality of their faculties and their educational programs deteriorate.*

For their part, state governments have also acted largely out of fiscal necessity. Since they are required to balance their budgets, many states have taken advantage of federal increases in Pell Grants and guaranteed loans by trimming the subsidies they give to their public colleges and universities, causing the latter to raise their tuitions and nullifying the efforts of Washington officials to lower college costs for needy students. This cannot be a welcome outcome for federal officials who are severely challenged themselves in trying to curb the huge deficits in their budget.

However state and federal officials resolve their differences, public flagship universities are not likely to play a decisive role in educating the added cohorts of students who will be flocking to the nation's colleges in the next decade or two. True, they could redirect much of their merit aid to increase the amount of need-based assistance. But the numbers of students affected by this shift would make up only a small fraction of the total needed to increase current attainment rates. The responsibility for educating these additional young people, therefore, will have to fall mainly on the comprehensive universities, community colleges, and for-profit institutions that already enroll the vast majority of students with limited resources.

---

*It is not clear how much harm has been done to flagship public universities by the decline in state support. See, e.g., Stephan Vincent-Lanerin, "An OECD Scan of Public and Private Education," in John A. Douglass, C. Judson King, and Irwin Feller (eds.), *Globalization's Muse: Universities and Higher Education Systems in a Changing World* (2009), p. 15. In 2011–12, only 11.6 percent of chief academic officers at public research universities believed that "budget cuts initiated by my institution in the past 3 years have done major damage to the quality of our academic programs," and more than 90 percent rated the academic health of their institution as "good" or "excellent." Kenneth C. Green, *The 2011–12 Inside Higher Ed Survey of College and University Chief Academic Officers* (2012), pp. 6, 15. Nevertheless, now that many measures to cope with declining state support have already been taken, it is questionable whether these institutions can continue to withstand further cuts in state support without suffering significant damage to the quality of their programs.

COMPREHENSIVE UNIVERSITIES
AND COMMUNITY COLLEGES

Comprehensive public universities and community colleges spend the least amount per student of the several types of degree-granting institutions—on average, roughly $11,000 per year for comprehensives and $9,000 for community colleges, compared with $14,000 for flagship public universities, and $33,000 for private research universities.[9] By virtue of their low tuitions, easy admissions policies, and experience in educating low- and moderate-income students, they might appear to be well positioned to help achieve the goal of accommodating larger enrollments and raising educational attainment rates. For various reasons, however, most of these institutions turn out to be less than ideal candidates to help the federal government achieve its purpose.

The Obama administration has invested heavily in increasing Pell Grants in order to make colleges more affordable and enable students to remain enrolled until they graduate. As previously mentioned, however, many state governments, under heavy pressure to cut expenses, have apparently capitalized on these increases in recent years to reduce their subsidies to comprehensives and community colleges and thus force the latter to raise their tuitions. If states continue this policy, they will keep increases in Pell Grants from making college more affordable and use them instead to shift more of the cost of higher education from their own budgets to the federal government.

Another problem with relying on community colleges (and, to a lesser extent, comprehensive universities) is that their dropout rates tend to be very high. Only a small fraction of students entering community colleges earn a degree or a certificate of completion within three years. Although additional students may graduate at a later time or transfer to a four-year college without earning a community college degree, the most careful study to date suggests that even six years after entry, only 36 percent of students entering community colleges have either earned an associate's (two-year) degree or gone on to graduate from a four-year college.[10] To make matters worse, a significant fraction of the students who drop out prior to completion eventually default on repaying the federally guaranteed loans they have accumulated in the course of their unsuccessful effort to earn a degree.

In theory, comprehensives and community colleges could raise their graduation rates substantially even without receiving much additional government support. According to the previously mentioned McKinsey report, these institutions could enroll and graduate enough additional students per year to meet President Obama's goal *at no increase in cost* if they could match the performance already achieved by the most successful 25 percent of colleges with student bodies of similar socioeconomic backgrounds.[11] In order to do so, they would need to concentrate on several things: on the one hand, lowering dropout rates by offering simpler, more highly structured programs and by providing more effective remedial education and better counseling and job placement services; and, on the other hand, reducing costs by eliminating nonessential activities (such as intercollegiate athletics), making greater use of online courses and part-time instructors, and instituting more effective ways of keeping students from taking more courses than they need in order to graduate.[12]

As a practical matter, however, implementing these measures to a sufficient extent to absorb the entire cost of graduating one million more students per year would be extraordinarily difficult. Having all comprehensives and community colleges duplicate the successful practices of the highest-performing members in their peer group seems unlikely, since it is unrealistic to imagine that leaders and their staffs throughout the sector will be as skillful and determined as those of the most successful institutions.* Resistance from faculty and students may block some of the reforms. Moreover, even if all of the improvements recommended in the report have proved effective for some institutions under some conditions, there is no guarantee that they will work as well or even be feasible at other institutions under different conditions.

Some of the reforms suggested by the report could even turn out to diminish the effectiveness of education.[13] For example, the use of part-time instructors undoubtedly lowers costs, but it has also been found by some analysts to contribute to grade inflation, higher dropout rates, and other adverse effects on quality.[14] Online education is a promising possibility, but experience to date suggests that it produces better results than traditional instruction in some cases but worse results in others.[15] Until more is known about just how to achieve improved learning and lower dropout rates, there is no guarantee that colleges will offer only online programs that work well. Improved methods of remedial education are also unlikely to become widespread until careful research and experimentation can demonstrate what forms of instruction yield better results.

In short, what the McKinsey report reveals is that substantial improvements in graduation rates and costs per student have proved possible in some

---

* For example, Kim Clark, the president of one of the six exemplary institutions singled out for analysis in the McKinsey report, previously served as the highly successful dean of the Harvard Business School and moved to his current post bringing several of his colleagues with him at the urging of the Mormon Church hierarchy. Such opportunities are not likely to exist for the vast majority of community colleges.

successful, well-run institutions. Such achievements offer real hope that similar measures can eventually succeed in lowering dropout rates and raising educational attainment levels at a lower cost. Yet accomplishing these results on a system-wide basis will surely be a difficult task. Under the best of circumstances, it will probably require at least a generation or more to achieve.

FOR-PROFIT UNIVERSITIES

For-profit universities have been the most inventive in developing a no-frills educational model tailored to the special needs and circumstances of working adults. More recently, they have been aggressively utilizing online programs to provide even more convenient instruction for employed students. By dint of these initiatives, reinforced by aggressive recruitment, for-profits have enjoyed the fastest growth of any segment of higher education.

Such accomplishments might seem to make for-profits an ideal vehicle for educating the additional students who will need to graduate from college over the ensuing years if increased attainment levels are to be reached. For several reasons, however, these institutions are a problematic partner for government officials seeking to achieve this goal. To begin with, for-profit programs are not uniformly successful in equipping students for the jobs they hope to fill. The better ones appear to be successful in keeping abreast of opportunities in the job market and helping their graduates find appropriate employment.[16] Other for-profits, however, perform poorly. As a result, if officials plan to count heavily on for-profit colleges, they will have to find a way to make sure that the programs they support can actually deliver the quality needed to meet the needs of their students.

Dropout rates are also a problem, at least for students enrolling in four-year programs leading to a BA degree. According to a recent report prepared for the Gates Foundation by the Education Trust, only 22 percent of the students entering such programs in for-profit institutions graduate within six years.* For-profits dispute these findings, pointing out that the working adults they serve tend to enroll only on a part-time basis and often take more than six years to

---

* Mamie Lynch, Jennifer Engle, and José L. Cruz, *Subprime Opportunity: The Unfulfilled Promise of For-Profit Colleges and Universities*, The Education Trust (November 2010). The Education Trust report makes much of the fact that six-year graduation rates of for-profits are far below the average rates of 55 percent for public four-year colleges and 65 percent for private colleges. Such comparisons are plainly misleading, however, since the average graduation rates for nonprofit colleges include large numbers of institutions with student bodies whose family incomes, SAT scores, and prior preparation are far better than those of the students attending for-profit colleges. More meaningful comparisons involving nonprofit colleges that have student bodies with similar backgrounds would doubtless show much smaller differences in graduation rates.

graduate. Thus, the largest for-profit, the University of Phoenix, claims that its graduation rate is actually much better than the 9 percent reported by the Education Trust.[17] The true figure, according to Phoenix, is 30 percent. Even if the corrected figure is accurate, however, it is still a disturbingly low graduation rate.

For-profits seem to do much better at graduating students in their two-year programs. According to the Education Trust, 60 percent of the students entering these programs earn an associate's degree or a certificate of completion for a vocational program within three years.[18] This figure is much higher than the completion rates for community colleges in most states.[19]

High dropout rates waste substantial amounts of the public's money, since students entering for-profit programs, like those attending community colleges, pay much of their tuition costs from federal grants. Students who drop out are also more likely to default on repayment of their federally guaranteed loans.* Whereas for-profits enroll only 10 percent of all undergraduates, they account for a whopping 43 percent of all educational loan defaults.[20] Of course, their students tend to have limited incomes and hence are more likely to default than undergraduates from highly selective colleges. Even so, 27 percent of their students default within four years compared to only 16.6 percent of community college students.[21]

There is one final drawback to a strategy that relies on for-profit colleges to educate a large share of the growing cohorts of undergraduates expected in future years. For-profits, by their very nature, owe their primary responsibility to their shareholders. The vast majority of their revenues comes from student aid provided by the federal government. As a result, if Washington tries to make college more affordable by increasing Pell Grants, for-profits may respond by raising their tuition to increase profits, thus nullifying much of the hoped-for benefit to students. Like community colleges and comprehensives, then, while for-profit universities could make a real contribution to increasing completion rates at a reasonable cost, they are not as reliable or as effective a partner as one might think for helping the government raise the levels of educational attainment.

GUIDELINES FOR POLICY

The preceding discussion makes clear that financial aid is a very leaky bucket with which to increase the numbers who go to college and earn degrees.

---

*The drain on the federal treasury caused by loan defaults is mitigated by the fact that the government recovers a remarkable 80 percent of the loans that go into default. To accomplish this result, however, the government spends well over $1 billion per year to hire private agencies to collect the money owed.

Because of inadequate programs of instruction, frequent student dropouts, rising tuitions, and cutbacks in state subsidies, much of the money provided by Washington can disappear without accomplishing its intended purpose. Faced with this prospect, government officials have little choice but to look for ways to try to plug the holes in order to waste as little money as possible. In doing so, it is likely that they will gradually find themselves drawn into exercising more and more supervision over the performance of for-profit and nonprofit institutions with student bodies that are heavily dependent on Pell Grants and guaranteed loans.*

Government efforts to increase graduation rates can easily backfire. Pressuring campus leaders to cut their costs and reduce their tuitions may cause them to lower the quality of the education they provide. Refusing to authorize financial aid for colleges that do not meet minimum graduation rates may likewise cause offenders to sacrifice their academic standards and credential students who lack the necessary skills. Nevertheless, the government cannot stand idly by if its efforts to raise educational attainment by increasing financial aid are routinely nullified by higher tuitions and diminished state subsidies, or wasted through programs of insufficient quality.

The preceding discussion suggests several principles for policy-makers to bear in mind in considering a strategy to increase the levels of educational attainment.

To begin with, it will not be possible to raise the number of students earning higher education degrees simply by pouring more money into the system. Such a strategy will fail to address all facets of the problem and, in any event, will prove too expensive to be feasible in these times of fiscal stringency. A viable strategy must include vigorous efforts to improve the efficiency of existing programs by limiting their cost (without impairing the quality of education) and by encouraging efforts apart from granting additional financial aid to reduce existing dropout rates.[22] The key figure to bear in mind in considering how to proceed is the cost to the government per additional graduate. All options should be considered, including assisting for-profit institutions (and

---

*The Department of Education has already issued regulations requiring institutions to meet at least one of the following three standards in order to be eligible to receive federal financial aid:

1. At least 35 percent of former students must be repaying loans (at least one dollar in the past year).
2. Annual loan repayments must not exceed 30 percent of a typical graduate's discretionary income.
3. Annual repayments must not exceed 12 percent of a typical graduate's earnings.

nonselective private colleges) if they can educate additional students properly at a lower cost per graduate than other types of institutions.*

A second principle is that achieving higher levels of educational attainment is unlikely if the principal actors involved—Washington, state governments, colleges, and schools—are allowed to proceed independently. Left to their own devices, state legislators and for-profit institutions may use increases in federal aid to improve their own financial position instead of allowing them to make college more affordable for needy students. Many colleges will continue to allocate too much money to merit awards in an effort to lure talented students from other states and institutions instead of allocating the funds to needy applicants who might otherwise be unable to enroll and earn degrees. High schools may keep on encouraging poorly educated students to go to college if only because they do not have the staff to provide the teaching and counseling needed to ensure that those who apply to college are truly prepared to succeed.†

A third guiding principle is to avoid shifting more of college costs to students from low- and moderate-income families by charging higher tuitions without compensating increases in need-based aid. Existing cost burdens (as a share of family income) are already very high for the low- and moderate-income families whose children will have to complete college in larger numbers to enable the nation to achieve higher levels of educational attainment.‡ Levels of student indebtedness are likewise at or near the limits of feasibility if dropout rates are to fall.

Finally, in the effort to increase college enrollments and graduation rates, it will be important to take steps to ensure that "success" is not achieved by lowering the quality of education in order to make it easier for students to graduate.

---

* In one study (funded by a for-profit university, Kaplan, Inc.), the authors found that the cost per capita to the government of educating students in a for-profit institution was substantially less than in nonprofit or public two- or four-year colleges. Robert J. Shapiro and Nam D. Pham, *Taxpayers' Costs to Support Higher Education: A Comparison of Public, Private Not-for-Profit, and Private For-Profit Institutions* (September 2010). Because of higher drop-out rates, however, the cost-per-degree appears to be greater at for-profit colleges (and at community colleges) than at research universities or comprehensives. See Richard D. Kahlenberg, "Community of Equals?" *Democracy Journal* (Spring 2014), p. 47.

† The exceptional decentralization of American higher education and the consequent lack of any comprehensive national plan for its development have often been looked upon as an advantage of our system. In view of current efforts to achieve a substantial increase in educational attainment, it may be more accurate to say that the absence of a national plan may avoid big mistakes but may also make it more difficult to achieve optimum results.

‡ In 2007, college costs (net of financial aid) at four-year public colleges amounted to 55 percent of family income for families in the lowest income quintile and 33 percent for the next lowest quintile, compared with only 9 percent of income for families in the highest quintile and 16 percent for families in the second highest quintile. William Zumeta, David W. Breneman, Patrick M. Callan, and Joni E. Finney, *Financing Higher Education in the Era of Globalization* (2012), p. 22.

It will do no one any good to raise the number of Americans with degrees if the added graduates lack the knowledge and skills that such credentials are meant to provide.

Policies to achieve higher levels of attainment ought to be shaped with the foregoing principles in mind. While it is beyond the scope of this book to try to set forth a precise blueprint for policy-makers, the following suggestions are illustrative of the type of steps that are needed.[23]

- Every state should try to set goals for increasing educational attainment and work with schools, colleges, and universities, along with federal officials, to plan how the goals can be achieved.
- The federal government should try to make more effective use of its resources by offering additional aid in the form of matching grants to the states instead of simply increasing Pell Grants. In order to qualify for additional aid, states should have to match the added funds with need-based grants (rather than merit awards or athletic scholarships) and agree to keep public tuitions from rising faster than increases in need-based aid. Ideally, the federal government should find some way to come to an agreement with the states on how to share the cost of educating students in public universities so that state legislatures do not continue to reduce the per student support they give these institutions.
- Further aid to for-profit institutions should likewise be conditioned on agreements to keep tuition increases within reasonable limits.
- States should be encouraged through appropriate financial incentives to establish common standards and tests to determine which students will be assigned to remedial courses. Public schools should be required to administer the tests commencing no later than the tenth grade so that all students will have timely warning of the basic skills they need to possess in order to qualify immediately for regular college classes.
- Federal and state support, both for colleges and for financial aid, should be structured to provide appropriate incentives for institutions to achieve higher graduation rates and for students to persevere toward a degree.
- The federal government (along with private foundations) should support research and experimentation to improve efficiency and increase graduation rates—for example, through efforts to develop, evaluate, and improve online educational programs and methods of remedial instruction.
- The federal government should encourage accreditors (or other appropriate bodies) to pay close attention to graduation rates, not just in deciding whether to accredit institutions, but in helping all kinds of colleges to review their procedures and adopt best practices developed by successful

institutions serving comparable types of students. Accreditors should also make efforts to ensure that higher graduation rates are not achieved by relaxing academic standards.

THE ROLE OF COLLEGES

The discussion thus far has focused mainly on the choices open to the federal government in seeking to raise completion rates dramatically. Nothing that has been said, however, should be taken to imply that colleges themselves have no useful part to play. Quite the contrary is true. Whether or not policy-makers implement the kinds of reforms just mentioned, individual colleges can do a lot on their own to raise the levels of educational attainment. The most effective measures, however, are not necessarily the ones the public has in mind when thinking about the subject.

COST CUTTING

If one were to take a poll on ways to increase college enrollments and graduation rates, most people would put cutting costs and lowering tuition at the top of the list. Large majorities of the public feel that tuitions are too high and could be reduced without diminishing the quality of education colleges provide.[24] Resentment over mounting tuitions may be eroding much of the goodwill that colleges have long enjoyed in this country. Even so, there is no simple way to determine how much unnecessary expenditures inflate tuition levels or what university officials can do to improve matters.

Critics often allege that universities, unlike corporations, lack the incentive to keep costs to a minimum, since they do not face any pressure from investor-owners to maximize profits.[25] Such statements are an oversimplification. Businesses are not constantly motivated to keep costs to a minimum; if they were, they could not slash expenses dramatically and lay off large numbers of employees as they do periodically when pressed by some event such as a recession, a new competitor, or a hostile takeover. Conversely, there are times when universities can be highly motivated to lower costs, either because the state legislature has cut their appropriation or because conditions in the stock market have reduced the payout available from their endowment.

Responding to such pressures, academic leaders over the years have undertaken a number of significant cost-cutting measures. The advent of computers has led many universities to reduce their secretarial staff; most campuses have outsourced functions, such as building maintenance and food service, to companies that can do the work more cheaply; and most comprehensive universities and community colleges have replaced large numbers of retiring professors with part-time instructors who are willing to teach for much less money.

Observers have pointed to several other ways by which universities could lower expenses and thereby reduce the cost to students of earning a degree. Each of these suggestions needs to be examined separately, since the prospects for realizing savings vary widely depending on the type of institution and the nature of the expenditure involved.

A favorite target for critics is the campus bureaucracy.[26] For many decades, the number of administrative employees in most universities has risen more rapidly than either the student body or the faculty. For every dollar devoted to instruction, the amount spent on administration has likewise increased over the years from 19 cents in 1929 to 33 cents in 1959–60 to almost 50 cents by the end of the century.[27] Since the primary mission of colleges and universities is education, there is something instinctively troubling about the constant growth of administrative costs and personnel.

Of course, many staff increases are defensible. The growth of government regulation in matters ranging from laboratory safety to environmental rules and affirmative action has forced universities to hire more people to ensure compliance with the rules. Student demand for more and better support services, such as psychiatric counseling and job placement help, has resulted in additional costs. The use of information technology, which has improved teaching and research (as well as administration), has required ample numbers of technicians to keep the equipment operating satisfactorily. The effort to increase private giving has led to ever-larger and more sophisticated development staffs, whose presence seems justified so long as the extra personnel enable the institution to raise more than enough additional dollars to cover the incremental costs.

While specific expenditures such as these may be appropriate, one must still have misgivings over the relentless tendency for administrative costs and personnel to grow more rapidly than spending on education and much more rapidly than increases in the faculty and student body. But suspecting administrative bloat and knowing how to root it out are very different things. The latter task is far more difficult than most critics are willing to acknowledge. At least, that was my experience when I tried to do something about the problem.

After I had completed several years in office, I discovered to my chagrin that expenditures by the central administration had consistently risen more rapidly than those of the several faculties. That was hardly the example I wanted to set.

I resolved then and there to reverse the trend and make sure that the cost of central services rose more slowly than expenditures in the rest of the university during my remaining years in office.

I began by asking to examine the increases in costs and personnel for the hundreds of offices and programs that were part of the central administration. My naive hope was that growth would be concentrated in a few areas that could then be carefully scrutinized one by one in an effort to discover why the increases had occurred. It soon became clear, however, that persistent cost increases and additions to staff were not confined to just a few areas but existed throughout the entire central administration. Analyzing them all would be a Herculean task. Moreover, I knew enough by then to realize that every office and program would have a seemingly plausible explanation for its growth, making the task of discovering unjustified bloat extremely difficult.

I settled instead on a much cruder approach to the problem. I decided simply to inform our five vice presidents that, hereafter, their budgets could rise only by a percentage slightly higher than the anticipated rate of inflation but below the average rate of increase in the budgets of the several faculties. If a vice president felt that there were compelling reasons for increasing expenses more rapidly than the target figure, he or she would have to persuade the other vice presidents to lower their costs to absorb the increase. If no agreement could be reached, the problem would come to me for resolution.

Over the next decade, the system worked as planned. The central administration budget absorbed a gradually diminishing share of total university expenses. Thanks to an exceptional group of vice presidents, I was almost never called upon to resolve a budgetary impasse.

While my effort to restrain cost increases was successful, the method used was an extremely blunt instrument, and its weaknesses are all too obvious. It is quite conceivable that more could have been done to lower costs without significant harm to important university goals. It is likewise possible that some expenditures were forgone that would have been worth the expense. At best, my method was only a temporary fix until other means could be identified.

Fortunately, there are better ways of seeking out economies in administrative costs.[28] In a number of universities, outside consultants have found ways to lower costs substantially by consolidating small administrative offices and centralizing functions such as purchasing and human resources. Individual units on campus like the freedom to control their own administrative services and stoutly resist giving them up. At a time of understandable concern over the cost of higher education, however, it is unreasonable for individual programs and faculties to insist on enjoying administrative independence at the cost of giving up substantial economies of scale.

In other universities, consultants have claimed that significant savings could be achieved through the elimination of unnecessary layers of supervision. Still other efficiency experts have suggested that campus authorities could lower costs by organizing teams to study various administrative processes and determine whether the desired objectives could be achieved with fewer steps and fewer people.[29] Of course, estimates of potential savings are one thing and actual savings quite another. Before employing a consultant, campus officials would do well to check and see whether previous reports for other universities have resulted in real cost reductions. With that caveat, however, there are doubtless economies achievable through the judicious use of outside experts. Such efficiencies are important and well worth making. Still, they are not a panacea but simply onetime measures that will slow the steady rise in costs temporarily. Moreover, the savings involved, though sometimes amounting to millions of dollars, will usually represent only a tiny fraction of a large university's total budget.

A number of other proposals have been made for reducing particular expenditures other than administrative costs. While some of them seem impractical or unwise, others hold considerable promise, at least for certain kinds of institutions.

A favorite target for critics is the money spent by highly selective institutions to upgrade their student residences, improve the quality and variety of food in student dining halls, and provide better amenities such as elaborate exercise rooms. Without a doubt, undergraduate living arrangements on many of these campuses are more attractive and more costly than they were when students' parents went to college. But why should this fact merit criticism? Many other goods and services in America are also more expensive and higher in quality than they were a generation ago, yet judgments about their reasonableness are normally left to the marketplace. It is not obvious why room and board costs should be treated differently. Selective colleges compete vigorously with one another for students. The reason why they have improved their food and residence halls is that better food and lodgings have proved to be an effective way of attracting applicants and persuading them to enroll.

In this respect, the elaborate dining options, upgraded bedrooms, and modern health clubs are much like leather upholstery, extra chrome, and other luxury items in higher-priced automobiles. No one criticizes the manufacturers of Lexus, Acura, and other upscale models for making wasteful expenditures that needlessly inflate the price of their cars. People assume that the market validates such decisions and that customers prefer the added luxury despite having to pay more. Upgraded student dorms and dining halls seem much the same. As a practical matter, few selective colleges would dare to offer student amenities that were no better than they were a generation or two ago (at a commensurately lower cost) for fear of losing applicants to their competitors.

A different way to reduce costs (and tuitions) would be to drop intercollegiate athletics. While a handful of universities make money on their athletic programs, the vast majority lose substantial sums averaging millions of dollars per year. Such expenditures have nothing to do with teaching students and thus could be eliminated or greatly reduced without any ill effects on the quality of education. Moreover, unlike the provision of better food and upscale residence halls, it is doubtful that enrollments would suffer at most colleges if they transformed their intercollegiate sports to do away with large coaching staffs, long-distance travel, athletic scholarships, and other expenses associated with high-powered programs. Emory, Cal-Tech, MIT, Johns Hopkins, and other schools with low-key programs do not lack for talented applicants.

The practical question that any college must consider in contemplating such a step is whether the opposition will be so intense as to make such a change impossible or too costly to be worth undertaking. There is little doubt that withdrawing from intercollegiate athletics would be unthinkable on most campuses with big-time, high-budget programs. If Alabama, Ohio State, or any other major public university tried to abandon football or basketball, governors and state legislators might well veto the move. In most private colleges and universities with high-profile programs, either the trustees would be opposed or the uproar from outraged students and alumni would suffice to dissuade the hardiest president from making the attempt. Even Tulane, which is hardly a major football "power," had to withdraw a proposal to deemphasize its program in the face of adverse publicity and angry protests.

The prospects for downgrading athletics, however, could be considerably brighter for colleges with much less visible athletic programs. In many of these institutions, such a move would not incur anything like the intensity of opposition in universities with high-profile teams. Intercollegiate athletics should be a tempting target for cost savings, the more so since such programs often bring a host of dubious practices in their wake, such as recruiting violations, lower admissions standards for athletic prospects, and easier courses or even special majors to accommodate athletes who might otherwise be unable to complete their coursework successfully.

Another way to reduce costs might be to eliminate the marginal programs of research and graduate education that many institutions have launched in an effort to gain prestige and attract federal grants. Such efforts are expensive since they require higher faculty salaries, lower teaching loads, and added outlays for libraries and laboratory facilities. In return, they frequently fail to achieve distinction while contributing to a surplus of PhDs and a flood of unremarkable, uncited articles. For all their weaknesses, of course, it is by no means easy to do away with such initiatives once they are well established. Faculty members hired with the expectation of building research programs and having graduate students will not willingly abandon these endeavors. Presidents who have made research a hallmark of their administration will resist admitting defeat. Even so, the severe economic pressures that so many institutions are now facing should force some university leaders to abandon such efforts and cause state boards to become less willing to authorize new PhD programs in the future.

There are other ways to achieve cost savings that are easier to implement than abandoning intercollegiate athletics and eliminating marginal research and PhD programs. One possibility is to move to year-round operations so as to spread the cost of facilities over a larger student population. Another way to lower the cost to students is to reduce the number of unneeded courses that students take to complete their college studies.* Undergraduates in most colleges currently take an average of one semester more than the necessary four years, because of either poor advising, or overly complicated course requirements, or an administrative reluctance to grant credit for courses taken by students who change majors or transfer from another institution. Unnecessary credits add a lot to the cost of a college degree if one takes account of forgone earnings as well as the added tuition. Experience suggests that it is possible to reduce the number of excess courses substantially through better advising and

---

* A related step that some observers have praised is to move to a "competency-based" education in which students gain the necessary credits, not by completing a certain number of class hours and passing an exam, but by demonstrating the requisite competence in various prescribed skills or tasks. Under this system, students can proceed at their own pace, and those who have gained the necessary skill through previous experience or who can master the necessary competencies in a shorter period of time can graduate sooner at less cost to themselves and to the taxpayer. Proponents claim that employers will gain by being able to read transcripts and tell what college graduates can do, not merely how many hours they have sat in different classrooms.

Competency-based programs may work well enough for training people to fill jobs that can be readily broken down into a series of well-defined skills. It is also at least arguable that students who can demonstrate sufficent competence in subjects such as expository writing, mathematics, statistics, or reading and speaking a foreign language should be able to receive credits toward graduation just like students who do well at high school in advanced placement courses. Yet the competency-based approach has limitations. Not all material lends itself well to such methods. Many capabilities are sufficiently amorphous that they will be evaluated differently depending on the college and the instructor. As a result, employers will still not be able to look at a transcript and know what a graduate can do. Moreover, not all the values of a good college education can be reduced to testable competencies or acquired by students sitting alone in front of a computer completing reading assignments, doing problem sets, and taking exams. Developing empathy, creative imagination, or lasting intellectual interests are examples of qualities that may require more discussion, more face-to-face teaching, and more informal human interaction than a competency-based program is likely to offer. Finally, it is doubtful whether a competency-based system can achieve sufficently high graduation rates to contribute much to the goal of raising the levels of educational attainment in America.

computer programs that make it easy for students to keep track of the courses they need to qualify for graduation.[30]

The measures just described, however, will work well only for institutions that have more qualified students applying than they can accommodate. Year-round operation, for example, will scarcely be feasible if there are no additional students forthcoming to spread the cost of college facilities. Eliminating excess credits will reduce revenues if colleges are unable to attract more students to take up the slack. Nevertheless, if history is any guide, the number of students seeking college degrees will continue to grow in the future, especially if the government persists in its effort to increase the number of younger Americans with college degrees. The key question will be how to accommodate the additional students at the least cost. Year-round operations and better course management are promising steps in the right direction.

Still remaining is the possibility of achieving major cost reductions through the use of online courses. It is quite possible that technology will permit colleges to offer an education of equal (or better) quality with fewer professors and thus bring the same type of cost savings to higher education that industry has long enjoyed through substituting machines for human labor. At the very least, online learning may allow colleges to accommodate increasing numbers of students without the expense of building additional classrooms and dormitories.

Media accounts of online courses enrolling thousands of students at a modest cost have raised the hopes of many people that technology alone will provide the remedy for mounting college costs. Yet it would be premature to count on such a happy outcome. Although one can point to some promising experiments, there are virtually no rigorous studies offering convincing proof that online classes can lower costs substantially with no increase in student dropouts or loss of educational quality.[31] On any agenda for cutting college costs, therefore, a high priority should be given to carrying out carefully controlled, large-scale tests to determine whether online courses can actually lower costs without reducing completion rates or student learning.*

---

*Much the same point could be made about another cost-cutting measure that has already been implemented on a massive scale—the use of part-time adjunct instructors in place of tenured faculty. Although there are few careful studies of the effects on the quality of education of using adjuncts, some researchers have found that adjuncts contribute to higher dropout rates. E.g., M. Kevin Eagan and Audrey J. Jaeger, "Closing the Gate: Part-Time Faculty and Instruction in Gatekeeper Courses and First Year Persistence," in John M. Braxton (ed.), *The Role of the Classroom in College Student Performance* (2008), p. 39. But see Iryna Y. Johnson, "Contingent Instructors and Student Outcomes: An Artifact or a Fact?" 52 *Research on Higher Education* (2011), p. 761 (finding that using part-time instructors does not increase dropout rates but does cause grade inflation). Surely these questions deserve more study than they have received. As much as we need to reduce unnecessary costs, higher education already has enough difficulty with retention rates and student learning without making the problems worse through ill-considered efforts to increase efficiency.

Using Cost Savings Effectively

If campus officials do manage to lower costs significantly, it is still not clear that they will use the savings to make college more affordable. Indeed, there are often strong incentives to do otherwise. In many sectors of higher education, academic leaders rarely feel that they will be judged according to their success in holding down tuition. No wonder. Examining media accounts of the accomplishments of retiring college presidents, one never finds much mention of what happened to costs, tuitions, or financial aid during their term of office. Rather, the emphasis is all on achievements such as new programs started, additional professors hired, and higher SAT scores for the entering classes. Trustees often favor the same priorities. Under such conditions, leaders on many campuses are likely to use any savings they make to add merit scholarships, recruit more professors, and launch new programs unless market forces or other incentives induce them to lower student costs instead.

Fortunately, the tendencies just described are less prevalent in the community colleges and comprehensive universities that will bear the brunt of educating the additional students needed to raise levels of educational attainment and promote economic growth and social mobility. Yet even in these institutions, campus officials may not choose to utilize cost savings to lower tuitions or even to increase financial aid. Instead, they may be more inclined to improve student services or increase the quality of instruction. Such choices are not necessarily inappropriate. Many of our community colleges and comprehensive universities have been starved for resources for so long that improvements in academic programs and student services could turn out to reduce dropouts and enhance the value of the education provided so as to yield greater benefits to students and society than those achievable through lowering college costs.

Even if academic leaders utilize their cost savings to ease the financial burden of their students, they must still decide how to use the cost savings most effectively. Many members of the public and some lawmakers as well seem to assume that the proper course is to lower tuitions, or at least slow their future growth. However, this alternative may not be the best way to produce a million more college degrees per year at an affordable cost.

The most efficient use of cost savings would be to increase financial aid for students who actually need it to stay in college. There is no evidence that lower tuitions will increase graduation rates among students from families in the upper half of the income scale.[32] As a result, if campus authorities use cost savings to lower tuitions across the board, much of the money may go to families who would have sent their children through college anyway. In colleges with substantial numbers of higher-income students, therefore, it would be far better to use the savings to increase financial aid for students from families with low and moderate incomes who actually need such help in order to enroll and stay enrolled until they graduate.

PREVENTING DROPOUTS

Reducing costs and increasing financial aid are not the only ways to raise graduation rates. In fact, they may not even be the most important. There are other reasons for dropping out of college that are at least as significant.

The preceding chapter identified a number of things that colleges can do to improve their graduation rates. The recent McKinsey report has done the same by pointing to the various steps that high-performing colleges have already taken, such as providing clearly structured programs with fewer options, better counseling and support services, and more proactive job placement efforts.[33] While no one improvement may bring dramatic results, the cumulative effect of several of these measures can be quite substantial.

As the preceding chapter also indicated, many colleges could work with local high schools to inform their students about the knowledge and skills they need to have so that fewer young people come to college only to find that their past studies have not prepared them adequately to cope with the academic demands at the next level. A further step would be to search for ways to improve remedial education so that more students who come with insufficient skills can be brought to a level high enough to enroll and complete regular courses.* Still another subject that needs attention is the sensitive topic of academic underperformance and high dropout rates among minority males, especially Hispanics and African Americans.[34] Since minorities will make up a growing proportion of additional entrants to college, it will be hard to increase graduation rates substantially without figuring out how to improve the level of academic achievement of this important segment of the college-going population.

How can colleges be persuaded to take these steps? Cutting off federal aid to institutions with abysmal dropout numbers is an obvious method, but extensive use of such a drastic sanction may simply cause colleges with low graduation rates to exclude high-risk applicants or relax academic standards and pass students through. As a result, such remedies must be used sparingly.

---

*Of course, colleges cannot do anything to improve remediation if they are situated in one of the states that forbids such instruction. Legislative prohibitions of this kind seem excessively harsh. One can understand why taxpayers would bridle at having to pay twice for teaching students skills they should have learned in high school. Nevertheless, it is hardly fair to deny students a chance to earn a college degree because of educational failings for which they may not be at all responsible.

A better approach that most accreditors use is to make a serious effort to help institutions raise graduation rates when they conduct their periodic college reviews. Even institutions that are not at risk of losing their accreditation tend to pay close attention to issues that are known to be of particular concern to accreditors. If graduation rates are emphasized, campus officials will look carefully at their existing programs to increase student retention when they prepare the required self-study prior to the accreditation visit. Inspection teams can call attention to additional steps that other institutions have found helpful in reducing attrition. Where significant deficiencies exist, accreditors can recommend corrective measures and call for a follow-up visit a year or two later to evaluate progress made since the initial review. Since most colleges want to perform well, if only as a matter of self-respect, their leaders will normally respond to such suggestions by making efforts to improve.

To complement the gentle pressure of accreditation, public officials and foundations can offer encouragement by funding promising research projects and experiments aimed at raising graduation rates. The efforts already being made by several major foundations to improve remedial education are a valuable step in this direction. Further research and experimentation might also help to develop new and better methods for keeping students enrolled. One example of the kind of innovation needed is a recent experiment for coaching at-risk students that appears to reduce dropout rates by up to 4 percentage points.[35] Another is the work being done to develop computer programs that can sift large amounts of information from student records to provide an earlier identification of undergraduates in danger of leaving so that colleges can intervene while there is still time to offer effective assistance.

PROSPECTS FOR SUCCESS

In light of everything said thus far, what are the odds of achieving President Obama's goal of regaining America's longtime leadership in the educational attainment of young people? By any honest calculation, the chances of success by 2020 seem very slight at best. On the positive side, the percentage of twenty-four- to twenty-nine-year-olds with college degrees has risen significantly since 1995, albeit not at a rate fast enough to keep pace with the ambitious target set by the president. High school graduation rates have also moved higher, as have the percentages of high school graduates who enroll in college. Even college graduation rates have had an uptick in the last few years.

These welcome changes, however, are largely due to conditions external to universities that may not continue for very much longer. The rising numbers of high school graduates have been helped along by a rapid increase in the teenage population, a trend that is expected to slow appreciably in the next few years. The recent growth in high school and college graduation rates may well be in part a reaction to the current depressed job market and could diminish as the economy improves.

The prospects for college efforts to boost graduation rates are equally uncertain, especially during the coming years when public funding is likely to be limited. The challenge of developing a more effective plan for providing financial aid to colleges will not be met quickly. The development and implementation of better methods of remedial education will also be a slow process. The exemplary practices identified in the McKinsey report that could increase graduation rates without large additional costs are unlikely to spread throughout the ranks of community colleges and comprehensive universities in less than a generation. These difficulties by no means justify abandoning the effort to have a more highly educated population. On the contrary, they caution against declaring failure if the hoped-for results do not materialize within a few years.

An equally important question involves the prospects for containing college costs. The tendency for these costs to keep rising at rates that consume a larger and larger share of family income seems impossible to sustain for much longer. Similarly, the efforts by states to minimize their financial commitment to public higher education cannot go on without impairing the quality of state universities or saddling the federal government with financial responsibilities that Washington may be unable or unwilling to assume. How, then, might the current system become sustainable?

Five possibilities are conceivable. The first is that students will eventually balk at paying higher tuitions and taking on increasing debt and either gravitate to lower-cost colleges or abandon plans for college altogether. In this event, campus authorities will have to curb their prices even if it calls for painful budgetary cuts. Indeed, that is what many private colleges are already doing by offering deep discounts to middle-income applicants to induce them to enroll. Eventually, this practice will either diminish the quality of education in a large number of institutions or force them to shut down. Neither result would benefit students or the public.

A second possible outcome is that federal officials will try to restrain the rising cost of college by withholding their financial aid from universities that do not moderate their tuition increases. While Washington clearly has the power to implement such a policy, government price controls seldom produce a satisfactory outcome, and efforts to limit tuitions are unlikely to prove an exception. The most probable result will be a decline in educational effectiveness. Quality is bound to suffer in public universities if states continue to reduce their support while federal officials block attempts by colleges to increase tuition revenues. Moreover, if community colleges and comprehensives cannot raise their tuitions significantly, they may not be able to boost levels of educational attainment by enrolling additional cohorts of poorly prepared students without lowering the quality of the instruction they offer. Since declines in the quality of education are so hard to measure, it will be all too easy for government officials to allow such erosion to occur in order to lessen the demands on the federal budget.

The third alternative is for the economy to resume the pattern that existed from 1950 to the mid-1970s when the gross domestic product (GDP) grew at a healthy rate and the gains were quite evenly distributed throughout the working population. (Note that blue-collar wages rose slightly *faster* over this period than CEO compensation.) Since 1975, however, four-fifths of American families have experienced real income growth no greater than 1 percent per year, and three-fifths have seen their incomes rise at an annual rate of only 0.5 percent or less.[36] Thus, whereas college costs increased without claiming a rising share of average family income during the early postwar decades, the opposite has been true since the mid-1970s. As a result, the public has grown increasingly upset about college tuitions, and many students have acquired excessive levels of indebtedness.

If the pattern of 1950–75 could somehow be repeated over the next generation, college costs could again rise moderately faster than the cost of living without taking a greater share of family income. Tax revenues could also increase, making it possible for governments to maintain their share of support for higher education and even help to finance the increased growth in college enrollments needed to raise educational attainment levels significantly.

This scenario is a happy one, but the odds of its occurring are doubtful at best. For one thing, organized labor is much weaker than it was in the 1950s, thus dimming the prospects for sharing the fruits of economic progress more evenly. Moreover, achieving robust economic growth with a more equal distribution of the benefits seems unlikely without raising levels of educational attainment to meet employer needs and provide higher earnings to low- and middle-income families. Thus, a catch-22 situation may exist. Middle- and lower-level incomes will not rise without a more educated workforce, but a more educated workforce may not be achievable without an increase in the incomes of low- and moderate-income families.

The fourth possibility is that, one way or another, government and college officials will arrive at an arrangement whereby federal and state governments agree to finance at least a slow growth in the undergraduate population through increased institutional support and student aid in return for reasonable restraint in the growth of tuitions. Governments might seek such an outcome recognizing that rising levels of educational attainment are a prerequisite to balanced and sustained economic growth. Universities might agree because the alternative of continuing on the current path is simply not possible and the arrangement just described seems the best feasible alternative.

This scenario seems much happier than the first alternative and a more likely prospect than the second. Yet it too has problems. In the present fiscal climate, governments may find it difficult to keep their end of the bargain. Universities may not be able to moderate tuition increases significantly by eliminating waste and may suffer some loss of quality. And in trying to make the arrangement work, public officials may seek to exercise a degree of supervision over colleges and universities that many will find objectionable.

The fifth and final possibility is that online education and related technological advances will produce enough cost savings to remove the need for unsustainable tuition increases while greatly reducing the expense of educating the larger cohorts of students required to raise current levels of educational attainment. This would indeed be a welcome turn of events. Whether it is a likely outcome, however, or even a realistic possibility, is a subject considered in more detail in chapter 7.

CHAPTER SIX

ENTERING THE RIGHT COLLEGE

|||||||||||||||||||||||||||||||||||||||||||||||||||||||||||||||||||||||||||||||||||||||||||||||||||||||

MANY YOUNG PEOPLE ARE not only interested in going to college; they are keenly concerned with *which* college they can enter. Such concern is especially likely to become intense in countries like the United States where great differences exist between the resources of richer and poorer colleges.

In an ideal world, all students would be able to attend the institution of their choice provided they were suitably qualified, and all would be well enough informed to choose the school best equipped to help them acquire the learning, self-knowledge, and other capabilities needed to lead full and rewarding lives. A world so arranged could maximize not only the opportunities for young people but the gains provided to society as a whole. As a practical matter, of course, this goal is unattainable. Even well-informed high school seniors cannot tell in advance which colleges will help them learn and develop the most. And even if they did know, they might have personal reasons for preferring some other college, or the school they coveted might have so many applicants that not all who wished to enter could do so.

Under these conditions, the best one can hope for is that as many students as possible are able to make a reasonably informed choice and as few students as possible are denied the college of their choice because they cannot afford the cost or for some other reason apart from their intellectual and personal qualifications. Achieving this goal would require providing enough financial aid to allow all deserving students to go wherever they chose to enroll. It would also require finding ways to give all young people enough information to help them choose which colleges they are qualified to enter and which seem most likely to fulfill their needs and aspirations.

Once students decide where they want to go and submit an application, it is up to admissions officers to judge all applicants on valid educational grounds and not be swayed by arbitrary or unrelated reasons. This process is seldom a problem for colleges that accept nearly all the students who apply. But it does raise difficult questions for colleges fortunate enough to receive many more applicants than they can accept. About 15 percent of four-year colleges regularly reject more students than they admit. Only a handful, mainly private research universities or leading liberal arts colleges, have many applicants for every place; a half dozen or so could even fill their entire entering class with high school valedictorians if they wished.

The students who succeed in gaining entry to these highly selective institutions are widely believed to represent a sort of meritocracy with much-improved prospects for achieving significant success and prosperity in later life.[1] There is some basis for this belief. One recent tabulation has revealed that a mere dozen institutions—Harvard, Princeton, Yale, Stanford, Chicago, Columbia, MIT, Cornell, Johns Hopkins, Northwestern, Pennsylvania, and Dartmouth— have educated 54 percent of the CEOs of large corporations and 42 percent of the nation's top government leaders.[2] Not surprisingly, then, the competition to enter such colleges is intense and the criteria used to decide which applicants to admit are matters of great interest not only to students and their parents but to the media and to social critics as well.*

Despite all the effort and anxiety that accompany the attempt to get accepted by the college of one's choice, it is still not entirely clear how much difference such decisions will actually make to the later lives of the students involved. It is certainly true that the more selective the college, the more successful its graduates tend to be. But those results could merely reflect qualities of mind and character that freshmen brought with them when they arrived on campus rather than anything they learned thereafter from the teachings and extracurricular life of the college itself. It is by no means easy to disentangle these influences. Although many investigators have tried to discover what turns on which college one attends, they have often arrived at different conclusions, and the variables they manage to measure rarely provide a full explanation of the results.

In fact, there is surprisingly little evidence that attending a highly selective college with impressive average SAT (ACT) scores produces exceptional improvement in the cognitive abilities of students. However, the selectivity

---

*The admissions policies of selective colleges have attracted even closer scrutiny in recent years because of concerns over the growth of inequality in American society. Richard Kahlenberg, introduction to Richard D. Kahlenberg (ed.), *Rewarding Strivers: How Increasing College Access Is Increasing Inequality, and What to Do about It* (2010), pp. 11–12. The share of total adjusted gross income received by the top 1 percent of Americans grew from 11 percent in 1986 to 17 percent in 2009, reaching levels not seen since the 1920s. "The Paradox of the New Elite," *New York Times* (October 23, 2011), pp. 1, 6; Joseph E. Stiglitz, "Of the 1% for the 1%," http://www.readersupported news.org/opinion2/275-42/8017-focus-of-the1-by-the1-for-the1. Such wealth carries a risk that rich families will become a hereditary aristocracy by giving their children the finest schooling, special tutoring, and other advantages that other applicants cannot match, thus assuring them an edge in competing for admission to elite colleges. In a country dedicated to equality of opportunity, such a prospect understandably causes concern.

of a college does appear to have a significant effect on graduation rates. With considerable regularity, the higher the average scores of entering students, the greater the percentage of them earn a degree, even after investigators control for their higher scores, their socioeconomic background, and their race and gender.[3] Although the reasons for these results are not completely understood, several factors are probably responsible, including the greater ambitions of the students, the higher expectations of the institution, and the more generous financial aid and added counseling and other student services that selective colleges are able to provide.

Researchers have come to differing conclusions on the impact of attending a selective college on later life earnings and career success. The weight of the evidence suggests that selectivity has a positive effect (again, controlling for the differences in the academic aptitude, socioeconomic background, race, gender, and other qualities that students possessed when they entered).[4] Based on a number of studies, a difference of 100 points in the average SAT scores of a college's students seems to be associated with an advantage in average earnings of roughly 2 to 4 percent, and the premium appears to grow over time.[5] Graduates of more selective colleges also tend to receive more job offers and are more likely to earn graduate degrees in law, medicine, and business than those attending less selective institutions.[6]

There is some evidence, however, suggesting that these differences are mainly attributable to a smaller subset of colleges—the extremely selective schools that attract students with SAT scores in the top 1 or 2 percent of entering freshmen.[7] Moreover, the studies involved rarely control for differences in the levels of ambition that students bring to college, thus leaving open the possibility that the higher earnings of graduates from the most selective colleges reflect a keener desire for success rather than any special benefit from attending the colleges involved.

Whatever the actual effects of colleges on their students, the fact remains that many applicants and their parents set great store by being admitted to the most selective institution they can enter, and for understandable reasons. The more selective colleges spend much larger amounts per student than the less selective institutions.[8] They provide more scholarships, better-known professors, more extracurricular activities and traveling fellowships, brighter classmates, handsomer facilities, and more. No one may know for sure what difference these characteristics will make to the later lives of students. Even so, many young people and their parents are plainly willing to assume that greater selectivity and additional resources will translate somehow into a more satisfying undergraduate experience and a more successful career thereafter.

CHOOSING STUDENTS

In view of the keen desire of many students and their parents to gain admission to the college of their choice, it is important to consider what criteria such colleges ought to use in choosing their entering class. A frequent answer is that applicants should be accepted or rejected "on the merits." But what are "the merits"? Many people assume that they simply mean high school grades and test scores, but this is surely an inadequate answer. Grades and scores are the best-known predictors of academic success, but they are very crude. A difference of 100 points in SAT scores is associated with a difference of only 5.9 percentage points in eventual class rank and explains still less of any differences in later life success. As a result, to base admissions decisions on grades and test scores alone without regard to other aspects of an applicant's background and accomplishments would be a narrow approach indeed.*

To be sure, no one denies that admissions committees should give substantial weight to academic ability. They should take particular care not to admit anyone whose intellectual capacities seem marginal enough to raise a serious risk of flunking out. To most experienced admissions officers, however, the quality of a freshman class is much more than the sum of its test scores. Students learn a great deal from their classmates, and much that they learn is not strictly academic. They are likely to gain the most from one another if their classmates are diverse in interests, experience, talents, and beliefs. As a result, it may be more important to admit an applicant who grew up in another country, or has a special talent for music or poetry, or belongs to a different religion, or has enjoyed unusual life experiences than to enroll someone with slightly better high school grades or SAT (ACT) scores.[9]

The proper way to choose students, then, is to examine each application taking account of all the relevant information in order to assemble a class that,

---

*Most studies that measure cognitive improvement in college find that differences among students in any given institution vary much more than average differences between institutions. E.g., Richard Arum and Josipa Roksa, *Academically Adrift: Limited Learning on College Campuses* (2011), finding that the 10 percent of students who improved the most in critical thinking gained 1.5 standard deviations, more than three times as much as the average student, while a substantial minority of undergraduates made no significant improvement at all. Students making exceptional progress could be found in all kinds of colleges, not just in selective institutions. Such findings suggest that test scores, such as the SAT and ACT, do not do much to identify applicants who will improve the most in college. In view of this fact, several universities and researchers are currently seeking ways to improve their admissions procedures by identifying the noncognitive traits that contribute to greater growth and higher performance in college. Eric Hoover, "Colleges Seek 'Noncognitive' Gauges of Applicants," *Chronicle of Higher Education* (January 18, 2013), p. A1.

collectively, will best fulfill the educational mission of the college. Although the criteria used may vary according to the special interests and priorities of different colleges, most admissions offices will be primarily interested in three qualities: the intellectual capabilities of applicants, how likely they are to contribute to society in worthwhile ways after they have graduated, and how much their presence promises to add to the life of the college and their fellow students if they are admitted. These criteria are admittedly vague and can be hard to apply in practice. Drawing fine-grained distinctions between young people with different backgrounds and accomplishments is bound to be an arbitrary process. Some issues, however, occur frequently and raise questions of policy and fairness that give rise to heated differences of opinion.

APPLICANTS WITH WEALTHY PARENTS

One practice in most selective colleges is to favor children from families wealthy enough to make a substantial donation. Fund-raising staffs usually notify admissions committees of applicants with rich parents, and admissions officers are typically aware of who these parents are when they decide which students to admit. How much difference this makes in admissions decisions is not widely known and probably varies considerably from one college to another, but it clearly makes *some* difference almost everywhere.

College officials defend this practice on the ground that a "wealth preference" will surely lead to higher levels of giving that in turn can be used to improve the college for everyone else and thus advance its educational mission. John McCardell, former president of Middlebury College, put the argument with unusual candor. "If a handful of slots go to deserving applicants whose families can at least have the potential to improve in dramatic ways the quality of education at Middlebury College, we would not be fair to our successors or predecessors if we were to overlook that reality."[10]

From a purely utilitarian standpoint there is something to be said for McCardell's argument. Students with very wealthy parents will normally make up only a small percentage of the entering class. As McCardell implies, such applicants will be admitted only if they are judged to be at least capable of doing the work. (After all, no one will gain, least of all the development office, if the students accepted under this theory flunk out.) Once these young people enroll, even if only a fraction of their parents make a handsome gift, the entire student body and faculty may be better off.

Utilitarian arguments of this kind, however, do not necessarily provide a fully satisfying answer. One could make the same point to defend a practice of auctioning off places in the class to the highest bidder or reaching an agreement with a wealthy family to admit a child in exchange for a gift of one million dollars. Yet when individual cases of this kind come to light, they are invariably greeted with widespread condemnation. Is there any real difference between making such an arrangement and admitting students because their parents have the capacity to make substantial gifts? In both cases, the university is undermining the principle of equal opportunity and helping to perpetuate differences in wealth from one generation to the next. In both cases, students are being admitted not simply on the basis of their own intellectual and personal qualifications, but in the expectation of the institution's receiving money from the parents. The only difference is one of probabilities, not of principle. If it is wrong to accept students because their parents have promised a handsome donation, it seems just as wrong to admit applicants because their parents *might* make a gift.

LEGACIES

A related set of cases involves the children of alumni—the so-called legacy cases. Most private colleges give *some* weight to applicants whose parents attended the institution. The reason given is sometimes said to be tradition—the value of educating generations of students from a particular family who will presumably develop a special loyalty to the institution. Other admissions officers point out that colleges often receive voluntary services from alumni in the form of helping to organize reunions, interviewing local high school students applying to the college, or raising money from classmates. Surely, one might say, such loyalty deserves *some* recognition in the admissions process.

The favored treatment given to the children of alumni has attracted increasing attention of late. The reaction has not been positive.[11] Preferences of this kind run counter to a widespread belief among Americans that opportunity should be available on the basis of merit rather than ancestry. Among the public as a whole, 75 percent are opposed to the practice.[12]

It is not always clear how strong an advantage legacies enjoy. Those who oppose such preferences often stress the fact that the percentages of legacy applicants accepted by selective colleges tend to be much higher than those of the remaining applicants whose parents did not have the foresight to graduate from the institution their children hope to attend. But statistics of this kind are misleading, since the children of alumni frequently have better grades and test scores, on average, than the other applicants. Once this difference is accounted for, the actual preference may turn out to be rather slight. At one highly selective university that is often singled out for criticism on this score, alumni children who were admitted actually had higher SAT scores as a group than the average for other students in the entering class in half or more of the preceding ten years. In another study covering a group of selective colleges, legacies turned out to finish only 1.5 points below the average rank in class for the class as a whole.[13] In such colleges, legacy status seems to be at best only a tie-breaking factor in choosing among candidates of equal promise. When the preferences are as modest as this, the practice seems hardly worth complaining about. Quibbling over such small differences in prior grades and test scores, which are too minor to have a significant predictive value, gives greater importance to these crude academic measures than they deserve.

In still another study, however, investigators found that being a child of an alumnus in a sample of selective colleges was equivalent to 160 points on the combined SAT test.[14] If the advantage grows this large, arguments about maintaining continuity from one generation to another seem a weak reed on which to base decisions of considerable importance to the applicants involved. The case for rewarding alumni loyalty and service is equally shaky. Granting admission in exchange for parental services is not self-evidently different from accepting students in exchange for parental donations. In both cases, it seems better to base admissions decisions on the qualities of the applicants rather than the generosity of the parents. Doing so may well not cause any demonstrable harm to the institution. Several schools that have dropped their legacy preference did not appear to suffer any perceptible decline in alumni giving thereafter.[15]

ATHLETES

Other familiar admissions practices can confer even larger advantages on favored groups of applicants. A well-known example is the preference given by selective colleges to promising athletes. In some selective colleges, many members of the varsity football and basketball teams have average SAT scores that are two or three or even four hundred points below the average for the entire student body.[16] Once these applicants are admitted, their grades tend to be much worse than those of their fellow students. According to one especially rigorous study involving a number of selective colleges, the average rank in class of recruited athletes in the major sports turned out to be far below even what their high school grades and test scores would have predicted.[17] Often, athletes remain academically eligible only because they receive special tutoring at the university's expense, take the easiest courses, or choose a major specially created to provide an undemanding path to graduation (or at least to continued eligibility).

Many dubious reasons have been given to justify athletic preferences. They are often said to be warranted because college athletes display unusual leadership abilities in later life, or are particularly likely to become active in alumni affairs, or because good teams attract a larger number of applicants and increase alumni contributions to the university. Careful studies by several scholars have not found any of these rationalizations to be well supported by the facts.[18] Nor are athletics an important source of funds for most universities. High-profile sports such as football and basketball may regularly yield a profit, but even that is often not the case if one accounts properly for the capital costs of a football stadium or a basketball arena plus the money spent on the practice fields, weight rooms, recruiting budgets, and large, well-paid coaching staffs that are considered essential for serious competition in these sports. Only a handful of universities make enough money from their high-profile teams to pay for their entire intercollegiate athletic program with its array of other sports, such as track, tennis, and field hockey, that do not generate sufficient revenue to cover their costs.

In the end, therefore, there is little to be said in defense of athletic preferences. As with so much else in big-time intercollegiate athletics, the treatment accorded to prospective athletes has become more and more embarrassing and difficult to justify. The real reason for continuing the practice is simply that the cost of abandoning a high-profile sport—in both practical and political terms—is now too great for the colleges involved to contemplate. Robert Hutchins managed to abolish football when he was president of the University of Chicago. But that was in the 1930s. Today, no president of a Division IA school would even make such an attempt. Many would lose their jobs if they did. As a result, the current system continues even though college presidents, faculties, and even majorities of students and alumni tend to agree that the situation has gotten out of hand.[19]

RACIAL PREFERENCES

Far more controversial than athletic preferences is the policy in selective colleges of favoring the admission of underrepresented minorities, chiefly African American and Hispanic applicants. At many institutions, the preferences given such students are almost as great as those received by athletes. According to opinion polls, most Americans disapprove of the practice.[20] In eight states, including Michigan and California, voters have approved referenda outlawing such policies in public colleges and universities. Even so, racial preferences are virtually universal among selective colleges except in states where they are forbidden by law. Though periodically the subject of legal challenge, they were narrowly upheld by the Supreme Court in 2003, provided that admissions committees did not impose quotas but instead considered race as only one of a variety of factors in making individual judgments to determine which applicants to admit.*[21]

Much confusion has arisen over the reasons for racial preferences. For a long time, commentators seemed to assume that the policy was meant as atonement for slavery, segregation, and other past injustices. This was clearly a weak rationale, however, since most white students who are denied admission owing to racial preferences bear no responsibility for the sins of the past, while many minority students who benefit from preferences may have suffered relatively little from discrimination. In practice, most minorities admitted to selective colleges today come from solidly middle-class families, and many are children of immigrants whose ancestors were never slaves in the antebellum South nor even lived under racially segregated conditions.

The more persuasive reasons for the policy were finally articulated clearly by Justice Sandra Day O'Connor in the Supreme Court case of *Grutter v. Bollinger*.[22] As Justice O'Connor pointed out, minority preferences benefit the society in two important ways. They contribute to the diversity of the student body by bringing different perspectives and experiences to the campus that broaden the understanding of all students and help them learn to live and work effectively with persons different from themselves. Since large numbers of white students have grown up in predominantly white neighborhoods and attended predominantly white schools, college is often the first experience they have to live and work with students of other races. In addition, said Justice O'Connor, admitting minorities to selective colleges will eventually help to diversify the leadership class to make it more representative of the population as a whole and thereby increase the legitimacy of the government, the judiciary, and other important institutions and professions. Accomplishing this objective calls for admitting the most academically talented minorities who apply even if they come from relatively well-to-do families.

Although few opponents of racial preferences have been convinced by these arguments, there is considerable evidence to support both of the rationales enunciated by Justice O'Connor. In the 1990s, Bill Bowen and I published a detailed study of more than eighty thousand graduates of twenty-nine selective colleges who had matriculated in the fall of either 1951, 1976, or 1989.

---

*In 2013, the Court again upheld the use of racial preferences but ruled that such practices must be "narrowly tailored" to acheive the benefits of diversity with the least possible disadvantage to applicants with higher grades and test scores. *Fisher v. University of Texas*, 133 S. Ct. 2411 (2013).

Substantial majorities of alumni from each class, both whites and blacks, felt that current policies of race-sensitive admissions either were correct or should be emphasized more, with support becoming greater in the more recent classes.[23] Seventy percent of blacks and 63 percent of whites from the most recent classes felt that their college experience had contributed either "a great deal" or "quite a bit" to their ability to "work effectively and get along well with people from different races/cultures."[24]* As for the value of encouraging a more diverse leadership, it is clear that the larger cohorts of black and Hispanic students who began graduating from major universities thirty-five years ago have helped bring about appreciable increases in the numbers of minority judges, legislators and other elected public officials, military leaders, corporate executives, and other persons in positions of authority.[25] It is impossible to assess the value of these developments in any exact way. But the fact that many prominent corporate CEOs and retired generals and admirals signed amicus briefs in the *Grutter* case supporting preferential admissions testifies to the importance attached by knowledgeable people to a leadership more representative of America's increasingly diverse population.

Several other arguments against racial preferences have now been refuted quite convincingly.[26] For example, many critics have insisted that preferences hurt the very people they are meant to help because minority students admitted by affirmative action would be unable to keep up with their classmates and would either flunk out or suffer from being stigmatized as intellectually inferior. In fact, it turns out that minorities admitted to highly selective colleges are much more likely to graduate than minorities with similar high school grades and test scores who attend less selective institutions. They also tend to be more enthusiastic about their college experience and to earn higher salaries after they graduate.

A troubling aspect of race-sensitive admissions is the tendency of most minority students to perform less well academically than their high school grades and admissions test scores would predict.[27] This is exactly contrary to what many advocates of affirmative action expected, since they had long argued that standardized tests were culturally biased *against* minority students and thus tended to *under*estimate their academic potential. The reasons for the

---

*After reviewing a number of studies on the effects of racial diversity on students' tolerance and racial understanding, Ernest Pascarella and Patrick Terenzini declared that "the more recent evidence seems conclusive in indicating that college attendance, independent of numerous other factors, promotes racial understanding and openness to diversity." *How College Affects Students*, vol. 2, *A Third Decade of Research* (2005), p. 581. Even more recent studies have found that "interacting with students of other races increases critical thinking skills." Dan Berrett, "Diversity Aids in Critical Thinking, 4 Studies Find," *Chronicle of Higher Education* (November 30, 2012), p. A-3.

weak academic showing of many black and Hispanic undergraduates are not entirely clear. Although there are a few examples of successful efforts to help minority students to perform at their predicted level, no widely applicable remedy has yet appeared that has been shown to be capable of achieving the desired results at a moderate cost.

In the end, no amount of evidence is likely to resolve the argument over racial preferences, and one can understand why. Despite the cogent arguments in support of the practice, there is something intuitively troubling about the notion that some students should be able to gain admission not for any accomplishment of their own but simply because of their race. It is especially galling to critics of the policy that minorities from well-to-do homes can be admitted in preference to white applicants from less affluent families who have better academic records. Granted, athletes also receive favored treatment even when they have very modest academic credentials, but one misguided practice hardly offers a convincing reason for favoring another. Moreover, athletes at least gain admission by virtue of their own abilities even if those talents have little to do with the educational mission of the college.

Arguments about affirmative action cannot be proved or disproved by logic alone. One may disagree strongly with opponents of preferential admissions yet still acknowledge that at bottom, the issue involves values, not merely facts. Like debates about abortion, therefore, arguments over racial preferences will continue until the practice is either no longer needed or prohibited by law. At some point, the policy will almost certainly be abandoned. Recent rulings of the Supreme Court suggest that the end may come sooner rather than later. Even so, it is likely that selective colleges will find some constitutionally permissible substitute which will allow them to continue admitting a significant number of minority students.

INCREASING ENROLLMENTS
OF LOW-INCOME STUDENTS

One final question about the methods of choosing applicants is whether more should be done to enroll students from low-income families. This issue has risen to prominence recently because of a growing awareness of the yawning gap between the percentages of students from rich and poor families who attend college and eventually graduate. Of course, one would expect to find *some* differences of this kind, because children from low-income families tend to do less well on tests of academic ability than children from wealthier families. SAT scores climb relentlessly as one moves from the bottom of the income scale to the top.* Yet differences in test scores cannot explain everything. Investigators have found that even if one restricts the comparison to students ranking in the highest 25 percent of test-takers, children of wealthy families are much more likely to go to college and likelier still to graduate than children from poor families.[28] The effects of wealth are especially striking in the most selective colleges.

There are good reasons why admissions committees should want to increase the numbers of academically qualified applicants from low-income families. Public colleges are supposed to serve all the qualified residents of their state, rich and poor alike. Private colleges pride themselves on welcoming talented students from every quarter instead of becoming bastions of the rich. Besides, accepting more low-income applicants will increase the diversity of the student body and enrich the educational process for all, since students from poorer families, like minorities, bring different experiences and perspectives to the campus.

WHY FEW LOW-INCOME STUDENTS APPLY TO SELECTIVE COLLEGES

One reason why so few low-income students enroll in selective colleges is that very few apply even if they have the academic qualifications to be admitted. Chris Avery and Caroline Hoxby surveyed 32,416 low-income high school seniors who scored in the top 10 percent of all those taking the SAT (or ACT) exams.[29] Of these highly qualified students, only 5,445, or approximately one in six, sent so much as a single application to a selective college, and only 4,775 ended up enrolling in such a school.† Ironically, because of the generous finan-

* The following figures make this tendency clear.

Family Income	SAT Critical Reading	SAT Math	SAT Writing
Less than $20,000	434	456	430
$20,000–$40,000	462	473	453
$40,000–$60,000	488	466	477
$60,000–$80,000	502	510	490
$80,000–$100,000	514	525	504
$100,000–$120,000	522	534	512
$120,000–$140,000	526	537	517
$140,000–$160,000	533	546	525
$160,000–$200,000	535	548	529
$200,000 +	554	570	552

† As this book went to the printer, Hoxby and Avery published an even more comprehensive study covering all of the students who took the SAT or ACT test in a given year. The authors confirmed that at least 25,000 and probably close to 35,000 students from families in the bottom

cial aid policies now in place in some highly selective colleges, these students could have attended such schools for less money than it costs them to study at a nearby community college or comprehensive university.

The reason why so many capable students from low-income families do not apply to a selective college is that they are poorly informed. They tend to exaggerate the cost of attending and do not realize how much financial aid they could receive. Because they do not know that most selective colleges routinely waive the $50 or $100 application fee, many of them feel that they cannot even afford to apply. As pointed out in chapter 4, although they can supposedly seek the help of high school career counselors, most advisers in public schools populated by low-income students are overworked and typically know very little about selective colleges, since the students they serve rarely ask about them. Parents and friends know even less and seldom offer much encouragement. If low-income students do apply and are accepted by a selective college, they may not seek financial aid from the federal government because the detailed form, though now somewhat simpler, can still leave students confused or unable to supply the needed data. Without a grant, they may not feel financially able to accept an offer of admission even if they receive one.

Persuading Low-Income Students to Apply

As Avery and Hoxby make clear, thousands more academically talented students from low-income families could qualify for admission to selective colleges if they would only submit an application. Those who do apply graduate at virtually the same rate as their classmates and at at a substantially higher rate than they would at a nonselective institution.[30] To be sure, not all of these students would be accepted if they did apply, since many of the selective colleges lack the money to enroll more low-income applicants, who typically require a lot of financial aid to attend and graduate. Still, a substantial number of schools

---

income quartile score in the top 10 percent of all test-takers. Low-income students constitute 17 percent of all students scoring in the top 10 percent, a number considerable larger than most college admissions officers realize, presumably because these students are not concentrated in the high schools frequented by admissions officers but are mostly enrolled in schools widely scattered throughout the country. According to Hoxby and Avery, the dominant reason why so few of them enter selective colleges is that they are much less likely than their high-income counterparts to apply. Specifically, "for every high-achieving, low-income student who applied [to a selective college], there are about 15 high-achieving high-income students who apply." Caroline M. Hoxby and Christopher Avery, *The Missing "One-Offs": The Hidden Supply of High-Achieving, Low-Income Students*, National Bureau of Economic Research, Working Paper No. 18586 (December 2012), p. 6.

could afford to take more, and additional schools will presumably be able to do so in time.

Merely getting these students to apply, however, is no easy feat. Because they are widely distributed among the nation's 42,000 high schools, it will be difficult merely to locate them, let alone inform them properly and encourage them to file the necessary papers.

Conceivably, this problem may eventually be solved, like so much else, with the aid of the computer. It is possible to imagine something akin to a massive dating service in which a central entity collects reams of information about millions of high school students revealing their interests, abilities, academic records, extracurricular activities, and other background data with which to match them systematically with appropriate colleges. Colleges could mine the information for just the right kind of students to fit their needs and contact them years before they have to apply. Students, even in middle school, could discover the names of colleges they should consider. With the aid of the computer, they could receive detailed information about these colleges and learn the courses they should take and what else they could do to maximize their chances of admission.

As it happens, one company, ConnectEDU, has already embarked on a project of this kind and has signed up hundreds of colleges and public schools with which to generate and share the appropriate information.[31] If this venture succeeds, many low-income teenagers with the ability to attend a selective college may have an easy way to discover (or be discovered by) a college fitted to their abilities and aspirations.

An undertaking of this kind may take years to develop and achieve comprehensive coverage, if indeed it can succeed at all. In the meantime, the organizations that administer the SAT and ACT might consider supplying colleges with the names and contact information of high school students from low-income families who score above a certain level. Such information was once solicited from test-takers on an optional basis, but the practice ended because many students chose not to answer and the answers given were not thought sufficiently reliable. However, since low-income, high-scoring students are so hard to locate, even incomplete and sometimes inaccurate information would be better than none at all. With such data, interested colleges could at least contact many of the students they seek and send them relevant information by letter, e-mail, and even social media, together with assurance that the college is truly interested in having them apply and that application fees will be waived.

By themselves, written communications will often be insufficient to persuade low-income students to consider colleges they may never have regarded as remotely possible. Some personal contact will be needed to overcome doubts and awaken interest. Arranging such meetings, however, will be difficult. It would be hugely inefficient for each college to mount its own recruitment program. A collaborative effort by interested colleges would be much more sensible. Under such a plan, participating institutions could send a representative to meet with low-income students in a given area and talk about the reasons for considering selective colleges, the extent of financial aid, and other relevant subjects. Representatives could then send accounts of their visits to participating colleges. In addition, the collaborative could arrange meetings with high school guidance counselors and inform them of colleges interested in having low-income, high-scoring students apply while giving them contact information to obtain prompt answers to students' questions about specific schools.

INCOME-BASED PREFERENCES

If selective colleges are to increase the number of low-income students substantially, they may have to go beyond financial aid and aggressive recruitment to give such applicants a preference in the admissions process just as they already do for minority students.[32] The reasons for doing so seem at least as persuasive as those used to justify minority preferences, if not more so. Aside from the value of increasing student diversity, such treatment would be an appropriate way to level the playing field and give low-income students a fairer opportunity for admission.

As things now stand, needy students have many disadvantages in competing for a place in a selective college against students from well-to-do families. They can seldom afford to enroll in a test-prep course to improve their College Board scores. They will not have the benefit of a high-priced private counselor to help them assemble a strong résumé or write a persuasive college essay. They rarely have the opportunity to attend the summer schools and other enrichment activities that so many upper-middle-class students enjoy.* Their schools will typically be of lower quality with peer pressures that are much less supportive of academic achievement than those experienced by students in higher-income communities. If one believes in the American Dream that all young people deserve an equal chance to fulfill their ambitions to the best of their ability,

---

*According to figures supplied by Martha J. Bailey and Susan M. Dynarski of the University of Michigan, rich families spent an average of $8,872 in 2005–6 on enrichment activities for their children, while poor families spent an average of only $1,315. "Inequality in Postsecondary Education," in Greg J. Duncan and Richard J. Murnane (eds.), *Whither Opportunity: Rising Inequality, Schools, and Children's Life Chances* (2011), p. 171.

admissions officers may need to put a thumb on the scales for low-income applicants simply to compensate for the handicaps these students bear that currently put them at a serious disadvantage in the fierce competition to enter selective colleges.*

At the very least, admissions officers could place more emphasis on high school grades and less on SAT scores. Traditionally, test scores have been viewed as the best way of judging the true academic potential of students attending little-known high schools, especially those in rural or inner-city communities that send very few students to selective colleges. Recent research, however, has disclosed the surprising fact that high school grades, even from schools of doubtful quality in poor neighborhoods, are better predictors of academic performance and graduation than SAT results.[33] Thus, emphasizing test scores tends to make low-income students appear less promising than they really are.

Selective colleges would run much less risk than they may think by doing more to enroll low-income students. Studies have shown that if such students performed well in high school, they are unlikely to fail academically despite the deficiencies of the schools they attended.[34] They appear to graduate from selective colleges at virtually the same rate as their classmates and show little sign of the underperformance that so often drags down the academic records of minorities and recruited athletes in the major sports. As a result, while students from poor families will require large amounts of financial aid, admitting them even if they have slightly lower grades and test scores than their classmates need not compromise the academic standards of highly selective colleges.

THE EFFECT OF FINANCIAL AID POLICIES

The most enlightened admissions policies will accomplish little if they are not backed by enough financial aid to allow admitted applicants to enroll and earn a degree. In recognition of this fact, some of the most selective, most expensive colleges have taken major steps in recent years to make themselves more affordable for families with modest incomes. A few have gone so far as to make it

---

*Many selective colleges also disadvantage poor applicants by adopting an "early decision" policy whereby prospective students can be admitted months earlier than the normal spring decision date if they commit to attend the institution extending the offer. Students who gain admission in this way have a significant advantage over those admitted later. Yet needy students find it hard to do the same, because they would have to commit themselves to attend without knowing how much financial aid they will receive. Christopher Avery, Andrew Fairbanks, and Richard Zeckhauser, *The Early Admissions Game* (2003).

possible for families with incomes below $60,000 or $65,000 per year to enroll their child at no cost to themselves and without forcing their children to incur any indebtedness during their undergraduate careers. Scores of other institutions have increased their financial aid substantially to make themselves more affordable even to the neediest families.

While initiatives of this kind are commendable, few colleges, perhaps no more than twenty, have the resources to maintain a truly "need-blind" aid policy that allows all applicants who deserve admission to enroll and graduate regardless of their financial circumstances. The rest can afford to give only a limited amount of scholarship aid each year. Unfortunately, in deciding how to allocate these funds, more and more colleges have adopted policies that disadvantage applicants who need the most financial help. As a result, although a number of elite colleges have significantly increased the percentage of their students from low-income families, thousands of children from such families are discouraged from entering other selective colleges for which they are academically qualified.[35]

Many colleges with limited scholarship budgets currently pursue a strategy of "tuition discounting" designed to attract the most students they can with the limited funds available. Rather than distribute their financial aid in accordance with the academic and personal qualifications of the applicants, they favor applicants they believe will accept if given a relatively modest financial inducement. For colleges that struggle to fill their entering classes and avoid running deficits, such a policy can allow them to enroll all the students they seek at the least cost in financial aid. The result, however, is to deny assistance to many of the poorest applicants, even if they have stronger academic records, because they will require too much money.[36] In these colleges financial aid looks less and less like a way to offer access to qualified students of limited means and more and more like a method for maximizing tuition revenues by enabling colleges to charge very high amounts to wealthy parents without making the college unaffordable for children of upper-middle-class families that are merely well-to-do but not truly rich.

Other colleges use much of their financial aid to attract candidates they particularly covet even though these applicants may not need as much assistance as they are offered or even require any assistance at all. The most prominent examples are merit scholarships awarded to students with outstanding academic credentials whether or not they have financial need. Athletic scholarships are another well-known example. Some institutions also give grants regardless of need to outstanding musicians or other applicants with special talents.

In recent decades, colleges have devoted increasing amounts of financial aid to such awards. From 1996 to 2012, the share of grant aid public universities gave to students in the bottom income quartile fell from 34 to 25 percent, while the share for top quartile students rose from 16 to 23 percent.[37] Whatever the form such scholarships take—whether they are given for academic ability or some other special quality—they tend to divert funds that could have been used to help those who truly need it in order to enroll applicants coveted for other reasons. As a result, they add to the financial barriers that prevent low-income students from attending the college of their choice.

Are colleges justified in allocating financial aid in the ways just described instead of using it to assist admissible students with real and serious financial need? It is impossible to answer this question categorically. Much depends on the reasons that gave rise to such a policy and account for its persistence.

Some colleges spend part of their financial aid on merit scholarships merely to improve their position in the highly publicized college rankings such as those appearing in *U.S. News & World Report*. Others limit need-based aid in order to free up more money for athletic scholarships in the hope of achieving greater success on the playing field. Such practices seem highly questionable.

Many colleges, however, use merit awards for more substantial reasons. They may have few applicants with high academic ability and believe that attracting a larger number will improve the quality of classroom discussions and help to set a standard of academic achievement that will encourage classmates to work harder. Other colleges may reluctantly conclude that offering modest grants (or strategic tuition discounts) to applicants they think they can attract is the only affordable way by which they can enroll enough students to fill their classes and survive financially. It is difficult to fault such decisions categorically, notwithstanding the virtues of need-based assistance.

The irony in even the most reasonable uses of tuition discounts and merit awards is that they often prove to be self-defeating. Once the first few colleges have adopted these methods, competing colleges feel compelled to do the same. The result is something of a price war in which few institutions end up gaining an advantage, since their competitors employ the same tactics. According to one comprehensive study of tuition discounts, 44 percent of the public colleges and 45 percent of the private colleges that used this practice ended up with *lower* average SAT scores for their entering class than they recorded before initiating the policy.[38] Although a small majority of colleges managed to raise their average SAT scores, only 20 percent of private colleges and 17 percent of public institutions enjoyed a significant increase (i.e., more than ten points).

In much the same way, while athletic scholarships may attract some students who might not otherwise have attended any college, much of the money simply goes to avoid being outbid by rival institutions. Merit scholarships may likewise wean away some high-achieving students from the small minority of selective colleges that do not give such awards, but most of the money will merely counter the merit awards of competing institutions without giving much advantage to any. Once the practice spreads, however, while one can criticize it as misguided or ineffective, no individual school can afford to abandon the policy if its principal rivals will not follow suit.

Overall, though some colleges depart from strictly need-based aid for insubstantial reasons, most probably do so either to achieve legitimate aims or to avoid being placed at a competitive disadvantage. Under these conditions, appeals to institutional responsibility will usually be fruitless. While many college officials may regret the results, few will feel able to do much, by themselves, to improve the situation. If groups of competing colleges could agree to give up tuition discounts and merit aid, and allocate scholarship funds in strict accordance with need, they might have more to give the neediest applicants without spending additional funds or lowering the academic quality of their student body significantly, if at all. However, persuading all or nearly all competing colleges to accept such an arrangement would be a tall order. Moreover, such agreements would run a substantial risk of violating the antitrust laws. Unless Congress creates a clear exception for arrangements of this kind, there can be little hope of reallocating the institutional aid that is currently spent on students who do not need it to complete their college studies.

CAN WE AVOID THE ADMISSION FRENZY?

At this point, many readers may object that after all the discussion about so many issues no mention has been made of the greatest problem with the current method of choosing which students to admit to selective colleges. Surely, they will argue, the entire process has gotten completely out of hand. Colleges spend large sums of money traveling around the country encouraging talented students to attend their college rather than some other institution. High school students (and their parents) become increasingly anxious and distracted wondering whether they will be accepted by the college of their choice and how they might improve their chances of admission. Many applicants turned down by colleges they hoped to attend consider their rejection a personal failure and become despondent as a result. All this effort and worry might be worthwhile if it helped high school seniors to predict which colleges would serve them best. But there is little reason to believe that most students, even with the help of an experienced counselor, can possibly know enough to answer such a question in advance.

These disadvantages are real, and it would be nice to be rid of them. But condemning the current process is one thing, and devising a better alternative is quite another. It is hard to think of a cure that would not prove to be a good deal worse than the disease.

It is possible, of course, to imagine some form of lottery for allocating students among colleges that would avoid many of the problems with the current system. For example, selective colleges could distribute relevant information (including their tuition and financial aid policies) and even visit high schools as they currently do to talk with groups of students and answer their questions. Each college could publish the financial aid that students with varying family incomes could count on obtaining and also set minimum SAT (ACT) scores and high school grades that students must receive to qualify for admission. At a specified time, interested students would choose up to a stipulated number of colleges they would like to attend in order of their preference. In the case of colleges receiving more first-place applications than the number of places available, acceptance would be determined by lottery. Students not assigned to their favorite school would be offered admission to another of the colleges they ranked in such a way as to permit them to attend their highest-choice school with places available to accommodate them.

Under this scheme, colleges would no longer be able to give preferences to legacies or children of wealthy parents. Nor would they have to spend time and money trying to persuade attractive applicants to choose their institution over others or compete for students by the questionable method of offering strategic tuition discounts. As for the students, almost all would at least be admitted to one of their favorite colleges. Those who did not get accepted by their number one school might feel unlucky but would not consider themselves a failure. Moreover, in view of how little applicants know about which school will turn out to serve them best, they could well end up learning as much and enjoying the experience as fully under a lottery scheme as they would under the current system.

Notwithstanding these advantages, schemes of this kind give rise to a host of problems. To begin with, selective colleges would still spend large sums of money visiting high schools and distributing literature in an effort to persuade as many students as possible to list their college as a preferred choice. They would likewise continue spending on better dorm rooms and other expensive amenities in an effort to attract more and better applicants and more first choices in the lottery.

A more serious problem for selective colleges would be the dilemma they would face in trying to decide on the minimum grades and test scores required to qualify for admission. Should they set as high a threshold as possible in the hope of ending up with an academically talented class? Or should they set a lower minimum to increase their chances of enrolling a desirable number of accomplished athletes, minority students, and members of other special categories? Whatever choice they made, they would be likely to consider themselves worse off than they are under the existing system.

Many selective colleges would likewise object strenuously to losing their chance to craft a class with a desirable mix of talents and backgrounds and interests. Coaches (not to mention football and basketball fans) would be particularly incensed at the prospect of having their rosters determined by lottery, with the consequent risk of finding themselves without a talented quarterback or anyone tall enough to play center on the basketball team. Directors of student orchestras would be distraught if the lottery failed to produce any trumpet players, while science faculties would be upset if the entering class yielded few, if any, students interested in chemistry or biology. Colleges would also balk at losing control over their financial aid costs. If the lottery happened to assign them an exceptional number of needy students, they would presumably have to provide the funds they advertised regardless of the impact on the rest of their budget.

Students have reasons of their own for disliking a lottery system. Many would find it very difficult to decide whether to give their top preference to a particularly popular college where their chances of success might be low or give it instead to a satisfactory but less desirable college where their prospects for admission might be better. (Bear in mind that an applicant who gave first choice to a highly selective college and failed to gain admission would automatically be excluded from all other schools that received more first-place choices than they had room to accommodate.) Those who wanted to enroll in a particular institution to join an older sibling, or go to the same college as their high school sweetheart, or play football under a favorite coach would hardly be impressed by judgments from on high that they could not really know what college would be best for them and hence would be better off with a lottery.

Finally, there is a strong likelihood that any agreement to establish a lottery system would be declared illegal under the antitrust laws unless Congress granted an exception. In circumstances where decisions must be made about which college to attend—or which soap to buy or which car to purchase—lawmakers have long preferred to have the results determined by competition and free choice rather than by agreements among suppliers. Arguments that particular goods and services are special or that suppliers have acted for benign reasons have seldom been looked upon favorably by legislators or by judges.

For all these reasons, then, it is doubtful that the current methods of admitting students to selective colleges will be replaced by lotteries anytime soon. Nor is it at all clear that a lottery system would improve matters.*

---

*Another way that is often mentioned to relieve the pressures and anxieties of college admissions is for highly selective colleges to expand the size of their student body. This proposal seems

THE BOTTOM LINE

What judgment, then, can one make about the fairness of the methods used by selective colleges in choosing which applicants to admit? It is easy to single out policies to criticize. Some colleges admit certain students ahead of more deserving applicants because their parents are alumni or possess the wealth to make a substantial gift. Others allocate large parts of their scholarship funds on the basis of athletic prowess, academic ability, or other grounds unrelated to financial need, leaving too little aid to allow poor but worthy applicants to enroll. Such practices, together with the sharp increase in strategic tuition discounting, have struck especially hard at students from low-income families.

In addition to these practices, in the fierce competition for students, more than a few admissions offices engage in recruitment practices that are more akin to those of a used car salesman than to methods appropriate to a profession ostensibly seeking to help students choose the right college. For-profit universities are the worst offenders. Yet many nonprofitt colleges under pressure from above to produce more applicants and higher SAT scores, engage in inflated advertising, early decision programs, and unseemly public relations campaigns to "rebrand" their institution, not to mention the shady methods employed by some colleges to manipulate the data that go into determining a college's place in the media rankings. Such tactics, even by a minority of institutions, chip away at the trust and respect with which the public views higher education.

While practices of this kind are unfortunate and deserve the criticism they receive, they should not be allowed to obscure the progress that most selective colleges have made over the past fifty years, both in doing away with practices that once excluded large groups of deserving students, such as women, Jews, minorities, and openly gay applicants, and in reducing the preferences given to children of alumni. Nor should one overlook how hard many colleges have worked, and continue to work, to raise as much scholarship money as they can, much of it still awarded according to financial need. On the whole, therefore, while there is clearly room for improvement, most admissions committees do

---

even less satisfactory than a lottery scheme. To have any appreciable effect, the expansion would have to be substantial. Not only would the resulting cost be very great; the consequences for the atmosphere of the college and its capacity to give individual attention to students and avoid the impersonal bureaucratic "feel" of much larger institutions would be significant. Worse yet, it seems unlikely that such a change would have its intended effect. If the Ivy League, for example, agreed to expand enrollments by 50 percent, the probable result would simply be to increase the number of applications. And even if applications did not rise, the odds of being admitted would still be low, and students would still feel much the same anxiety and pressure wondering whether they would gain acceptance to their favorite school.

a better job of choosing students on the basis of their academic ability and appropriate personal qualifications than they did several decades ago.

The last and greatest unrealized opportunity for selective colleges is to enroll larger numbers of students from low-income families. Progress toward this goal will be hard to achieve. It will cost money. Finding a way to reach talented low-income students and persuading them to apply may prove to be difficult. Giving them the confidence and the support to persevere and graduate once they have enrolled will also be a challenge.* In view of these obstacles, the immediate prospects for success seem doubtful at best. Even the most selective colleges are feeling hard-pressed financially. Many others find themselves locked into an expensive competition that causes them to shift much of their financial aid budget to merit awards and strategic tuition discounts in order to counter other institutions in the struggle to raise the test scores of the entering class.

Even so, the conditions that seem so daunting today will not always remain the same. Financial circumstances may improve. The grip of media rankings, which underlie so much of the current, costly competition for students, may eventually ease. Gradually, if they think it important enough, more and more colleges should be able to accumulate the resources to enroll more low-income students and find ways to reach out to them and persuade them to apply.

Such an accomplishment will not be sufficient by itself to make the American Dream a reality. Nevertheless, it is the most important step that selective colleges can take toward the realization of that noble goal. Such progress, when and if it comes, will surely represent the crowning achievement in the long and honorable effort to give all young people, regardless of their circumstances, a fair opportunity to attend any college they are qualified to enter.

---

* For a detailed account of the many obstacles and pitfalls that can derail the aspirations of lower income students attending a large selective university, see Elizabeth A. Armstrong and Laura T. Hamilton, *Paying for the Party: How College Maintains Inequality* (2013).

CHAPTER SEVEN

THE EXPANDING AUDIENCE FOR HIGHER EDUCATION

|||||||||||||||||||||||||||||||||||||||||||||||||||||||||||||||||||||||||||||||||||||||||||||||||||||

ONE OF THE MOST PROFOUND changes that has occurred in higher education over the past forty years has been the huge increase in the number and variety of people seeking some form of learning from our colleges and universities. For the most part, these new audiences are not made up of students between the ages of eighteen and twenty-five who attend full-time and leave with a degree on graduation day. Many are over thirty. They may be doctors or lawyers who come to a campus for only a few days to catch up with recent developments in their field. They may be business executives or diplomats who will spend several weeks or months preparing for a substantial change in their responsibilities. They may be employees or housewives studying part-time to upgrade their skills or reinvent themselves for a different, more rewarding career.

Other nontraditional students are coming to universities, not for vocational purposes, but simply to learn something new or deepen their knowledge about a subject that has aroused their interest. Some are young adults wanting to learn a foreign language in anticipation of traveling abroad, or fifty-year-olds who have developed a passion for studying theology or the Civil War. Others are retired men and women in their sixties and seventies with a lot of leisure time in which to learn about world politics or discuss literature. Many universities sponsor very popular noncredit programs for these older students.

Together, this varied assortment of nontraditional students is living proof of the fact that the audience for higher education now extends from the freshman year to the end of life. Universities are by no means the sole providers for this vast population. Corporations spend billions of dollars on training their own employees and managers. Enterprises such as The Teaching Company hire accomplished professors to give lectures on video and audio discs for adults wishing to learn something about a new subject while relaxing at home or driving to work. Resort hotels and business groups pay handsome sums to well-known authors and commentators to give talks on subjects of broad interest.

None of these organizations, however, can match universities in the sheer variety of courses they give or the number of different adult audiences they reach—on campus, online, in remote locations, even aboard luxury cruises in distant waters where faculty members talk to alumni about European history, Asian art, or ancient civilizations. By now, a little-known fact in some universities is that nondegree learners far outnumber all of the regular undergraduates and graduate and professional school students put together.

THE FAR-FLUNG REACH OF
MODERN TECHNOLOGY

Thanks to the Internet, the audience for higher education has also expanded geographically far beyond the campus. To be sure, distance education is not an entirely new development. Several universities developed flourishing correspondence courses almost a century ago. Later on, educators began reaching far-off audiences via radio and television, though these efforts met with only limited success. With modern technology, however, everything has changed.

Once the Internet appeared, professors could communicate easily with all their students to distribute syllabi, homework assignments, and other announcements. Before long, entire courses were delivered online, solving a variety of practical problems for students. Such courses proved particularly helpful for those who could not come to class regularly, those who wanted to take two courses that were scheduled at the same hour, or those who would otherwise be shut out of overcrowded classes that they needed to take. The growth of students taking one or more courses at least partially online has been huge—from 1.6 million students in 2002 to more than 5 million today. By now, more than half of all colleges and universities consider such instruction to be a necessary part of their long-term institutional planning.[1] Three students in ten are currently taking at least one course online.

Online teaching is now being used to do much more than simply add greater convenience for students who otherwise live traditional undergraduate lives.[2] Duke University and the University of Massachusetts, among others, have successfully created entire business schools on line. The University of Maryland provides a wide assortment of courses for almost one hundred thousand students, offering a BA degree with more than fifteen majors along with several master's programs, all of them online with most of the classes interactive. Rio Salado Community College in Arizona is a largely online institution serving more than forty thousand students, many of them living in remote areas where they cannot come to a campus to attend classes.

Technology is also extending the reach of universities to students far beyond the borders of the United States. Michael Porter at Harvard gives a course on corporate strategy in cooperation with more than one hundred business schools around the world. Students use his syllabus, watch his lectures on video, and then engage in discussions led by local faculty armed with teaching notes supplied by Professor Porter along with Internet access to instructors in Cambridge to answer any questions about the material. Stanford professors have gone even further by offering online classes on artificial intelligence, machine learning, game theory, and other subjects that are attracting audiences in excess of 100,000 students worldwide. Impressed by these results, new companies founded by professors and by consortia of major universities are producing courses available to learners everywhere. For those with the motivation to study independently, instruction heretofore reserved for students at the most selective institutions is now available even in remote regions of the globe where local colleges and universities are overcrowded and underdeveloped.

The Effect of the New Technology on Teaching

The advent of the computer is not the first technological breakthrough in the past century to provoke visions of revolutionary change. Both radio and then television gave rise to extravagant claims about their likely impact on colleges and universities. In the end, these predictions proved to be groundless, and colleges continued to operate much as they had before.

Conceivably, information technology could suffer the same fate. Yet computers and their accompanying innovations have important capabilities that radio and television did not possess. In particular, the new technology is interactive and hence has the potential to engage students in a variety of new and fruitful ways. Instead of merely listening to a disembodied voice on the radio or watching a "talking head" on a television screen, students can ask the computer questions and receive immediate answers. Members of an online class can discuss course material with one another in a "chat room" with or without the participation of the instructor. Carnegie Mellon University has even developed programs for a variety of courses that can tutor individual students by asking them questions, responding to the answers, and offering helpful hints and additional queries whenever the responses reveal a failure to understand the material.

The Long-Term Impact of New Technology

The powers of modern technology have inspired much speculation over the eventual effects on the shape and nature of higher education. Some commentators envisage a world dominated by a limited number of famous instructors teaching millions of people via the Internet while rendering superfluous the tens of thousands of professors who continue delivering their lectures to steadily dwindling student audiences. In 1997, anticipating the vast potential of online teaching, Peter Drucker even proclaimed that the traditional college campus would become as obsolete by 2020 as the typewriter and the quill pen.[3] Such radical visions are arresting. Nevertheless, predictions of empty classroom buildings and vacant dormitories overlook many of the subtler benefits that a campus-based undergraduate education can provide.

Modern technology may allow many professionals to work at home, but it has not made cities disappear. On the contrary, as economists such as Ed Glaeser point out, dense urban centers promote creativity and entrepreneurial vigor by increasing the kinds of personal interaction that spark new ideas and lead to innovative solutions to knotty problems.[4] Living together in a campus community may offer similar advantages. Looking back, most college seniors claim that the experiences that proved most valuable for them took place outside of regular classes, often in unexpected ways from chance human encounters. The benefits are manifold.

- Students frequently gain most in tolerance and understanding of other backgrounds, cultures, and beliefs from casual conversations and experiences with fellow students, either in residence halls or through extracurricular activities. The growing presence of minorities and overseas students continues to enrich these opportunities.
- The close communities common to residential campuses that enable students to live, work, and play together create social bonds that contribute to graduation rates significantly higher than those achieved by colleges whose students commute from homes and apartments.
- Informal conversations with faculty members outside of class are often a source of new interests, insights, and perspectives on oneself and one's future.
- Unstructured discussions with classmates can also be critical in helping students develop career plans.
- Working with other students in community service programs—when integrated with regular courses—can often do more than any online class

or seminar to foster civic engagement, empathy with others, and citizenship skills.

- More generally, the impressive array of extracurricular pursuits and other opportunities made possible by the coming together of undergraduates can allow students to experiment, at little risk to themselves, with lifestyles, beliefs, and activities that help them decide what sort of person they want to be and what kind of life they want to lead.
- Finally, one should not overlook the success of residential colleges in creating an experience for countless young people that ranks among the most enjoyable of their lives. The enthusiasm of alumni at class reunions suggests the enduring place these four years occupy in the minds and memories of many graduates. The shared experiences and human relationships that make this time so memorable are not reproducible by a computer.

These advantages by no means rule out an expanded use of technology to enhance instruction and even to convert existing courses to a heavily online format. But the benefits of the traditional undergraduate experience seem substantial enough to guarantee a future for the selective colleges populated by students of traditional age who live on campus and participate in its rich extracurricular life.

At the same time, students attending colleges of this type now make up less than 20 percent of the total undergraduate population. The vast majority of today's students have jobs, live in off-campus apartments or with their parents, and take considerably longer than four years to graduate. Their number is likely to increase as federal and state officials encourage more people to go to college. For them, the convenience of studying at home at their own pace during hours away from work could make a decisive difference. For governments strapped for funds, the Internet may provide a welcome way to accommodate growing enrollments without having to build new classrooms or entire campuses. These possibilities invite the question whether technology will be able to solve the critical problem of achieving significantly higher levels of educational attainment at a cost that governments and families can afford to pay.

For-profit universities have already had great success in using online education to reach this older, working audience. Many thousands of such students are now enrolled in online programs offered by the University of Phoenix, Kaplan, DeVry, and other major providers. Another successful newcomer to the field is the nonprofit Western Governors University (WGU). Founded in 1995 by nineteen state governors, WGU started very slowly with only a handful of students. After the institution was accredited in 2003, applications picked up, and enrollments rose to exceed twenty-five thousand students by 2012, following a growth rate of 30 percent per year. The curriculum is narrow and heavily vocational (much like that of the for-profits), but this is apparently what many working adults prefer.[5] Degrees are offered in four subjects: education (teaching), business, information technology, and health professions. Course materials are purchased from commercial providers, such as McGraw-Hill, and grades are limited to pass-fail.

Without the need to make a profit or engage in expensive marketing, WGU can charge less than half the tuition of the large for-profits. Defaults on student loans are said to be low, and graduation rates appear to be improving. Impressed by these results, the governor of Indiana has signed up with WGU to absorb future increases of students wanting to enroll in state colleges. The University of California has likewise indicated interest in creating a new online university of its own to absorb future growth. Florida officials have made a similar proposal.

While the examples just described are encouraging, plenty of hurdles remain before proponents of online teaching can demonstrate its capacity to educate and graduate an expanded student population at an affordable price. First and foremost, it is essential to prove through rigorous assessments that online courses can achieve the hoped-for goals of lowering dropout rates, increasing learning, and cutting costs. At present, university professors may be attracting extraordinary numbers of students through their online courses, but far fewer persevere to the end. More than 100,000 people worldwide signed up for a course on machine learning but only 13,000 completed the course. Introduction to Data Bases drew 92,000 enrollees but only 7,000 finished. Western Governors University does much better, but its six-year graduation rate is still well below those of most traditional nonprofit colleges. Dropout rates are also heavy in the online programs of community colleges and for-profits. At present, therefore, only highly motivated, disciplined students seem to complete online courses with any regularity. It is not yet clear that such offerings can succeed in sustaining the interest and commitment of the legions of poorly prepared young people from mediocre high schools whom we will have to educate in order to raise the number of college graduates to meet President Obama's goal.

We also do not know for sure how much students will learn by taking all their courses online and how these results will compare with those of students of similar ability and background in traditional classrooms. Although more than one thousand reports have appeared on the effects of online courses, the conclusions are mixed, and very few of the studies have been rigorous enough to yield reliable results.[6] Still other problems are likewise not resolved, such as how to give reliable grades in classes enrolling thousands of students, or how to minimize cheating and plagiarism when students in widely scattered locations write exams and papers and submit them over the Internet instead of being physically on campus.[7]

Even if online teaching proves to be effective, there are still more problems that must be overcome before it can succeed in spreading widely throughout higher education. Millions of people throughout the United States do not have the high speed access needed to take advantage of the new online courses. This problem is especially prevalent among the lower-income and minority communities from which the bulk of the new students will have to come if levels of educational attainment in America are to rise.

In addition, universities will need to provide the initial investments, technical assistance, and released time to enable faculty members who are not technologically adept to convert their courses to an online format. Furthermore, ways must be found to overcome the opposition of many professors to the new technology. This may not prove difficult in for-profit institutions or in not-for-profit community colleges where most instructors are part-time and seldom in a position to resist. In most four-year colleges and universities, however, where the faculty has more authority over teaching, professors will need to be persuaded that technology is not going to replace them entirely or reduce them to robots mechanically carrying out instructional duties defined by experts they have never met.

Professors may not object to online teaching merely because they will have to use material devised by others. After all, faculty members have long used textbooks authored by other scholars. As previously mentioned, more than one hundred business schools currently use the online lectures and materials prepared by Michael Porter in his course on business strategy. Yet professors are likely to resist any arrangement that denies them the opportunity to supplement and adapt online material to suit the particular needs and circumstances of the students in their course.

Despite the obstacles that cloud the future of new technology, the Internet is already having subtle effects on the way in which classes are taught in colleges and universities. The prospect of reaching much larger student audiences has caused many respected members of the faculty to offer online courses. Their involvement has helped to arouse a wider interest on campus in experimenting with new ways of teaching. The experience of working with media experts and technicians to prepare a massive open online course (MOOC) is causing these professors to engage in a more careful and collaborative process of thought about how to best present their material than they have typically employed in preparing conventional courses.

The ready availability of MOOCs is also likely to hasten the day when lecturing ceases to be the predominant method of teaching large classes. Why continue this practice when students can sit before their computer at the time and place of their choosing and watch any of several well-known experts teach the same material? Rather than lecture, more and more instructors will probably assign a MOOC much as they now assign a textbook and use their classes to engage students in more active forms of learning, such as discussions, problem-solving, and team projects.

Other instructors are already converting large, introductory courses into "blended" offerings that include fewer lectures and more problem-solving sessions in small groups staffed by graduate students to help participants when they encounter difficulties. Careful assessments have found that undergraduates who take these courses are often able to learn the material much faster at significantly less cost to the university.

Chat-rooms accompanying online classes and computer-assisted exercises can also give instructors a wealth of information about how students are grappling with the subject matter and where they have trouble understanding the material. By examining print-outs of student responses, professors can discover much more about the impact of their courses than they have previously known and can thereby become more proficient teachers. Some of them are likely to find that the class is not learning as much as they had assumed and will be moved to make major changes in their methods of instruction.

At the same time, computers can help undergraduates learn more effectively by giving them instant feedback about how well they have mastered the material of their courses. Answers to questions in math, statistics, and other highly structured material can be submitted online, graded by machine, and returned immediately to students. In this way, computers will provide the rapid feedback that has repeatedly been shown to be important for successful learning.

Finally, technology can help instructors make their courses more engrossing so that students will devote more effort to learning the material. Members of an art history class can make "virtual" trips to the great museums of the world and inspect their masterpieces in detail. Archeology students will be able to "visit" important sites and observe them at various stages in their excavation. Business majors can engage in computer games in which teams representing rival firms devise strategies, negotiate deals, make decisions and instantly observe the consequences for their companies. Videoconferencing can bring students from other countries into seminar discussions with their American counterparts and thereby expand the global understanding and cultural awareness of all participants.

Apart from its impact on teaching, technology is also beginning to affect the way students make important decisions about their education. Already, the Internet gives high school juniors and seniors ready access to a wealth of information about the colleges they are thinking of attending, and the quality of the data will undoubtedly improve as time goes on. Once enrolled, undergraduates can use their laptops to obtain immediate answers to a host of routine questions that formerly required an appointment with their faculty advisor. They can also summon abundant information to help them choose a major. Computer programs can even alert them to the remaining courses they must take in order to graduate and warn them against taking classes that will prolong the time they have to spend to earn their degree. Meanwhile, by sifting quickly through masses of available data, computers can give college officials early warning of students who are floundering and at risk of dropping out unless they receive timely help.

The innovations just mentioned are only the ones already visible. For all their power, they may not massively disrupt the shape of higher education or destroy hundreds of existing colleges and universities. But they are already causing campus officials to unbundle the complex of activities performed by the university and outsource a number of specific functions. Lectures can be farmed out to well-known professors with massive open online offerings. Commercial companies are already supplying course management systems to simplify the task of communicating assignments and other material to students and collecting homework from them. Computers are beginning to take over more and more routine advising, allowing campus personnel to focus their efforts on the kinds of advice that require person-to-person communication.

In time, technology may conceivably come to have even more dramatic effects on higher education.* At this point, however, trying to foresee the results of such a powerful new force is probably a fruitless enterprise. In the words of James Duderstadt, former president of the University of Michigan and himself a scientist and engineer, "who can predict the impact of exponentiating

---

*Some analysts claim that for-profit universities will eventually drive out community colleges and comprehensives altogether. Clayton Christenson, Michael Horn, Louis Calderon, and Louis Soares, *Disrupting College: How Disruptive Innovation Can Deliver Quality and Affordability to Postsecondary Education* (2011). It is not clear, however, that online education will be sufficiently cheap and effective to displace the heavily subsidized public colleges or that Congress, which provides 75 percent of for-profits' revenues, will allow this to happen.

technologies on social institutions, such as universities, corporations, or governments, as they continue to multiply in power a thousand-, a million-, and a billion-fold."[8] Rather than speculate, the wiser course at present is surely to invest in rigorously testing applications of the new technology so as to avoid spending large amounts of money on unproven innovations without first showing that they can truly deliver the hoped-for results.

OVERSEAS INITIATIVES

In addition to reaching foreign audiences through the Internet, American universities have begun offering programs of instruction in overseas locations. Several business schools conduct executive programs for midcareer managers in cities such as Hong Kong, London, and Singapore. More recently, prominent universities have begun to build new campuses in foreign countries. The oil-rich Emirates are fast becoming a major outpost for American universities. Cornell, Texas A&M, Carnegie Mellon, Northwestern, Georgetown, and Virginia Commonwealth offer degree programs in a variety of fields in Qatar. Meanwhile, New York University has created an entire new university in Abu Dhabi using NYU faculty and offering NYU degrees, while another NYU campus in China is nearing completion. Dozens of other institutions are giving joint degrees in collaboration with Chinese universities. Yale is starting a new liberal arts college in Singapore. All in all, more than 160 universities, most of them American, are operating branch campuses in other countries. And the list grows longer every year.

SERVING THE EXPANDED AUDIENCES

Together, continuing education, the Internet, and overseas campuses have extended the reach of American colleges and universities to include all learners, regardless of their age, wherever they reside in the world. With such a huge potential market, questions abound. How is a university to decide which types of education to offer and which markets to pursue? On what terms will these new ventures be conducted? What benefits and risks arise from entering these new waters, and how should these possibilities affect the choices made?

FOR-PROFIT OR NONPROFIT?

At present, there are two separate movements trying to serve the expanding audience for American higher education. One of them seeks to increase worldwide access to quality education by providing learning opportunities at cost or free of charge throughout the world. The Massachusetts Institute of Technology (MIT) has led the way by putting the materials for many hundreds of its courses online for free use by students and universities everywhere.[9] Postings for many of these courses include only a syllabus and a reading list, but some also provide videotaped lectures by the professor.

Scores of other universities have now joined the effort to offer free content to the public. Yale, Harvard, and the University of California, among others, have put a number of their most popular undergraduate courses online for anyone to watch without charge (unless they wish to receive credit, take examinations, and participate in small group online discussions led by regular instructors). More recently, Harvard, MIT, and several other universities have joined a consortium to offer free noncredit online courses for students throughout the world. MIT has developed computerized laboratories that can allow students in Africa and other distant countries to carry out experiments using MIT facilities.

Other organizations have contributed to open access in different ways. The Mellon Foundation has created JSTOR, which offers universities and other institutions an opportunity for a modest fee to download articles from scores of academic journals. Mellon has also created ARTstor, which gives universities ready access to slides of the highest quality from museums around the world to enrich their teaching and research. Google, in cooperation with several university libraries, is bringing millions of books online for students (and others) to read. Together, these efforts are making an impressive collection of educational resources available free or at cost to the entire world.

The other, more prevalent method of reaching nontraditional or distant audiences is to offer courses on a for-profit basis, using much of any surplus earned to supplement the regular university budgets. Business schools make millions of dollars every year from their midcareer programs for corporate executives. Most medical schools earn a profit from their programs of continuing education. Extension schools serving nontraditional students are increasingly operated on a for-profit basis. Almost all of the efforts to create universities abroad have been undertaken with a view to earning money that can be repatriated to augment the sponsoring institution's resources. New York University reportedly received an initial payment of $50 million from Abu Dhabi in addition to being paid for the cost of building and operating a brand-new campus in that country. Cornell, Johns Hopkins, Carnegie Mellon, and other universities have also sought to harvest surpluses from their overseas programs.

It is reasonable to ask whether universities that normally operate as not-for-profit institutions should try to serve the vastly expanded audience of older and geographically distant students on a for-profit basis. This question deserves careful thought, the more so now that traditional boundaries between commercial enterprise and public service have begun to blur with the growth of for-profit hospital chains, not to mention the rapid, recent expansion of for-profit universities.

There are familiar and important advantages to a for-profit system. The desire to make money creates a powerful incentive to improve quality and lower costs. When adequately channeled by market forces, it can generate great energy and initiative in finding new and better ways of satisfying human needs. The benefits are not confined to ordinary commercial markets. They have been manifest in the success of for-profit universities in finding inexpensive and convenient ways to serve the vocational needs of adult workers who want to prepare themselves for better careers but cannot accommodate to the class schedules of nearby colleges.

The question arises, then, why governments everywhere have traditionally chosen to forgo these advantages and organize their educational systems predominantly on a nonprofit basis. If the for-profit enterprise is the basic organizational unit for the commercial markets that provide the great bulk of all goods and services, why has education been an exception?

One reason, surely, is that education benefits the entire society, so society has an interest in giving all qualified young people a chance to enroll instead of restricting access to those who can afford to pay the price that for-profit companies would charge. Because a college education is a prerequisite for so many desirable occupations, countries such as the United States that are committed to equal opportunity for everyone have wished to give all young people who are capable of doing the work a chance to earn a college degree whether or not they can afford the cost.

If there were no other reason to prefer nonprofit colleges, it would be a simple matter to allow governments to preserve the energy and ingenuity unleashed by the profit motive while still providing educational opportunities to all. Legislators could simply give financial aid to needy students and make such assistance available to students regardless of whether they attended for-profit or nonprofit institutions. In fact, that is precisely what the federal government has done. Had they refused to do so, major for-profit providers, such as the University of Phoenix, would never have been created, since these mega-institutions rely on federal financial aid for 75 percent or more of the revenues they receive in tuitions from their students.

There are other reasons, however, why governments may still choose to have education provided primarily on a not-for-profit basis. Whereas competition drives commercial firms to try to satisfy the desires of consumers, there are other ends one might wish to achieve through education. For example, society has an interest in educating its young people to act in accordance with ethical principles and to be active and informed citizens. Because many students are not interested in taking courses on these subjects, one cannot assume that for-profit colleges will provide them. More generally, students eighteen or nineteen years of age are often poor judges of what kinds of learning will prove reward-ing in later life. As a result, there is reason to favor putting education in the hands of people who may be more capable of making wise decisions about the kinds of courses students should take in college.

In addition, education differs significantly from most other consumer goods: young people cannot easily judge in advance what kinds of classes and instruc-tional methods will help them learn the most of what they need to know. If uni-versities were created as profit-seeking businesses, their sponsors might exploit this weakness and take unfair advantage of students by selling them a superfi-cially attractive but inferior education. Officials could try to prevent such tactics by some sort of regulation, but this is not easy to do successfully. Even simple measures, such as forbidding false and misleading methods of persuading stu-dents to enroll, can easily bog down in costly efforts by regulators to distinguish between materially false statements and mere exaggerations and puffery. The more serious problem is that commercial firms will tend to provide the methods of education that make the most money rather than those that are most effective. Since students will frequently be unable to tell the difference, the profit motive provides no assurance that the best methods of instruction will be used.

One can perceive these disadvantages more concretely by observing the experience of for-profit universities in the United States. Despite the initiative displayed by these providers in finding more convenient and effective ways of preparing working adults for better jobs, few people would give high marks to for-profit universities for their courses in moral reasoning or for their efforts to prepare active and knowledgeable citizens. By and large, they have focused their efforts on offering vocationally oriented programs and have provided only the minimum of general education courses needed to obtain accredita-tion and thereby qualify for access to federal aid. Moreover, there is evidence that a substantial number of for-profits have resorted to dubious tactics to persuade people to enroll in their programs. A General Accounting Office investigation of fifteen of these universities found that all of them had made misleading statements to prospective students and that several had made pa-tently false representations in an effort to enroll larger numbers of paying customers.[10] In sum, while for-profit institutions have added something valu-able in meeting the needs of an important segment of the population, there are reasons to be wary of entrusting them with the task of educating under-graduates, especially the younger students who make up the bulk of those who enroll in college.

Do the same reasons apply with equal force to older Americans seeking midcareer education or to nonprofit colleges and universities that are trying to reap a surplus from programs for nontraditional students? Certainly, serving these audiences strictly on a for-profit basis will effectively exclude many people who cannot afford to participate. Midcareer programs in the United States will be readily available for corporate executives and government officials but rarely for managers of small businesses or leaders of struggling nonprofits doing valuable work on the environment or human rights. Universities will offer alumni a chance to take expensive cruises and listen to professors lecture on intriguing subjects, but only their well-to-do graduates will be able to enjoy these opportunities. The prospect of earning a surplus may lead American universities to build new campuses and offer executive programs in Qatar, Singapore, and Hong Kong, but it will not necessarily cause them to do the same in Kenya, Guatemala, or Bangladesh where American expertise and experience might make an even greater difference. Colleges that operate abroad on a for-profit basis are also unlikely to offer generous scholarships that make it possible for students of limited means to attend unless the governments involved agree to cover the cost.

Of course, nontraditional audiences differ in important ways from the eighteen- to twenty-five-year-old students enrolled in regular degree programs. Whereas public policy in the United States has embraced the goal of offering educational opportunities to all young Americans, no analogous policy exists for extending such privileges to students throughout the world. Nor do the reasons that cause governments to favor nonprofit education for our youth seem applicable to older alumni enjoying a luxury cruise to explore ancient Greek temples or gaze upon Asian art.

At the same time, not all nontraditional audiences can be brushed aside so easily. For example, attaching less importance to educational opportunities for older students simply because they are older seems anachronistic and out of step with the conditions of modern life. Vocational preparation is valuable not just for young adults or older individuals who can afford to pay for it. Most people today change jobs several times in the course of their careers, and education of some sort at these transitional moments is often necessary for success or simply for survival. Such midcareer training can contribute to productivity and growth much as education does for younger audiences. In time, policy-makers may provide a way to make this instruction affordable to all who need it.

Some of the other aims of undergraduate education may also be better achieved at later stages of life. Adults who disdained politics and civic affairs in their youth may become genuinely interested and involved in their middle years. College graduates who slept through required courses in literature, history, or science may develop serious interests in these subjects at later stages of their lives. Students may not feel any desire to study a foreign language until their adult years when they encounter a specific need to do so. It is at least worth considering whether such people should be allowed to satisfy their late-blooming interests on the same terms as those offered their younger compatriots, rather than being treated as a profit center. If their incomes are too low, might they not deserve some amount of financial aid as well?

Educating students in other countries raises different issues. Clearly, it would be utopian to argue that our universities should feel obliged to extend educational opportunities to the rest of the world on the same terms offered to young Americans. The fact that public and private universities in this country receive all manner of subsidies and tax-supported benefits creates obligations toward domestic students that do not extend to people overseas. After all, public universities are not even expected to offer the same low tuitions to out-of-state students as they charge to local residents.

While this argument has merit, it hardly disposes of all the issues that arise in considering how to extend educational services to students around the world. Universities, after all, are not governments; they tend to look upon their values as universal rather than bounded by nationality. With this in mind, is it ethically proper for elite universities to earn a profit from educational programs in countries much poorer than our own in order to benefit students and faculties in this country? Should American institutions that open colleges abroad accept students only from families rich enough to pay the full tuition so that they can earn a surplus to finance programs on their own campus here at home? If they raise money to offer scholarships for needy students in this country, should they not use the surpluses earned by their foreign operations to do the same for poor but talented students overseas?

What about the risk that universities seeking profits will exploit unwary students? Alas, one cannot reject this possibility out of hand. In the 1920s and 1930s, Columbia, Chicago, and other major universities made a handsome profit from correspondence courses. Subsequent research has revealed that these profits depended on a policy of charging tuition up front and denying refunds to those who dropped out subsequent to an early cutoff date.[11] Since most of the expense of giving these courses resulted from paying graduate students according to the number of papers they corrected, students who left the program after the cutoff date lowered the university's costs but did not reduce its revenues. The more dropouts, the greater the profit. As attrition has always tended to be high in correspondence courses, this policy earned a tidy sum for the sponsoring institutions. Such an episode suggests that universities are not immune from the temptation to exploit the human frailties of students in order to make a profit.

Intercollegiate athletics represents a more current example of exploitation. Scores of colleges and universities recruit promising athletes who can help their football and basketball teams earn a profit to support the rest of the athletic program. Such students are admitted with academic qualifications well below those of their classmates. They are frequently encouraged to take easier courses and receive an inferior education while devoting thirty hours a week or more to team practice, travel, and other activities related to their sport. Once their eligibility is exhausted, they either graduate or drop out. In either case, they frequently leave poorly prepared to succeed in their chosen careers.

Will universities today take advantage of their new audiences when they operate educational programs at a profit? Not necessarily. Some customers can protect themselves against exploitation. Several business schools make millions of dollars from their executive programs. Even so, one would assume that large corporations are well equipped to judge what they are getting for their money and will be quick to switch to alternative providers if they find that a university's programs are not worth the price. Much the same is presumably true of government agencies that send mid- and high-level officials to universities for advanced training.

Yet consider the development of online programs that charge young people seeking to earn degrees. It is likely that distance education will produce the same educational benefits as traditional courses only if it provides ample opportunities for interactive learning. Students need to have the chance to discuss problems in small groups with qualified instructors to guide the discussions and offer help to individual participants and useful feedback on student papers. This form of education, however, is expensive. A university seeking to maximize profits might prefer to attract students by spending large amounts of money up front to create polished lectures on popular subjects with attractive visual aids while minimizing added expenditures for individual tutoring, small discussion groups, and the like. In this way, once enough people enrolled to cover the initial cost, tuitions from additional students would provide almost pure profit.*

Such a practice would seem to illustrate the same sort of risk that has traditionally led governments to rely on nonprofit organizations to provide educational services. The danger seems no less troubling when universities choose to offer online courses on a for-profit basis. When universities engage in academic activities to earn a profit, they introduce a motive far different from their

---

*It is possible, of course, that for-profit providers will offer courses free of charge but earn a surplus by carrying paid advertising. Even so, the desire to make a profit will still give an incentive to develop courses that attract students but do not provide the kinds of personal attention that promote learning.

customary intent to contribute to knowledge or enhance the development of students. By doing so, they create a conflict of interest just as surely as individuals who acquire any other financial motive that conflicts with their professional responsibilities.[12]

ADDITIONAL RISKS IN REACHING FAR-FLUNG AUDIENCES

Profit seeking may also lure universities into academic ventures that cause serious problems even if they do not involve any exploitation of students. One thought-provoking example is the creation of campuses abroad. In order to attract the talents and prestige of a major American university, foreign governments may offer a large sum of money in exchange for a commitment to plan, construct, and administer a college, a business school, or even an entire university. As previously mentioned, several American universities have already tested these waters in Singapore, Abu Dhabi, and other locations. Building an overseas campus can do much good. It may give a superior education to many students in the host country while providing a model that could lift the quality of higher education in the rest of the region as well. There may arguably be little danger of exploitation in such ventures, since foreign governments should be capable of judging the value of what they are getting. Even so, such ventures can sometimes prove unwise even if they are not unethical.

There are special challenges in administering an academic program successfully when it is located far from the rest of the institution. Visual inspection and informal consultation can occur only infrequently so that problems take longer to be noticed. Additional risks are compounded in countries with autocratic regimes of the type common to many developing nations with enough money to attract American universities with an international reputation. Student riots, political upheavals, devaluation, and countless other unforeseen crises may occur that will demand the personal attention of top officials at the parent university. The host governments may not share the American tradition of university autonomy and instead may interfere repeatedly with academic matters. Foreign officials may discriminate against students and faculty who are homosexuals or belong to religious or racial minorities. They may make subtle efforts to discourage writings critical of the host country's regime or urge the nonrenewal of instructors who oppose government policies. Radical students may be punished or put in jail. Such practices conflict with basic academic values and could result in embarrassing publicity and protests on the home campus in America.

Finding and retraining a highly qualified faculty to teach in a distant country and culture are also likely to cause problems. Once the first cohort of internationally minded professors have completed an initial tour of duty, it may be hard to recruit replacements, especially among professors who have children in school and spouses with careers of their own. On top of these difficulties, faculty and alumni in the United States may question whether it is wise for their university to risk depreciating the value of its "brand name" by awarding degrees to foreign graduates who may not receive an education of the quality normally associated with the home institution.

Already, mounting administrative and financial duties have forced most presidents to limit their active involvement in the academic affairs of their institutions. Why would one want to undertake the added burdens of developing and maintaining satellite campuses in distant lands with all the travel, oversight, and crisis management that ventures of this kind are likely to entail? If academic leaders want to encourage their students to spend time abroad, they can establish exchange programs with foreign universities. If they wish to spread the benefits of American higher education overseas, they can readily do so by training the professors charged with planning a new foreign university, sharing curricula and course materials, even recruiting volunteers from their own faculty to teach in the new institution for the first few years. Efforts of this kind have already helped American universities to build successful colleges and professional schools in Africa and Asia without exposing themselves to much risk.

On further reflection, one can conjure up additional reasons for operating branch campuses overseas. Conventional programs for study abroad often lead students to spend much of their time congregating together instead of immersing themselves in the life of the host country and its people. Perhaps a wholly owned foreign campus with a student body drawn from many countries could be administered in such a way as to provide a more truly cosmopolitan experience appropriate for preparing students to live and work in a globalizing world. Building a new university overseas may also provide opportunities for the sponsoring institution to experiment with bold new ideas for curriculum and teaching that would not be possible on the home campus with its well-established habits and entrenched interests. Such an institution could even provide a uniquely stimulating atmosphere for professors who, thrust into a new environment markedly different in nature and population, may arrive at insights and ideas that might otherwise have failed to emerge. Athens, Florence, and other great creative centers of thought throughout history benefited from a lively convergence of different cultures and intellectual traditions, and overseas campuses might accomplish similar results.

These possibilities are real, although they are highly speculative. But are they worth the risks and burdens that such foreign ventures would entail? There is no sure answer to this question. Yet one point does seem clear. The stakes involved are very high. Both the possibilities and the hazards could have large and lasting consequences. Under these circumstances, the prospect of pocketing a tidy profit could well exert a decisive influence on a judgment of great difficulty and importance that would be better made on academic grounds alone. To introduce the lure of money into such a major decision is surely to venture forth on very thin ice.

WHERE SHOULD PROFITS GO?

Regardless of the wisdom of such initiatives, some universities will continue to operate a variety of educational programs on a for-profit basis. Even in such cases, however, it is not always clear that using surpluses earned from such activities to fund the regular budget of the university is the wisest use of the money. For example, surpluses gained from midcareer programs for corporate executives could provide the funds for similar programs to teach much-needed management skills to officials of nonprofit, nongovernmental organizations in fields such as the environment or human rights. Profits earned from campuses overseas could be used to fund scholarships for talented students in the host country who lack the money to attend on their own.

Online education, executive programs, and extension schools are also operating on a vast and promising frontier that offers plenty of useful opportunities for further experimentation and improvement. For example, while some professional schools earn millions of dollars from executive programs, surprisingly little is known about how much learning of lasting value actually occurs in these brief encounters and how such learning could be increased. Further study is also needed to identify differences in the way older students learn and decide how educational programs can best be adapted to their needs. Even greater possibilities exist for developing and improving the uses of technology to reach distant audiences. Apart from experimenting to discover how to use the Internet in new and more effective ways, universities could invest substantial sums simply to give professors the support they need to employ technology to enhance the courses they already teach.

A farsighted university might do better to invest its surpluses in efforts of this kind instead of using them to benefit traditional programs that are already heavily subsidized. To be sure, the latter programs are the ones on which the university's reputation currently depends. Their constituencies are often more powerful. Moreover, many institutions are facing hard times and doubtless find it easier to appropriate surpluses from nontraditional programs than to cut their budgets for well-established activities. Even so, although such choices are understandable, they are not necessarily wise. In the long run, using surpluses to discover how to serve new audiences in more imaginative and effective ways may well make a greater contribution to teaching and learning than diverting the money to give even larger subsidies to traditional programs.

A TENTATIVE ASSESSMENT

Looking back, what judgment can we make about the response of universities to the vast growth in the pool of of potential learners? There have surely been promising initiatives; MIT's Open Source program is a notable recent example. A host of useful educational ventures have also been launched to reach new audiences, some of them highly imaginative and successful. All sorts of mid-career programs now exist to meet the needs of corporate executives, doctors, journalists, public officials, and many others. Modern technology has brought first-rate teachers into virtual classrooms and seminars to learners in remote locations around the world. All in all, the expanded reach of our universities has elicited an abundance of venturesome and creative initiatives in the best tradition of American higher education.

While experimentation of this kind is both admirable and necessary, one might have expected that the ability to reach persons of any age in every corner of the world would provoke a more spirited public conversation over the appropriate priorities and responsibilities of universities. What should the ideal university of the future look like? Whom should it serve, on what terms, and with what educational purposes in mind? Which audiences are underserved and which are most worth serving? Thus far, the only item on this large agenda that has provoked a lively discussion is the likely impact of modern technology on higher education. Even here, most of the commentary has been speculative in nature without much empirical support with which to evaluate potential changes or calculate their risks. Fundamental questions such as whether to reach the new audiences on a nonprofit or for-profit basis, or what the benefits and disadvantages of operating overseas might be, have yet to be subjected to a vigorous public debate. On some campuses, such matters have been resolved by the administration without much opportunity for the faculty to participate in a careful examination of the issues.

In the absence of such a discussion, the responses thus far to the huge increase in the numbers of potential students have often seemed ad hoc and opportunistic rather than the product of careful thought. Experimental programs using new technologies continue in use without being rigorously evaluated. Some overseas campuses and online ventures appear to have been initiated more to develop an added source of revenue for traditional programs than to discover how to serve new audiences in novel and effective ways. The conflicts of interest that arise from initiating educational programs on a for-profit basis have yet to be debated thoroughly.

Without a more thorough discussion of the future, there is a possibility that financial pressures and other immediate demands will inhibit universities from responding both imaginatively and wisely to the vast new audiences that are now within their reach. Rarely has such a wealth of new opportunities existed for academic leaders and their faculties. Surely the moment calls for the fullest discussion of the possibilities, coupled with a careful testing of the results, before decisions are made that may prove difficult to undo once commitments have been made and plans put firmly into place.

CHAPTER EIGHT

WHAT TO LEARN

||||||||||||||||||||||||||||||||||||||||||||||||||||||||||||||||||||||||||||||||||||||||||||||||||||||||||

NOTHING REVEALS THE EDUCATIONAL goals of a faculty as clearly as the curriculum or conveys as much about the means by which these ends are meant to be achieved. Throughout the history of American higher education, the great majority of colleges have adopted a similar curricular structure, although its nature has greatly changed over time. From the colonial era through the Civil War, most colleges embraced a highly prescribed course of study known as the classical curriculum.[1] It emphasized mental discipline attained through a rigorous study of classical subjects and texts coupled with moral discipline achieved with the aid of a strict disciplinary code, compulsory chapel, and a capstone course on practical ethics often taught to the senior class by the college president.

In colleges of the seventeenth and eighteenth centuries, Greek and Latin were compulsory subjects. A typical class in these languages consisted of recitations in which students would translate short passages and answer detailed questions from the instructor about their meaning and construction. Though seemingly archaic, this form of instruction had a clear purpose. "The college course," explained Yale president Noah Porter, "is preeminently designed to give power to acquire and to think rather than to impart special knowledge or special discipline."[2] According to one instructor, "the student who has acquired the habit of never letting go a puzzling problem—say a rare Greek verb—until he has analyzed every element and understands every point in its etymology, has the habit of mind which will enable him to follow out a legal subtlety with the same accuracy."[3]

As time went on, however, efforts arose in various quarters to break the mold of the classical model. American professors who had studied in Europe returned eager to introduce the study of modern languages. Scientists pleaded for opportunities to teach their subjects. State universities were encouraged to offer practical courses on such down-to-earth subjects as farming, home economics, and the mechanical arts. Students chafed at the paucity of electives.

In the latter half of the nineteenth century, the classical curriculum began to give way at last under the weight of these demands. A new model eventually emerged that has continued more or less to this day. Yet once again, as we will discover shortly, signs of strain have begun to appear. Pressure is mounting to break the bonds of the prevailing structure and make more room for new knowledge and new competencies that students need in order to flourish in the contemporary world. Meanwhile, empirical research is casting doubt on whether the familiar course requirements are accomplishing all that educators have long assumed. In short, the current curriculum is ripe for a careful reexamination.

THE AIMS OF A COLLEGE EDUCATION

For almost a century, undergraduate education in the United States has pursued three large, overlapping objectives. The first goal is to equip students for a career either by imparting useful knowledge and skills in a vocational major or by developing general qualities of mind through a broad liberal arts education that will stand students in good stead in almost any calling. The second aim, with roots extending back to ancient Athens, is to prepare students to be enlightened citizens of a self-governing democracy and active members of their own communities. The third and final objective is to help students live a full and satisfying life by cultivating a wide range of interests and a capacity for reflection and self-knowledge.

These ends are very general. As it happens, however, there is a strong consensus among American professors on a number of specific goals that can contribute to one or more of these larger purposes.[4] Over 99 percent agree that teaching students to think critically and to evaluate the quality and reliability of information is either an "essential" or a "very important" goal. More than 90 percent feel the same about increasing students' capacity for self-directed learning, mastering knowledge in a discipline, and developing an ability to write effectively. More than three-quarters believe in preparing students for employment (78.3 percent), fostering a tolerance for other beliefs (78.9 percent), and developing students' creative abilities (79.4 percent). Smaller but still solid majorities are in favor of improving racial understanding (70.4 percent), fostering a breadth of learning and an appreciation for the liberal arts (66.7 percent), and developing moral character (68.8 percent). Although there are no comparable figures measuring faculty support for additional aims, a glance at college brochures suggests a commitment on the part of many institutions to achieve such other goals as helping students to become enlightened, engaged citizens, teaching them basic quantitative skills, and introducing them to other countries and cultures in order to prepare them to live in an increasingly interdependent world.

It would be hard to disagree with any of the objectives just mentioned. One can make a plausible case for including all of them within the undergraduate course of study, provided the faculty knows how to achieve them and there is enough time and space in the curriculum to pursue each one effectively. At present, however, over 80 percent of the public believe that "at many colleges, there is too much of a disconnect between the courses offered and students' career goals."[5] Prominent government officials, many for-profit colleges, a large body of students, and a number of commentators as well seem to assume that while a broad liberal arts foundation may be fine for those who want it, all that the nation really needs to accomplish in seeking higher levels of educational attainment is to give students the skills they have to master to get a job and help America compete effectively in the global economy. Those who share this opinion question whether it is either necessary or feasible to compel every student to study literature or history or foreign cultures when all that many of them really want from college is the training and the credential for a desirable career.[6]

The latter view cannot be brushed aside as merely the attitude of Philistines and Babbitts. After all, the liberal arts curriculum was designed for the education of an elite and not for the current era of universal higher education. The thought of classrooms populated by sullen students with limited intellectual ambitions who are forced to labor over Shakespeare sonnets or struggle with differential equations is not an especially happy one. Might we not be sacrificing the time and money of countless undergraduates to the vision of educators who have little in common with those they are teaching? How much difference is there between these students and the luckless farm boys and merchants' sons in the eighteenth century who were forced to study Latin and Greek to satisfy believers in the classical curriculum?

The pressure for a narrowly vocational education has gained ground in recent decades with the rise of for-profit colleges and the growth of certificate programs that train students for specific jobs and last for only a year or less. There is undoubtedly value in such programs. Many high school graduates, especially those who are older and already employed, may not be willing to go to college if it requires spending many hours in classes studying subjects that seem to have no immediate practical relevance. Many others may simply be unable to satisfy the minimum requirements in mathematics that they must meet to start getting credit in courses at a community college. It is surely better for such students to earn a certificate or complete a vocational program than obtain no further education whatsoever.

It would be a mistake, however, to assume that America can achieve all the benefits of increased levels of educational attainment on the cheap by substituting shorter, less expensive vocational programs for conventional undergraduate curricula. College degrees have traditionally served a broader set of aims than merely preparing young people for a job. The case for continuing to do so is considerably stronger than most enthusiasts of vocational programs are wont to admit.

According to employment experts Anthony Carnevale and Donna Desrochers, companies find that graduates who have completed a broader, more traditional program tend to adapt more easily to changes in the nature and skill requirements of their jobs and to be more "trainable" for evolving occupational demands than those who have received a narrower vocational training.[7] Business leaders also seem to favor a curriculum that embraces a variety of goals extending well beyond a strictly vocational program. Thus, when employers were asked in a recent survey what qualities they would like colleges to emphasize more, large majorities expressed strong support, not for more technical skills, but for such familiar liberal arts goals as thinking critically, communicating effectively both orally and in writing, acquiring a sensitivity and concern for ethical issues, and learning to understand and work effectively with people of different cultures, backgrounds, and races.[8]

In addition, the public has good reasons to demand more from a college degree than merely vocational training. Most undergraduates will be citizens whether they choose to be or not, and the society has a natural interest in preparing them to vote in an informed manner and to participate in the political process and the civic life of their communities. Moreover, everyone has a stake in having colleges contribute to the moral development of students by heightening their awareness of ethical issues and the reasons for respecting ethical principles. The efforts made by many colleges to foster greater tolerance and an ability to live and work effectively with a wide variety of people are likewise important to a society growing steadily more diverse and still grappling with deep-seated divisions on matters of race, gender, and sexual orientation.

Interestingly, while a substantial fraction of entering students may think of college chiefly as preparation for a good job, support for a wider set of goals seems to increase over the four undergraduate years. According to Ernest Pascarella and Patrick Terenzini, after reviewing dozens of studies on how undergraduates change during college, the number of students who believe that there is an intrinsic value in a broad liberal education rises as much as 25–30 percentage points by their senior year.[9]

It is possible that some proponents of the liberal arts curriculum go too far in their defense of the traditional model. There may be a few familiar requirements that are of doubtful value for colleges whose students have a markedly vocational orientation. Insisting that all undergraduates acquire a basic competence in a foreign language, for example, is open to question in institutions such as these.[10] Granted, some students may graduate and later find that being fluent in a particular language would have helped them to qualify for a desired job or visit a foreign country. Even so, the odds that the language they study in college will be the one that proves useful to them in later life seem small enough to offer some justification for omitting the requirement, as many colleges have done. With such occasional exceptions, however, the goals of undergraduate education supported by large majorities of the faculty seem valuable enough both to society and to the long-term interests of young people themselves that almost any college would do well to pursue them.

A more troublesome question, however, and one that is too rarely discussed, is whether colleges that claim to set great store by a wide variety of aims are actually pursuing them all with sufficient seriousness to warrant the requirements imposed in their name. As a growing number of goals vie for space in a crowded curriculum, it is possible that some of the requirements agreed to by the faculty are uneasy compromises that threaten to produce the worst of both worlds—making enough demands on students' time to represent a burden but not enough to afford much chance of actually achieving the hoped-for results. It is this possibility that occupies much of the remaining discussion in this chapter.

THE PREVAILING STRUCTURE
OF THE CURRICULUM

To achieve its several aims, the traditional curriculum, like Caesar's Gaul, is divided into three parts: the major, which normally consumes 40–50 percent of the total undergraduate course load; electives, which claim up to 25 percent; and general education, which occupies, on average, approximately 30 percent. The major may consist of courses within a single academic discipline or an interdisciplinary subject, or it may be explicitly vocational by offering a preparation for business, engineering, or some other occupation.* The elective portion of the curriculum is meant to give students ample opportunity to pursue their own intellectual interests. The remaining portion of the curriculum is devoted to general education and typically encompasses a variety of aims, such as acquiring a breadth of learning by sampling courses in the sciences,

---

*Colleges that offer only or mostly discipline-based majors are often said to provide a "liberal arts education" or to be "liberal arts institutions," in contrast to colleges that provide a variety of majors to prepare students for specific careers or occupations. Yet even the latter colleges typically have general education requirements and offer discipline-based as well as vocational majors.

social sciences, and humanities, achieving proficiency in English composition, obtaining a rudimentary grasp of a foreign language, and gaining some understanding of ethical principles, quantitative reasoning, and other races, religions, and cultures.

Although each college makes its own curricular choices, most faculties accept the tripartite division just described and the underlying rationale for each component. Most agree that a major is an appropriate way to ensure that students go far enough into a field of knowledge to explore it in some depth, whether by preparing for a vocation or by studying a particular discipline or field such as physics, economics, or philosophy. Electives offer an opportunity for an increasingly diverse student body to explore individual interests or experience especially stimulating teachers. General education was originally designed to provide the breadth required to prepare enlightened citizens and to awaken intellectual interests that could endure and enrich one's later years. More recently, it has expanded to become a kind of curricular catchall for courses designed to nurture the growing list of specific competencies that faculties believe students need in order to function well in the contemporary world.

At first glance, this form of organization may seem to provide a reasonable structure through which to achieve the various purposes and needs that a curriculum is supposed to serve. In fact, however, the tripartite division, in its usual form, conceals a host of difficulties.

Requiring students to explore one field of knowledge in depth is widely accepted as an appropriate way to train the mind and avoid the superficiality of acquiring only a smattering of knowledge about a variety of different subjects. As currently designed, however, vocational majors have attracted serious criticism. For example, the National Alliance for Business has complained that "the majority of [college] students are severely lacking in flexible skills and attributes, such as leadership, teamwork, problem-solving, time-management, adaptability, analytical thinking, global consciousness, and basic communications, including listening, speaking, reading, and writing."* Researchers have also found that some of the most popular vocational majors tend to undermine other important aims of undergraduate education. For example, Alexander Astin's longitudinal study of twenty-four thousand undergraduates revealed that majoring in engineering was associated with declines in writing ability, cultural

---

*See Association of American Colleges and Universities, *The LEAP Vision for Learning: Outcomes, Practices, and Employers' Views* (2011), pp. 23–27. There appears to be some confusion, however, about what employers truly value in a college education. Top corporate executives often favor the broad intellectual capabilities cited in the quoted passage. Company recruiters, however, seem more inclined to stress the practical knowledge and skills needed to function effectively in one's first job.

awareness, and political and civic participation; that education majors became less proficient in problem solving, critical thinking, and general knowledge; and that science majors wrote less well as seniors than they had as freshmen and were less inclined to participate in civic affairs.[11]

The liberal arts (or discipline-based) major has problems of its own. It has been a fixture for so long that few professors give much thought any longer to its underlying purpose. Yet its rationale is far from clear. Departments typically design their concentration to provide an introductory course or two, followed by a study of the characteristic methods of inquiry in the discipline, leading to either a choice among a variety of specialized courses or an exposure to each of the principal subfields or subject areas in the department. Although this progression may lay a suitable foundation for graduate study toward a PhD, only a tiny proportion of students in most majors take this route. Exactly what faculties hope to accomplish for all the other students is often left unclear.*

A common assumption is that studying a subject in depth by majoring in a discipline is a good way to improve critical thinking. Yet evidence of the effects of completing such a major casts doubt on whether this aim is actually achieved. In their review of a vast number of empirical studies on undergraduate education, Pascarella and Terenzini "found little evidence that one's major has more than a trivial impact on one's general level of intellectual or cognitive outcomes."[12] The experience that could best teach students how to think in depth is the completion of a senior thesis, yet surveys show that fully half of all college seniors go through their final year without writing a single paper of twenty pagers in length.[13] If provision for a senior thesis exists, it is often reserved for honors candidates, as if only the better students needed the opportunity.

The role of electives is also open to question. Almost everyone accepts the general proposition that a diverse group of undergraduates needs an opportunity to roam freely through the course catalog in order to pursue special interests and satisfy individual needs. But little is known about how this freedom is actually used. Are students exploring genuine interests or are they simply taking easy courses that leave them more time for extracurricular pursuits?

---

*The most detailed study of majors was carried out by teams of professors in different fields under the auspices of the Association of American Colleges and Universities. According to the final report, "the major in most colleges is little more than a gathering of courses taken in the department, lacking structure or depth, as is often the case in the humanities, or emphasizing content to the neglect of the essential style of inquiry on which the content is based." Association of American Colleges, *Integrity in the College Curriculum: A Report to the Academic Community* (1985), p. 2. It is possible that departments will improve upon this description now that accrediting agencies have begun to press colleges to develop clear learning objectives for their majors.

Are they sampling a wide variety of subjects, or merely using electives to take more courses to supplement their vocational major? Looking back, do seniors value the electives they have taken more than courses in general education or the major? Answers to these questions might help faculties decide whether the elective portion of the curriculum should be expanded, contracted, or altered in some way. In practice, however, such inquiries are seldom made. Just as concentrations are left to the departments, so are electives abandoned to the students.

General education has serious problems of its own. It suffers from the fact that it has become the repository for all the purposes not normally fulfilled through majors or electives. Over the years, the list of aims to be achieved has gradually increased. Newer goals, such as acquiring "global competence" or basic quantitative skills or a tolerance for diversity have been tacked on to the traditional aims, such as acquiring a breadth of knowledge, learning to write more skillfully, and gaining at least a rudimentary ability to speak and read a foreign language. The net result is that general education is now expected to do more than it can possibly accomplish within the 25–35 percent of the curriculum normally allotted for the purpose.

How have faculties dealt with this problem? The attempt to instill a proper breadth of learning has received the most attention, and several models have been widely discussed over the years. One approach is to offer an intensive study of the greatest masterpieces ever written in various fields of knowledge and literature. Another seeks to encourage students to continue learning on their own by acquainting them with the distinctive methods of thought utilized by different disciplines. For a time, a number of colleges tried yet another way of achieving breadth by developing special courses focused on important problems facing society. Still others sought to broaden their students by requiring them to take a series of survey courses covering vast areas of human experience and knowledge.

Each of these approaches has obvious strengths, but each has serious weaknesses as well, and none enjoys widespread support among college faculties.[14] Instead, the vast majority of colleges have settled on some form of distribution requirement whereby students are required to take a specified number of courses from each of several designated categories. Under the simplest and most common structure, all students must complete at least two or three courses from each of the main divisions of knowledge—sciences, social sciences, and humanities. There are many variations on this model. Some colleges have designated only certain courses that qualify to fulfill the requirement. Others carve up knowledge into more than three categories, and many have their own special titles to define the different components. All in all, however, more than three-quarters of all four-year colleges have adopted some version of a distribution requirement to achieve the desired breadth of knowledge.

At first blush, the popularity of such a requirement is hard to fathom since it does not embody any coherent notion of how "breadth" is to be achieved but simply allows students to choose from a long list of courses, most of which were never designed to achieve the aims of general education. Just how professors can best engender a lasting interest in science or in the study of society and government or in literature and art is far from obvious. Yet most faculties rarely discuss such questions explicitly; they seem to assume that the purpose will be adequately served if students are required to fulfill the distribution requirement. One or two writers have suggested that giving students such wide freedom of choice ensures that they will gravitate to subjects they enjoy and thus will be more likely to develop enduring interests, but this claim has never been tested empirically.[15]

Meanwhile, the remaining aims of general education—developing a competence in writing, speaking, quantitative methods, moral reasoning, global understanding, civic knowledge, and the like—must be accomplished in whatever curricular space is left over after the major, the electives, and the distribution requirements have all received their allotted share. In many cases, the means by which the remaining goals are supposed to be achieved are never debated in any detail. One looks in vain for serious faculty discussions of how to achieve such widely supported goals as increasing a capacity for self-directed learning, developing moral character, or fostering creativity. Instead, these questions are all too often disposed of through a series of heroic assumptions. For example, faculties assume that students will develop oral communication skills and acquire an adequate civic education simply by completing the four-year undergraduate program, or that competence in moral reasoning or expository writing can be attained in a single course, or that these capabilities (along with other aims, such as the development of "global awareness" or quantitative skills) will be achieved if the faculty is urged to incorporate the necessary material into their existing courses.* The validity of these assumptions is seldom put to a rigorous test, but the curriculum itself is approved nonetheless.

---

*E.g., to quote a recent report by a committee to review the curriculum at one elite college: "Although we have chosen not to impose a specific course requirement in ethical reasoning, we recognize our responsibility to educate morally responsible leaders and citizens. We encourage faculty and departments to incorporate an appropriate range of ethical questions and case studies into their courses and majors." The curriculum committee from another elite college gives the following explanation for the lack of any required course on writing: "[W]e envision serious writing training as being available in scores of courses in many disciplines." No evidence is cited in either report to demonstrate whether the hopes expressed were actually being fulfilled.

THE FAMILIAR CRITIQUE
OF THE CURRICULUM

Critics have launched many attacks on the prevailing college curriculum. With few exceptions, however, they have not challenged the conventional tripartite structure that has been adopted almost everywhere. Nor have they objected very often to electives or to undergraduate majors. Almost all the complaints are directed at the remaining portion, the general education segment, of the curriculum. How can faculties justify requiring only two semesters of a foreign language? Why don't more colleges build their general education program around a study of the "Great Books"? How can any self-respecting college allow its students to graduate without having taken a single course on economics, . . . or Western civilization, . . . or American history, . . . or without reading a single play by Shakespeare or a word of Plato?[16]

One can respond to such concerns by pointing to the practical problem of staffing mandatory Great Books courses or by questioning the lasting impact of making students study this or that particular author or subject. However, there is a much more fundamental problem with these complaints. Those who express them overlook how much easier it is for individuals like themselves to insist on their particular version of the ideal college curriculum than it is to persuade a large body of highly educated scholars with widely varying educational views to agree on how to accomplish a long list of worthy goals within a limited number of classroom hours. It is the sheer difficulty of such a task that explains why faculties settle so often for a curriculum that seems to rest on a series of unexamined premises, implausible assertions, and unrealistic hopes.

THE PREVAILING CURRICULUM
AS A PRACTICAL COMPROMISE

Criticizing a faculty for not agreeing on a single "ideal" model of general education is akin to condemning the United States Congress for not enacting a universally agreeable tax code. There are simply too many issues to resolve, many of which are matters on which thoughtful educators have disagreed for generations. Professors lack the time to discuss such thorny questions in detail. Efforts to do so could easily degenerate into long-winded debates punctuated by unseemly struggles among departments to secure themselves an ample niche within the final array of course requirements. Rather than engage in such a fruitless and disagreeable exercise, faculties are generally willing to settle for a practical compromise that enables them to emerge after a reasonable time with a superficially plausible result that does not sacrifice the vital interests of any of the parties involved.

Judged from this perspective, the typical college curriculum may lack a convincing rationale, but it succeeds brilliantly in satisfying the concerns of all the principal interested groups. It allows members of the faculty to devote virtually all of their teaching efforts to courses within their particular area of expertise. It makes minimal inroads on the cherished right of individual professors to teach the classes they prefer in the manner they choose without having to bow to the dictates of a well-intentioned but intrusive majority. It offers a breadth of learning by providing a distribution requirement that simply asks students to choose among courses professors are teaching anyway. While the curriculum often requires courses to achieve several other specific goals, most of these— notably, classes in writing, basic quantitative skills, and foreign languages—can be taught by graduate students or untenured instructors without forcing the regular faculty to participate. At the same time, the agreed-on requirements are reasonably satisfactory to students, since they give undergraduates extensive freedom to choose the courses they want while often leaving them ample opportunity to prepare for the vocation of their choice. Finally, the standard curriculum offers assurance to the administration that nothing proposed will demand the hiring of a lot of additional faculty or require new programs costing significant amounts of money.

In short, the curriculum that emerges from the process just described can be best understood as a political accommodation rather than a carefully considered framework for achieving the lengthy list of generally accepted educational goals. The basic structure is more noteworthy for the interests it serves than for the academic purposes it achieves. The requirement of a major, which corresponds so neatly to the intellectual interests of the faculty, is allowed to take up nearly half the curriculum even though the underlying rationale for disciplinary majors is poorly understood and its contribution to critical thinking has not been confirmed empirically. The provision for electives, which helps to satisfy the student desire for choice, rests on shaky ground, since few institutions have investigated the choices students make or considered how they contribute to important educational goals. The distribution requirement makes no new demands on the faculty but rests on the implausible assumption that students can achieve intellectual "breadth" or develop lasting interests in science, social science, and the humanities by simply taking any two or three courses that they happen to choose among a long list of offerings created with different purposes in mind. Meanwhile, other important aims are left with so little space that several are but skimpily addressed while others are not specifically addressed at all.

HOW WELL DOES THE PREVAILING CURRICULUM SUCCEED?

Fortunately, the lack of a convincing rationale for the typical curriculum does not mean that no real learning takes place. Although the weaknesses previously described may keep students from fully achieving the aims that colleges claim to embrace, there are abundant opportunities for undergraduates to learn and make at least *some* progress toward most of the familiar goals of a broad liberal education.

For example, majors often contribute to other specific goals apart from teaching students to think in depth. In studying literary texts, English majors learn to read more carefully and write more clearly and gracefully. Science majors develop quantitative skills as well as knowledge of a scientific field. Philosophy concentrators can acquire greater powers of critical thinking and moral reasoning. Moreover, although the major occupies up to half of the available classroom hours, it allows professors to devote the bulk of their undergraduate teaching to the subjects they know best and enjoy the most. Surely, there is value in that.

As for the year's worth of elective courses, there is something to be said for student choice. Undergraduates may use their electives to choose easy classes or lenient graders, or simply to add one more vocational course, but most presumably pick subjects that interest them enough to cause them to study more conscientiously. Similarly, many students will satisfy their distribution requirements by choosing courses with instructors who are known to be good teachers. A well-taught course on almost any serious subject can inspire more interest and evoke more effort than a dull offering designed to achieve some carefully prescribed educational purpose.

It is also worth noting that much student development comes not from courses but from extracurricular activities. Ask seniors to name the college experience that contributed most to their personal growth and they will usually mention something that took place outside of class.[17] As one professor concluded after spending a year studying and observing undergraduates, "the median response of students polled was that 65 percent of learning occurs outside of classes and class-related activities while 35 percent occurs within."[18] Thus, even if the curriculum does not do a great deal to prepare students to be knowledgeable and engaged citizens, participation in student government, political clubs, and community service can spark many students' interest in policy and politics and inform them about the political process. Similarly, undergraduates will often develop greater tolerance and gain a more lasting understanding of racial differences and other cultures by interacting with classmates of other backgrounds, races, and nationalities than they would derive from taking a single course on Japanese culture or European politics.

While students have many opportunities in college to learn and to develop, the critical question is *how much* progress they make during their college careers. Until recently, no one could supply a reliable answer. In the last few decades, however, researchers have conducted literally hundreds of studies to measure the effects of a college education on students. Their findings tend to confirm that most undergraduates make at least *some* progress toward most of the goals that faculties claim to share.

The most optimistic accounts of student improvement come from surveys asking college seniors how much they *think* they have progressed toward various learning goals. For example, according to the senior survey conducted by the National Survey of Student Engagement (NSSE) in 2010, 84 percent of seniors opined that college had contributed "very much" or "quite a bit" to their broad general education.[19] An even higher percentage answered "very much" or "quite a bit" to a question on the impact of the college experience on their critical thinking, while 78 percent felt the same about their progress in writing clearly and effectively, as did 76 percent with respect to analyzing quantitative problems.[20]

These self-reports are interesting but of doubtful validity. More revealing are the results of direct efforts to measure student progress during college. The following table indicates the estimated gains students make based on an exhaustive analysis by Ernest Pascarella and Patrick Terenzini of the many studies that seek to measure how much learning occurs during college. (The improvements listed below are expressed as fractions of a standard deviation. A gain of one full standard deviation signifies that entering freshmen scoring at the median, or 50th percentile, of their class will graduate four years later capable of scoring at the 83rd percentile if they were to take a similar test again with a comparable group of freshmen.)

While these conclusions may seem reassuring, it is only fair to add that most of the gains reported by Pascarella and Terenzini are fairly modest and probably fall short of what students *could* be learning. For example, the ability to reason critically improves through college but only by an average of half a standard deviation. What this means is that freshmen who scored at the 50th percentile of their entering class on a test of critical thinking would score at the 67th percentile if they were to take such a test again at the end of their senior year with a comparable group of freshmen. This is progress but hardly great progress toward developing the competency that faculties claim to value above all others.*

---

*Recent studies of critical thinking have reached results similar to those of Pascarella and Terenzini. See, e.g., Richard Arum and Josipa Roksa, *Academically Adrift: Limited Learning on*

Estimates of Freshman-to-Senior Gains in the 1990s

Goals	Progress
Critical thinking	.50
Reflective judgment (use of reason to address ill-structured problems)	.90
English—reading, writing	.77
Math—quantitative skills	.55
Science	.62
History, social science	.73
Decline in authoritarianism, dogmatism	.70–.90
Decline in ethnocentrism	.40
Moral reasoning	.77

Ernest T. Pascarella and Patrick T. Terenzini, *How College Affects Students*, vol. 2, *A Third Decade of Research* (2005), 574.

While tests of students' ability to reason about practical problems have shown larger average gains approaching one full standard deviation, two prominent experts on reasoning have concluded from careful observation that the vast majority of graduating seniors are still "naïve relativists" who "do not show the ability to critique their own judgments in analyzing the kinds of unstructured problems commonly encountered in real life."[21]

In addition, some of the gains made during the undergraduate years cannot be attributed to education; they would have occurred anyway through normal processes of maturation even if students had not gone to college. After taking account of the expected maturation effects, Pascarella and Terenzini estimate that the progress in critical thinking and reflective judgment remains largely unchanged, but that gains in writing and reading diminish by more than half, those involving mathematics and quantitative skills drop by 40 percent, and those attributable to science, history, and social science shrink by approximately one-third.[22]

Other recent assessments are even more troubling. For example, the Educational Testing Service has compared the degree of proficiency displayed by freshmen and by seniors in several important competencies. The following table reveals the average results over the period from 2006 through 2011.[23] The results do show consistent improvement from freshmen to seniors, but the progress is modest, and the levels of proficiency achieved by seniors, together with the large majorities who are still not proficient, seem downright

College Campuses (2011); Charles Blaich and Kathleen Wise, *From Gathering to Using Assessment Results: Lessons from the Wabash National Study*, Occasional Paper No. 8 (2011), p. 9.

		Percent of Freshmen	Percent of Seniors
Critical thinking	Proficient	3	8
	Marginal	10	20
	Not proficient	86	72
Written communication	Proficient	5	9
	Marginal	19	28
	Not proficient	77	63
Mathematics	Proficient	5	10
	Marginal	11	18
	Not proficient	84	73

depressing. To be sure, the figures are based on a single test, and there is no way of knowing whether the students involved put forth their best efforts. Still, the findings, taken together with the previous assessments, suggest that the progress made by most undergraduates may be much more limited than the students' own estimates.

Finally, levels of knowledge and competence displayed by past graduates of college leave a lot to be desired. Studies of adult reading comprehension show surprisingly low levels of achievement among alumni. The National Assessment of Adult Literacy in 2003 revealed that fewer than one-third of college graduates were proficient in reading and understanding prose passages or typical documents.[24] Surveys of employers show similarly low assessments. One study by an industry group, the Conference Board, found that employers felt that only 16 percent of recent graduates excelled at communicating in writing while only 28 percent excelled in critical thinking.[25] Another survey, conducted by the Association of American Colleges and Universities, found that companies rated only 26 percent of college graduates as very well prepared in writing and considered only 22 percent to be similarly qualified in critical thinking.[26]

On reflection, the results that have just been summarized are not entirely unexpected. If students take no courses in quantitative reasoning, they will seldom acquire much added competence on their own. If they take only a single course on expository writing and receive little feedback on their papers thereafter, one can hardly expect a large majority to develop much skill in expressing their ideas. Although undergraduates may learn valuable lessons about civics through extracurricular activities, what they learn will be haphazard and can hardly be considered a substitute for the knowledge they might gain from well-designed courses on American government and politics. And though a rich extracurriculum can be a valuable supplement to formal coursework for college students who reside on campus, the same is much less likely to be true for the large majority of today's undergraduates who live at home or in off-campus apartments, work for many hours each week, and often attend classes only part-time.

THE NEED FOR REFORM

What, if anything, can be done to improve upon the modest results just summarized?* Surely little will be gained by yet another attempt to specify "the one best curriculum." No such curriculum exists, especially one appropriate for all colleges and all student bodies. But every college should do its best to produce a curriculum that achieves far more than simply accommodating the parochial interests of its principal constituencies. At the least, faculties should agree on a set of requirements that give reasonable promise of enabling students to acheive most of the worthy objectives that large majorities of American professors agree are "essential" or "very important."

A satisfactory curriculum should not rest upon dubious assumptions such as the belief that one can prepare students adequately as citizens without requiring any specific courses for doing so or the proposition that most undergraduates can automatically acquire a lasting breadth of interest merely by taking any offerings they choose within broad categories of courses. Instead, faculties should at least be willing to reconsider the prevalent assumptions that up to half the courses required for graduation should be allotted to a major designed by the individual departments and that up to a quarter should be reserved for student electives, leaving only the limited time left over to achieve all the other aims the faculty claims to be pursuing. This familiar division imprisons the discussion in an iron cage that virtually forces the faculty to engage

---

*One proposal that has gained some traction in policy circles would almost certainly make matters worse: namely, cutting the length of time normally spent at college from four years to three. If the proposal is simply to compress the time to degree by causing students to attend year-round, little difficulty might arise, although not much money would be saved either. But eliminating a year of coursework would be another matter entirely. Such a change might lower the cost of going to college (although the savings could be offset if employers paid less of a premium for a three-year degree than they are willing to offer at present). But what are the other likely consequences? One result seems fairly clear. The effort to achieve many of the familiar purposes of college would become harder, much harder, than it is already. Most faculties would resist making deep cuts in the courses required for the major, since this is the part of the curriculum dearest to their hearts. Students would oppose inroads into their electives, since they enjoy the freedom to choose. General education would experience the strongest pressure to give ground, since it has the weakest constituency. As a result, it would become more difficult than ever to achieve the array of important aims and aspirations already crowded into this segment of the curriculum. For most undergraduates, the BA would probably become even more of a narrow vocational degree than it is already.

in wishful thinking in order to fit a growing list of plausible goals into the residuum reserved for general education.

Accomplishing these goals will admittedly pose a formidable challenge for the faculty. Issues will arise that are very difficult to resolve and often touch upon sensitive interests of professors and their departments. Completing such a review may well take several years. One can therefore appreciate why faculties would be loath to make the attempt and why so few have already done so. Nevertheless, perpetuating the status quo may have even greater disadvantages.

To begin with, the current curricular structure, with its untested assumptions and unexamined rationales, often fails to give students a clear and persuasive idea of what they should aspire to achieve in college and why. This is a serious shortcoming. Authors who have studied the thinking and behavior of undergraduates at first hand give dismaying accounts of student views toward their college experience.[27] A substantial group of undergraduates appear to believe that there is little worth learning in college courses and that the only reason for attending, apart from having a good time and acquiring social skills, is to get the degree that is a prerequisite to most well-paying careers. Others feel that the only subjects worth studying are those that will give them the practical skills and knowledge to find a good job when they graduate.

Under these circumstances, it is not enough to utter broad generalizations about the benefits of a well-rounded undergraduate education. College officials need to give a convincing account of what they hope students will gain from their four years and how the current course requirements will help them achieve these ends. A curriculum that is more a political accommodation of competing interests than a well-reasoned and coherent educational plan offers a poor platform for making the necessary arguments. It is hardly surprising, then, that many introductory speeches to college freshmen seem vacuous and that many students appear to have little understanding of what they can gain by attending college and why it is worth working hard at their studies.

Of course, there is more to improving our colleges than changing the curriculum and explaining its underlying rationale. As the following chapter will try to demonstrate, the methods of instruction used in many courses also help to account for the modest progress made by many students. Together, these deficiencies leave undergraduate education in a weakened state, hardly a desirable condition for the course of study that attracts the vast majority of students who attend our colleges and universities and constitutes for most of them their last sustained opportunity to educate themselves for a full and productive life.

CHAPTER NINE

HOW TO TEACH

‖‖

"[O]NE OF THE MOST sobering insights I had [was] how little intellectual life seemed to matter in college."[1] With these words, a young anthropology professor described her impressions from a year spent living in a college dorm masquerading as a student.[2] One of her dorm-mates expressed the prevailing campus sentiment in even more vivid terms. "Except for those pesky classes, why would I ever leave this life of friends and fun."[3]

Such attitudes are not new. They have reverberated throughout a century or more of accounts of residential college life. One historian of higher education describes a time early in the twentieth century when undergraduates across the country decorated their rooms with posters reading, "Don't let your studies interfere with your education."[4] According to a Yale official of that period, the typical student was "a careless boy-man who is chiefly anxious 'to have a good time' and who shirks his work and deceives his instructors in every possible way."[5]

It would be inaccurate, then, to suggest that there was ever a "golden age" when most college students were industrious and deeply absorbed by their coursework. Nevertheless, there are worrisome signs that the degree of disengagement may have grown worse in recent decades.

In 2010, Philip Babcock and Mindy Marks announced a startling discovery.[6] From 1961 to 2004, according to a series of self-reports from large samples of students, the average amount of time that undergraduates spent either in class or doing their homework dropped by almost one-third—from roughly 40 hours per week to only 27. Homework accounted for most of the loss, falling from 24.38 hours per week in 1961 to only 14.40 hours in 2004. Today, observed University of Chicago professor Ofer Malamud, "American students devote far less time to their studies than their European counterparts."[7]

The forty-year decline in the time spent preparing for class followed a period from 1921 to 1961 in which the number of hours devoted to coursework appears to have remained quite stable. While commentators were quick to offer reasons why this erosion might have occurred, most of their theories turned out to be unsupported by the facts. Yes, the nature of undergraduate student bodies had changed over the forty years as many more high school graduates entered college, and yes, many of the new cohorts of students may have had less aptitude and possibly less interest in academic learning than previous student generations. Still, the decline in studying was about as large in the kinds of institutions that attracted the most gifted undergraduates—liberal arts colleges and research universities—as in comprehensives and community colleges.

One might speculate that students need to spend less time studying, because they can write papers and do research more quickly than in earlier decades thanks to the computer and the Internet. Yet this explanation fails as well, because most of the drop in study time took place before the Internet existed. It is also true that many undergraduates today have less time for homework because they are working more hours per week at outside jobs. Nevertheless, working more explained little or none of the decline that occurred over the entire period. Nor could the trends be explained by larger numbers of students going to school part-time or taking longer to finish.

While there is no evidence to prove why students seem to be working less at their studies, certain trends in college life suggest one plausible answer. Consider, for example, the results of a recent survey of how undergraduates allocate their time at the University of California.[8] According to this investigation, students averaged 13 hours per week of studying, 12 hours socializing with friends, 11 hours using computers for fun, 6 hours watching television, 6 hours exercising, 5 hours engaging in hobbies, and 3 hours enjoying other forms of entertainment. In other words, undergraduates at these highly selective colleges spent more than three *times* the number of hours engaged in recreation and socializing as they spent preparing for class.

What these findings suggest is that faculties, whether they know it or not, are engaged in an intense competition for the time and attention of undergraduates. Among the competitors are older forms of entertainment, such as motion pictures and television, as well as newer arrivals, such as computer games, iPods, Facebook, Twitter, and the like.* These distractions are developed and promoted by highly intelligent people who are doing their best to capture an ever-greater share of the waking hours of young audiences. Over the years, it seems, their offerings have been gaining at the expense of the academic programs that are the principal raison d'être of college. College authorities may have unwittingly contributed to the problem by organizing all manner of absorbing extracurricular

---

*The National Survey of Student Engagement (NSSE) reports that over two-thirds of the almost 300,000 students in its 2012 survey used social media "sometimes" *during class*, while 39 percent of freshmen and 31 percent of seniors did so "frequently." *Promoting Student Learning and Institutional Improvement: Lessons from NSSE at 13* (2012), p. 18. On the effects of multi-tasking on learning, see Reynol Junco and Sheila Cotton, "No A 4 U," 59 *Computers and Education* (2012), p. 505.

activities, many of them wholesome and worthwhile, but all of them tempting diversions from the intellectual work of the college.* Meanwhile, the percentage of freshmen claiming to be bored by their college classes appears to have risen sharply.[9]

Students pay a price for their dwindling effort. Researchers have found that the amount of time undergraduates spend on coursework affects their progress in developing essential skills such as thinking critically and writing well.[10] Other investigators have found that the effort students devote to their studies has an effect on their level of earnings after graduation.[11] Since young people entering college attach great importance to making "a lot of money," these results should clearly concern them.

There is little sign that faculties, or their deans and presidents, have done a great deal to resist the decline in academic engagement among undergraduates. More than 80 percent of chief academic officers acknowledge that "student learning suffers because students do not spend enough out-of-class time studying."[12] Rather than trying to overcome the problem, however, recent research suggests that college instructors have yielded to the desires of students by making diminishing demands on their time. In a national survey from 2009, half of the seniors reported that they had not written a single paper over twenty pages in length during the entire year.[13] Thirty-two percent claimed that they had not taken any courses that demanded more than forty pages of reading per week.[14] Undergraduates have not been held to account for their diminished level of effort. On the contrary, grade averages have continued to rise even as the time devoted to homework has shrunk.†

Many college officials seem curiously complacent about these trends. According to a recent survey, only 16.5 percent of chief academic officers believe that "academic rigor has fallen at my campus in recent years," whereas 72 percent feel that "while my campus is doing well on rigor and quality issues, these issues pose real problems elsewhere in American higher education."[15] Similarly, only 30 percent of chief academic officers feel that grade inflation is a significant

---

* As early as 1909, Woodrow Wilson, then president of Princeton, was determined to shut down fraternities, eating clubs, and student athletic associations because they had become "so numerous, so diverting—so important, if you will—that they have swallowed up the circus, and those who perform in the main tent must often whistle for their audiences, discouraged and humiliated." "What Is a College For?" 46 *Scribner's Magazine* (November 1909), p. 576. I am indebted for this quotation to Professor Mark C. Carnes of Barnard-Columbia University.

† George Kuh has characterized the implicit bargain that students often make with their instructors: "You don't bother me, I won't bother you. I won't ask much of you as a faculty member, you don't ask much of me [as a student]." Quoted in Robert Zemsky, *Making Reform Work: The Case for Transforming American Higher Education* (2009), p. 31.

problem at their institution even though 65 percent consider it "a serious problem across higher education."[16]

The prevailing incentives do not favor taking tough stands for longer homework assignments and harder grading. Most colleges are actively competing for students, either for prestige or simply to survive. Under these conditions—and in today's student climate—gaining a reputation for hard work and stiff grading cannot strike many deans and presidents as a promising way to attract more applicants. As for the faculty, fewer and fewer members have tenure, while increasing numbers are either full- or part-time instructors on term appointments. Since members of both of the latter groups want to be promoted or reappointed, they are presumably anxious to receive high student evaluations of their classes. Teachers with these aspirations are unlikely to insist on tough grading and heavy assignments.

Reports of shrinking student effort will surely give added impetus to critics who are already calling for a halt to grade inflation and a return to more demanding requirements. In principle, there is much to be said for such proposals. In practice, however, reforms of this kind may not come easily, given that prevailing incentives do not encourage them. Nor are such policies easy to implement. Longer assignments often go unread, and even conscientious instructors may hesitate to give lower grades for fear of putting their students at an unfair disadvantage in competing for jobs with graduates of other colleges.

Negative sanctions are not the only way to encourage students to work harder. A better approach would be to improve the quality of teaching and, in particular, to adopt methods of instruction that will create more interest and elicit more effort from students. As it happens, promising methods already exist that may do just that.

THE PROBLEM WITH
UNDERGRADUATE TEACHING

It is often said by critics that the quality of college teaching is not nearly as good as it should be. Yet most of those who voice these complaints misconceive what is really wrong. The usual explanation is that universities and their faculties are so preoccupied with research that professors neglect their classes in order to spend more time in the library or laboratory. As it happens, however, American college professors spend much more time teaching while classes are in session than they do carrying out research, even at leading universities. By more than 2–1, they consider teaching more interesting and important.[17] In fact, surveys of faculty members from a number of countries have found that

American professors enjoy their teaching more than their counterparts in any of the other nations.[18]

Some of those who criticize the quality of teaching also complain that colleges have made increasing use of part-time instructors or adjunct (non-tenure-track) faculty to teach their students. Such a trend has clearly been underway for quite some time. By 2012, a large majority of college instructors were not on a tenure track.[19] There is no convincing evidence yet, however, that such teachers are less effective or engaging in the classroom. Student course evaluations find that part-time and adjunct professors are usually rated at least as highly as the regular tenure-track faculty, while the few studies that attempt to measure directly the effects of part-time instructors have come to mixed conclusions.*

Whether or not instructors are full-time or tenure-track, the methods they use are often poorly designed to achieve their goals. A remarkable 99.6 percent of college professors agree that developing students' ability to think critically is either "essential" or "very important."[20] More than 90 percent believe that it is *the most important* aim of undergraduate education.[21] Moreover, large majorities of college seniors report that their courses do in fact emphasize the analysis of ideas and theories and stress the application of theories and concepts to new situations and practical problems.[22] Nevertheless, the most common method instructors use in conducting their classes is the lecture, a method repeatedly shown to be one of the least effective means of developing higher-level thinking skills or helping students to achieve a deep comprehension of challenging subject matter.[23]

Lecturing appeals to instructors because it is the most efficient way to cover a lot of material. The catch is that students retain very little of what they hear. Studies suggest that students remember less than half of the information in a

---

*Eric Bettinger and Bridget Terry Long, *Do College Instructors Matter? The Effects of Adjuncts and Graduate Assistants on Students' Interests and Success*, National Bureau of Economic Research, Working Paper No. 10374 (2004). Student evaluations, however, provide an unreliable basis for comparing the effectiveness of adjuncts and tenure-track faculty, since they can be affected by such factors as whether instructors are easy graders or give lighter homework assignments. Moreover, some investigators have claimed that the use of part-time adjunct instructors does increase dropout rates, most probably because such instructors appear on campus only briefly to teach their classes and often have no offices or other facilities for counseling students. M. Kevin Eagan, Jr., and Audrey J. Jaeger, "Part-Time Faculty and Instruction in Gateway Courses and First-Year Persistence," in John M. Braxton (ed.), *The Role of the Classroom in College Student Performance* (2008), p. 39. On the other hand, another author, Iryna Y. Johnson, "Contingent Instructors and Student Outcomes: An Artifact or a Fact?" 52 *Research in Higher Education* (2011), p. 761, has concluded that the use of adjuncts does not increase dropouts but does lead to higher grades, presumably because part-time instructors are anxious to obtain higher evaluations in order to bolster their case for reappointment. Finally, Paul Umbach has found that part-time instructors challenge students less, interact with students less, and spend slightly less time preparing for class than other faculty members. "How Effective Are They? Exploring the Impact of Contingent Faculty on Undergraduate Education," 30 *Review of Higher Education* (2009), p. 91.

lecture by the time it ends and only about 20 percent a week later.[24] Of course, most students take notes, which they can subsequently review. But it is difficult to listen and take notes at the same time. Researchers find that students typically write down only about one-third of the information conveyed in a lecture.[25] Some of what they record is not even accurate. As one author reported after observing a variety of lectures and interviewing members of the class, professors "were amazed," when they saw the notes their students had taken, at "how different students' perceptions were from what [the instructors] thought they had presented in class."[26]

Listening to professors explain facts and concepts also offers no guarantee that students will be able to use the information in helpful ways. Applying concepts to new problems requires a thorough understanding of the underlying principles and active practice, not simply memorization. Lecturing alone does not do the job. According to one of the most widely read texts on the art of lecturing, "the balance of evidence favors the conclusion: use lectures to teach information. Do not rely on them to promote thought."[27]

Two professors of physics, Ibrahim Halloun and David Hestenes, gave a striking illustration of the drawbacks of lecturing after they began to suspect that students in their introductory course did not really understand the basic principles of physics covered in class.[28] Instead of putting their suspicions aside—as professors often do when temporarily assailed by dark thoughts about their teaching—they devised a test consisting of problems students could easily solve if they truly understood the basic concepts. They then gave the test to students prior to the first class. Since the course had not yet begun, the results were naturally abysmal. At the end of the course, however, when students should have mastered the basic concepts, the instructors gave the same test again. The results showed virtually no improvement. The students could recite the concepts, but they did not understand them well enough to apply them even to simple problems that differed from those taken up in class.

After reading about this experiment, another physics professor, Eric Mazur, decided to try the same sort of test in his class. Although he was an accomplished lecturer with high student evaluations, he too had been puzzled by some of the questions students put to him after class that seemed to indicate a lack of genuine understanding. Sure enough, the results he obtained from his simple exam were very similar to those found by Halloun and Hestenes. Bright as they were, his students did not truly grasp, nor were they able to apply, the principles of physics he had tried to teach them.

Experts in learning and pedagogy are largely in agreement on certain steps for instructors to follow if they wish students to gain a fuller, deeper understanding of the material.[29] Rather than lecture extensively, they should spend much of the time in class having students grapple with problems raised by their readings. In many subjects, students will gain more from such exercises if they work in groups where those having trouble grasping a concept or solving a problem can get help from fellow students. Often, being closer to one another in age and experience, classmates are better able than the instructor to intuit why a fellow student is encountering difficulty. By helping others, they also gain a deeper understanding of the material than they had before.

Because students may be unfamiliar with active, discussion-based teaching, professors should explain to students at the beginning of the course what they hope to have their students learn, why it matters, and why they consider the problem and discussion method to be the best way to achieve the desired result. Throughout the course, instructors should convey high expectations for their students and resist the temptation to reduce the amounts of reading or the difficulty of homework assignments.

Students should be given repeated opportunities to test their abilities and receive prompt feedback to help them recognize what material they have mastered and where they need improvement. Exercises of this kind ought not to count toward the final grade or carry other penalties or rewards but should be used simply to inform the students and the instructor. In working on problems or taking periodic tests, students should be encouraged to reflect on the thought processes and strategies they have used to search for answers so that they can develop alternative methods and learn how to adjust their learning strategies to suit the problem to be solved.

Finally, instructors should take pains to ensure that their teaching methods, the problems they assign, and their examinations are each tightly aligned with the objectives of the course. In this way, all of the efforts students make, including the questions they are asked to answer and the problems they are assigned, will be directed toward acquiring the knowledge and capabilities that the teacher is trying to nurture.

Measured by these criteria, many college courses are woefully inadequate. Lectures leave little room for a thorough discussion of problems; often, the instructor simply reserves a bit of time for questions at the end of the hour. Homework frequently consists mainly of reading limited quantities of text. Members of the class are typically not required or even encouraged to work at problems in groups even though dozens of studies have found that collaborative efforts to solve problems are usually more effective than simply studying alone.* Students are seldom helped to acquire habits of metacognition—the

*David W. Johnson, Roger T. Johnson, and Karl A. Smith, *Cooperative Learning: Increasing College Faculty Instructional Productivity* (1991), p. 38; Barbara J. Millis, *Cooperative Learning in*

capacity to reflect on how they are going about solving problems and how other strategies might serve them better. Feedback is belated and infrequent at best, often coming entirely from taking a midterm and a final exam and having them returned several weeks later with a few marginal comments. Worse yet, though professors proclaim the importance of critical thinking, studies show that the most common types of undergraduate tests are either multiple-choice or short answer.[30] Even essay exams often call upon students' memory or comprehension of material instead of testing their deep understanding of the material learned and their ability to apply this knowledge through reasoned analysis to answer questions and solve problems different from those covered in class.

In view of these weaknesses, why do so many instructors fail to use more effective methods of teaching? One reason, surely, is that most of them have never had training in pedagogy and are unacquainted with the research comparing lecturing with other, more active ways of teaching and learning. As a result, lacking better models, when new PhDs step into the classroom for the first time, they emulate the teaching they remember from their own days as a student.

There may also be a touch of self-interest in clinging to traditional methods of undergraduate instruction. Lecturing is the easiest form of teaching. In many subjects, once the instructor has prepared the syllabus and an initial set of lectures, only modest revisions are needed in subsequent years to keep the course up-to-date. Since surveys show that over 90 percent of professors believe that their teaching is above average, most instructors may see little reason to change—unless something occurs similar to what happened to Eric Mazur, something to make clear that well-delivered lectures with high student evaluations do not necessarily mean that students are learning much. Unfortunately, such epiphanies come all too rarely.

In theory, deans and provosts and other academic leaders should be aware of the research on student learning and use it to persuade their faculties to try other methods of instruction. Some do, but they are the exceptions. Few deans and provosts will have studied the empirical research on student learning or read extensively in the literature on teaching. After all, they were not specially trained for academic leadership; most of them are simply professors

---

Higher Education: Across the Disciplines, across the Academy (2010). Recently, however, Richard Arum and Josipa Roksa, *Academically Adrift: Limited Learning on College Campuses* (2010) have found that studying together has negative effects on student learning. This apparent disagreement probably stems from differences in how collaborative work is carried on. Studying by merely getting together to talk about homework may detract from learning. Collaboration works best when students are assigned problems to solve and have tried individually to resolve them before meeting to discuss the answers with other students.

who showed some executive talent and agreed to assume administrative responsibilities. Besides, from an administrator's perspective, the lecture does have one practical advantage. It is a relatively inexpensive way of teaching large groups of students—much more so, one would suppose, than offering tutorials to every undergraduate in the fabled Oxbridge manner or dividing students into small discussion groups and assigning a faculty member to each. Since money is always in short supply, especially in a time when states have been gradually reducing their appropriations for public colleges and universities, academic leaders understandably hesitate to do away with large lecture courses.

HOW TO IMPROVE TEACHING
WITHOUT PROHIBITIVE COST

While cost is a valid consideration, there are inexpensive ways to combine large classes with active learning that do not require more money and may even result in savings. One alternative is simply to teach by posing questions to the class and conducting discussions—either through dialogues with individual students in the manner made famous by Socrates or by prompting and guiding discussions among members of the class. Law school professors have long managed to teach socratically in classes of one hundred or more students, while many business school instructors carry on lively discussions of business problems in audiences of eighty to one hundred. Harvard's Michael Sandel, in his celebrated college course on justice, manages to make extensive use of Socratic discussion with eight hundred or more undergraduates. Although only a small minority may have a chance to speak in the course of an hour, the rest participate vicariously. When discussions are interesting, students continue them outside the classroom. Indeed, Professor Sandel's late morning course is famous for provoking continued debate over lunch after the class has ended.

Other teachers have found different ways of introducing more active learning into large classes at little cost. For example, students can be asked to write short papers on a question raised by the course and then meet in small groups to critique one another's work. Experiments have shown that students are highly motivated to write for their peers and believe that the comments they get in return are helpful.[31] To supplement the feedback, instructors can distribute model answers to give students a clear idea of what a thoughtful, well-crafted paper looks like.

At Indiana University, professors in the history department concluded that undergraduates were misconceiving what the study of history was all about. "Students come into our classrooms believing that history is about stories full of names and dates," explained one of the professors. "They discover that history is actually about interpretation, evidence, and argument."[32] The problem was that neither the lectures nor the exams given to students reflected this view of the subject. Instead, they reinforced the students' notion that history was all about facts and dates.

Accordingly, the faculty set about revising their courses to stress "interpretation, evidence, and argument." Instructors emphasized problems and analysis in their lectures. Assignments did not merely consist of readings but included questions that students needed to analyze every week. Both lectures and problems were designed to overcome common errors in student reasoning that professors observed in looking over answers to the homework assignments. Final exams consisted of problems of a similar kind to those emphasized during the course. By studying the exams and the papers students wrote, instructors could determine how successful they had been in improving students' thinking so that they could modify the course for future use when the results fell short of expectations.

Other professors have begun using technology to introduce active learning in large classes at no increase in cost. For example, after discovering how little his students understood the basic principles of physics, Eric Mazur made radical changes in his teaching.[33] He required his students to submit short answers to assigned questions prior to each class not only to ensure that they had read the assigned material but to alert him in advance to difficulties they had encountered so that he could adapt his teaching accordingly. He still lectured but stopped every fifteen minutes or so to put a question to the class to test their understanding. After allowing them to think for a short interval, he asked the students to choose the correct answer from a list of possible solutions and to indicate their choice by pressing the appropriate button on a handheld "clicker" given out at the beginning of the course. The responses were instantly tabulated electronically and displayed on a large screen. If a substantial number gave the wrong answer, he went back over the material and then asked the students to discuss the same question with classmates sitting next to them and answer it again. By now, he has given up lecturing almost entirely and uses class-time to coach groups of students working on projects related to the readings.

Mazur's technique embodies several lessons from learning theory. To begin with, his use of questions forces students to think carefully enough about the underlying principle of physics that they are able not merely to repeat it but to apply it to a problem that has not been discussed. Because students know that they will be asked to solve problems during class, they pay closer attention to the lecture. The instant feedback Mazur receives by the use of clickers tells him and his students whether or not real learning and understanding have been achieved or whether he should take more time to help students overcome their lingering confusion. The time spent in small student groups allows those with wrong answers to recognize why they erred and to think of better ways to approach the problem. At the same time, students with the right answer deepen their understanding by trying to figure out why their neighbors have erred and how they can be helped to understand why another answer is correct.

Of course, the decision to cut back on lectures and work at solving problems means that less material can be covered. This realization leads many instructors to protest that they cannot afford to use such methods. Yet instructors who cannot bear to sacrifice content take no account of how quickly information disappears if it is understood superficially, and how much longer students will retain material if they have learned it well enough to apply it to new problems. Thus, when Professor Mazur tested his students using his new method, they not only showed far greater understanding of the underlying principles; they also did somewhat better on questions requiring recall of material covered in the lectures.

Technology offers ways of enriching classes that are far more elaborate and spectacular than using clickers. In fact, when professors now meet to talk about teaching, the uses of technology often dominate the discussion. As one professor of Egyptology remarked: "In some of my classes, we take students to the Giza pyramids courtesy of a large screen, 3-D glasses, and a real time navigation system—not a linear video—that allows for visits to any part of the site. No two classroom sessions are ever the same." According to a historian of the British Empire: "To understand the imperial dimensions of World War I, . . . we 'visited' war memorials from Flanders and Gallipoli to Basra, Dar-es-Salaam, New Delhi, and Ottawa. To appreciate the sweep of decolonization, we 'traveled' to Kingston, Accra, and Kuala Lumpur and watched period footage of new citizens cheering their independence."

These feats of modern technology are intriguing. There is a danger, however, that instructors will be dazzled by technological innovations for their own sake and not ask hard questions about their use. I vividly remember on one occasion in the 1980s when a young assistant professor came to my office seeking a grant to capture the entire record of the classical age of Greece on a disc. As he described his project, with evident excitement, his disc would enable students to access instantly the complete works of Sophocles, Aristotle, Plato, and Thucydides, view the Parthenon from multiple vantage points at various times through history, and study the sculptures of Phidias and Praxiteles from every angle and perspective. Having listened to this account, I asked, "Exactly how will you use these discs to improve what students learn, and how will you know whether you have succeeded?" After a long pause, he confessed that he hadn't really thought about these questions.

Fortunately, many instructors today are asking these questions and thinking hard about the answers. A number of them, for example, have been experimenting with ways to utilize computers in large introductory courses to improve learning at less cost, especially in subjects that have definite answers, such as mathematics, statistics, or science.

Computers exercises offer several advantages. Learners can develop skills through repeated practice at solving problems with immediate feedback. Students can proceed at their own pace so those who learn quickly need not wait for others to catch up, while slower classmates can continue to practice without risk of being left behind. Artfully designed computer games can engage students' interest while helping them learn to reason more effectively. By studying computer records, instructors can discover points that are giving the class special difficulty and alter their teaching of their reading materials in order to help the students figure out how to overcome the problem.

For a time, conventional wisdom cast doubt on the value of online education. Many efforts failed because students lacked the self-discipline to persevere with no one to keep them company except their computer. Studies seemed to show that online courses were no more effective than traditional instruction, and that the better online offerings were no cheaper and often more expensive than conventional lectures. Even experienced practitioners maintained that technology could provide any two of the following—convenient access, higher quality, and lower cost—but it could not provide all three.[34]

More recent findings have called these conclusions into question. Courses that combine (blend) face-to-face *and* online instruction emphasizing collaborative problem solving may help to keep students from dropping out.[35] There is also reason to hope that well-designed online courses will increase learning. To be sure, the consensus from a number of studies has been that online instruction is no more effective for student learning than traditional instruction. But this generalization turns out to mask a wide variety of results. In one Department of Education analysis of dozens of prior studies, some online courses resulted in up to 48 percent less learning than a control course taught in conventional ways; in others, however, the online students learned up to 50 percent more.[36] Instructors in some experimental courses even claim to have lowered costs, kept dropout rates low, *and* achieved as great or even greater learning gains.

Carnegie Mellon University has produced an especially intriguing example of what technology might be able to accomplish in the form of a partially online introductory course in statistics.[37] Professors deliver only half as many lectures per week as they do in the traditional format, with the remaining time given over to problem solving in the computer lab. The lab makes heavy use of computer programs that pose questions and give students instant feedback. Drawing on years of close observation of how people learn, the programs are designed so that they adapt automatically to the particular weaknesses and learning styles of different individuals. The computer is programmed to recognize common errors and misconceptions and immediately offer hints and further questions that help faltering students understand where they went wrong and how they might revise their thinking. Thanks to the computer printouts, instructors also receive detailed feedback on how well the students are learning so that they can organize their lectures accordingly, either by devoting more attention to problems that students find especially difficult or by deepening the discussion to explore interesting questions related to the basic material.

In the most rigorous evaluation yet conducted of an online course, William Bowen and his colleagues found that students in dozens of courses who were taught statistics in the blended, Carnegie Mellon manner learned as much as those taught in the conventional lecture course format.[38] More important, Bowen et al. discovered that students in the online sections achieved this result while spending an average of 25 percent less time on the course, resulting in cost savings to the institution ranging from 19 to 57 percent compared with carefully selected control groups enrolled in courses with different types of conventional formats. (The estimates did not include the money saved by being able to enroll more students without having to build new classrooms.) These results hold much promise for teaching larger enrollments at lower costs, at least in well-structured subjects such as mathematics, physics, chemistry, and economics.

In another effort to use technology effectively, Carol Twigg has been working with colleges to reconfigure the way their professors teach large introductory courses in a variety of subjects ranging from chemistry and biology to English, fine arts, and sociology.[39] The principal method she employs (similar to the one used by Carnegie Mellon) is to diminish the number of lectures by (high-priced) professors while employing technology to allow more problem solving and active learning through the use of collaborating groups with graduate student tutors on hand to help when students get stuck.

With support from the Pew Foundation, Twigg was able to offer modest grants to institutions to defray the cost of trying to introduce her methods in large introductory courses in collaboration with faculty and staff. Thirty institutions offered to participate, including such large universities as Penn State and Wisconsin. The results Twigg reported seem encouraging. Comparing the outcomes of the redesigned courses with those of classes given in the same subject during the preceding year, she found that twenty-five of the thirty participating universities realized significant gains in learning. (The remaining five schools realized no improvement but no decline either.) Three-quarters of the schools found that fewer students dropped out of the newly reconfigured classes. At the same time, the cost of giving the courses dropped in all thirty institutions by amounts averaging 37 percent.[40]

THE ROLE OF ASSESSMENT

The growing number of experimental courses to improve undergraduate instruction is encouraging. Any serious attempt to improve the quality of teaching, however, must be accompanied by rigorous efforts to assess the results to determine whether progress has actually occurred. Without a reliable means of measurement, instructors wishing to increase student learning cannot be sure whether they have succeeded, and prudent administrators will be reluctant to invest the funds required to spread the use of promising innovations.

The development of online courses illustrates this point very clearly. Such offerings have great potential for lowering costs, especially for accommodating the expanded enrollments that President Obama favors and the economy badly needs. Still, despite scores of evaluations of one sort or another, truly reliable tests of the results are still hard to come by. Either past assessments included insufficient numbers of students, or the methods used did not employ well-enough constructed groups for comparison purposes. Often, the effects on course completion and instructional costs were not considered. Not surprisingly, therefore, conflicting and unreliable conclusions abound concerning such vital matters as dropout rates, student satisfaction, comparative costs, and, most of all, student learning. Until these questions are resolved through rigorous testing, it is not possible to know for sure how effective online courses will be in maintaining or improving current levels of learning, cost, and student retention.[41] In view of the effort and money required to implement such methods on a large scale, obtaining reliable answers to these questions is a matter of great urgency.

Testing of this kind is badly needed not only for evaluating new, experimental methods of teaching but for examining the effects of existing courses to identify weaknesses and areas in need of improvement. However, if assessments are to be accepted by the faculty, it is important that they be used to inform professors and students and help them improve, and not be required by government officials or other authorities for the purpose of imposing penalties or distributing rewards. Top-down efforts to measure progress for purposes of accountability almost always arouse suspicion and opposition from the faculty, and not without reason.* Those in charge typically employ standardized tests to measure student progress so that the results from different institutions can be compared with one another. Experience in the public schools suggests that tests of this kind are often crude and ill-suited to some of the classes in which they are used. Their use almost invariably provokes resistance from the faculty on the ground that the tests impose a single external standard of what students should learn, a practice that may be justifiable in public schools but is far less suitable for most university courses, especially in the humanities and softer social sciences. Using test scores to distribute rewards and penalties can also be unfair, since the progress students make may reflect not only the quality of teaching but differences in student motivation or intrinsic ability that lie beyond the power of instructors to control.

The use of mandated tests by public officials is also likely to distort the teaching efforts of the institution. Once assessments are used to impose penalties and provide rewards, colleges and their faculties will begin to shift time and energy from important subjects and skills that cannot be evaluated to concentrate on those that can. Worse yet, if the stakes are high enough, institutions and their instructors may even resort to manipulation and deception to improve results, just as some already do in an effort to move higher up the college rankings in media such as *U.S. News & World Report.*

Even if university officials propose the use of assessments and do so simply to help their faculties improve, the suggestion will often be rejected or simply ignored by the faculty either because the proposed measures are thought to be poorly designed or because they arouse suspicion that the administration is trying to interfere with how professors teach their courses. If assessment is to succeed, therefore, the faculty must play an active part in designing the instruments used, and professors who help in the design or in experimenting with different measures should be given released time to allow them to exert their best efforts. To allay distrust, academic leaders must also take pains to reassure the faculty that the purpose of assessment will be to improve student learning and not to provide a basis for rewarding or penalizing individual professors.

Fortunately, many forms of learning can be evaluated quite easily and reliably, particularly in subjects with reasonably definite answers, such as

---

*Laurie Fendrich has provided a colorful example of a frequent faculty response to proposals to assess student progress: "Outcomes-assessment practices in higher education are grotesque, unintentional parodies of both social science and accountability. No matter how much they purport to be about 'standards' or 'student needs,' they are in fact scams run by bloodless bureaucrats who, steeped in jargon like 'mapping learning goals' and 'closing the loop,' do not understand the holistic nature of a good college education." "A Pedagogical Straightjacket," *Chronicle of Higher Education* (June 8, 2007), p. B6.

mathematics, statistics, foreign languages, and much of science and engineering. Other important forms of learning may be harder to measure but can at least be evaluated accurately enough that the results can be of help in improving the quality of instruction. Critical thinking is a useful example, since faculties consider this capability to be so important. In recent years, researchers have developed an essay exam that poses realistic problems with extensive relevant information that students can use in order to reach a reasoned conclusion. The test in question—the Collegiate Learning Assessment or CLA—was developed with the help of a large panel of college professors.[42] It has been validated quite carefully and has now been used in more than one hundred colleges to measure progress in writing as well as critical thinking. By some miracle of modern technology, the essay answers can be graded electronically and thus can give immediate results to users.*

Tests such as the CLA can be helpful in at least two ways. Faculties can examine the results to identify particular categories of students who seem to be performing below their capabilities and hence require special attention. Since many colleges have already used the test, faculties can also discover how their students compare with those at other colleges and identify weaknesses in need of improvement.

If the CLA test is deemed unsuitable for one reason or another, it should be possible for colleges to assess the quality of student writing and critical thinking by enlisting the faculty to develop their own tests using well-trained graders to evaluate the results. Since faculty members often rely on graduate students to mark their exams, they can hardly claim that it is impossible to train graders to read paragraphs perceptively enough to arrive at reasonably reliable judgments of the writing and reasoning of undergraduates.

Although college-wide assessments are useful for some purposes, they need to be supplemented by efforts to measure student progress in individual departments and programs. These smaller units will usually have specific purposes of their own that cannot be captured in college-wide measures of proficiency in writing or critical thinking. Moreover, faculty members are much more likely to take an active interest in attempts to evaluate the work of their own department

---

*While the CLA may well be the most effective measure of its kind, it suffers from at least one weakness. As usually administered, it does not count for credit so that students lack much incentive to exert their best effort on the test. Although supporters of the CLA claim that this is not a serious problem, other studies have found that motivation can have substantial effects on the test results. See e.g., Lydia Liu, Brent Bridgeman and Rachel M. Adler, "Measuring Learning Outcomes in Higher Education: Motivation Matters," 41 *Educational Researcher* (2012), p. 352. It is likely, therefore, that the CLA and other similar tests need to be embedded in some way into regular course examinations to ensure that students are sufficiently motivated that the results accurately reflect improvements in their knowledge and proficiency.

or program, since they can participate personally in devising the assessment measures and discussing the results. They are also likely to feel a greater capability and responsibility to help remedy weaknesses in their own department than they will about trying to improve the writing or the critical thinking of the entire undergraduate student body.

Some opponents of assessment argue that instructors already evaluate the progress of their students by grading term papers and examinations. But there are many reasons why grading is no substitute for institutional assessment. Grade averages tell deans and provosts only how individual students compare with their classmates, not how much they have actually learned. In many courses, professors gain nothing from the grading process, because they do not read papers or exams but leave that chore to graduate teaching assistants. Even when they do read their exams, grades still reveal only what students knew at the time they took the test, not what residue of learning remains a week, a month, a year thereafter. Moreover, in many courses, exams do not evaluate the competencies that professors themselves consider most important. For example, survey after survey reveals that improving critical thinking is the goal that faculty members regard as the most important objective of undergraduate education. Yet in two careful studies of the content of college exams, John Braxton and his colleagues discovered that only a small fraction of the questions asked on exams in liberal arts colleges and research universities demanded critical thinking; most questions simply called upon the lower-level skills of memory and comprehension of material.[43] Such testing not only fails to give adequate feedback to instructors; it has an unfortunate effect on what students learn in the course, since most students studying for exams prepare for the kinds of questions asked by the instructor in previous tests.

Another problem with examinations and term papers is that they seldom measure other qualities and competencies that are increasingly recognized as important, such as a capacity to collaborate effectively with others, or to exercise imagination and ingenuity in carrying out complex tasks. Fortunately, federal agencies, foundations, and even some corporations are investing substantial sums to try to discover new methods of evaluation that can assess a wider range of important capabilities. Once again, technology may eventually prove to be an important part of the answer. Computer games, for example, may not only call upon students to display collaborative, creative, even leadership skills; they may also monitor the way participants play the game so that instructors can evaluate not just the quality of students' solutions but how they go about trying to solve the problem.[44]

In addition to departmental assessments, simple methods are available for use in a single class to measure the progress students are making. Instructors can test their students before they start and after they finish the course, as professors Hestenes and Halloun did in their course on introductory physics. Multisectioned classes offer further opportunities to compare the effectiveness of different teaching methods. One of the most influential efforts of this kind was Uri Treisman's well-known experiment in an elementary calculus class to see whether studying in groups would improve the performance of African American students.[45] By requiring students in one section to form small study groups while teaching another section without such a requirement, Treisman showed that the grades of African Americans who studied together were substantially higher than those of black students in the control section, and that the percentage of these students who went on to major in science was significantly greater as well.

The ultimate goal of any college intent on achieving the highest attainable quality of education should be to engage in a process of continuous assessment of learning at all levels—for individual courses, programs and departments, and the entire college. This does not mean that every course and program must be constantly evaluated. It does call for creating a culture of assessment and experimentation in which faculty members periodically evaluate particular areas of instruction to identify problems, which they then seek to overcome through a process of informed trial and error.

Carried out in this spirit, assessment need not give rise to the objections leveled at batteries of tests imposed from above and accompanied by rewards and punishments. Rather, it relies on a cooperative effort between faculty and administration to develop useful measures of learning that professors can employ to detect areas of weakness and evaluate efforts to improve. The ultimate aim is to nurture the same spirit of inquiry and discovery that animates the faculty's research and apply it to the process of teaching and learning in a continuing effort to find more fruitful methods of instruction.

Progress along these lines is slowly occurring on many campuses. Attempts to clarify learning objectives and measure improvement in achieving them have now become standard topics of discussion in accreditation visits and association meetings across the country. More colleges are experimenting with assessments to evaluate progress in writing, critical thinking, and other important skills. As yet, however, such efforts are still at an early stage. Whether they will spread to become a genuine movement of reform is a question taken up in the next chapter. The answer promises to have important consequences for the quality of undergraduate education over the next generation.

CHAPTER TEN

PROSPECTS FOR REFORM

|||||||||||||||||||||||||||||||||||||||||||||||||||||||||||||||||||||||||||||||||||||||||||||||||

ONE OFTEN HEARS THAT change comes exceedingly slowly in colleges and universities. According to a former Duke trustee, "If I learn that the end of the world is at hand, I will immediately come to Duke, because everything takes a year longer here."[1] In the same vein, faculties are often accused of urging reform for every institution save their own. As Francis Cornford put it in his famous satire on British academia, the response of the dons to any proposal to change the traditional practices of their college was "Nothing should ever be tried for the first time."[2]

While comments such as these are common, even the briefest look at the recent history of higher education reveals that American universities have often responded promptly to important challenges. After World War II, they quickly improvised to accommodate a host of returning veterans and then accomplished a vast transition from elite to mass higher education. They reacted in a timely manner to the civil rights movement of the 1960s by recruiting more minority students and creating a more hospitable environment for them. They expanded their research to meet a series of national needs during the 1950s and 1960s and moved even more swiftly after the Bayh-Dole Act of 1980 to speed the translation of discoveries in their laboratories into useful products and processes. Their schools and departments have been quick to add new courses and programs to prepare students for careers in a host of emerging fields such as computer science and environmental studies, while their professors have lost no time in making use of computers and other new forms of instrumentation that could aid their research.

On the other hand, universities have been much slower to improve the quality of undergraduate education. Faculties have clung to the traditional tripartite division of the curriculum—majors, electives, and general education—despite the growing difficulty in accommodating all the aims of undergraduate education within this framework. They have likewise been sluggish in adapting their teaching to embrace methods that have been shown to do more to help students to acquire the very critical thinking and analytic skills that professors claim to value above all others.

In view of this record, what are the prospects for overcoming the problems described in previous chapters? Are colleges destined to retain outmoded curricula and inadequate methods of teaching? Or is successful reform achievable, as it has proved to be in responding to many other needs and opportunities over the past half century?

PERSUADING FACULTIES TO IMPROVE THE QUALITY OF UNDERGRADUATE EDUCATION

Reforming education presents a special challenge to those seeking substantial change. Lasting improvements in curriculum or teaching cannot come about simply by issuing regulations and commands from above. Public officials can publish reports, make threats, and even provide financial inducements to try to bring about progress. In the end, however, professors must be convinced that current practices are not working as well as they should, and that their underlying rationales no longer apply, before they will agree to change their ways.

Fortunately, most faculty members do care sincerely about their responsibility as teachers to help their students learn. In fact, American professors seem to care more about this responsibility than their counterparts in other advanced nations in Europe and Asia.[3] They also have a healthy respect for facts. Once they are persuaded by credible evidence that the way they are teaching or the curriculum they have been using is not actually accomplishing what they thought it was achieving, they will usually try to change their methods without much prodding from outside.

Examples of this kind, however, do not occur very often. In this respect, college teaching differs sharply from research. The systematic testing of current beliefs is standard practice in most fields of inquiry, especially in the sciences where prior findings and propositions are routinely subject to verification and revision in the light of new evidence. The same process has not been common in the case of teaching and education. For a long time, in fact, little rigorous research of this kind was even attempted. Methods of teaching were largely matters for conjecture, intuition, and personal experience rather than careful testing.

In the last few decades, however, a flourishing process of educational research and assessment has emerged. Thousands of studies have been published on the effects of various methods of instruction, the development and behavior of college students, and other aspects of undergraduate education. Numerous books have been written making use of these findings and discussing their implications for colleges and for further research.

As yet, however, most professors are unaware of this large and growing literature. Instead, especially in the most prominent universities, faculties periodically debate changes in the curriculum without much sign that research findings have played any role in forming their opinions. The methods of education they use do not undergo anything like the constant process of testing and revision common to many fields of research in which they engage. As a result, faculties cling to familiar forms of teaching and curriculum for long periods of time without realizing that their accustomed practices have been challenged by new developments or undermined by persuasive evidence of their shortcomings.

Under these conditions, reform may be possible, but it generally requires an effort, typically from outside the faculty itself, to make professors aware that the methods of instruction they are using or the assumptions on which their course requirements rest are open to serious question in the light of emerging evidence. Attempts to call attention to such problems can come from a variety of external sources—government officials, professional organizations, or reform-minded writers. Most of the time, however, these voices go unheeded or are dismissed as inapplicable to the special conditions of one's own institution.

If change is to occur within a reasonable period, therefore, academic leaders must usually assume the responsibility of keeping abreast of the accumulating research on teaching and learning, and engaging their faculties with persuasive findings and arguments that call accustomed practices into question. This is not as easy as it sounds. Discussions about the inadequacies of instruction are not always welcomed by busy professors who are preoccupied with other matters and feel content to carry on as they have in the past. That is probably one reason why academic leaders hesitate to raise such issues with the faculty.

This lack of discussion is unfortunate. Getting professors to recognize that a conflict exists between their current educational methods and their deeper commitment to help their students learn is the most effective stimulus to reform. If assessment results show clearly enough that current practices are not helping students to learn and the effort required to take corrective action is not too great, professors are likely to reform without much argument. The conflict between the evidence and the faculty's underlying commitment as educators is simply too uncomfortable to be left unresolved. A concrete example helps to illustrate the point.

At Harvard during the 1970s, I arranged to have tests administered to freshmen and to seniors to measure the progress in writing that students made during their four years at college. The freshmen and seniors involved were sufficiently similar in background and aptitude to minimize the risk that the two groups were not comparable. Students from both classes were asked to write several paragraphs on given topics, and graders were trained to evaluate the papers so that their assessments were consistent with one another.

Once the tests were administered, the results were intriguing. They revealed that seniors who majored in the humanities wrote much better than the comparison group of freshmen, and that social science majors wrote considerably better than freshmen (though not as much better as humanities majors). In these respects, the results were reassuring though not unexpected. The surprising finding was that the writing of seniors who majored in science had actually deteriorated over the four years of college.

Further probing revealed the probable cause. Whereas humanities majors had to write a lot of papers and social science majors wrote a good many as well, science departments demanded very little writing of their concentrators. Even complete sentences were not always necessary. The important thing was to state the proper formulas and equations correctly. Four years of practicing such habits naturally undermined the students' writing.

After the results of the study were shown and the reasons discussed with the faculty, neither the dean nor I had to do anything more to bring about reform. The departments involved quickly deliberated and introduced substantial writing exercises into their courses. When I returned to the presidency for a year in 2006, the study was repeated. This time, seniors majoring in science showed substantial improvement in their writing.

The key to educational reform, therefore, lies in gathering evidence that will convince the faculty that current teaching methods are not accomplishing the results that professors assume are taking place. Once that is acknowledged, the underlying values of the faculty will usually persuade them to seek corrective action, especially when the administration offers released time and other support to ease the burden of making the necessary changes.

REFORMING THE CURRICULUM

The prevailing college curriculum, with its timeworn tripartite division, may now have become as outmoded and unsuited to the times as the classical curriculum at the end of the Civil War. Nevertheless, of all the changes one might propose for the contemporary university, reforming the undergraduate curriculum in more than cosmetic ways is surely among the most difficult. It is one thing to persuade individual professors to try new teaching methods and quite another to convince an entire faculty drawn from a wide variety of disciplines to agree on questions as controverted and value-laden as those involved in deciding what undergraduates should learn and which courses will help them most. Should the general education program consist of a distribution requirement, or a Great Books program, or something else entirely? Exactly what sort of education do students need in order to prepare to be active and enlightened citizens, or to be ethically perceptive and empathetic human beings, or to function effectively in an increasingly interdependent world filled with different cultures and traditions?

Such questions have no definite answer, especially when they are discussed without much knowledge of existing evidence that might throw light on the subject. For an entire faculty to consider all of the issues in a curriculum at once, examine them with care, and resolve them by collective agreement is a well-nigh impossible task, save perhaps in a small, highly cohesive college whose professors are exceptionally dedicated to teaching undergraduates. In most institutions, such an undertaking seems destined to result in superficial reviews and minor changes in a set of requirements needing a much more searching reexamination.

If there is to be any hope of major changes in the basic structure, academic leaders will have to divide the task into separate pieces to be taken up in sequence over an extended period. In this way, faculties can consider each educational objective and take the time to read the most thoughtful writing on the subject together with any relevant empirical evidence regarding the goal being examined.

Faculty committees with administrative support might begin such a review by trying to discover how much progress students are making toward a few measurable goals, such as the capacity to write with clarity and precision, speak and read a foreign language, or utilize quantitative methods to analyze practical problems. To accomplish this task, the administration will first need to work with faculty members to develop tests to determine whether students have achieved the desired levels of competence. The committee must then find a way to administer the tests in such a manner that students are motivated to exert their best efforts in answering the questions so as to demonstrate reliably how much they have learned. The committee might perhaps embed the questions in examinations given in regular courses. Alternatively, students could be required to pass the test or else do supplemental work to try to achieve the desired level of competence.

If student progress proves to be less than satisfactory, committees can then consider ways in which the existing requirements could be changed to achieve better results. Should students be asked to do more writing in other courses? Should they be required to continue studying a foreign language until they can demonstrate the desired level of competence instead of merely having to complete a fixed number of semester-long courses? Would computer-assisted learning help undergraduates acquire a basic competency in quantitative reasoning in a shorter period of time? Having considered such questions as these, committees can test possible changes by creating pilot programs and evaluating the results before recommending their adoption by the full faculty.

Once the simpler objectives have been addressed, the president and dean can appoint similar committees to consider more complicated goals of general education, such as developing a capacity for moral reasoning, or nurturing lasting interests in a variety of different fields, or acquiring the knowledge and skills to become engaged and thoughtful citizens. Once again, each committee can be given a sample of the best writings on the subject along with the results of existing studies of the progress students have made toward the desired goals both in the college doing the review and at other institutions. If no suitable instruments exist to measure progress directly, recent graduates can be surveyed to examine how they believe their behavior has been affected by courses or other experiences in college. How regularly have they voted and how have they participated in the political and civic life of their community? To what extent have they acquired the lasting intellectual interests that distribution requirements are supposed to nurture? How have they benefited from or made use of the foreign language they were required to study? The committee might supplement such surveys by inquiring of seniors and recent alumni how much they think they progressed during college toward the goals being reviewed, and which courses and activities they feel contributed the most.

To support the committees, representatives of the administration can work with the other members to procure the relevant information and administer any tests and surveys that the committee believes would be helpful. In so doing, they can try to see to it that difficult questions are not evaded or troubling data brushed aside with facile arguments and rationalizations. To be sure, no curriculum can be built entirely on clear and certain facts; requirements must usually rest on informed judgment rather than proven truths. Still, conclusions should at least be consistent with the best obtainable evidence. And where the available data is truly weak and inconclusive, it may be better to abandon a goal rather than continue subjecting students to requirements based on guesswork and lofty hopes unaccompanied by any evidence that the prescriptions are truly benefiting the patient.

Once the several committees have completed their work on the various aims commonly grouped under "general education," one of two outcomes is likely to have emerged. Either the committees will have concluded that some of the goals are not likely to be achieved, given the current state of knowledge, and should therefore be abandoned, or they will recommend new requirements that call for more courses than the existing curriculum can accommodate. If the latter occurs, as may well be the case, the time will be ripe to examine the other two components of the typical undergraduate curriculum, the major and electives.

As faculty committees begin to consider the major and electives, it will again be important for representatives of the administration to assemble as much relevant data as possible. Discipline-based majors have existed for so long as a basic element of the curriculum that their objectives are typically accepted without discussion or passed over briefly with a sentence or two about such things as the importance of giving students the experience of learning "what it means to think deeply about a subject." Surely something more than this is required to justify a requirement that occupies up to half the undergraduate curriculum. The goals should at least be defined more precisely and student progress, if possible, tested empirically. If the stated aim is truly to help students learn to think more deeply, what does "think deeply" really mean? To what extent is such a capacity transferable from the discipline of the major to other fields of thought and experience? Are students actually developing the hoped-for ability or are Pascarella and Terenzini correct in stating that there is "little evidence that one's major has more than a trivial impact on one's general level of intellectual or cognitive outcomes"?[4]

The justification for vocational majors seems more straightforward. Undergraduates need to prepare themselves to pursue the occupation of their choosing. Even this rationale, however, is open to question at colleges in which very high proportions of the senior class go on to earn a graduate or professional degree. If large percentages of the undergraduates who major in business subsequently attend a business school, it is hard to see what valid educational purpose is served by studying the same subject twice. For students who go on to pursue some other form of rigorous professional training, such as law or medicine, one can legitimately ask why that experience will not be enough to equip them to make a living without having them spend up to half their college courses fulfilling the requirements of a vocational major.

In colleges where fewer students attend a graduate or professional school, the need for vocational majors is more compelling. Students who plan to start working as soon as they graduate have to be adequately prepared, and vocational programs may serve the purpose well. Even here, however, recent evidence has exposed enough signs of difficulty to warrant a serious effort by college faculties to collect the available data and consider how well such majors are succeeding. Some studies have found that student progress toward basic goals such as critical thinking and competent writing tends to be more modest in vocational programs than it is among students completing traditional liberal arts majors.[5] At least one large-scale inquiry has concluded that many vocational majors appear to demand less work from their students than discipline-based concentrations.[6] Still other studies have revealed troubling indications that some of the most popular vocational majors actually have a negative effect on other familiar aims of undergraduate education, such as civic engagement and understanding other races and cultures.[7]

In addition, as previously noted, employer surveys reveal considerable dissatisfaction with graduates who have taken vocational majors, not over any failure to acquire needed technical skills, but because of deficiencies in the very qualities general education is supposed to provide.[8] If such concerns are genuine, they suggest a need either to revise the content of courses and the teaching methods used or to reduce the number of required courses in order to leave more room for general education classes that can develop the missing capabilities.

Problems of this kind point up the danger of leaving majors entirely to the sponsoring schools and departments. It would be far better to have them reviewed by committees that include faculty outside the major as well. If the review, enlightened by the best empirical evidence available, reveals deficiencies of the type mentioned above, that finding alone should provide sufficient impetus for a careful reexamination followed by suggestions for reform.

Electives are in need of much the same critical scrutiny. To what extent do students use their freedom to explore new interests? To seek out easy courses? To supplement their major in an effort to get a head start on graduate or professional school? Do students work harder or less conscientiously in elective courses than they do in their major or in general education classes? In course evaluations, do students rate their electives more highly or less highly than other classes? After gathering information on these points, a committee can then consider what purposes electives are meant to serve, how well the choices students make are achieving these purposes, and, finally, whether the number of electives allowed should be increased or diminished.

Having come this far, the faculty can then consider how best to accommodate all the courses needed to accomplish the goals it wishes to pursue in educating undergraduates. Several strategies are possible to provide more space in the curriculum in the event that this seems necessary to achieve all of the important aims currently lumped together under the rubric of general education. The number of electives could be cut back moderately. The requirements for the major could be somewhat reduced. Finally, some aspects of general education could be integrated into appropriate majors. For example, students could be given credit for civic education by completing a major in political science or they could satisfy a quantitative reasoning requirement by completing a designated social science or natural science major. Conversely, business majors could receive credit toward their concentration by taking certain general education courses on foreign cultures or ethics and moral reasoning or expository writing, since CEOs have expressed a desire for graduates with a greater understanding of these subjects. In the end, the most feasible solution may well be to combine these three approaches rather than rely on a single method to make room for all of the objectives that faculties consider necessary for a suitable undergraduate education.

These are only some of the issues that faculties could explore in examining the several parts of the curriculum. Others will doubtless come to light in the course of the review. The essential point is to take one part at a time and examine it in the light of whatever evidence can be found in order to test its underlying assumptions and cast a clearer light on how well or how badly the current program is achieving its intended objectives.

There is no denying the political difficulty involved in such a process. Several years and much effort will be needed to carry out such a review. In most colleges, faculty members will resist any attempt to cut the number of courses allocated to majors, while students will oppose any reduction in the number of their electives. Still, if the basic structure of the curriculum is ever to be modified, and its ends and means brought into better alignment, the task will surely require the patience to assemble enough evidence to identify weaknesses in the current framework and in the rationales used to justify it.

The end result of this process may not be a curriculum guaranteed to accomplish all the faculty's goals. No such curriculum exists, nor is there evidence enough to prove conclusively which set of requirements will work best. But some evidence is better than none. Enough useful data can surely be gathered to expose shortcomings and develop requirements better designed to achieve the faculty's goals and easier to explain convincingly to students than the arrangements now in place in most colleges. This prospect should be justification enough for devoting the time and effort required for such a review.

IMPROVING TEACHING

Despite much recent talk about new methods of teaching and the shift to a learner-centered pedagogy, the pace of progress over past decades has been very gradual in most colleges. Many courses are still being taught in virtually the same way as they were fifty or sixty years ago. The principal roadblock has rarely been overt opposition from a powerful group but rather the lack of any strong pressure to change. Faculties have seen no compelling reason to alter their traditional methods of teaching, nor are students clamoring for more effective instruction. University presidents and provosts are usually preoccupied with other duties and reluctant to interfere in a domain that faculty members regard as their prerogative. The challenge, therefore, is to conceive an effective strategy to overcome this inertia and begin a serious process of reexamination and reform.

EFFORTS FROM OUTSIDE

Impatient with the sluggish pace of change, both federal and state officials have manifested interest in improving the quality of undergraduate education. Over the past twenty years, they have repeatedly expressed a desire for more accountability and demanded to know what citizens are getting in return for all the money contributed to colleges in tuitions and taxes.[9]

Dissatisfied with the answers they have received, officials have experimented with more intrusive strategies to try to induce educators to act. During the 1990s, a number of states tried to use the power of the purse to encourage their public colleges to become more accountable and improve their performance. The most ambitious of these efforts utilized a method known as "performance budgeting" through which states would set aside a certain percentage of their higher education budget every year and allocate it among institutions depending on how much progress they made toward prescribed objectives. For example, budget allocations might reflect the percentage of entering students who earned a degree, or the success of recent graduates in finding jobs, or how much improvement colleges could demonstrate in raising scores on measures such as the Graduate Record Examination (GRE) and other standardized tests of student achievement.

For a time, this idea proved politically popular, and growing numbers of states hurried to climb on the bandwagon. A decade later, however, the practice had been abandoned by almost all the legislatures that had adopted it. By 2005, little performance budgeting remained.[10] While several states have now renewed the practice, the emphasis is more on matters such as access and graduation rates rather than the quality of instruction.

What went wrong? To begin with, some of the measures used were poorly chosen. For example, merely looking at how many students graduated or at the scores of seniors on prescribed tests could not prove much about the quality of education; rather, such indicators either tended to reward institutions that enrolled the brightest freshmen, or, in the case of the employment records of recent graduates, reflected the state of the economy more than the nature of the education students received.

Deficiencies such as those just mentioned could be corrected. But even states that used more plausible measures found that giving money to the best-performing colleges and taking funds from the weakest performers was not an ideal way of bringing about educational reform. Often, the least effective colleges needed more money to improve; reducing their state appropriations could simply weaken them further. As for successful universities, performance budgeting did not necessarily reward the faculty, who were primarily responsible for student learning. More often, states simply sent money to the institution. As a result, professors saw no advantage in helping to improve student performance. In fact, surveys showed that most faculty members did not know the program existed. Even department chairs tended to be ignorant of the government's efforts. So constructed, the incentive scheme was bound to fail.[11]

After the turn of the century, performance budgeting fell victim to the political realities of state finances. The system seemed attractive to lawmakers during good economic times when state revenues were rising. It was not nearly so enticing when a recession came along and state resources were shrinking. As political analysts often observe, "incentive funding is invariably the first casualty of hard times." Sure enough, when hard times arrived in 2000 and 2001 and state governments had to cut appropriations, performance budgeting schemes were among the first programs to feel the ax.

During the administration of George W. Bush, Secretary of Education Margaret Spellings flirted with another strategy for bringing about reform.[12] In 2004, she formed a Commission on the Future of Higher Education to review the performance of universities. At one point, the commission became intrigued with the possibility of mobilizing market pressure to produce change. If the government could require colleges to measure the amount of improvement by their students and publicize the results, applicants could compare the findings and choose the school where they would learn the most. Colleges that could not show much student progress would then feel compelled to change their methods in order not to risk losing applicants to other institutions.

Despite its intuitive appeal, this strategy too has major weaknesses. For one thing, no one knows how students would react to what could turn out to be rather modest differences in student learning. Would applicants pass up going to Stanford or Cornell simply because students seemed to be making a bit more progress in critical thinking and quantitative reasoning at Grinnell and Middlebury? Mandating a single test for all colleges could also discourage efforts to experiment with new and potentially superior ways of assessing learning. Having had no part in choosing the test, faculty members and university officials would be bound to criticize it instead of cooperating with the program.[13] Since there is no perfect way as yet to measure learning, such criticisms would probably have some merit, thus undermining the public's confidence in the reliability of the tests and further weakening their effect.

In addition, methods of assessment that are even minimally adequate for comparative purposes currently exist for only a few forms of learning, mostly skills such as writing and critical thinking. If test results were made public and if poor scores did cause colleges to have fewer applicants, faculties might well respond by spending more and more time trying to raise the scores for these measurable skills at the expense of other educational aims that are harder to evaluate. That has apparently been the result in public schools following the introduction of mandatory testing of science, math, and reading.[14] Some colleges might also try to game the system (as they have with the highly publicized institutional rankings) by finding ways to improve test scores without actually teaching their students more effectively. Such tactics would hardly help to improve undergraduate education, let alone win the confidence and support of either faculty members or the public.

Under heavy criticism, the commission wisely backed away from mandatory tests and simply issued a plea to colleges to develop their own means of assessing student learning.* In an effort to achieve this result, Congress has chosen

---

*Efforts to make comparative data publicly available, however, have hardly disappeared. In his 2013 State of the Union address, President Obama indicated his intention to have the government publish information about the cost of attending each of America's colleges, along with data on the employment records and other outcomes for recent graduates of each institution. No sensible person would quarrel with the intent of such proposals to give college applicants more accurate and complete information about the various institutions they might be thinking of attending. Nevertheless, there are substantial problems in achieving this objective. For one thing, it is difficult to provide applicants with useful information about what it will cost to attend a given college, because the amounts of scholarship aid provided tend to vary widely from one student to another depending on a variety of factors, such as the applicant's academic record, financial circumstances, and special talents (e.g., athletic ability). It is even harder to provide useful data about the "outcomes" of students graduating from different institutions. Attempts to present information about how much students learn are handicapped by the lack of reliable tests to measure most types of learning and by the possibility that differences in the amount students learn may result from factors other than the quality of instruction they received at college. Employment and earnings records of a college's recent graduates may be useful for applicants considering predominantly vocational institutions, such as most community colleges and for-profits, although even there, the results will often vary widely from one occupation to another and may reflect differences between colleges in the native abilities of their students or variations in local employment conditions more than the quality of a college's education. Such information is likely to be even less helpful in the case of selective colleges, since many of the graduates of these institutions do not seek jobs immediately but attend a professional school, and because their earnings record often becomes truly meaningful only after a decade or more following their graduation from college.

a different strategy. Lawmakers have urged accrediting organizations to press faculties to define their learning objectives and develop methods of evaluating the progress of their students rather than concentrate on inputs, such as the amount of money per student spent on instruction or the number of books in the library. In the bill reauthorizing the Higher Education Act in 1998, Congress even stipulated that accreditors give their highest priority to persuading colleges to measure student learning.[15]

Accrediting organizations have since proceeded to urge every inspection team to review the efforts of the college to define its learning objectives and assess the results in achieving these goals. They have not sought to impose particular standardized tests on colleges but have let each institution devise its own methods of measurement. University officials in many institutions have responded by describing what they want their students to learn and have even begun conducting some assessments to measure student progress. But accreditors have had less success persuading academic leaders to discuss the results with their faculties in order to identify weaknesses and search for ways to overcome them.[16] Even voluntary efforts at assessment quite apart from accreditation have encountered similar resistance. In one elaborate effort to measure student learning by a group of nineteen colleges and universities, a follow-up study revealed that "nearly 40% of the institutions have yet to communicate the findings of the study to their campus communities, and only about a quarter of the institutions have engaged in any active response to the data."[17]

As of now, therefore, assessment data have piled up in administrative offices, but few campuses can report much progress in actually using the information to improve the quality of education. In fairness, it is still too soon to know how much success accreditors will eventually have in persuading colleges to use assessment results to increase learning. On the other hand, it is also too early to label the effort a success.*

---

*Many critics dismiss accreditation as toothless and ineffective. Nevertheless, it is not insignificant that the great majority of colleges have now defined their learning objectives and are using at least several methods of assessment. In a recent survey, moreover, 69.2 percent of chief academic officers agreed that "regional accreditation makes a significant contribution to the quality of our academic programs." Kenneth C. Green, *The 2011–12 Inside Higher Ed Survey of College and University Chief Academic Officers* (2012), p. 15. It is true that accreditation has had less success thus far in getting college officials to use assessment results to encourage serious faculty consideration of improvements in teaching. In engineering, however, efforts to induce faculties to comply with ambitious new standards for accreditation appear to have made significant progress in achieving changes in curriculum and student performance. J. Fredericks Volkwein, Lisa R. Lattuca, Betty J. Harper, and Robert J. Domingo, "Measuring the Impact of Professional Accreditation on Student Experiences and Learning Outcomes," 48 *Research in Higher Education* (2007), p. 251.

WHY REFORM WILL OCCUR
DESPITE THE PROBLEMS

Underlying the efforts of government officials and accrediting organizations to bring about reform is a quiet war between two different cultures. The first culture, shared by reformers, is an evidence-based approach to education. It is rooted in the belief that one can best advance teaching and learning by measuring student progress and testing experimental efforts to increase it. The second culture rests on a conviction that effective teaching is an art which one can improve over time through personal experience and intuition without any need for data-driven reforms imposed from above. This has long been the prevailing belief among most faculty members. Their instinctive response to the reformer brandishing tests and empirical studies is to retreat into silence and withhold cooperation.

Observing this clash of cultures, one could easily conclude that the prospects for reform are rather dim. Faculty members must believe in the evidence-based approach if it is to have any hope of succeeding. In the minds of skeptical professors, however, such methods conjure up visions of the government's attempts to improve the public schools—crude standardized tests, bonuses for teachers to reward demonstrated improvement, and an emphasis on workplace skills coupled with a neglect of the arts and humanities and other fields of study that do not help the economy or lend themselves to standardized measurement. To professors who passionately believe in a wider, subtler set of educational goals, who treasure their autonomy in the classroom, and who are already stretched thin by their existing duties, the language of reformers is bound to seem threatening. Sensing this hostility, many academic leaders shrink from initiating discussions concerning the need for educational reform for fear of arousing faculty resentment.

Surprisingly, however, notwithstanding these difficulties, there is reason to believe that major improvements in teaching will eventually take place. In fact, they have already begun to occur. In the past decade or two, more and more colleges have chosen to participate in national programs that seek to measure the progress of their students in acquiring important skills, notably critical thinking, or to determine how much use is made on their campus of proven methods to increase learning.[18] Faculty surveys also suggest that the amount of lecturing has begun to recede, albeit slowly. Take any of the tested methods to improve undergraduate instruction, such as collaborative working groups, student research, computer-assisted learning, or problem-based teaching, and one is likely to find that their use is gradually increasing.* The interesting questions, then, are not whether change will ever come, but why a transformation has finally begun and how long the process will take.

How did this process start? Part of the explanation lies in the gradual accumulation of evidence that lecturing is not the ideal way to teach students and could be improved upon by greater use of class discussion, problem solving, collaborative learning, and the like. Associations of colleges and universities published accounts of such findings and held conferences to discuss them with interested faculty. Meanwhile, accreditors, as already noted, were being ordered by lawmakers to insist on some means of assessing the actual effects of university instruction.

These developments did not meet with instant interest and approval on the nation's campuses. But in a system of higher education as decentralized as ours, concerns about the effects of college teaching did not go entirely unheeded. Here and there, academic leaders, often from small, less prominent colleges, took a special interest in improving the quality of education and initiated efforts to put some of the research findings into practice.[19] Faculty members, especially those active in professional organizations such as the Association of American Colleges and Universities, took part in conferences and workshops to discuss the growing literature on student learning. Other professors became aware of these developments and began to experiment with new methods in their own classes. Particularly striking findings, such as those from the work of Uri Treisman and Eric Mazur described in chapter 9, were widely noticed and

* Faculty Surveys of Four-Year Colleges on Methods of Instruction Used in All or Most Undergraduate Courses Taught

	1991–93	2010–11
Extensive lecturing	54.2	47.4
Class discussions	69.4	80.7
Cooperative learning	31.7	53.7
Experiential learning / field studies	19.8	23.4
Group projects	21.6	30.4
Multiple drafts of written work	14.4	21.7

Eric L. Dey, Claudia Ramirez, William S. Korn, and Alexander W. Astin, *The American College Teacher: National Norms for the 1992–93 HERI Faculty Survey* (1993), p. 36; Sylvia Hurtado, Kevin Eagan, John H. Pryor, Hannah Whang, Serge Tran, *Undergraduate Teaching Faculty: The 2010–2011 HERI Faculty Survey* (2012), p. 25. The National Survey of Student Engagement (NSSE) also reports significant progress among its participating colleges in the percentage of institutions adopting more effective instructional methods in the freshman and senior years over the past dozen years. NSSE, *Promoting Student Learning and Institutional Improvement: Lessons from NSSE at 13* (2012), pp. 12–13.

adopted by hundreds of instructors around the country. Although the process of change is still at an early stage, it is now too obvious to be ignored.

Will the process continue? Probably yes. For one thing, the forces pressing for accountability and improvement are powerful, and the reasons for their existence are not likely to disappear. The cost of higher education is now so great that policy-makers are bound to continue insisting on some effective form of accountability to give assurance that the taxpayer's dollar is being well spent. Employers too are likely to press for improved methods of education to help them succeed in increasingly competitive global markets.

Competition will also serve to force more colleges to experiment with new methods to improve the quality of their teaching. The largest, most successful for-profit universities routinely use research and assessment for this purpose.[20] As they continue to expand and vie for students with community colleges and comprehensive universities, the latter may feel compelled to introduce similar methods in order to hold their own. Once individual colleges begin to move down this path, associations and enterprising journalists will publicize their efforts, and other institutions will be more inclined to follow suit.

As more colleges focus on increasing the quality of their programs and evidence continues to emerge that casts doubt on how much students are learning, many academic leaders will decide that educational reform could be a more promising strategy for their institution than expensive efforts to encourage research or start additional master's and doctoral programs. More faculty members will learn about new methods of instruction and attempt to use them in their own teaching. The increased use of improved measures of student learning will give academic leaders tangible goals to strive for. Once they can measure the results of their efforts, individual faculty members may come to take the same interest in experimenting to discover more effective methods of teaching that scientists have long felt in searching for solutions to unresolved questions in their own fields of inquiry.

Still other institutions may be moved to act by the prospect of using new teaching methods to save money. As Carnegie Mellon and other universities are discovering, blending online instruction with face-to-face teaching may allow them to lower the cost of their larger classes.[21] By now, more than one hundred institutions have experimented with similar methods to change the way large introductory courses are taught. As college enrollments continue to increase, academic leaders will feel great pressure to utilize online instruction to avoid the necessity of adding expensive new classroom buildings. The governor of Indiana has already agreed to use the online Western Governors University to absorb the expected increase in student enrollments, and several other efforts are underway to create inexpensive models of undergraduate education using online instruction.

The growth of online education could help in several indirect ways to persuade faculty members to adopt a more deliberate, experimental approach to teaching and learning. Some of the pioneers in the development of massive open online courses (MOOCs) appear to be acting out of a desire not only to expand the audience for their courses but to develop a new, more active model of learning. As the *Chronicle of Higher Education* describes it, "Sebastian Thrun . . . whose free online course in artificial intelligence attracted 160,000 students worldwide, says he founded Udacity [a new company] to develop a MOOC model in which students learn by solving problems, not by listening to a professor tell them how to solve them."[22]

The prospect of reaching larger audiences has attracted the attention of many faculty members and led them to devote much effort to developing online offerings of their own. Professors who create such courses will work with technical advisers to think explicitly together about how best to adapt the course materials and methods of instruction to fit the new medium. Technology will provide instructors with abundant information about how much their students are learning, what kinds of material and what concepts are hard for them to understand, and how they go about thinking through the questions and problems they are asked to consider. Prudent universities are likely to insist on evaluating the results of online teaching before agreeing to invest substantial sums. In all these ways, professors will become accustomed to a more deliberative, evidence-based, collaborative approach to teaching instead of the traditional practice of leaving course development and content solely to the discretion of the instructor.

Further stimulus for reform has arisen through the development of two new instruments for measuring the quality of education. The first of these, the National Survey of Student Engagement (NSSE) uses an indirect approach by surveying the students in participating colleges to determine how often they experience educational practices (such as rapid feedback, active discussion, collaborative problem solving, and the like) that research suggests will improve learning. College officials then receive a summary showing the extent to which these exemplary practices are used on their campuses and how their usage compares with that of other institutions of a similar type. More than five hundred institutions are currently participating in the survey every year and more than a thousand have used it at least once.[23] The results will again provide tangible goals that faculties can try to meet.

The second measure, the Collegiate Learning Assessment (CLA), seeks to measure two basic skills, writing and critical thinking.[24] A signal virtue of these tests is that they are not true-false or multiple-choice but consist of problems accompanied by a summary of facts and other evidence that may bear on a solution. Students are asked to respond by writing a short essay stating their conclusion together with supporting arguments. Although the tests were previously scored by trained readers, they are currently gradable by machine, making the process both cheaper and quicker to transmit results. By now, more than five hundred colleges have used the test to determine the extent of improvement in student writing and critical thinking from the beginning of college to the end.

Of course, if the colleges that administer these surveys and measures do not share the findings with their faculty, little will come of the exercise. As Talleyrand once said of bayonets, however, you can use data for anything except to sit on. In time, faculty members who know about the tests will be curious to see the results. State lawmakers will demand that the findings be disclosed. Even now, studies have appeared that report the aggregate findings of NSSE surveys and CLA tests (without disclosing the results for individual colleges).[25]

It is studies like these that have revealed the modest progress that many students are making in critical thinking and writing and the shrunken homework assignments that most instructors give their classes. The resulting findings have been duly reported in the media and repeated by widely read commentators. Already, more and more people are becoming aware that existing methods of teaching may not be doing all they should to help students learn. In the future, more innovations in teaching will emerge and be publicized. Research may also show that better methods of instruction can help bring about other changes of importance to society, such as lowering dropout rates and causing fewer talented undergraduates to abandon plans to major in science.

As word of these developments spreads, continued unwillingness by faculties to evaluate progress and initiate change will increasingly seem unreasonable and engender disapproval. If the accumulating evidence continues to reveal the modest intellectual progress of many undergraduates, more and more professors will perceive a conflict between their current methods of teaching and their deeper commitment to trying to help their students learn. Once these conflicts become widely recognized, raising questions about teaching methods will be less likely to provoke resistance from the faculty and seem less hazardous to academic leaders.

Government agencies and other external organizations cannot force this process to accelerate, but they can refrain from getting in the way and even help to speed the rate of change. As previously mentioned, public officials need to avoid efforts to compel reform by mandating particular tests and publicizing the results. Such tactics could easily provoke resistance, inhibit efforts to improve upon existing assessment measures, and weaken the hand of professors and academic leaders who are interested in improving teaching and learning.[26]

A better strategy for government and foundations would be to support promising efforts to improve teaching, such as the work of Carnegie Mellon in combining technology with traditional lectures to increase learning and reduce costs. An even more helpful step would be to fund research to find better ways of measuring student progress, since credible measures are essential to reveal the weaknesses in existing practices and demonstrate the superiority of new and improved methods of instruction. Since studies of student progress regularly find that differences *among* students in any given college are much greater than aggregate differences *between* colleges, another inquiry worth encouraging would be to study why some undergraduates seem to make so much more progress than others. Financial support for research of this kind costs relatively little and could eventually help to discover valuable ways to improve student learning.*

Of the several kinds of reform needed to strengthen undergraduate education, the introduction of more effective methods of instruction seems the one most likely to succeed. Efforts of this kind are less expensive than raising graduation rates. They do not threaten the interests of the principal parties involved to nearly the same extent as attempts to change the basic structure of the curriculum. The systematic effort to assess current practices and experiment with new and potentially better methods of teaching is a process similar to the one most faculty members use in conducting their research and hence is aligned with their deep-seated beliefs about how to solve problems. As a result, although the needed changes may prove time-consuming for busy professors, their basic commitment to helping students learn coupled with society's pressing need for better education seems likely to win out eventually and bring about widespread reform.

---

* Another means of speeding reform would be to change existing accreditation procedures slightly to encourage accreditors to offer some form of special recognition to colleges making exceptional progress in defining learning objectives, assessing learning, and experimenting with new and better methods of teaching. Colleges could then publicize this recognition in communicating with alumni, prospective students, and other interested audiences. Such a procedure would probably provide a significant inducement to colleges to initiate reforms in order to be recognized. The danger is that such a procedure could alter the relationship between colleges and accreditors by making campus officials less candid in revealing weaknesses in their educational programs in order to enhance their chances of gaining recognition, thus undermining the quality and usefulness of the accreditation process.

AFTERWORD (II)

IIIIIIIIIIIIIIIIIIIIIIIIIIIIIIIIIIIIIIIIIIIIIIIIIIIIIIIIIIIIIIIIIIIIIIIIIIIIIIIIIIIIIIIIIIIIIIIIII

Two problems facing colleges overshadow all the others. The first—persistently low graduation rates—has become apparent only in the past thirty years. Prior to that time, the United States had long had the highest percentage of citizens with high school diplomas and college degrees of any nation in the world. Now that more and more countries are overtaking us in the share of young people graduating from college, and the implications of this fact for economic growth and competitiveness have become more widely understood, political leaders have grown concerned and set ambitious goals for raising our levels of educational attainment over the next few years.

The second problem, involving growing doubt over the quality of education, has also become apparent only relatively recently. For a long time, debates about quality consisted mainly of arguments about the nature of general education requirements and revolved for the most part around complaints by conservative critics about the lack of attention paid to the Great Books. Within the past few years, however, studies have appeared providing troubling evidence of declines in the amount of time undergraduates spend studying for their classes and the limited gains that most of them make in improving such basic competencies as writing and critical thinking. These reports make clear that we need to be concerned not just with expanding the numbers of students who graduate but with increasing the amount they learn while they are enrolled.

At this point, however, perceptive readers may observe a difficulty in simultaneously trying to improve both graduation rates and the quality of a college education. Efforts to address the first of these problems may conflict with attempts to deal with the second. Many of the undergraduates who are most likely to drop out of college tend to be less motivated and less capable academically than those who persevere and graduate. If colleges demand more work and tighten their academic standards to increase learning, these students may be even less likely to earn a degree. Conversely, if colleges are pushed too hard to increase graduation rates, they may respond by lowering their requirements and accepting less effort from their students, thus dimming the prospects for improving the quality of education.

At present, the latter outcome is more likely. Efforts to increase the percentage of young Americans with college degrees (and lower the costs of educating them) are attracting far more high-level attention than attempts to maintain and increase the amount they learn along the way. The lack of widely accepted measures of student learning exacerbates the risk of neglecting quality. Since dropout rates are easy to calculate while improvements in the effectiveness of education are not, there is an obvious danger that colleges will lift their graduation rates while gradually allowing their academic standards to deteriorate. Without adequate means of assessing student progress, neither college authorities, nor students, nor the government and the public may even be aware that such a slippage has occurred. As a result, America could easily end up with a two-tier structure of undergraduate education: an expensive, quality tier primarily for those who can afford it, and a low-cost, heavily vocational education of marginal quality for all the rest. Such an outcome would be most unfortunate. There is little to be gained by raising the levels of educational attainment if the result is simply to increase the number of young people who complete their studies without acquiring much knowledge or mastering essential skills such as critical thinking and writing.

In contrast to past generations of college students, undergraduates today will be entering a world in which jobs are becoming more demanding. Information technology is making them compete for many positions, not just with other young Americans, but with college graduates throughout the world, many of whom are willing to work for much less than BAs in this country would accept. Already, hundreds of thousands of American tax returns are being made out, not by public accountants in America, but by college graduates in India. Thousands more computer programmers for American industry now reside in Asia. Major US corporations have located research laboratories in Russia and China where they can hire capable scientists for much lower salaries than they can in the United States. Altogether, according to one recent analysis, eight million white-collar jobs, including positions such as software engineers, accountants, and auditors, are at high risk of being outsourced overseas, while another sixteen million jobs are at medium risk of being exported.[1] The influx of highly educated professionals from other countries, whose entry is encouraged under our immigration laws, creates still another source of competition. As a result, if American college graduates are to compete successfully for desirable jobs, they will increasingly need an education that is qualitatively superior to what their foreign counterparts receive.

The importance of improving student learning goes well beyond competing successfully for employment. Jobs are not the only things that are steadily growing more complicated. Problems of everyday life, such as choosing a health-care plan, making out one's income tax returns, or providing for one's retirement, require much more analytic skill and reading comprehension than they did only decades ago. Understanding developments in the society that affect our lives, such as economic trends, or the state of the environment, or the problem of health-care costs, calls for abilities of comprehension greater than those required of earlier generations. Merely to cast an intelligent vote in elections requires more knowledge than was needed only decades ago. In short, if young Americans are to understand the world around them, conduct their affairs competently, and be reasonably informed and discerning citizens, they will not merely need to earn college degrees; they will have to be better educated as well.

The tension between the quantity of college graduates and the quality of what they learn is real. Resolving it will be a challenge. Still, it should be possible to raise graduation rates and improve quality at the same time. For one thing, many students who drop out are not less capable or less motivated than their classmates. Highly qualified undergraduates from low- and moderate-income homes also leave college at higher than average rates. If they could receive adequate financial aid, and if they were properly advised and encouraged to attend the most selective institution that will take them, more of them would earn a diploma. If colleges improved their support services and increased their efforts to integrate students into campus life, dropout rates would decline. If they could improve remedial instruction and high schools could align their courses properly with the demands of college work, more students would enter adequately prepared and fewer would become discouraged and leave. All of these steps can be taken without any sacrifice in the quality of education.

Academic leaders and their faculties could also make greater efforts to persuade their students of the long-term benefits they can derive from a college education. Today, large majorities of undergraduates understand that college is the essential path toward a successful career and a comfortable lifestyle. But a significant fraction believe that getting a degree is all that truly matters.[2] Another substantial number think that the only courses that really count are those that specifically prepare them for a good job. They are not likely to change their minds as a result of listening to platitudes of the kind that often fill encomia to a liberal education. A more thoughtful, empirically informed account is required to get students to appreciate the reasons why investing time and effort in a well-rounded education, a particular major, or an individual course could make a difference to their lives both during and after college.

Students who leave college prematurely or do the minimum to pass their courses often do so not because they cannot do the work but because they are bored by listless teaching or do not see the point of learning what their professors are trying to teach them. There is considerable evidence that clearer, better organized instruction and more active and collaborative methods of teaching can motivate and engage such students and thereby reduce dropout rates.[3] Recent surveys have also revealed that undergraduates who are more engaged in active learning—applying knowledge to solve problems, discussing ideas in and out of class, integrating insights from various sources, and examining their own methods of thinking—spend more time than their classmates preparing for their courses.[4] In these ways, effective teaching can help to minimize any conflict that exists between the two most necessary improvements in undergraduate education.

The preceding chapters make abundantly clear how important it will be to succeed in reconciling these two objectives. Enrollments and graduation rates undoubtedly need to rise in order to increase opportunity and allow more young people to live fuller, more rewarding lives. At the same time, now that many other countries have moved successfully to a system of mass higher education, the United States will be hard-pressed simply to keep up. Even if we succeed over the next decade in recapturing our traditional lead in educational attainment, we are unlikely ever again to enjoy the huge advantage we once possessed that helped the nation sustain its unrivaled prosperity throughout most of the twentieth century. If America is to regain a significant edge, educators and public officials will have to concern themselves not only with the *quantity* of higher education but with its *quality* as well.

Many American colleges currently offer a better education than most foreign universities, which have long tended to be chronically overcrowded and underfinanced. However, more countries have now recognized the importance of higher education and are investing more in their universities. Many governments have initiated reforms to hold faculties more accountable for the quality of education they are providing. As a result, any advantage we currently possess could easily vanish if our colleges do not make a serious effort to improve the way in which they teach undergraduates. Fortunately, as the chapters in this section have tried to make clear, there are plenty of ways to do a better job.

The prospects for sustained progress in the quality of undergraduate education will depend not only on the willingness of current faculty members to embrace reforms but on the training given to those who are preparing to teach college students in the future. Because of advances in cognitive theory, improvements in our ability to assess student learning, and the pedagogic possibilities offered by new technology, the need to give PhD candidates a serious preparation for teaching is more compelling than ever. Already, Australia, New

Zealand, and several other countries have initiated programs of this kind. Thus far, however, graduate schools in the United States have not done enough to equip future professors for their responsibilities in the classroom. Just why this is so and what might be done to improve matters are the subjects of the following chapter.

CHAPTER ELEVEN

GRADUATE EDUCATION

||||||||||||||||||||||||||||||||||||||||||||||||||||||||||||||||||||||||||||||||||||||||||||||||||

THE TREATMENT OF GRADUATE EDUCATION occupies an anomalous place in this book, sandwiched between a section on undergraduate education and another on professional schools without being incorporated into either one. The location is not accidental. PhD programs have too close a relationship both to colleges and to professional schools to be lumped together with either one. The faculty members responsible for doctoral training teach undergraduates as well, and graduate students themselves often assist professors in teaching large college courses. At the same time, graduate programs are much like professional schools in that their mission is to prepare college graduates for specialized careers as researchers in corporations and government agencies, but most of all as professors for the nation's colleges (and for several professional schools as well). Whatever part of the university they resemble most, PhD programs are by far the leading source of new faculty members. As a result, the training they provide has important effects on the performance of colleges and universities and hence deserves careful scrutiny in any study of the problems and future needs of American higher education.

Several hundred universities award PhDs, although a mere sixty or so account for over half of all the degrees. The basic structure of the programs is similar in all universities and disciplines. Students typically spend the first year or two completing coursework (mostly advanced seminars), followed by some sort of comprehensive exam to demonstrate competence in their discipline or field of study. Thereafter, they devote themselves to writing a thesis, which may consist of a book-length manuscript or a series of short papers, depending on the field. The average length of time to degree varies widely by discipline; it typically ranges from 5 to 7 years in the sciences, 6 to 9 years in the social sciences, and 8 to 10 years, or even longer, in the humanities. In the course of completing the program, however, most graduate students work part-time for several years, helping a professor as a research assistant or serving as a teaching assistant by conducting one or more weekly discussions with groups of undergraduates in a large lecture course.

TRENDS IN GRADUATE
STUDENT ENROLLMENTS

One of the puzzling facts about graduate education in the United States is that the demand for such training has continued to rise since the mid-1970s even though career prospects in most fields of study have gradually worsened.[1] During the last four decades, academic salaries have fallen some 30 percent below the compensation earned in other professions requiring advanced study. Tenure-track jobs have been hard to find. Nevertheless, the number of PhD degrees awarded has kept on growing at a pace far exceeding the number of faculty positions available. From 1981 to 2011, the number of PhDs awarded rose from 31,355 to 49,010.[2] Over the same period, however, increasing numbers of freshly minted PhDs have graduated without definite jobs. Many who aspire to permanent faculty positions have been forced to teach part-time or on a fixed-term contract with uncertain chances of ever being considered for tenure. Many others have had to find employment in other occupations.

What accounts for the growing demand for graduate training? Part of the explanation lies in the changing aspirations of women, who have chosen increasingly to pursue careers in academe as well as in law, business, and medicine. Having made up little more than 10 percent of newly graduated PhDs in the 1950s, they now account for more than half of all new doctorates. Foreign students are another part of the answer; their proportion of the graduate student population more than doubled from 1980 to 2009, from 12.2 to 28.3 percent. Minorities have been a further source of growth. The number of Asian American graduate students increased by 162 percent in the past twenty years. The ranks of Hispanics grew even faster—by 189 percent—while the number of black students rose by 69.2 percent.[*]

By all appearances, the market for PhD training does not seem to react automatically and rationally to changes in demand. Not only have the numbers of applicants and graduate students failed to decline in the face of worsening conditions; when graduate schools have responded by shrinking the number of students they accept, it is not always the weakest departments that have

---

[*] Despite their recent growth, the percentages of graduate students who are black or Hispanic are still much lower than their share of the total population. In 2009–10, the percentage of blacks receiving PhDs was 6.3 while that of Hispanics was 5.9. In both cases, the percentages are also a bit lower than the percentages of blacks and Hispanics receiving BA degrees in the same year. In their study of minorities in graduate school, however, Stephen Cole and Elinor Barber found no evidence of discrimination. *Increasing Faculty Diversity: The Occupational Choices of High-Achieving Minority Students* (2003), pp. 138, 234.

acted. More often, the larger, more highly rated programs have been the ones to cut back.

On closer analysis, it is not altogether clear how concerned graduate schools should be about the persistent glut of PhDs. The few studies that have surveyed graduates who have not found teaching jobs find that almost all are employed in other fields, often at a higher salary than their classmates teaching in universities. Although they regret not having a faculty position, they are, on average, just as satisfied with their work as their contemporaries in tenure-track positions, and few regret having gone to graduate school.[3] More troublesome is the plight of PhDs who settle for part-time (adjunct) teaching jobs at low wages and often without the normal amenities of a faculty member, such as a suitable place to meet with students or even a telephone or a computer. Although they enjoy their teaching, they are less satisfied with their careers than their tenure-track contemporaries and less sure they would choose to earn a PhD if they had the choice to make again.[4]

It is hard to argue that graduate schools are at fault for continuing to accept so many PhD candidates. What does seem clear is that every department should take care to convey an accurate picture of the job prospects to all applicants for admission, including a summary of the employment records of all of its recent graduates, so that those who enter will do so with their eyes fully open. By all accounts, only a minority of schools currently provide such information.

The most important question to ask about the trends in graduate school enrollments is not simply whether the numbers have been rising or falling but whether the quality of doctoral students has declined. In their comprehensive study of American faculties, Jack Schuster and Martin Finkelstein assembled a substantial body of evidence on this question.[5] One indicator they used was the percentage of Phi Beta Kappas choosing academic careers. The trend turns out to be uneven, having exceeded 20 percent from 1945 to 1970 before plummeting to 7.9 percent during the 1970s, then rising once more to 17.7 percent in the 1980s, and falling back again to 13 percent in the 1990s. Overall, there is some evidence of a downward trend, but the numbers are too volatile to support any firm conclusions.

In search of more definite answers, Schuster and Finkelstein conducted a large-scale survey of chairs in the leading academic departments where the quality of graduate students is most crucial to the future of research. In almost all fields, chairpersons rated the quality higher in 2000 than they did in a similar poll in 1983–87. The greatest improvement, surprisingly, was in the estimates for the humanities, where employment prospects are generally thought to be the bleakest. Evaluations from chairs in the physical sciences were slightly less favorable than they had been in the earlier survey, although respondents were still more likely than not to think that the quality had improved. Overall, then, the evidence shows little indication of a significant drop in quality despite the poor career prospects for would-be academics.

Amid these hopeful assessments, however, a number of observers have found one source of concern. In the sciences, where the quality of faculty is especially likely to affect the nation's growth and prosperity, there are signs of potential trouble. Since 1966, the percentage of college freshmen indicating a probable career in scientific research has dropped by approximately half (although it has remained at 2 percent or slightly below since 1980).[6] During college, moreover, some 40 percent of the freshmen who declare an intent to concentrate in the sciences end up choosing a different major, while virtually no students move in the opposite direction. By 2010, at least twenty-six economically advanced countries in Europe and Asia ranked above the United States in the percentage of college students earning bachelor's degrees in sciences and engineering.[7]

These trends have led several high-level committees to conclude that the United States is at risk of producing too few scientific researchers to meet America's future needs.[8] Corporate executives, government officials, and scientists themselves have all warned of impending shortages and the consequent danger for the economy. One reason often cited is that public schools have too few teachers trained in math and science and use outmoded and inadequate textbooks. But science departments in colleges and universities must also be held responsible for the heavy attrition of students who come to college as freshmen with the intention of majoring in science and then switch to another department. Poor teaching is one of the most common reasons undergraduates give for moving to other fields of concentration.[9]

A more careful examination of the facts suggests that though the nation may need more college graduates with scientific training, talk of a looming dearth of research scientists may well be misconceived.[10] In fact, the labor market for PhDs in science and engineering shows little sign of a shortage. Quite the contrary. Roughly three times as many scientists and engineers graduate each year than there are available job openings. Entry-level salaries for PhDs in science have not been rising, as they would if the supply were truly lagging behind demand. Instead, compensation levels for young scientists and engineers have been gradually falling further behind those of young MDs, JDs, and MBAs. Moreover, unemployment rates for science and engineering doctorates increased in most fields during the years prior to the recent recession, even as jobless levels were declining for the workforce as a whole—just the opposite of what one would expect if there truly were too few science PhDs.

The real danger for science, then, is not a looming shortage of research scientists and engineers but the discouraging state of the job market for those starting out in these fields. Not only do many recent PhDs who aspire to academic careers have to take postdoctoral positions at low salaries; they tend to remain in them for longer and longer periods of time, fattening their publication records while they wait in hopes of obtaining a junior faculty position.* In the end, only a quarter of them succeed. Meanwhile, their stipends as postdocs are modest at best, generally varying between $25,000 and $50,000 per year. According to one study covering thirty universities, only 52 percent of these institutions provided paid vacations, while only 45 percent offered paid sick leave.[11]

The glut of research scientists and engineers offers tangible benefits for some interested groups. Companies can hire well-trained people for relatively low salaries. Established university investigators can staff their research groups with competent assistants for little money. In the longer run, however, the current situation does not augur well for the future of science. Even the fortunate minority who find an academic post have difficulty getting started. From 1980 to 2001, the proportion of NIH grants awarded to scientists under the age of thirty-five dropped from 23 to 4 percent. Despite repeated efforts to correct the problem, the average age at which scientists finally receive a grant to do a research project of their own remains uncomfortably high at above forty. Many leading researchers today had already done their best work at a younger age. As Bruce Alberts remarked in his presidential address to the National Academy of Science: "Many of my colleagues and I were awarded our first independent funding when we were under 30 years old. [Now] almost no one finds it possible to start an independent scientific career under the age of 35."[12]

For young college seniors majoring in science who are qualified for admission to a doctoral program in a first-rate department, these prospects cannot seem inviting. As a result, only approximately 30 percent of undergraduates majoring in science and engineering elect to enter a graduate program in those fields, a much lower figure than was true only twenty-five years ago.[13] From 1970 to 2005, the number of US citizens earning PhDs dropped by 23 percent in engineering, 44 percent in the physical sciences, and 50 percent in mathematics.[14] The decline extends even to the ablest science and engineering majors.[15] Some find jobs in industry. Others leave science entirely to enter a professional school or take a job outside of science where their prior training may prove advantageous. By all indications, then, if too few promising students

---

*In 1973, 55 percent of PhDs in the biological sciences secured tenure-track positions within six years of obtaining their degree, and only 2 percent were in a postdoc or other nontenured position. By 2006, only 15 percent were tenured within six years, while 18 percent were in a nontenured position. David Cyranoski, Natasha Gilbert, Heidi Ledford, Anjali Nayar, and Mohammed Yahia, "The PhD Factory: The World Is Producing More PhDs Than Ever Before: Is It Time to Stop?" 472 *Nature* (April 21, 2011), pp. 276, 277.

are entering doctoral programs in science and engineering, it is not a failure of the educational system that is mainly responsible but a shortage of attractive, long-term careers.*

Up to now, the paucity of talented young Americans seeking graduate degrees in science has been offset by the desire of many students from abroad to enter doctoral programs in the United States. From 1977 to 2008, the share of all new PhDs in science and engineering coming from other countries grew from 19.3 percent to 46.7 percent.[16] After graduation, a large majority of these students remain to work in the United States, at least for a period of years. As a result, the proportion of immigrants among America's scientists and engineers has grown from 7 percent in 1960 to well over 25 percent today.[17] While this trend has removed any immediate threat of a shortage, the possibility remains that in the future, other nations will improve their graduate programs and science careers, especially in rapidly developing countries, such as India and China. In this event, fewer students from these nations may seek training in the United States, and more foreign scientists currently working in America may return to their home countries. Thus far, however, there is little sign of such tendencies. If anything, the proportion of foreign PhDs who hope to remain to work in the United States seems to be increasing.[18]

THE STATE OF GRADUATE EDUCATION

The current condition of our graduate schools depends very much on what is being observed. From one perspective, they are a jewel in the crown of American higher education, attracting talented students from everywhere in the world. Over the years, tens of thousands of PhDs have graduated and gone on to enjoy successful careers in science and scholarship. Indeed, from 1997 to 2009, more than half of all Nobel Prize–winners in the sciences and economics received their graduate training in the United States.

If one examines how PhD programs actually operate in practice, however, there is a plausible argument that graduate schools are among the most poorly administered and badly designed of all the advanced degree programs in the

---

*Apart from the aggregate problem of supply and demand, a variety of factors may keep excellent students from earning a doctorate in science or engineering in the United States. Some outstanding young people from other countries are discouraged by the delays and restrictions in obtaining visas to enter the United States. Only 20 percent of PhDs in engineering are awarded to women, although women make up 57 percent of all doctoral students. Other highly promising students drop out of PhD programs for lack of good mentoring or for other reasons described in the subsequent section on attrition.

university. Of course, these are very broad generalizations. Some individual departments undoubtedly offer training that does not deserve such criticism. Nevertheless, the generalizations hold for most graduate programs even in the best universities. Why this is so and what can be done about it are the questions addressed in the pages that follow.

Most of the problems with graduate education have a long history. Three seem especially serious: the excessive length of time that many graduate students take to receive their degree; the high rate at which graduate students drop out before earning their degree; and the failure on the part of PhD programs to prepare students adequately for their responsibilities as teachers and faculty members.

THE LONG TIME TO DEGREE

Completing a doctoral program has rarely been a quick and easy process. Throughout the history of graduate education, most students have taken at least four or five years to earn their degree, and the time required has often been considerably longer, especially in esoteric fields, such as Near Eastern civilizations, where students need to master forbiddingly difficult languages such as Akkadian or Hittite. Although the time to degree has recently declined a little, it is still very long in most fields, especially those outside the sciences. In social science departments, nearly 30 percent of recent PhDs now take more than seven years to finish. In the humanities, the figure is closer to 40 percent. Such extended periods of study are expensive—for students in terms of mounting opportunity costs and for universities through whatever funds and services are devoted to helping students complete their studies.

It should be possible in most departments to shorten the number of years to graduation. How concerned faculties are to make this happen, however, is not entirely clear. Departments may enjoy having a larger pool of graduate students available as teaching assistants to ease the burden on professors of mentoring undergraduates and grading their exams. Similar motives may lead a department to allow its graduate students to teach too much and thus prolong their studies. Still other PhD candidates take longer to graduate simply because they are slow to choose a suitable thesis topic or to bring their thesis to a satisfactory conclusion.

Some professors may consider it a good thing in today's bleak job market for graduate students to delay their degree and take more time to strengthen their résumés by polishing their thesis and publishing more articles. Recent evidence, however, casts doubt on such reasoning. Even after controlling for differences in students' abilities and the quality of the university and department in which they study, those who take more than seven years to finish have diminishing success in finding a tenure-track job within three years.[19] Moreover, they do not tend to publish more than students who earn their degree in seven years or less.[20] All things considered, then, departments would be well-advised not to make it easy for students to delay graduation beyond seven years but to encourage them to complete the PhD *and* publish within a seven-year period.

The problem is how to implement such a policy effectively. Departments can establish clear expectations for the time within which students should complete the program. Universities, if they can afford it, can provide the funds to enable students to have a year without other employment to concentrate on finishing their thesis. These measures can help, but they will not solve all problems.

Many students are bogged down writing their thesis either because they become discouraged with their topic and switch to another, or because they have difficulty writing and are easily diverted to other pursuits. In theory, of course, departments can get tough with laggards and grant extensions of time only for compelling reasons. In practice, however, few departments are prepared to enforce such rules, and one can understand why. Once students have spent six to eight years working toward a PhD, it is very difficult to refuse them extra time if there is any chance that they will eventually finish the job. As a result, though one can legitimately ask for reasonable steps to encourage timely graduation, there is not much chance that departments, especially in the humanities and social sciences, will ever succeed in having all, or even nearly all, of their graduate students complete their work within a prescribed period of years.

One final, potentially fruitful step that graduate departments could take is to review their thesis requirements to determine whether they have been allowed to grow gradually more demanding in length and scope. "Thesis creep" may be part of the explanation for why graduate students in many departments are taking longer to graduate. The underlying problem, however, is actually much larger and harder to fix. Put bluntly, the traditional design of PhD programs, at least in the humanities and social sciences, has come to be woefully out of alignment with the career opportunities available to graduates. The requirements for such programs are constructed primarily to prepare graduate students to serve on the faculties of research universities. The difficulty is that only a minority of graduates eventually find permanent faculty positions in institutions of this kind. For the rest, doctoral programs often require students to spend years preparing for work that most of them will never have to perform.

In the sciences, most graduates who do not teach find employment in corporate laboratories or government agencies where they can make use of the research skills they learned in obtaining their degree. In many social science departments, however, and even more frequently in the humanities, most PhDs end up in careers that call for little or no scholarly inquiry. Some of them teach in institutions where research is not encouraged. Others become adjunct or term-limited instructors and are not expected to publish. Still others find jobs in a wide variety of fields in which the experience of writing a lengthy thesis, if not wholly irrelevant, demands far more time than its ultimate usefulness deserves.

Unfortunately, it is much easier to state the problem than it is to think of a viable solution. It would no doubt be helpful if graduate schools accepted many fewer students so that fewer graduates would have to take jobs other than the tenure-track faculty positions that they came to graduate school hoping to fill. Nevertheless, this step seems highly unlikely, since each university acts independently in deciding how many graduate students to admit. It would be still more helpful if universities with mediocre graduate schools closed down their programs, but such a drastic remedy seems even further beyond the range of possibility.

Another alternative might be to create a graduate teaching degree that would emphasize pedagogy while no longer requiring a lengthy thesis. Such a degree would seem ideally suited for those who teach in institutions at which research is either not expected or at least not emphasized. The problem with this solution is that most graduate students do not know they will end up in such positions and hence would rarely choose a teaching degree even if one were available. In fact, efforts to introduce such degrees have been tried in the past with foundation support and failed, chiefly because "teaching doctorates" were looked down upon as second-class and therefore failed to win widespread recognition.

As matters now stand, therefore, the PhD degree in numerous fields continues to require an education that is not well suited to many of the careers that its recipients will ultimately pursue. The remedy that seems most feasible is to shorten the time to degree by limiting the scope of the thesis requirement in departments in which it has gradually increased over the years. Some professors will object even to this modest reform, fearing a decline in the standards of future scholars. But rigorous standards can be used to evaluate student research without demanding a book-length manuscript. Besides, there is ample opportunity to impose more exacting standards on those who actually secure a tenure-track position before awarding them a permanent appointment.

Other departments may hit upon alternative ways of shortening the time to degree. Thus, one must hope that universities such as Stanford, which is currently trying to create a five-year PhD, will succeed in doing so and that other graduate schools will follow suit. This reform will not succeed in aligning doctoral education with the needs of the job market, but it will at least save students years of study that now turn out to be unnecessary for all too many graduates.

The Problem of Attrition

Very early in my presidency at Harvard I came across a study of doctoral education in a leading public university. I was startled to discover that graduation rates from PhD programs in this institution varied from a barely respectable 70 percent or more in the sciences to less than 20 percent in language and literature departments. Concerned by these findings, I began asking our department chairs in the social sciences and humanities about their own graduation rates. I was initially comforted to hear that our figures seemed to be well above those I had just read about. Closer analysis of the official records, however, convinced me that the estimates from most of our chairs were greatly inflated. Apparently, few members of our faculty were even aware that a serious problem existed.

Over the intervening years, the situation nationwide seems to have improved somewhat but not by nearly enough to suggest that the problem is solved. According to a Graduate School Council report in 2009, only 57 percent of a large sample of doctoral students who began their studies in 1998–99 completed the program within ten years after they began.[21] Completion rates averaged 49 percent in the humanities, 55 percent in the physical sciences and mathematics, 56 percent in the social sciences, 63 percent in the life sciences, and 64 percent in engineering (where almost two-thirds of the students come from outside the United States). Even in some of the best universities, a majority of graduate students outside the sciences drop by the wayside.

Attrition varies greatly both among departments in a single institution and among different institutions. A study of ten departments in two universities found that dropout rates among the departments in one of the institutions ranged all the way from 19 percent to 82 percent, and that one of the universities had an overall dropout rate (68 percent) more than double that of the other (32 percent).[22] Such wide variations are not unusual. In their detailed study of graduate education in ten leading universities, William Bowen and Neil Rudenstine found that attrition was fully twice as high in some institutions as it was in others.[23]

These dropout rates greatly exceed those of the major professional schools in leading universities where over 90 percent of the entering students normally graduate. In these schools, attrition levels of 50 percent would be regarded as a catastrophe. Yet year after year, graduate departments in the same universities have accepted such losses with equanimity even though many thousands of dollars in fellowship money are wasted, not to mention years of students' lives.*

---

* Some may argue that it is unfair to compare graduate schools with professional schools. In law or business, students who decide they do not want a career in these fields may rationally conclude

One reason why faculty members who teach graduate students continue to tolerate such dropout rates is that few of them are aware of the severity of the problem. The estimates I received from our department chairs were not unique. Several studies have confirmed that professors often estimate the attrition in their own departments at only half the actual level.[24] Part of the explanation may be that 40 percent of the dropouts typically occur during the first year or two of graduate study when students are mainly taking courses and are less likely to be noticed by faculty in their department.

Another reason for the persistence of high attrition rates in some departments is a belief among professors that since it is difficult to know in advance who will turn out to have exceptional talent, the wisest strategy is to enroll large numbers of students in order to increase the odds of ending up with a reasonable number of outstanding prospects. Such a policy is highly questionable. It consumes years of students' lives, especially in the humanities, where most dropouts remain for extended periods before eventually leaving the program. In addition, it wastes large amounts of the university's (or the government's) money, since entering graduate students usually receive generous scholarship support. Perhaps the underlying rationale might be more defensible if departments tried hard to evaluate students carefully during the first year or two to determine which ones showed enough promise to remain and which did not. Since most dropouts occur after completion of two years of study, however, current efforts seem ineffective. In many departments, there is little evidence that a rigorous early evaluation even occurs or that most of the students who do drop out leave at the urging of the department.

When faculty members do notice the loss of students, they tend to give highly questionable explanations. In one study, most professors who were asked about the problem blamed the students.[25] Either they were said to lack the ability to succeed in an academic career, or they didn't work hard enough, or they weren't sufficiently committed to a life of scholarship and should never have enrolled in the first place. Such explanations, however, seem suspect, since the academic credentials of graduate students who drop out turn out to be at least as strong as those of the students who stay the course.[26]

Interviews with students who dropped out of graduate school suggest very different reasons from those given by professors. Of course, some had personal problems or lacked the commitment to continue. But many spoke of the poor

that it is worth persevering for a year or eighteen months to earn a degree, while graduate students understandably drop out rather than soldier on for years to obtain their PhD. While this argument may be valid for some students in law or business, it does not explain why some 96 percent of entering medical students complete their MD within ten years. Nor is it even very plausible for law schools, where tuition costs often exceed $50,000 per year.

advice and inadequate information they received when they were deciding whether to apply to graduate school.* Others stressed the lack of faculty contact once they arrived and complained of feeling invisible and abandoned. Poor advising was one of the two factors cited most frequently by dropouts. As the authors of one study pointed out, "a student's relationship with his or her adviser is probably the single most critical factor in determining who stays and who leaves."[27]

One might also suspect that lack of money must be a common reason for dropping out, since PhD programs take so long to complete. Yet financial problems turn out to have little to do with leaving graduate school. Although foundations have supported experimental programs to see whether attrition can be reduced through the awarding of generous multiyear fellowships, these efforts have failed to raise completion rates significantly.[28]

The reasons graduate students give for dropping out suggest several other steps that could do more to lower attrition. Since many of those who leave claim that they didn't know enough about the program when they applied, there may be room for improvement in the literature that departments send to prospective applicants.[29] Does it provide a full and accurate picture of the nature and requirements of the program, the average time students take to graduate, the attrition rate for the program, and the jobs obtained by students who have graduated during the last several years? Full and candid answers to questions such as these could help to deter college seniors who wander into graduate programs with far too little understanding of what their choice will entail.†

Entering students are also likely to fare somewhat better if they have a clear set of expectations about how long they should normally take to earn their degree and how much progress they should make in each year of study. Such

---

* According to an extensive survey of graduate students, "[s]tudents reported that they decided to enter a doctoral program without having a good idea of the time, money, clarity of purpose and perseverance that graduate study entails. . . . The responses suggested that students often enroll in a PhD program at the encouragement of a favorite undergraduate professor without considering the full range of alternatives and without developing a clear understanding of why they are doing so." Chris Golde and Timothy M. Dore, *At Cross Purposes: What the Experiences of Today's Graduate Students Reveal about Graduate Education* (2001), pp. 29, 31.

† Providing ample opportunities for undergraduates to engage in research may also help students appreciate both the joys and disadvantages of life as a scientist or scholar. There is considerable evidence that undergraduate research programs under close faculty supervision do in fact have this effect, encouraging some undergraduates to enter graduate school and dissuading others. See, e.g., Joyce Kinkead, "Learning through Inquiry: An Overview of Undergraduate Research," *New Directions in Teaching and Learning*, no. 93 (Spring 2003), p. 5; Elaine Seymour, Ann-Barrie Hunter, Sandra L. Laursen, and Tracee Deantoni, *Establishing the Benefits of Research Experiences for Undergraduates in the Sciences: First Findings from a Three-Year Study*, http://wiki.biologyscholars .org/@api/deki/files/165/=Seymour_UG_ressearch.pdf.

expectations are well understood in every other major professional school. Yet a survey of 27 graduate schools conducted by the Pew Charitable Trusts found that "how long the student would be a student and what the criteria are for readiness to graduate—are the subject of considerable confusion."[30] Only 45.4 percent of graduate students reported that they knew the requirements for graduation, and only 30.9 percent felt that they understood how long they should take to complete the program.

Another useful step would be to review the existing incentives to make sure that departments are encouraged to try to reduce attrition rates. In the public university whose abysmal completion rates first alerted me to the problem, the number of faculty positions allotted to departments depended on the number of graduate students they enrolled. This practice is perverse since it encourages departments to admit more students whether or not they ever graduate. It would be far better to make the number of students a department can enroll depend in part upon its graduation rates so that departments would have an incentive to pay more attention to attrition and try to do something about it.

In addition to creating proper incentives, universities could work with departments to improve their methods of advising new graduate students. As Michael Nettles and Catherine Millett point out in their study of graduate education, "the overwhelming evidence is that advisers play an important role for students and that the quality of their relationship has consequences."[31] Graduate school officials could also encourage department chairs to find ways of integrating students into the life of their department at an early stage. Several studies of attrition suggest that students are less likely to drop out in the first two years if they have had opportunities to take part in activities in their department.[32] Especially helpful are regular occasions when faculty and graduate students gather to discuss important topics in their field.

Of course, an ideal way of reducing attrition would be to discover better ways of selecting students. By most accounts, scores on the Graduate Record Examination and college grades are both weak predictors of future success, and rankings of students by their department before they enter seem to bear little relation to their eventual success in graduate school and thereafter.[33] These findings suggest a need for research to discover more reliable ways of evaluating applicants. There is little evidence as yet, however, that universities have made much effort along these lines.[34]

As the preceding discussion makes clear, there are many reasons for the high attrition rates, and progress over the years has been slow in coming. Recently, however, there seem to be signs of growing concern about the problem. There are even scattered indications that dropout rates are beginning to fall.[35] If so, improvements may at last be on the way, although much remains to be accomplished before graduate schools can be confident that they have done all they can.

Preparing Graduate Students as Teachers and Faculty Members

Most PhD students who earn their degree will have learned a lot about research methods in their discipline. If they have been mentored conscientiously by a sympathetic and engaged thesis adviser, they are likely to have developed strong values and high standards for scholarly work. They will also have accumulated a great deal of knowledge about their specific field of study and will probably have acquired a reasonable understanding of the other subfields in their discipline. They may have broadened their preparation even further by taking a few courses in other departments, especially if they attended graduate school within the last decade. Now that faculty members have become more interested in interdisciplinary approaches in their own research, many graduate programs have made it easier for students to move more freely across departmental lines.

The knowledge that students acquire in graduate school is clearly valuable for aspiring researchers, and few, if any, universities in the world do as good a job of conveying it as America's leading research universities. What is done less well, however, is preparing graduate students to teach. In most programs, there is no required course of study to acquaint them with what is known about effective pedagogy, motivating students, or preparing examinations. This is a regrettable deficiency since studies consistently show that teaching occupies more time in the average workweek of professors than any other activity, whether in research universities, comprehensive institutions, or liberal arts colleges.[36] Moreover, surveys find that interest in teaching is by far the most frequent reason why college seniors decide to attend graduate school in the first place. In one survey of more than four thousand graduate students, over 80 percent reported "enjoyment of teaching" as a reason for being attracted to an academic career.[37]

It is true that graduate students have long had opportunities to serve as teaching fellows in large lecture courses. These positions typically entail conducting weekly discussions with groups of undergraduates and, quite often, preparing examinations and grading student papers. Such activities clearly help to develop teaching skills. In performing these functions, however, only 40 percent of teaching assistants in one large-scale study believed they received careful supervision by a faculty member.[38] Worse yet, many graduate students report that professors in their department have advised them not to spend much time on their teaching duties lest they be distracted from the more important task of writing a thesis. Indeed, one suspects that the growing use of teaching fellows owes more to an eagerness on the part of the faculty to escape some of the burdens of teaching and grading than it does to a desire to prepare graduate students for their role in the classroom.

By now, fortunately, most universities have created teaching centers where graduate students who are so inclined can find helpful guidance in how to give lectures or manage discussions in sections of large courses. These centers give orientation programs to prepare new teaching fellows for their duties. They often arrange discussions about topics of interest to teachers. They usually offer opportunities to have classes videotaped so that graduate students can watch themselves teaching and receive a friendly critique from an experienced coach. Almost two-thirds of all graduate students report that they have access to such a center, although participation is seldom required.[39] More than half can attend a workshop on teaching in their discipline or a program on how to perform the functions of a teaching assistant.[40]

These centers are a great improvement, and many graduate students take advantage of them. Nevertheless, the help most centers provide covers only a fraction of what future faculty members need to know in order to prepare for an academic career. Few graduate students learn about the implications of cognitive research for teaching and learning, or the uses of technology, or the empirical evidence on the effectiveness of different methods of instruction. Even fewer become informed about the ethical obligations of instructors, or the history and competing conceptions of undergraduate education, or the organization and governance of universities. One large-scale survey found that only 29.1 percent of graduate students reported the existence of a seminar on research ethics, and only 6.4 percent recalled a workshop on the history or the mission of higher education.[41]

In several respects, therefore, the opportunities now available in most universities do not provide a sufficient preparation for a faculty career. The consequences of this deficiency are more important now than in the past. Graduate students today will begin their academic careers at a time when many colleges will be shifting from a teacher-centered to a student-centered curriculum. In this new world, professors are likely to spend less time lecturing and more time designing course materials that challenge students to learn for themselves by assigning them interesting problems with appropriate guidance when they need help. To function effectively in this environment, beginning faculty members will not be able to succeed by simply calling on skills they learned as section leaders or by emulating the professors who taught them.

Cognitive scientists have discovered a lot about how students learn, and much of what they have found is applicable to teaching.[42] An ample stock exists of findings and suggestions about how to motivate students, how to overcome the faulty preconceptions many students have that interfere with learning, how to teach students to transfer the concepts they study and apply them in other settings, and how to promote a deep rather than a surface understanding of material. Education researchers have also produced a large body of work evaluating the progress students make in college and measuring the effectiveness of different methods of teaching. There are literally scores of studies comparing collaborative versus individual learning or the impact of lectures versus problem-based instruction. Meanwhile, computers and related technologies have given instructors new possibilities for enhancing student learning. Although many graduate students may be adept at using a computer, few of them are likely to have any idea of how to develop an online course, or manage synchronous and asynchronous interactive discussions, or blend technology with traditional face-to-face instruction for maximum effect on student learning.

The evidence is mixed on how confident advanced graduate students feel about their competence as teachers. According to a study in 2001 by the Pew Charitable Trusts, only 36.1 percent of graduate students considered themselves prepared to teach a lecture course, only 26.6 percent believed that they could develop and articulate a teaching philosophy, and only 14.1 percent felt capable of using technology in their classrooms.[43] A more recent Carnegie survey found much higher percentages of graduate students in some departments who felt confident of their ability to design and teach a course, but low percentages in others.[44] Such surveys, of course, tend to reflect how confident graduate students are about their ability to teach in conventional ways rather than how capable they are of using newer methods that may be more effective in promoting learning.

The need for more thorough preparation takes on added urgency in view of the kinds of positions recent PhDs are increasingly likely to fill. No longer can graduate students, even in the most eminent programs, count on finding a tenure-track position in a major research university with a highly select student body. Only one-quarter of new PhDs who take an academic position obtain a job in a research university of any kind. The rest either accept offers from colleges that are primarily devoted to teaching or find themselves in term-limited positions where research is not expected. Often, the students in their classes will be quite different from those they knew in the elite colleges and graduate schools they attended and will require different pedagogic strategies. Even in highly selective institutions, as pointed out in chapter 9, undergraduates spend fewer hours per week studying and are less engaged by their classes than they were a few decades ago.[45] To motivate these students, instructors will have to know more and be able to call upon a wider array of teaching strategies than their predecessors. A graduate program that does not offer adequate preparation for teaching will leave many of its new PhDs ill-equipped for the challenges they will face once they begin their academic careers.

Fortunately, there are a few recent signs of experimentation in several major graduate schools to introduce some of the training needed to correct these deficiencies. With encouragement from the Association of Graduate Schools and funding from the Teagle Foundation, pilot programs have been created at Stanford, Columbia, Princeton, and other leading universities on subjects such as the uses of technology in instruction or the findings of cognitive science and their implications for teaching.[46] Several universities are also making efforts to teach graduate students about methods of assessing student learning. These initiatives are encouraging, but they are still only scattered, experimental efforts reaching limited numbers of students. Only time will tell whether they can take root and become part of the standard preparation of those seeking academic careers.

If progress is to occur, it is important to recognize that the departments, which have traditionally been in charge of constructing graduate programs, cannot be expected to take primary responsibility for carrying out the reforms that need to be made. Professors in most departments lack the knowledge or the training to teach their graduate students all they need to know about teaching. One can hardly expect that chemistry professors, or sociologists, or literature scholars will be well acquainted with recent research in cognitive science or the uses of technology in the classroom. Even graduate schools are not staffed to supply all the needed instruction. That is doubtless an important reason why so few departments and graduate schools have included such material in their programs. If future college teachers are to learn what they need to know, deans and provosts, not individual departments, will have to take the lead in working with the faculty to organize and staff the necessary instruction.

It is not immediately obvious, however, which university should assume this responsibility: the one in which students earn their doctorate or the one in which recent PhDs take their first teaching position. There are reasons for choosing either of the two. The university where students receive their doctorate might seem to be the natural choice, since such training is part of the necessary preparation for a teaching career. Nevertheless, only half of all PhDs become college teachers; the rest often choose to work in corporate laboratories or in some other setting. The latter could justifiably object to having to study the applications of cognitive science or discuss the ethical issues that professors may confront.

At the same time, many graduate students who do not eventually enter academic life still serve as teaching assistants in the course of studying for a PhD. While such students may not need to learn all they ought to know to be a faculty member, universities can legitimately insist that they learn something of the skills of pedagogy before they begin to teach undergraduates. Besides, since most employers outside the academy complain that the PhDs they hire lack good communication skills, such training is likely to prove useful even to those who never take a teaching position.

The best solution, then, would be for colleges to require all would-be teaching assistants to complete a program designed by the teaching and learning center that will prepare them to conduct discussions in sections of large lecture courses and to construct and grade exams. Once students earn their doctorate, those who accept an academic position could be required by their new university to take a specially designed course that will teach them more of what is known about methods of instruction and the design of courses, including material on the uses of technology in teaching, along with readings on the ethical responsibilities of instructors and researchers, the history of undergraduate education, and the organization and functioning of universities. Such a course would go well beyond the basic skills required of teaching assistants to convey the added knowledge that will be useful to those embarking on an academic career.

A yearlong course for new members of the faculty could include all of these topics, and capable instructors could be recruited from the entire university to do the teaching. (New part-time faculty could also be required to attend at least such portions of the course as are appropriate to their duties.) The classes would necessarily provide rather cursory coverage, given the range of material involved, but assistant professors are mature enough to probe more deeply once they receive appropriate readings to study and ample opportunities to practice new skills. If beginning instructors are thought to have too much else to do in their first year, they could be given a lighter teaching load. Any short-term costs resulting from a temporary reduction of their teaching should be more than repaid in future years through their improved preparation to carry out their responsibilities as faculty members.

These steps may seem a radical departure from conventional practice. Yet there is scant basis for serious faculty opposition to such proposals. Deans and presidents have every right to insist that teaching fellows be adequately prepared before they are allowed to teach undergraduates. Asking beginning assistant professors to take an introductory course when they arrive may be a more novel step, but universities surely have a legitimate interest in trying to ensure that new faculty members are properly equipped to carry out their responsibilities as educators and as knowledgeable members of a self-governing institution.

As a practical matter, of course, the prospects for initiating such reforms will be bleak indeed if senior professors consider them a waste of time. Yet departments may not resist such reforms if interested members are given an opportunity to participate, or at least be consulted, in the creation of the new introductory courses. Departments can rarely be forced to take on additional responsibilities unless they wish to do so, nor should they be prevented from supplementing faculty-wide instruction with preparation in matters of special relevance to their discipline. Yet the senior faculty must finally recognize that the case for providing suitable preparation has now become compelling. The body of information about teaching and learning—including the findings from empirical studies of student learning and motivation, the uses of technology, and the more thoughtful writing on curriculum—has simply become too large and too important to expect new faculty members to acquire it on their own.

The critical challenge will be to develop programs for new instructors that are genuinely informative, interesting, and relevant. If the material offered is superficial and inexpertly taught, graduate students and new assistant professors will quickly lose interest and complain. Their senior colleagues will surely give them tacit support, and the entire effort is likely to fail.

With sufficient care, however, those who design the new programs should be able to avoid such a fate. Graduate students about to teach undergraduate sections for the first time are anxious to learn whatever will help them perform well in their new and challenging task. Recently appointed assistant professors at the threshold of their professional careers are normally interested in anything that will inform them about their new responsibilities. The material now available about the educational uses of technology and the effectiveness of different teaching methods is challenging and relevant enough that a thoughtfully prepared and skillfully presented course of instruction should succeed in capturing the interest of these audiences.

In the end, despite the failures of the past and the pitfalls that remain, there are reasons to anticipate that efforts to improve the entire process of teaching and learning and offer better preparation to graduate students will eventually take root and gather strength in the years to come. The arguments for reform are persuasive. The aims are aligned with the deeper professional values of the faculty. Some hopeful experiments are already underway. The existence of so many graduate schools increases the likelihood that some of them will make a serious effort to respond so that the power of example can help persuade other programs to follow suit.

THE SLUGGISH PACE OF REFORM

This brief survey of graduate education should help to explain why PhD training in the United States can be the envy of the world yet still be judged to be seriously deficient in preparing aspiring faculty members for the duties of their profession. On the one hand, despite its weaknesses, graduate education in America does a better job of training researchers than similar programs in other leading countries of the world. Many professors in the United States take their work with graduate students very seriously, especially with students who show real promise as future scholars and scientists. The homage professors often pay to their mentors by presenting them with festschrifts late in life testifies to the respect and affection felt by many faculty members toward those who trained them. Moreover, unlike the traditional European model in which would-be researchers took all their training under a single professor, graduate education in the United States has long been conducted by departments so that graduate students can take a variety of courses and seminars in their field and obtain a broader foundation of learning to support their future work. With these advantages, along with their excellent facilities and accomplished faculties, it is little wonder that American universities have long been the venue of choice for highly talented students from abroad, and that many other countries have adapted their methods of training scientists and scholars to resemble those in the United States.

On the other hand, the weaknesses of American graduate schools in preparing their students to be teachers and faculty members are equally apparent. Discussions of these deficiencies have gone on for many years without resulting in much change. As previously mentioned, part of the problem today may be that much of what is needed is no longer within the competence of individual departments. That being so, with so much to gain from reforming graduate education, one wonders why presidents, deans, and other academic leaders have not done more to initiate the needed changes. The arguments for reform are compelling. The failure to train students adequately for their teaching responsibilities has doubtless contributed to the sluggish rate of change in undergraduate education. Unless these deficiencies are corrected, progress in improving the quality of teaching will continue to come slowly if indeed it comes at all.

Presumably, one reason why academic leaders are reluctant to involve themselves in the preparation of PhDs is that graduate education has long been regarded as the special preserve of academic departments. Presidents and deans in research universities may be hesitant to depart from this tradition, since it is in these institutions that faculties are the most powerful. Efforts to intervene might prove embarrassing by provoking professors and stirring up controversy, overt resistance, and unfavorable publicity.

There is no compelling reason that would drive academic leaders to take these risks. The liberal arts colleges and comprehensive universities that employ many PhDs may grumble—as they sometimes do—that the graduates they hire are not well prepared for teaching, but there is nowhere else they can turn to recruit new members of their faculty. Graduate students seldom complain, since existing methods of doctoral training are so well established that they are simply taken for granted. The senior faculty in research universities who control graduate training are the least likely to feel any pressing need to change the content of their programs. If they perceive any problem with graduate education, it is likely to be that students take too long to finish—hardly a weakness that would cause them to favor adding further requirements for graduate students to fulfill.

In principle, of course, professors want their students to be properly trained. But many senior professors are not convinced that teaching is something that needs to be taught. They have long considered it a skill that one learns by doing and improves with practice to the extent that one's natural gifts allow. After all, that is how *they* learned to teach. Since more than 90 percent of American college professors believe that they are above-average teachers, they have little reason to feel that their graduate students need to prepare any differently.

This state of inertia calls attention once again to a weakness in the way research universities currently function. Many academic leaders, at least in research universities, appear to have accepted too limited a role in influencing educational policy. Burdened as they are with heavy administrative and fundraising duties, they seem inclined to leave much of the responsibility over academic matters with the departments. Faculties, of course, are perfectly content to allow this to occur. As a result, as pointed out in chapter 3, shared governance has evolved to give more and more influence to the faculty in matters of curriculum and pedagogy.

No one can deny that decisions about teaching and curriculum must ultimately be made by the faculty. Those who actually do the teaching have to agree with educational policies and requirements, since they are the ones who must carry them out. Even so, unless academic leaders are well informed about issues of teaching and learning and feel free to discuss such matters frankly with the faculty, there will continue to be too much inertia in the system. This problem is most acute in research universities, where professors are the busiest and feel least willing to take the time to give serious consideration to basic changes in their accustomed way of teaching. Yet it is in these same institutions that improvement is most important, since their departments are the ones most likely to attract attention, inspire emulation, and thereby speed the process of reform.

At present, most of the initiative for improving the quality of education is coming from sources outside the universities—from government, from foundations, from higher education associations and education researchers. These voices are useful, but not sufficient. Foundations, associations, and education researchers are simply not powerful enough to bring about substantial change within universities, however helpful they may be in offering money, sharing information, and contributing ideas. Governments, on the other hand, have plenty of power, but they are often inadequately informed, and their intervention is more likely to provoke suspicion and resistance than persuade universities to change. As a result, there is no adequate substitute for presidents, provosts, and deans who are knowledgeable and willing to take the initiative to raise educational issues, such as the appropriate training of graduate students, and persuade the faculty with credible evidence that problems exist which require their best efforts to overcome.

PART III

PROFESSIONAL EDUCATION

FOREWORD (III)

||||||||||||||||||||||||||||||||||||||||||||||||||||||||||||||||||||||||||||||||||||||||||||||||||||||||

America has long since entered what some commentators describe as "the age of experts." As knowledge continues to expand in volume and complexity, ordinary citizens have come to depend on competent specialists to guide them through even the most commonplace procedures such as preparing tax returns, selling a home, or applying to college. Familiar ailments that were once borne stoically as the inevitable inconveniences of advancing age are now considered illnesses to be treated by highly trained health professionals.

At the same time, the work that professionals do has steadily grown more exacting and difficult. Doctors have to know much more and use far more sophisticated technology. Lawyers need to keep abreast of an ever-changing, ever more unwieldy mass of statutes, regulations, and precedents. Corporate executives preside over far larger, more complex organizations with operations that frequently stretch across the globe.

For universities, then, the training of experts has acquired a vital importance not only for the growing numbers of students preparing to enter a profession but for all the members of the public who depend on their expertise. The role of professional schools, and their size and stature within the university, have consequently reached such a point that no thorough treatment of higher education can ignore them. Yet any attempt to include them will quickly encounter a dilemma. There are now so many kinds of schools preparing students for such a wide variety of occupations that it is hardly possible to cover them all, let alone convey a full understanding of professional education as a whole. This difficulty may explain why one rarely finds a book about higher education that gives the subject more than a passing mention.

The following chapters try to deal with this problem by limiting the discussion to three of the most powerful and influential professional schools—those of medicine, law, and business.* This choice admittedly leaves out some

---

*Some readers may protest that business is not a profession in the strict sense. Nevertheless, business schools are included here, because they offer sustained preparation and specialized

important faculties. Still, both the accomplishments and the problems of the three that are discussed have enough in common with the rest of professional education to make the limited coverage defensible, if not ideal.

All of the three schools discussed have experienced remarkable growth over the past several decades. Since 1951–52, the number of students attending American business schools has risen more than fiftyfold, resulting in 177,000 master's degrees awarded in 2010.[1] Law school enrollments have likewise increased many times over, with nearly 50,000 matriculants in the fall of 2009.[2] The ranks of medical students have grown more slowly since the number of schools is limited by their enormous cost, leaving many would-be doctors unable to gain admission anywhere in the United States. But enrollments in MD-PhD programs, along with the numbers of postdoctoral students, have risen markedly, propelled by the growth of medical research made possible by massive funding from the National Institutes of Health (NIH). The ranks of part-time clinical faculty have expanded even more rapidly in the wake of Medicare and Medicaid to the point that professors with appointments in the medical school and its affiliated hospitals often outnumber the faculty members of all the other parts of the university combined.

Schools of law and business, like those in medicine, devote much effort to research. To strengthen the quality and rigor of their work, schools for all three professions have drawn increasingly on graduates of arts and sciences departments. Basic science faculties in medical schools also include numerous PhDs. Leading business schools no longer hire many faculty from their own doctoral programs but look in the main to recent PhDs in the social sciences for their professors. Law schools are seemingly an exception; their faculties continue to be made up almost entirely of legally trained scholars. Nevertheless, more and more law professors today begin their teaching careers after earning an advanced degree in philosophy or one of the social sciences in addition to their legal studies.

By now, professional school faculties are more than holding their own with their arts and sciences colleagues. In several major universities, the most distinguished researchers in the biological sciences are found in the medical school and its affiliated hospitals rather than in arts and sciences departments. Over the past half century, business schools have improved their research capabilities to such a point that their professors have been winning a substantial share of the Nobel Prizes in economics. No longer, then, are professional school faculties looked down upon as mere applied practitioners.

---

knowledge for demanding careers and have well-trained faculties that engage in rigorous academic research relating to their field.

The quality of students has also improved markedly, at least in the better-known professional schools. Now that so many young people are enrolling in college, earning a degree in medicine, law, or business has become the preferred next step for more and more of America's brightest, most ambitious college seniors. As a result, many schools in all three professions have enjoyed impressive increases in the test scores and college grade-point averages of their entering classes.

Student bodies in all three professional schools have also become much more diverse over the past several decades. In the 1950s and 1960s, almost the entire graduating class at leading schools consisted of white males. Today, up to half of all medical students are women, as are at least 45 percent of the students in law and more than one-third in business.[3] Underrepresented minorities are also far more numerous. Whereas only 2.4 percent of graduating medical students were African American in 1971–72, 6.9 percent received MD degrees in 2007–8.[4] Blacks constituted 7.3 percent of law school students in 2008.[5] Business schools have lagged behind their sister professional schools, with the total number of blacks, Hispanics, and Native Americans combined often making up less than 10 percent of enrollments in leading schools.[6]

The situation is reversed in the case of income diversity. The striking fact in schools of law and medicine is the dearth of low-income students.[7] Because of the length of time to degree and the high cost of medical training, the average debt of graduating MDs is now over $150,000. This is a daunting obstacle for college graduates of modest means who typically leave college already owing a considerable sum. As debt loads have increased, the percentage of medical students from the lowest income quintile has declined, although even in the best times, it never exceeded 5.5 percent. In contrast, 55 percent of medical students in 2005 came from families with incomes in the highest quintile. Very few medical schools have the resources to solve this problem with financial aid, and, in any case, many of them distribute the scholarships they have largely on the basis of merit rather than need.

Law school students face a somewhat similar problem.[8] Starting in the late 1980s, tuitions rose rapidly, not only in elite schools but in many others as well. From 1987 to 2009, the average charge per year at public law schools for in-state students jumped from $2,398 to $18,472. At private law schools, the average increase was equally dramatic—from $8,911 to $35,743. In several leading schools, along with others located in large cities, tuitions now top $50,000, well above even the amount charged by Ivy League colleges.*

---

*There are many reasons for the steep rise in law school tuitions. Some are justifiable. In response to mounting criticism from the bar that newly graduated attorneys lacked sufficient

To pay for a legal education, almost 90 percent of all law students borrow. Because of high tuitions, the average debt per graduating student has now grown to exceed $70,000 for public law schools and more than $120,000 for private law schools. Such heavy indebtedness is not a great problem for graduates of elite schools, since most of them go to work in large law firms where starting salaries for attorneys will often be above $150,000. Outside the top twenty-five schools, however, only about 10 percent of graduating students are offered such positions, and many of their classmates have been encountering difficulty finding any kind of work in the profession. Because so many law students have very high debt loads, even those who do find legal jobs often have repayment obligations well beyond the limit that financial advisers recommend.

These developments have made it hazardous for students with limited resources and lower-income parents to enter law school. In the ten highest-rated schools, 57 percent of the students now come from families in the top 10 percent of the income scale. Even in the one hundred *lowest*-ranked schools, 27 percent of students have parents in the top income decile. While various factors help to account for these results, the combination of high debt loads and uncertain job prospects must surely be discouraging to prospective students who know they cannot count on parental support if they find themselves in dire financial straits.

Business schools have largely escaped the problem of excessive debts. Only two years are needed to earn a degree, and many students can find lucrative positions in the summer after their first year to reduce their educational loans. Those who are less likely to land highly paid jobs can usually find schools that charge lower tuitions, since accreditation is not essential, freeing schools from

---

practical know-how, law schools have hired additional faculty to teach basic skills and supervise students delivering legal services. Because of rapid increases in the starting salaries paid by well-established firms, law schools have felt compelled to raise their own salaries to attract highly qualified young lawyers to their faculties. Like state colleges and universities, moreover, many public law schools had to raise tuitions to offset declining state support.

Other reasons for the rapidly rising tuitions are harder to justify. In the relentless competition to rise in the annual rankings in *U.S. News & World Report*, law schools have engaged in fierce bidding wars for well-known professors, which have resulted in escalating salaries. Efforts to improve their "research profile" have caused schools to lower teaching loads and hence hire additional faculty. In order to raise the average admissions test scores of their entering class—an important factor in the rankings—schools have increased their merit scholarships.

Finally, the accreditation process—administered jointly by law professors and the American Bar Association—has established standards that make it more difficult for schools offering lower-cost education to enter the field. Rules requiring students to complete three years' worth of classes have inhibited experiments with a two-year law degree. Other requirements dealing with the size of law school libraries or mandating a predominance of tenured faculty have a similar effect. For a more complete discussion of law school costs, see Brian Z. Tamanaha, *Failing Law Schools* (2012).

having to comply with costly requirements. As a result, graduate business education is much more accessible to low- and moderate-income students than law schools or medical schools.

The curricula for the three professions naturally differ greatly. Nevertheless, all three schools share the same underlying tasks in attempting to prepare their students for practice. Their initial, and perhaps most important, responsibility is to instill a special mental discipline, a particular form of analytic thinking about the characteristic problems of the profession. In medical school, it is a "clinical habit of mind"; in law school, "thinking like a lawyer"; in business school, "the administrative point of view."

These habits of mind demand an acquaintance with the basic knowledge and principles of the professional field, but, more than that, they require an instinctive ability to reason carefully and precisely about the kinds of practical questions that professionals repeatedly face. Developing this mental discipline is typically an arduous, all-consuming process. It is no accident that books about professional schools by former students, such as *One L* by Scott Turow or *Gentle Vengeance* by Charles LeBaron, often read like personal odysseys in which the authors endure a series of harrowing trials and tribulations on the way to some imagined Ithaka, which they eventually reach not quite knowing where they have landed or how they may have changed along the way.[9]

The second important responsibility of every professional school is to help students acquire the specialized knowledge they require in order to practice. Faculties in each of the three professions have had to cope with a constantly growing and changing body of relevant information that practitioners need to know and use in their work. As a result of generous funding from both government and private sources, the corpus of scientific knowledge relevant to medicine has expanded massively since World War II. In addition, medical faculty must take account of the impact of the environment and personal lifestyles on human health as well as the effect of health-care policies on the availability and cost of medical services. The law is likewise fed by an unending stream of new statutes, new regulations, and new judicial rulings that legal scholars need to keep abreast of in order to do their research and teach their students. Business school professors must also acquaint their students with an ever-changing and ever more complex environment filled with new products and methods of production, new markets domestic and foreign, and new laws and political issues affecting business. Since the length of time required to earn a professional degree is usually fixed, professional faculties are constantly challenged to figure out what knowledge students most need to have and how to fit it all within the time available for instruction.

A third task for schools serving all three professions is to help their students acquire the skills practitioners need, such as drawing blood from a patient, writing a legal brief for a client, or developing a business plan for a new company. In carrying out this task, faculties typically wrestle with the problem of deciding which competencies to teach and which ones to leave to be learned on the job. When faculties assume the task of teaching skills, they cannot always succeed through the usual methods of classroom instruction. No one ever learned to drive a car by simply reading a manual, nor has anyone ever become an accomplished baseball player merely by listening to lectures on the fine points of the game. Instead, students learn most skills by doing and not merely by listening and reading. In seeking to help students acquire the necessary competencies, the three professional schools have responded in different ways and with differing degrees of success.

Finally, all professional schools must try to imbue their students with the ethical standards and professional responsibilities that practitioners need to observe in carrying out their work. It is these commitments that set true professionals apart and help to earn the public's trust and justify the faith that laypersons place in their expert judgment. As a result, organizations such as the American Bar Association and the American Medical Association, as well as prominent business leaders, regularly stress the importance of ethics and professional responsibility in serving the public and earning its trust. Yet instilling these values is one of the most difficult challenges that educators have to face. Defining the nature of professional responsibility and the ethical standards and social obligations it entails, and deciding when these duties take precedence over the interests of patients, clients, and shareholders, are difficult intellectual tasks in themselves. Helping students develop the strength of character to honor their obligations to others even when they conflict with the wishes of clients and employers presents a still greater challenge. It is little wonder, then, that all three professional schools have struggled in their attempt to achieve these goals.

In carrying out their common tasks, faculties in each of the professions have had to strike a balance between the practical needs of the calling they serve and the standards and values of the academic community to which they belong. Good professional schools are rarely content to be trade schools catering only to the immediate practical needs of their calling. At the same time, they will serve neither their students nor their profession by becoming too detached and academic in their interests. Finding a proper balance between these extremes is no easy matter. The path of least resistance is to move predominantly toward one or the other. At any given point, therefore, all three schools may hear criticism either from the profession or from the academy that they have veered too far in the opposite direction.

Although all of the challenges and responsibilities just discussed are common to schools of medicine, law, and business, each of the three faculties has responded in different ways. Some of the variations result from peculiarities in the nature of the three professions. Others may be due to differences in the organization and resources of the schools themselves. In some instances, however, schools in one profession have achieved success by using methods that the other faculties could usefully consider. For this reason, the afterword to these chapters will try to compare the responses of the three types of schools to the common challenges they face and suggest why some schools have made more progress than others.

CHAPTER TWELVE

MEDICAL SCHOOLS

||||||||||||||||||||||||||||||||||||||||||||||||||||||||||||||||||||||||||||||||||||||||||||||||||||||||

THE EDUCATION OF DOCTORS is a remarkable achievement. Medical schools welcome bright young men and women recently graduated from college and transform them over a period of years into specialists capable of performing open-heart surgery, replacing arthritic knees, or using highly sophisticated technology to diagnose illnesses and prescribe appropriate treatments. Acquiring such expertise does not come easily. More than any other form of professional education, medical training forces students to witness death and suffering, dissect cadavers, and perform other acts that would be repellent to most ordinary people. Often, the process demands that students work exceptionally long hours and experience extreme fatigue. To function effectively, they must learn to steel themselves against the pain and anguish they see all around them. It is little wonder, then, that most doctors who write about their years in medical school pay close attention not only to their struggle to learn all they needed to know but to the effects the training had on their personalities, fundamental values, and outlook on life.[1]

Becoming a doctor has not always been this arduous or this successful. A century and a half ago, when William James entered Harvard Medical School, the course of study was entirely different.

> Students were expected to attend lectures for two terms, perform a few recitations, make a few visits to hospitals, and present a brief thesis. It was possible to get through the whole thing in a year. When a candidate had completed the two terms, had a short thesis in hand, and had paid a fee of thirty dollars, he took his one and only examination. . . . The exam was brief, oral, and covered nine subjects. A student who passed five out of the nine got an M.D. degree and a license to practice. New doctors could thus be set loose on the public lacking basic knowledge of almost half the subjects of their profession.[2]

In the 150 years that have elapsed since then, the training has become much longer and more intense. A vast body of knowledge has accumulated about the human body and the ailments that afflict it. No student can learn it all, but most absorb a remarkable amount while engaging in constant practice to learn how to use the knowledge effectively.

Today, there are some 140 medical schools in the United States that award a total of approximately 15,000 MD degrees each year. They have long been able to accept fewer than half the students who apply. Their faculties typically include basic scientists who spend most of their time on research, together with clinical faculty, made up chiefly of practicing physicians based in teaching hospitals that are either owned by the school or, more often, affiliated with it. Because of generous funding for research from the National Institutes of Health, along with large sums of money earned from patient care delivered by the clinical professors, medical schools have been able to assemble faculties numbering in the hundreds or even thousands. Most of them, however, are only part-time professors who spend the bulk of their working days caring for patients and training residents, with only a few hours each week devoted to teaching and research.

WHAT TO TEACH

The process of learning to become a doctor has long followed a standard sequence. Undergraduates have begun by taking a series of premedical requirements consisting of basic courses in biology, chemistry, mathematics, and physics. Those who are subsequently admitted to a medical school normally devote much of their first two years to learning more basic science and studying human anatomy and the various organ systems and diseases. The final two years of medical school are largely spent on the hospital wards observing and assisting hospital staff and faculty physicians in a variety of specialties such as surgery, pediatrics, internal medicine, and the like. Once they have earned an MD degree, graduates spend several more years as interns and residents acquiring specialized training in the field of their choice. At this advanced stage, they also serve as members of a hospital staff taking care of patients and helping to teach medical students under the general supervision of attending physicians, who typically hold faculty appointments.

A peculiarity of this sequence that distinguishes medical education from legal training is that control over the several stages of learning is divided among several entities instead of being administered entirely by the medical schools.

The latter are responsible only for the four-year programs leading to the MD degree, and even then, teaching hospitals supply the venue and share responsibility for the last two years. Premedical education is provided in courses taught by the college faculty, while the training of interns and residents is the responsibility of the teaching hospitals according to specifications established by the boards of the various medical specialties, such as internal medicine and surgery. As one might expect, the fragmented authority over the preparation of doctors has complicated the task of creating a fully satisfactory, smoothly integrated system of education.

Over the past generation, the curriculum for educating doctors has undergone several major changes. The first of these involved the relationship of basic science and clinical instruction. Students complained for years about the two first years of medical school, because the constant diet of basic science lectures was not only boring but often seemed unrelated to real patients and real diseases. In response to these complaints, many schools have begun in recent decades to combine the basic sciences with clinical medicine by reducing the number of lectures and providing time for students in small groups to discuss the application of science to actual cases of illness and disease. Efforts are also being made to integrate basic science more closely with clinical care during the final two years. As a result, the wall that once separated the teaching of scientific knowledge in the first two years from the emphasis on diagnosis and treatment in the third and fourth has now been breached at several points.

A more recent change has involved the so-called premedical requirements that all college students need to complete in order to qualify for admission to a medical school. As biomedical knowledge has evolved, the familiar premed courses have grown less and less suited to the needs of modern medicine. Much of the material covered in organic chemistry is no longer as relevant to medicine as it once was, while essential aspects of biochemistry are now much more important. Some of the time that premeds have traditionally spent on physics could be better used studying statistics. For many years, however, the content remained pretty much the same, because no single college felt free to change the required courses very much without putting its students at risk in applying to other medical schools.

Only a collective effort to alter the requirements for all colleges and medical schools could overcome this problem. At long last, fortunately, such an attempt has been made. Under a plan proposed by a joint task force of the Association of American Medical Colleges and the Howard Hughes Medical Institute, applicants to medical school will no longer have to take the traditional set of premed courses but will simply prepare for a newly revised entrance exam to demonstrate that they have mastered a body of carefully defined knowledge considered essential for studying to be a doctor. Once the new test is introduced in 2015, a long-standing problem should be largely resolved.[*]

A third source of change in the content of medical education is the persistent and rapid growth over the past half century in our understanding of human biology and health. The knowledge of subjects such as genetics and the effects of environment and lifestyle on health have expanded enormously. This intellectual ferment has forced many medical schools to make major revisions in their course of study. For example, the Johns Hopkins Medical School recently announced an entirely new curriculum.[3] After extensive study of how medicine will be practiced ten years hence, a faculty committee concluded that "the next generation of physicians will require a new conceptual foundation of health and disease that focuses on individual [genetic] characteristics and that explores how they interact with accrued environmental experiences."[4] As members of the committee explained, based on "principles of biologic and environmental individuality, [a] major goal of this new curriculum is to reframe the context of health and illness more broadly to encourage medical students to explore the biologic properties of an individual's health in the light of a larger integrated system that also includes social, cultural, psychological, and environmental variables."[5] To implement the new curriculum, the medical school has constructed a building specially designed to accommodate smaller-group instruction and introduced new methods of compensation and evaluation to give teaching and learning a status equal to research.

Not every medical school has undertaken quite such a comprehensive reform. But all faculties are constantly revising their lectures and creating new courses to keep up with the evolving stock of relevant knowledge. As the storehouse of useful information continues to grow, there are inevitably complaints that one subject or another is not receiving enough attention. Some critics have pointed out that most doctors do not know enough about the treatment of chronic pain, causing millions of patients to suffer needlessly.[6] Others argue that general practitioners understand too little about mental illness, which helps to explain why only one in three among clinically depressed Americans who see a doctor receives appropriate treatment.[7] Still others claim that students have too little exposure to the public health dimension of medical care, or to information technology and the techniques of data retrieval and manipulation.[8]

---

[*] Students applying to medical schools have long had to take an entrance exam, the Medical College Admissions Test or MCAT. The MCAT has recently been revised to incorporate current thinking about what students need to know before entering medical school. For a set of articles about the new MCAT, see Association of American Colleges and Universities, *Peer Review* (Fall 2012).

Changes in health-care policy and the delivery of care have also had an effect on the content of medical education. The laws Congress has enacted to deal with the mounting cost of care and the consequent rise of health maintenance organizations and other new ways of providing services have transformed the way physicians practice their profession. Doctors cannot remain ignorant of these developments if they are to adapt to this new environment, nor will the problems of our system for delivering care ever be fully overcome without the willing and knowledgeable cooperation of practicing physicians.

Medical faculties have responded by developing courses in health economics and health policy. By now, such offerings exist in every school. Nevertheless, teaching this material in schools dominated by a preoccupation with scientific medicine has proved to be more of a challenge than medical schools anticipated. A recent survey revealed that almost half of the students polled were dissatisfied with the available classes, and nearly 90 percent expressed a desire for more exposure to the subject.[9] Another recent study found that over one-quarter of the doctors surveyed did not know that the United States had the most costly system in the world; almost one-third thought that Americans enjoyed the longest life expectancy in the world; and 40 percent seriously underestimated the percentage of Americans who lacked health insurance.[10]

The internship and residency programs (which make up what is known as graduate medical education) provide a further opportunity to prepare young doctors to help address the major problems of our health-care system. At the least, one might expect that interns and residents would be carefully mentored to help inculcate habits that could counter the steady rise in health-care costs such as ordering fewer diagnostic tests and relying more on evidence-based diagnosis and treatment.* One would also suppose that special efforts would be made to improve the quality of care by training residents to minimize the medical errors that currently result in an estimated ninety-eight thousand unnecessary deaths every year.[11] Nevertheless, recent reports by distinguished panels of experts point out that graduate medical education still falls short of accomplishing these results.[12]

A final set of problems for the curriculum concerns the treatment of topics such as medical ethics and the human relations aspects of patient care. For many years, it was assumed that these subjects could be transmitted without formal courses through the examples set by the senior physicians who taught students

---

*According to Harvard professor Joseph P. Newhouse, between one-sixth and one-third of medical procedures performed in the United States are "demonstrably inappropriate," while a substantial additional number are "equivocal." "Why Is There a Quality Chasm?" 21 *Health Affairs* (2002), pp. 13, 15.

in the hospital wards. Eventually, however, this assumption broke down under a multitude of pressures. Ethical problems became more prominent and complex in the wake of conflicts over abortion, euthanasia, cloning, and stem cell research. At the same time, as researchers discovered the impact of diet, exercise, and smoking on health and revealed the dismaying numbers of patients who failed to follow their doctor's advice, communication skills began to seem too important to be left to the goodwill and common sense of physicians.

Teaching these subjects effectively, however, has proved to be a problem. The field of bioethics has developed to a sufficient point that students can be taught to recognize complex moral questions when they arise and to analyze them carefully in light of the various competing considerations. Much has also been learned about the needs of patients and the reasons why they often fail to follow doctors' prescriptions or adopt a healthier lifestyle. Nevertheless, it is one thing to convey such knowledge and quite another to change students' behavior so that they actually practice higher ethical standards and display greater sensitivity to the psychological needs of patients and the subtle cultural differences of an increasingly diverse population. A threshold challenge is simply to convince students to take these subjects seriously in an academic culture dominated by the ethos of scientific medicine. In this environment, students can easily look upon courses in ethics or human relations as so much fluff, diverting them from the overriding need to master an enormous body of scientific knowledge and medical know-how.

A further complication in trying to teach ethics and human relations effectively is that the lessons conveyed in such courses are often contradicted by the behavior students observe on the hospital wards. In surveys given to medical students and interns, large percentages report having seen multiple cases of hospital personnel falsifying medical records, speaking harshly to subordinates or insensitively to patients, taking credit for work performed by others, even using drugs or alcohol while on duty.[13] In one study conducted in six Pennsylvania medical schools, 61 percent of the students who responded claimed to have witnessed behaviors of this kind.[14]

In earlier decades, most medical schools had a few great figures—physician-teachers whose character and behavior toward patients were models of responsible care and humane concern. Today, such persons undoubtedly exist, but they tend to be swallowed up in vastly larger faculties where few senior physicians still have frequent, continuing contact with medical students. In the modern medical school, the examples set by the clinical faculty are uneven at best. According to one survey of residents and interns, only 42 percent of attending physicians in teaching hospitals were regarded as excellent role models.[15]

In view of these difficulties, it is not surprising that surveys reveal serious deficiencies in the professional norms of physicians. Almost half of the doctors in one study admitted knowing of an incompetent or impaired colleague without notifying superiors about the problem.[16] Large numbers did not see a problem in referring a patient for tests by a facility in which they held a financial interest.[17] More than one-third of the respondents admitted that they would order a medical test if their patient really wanted it even though they considered it wasteful and unnecessary.[18]

All in all, then, medical schools appear to have done a good job of keeping up with the rapid growth of new knowledge and giving students the technical know-how and competence to diagnose and treat their patients. They have been less successful in going beyond medical science to prepare students to be active collaborators in improving the health-care system or to nurture the values and human relations skills that students will need to be fully effective and responsible members of their profession. At one time, such deficiencies may have seemed rather minor. In contemporary America, where lifestyle is perceived to be as important to health as viruses and genes, where the patient population has become far more racially and culturally diverse, and the cost of health-care has become the principal challenge for America's fiscal policy, correcting these weaknesses has acquired a much greater urgency than in earlier generations.

HOW TO TEACH

There is much to admire about the efforts medical schools have made to improve their methods of instruction. Within the past few decades, most faculties have transformed the way they teach first- and second-year medical students. Instead of imposing the heavy diet of lectures on basic science that earlier generations of students endured, most faculties today spend much of the class time in small groups discussing the application of science to real cases of illness and disease. In these sessions, students grapple with the problems of actual patients in order to learn what they need to know and how to find the information and use it to diagnose illnesses and prescribe appropriate treatment.

The new method has not only proved to be more interesting to students; it employs many suggestions from contemporary cognitive theory such as the use of active learning and collaborative problem solving. Many schools supplement their teaching by using computer-driven simulations that offer students opportunities to practice their diagnostic skills.[19] These exercises combine the use of film or lifelike manikins with computer technology to create a simulated patient with a variety of symptoms. Students can ask the "patient" questions and receive instant answers or order simulated tests and obtain immediate results until they succeed in making an accurate diagnosis.

After the first two years, students experience a different type of learning by serving an apprenticeship in a hospital where they watch physicians question patients and perform medical procedures. After a time, they begin to do some of the simpler tasks themselves. The process of learning medical procedures—vividly captured by the familiar mantra "See one, do one, teach one"—echoes the findings of cognitive experts that performing tasks and teaching them to others are the best ways of truly mastering a skill.

Despite these admirable features, the current methods of instruction in medical schools are hardly free from criticism and controversy. The deepest, most fundamental question involves the nature of expertise and how it can best be acquired. How do experts know how to solve a problem? In particular, how is it that they often seem to intuit the likely answer to a problem immediately without spending hours sifting through information and testing a long series of possible solutions? Presumably, experience helps them perform in this way, but how, exactly, does expert judgment work and how can good teaching help students to acquire it?

More and more medical schools have answered this question in the manner previously described—by having first-year students start quite soon to discuss real medical problems and discover what information they need, where to find it, and how to analyze it to arrive at the right solution. Not everyone, however, agrees that this procedure is optimal. Some traditionalists believe that too rapid an immersion in clinical problem-solving gives students an inadequate grounding in basic science, and that the older method of beginning with lectures, however boring or irrelevant they may seem, provides a better factual foundation from which to begin analyzing symptoms and diagnosing illness.[20]

Efforts to resolve this argument empirically have thus far been inconclusive. At least one team of investigators has found that medical students who learn their basic science the old-fashioned way are more efficient and accurate in diagnosing illness than others who have started very early to analyze clinical problems.[21] According to these researchers, a solid grounding in basic science offers concepts that help students to organize relevant information in their minds and process the clinical data rapidly to make an accurate diagnosis. Defenders of the newer method respond by citing evidence that students who begin by discussing clinical problems are more interested in their studies, remember relevant information longer, and do almost as well on national tests of basic science as those who studied under a more traditional curriculum.[22]

A related dispute has emerged between those who believe that doctors should make decisions on the basis of proven rules of thumb—or algorithms—derived from scientific and empirical data and those who worry that an "evidence-based" approach ignores the inconvenient cases that cannot be resolved in this fashion. In the latter cases—often estimated to make up at least 10–15 percent of the total—a doctor needs to consider all kinds of information, including details elicited by close physical observation and careful questioning of patients even about the seemingly irrelevant personal details of their lives.[23] According to this view, doctors who learn to rely heavily on algorithms and data obtained from multiple laboratory tests may miss the clues that could disclose the true nature of the patient's illness.

This dispute, like the argument over how to combine basic science with clinical problem solving, is not yet resolved. It is possible, of course, that both sides are correct. Although evidence-based medicine may not cope well with unusual cases, it may still improve the diagnoses of doctors as a whole, many of whom are not completely up-to-date in their knowledge or proficient enough to diagnose illness accurately within the limited time available to see individual patients under managed care plans. Until the controversy is settled, however, doubts will remain over how best to teach diagnostic skills to students.

The issues just discussed underscore the importance of measuring how much students are learning in order to discover by enlightened trial and error which methods of instruction are most effective. Hospitals are already making increasing use of careful assessments of this kind in order to discover which treatments seem to work best in curing different diseases and which drugs have the fewest side effects. Through work of this kind, methods of practice and patient outcomes have improved significantly. As several recent reviews of medical education have pointed out, faculties should routinely use similar methods to assess and improve the quality of their teaching and to evaluate the effectiveness of the entire curriculum.[24]

THE SETTING FOR CLINICAL TRAINING

A final set of problems has arisen from the vast changes in the settings where clinical instruction takes place. Prior to World War II, most medical schools were quite modest in size. Their teaching hospitals restricted the intake of patients to make sure that training medical students and residents remained their primary concern. Teaching staffs were likewise small, and members were paid considerably less than doctors in private practice. Although eminent physicians often served on clinical faculties, many of them could afford their modest academic salaries only because they had independent means. They had extensive contact with their interns and residents and devoted much time to instructing third- and fourth-year medical students in the wards and through the periodic "grand rounds" at which interesting cases were discussed. As noted earlier, the best of these professors became well-known role models and had a lasting effect on those they taught.[25]

This way of life began to change during the postwar period. The National Institutes of Health (NIH) were founded, bringing large research grants to medical schools and their faculties. From its modest beginning dispensing a few million dollars a year in the late 1940s, the NIH grew to distribute almost thirty billion dollars by 2010, most of it to universities. With the aid of this support, medical schools and their teaching hospitals increased their research effort enormously while constantly adding new laboratory space complete with state-of-the-art equipment. Research took increasing priority over teaching, and basic scientists had less time to spend with medical students.*

In 1965, Congress enacted Medicare and Medicaid. Together with the spread of private health insurance, these programs brought vast new sources of income to the medical profession. For the first time, patient care became profitable for academic health centers. Doctors on the faculty banded together to form practice plans, bringing new streams of revenue to medical schools and their teaching hospitals. From 1965 to 2010, this source of support grew from a modest total of $49 million per year to $36 billion, contributing nearly half of all income received by academic health centers.

To accommodate this growth, medical schools and their hospitals had to transform the way they carried on their work. Success in research depended on maintaining a large volume of grants to pay investigators and gain the over-head to fund the new laboratories and the growing support staff needed for a vastly expanded program. Financing teaching hospitals depended on expanding the flow, or "throughput," of patients. As a result, administrators struggled to attract larger numbers of patients and discharge them more quickly to make room for new ones. To achieve this growth, medical schools began giving faculty appointments to practicing physicians, some of whom lacked any teaching or research experience, so long as they brought their patients with them. Many of these new recruits did little or no teaching and had little contact with medical students. In fact, clinicians came to spend less and less time in the hospitals where third- and fourth-year students did their work. Instead, they examined

---

* Basic scientists in medical schools do continue to give lectures to first- and second-year students and also spend much time training graduate (PhD) students, whose numbers have increased rapidly in recent decades.

patients in their offices, referring to the hospital only those ill enough to require the expensive treatments available in academic health centers.

These developments had a marked effect on the nature of clinical education. With the average length of hospital stays sharply reduced, students could no longer observe the progress of illness and treatment in the way they did in earlier times. As more people came to be treated in doctors' offices and clinics, teaching hospitals no longer attracted many patients suffering from the chronic diseases that had become the most prevalent type of health problem in the United States. As a result, teaching hospitals ceased to provide the ideal educational setting they had once offered.

Medical schools have responded by trying to develop relationships with community hospitals and outpatient clinics where students can observe a wider variety of illnesses. This strategy has had some success. But doctors in these newer settings are under pressure to work efficiently by seeing more patients and spending less time with each. Government regulators and managed care providers have also forced physicians to do additional paperwork and meet other administrative demands. As a result, clinical professors have less time to spend with students. Many clinics will not even agree to teach medical students or will allow them only to observe instead of helping to provide care.

With doctors spending less time in teaching hospitals, students have come to rely increasingly on interns and residents for their education. Accompanying doctors on the wards as they visit patients is often too hurried a process to allow much learning to occur or to provide suitable opportunities for students to observe how the science they learned connects with the care of the sick. Fewer students or even house staff have the chance to eat lunch regularly with eminent physicians on the faculty and discuss interesting cases informally. More recently, teaching hospitals have begun to hire young doctors, called hospitalists, to take charge of entire floors and oversee the education of medical students while also making sure that patient care is properly coordinated and carried out efficiently.[26] Although hospitalists have apparently improved patient care, they often lack the experience or even the time to serve effectively as teachers and mentors.

The increased size and wealth of the modern teaching hospital has also brought a pervasive preoccupation with money. Fund-raising occupies more of the time of top hospital officials. Administrators have to work continuously to keep budgets balanced by maintaining a sufficient flow of patients and streamlining the care they receive. Changes in federal legislation have diminished the ability of hospitals to support medical education with surpluses earned from Medicare patients.

Meanwhile, many members of the clinical faculty can now earn large sums of money and supplement their income by consulting with pharmaceutical, biotech, and medical device companies and giving paid promotional speeches to professional groups. In this environment, cases of conflict of interest and incomplete reporting of outside income crop up repeatedly. Meanwhile, drug company representatives roam the floors dispensing gifts while giving free lunches to residents and interns in order to talk about their products and hopefully sow the seeds of future sales.* At the low end of the hospital hierarchy, medical students worry increasingly about making enough money to repay educational loans that often exceed $150,000 or even $200,000.[27]

Such changes in the teaching hospital environment could hardly fail to have an effect on medical education. Without doubt, decades of intensive research have greatly increased the knowledge conveyed to students about the treatment of illness and disease. At the same time, now that education is no longer the primary function of the teaching hospital, something of value has been lost. Having less contact with senior physicians, students find fewer opportunities to absorb the professional values that successful role models can convey. When doctors are added to the clinical faculty with little regard for their academic accomplishments and the leading physicians in the school are no longer as visible or as accessible as they once were, students are more likely to become cynical as they see things on the wards that contradict what professors try to teach them about ethics and the responsibilities of a doctor to patients and society.[28]

Graduate medical education has also suffered from the transformation that has occurred in the teaching environment. A series of reports on the state of medical education have criticized hospitals for neglecting their educational responsibilities.[29] In the current environment, with its stress on maximizing the "throughput" of patents and its preoccupation with matters of money and finance, interns and residents have limited time to engage in teaching and learning, while clinical faculty spend less time mentoring them. Thus, a recent survey of internal medicine trainees found that 46.3 percent felt that they were given insufficient time to participate in learning activities and that "limited educational activities are the weakest part of the average inpatient rotation."[30]

These conditions are not new; critics have complained about them for at least fifty years. Progress is slow in coming, however, because powerful interests benefit from keeping things as they are. Hospitals rely on interns and residents as a source of inexpensive labor to perform many routine tasks serving patients and performing administrative chores. The clinical faculty likewise favor the status quo since it frees up time for them to spend on research or on additional private patients to swell their incomes.[31] As a result, the education of residents continues to suffer.

---

* In recent years, a number of schools have prohibited or severely curtailed this practice.

The challenges posed by the modern academic health center are widely recognized. Medical schools are actively seeking ways to address them that will at least mitigate their undesirable effects. One of many examples is the integrated clerkship for third-year medical students recently agreed to by the Harvard Medical School and its independent affiliated teaching hospitals.[32]

The primary objective of the new clerkships is to provide a continuity of teaching and learning for third-year students instead of a disjointed series of monthlong stays in each of the major clinical departments—medicine, surgery, obstetrics/gynecology, pediatrics, radiology, neurology, psychiatry, and primary care. In the past, these separate clerkships have typically taken place in different hospitals and lacked the coordination among the different departments that is needed to keep track of the professional development of individual students or allow them to observe patients over an extended period of time. To address these problems the medical school and the hospitals have agreed to create single teams of instructors to take responsibility for cohorts of students and guide them throughout the entire third year.

In one participating community hospital, a physician team with members from each of the clinical departments involved has agreed to do all the teaching of a cohort of students who can then remain with a single group of patients throughout the entire year. In this way, students have an ample opportunity to watch how the condition and treatment of patients evolve over an extended period and how doctors from different specialties contribute to their care. The students also come to know and interact closely with their team of senior physicians. The latter act as role models while monitoring the progress of the students and helping to remedy weaknesses in their development.

Other Harvard teaching hospitals have chosen not to make a single team of instructors responsible for all of the teaching during the year. But they have arranged to have all the monthlong clerkships take place in one hospital and to have a single group of faculty meet with students for several hours each week throughout the year. These physicians assume responsibility for ensuring proper coordination of the separate clerkships and for mentoring the students and helping them overcome any deficiencies in their development. In this way, students can develop close relationships with several senior faculty, who in turn will "take ownership" of the group to make sure that they make appropriate progress. In addition, the core faculty can use the weekly sessions with students to reinforce earlier themes in their training such as the relationship of science to clinical care and the importance of ethics to the practice of medicine.

The new integrated clerkships require a significant amount of the time of participating faculty that must be paid for in some fashion. To make this commitment possible, the medical school, the hospitals, and the departments have agreed to share the expense. The amounts provided are not sufficient to cover the entire cost, but they are substantial enough to persuade the departments and the professors to participate willingly in the new clerkships. Because the clinical faculty is so large, it has been possible to recruit senior physicians who enjoy working with students and are well-qualified to serve as mentors and role models. To reinforce their efforts, the medical school has sought to emphasize the importance of teaching by giving it greater prominence in promotions and establishing a center for improving instruction similar to those created in many colleges.

In order to evaluate the new approach, the integrated clerkships were initially conducted on a pilot basis so that the experience of participating students could be measured against the progress of a carefully selected control group of students enrolled in the traditional clerkships. These assessments revealed high levels of satisfaction among both students and faculty in the pilot programs. Professors enjoyed the chance to work closely with students over an extended period. Students appreciated the mentoring they received and the chance to come to know senior faculty members well. Of particular note is that students in the new system did not exhibit the loss of empathy and the growing cynicism observed in several previous studies of third-year medical students.

Apparently, then, the new clerkships are succeeding in accomplishing the goals for which they were created. Other medical schools are finding ways of their own to achieve these ends. These innovations offer hope for overcoming the hectic pace of the modern hospital, the dwindling presence of senior role models for students, the shorter stays of patients, and other problems arising from the changes in medicine and the delivery of care that have so profoundly altered the setting for teaching.

THE ROAD AHEAD

The transformation of recent college graduates into competent physicians is an achievement unsurpassed by any other form of professional training. Difficulties remain, however, many of which are the product of the massive changes in the way health care is provided and paid for in our society. Some of them, such as the shortcomings of graduate medical education, are largely under the control of the teaching hospitals and hence are difficult for medical schools to correct. Other deficiencies, however, involve the MD curriculum and hence are the direct responsibility of the medical schools.

With respect to the latter problems, there are grounds at least for cautious optimism.[33] The willingness of medical schools to work in concert to revise premedical requirements after many years of neglect is a constructive step. So is the transformation that has occurred in the preclinical years with the growth of problem-based teaching. The creation of courses on ethics, human relations, and the health-care system, though not yet fully effective, at least show a genuine concern for the professional responsibilities of physicians. Experiments such as the integrated clerkship, the new Johns Hopkins curriculum, and the use of computerized simulations, among others, demonstrate a continuing willingness to innovate. All in all, therefore, medical schools seem well aware of the challenges they face and willing to make impressive efforts to respond constructively. In considering the current state of medical education, therefore, one can at least entertain the hope that a system of professional training that has come so far since the time of William James will succeed in finding ways to surmount the problems that still remain.

CHAPTER THIRTEEN

LAW SCHOOLS

IIIIIIIIIIIIIIIIIIIIIIIIIIIIIIIIIIIIIIIIIIIIIIIIIIIIIIIIIIIIIIIIIIIIIIIIIIIIIIIIIIIIIIIIIIIIIIIIIIIIIIIIIIIIIIIIIIIIIIIIIII

COMPARING LEGAL EDUCATION to the training of doctors, one is struck more by differences than by similarities. Law faculties usually number fewer than one hundred members, while most medical school faculties are many times larger. Law professors devote a lot of time and effort to teaching, whereas most faculty members in medical schools do little teaching and spend the bulk of their time on research or patient care. Much of the instruction in law schools takes place in large or medium-sized classes, while more of the teaching in medical schools occurs in small groups. Law students are usually challenged by the first year but are less engaged by their coursework thereafter, whereas medical students grow increasingly absorbed as they move from the lecture room and the laboratory to the hospital wards to work with patients and learn the rudimentary skills of medical care.[1]

THE HIERARCHY OF SCHOOLS

There are currently roughly two hundred accredited law schools in the United States. Virtually all of them use the same type of text, or casebook, and the same methods of teaching. Where law schools differ most is in the academic qualifications of their students and the kinds of legal practice their graduates enter. The leading schools draw students from all across the country and accept only a small fraction of those who apply. Unlike medical schools, however, where almost every entering student has long been intent on becoming a doctor, the most selective law schools are a magnet for students with excellent college records who decide on a legal education late in their college careers, not from conviction but for want of a better alternative. Many have no idea of what kind of practice they would like to have, and a substantial number are quite uncertain whether they will ever practice law at all. Once they complete their studies, however, the vast majority move to a good-sized city and spend at least a few years working in one of the established law firms that specialize in representing major corporations.[2]

Less prominent law schools tend to draw most of their applicants from the same state or even the same metropolitan area. Students in these schools will usually enroll with a clear expectation of practicing law, and the courses they take will tend to be more practical than those offered in the elite schools.[3] They will spend more hours helping to represent clients in real cases and less time studying jurisprudence and other theoretical approaches to law. Rather than wondering whether to pursue a legal career, they are more likely to worry about passing the bar exam and finding a job with a high enough salary to allow them to repay their student loans.

Only a small minority of the graduates of these schools (usually 10 percent or less) tend to receive offers from one of the large, well-established firms. Others practice in different settings. Many work in a government department or a corporate in-house legal office. Others join a small firm representing individual clients and small businesses or specializing in a particular type of practice, such as representing persons accused of a crime or injured at work or in an automobile accident. Still others end up practicing alone, perhaps in a small community, writing wills, drafting contracts, working on tax matters, and helping to resolve a variety of legal problems involving local residents and small businesses.

A disturbing number of graduates from these lower-tier schools will not find any legal job at all. According to the Bureau of Labor Statistics, there were roughly 275,000 job openings for lawyers from 2000 to 2010.[4] During this period, however, 400,000 students graduated from law school. In the class of 2009, of the 42,854 graduates, only 28,167 had secured a legal job within nine months.[5] While 2009 was a particularly bad year for the economy, projections for the next five years predict a continuing glut of lawyers even after economic conditions improve.[6]

Law schools have not responded effectively to this problem, at least not yet. Although they are fiercely competitive, the competition has not resulted in lower costs but has led instead to an expensive struggle to attain a loftier position in the U.S. News & World Report rankings.* As has been true of so many

---

*In many cases, schools have resorted to shameful tactics to improve their ranking, such as inflating the job placement records of their recent graduates, artificially lowering their faculty-student ratios, and manipulating their admissions policies to boost the test scores of their entering class. In order to improve their faculty-student ratios, some schools have required their professors to take their sabbaticals in the spring, since ratios depend on the number of faculty in residence at the beginning of the academic year. To increase the average test scores of their entering class, schools have shrunk the size of their first-year enrollment and made up the loss of tuitions by

colleges, the effect has been to intensify the competition to hire well-published professors and to attract outstanding students in order to raise the average test scores of the entering class. As a result, the rankings competition has inflated faculty salaries, increased tuitions unnecessarily, and massively shifted financial aid from need-based grants to merit scholarships.

Despite the problems caused by the struggle for prestige, the prospects for abandoning this wasteful competition are slim. Publishers will not stop issuing rankings, despite their obvious flaws, since they are commercially very profitable. Few, if any, law schools can stop paying attention to their standing, since a drop in the pecking order often leads to fewer applicants, lower test scores, and concerns on the part of alumni. More than one dean has had to resign following a fall in the rankings. Meanwhile, schools on lower rungs of the ladder find themselves in an unsustainable position, with many of their graduates unable to find legal jobs and many more forced to take positions at salaries too low to allow them to repay their educational loans.

WHAT TO TEACH

Regardless of its place in the hierarchy, virtually every law school requires its first-year students to take a series of basic courses such as civil procedure, contracts, property, and criminal law. In the second and third years, the curriculum is much less heavily prescribed, and catalogs bulge with electives devoted to all kinds of specialized subjects. On the whole, faculties have been quick to respond to emerging fields of law. Courses on environmental regulation began popping up soon after Earth Day began and the Clean Air Act became law. With increasing globalization, most faculties offer a variety of courses on aspects of international and comparative law. The growth of the Internet and other new forms of communication technology have already given rise to courses on the legal problems posed by these innovations. Name a significant controversial subject, be it immigration, health-care delivery, or women's rights, and you will find the legal rules and pertinent cases being taught in at least some law schools.

---

increasing the number of transfer students in the second and third years. Earlier efforts to raise test scores by requiring applicants with low scores to register as part-time students (and thus not be included in the computation of the averages) were halted only when *U.S. News* changed the method of counting students. To improve the job placement statistics for recent graduates, one highly ranked school actually hired a number of recent graduates temporarily at $10.00 per hour so it could count them as being employed in legal jobs. For more details, see Brian Z. Tamanaha, *Failing Law Schools* (2012), pp. 71–99. (The author of this study is a law school professor and erstwhile acting law dean.)

Notwithstanding its richness of content, the typical curriculum has been the subject of a number of complaints. Few of the criticisms are new. Most of them have existed for decades without being satisfactorily resolved.

MAINTAINING STUDENT INTEREST
THROUGHOUT THE THREE YEARS OF STUDY

In many ways, the first year of law school has been a great educational success. Students encountering legal materials for the first time have found themselves prodded in class to think carefully about an endless series of problems rather than simply having to remember and organize large quantities of information. A perennial difficulty for law faculties, however, has been to figure out how to build on this foundation by challenging students in new and different ways as they progress through the second and third years. Despite decades of effort to overcome this problem, the first year continues to be a hard act to follow. Although second- and third-year students have a wide variety of courses to choose from, few of them find that they are engaged by their classes to nearly the same extent as in their initial year of study.

As interest in coursework declines, the amount of time most students spend preparing for class drops by at least half from the first to the third year.*[7] One recent study found that over 40 percent of students who were about to graduate felt that "the third year of law school is largely superfluous."[8] Not surprisingly, then, what little evidence exists on the intellectual development of law students tends to confirm what graduates have long suspected—that improvement in their powers of legal reasoning slows markedly in the later stages of their law school training.[9]

In view of these problems, proposals have been made periodically to shorten the required period of study from three years to two.[10] Current accreditation requirements, however, stipulate that students must accumulate the equivalent of three years of course credit. Changing the rule to two years could drastically reduce the revenues of law schools at a time when many of them are struggling to make ends meet. Even so, now that tuitions have risen to sky-high levels and many students are graduating with very large debts, support for such a reform seems to be growing.

---

* There is no invariable tendency for students to study less as they progress through their course of study. For example, college seniors apparently study slightly *more* than college freshmen. Philip S. Babcock and Mindy Marks, *The Falling Time Cost of College: Evidence from Half a Century of Time Use Data*, National Bureau of Economic Research, Working Paper No. 15954 (2010), p. 7.

Whether or not a two-year law school becomes a reality, there are other possibilities worth considering to make the third year more useful. One alternative would be to improve and increase the opportunities for students to represent real clients under the supervision of experienced lawyer-teachers in order to develop their practice skills. Another would be to draw upon the teaching resources of business schools and public policy and public administration faculties to provide a better preparation for law students interested in a corporate position or a career in government or politics. Still another alternative would be to create concentrations in different legal specialties, such as litigation, antitrust, or securities law, for those who have already decided on the type of law they intend to practice.* These possibilities are not mutually exclusive. Together, they provide a variety of ways to sustain students' interest and give them a more useful training during their final year of law school. The appropriate mix would presumably vary in accordance with the types of legal careers that students in each school were most likely to pursue.

TEACHING LEGAL SKILLS

At one time, law schools were criticized for concentrating too much on the analysis of appellate cases and the reasoning of judges while neglecting other legal institutions, such as trial courts and administrative agencies, and alternative ways of settling disputes, such as mediation, arbitration, and negotiation. By now, law schools have succeeded in introducing these previously neglected subjects into the curriculum. However, faculties have been slower to give adequate attention to the full range of skills students require to become effective practitioners.

For many decades, law teachers concentrated chiefly on developing the ability to use inductive, deductive, and analogic reasoning to resolve legal disputes. Students were given occasional opportunities to practice other competencies, such as writing moot court briefs or arguing a mock trial before a judge, but these and other lawyering skills were mainly left for students to learn from experienced colleagues once they graduated and began to practice. While leaders of the bar often grumbled, this system seemed to work well enough, at least for

---

*As competition intensifies among law firms and other providers of legal services, specialization among lawyers is likely to increase. Persuading law students in their first two years to decide on a preferred specialty, however, will be difficult, especially for law schools with many students who are uncertain on entry about what they hope to do with their legal education. It may well be, therefore, that law faculties will need to do more at an early stage in law school to acquaint students with the various career possibilities and the advantages and disadvantages of each.

those who began their legal career in a law firm or enjoyed some other form of close association with seasoned practitioners.

In recent decades, however, law firms have become much larger and more businesslike.[11] Many corporate clients now refuse to pay for work done by untrained young attorneys. In this environment, partners are less willing to hire recent graduates who do not know how to file a complaint, draft a will, or take a deposition. Consequently, pressure has mounted to have law schools assume more of this responsibility.[12]

By good fortune, these growing demands did not catch law faculties wholly unprepared. Most schools had long included extracurricular programs in which interested students could represent clients who lacked the means to pay a practicing attorney. Under pressure from socially conscious students in the late 1960s, these activities were enlarged. Many of them began to receive academic credit, and experienced attorneys were hired to help supervise the students.[13] Over time, more programs of this kind were added, creating opportunities to work in a wider variety of legal settings. Before long, law students were helping to represent poor tenants facing eviction, defendants in criminal misdemeanor cases, immigrants threatened with deportation, couples seeking mediation in divorce cases, and clients needing a variety of other legal services.

At the same time, law schools began to develop ways apart from the legal clinic to teach lawyerly skills. Students developed their litigation capabilities through various kinds of simulation exercises. Instructors started to use role-playing to help students learn how to negotiate. Law schools beefed up their legal writing courses in which students had to prepare a series of legal documents carefully critiqued by the instructor.

Methods of these kinds have unquestionably helped to impart a broader range of competencies. Even so, few law schools have succeeded in preparing their students well in all of the fundamental skills they need to practice effectively.* Most courses are still chiefly concerned with substantive law. As a result, law firms continue to complain that many of the graduates they hire

---

*Some writers suggest that practical skills are better left to be learned in practice. See, e.g., Thomas D. Morgan, *The Vanishing American Lawyer* (2010), pp. 2002–3. Yet even though some young lawyers receive excellent mentoring in practice, relying on senior practitioners to shoulder the entire burden of teaching lawyerly skills is too unreliable and hit-or-miss to serve the purpose adequately. Were this not so, leaders of the bar and sitting judges would not continue to complain about the basic deficiencies of many attorneys. On balance, therefore, while lawyers, like all professionals, will continue to develop their skills as they gain more experience, the wisest course is to have the law schools give their students a solid foundation of practical competencies on which to build after they graduate. The nature of these skills and the relative emphasis they receive in law school should presumably vary according to the kinds of legal careers that most students in each school tend to pursue.

are insufficiently trained in such practical matters as drafting legal documents, interviewing witnesses, arguing before a judge or jury, and counseling clients.[14]

ETHICS AND PROFESSIONAL RESPONSIBILITY

The last major criticism of law school curricula has been that faculties are not doing enough to nurture professional responsibility and proper ethical standards.[15] In recent decades, the reputation of lawyers for integrity has fallen further in the eyes of the public, and the amount of pro bono (public service) work supplied by leading law firms has declined even as their incomes have risen.[16] Prompted by these trends, the American Bar Association revised its standards for entry to the bar in 1996 to insist that every student take at least one course on legal ethics and professional responsibility.[17] Although law schools have complied with this requirement and some individual professors have created excellent courses, the results have fallen short of expectations. In many schools, students seem to regard the obligatory course as a "feel-good" requirement that diverts them from the real work of preparing to be a lawyer.[18]

Faculty members have encountered several difficulties in trying to teach ethics. Confusion has arisen over whether to offer courses that simply teach the Bar Association's rules of professional responsibility, or whether courses should concentrate on teaching students to apply general ethical principles to problems of the kind lawyers frequently encounter in their practice. Regardless of how the subject is taught, a single course is likely to have little effect unless it is reinforced in other classes by discussions of ethical problems arising in the various fields of law covered in the curriculum. Progress on this front has been spotty at best. Notwithstanding periodic pleas to integrate the study of ethics into the entire curriculum, the overall response has been disappointing. Many professors either feel unqualified to deal with such issues, or they believe they have enough trouble covering the essential material in their courses without wandering further afield in discussions of ethics and professional responsibility.

The lack of ethical discussion in the rest of the curriculum not only fails to reinforce the basic course; it conveys an implicit message to students that the subject itself is not considered important by most members of the faculty.* Not surprisingly, then, studies of the effects of law school on students have gener-

---

*A former dean of the Yale Law School, Anthony Kronman, has made the further point that the two most prominent theoretical approaches to law in the past thirty years—critical legal studies and law and economics—both make assumptions about lawyers' behavior that tend to undermine ideals of ethically minded practitioners. For this among other reasons, he concluded, "the collapse of the lawyer-statesman ideal, which shaped the American legal profession for so long, is now in

ally found no improvement in ethical values.[19] Even more troubling are studies concluding that despite the courses on professional responsibility and the wide variety of clinical programs to represent the poor and underprivileged, students tend to leave law school with more cynicism about the law and less commitment to public service than they had when they entered.[20]

HOW TO TEACH

Turning from subject matter to teaching methods, law schools can boast of one towering pedagogical achievement. Among the major professional schools, they were the first to discard the traditional lecture for a more active form of learning. Instead of trying to have students master an ever-larger and more unwieldy mass of substantive and procedural rules, Harvard's law dean Christopher Columbus Langdell had the insight to recognize in the 1870s that law schools should simply teach their students how to look up the rules and applicable precedents for themselves. Professors could then use their classes to help students develop the capacity for legal reasoning by questioning them in detail about how the appellate court opinions they read might apply to new factual situations, what arguments lawyers could make on either side of the case, and how a judge would be likely to decide. Using this "Socratic" method to analyze judicial opinions turned out to be a stunning success. Before long, it had become the dominant method for teaching law, a distinction it enjoys to this day.

Apart from helping students "to think like lawyers," the Socratic method of teaching had one other consequence, perhaps unanticipated by its creators. Preparing for a discussion proved to be harder than planning a lecture. The instructor was less in control of what happened in class, and more likely to encounter unexpected comments and unplanned deviations from the intended course of the conversation. At the same time, the experience of teaching a bad class was more unpleasant than it was in the lecture halls of the college. If professors were stymied by an unanticipated answer, they lost face in the eyes of their students. If their questions failed to arouse the interest of the class and

---

full retreat. It is losing its hold on lawyers everywhere." *The Lost Lawyer: Failing Ideals of the Legal Profession* (1993), p. 354.

It is not entirely clear, however, whether the lawyer-statesman ideal was ever widely realized in law practice. If it was, factors other than law school theorizing were probably more responsible for its demise, such as the growing preoccupation in law firms with the earnings of partners and the decline of long-term relationships between senior partners and chief executives of corporate clients. See, e.g., Russell G. Pearce, "Lawyers as America's Governing Class: The Formation and Dissolution of the Original Understanding of the American Lawyer's Role," 8 *Roundtable* 381 (2001).

provoke a lively spontaneous discussion, the effect was much like giving a life-less cocktail party. Rather than risk such a disagreeable experience, law teachers tended to prepare more carefully for each class than college instructors delivering their customary lectures year after year.*

By asking questions instead of giving answers, professors forced many students to think much more carefully and precisely than they had previously done during college. For those accustomed to memorizing college lecture notes and assigned texts, the classroom discussions were a formidable challenge. The process was arduous and could even be unpleasant when professors resorted to ridicule or disdain to emphasize flaws in a student's reasoning. Yet most aspiring lawyers emerged feeling much as many ex-marines feel about their weeks in boot camp—hardly a happy experience but one that helped them to think more clearly and contributed greatly to their subsequent careers whether within or outside the legal profession.

Much has changed in the typical law school classroom since the days made famous by the fictional Professor Kingsfield who humbled and ridiculed his students in the television series *The Paper Chase*. The harsher forms of Socratic teaching have largely disappeared as students have become more willing to push back and the drawbacks of such methods have been more widely understood. Professors seldom hector their students or make fun of them in class. Grading systems have become less precise and class rankings deemphasized. In one survey of recent law school graduates, 64 percent considered the classroom atmosphere "supportive" or "hospitable" while only 8 percent considered it "hostile" or "inhospitable."[21]

While the Socratic method continues to have great virtues, it has not been an unalloyed success. For one thing, its constant use in class after class grows tedious and contributes to the flagging interest of students in the second and third years. Aware of this problem, many law professors have varied the routine by using other methods of instruction. Some teachers offer computer exercises to supplement class discussions. Others use simulations and role-playing, especially in second- and third-year courses. More textbooks are going beyond the analysis of appellate opinions to focus on legal problems that require students to consider not just the facts of a case and the applicable rules and precedents, but the larger human or business context in which the legal issues have arisen.

---

*It is interesting to speculate whether the appreciation of the first-year experience will continue if colleges change their methods of instruction and become more successful in teaching critical thinking by making greater use of active learning and problem solving. It is possible that the success of the first year of law school owes more to the overuse of lecturing in college and the consequent novelty and challenge of the Socratic technique than to any special interest engendered by the law itself.

Class discussions are then used not only to determine how judges might respond to a lawsuit, but to consider ways in which a wise counselor can help clients achieve their aims without running the risk of incurring legal sanctions or the expense of having to go to court.

Despite these promising developments, the process of change in the way traditional courses are taught has hardly been swift or comprehensive. While some professors have introduced new and promising teaching methods, many others have reacted to student boredom in the last two years of law school by resorting increasingly to lecturing, a response that seems more of a regression than an improvement. Together, Socratic discussion and lecturing continue to be the most common forms of teaching throughout all three years, thus contributing to the nagging problem of increasing apathy, especially in the third year.

The successes of the discussion method have also made it easier for law faculties to overlook its pedagogic deficiencies. The growing interest in cognitive science and its application to teaching and learning has exposed several weaknesses and given added legitimacy to several long-standing student complaints. As practiced by most law schools, classroom teaching motivates students less by instilling a love of law and a curiosity about its complexities than by creating anxiety—a fear that they might be called upon in class and that they might flunk out or fail to do well enough academically to land a job with an adequate salary.[22] Although research has found that students learn more effectively when they have a reasonable level of confidence, law teaching often undermines self-esteem, especially during the crucial first year.[23]

Other law school teaching practices also inhibit learning and increase student insecurity. In particular, students receive remarkably little feedback to let them know how they are progressing and where they most need to improve. In many courses, students submit no papers and take no tests until the final exam. The only information they get about the quality of their work comes weeks after the end of the course when their grades arrive in the mail unaccompanied by any explanation of why they did not do better.[24] This practice does not result from laziness on the part of the faculty. Unlike many of their colleagues in other parts of the university, law professors continue to read their own examination papers even in large classes, a process that can take several weeks per year of extremely tedious work. After all this effort, however, they have little inclination to spend additional time offering comments on examination papers, grading periodic quizzes, or taking other opportunities to let students know how they are progressing. Often, students do not even have their examinations returned. The marks they receive do not tell them much about the levels of competence they have achieved but merely indicate how they compare with their classmates.* All in all, the entire time-consuming grading system seems to be devised, not for the benefit of students, but to help prospective employers assess the relative abilities of potential recruits.

In addition to the frequent lack of feedback, law school teaching tends to ignore other principles associated with effective learning.[25] Many first-year instructors do not take enough time at the beginning of the course to explain why they are using the Socratic method and what they hope will be achieved thereby. Nor do most law faculties do enough to teach students to work collaboratively on papers and projects, even though the practice of law often requires practitioners to work effectively in teams.

Some schools do not even give much individual help to those who encounter difficulty learning "to think like a lawyer."[26] In every law school class, there are some students who "don't get it." Despite all the class discussions of individual cases, they continue to have problems spotting legal issues in a body of facts or figuring out whether legal rules do or do not apply to different factual situations. Law schools have made some progress in helping such students by introducing courses on lawyering and legal writing that provide more individual attention than the typical class.[27] But these courses, helpful as they are, may not deal with all the facets of legal reasoning. Even in those that do, instructors often find that helping students learn to think more rigorously is a formidable task and that some students are extremely hard to reach.[28]

In some respects, law schools have fallen behind other faculties in taking steps to improve the quality of pedagogy and enhance student learning. They have failed even to do as much as faculties of arts and sciences to prepare new professors for their responsibilities as teachers and educators. Lacking such preparation, beginning instructors tend to pattern their teaching after the most successful professors they remember from their own student days. This is hardly a recipe for innovation. It is difficult to believe that law professors would have continued for so long giving so little feedback to their students and ignoring other principles of effective teaching had they received some prior exposure to the growing corpus of writing and empirical research on how students learn and how they can be helped to learn more.

Law schools have also tended to lag behind other faculties in the university in attempting to measure the extent to which their students are acquiring the knowledge or the competencies they need to perform effectively as lawyers.[29]

---

*Some law school innovations have improved on this situation. For example, clinical programs allow students to work under supervision from experienced attorneys who can comment on their work. Legal writing courses often require frequent papers that are returned with the instructor's comments. Computer exercises also provide immediate feedback for certain kinds of legal material.

Of course, professors know how well their students have done on the final exam, but they have no way of telling how much the performance owes to the course itself and how much merely reflects abilities students possessed when they began.[30] They may be aware of how students rank academically in relation to the rest of the class, but know much less about how much the class as a whole has learned, or how much progress individual students have made, or in what respects and for what categories of students the educational program is falling short. As a result, neither the faculty nor its individual members may have the information to know where improvements in teaching are needed or whether new methods of instruction are succeeding.

In many schools, the most active locus of innovative teaching has been in the clinical programs. It is here that one is most likely to find the frequent use of role-playing, simulations, films, and collaborative learning to supplement classroom discussions. Here is where one sometimes encounters a special course on teaching for new instructors. It is also from the clinical faculty and teachers of legal writing that articles are appearing, usually in lesser-known law reviews, discussing cognitive theory and research on student learning and their potential application to law teaching.[31] Yet even though these initiatives are intriguing and potentially fruitful, clinical courses occupy a minor part of most students' program, and the innovative teaching methods one finds there are not uniformly used even by other clinical instructors. As a result, such contributions seldom suffice to make up for the deficiencies found in many of the traditional offerings.

The shortcomings just described call to mind the old adage "Nothing fails like success." The very triumphs of the Socratic method in fostering reasoning skills and engaging first-year students may have contributed to the lack of attention paid to other ways to foster effective teaching and learning. Because Socratic teaching requires conscientious preparation, and because law schools have long placed considerable weight on classroom skill in making appointments and promotions, faculty members may have assumed too readily that the quality of instruction was not a problem they needed to address.

THE ROAD AHEAD

The most serious problem facing law schools today is not primarily a matter of educational quality, nor is it one that law schools can solve by themselves. The crux of their predicament is that they are currently graduating far more students per year than the annual number of new legal jobs that are projected to materialize through 2018 as a result of retirements and new openings. Granted, not all of their graduates will wish to practice law. But enough of them will, based on past experience, to leave many of them unable to find a legal position even after the current recession ends, let alone a job with a high enough salary to allow them to repay their educational loans.

Some law deans dispute these projections and insist that the market for lawyers will improve, as it has following past recessions. If the deans are wrong, however, as most analysts predict, something will have to be done to remove the glut of lawyers.* Either college seniors will eventually respond to the dismal job market by abandoning their plans to enter law school, or the federal government, concerned by the numbers of law graduates who default on their student debts, will restrict the amount of guaranteed loans that law students can borrow, thus making it difficult, if not impossible, for many young people to finance a legal education. In either case, students with limited resources are the most likely to feel compelled to abandon their plans to earn a law degree, while many law schools below the first or second tier will be hard-pressed to enroll enough students to balance their budgets.

As matters now stand, the law schools that are at serious risk from the overproduction of lawyers have no easy means to protect themselves. They can institute a hiring freeze, increase teaching loads, and halt their expensive quest for higher rankings, but accreditation requirements will limit what they can do, and accreditation is a necessity since graduation from an approved school is required in forty-five states in order to practice law. According to the standards currently in force, every school must satisfy a number of conditions that drive up costs, such as requiring the equivalent of three years of study, maintaining a suitably low faculty-student ratio, providing a library of a sufficient size and quality, and limiting the use of part-time, adjunct (and lower paid) instructors.[32]

The federal government could try to help by offering debt relief for law graduates who cannot find well-paid jobs, and Washington has already taken steps in that direction. Nevertheless, such measures merely shift the financial burden to taxpayers while doing nothing to curb tuitions or to deter students from

---

*Several analysts have concluded that job openings in the legal profession began to slow before the current recession and are likely to continue at a lower level once normal economic conditions return. They attribute this trend to a major restructuring of the profession brought about by increased efforts by institutional clients to obtain legal services more cheaply either by forcing firms to compete for individual pieces of work or by assigning routine legal tasks to individuals in America and overseas who can perform the work more cheaply or by using technological methods that can replace lawyers entirely. See, e.g., William D. Henderson and Rachel M. Zahorsky, "Law Job Stagnation May Have Started before the Recession—and It May Be a Sign of Lasting Change," 97 *ABA Journal* (2011), p. 40; Bernard A. Burk and David McGowan, "Big but Brittle: Economic Perspectives on the Future of the Law Firm in the New Economy," *Columbia Business Law, 2011* (2011), p. 1.

incurring excessive debts in the mistaken belief that they will somehow succeed in finding one of the coveted highly paid positions in large law firm.

If little else changes, the glut of lawyers may disappear only when many would-be attorneys begin to choose other careers, forcing a number of law schools to shut their doors. Already, law school applications nationwide have dropped from 100,000 at the turn of the century to an estimated 54,000 in 2012–13, and enrollments have fallen almost 20 percent. This is the way markets work to adjust supply to demand. In the case of the law, however, no genuine glut of legally trained professionals exists. On the contrary, there is a huge unmet demand for legal services among poor and middle-income clients who cannot afford to hire a lawyer to help them with routine problems involving such matters as domestic relations, tax disputes, and landlord-tenant questions.[33] Students could be trained more quickly to perform many of these services adequately for an affordable price. Yet these needs currently go unmet, at least in part, because anyone providing such assistance must have completed an education conforming to the costly model defined by present accreditation requirements.

The measures needed to restructure these rules go beyond even sanctioning a two-year law school and will be very difficult to achieve. Doing so would require major changes in the way legal services are provided and by whom—and there are plenty of vested interests that will stoutly resist such reforms. Washington has recently decided to let persons with limited training perform some simple legal tasks, but it is unclear how many states will follow suit.

Aside from this structural problem, the current state of legal education presents a mixed picture. The use of Socratic discussions to analyze legal opinions remains its greatest achievement even though Dean Langdell initiated his reform almost 150 years ago. While this technique still provides an excellent training in legal analysis, it does not give students all the skills they need to practice effectively. Fortunately, law schools have done a lot to broaden their programs, not just in subject matter but in the competencies taught and the methods of instruction employed. Nevertheless, much remains undone. There is still too little feedback to help students improve. The methods of teaching that professors use and the skills they try to cultivate are not sufficiently varied to prepare students fully for legal practice or to retain their interest once they emerge from the rigors of the first year. Finally, law schools have done no better than other professional schools in fostering a commitment to high standards of ethical and professional responsibility.

For many schools, clinical programs offer the best opportunity for remedying these shortcomings. They can lend variety to the experience of law students, improve their lawyering skills, and expose them to the unmet needs and other deficiencies in the provision of legal services. By so doing, they may also offer a partial answer to the stubborn problem of sustaining student interest through the second and third years. The opportunity to represent real clients and practice new skills could serve this purpose well, just as it has in medical schools. As yet, however, clinical courses have not acquired the status in most law schools to realize this potential, nor are they varied enough in the skills they teach to prepare students for all of the specialized careers they may seek to pursue.[34] Until they are expanded and fully integrated into the curriculum to become a significant part of the law school experience for all or at least a large majority of students, one can hardly expect them to carry the entire burden of giving the second and third years a clear sense of intellectual progression.

The principal impediment to achieving the full potential of clinical studies is the skepticism on the part of many members of the core faculty as to whether the training itself or those who provide it fully meet appropriate academic and intellectual standards. In this regard, law schools have not been as successful as their sister schools of medicine. Since many tenured professors have little or no experience in legal practice and often regard it with indifference or even disdain, the contributions of the clinical faculty can easily seem pedestrian. It is true, of course, that clinical instructors do not, on average, publish as much or boast as imposing an academic résumé as most regular law school professors. Yet they possess a body of practical experience and a capacity to impart certain practical skills that the rest of the faculty seem either unwilling or unable to supply. More than a few clinical professors have also manifested greater willingness to innovate and think creatively about the process of teaching and learning than most of their more traditional faculty colleagues. On balance, therefore, the potential of clinical programs and their faculty to enrich legal education seems to justify a larger role than they are currently given in most law schools.

In fairness, however, though the rest of law school teaching may be slow to change, it is hardly frozen in place. New subjects are constantly being introduced, new methods of instruction are being tried, and new questions are being raised throughout the law school world. Some schools are trying to prepare students better for corporate law practice by making greater use of guest teachers from practice, role-playing exercises, and problem-based instruction.[35] Other schools are beginning to restructure their third year to emphasize programs of study that prepare students for the career paths they are most likely to pursue. While the status of clinical programs still leaves much to be desired, it has gradually risen and may continue to do so.[36] In the fullness of time, therefore, legal education may yet succeed in offering a useful and engrossing experience in all three years while providing every student with the basic competencies that successful law practice requires.

It is less certain whether law professors will discover how to help their students acquire greater ethical judgment and a firmer commitment to furthering the ideals of their profession and the interests of society. On this score, they face the same challenge as professors of medicine and business. It would be unjust, however, simply to blame the faculty. Law professors could surely do more to integrate discussions of ethics into regular courses and experiment with more effective methods of instruction. But teaching ethics to students is one thing; giving them ideals and strengthening their character are much more difficult. Whether any professional school can accomplish such feats remains a very open question.

CHAPTER FOURTEEN

BUSINESS SCHOOLS

||||||||||||||||||||||||||||||||||||||||||||||||||||||||||||||||||||||||||||||||||||||||||||||||||||||

BUSINESS SCHOOLS EMERGED MORE recently than their counterparts in law and medicine.[1] The Wharton School, founded in 1881 at the University of Pennsylvania, is generally thought to be the first graduate program in business, although in its early years, it consisted largely of social science classes rather than courses on commerce or management. No other venture of this kind emerged until the end of the century. From 1898 to 1913, however, no fewer than twenty-five universities created business schools, including the Universities of California, Berkeley, Northwestern, Michigan, Harvard, and Chicago.

From the beginning, controversy arose over the aims of business schools and whether these goals could be achieved. Most university leaders explaining the decision to start a business school spoke of lofty objectives. According to Dean Edward Jones at the University of Michigan:

> If we lament the prominence of the desire for material acquisitions in our civilization, we may hope to form an effective counteracting force, if within the domain of industry itself we can stimulate an ambition on the part of industrial leaders to realize . . . newer and more social ideals.[2]

Nicholas Murray Butler, president of Columbia University, was even more effusive:

> There is coming to be a philosophy of business just as there has been a philosophy of theology, of law, of medicine and of teaching, and it is through the door of that philosophy, that understanding of fundamental principles and higher standards, that the University seeks to lead men and women to prepare themselves for the capable and competent pursuit of this form of intellectual activity and public service.[3]

Not everyone, however, was convinced that management could be a proper subject of study in a university. Faculty members at Columbia, Harvard, and other institutions were strongly opposed to the idea. Melvin Copeland, a professor at the Harvard Business School from 1909 to 1953, remarked that "by many professors and by numerous Harvard alumni, it was deemed to be degrading for the university to offer instruction in the venal subject of business management."[4] The noted commentator on higher education Abraham Flexner even doubted whether Harvard deserved to be called a university once it decided to create a business school.[5] Looking back, historian Frederick Lewis Allen recalled the skeptical voices heard in many intellectual circles: "Business a profession? What an innocent notion! Business was a rough-and-tumble battle between men whose first concern was to look out for number one, and the very idea of professors being able to prepare men for it was nonsense."[6]

In their early years, faculty members themselves had difficulty agreeing on an appropriate course of study. They seemed torn between the emphasis of academic leaders on high ideals and scholarly subjects and the practical need for technical competence urged upon them by corporate employers. According to the dean of Northwestern University's business school in 1928, "Anyone who goes to the catalog of American collegiate schools of business expecting to get a clearly defined concept or any substantial agreement with regard to objectives is doomed to disappointment."[7] The only courses that were required by a large majority of prominent schools were accounting, law, English (business correspondence), and elementary economics. The practical nature of these courses prompted a few deans to complain that business schools had lost sight of their early ideals. In the words of Joseph Willis, dean of the Wharton School, in 1934, "Have we not put too much emphasis on turning out business technicians alone, and paid too little attention to the development of businessmen with a sense of statesmanship—men who would also be good citizens?"[8]

During the first few decades of its existence, graduate study in business was hardly a magnet for students. As late as the academic year 1939–40, only 1,139 MBA degrees were awarded in the entire country, and this was the largest number achieved up to that time. The published work of business school professors was meager at best. Several schools created research "bureaus," but these were typically devoted primarily to collecting information and statistics or performing contract research for corporations. Rigorous scholarship, such as the work of Edmund Learned or the well-known studies of the "Hawthorne Effect" by Elton Mayo and Fritz Roethlisberger, though highly influential, were decidedly exceptions to the rule.[9]

The Second World War marked a turning point in the history of business schools. The reputation of large corporations, badly tarnished by the Great Depression, rebounded following their impressive contributions to the war effort. Business leaders acquired a new importance as the United States found itself in competition with the Soviet Union economically as well as militarily and diplomatically. With a boost from the GI Bill, enrollments in business schools began a steady climb that continued for many decades.

The postwar period also brought a new source of support for business education. The Ford and Carnegie Foundations developed a keen interest in strengthening management education. To guide their grant making, each one launched a major study of American business schools authored by economists. In 1959, both reports were published—*Higher Education for Business* by Robert Gordon and James Howell for the Ford Foundation and Frank Pierson's *The Education of American Businessmen* for Carnegie.[10]

Each of the reports was highly critical of the quality of education and research at the nation's business schools, describing the prevailing standards as "embarrassingly low."[11] Both reports proposed similar remedies. They called for a larger research effort and a more rigorous curriculum rooted in a science of management based on quantitative methods and rigorous social science. To achieve these goals, the reports urged business schools to build strong doctoral programs that would prepare faculty members firmly grounded in the knowledge and skills required for first-rate teaching and research. The Ford Foundation, in particular, followed up its report by making substantial grants to a number of leading schools.

Unlike the celebrated Flexner report on medical education issued a half century earlier, the Ford and Carnegie reports did not succeed in bringing about the rapid disappearance of weak schools. Many unaccredited business programs continued, and many more exist to this day, either as schools to train students for lower-level management positions or, much worse, as little more than diploma mills. Business, unlike law and medicine, has not been able to establish educational requirements for entry into the ranks of management, a fact that has led some critics to question whether management can truly be called a profession. Nor could the organization representing business schools, the Association to Advance Collegiate Schools of Business (AACSB), succeed in enforcing minimum standards through accreditation.

The Ford and Carnegie reports did have a dramatic effect on the fifty to one hundred business schools that included the elite faculties, at universities such as Stanford, Pennsylvania, Chicago, and Northwestern, as well as a number of regional institutions that aspired to elite status. Almost all of these schools are accredited, and almost all are ranked each year by publications such as *Business Week*. They are the programs to which most commentators refer when they write about business schools and the education they provide.

The leading schools eagerly embraced the recommendations of the Ford and Carnegie reports and immediately set about to strengthen the quality of their faculties. Unable to find enough qualified graduates from their own doctoral programs, they began hiring recent PhDs from highly regarded social science departments. By the 1980s, PhDs made up roughly 80 percent of the faculties in major schools of business. Before long, most of these schools had succeeded in building much more rigorous programs of research that produced an impressive output of articles appearing in top academic journals.

For two decades, the new version of business education proved remarkably successful. Student enrollments surged. From 1956 to 1980, the number of MBA degrees awarded annually grew from 3,200 to more than 55,000.[12] Midcareer programs for corporate executives, which had led a modest and precarious existence for many years, expanded in numbers and enrollments. Supporting this growth were generous gifts from well-to-do alumni. More and more schools began to carry the name of some beneficent captain of industry in return for a large capital donation. The buildings and facilities of the leading schools often achieved a quality rivaling anything to be found elsewhere on the campus.

These achievements soon attracted the attention of foreign observers. In the 1960s, Jean-Jacques Servan-Schrieber wrote a best-selling book, *The American Challenge*, which attributed the success of American business to the quality of managers trained in leading business schools.[13] Soon, similar institutions began to appear throughout Western Europe. If emulation is the sincerest form of flattery, our business schools could revel in the emergence of programs in many nations that patterned themselves after the American model.

Despite these successes, storm clouds started to gather in the late 1970s, as American business encountered stiffer competition in global markets and the US economy suffered from stagflation and surging oil prices engineered by OPEC, the cartel created by oil-producing countries. The changing mood was exemplified by a widely read article written by two business school professors, Robert Hayes and William Abernathy, entitled "Managing Our Way to Economic Decline."[14] Hayes and Abernathy pointed to America's loss of economic competitiveness and criticized companies for emphasizing the kind of detached, analytic decision making taught in business schools rather than insights drawn from hands-on management experience, and for encouraging short-run cost reductions rather than the investments in technology needed for long-term growth. These criticisms were echoed in popular books, such as Thomas Peters and Robert Waterman's *In Search of Excellence: Lessons from America's Best-Run Companies*.[15]

Although American business rallied to become more competitive in international markets, the problems of the 1980s were followed by a series of highly publicized scandals and exposés that shook the public's confidence in corporate leadership. The dealings of financiers such as Ivan Boesky and Michael Milken in the late 1980s gave way to executive misdeeds leading to the bankruptcy of companies such as Enron and WorldCom at the turn of the century, and then to the high-risk behavior of investment banks and other financial institutions that contributed to the major recession of 2008.

Since a number of the corporate leaders involved in these misfortunes have been graduates of leading business schools, attacks on companies have been accompanied by a flurry of complaints directed at management education. Journalists, corporate leaders, and even business school professors have joined in the condemnation. No aspect of business education has gone unscathed. Critics have attacked the subject matter being taught, the methods of instruction used, and the theories of management and business behavior on which much of the teaching is based.

WHAT BUSINESS SCHOOLS TEACH

In the years since the Ford and Carnegie reports appeared, leading business schools have arrived at a fairly clear consensus on the list of basic courses that their students ought to take.[16] The core consists of eight subjects: financial accounting, finance, microeconomics, strategy, organizational behavior, operations, marketing, and decision science or statistics. These courses are either required or strongly recommended and taken by large majorities of students, mainly during the first year. The second year is a different story. It typically allows students to choose from a large number of courses, most of them elective, usually discipline-based, and often closely related to the research interests of the instructor. It is generally agreed that the second year is much less coherent than the first. Students tend to be less engaged by classwork. If they are not already employed, they are preoccupied with finding a good job and spend much of their time interviewing with recruiters and flying around the country to visit prospective employers.[17]

Whatever one may think of management education, one cannot say that the curriculum is out of date. A brief look at business school catalogs suggests that faculties have been quick to take up emerging problems in the corporate sector. Offerings on international business abound, as do classes on entrepreneurship. Not all new courses, of course, have equal standing. It is one thing to win a place in the curriculum and another to gain the respect of faculty and students as one of the "important" subjects being taught.[18]

The content of business education is currently undergoing intense ferment and introspection occasioned in large part by the concerns expressed by members of the business community. Some of the criticisms have to do with the capacity of MBAs to make sound business decisions.[19] Executives complain that business school graduates are deficient in their ability to think clearly and practically, their capacity to adapt to different cultures and values, their grasp of political and regulatory forces, and their sensitivity to moral issues confronting companies. Corporate leaders also question the ability of MBAs to implement decisions effectively or to appreciate the practical realities of the workplace. Business school graduates have been criticized for lacking leadership qualities, human relations skills, a capacity for effective collaboration, and even an ability to communicate clearly and persuasively.

This is a formidable bill of particulars. But business schools are now encountering an even more troublesome skepticism. Despite their rapid growth, their handsome facilities, and the scholarly distinction enjoyed by many members of their faculty, some corporate executives are beginning to question whether management education in its current form has enough practical value to justify two years of study.

At first glance, such doubts seem far-fetched. After all, more than 95 percent of graduating business school students say that they would "recommend graduate business school to someone else."[20] One survey (twenty-five years ago) found that 81 percent of corporate CEOs rated business schools as either "excellent," or at least "pretty good."[21] Even more telling is the popularity of executive courses for midcareer managers. Why would corporations continue sending their executives to these expensive programs if they did not feel that management faculties had useful knowledge to convey?

In response, skeptics have persuasive arguments of their own. Many of the most successful CEOs of large corporations, such as Bill Gates and Jack Welch, did not go to business school at all. Although enrollments have boomed in past decades and graduates seem to think well of their experience, these favorable signs may have little to do with the quality of a business education. Rather, the mere fact of being admitted to a leading school and the contacts one can easily make there could be what helps students to get good jobs and move ahead thereafter. Similarly, corporate recruiters may value business schools not so much for the knowledge they convey as for the role they play in collecting smart, ambitious candidates for companies to interview and hire. How else to explain why companies are increasingly making job offers to first-year students without waiting to find how well they have performed in their classes?

Even consulting firms, whose work seems ideally suited to the kind of detached analysis featured in business schools, regularly employ large numbers of bright students from other professional schools, such as law, public policy, or even medicine. Investment companies, private equity firms, and other financial institutions do the same. These students do not appear to suffer from their lack of management training. At the McKinsey consulting firm, although new hires without an MBA receive only a brief orientation course before they start to work with clients, those who stay with the company seem to perform just as well as their colleagues holding business degrees.[22]

Arguments over the value of business school training are far from being resolved, and the effects on business school enrollments are consequently uncertain. But there are definitely reasons to be concerned. The strong in-house training programs developed by many large companies provide an alternative to business schools that executives of these firms may consider preferable. Apparently, some financial organizations (along with some consulting firms) are no longer encouraging their recent college graduates to take two years' leave to earn a MBA, believing that able young recruits hired fresh out of college can develop as well or better by continuing to work in the company.[23] Since 40–60 percent of the recent graduates of leading business schools have sought employment in finance or consulting (at least prior to the recession of 2007–8), such a reaction represents a genuine threat to management programs.

Business schools are not about to give up or close down as a result of these nagging doubts about the value of their product.* Nor are they the only professional schools to encounter questions of this kind. While no one would dream of being operated on by someone without medical school training or think of completing a corporate merger without the help of a law school graduate, schoolteachers often perform quite well without attending an education school, and graduates of public policy programs remain the exception rather than the rule among high government officials. The useful role of business schools in attracting and ranking talented young people interested in management careers makes them valuable to recruiters and applicants alike regardless of what they teach. Still, the doubts expressed about the value of an MBA and the complaints now being voiced by corporate leaders have caused consternation among business school deans—and rightly so.

Ironically, the current problems of management education are in no small part unintended consequences of the Ford and Carnegie reports and the reforms these foundations helped to initiate. The efforts of business schools (enthusiastically supported by the two foundations) to increase the rigor of their research by hiring social science PhDs have placed the faculty in an unusual relationship with the profession they are meant to serve. In striking contrast to

---

* Already, however, enrollments in two-year MBA programs have declined in many schools outside of the top fifteen or twenty, while shorter programs, such as one-year MBAs and executive courses that allow students to continue their day jobs while taking courses at night or on weekends, seem to be gaining in popularity.

their counterparts in law and medicine, most professors of management have little or no training or practical experience in the calling they are supposed to teach.

In medical schools, basic scientists may never have cared for the sick, but they are seldom asked to teach about diagnosing and treating illness. That task is left to a huge clinical faculty composed of experienced physicians who are based in hospitals and actively engaged in patient care. Law school faculties do not have the depth of hands-on experience possessed by clinical professors of medicine, but they typically include a small clinical staff of seasoned practitioners. Moreover, almost all of their professors have at least graduated from law school. Most have served as clerks to judges, and many have spent a few years in practice.

In contrast, among the leading business schools, with the exception of a few former top executives hired as distinguished lecturers, most professors are PhDs with no training in how to run a company. Their study of management typically begins only after they join the faculty and start preparing to teach. Thereafter, they may acquire practical knowledge through consulting with companies or, perhaps, by conducting empirical studies of corporations and their leaders. In many cases, however, their research has little to do with the day-to-day work of management but focuses instead on theoretical problems or the analysis of large aggregates of data. The articles they publish are often aimed primarily at academics like themselves rather than corporate executives. Not surprisingly, many managers find these writings to have little practical relevance.

The academic background of business school professors and their lack of management experience also affect what they emphasize in the classroom. Despite the wide array of courses being offered, the subjects most frequently required by leading business schools are virtually all devoted to material that lends itself to rigorous, often quantitative analysis. Softer skills, such as human resource management, leadership, or negotiation, important as they are to managers, are typically required by only a third or less of the leading schools.[24] What students learn is heavy on the side of theory, analysis, and decision making and light on how to implement decisions and make them work.[25] It is only natural, then, that so many graduates of leading business schools take their first jobs in finance or consulting—sectors where analysis is central and implementation much less so. This is not to say that MBAs never end up occupying high management positions in manufacturing or retail companies. Yet when they do, their success usually owes more to natural aptitude and the experience they gained after graduation than to what they learned in business school.

The problems of the curriculum lie even deeper, however, and again, the difficulty has its roots in the Ford and Carnegie reports. The emphasis on social science research led to a growing influence of economics, widely regarded as the most successful of the disciplines in creating a value-free and rigorous "science" within its field of study. While some influential economists were still producing descriptive analyses of institutions at the time the Ford and Carnegie reports were written, work of this kind lost status thereafter and increasingly gave way to theoretical research and model building of a highly abstract and sophisticated kind.

Out of this work came essays on subjects such as the efficient markets hypothesis and agency theory, ideas that held great attractions for business school professors since they seemed to provide clear and plausible answers to important questions affecting corporations. According to these theories, corporations were in essence a network of contractual relationships.[26] One of the most important relationships was that of the shareholders (the principals) with the chief executive (their agent). In keeping with much mainstream economic theory, chief executives were assumed to be rational, self-serving individuals whose interests did not necessarily coincide with those of their principals, the shareholders. Left to their own devices, CEOs might pay too much attention to their outside interests or to the needs of workers and the surrounding community instead of concentrating on earning as large a profit as possible to satisfy the shareholders. The challenge for investors, then, was to create incentives powerful enough to keep the actions of the chief executive tightly aligned with their own profit-making objective.* That result, according to agency theorists, could best be achieved if CEOs were given large quantities of stock options so that their compensation would rise in direct proportion to the growth in the value of the stock.[27]

This line of reasoning proved appealing to corporate trustees and chief executives as well as to business school professors. Boards began giving lavish stock options to their CEOs that allowed top executives to earn many millions of dollars. Meanwhile, students learned to look upon "maximizing shareholder value" as the dominant goal for managers and to regard the use of stock options as the appropriate way to "incentivize" corporate leaders to exert their best efforts for the shareholders.†

---

*It is perhaps not entirely coincidental that academic economists favored this theory of the firm, since the models they build tend to work well only if one assumes a single objective for the firm rather than having it attend to the interests of several stakeholders.

†A recent survey by the Aspen Institute found that almost two-thirds of business school students selected, among ten alternatives, "maximize value for shareholders" as the primary responsibility of a company. Support for this objective tended to grow stronger as students progressed through the curriculum. Aspen Institute, *When Will They Lead? MBA Student Attitudes about Business and Society* (2008).

In retrospect, these theories overlooked much that should have been obvious. Offering huge incentives to achieve financial objectives gave chief executives a powerful temptation to cook the books, manipulate the compensation committee, or employ questionable strategies if legitimate business decisions failed to achieve the hoped-for results. All too often, stock options were structured to create the kinds of incentives that encouraged executives to overemphasize short-term gains or take imprudent risks of the kind that contributed to the financial crisis of 2007–8.[28]

The emphasis on maximizing shareholder value had another unanticipated effect on business education. It denied responsibility on the part of corporate leaders to take account of the interests of employees, local communities, and society as a whole unless doing so promised to further the interests of shareholders. These other constituencies were thought to be adequately protected by the play of market forces reinforced by appropriate laws and regulations without the need for special attention from the CEO.

This conception of the proper role of corporate executives raised troubling issues for business schools. How could a faculty that embraced such a theory pretend to be educating leaders of high moral principle and social responsibility, as many business school mission statements proclaimed? According to agency theory, top executives, far from being "corporate statesmen," were unreliable stewards of shareholder interests who had to be induced to behave properly by offering them huge financial rewards.*

The emphasis on agency theory also had a dampening effect on the teaching of ethics. The two fields are not necessarily incompatible. One can make a forceful argument that adhering to strong ethical standards will improve the bottom line, at least in most instances. Yet ethics has not had a prominent place in the writings of agency theorists, which can easily give the impression that moral considerations do not count for much. More generally, teachers of subjects such as ethics and corporate responsibility fit uneasily in a business school culture that emphasizes theories and skills of a more precise and seemingly rigorous nature using models and quantitative methods that appear to yield clear answers. By now, fewer than half of the top fifty schools even require students to take a course in ethics.[29] According to deans of schools that lack such

---

*In the words of a widely quoted statement by Stanford Business School professor Harold Leavitt, "The new, professional MBA-type manager began to look more and more like the professional mercenary soldier—ready and willing to fight any war and to do so coolly and systematically, but without ever asking the tough pathfinding questions: Is this war worth fighting? Is it the right war? Is the cause just? Do I believe in it?" Quoted in Rakesh Khurana, *From Higher Aims to Hired Hands: The Social Transformation of American Business Schools and the Unfulfilled Promise of Management as a Profession* (2007), p. 326.

a requirement, students complain that courses on ethics are "soft" and not as practical as other classes on subjects such as microeconomics and finance.*

ADDRESSING THE CRITICISMS

The discussion thus far suggests that business schools cannot satisfy their critics merely by adding new courses. Most of the skills in which MBAs are said to be deficient—leadership, moral reasoning, critical thinking, and the like—are already covered, at least as electives, in existing curricula. The solution, then, must involve not just *what* subjects are taught but *how* they are being taught.

Some of the specific weaknesses identified by corporate executives can be addressed fairly easily, at least in principle. With respect to critical thinking, for example, most business schools already devote a substantial number of classroom hours to considering "cases"—which in management education means elaborate descriptions of problems facing a company based on actual situations that corporations have experienced. At present, many business school professors use cases merely as examples to illustrate how economic analysis and other social science theories can be used to analyze a business problem. When skillfully taught through vigorous class discussion, however, cases provide ideal vehicles for teaching students to analyze problems rigorously and to develop skills of oral communication and persuasion.

Much is also known about how to teach students to write clearly and effectively and to identify ethical problems when they arise and reason about them carefully. The principal problem in developing these skills is not just to figure out how to teach them but to find capable professors willing to make the effort.

---

*The deemphasis of ethics seems unfortunate for several reasons. Surveys of college seniors intending to go to business school indicate that these students are much more interested in making money than the rest of their classmates, and are much more likely to acknowledge having cheated more than once or twice in college. Donald L. McCabe and Linda K. Trevino, "Cheating among Business Students: A Challenge for Business Leaders and Educators," 19 *Journal of Management Education* (1995), p. 205. According to one study, more than half of current MBA students admitted to cheating on exams while in business school. A. Hendershott, P. Drinan, and M. Cross, "Toward Enhancing a Culture of Academic Integrity, 37 *NASPA Journal* (2000), p. 589. See also Donald L. McCabe, K. D. Butterfield, and Linda Trevino, "Academic Dishonesty in Graduate Business Programs: Prevalence, Causes, and Proposed Action," 5 *Academy of Management Learning and Education* (2006), p. 294. While no one knows whether corporate executives or MBAs are less ethical than members of other professions, many people seem to think so. In one poll, only 47 percent of corporate employees considered their CEO a "person of high moral integrity." Henry Mintzberg, *Managers, Not MBAs: A Hard Look at the Soft Practice of Managing and Management Development* (2004), p. 144. Not surprisingly, then, prominent business school alumni, thoughtful CEOs, and the general public have long emphasized the need to teach ethics.

The economists, psychologists, and other PhDs who populate the faculty may not feel they were hired to teach writing, or moral reasoning, or even critical thinking. Their assignment, they believe, is to teach students how the knowledge and methods of their discipline can be used to understand business problems.

The simplest response to this dilemma would be to hire qualified instructors to teach these skills. Some schools have already chosen this approach to teach writing or critical thinking. The use of special instructors, however, may help to confirm the suspicion of many students that these courses are not truly important. Moreover, it is not possible to train students to speak and write well, or think critically, or analyze moral problems by simply having them take an introductory course any more than it is to teach someone to be a capable golfer or tennis player by merely having them take a set of beginner's lessons. In each case, lasting proficiency can be achieved only by repeated practice with ample feedback and opportunity for reflection.

The ideal solution, then, would be to have the entire faculty play an active part in developing the desired skills by providing opportunities in their courses to practice them. However, persuading professors to cooperate who have not been trained in this tradition can prove difficult. If they resist, the next-best solution would be to offer advanced classes in these subjects taught by specialists. The problem with that solution is that few students may choose to take such courses and instructors will feel isolated. Moreover, without participation from the rest of the faculty, it will be harder to convince students that such instruction is truly respected and considered important by the school. It may not even be possible to attract first-rate professors of writing or ethics to teach in such an environment.

Other needs identified by corporate executives pose quite different challenges. In the case of "intercultural competence," for example, there is currently no well-developed body of principles to suggest how corporate managers should operate in the other cultures in which they do business. Nevertheless, business schools have impressive resources to help them surmount this problem. Already, faculties have incorporated many international cases into their course materials, and several schools have established research centers in foreign countries to facilitate work on other markets and cultures. With more than a quarter of all professors in America's top fifty business schools having been born overseas, their faculties are well-equipped to generate useful insights into the effects of other cultures on business operations.[30] Since an average of one-third or more of the students in these schools come from other countries, it should also be easy to create diverse, collaborative study groups in which members can bring their different cultural perspectives to bear in discussing cases and problems with their classmates.[31]

Helping students to integrate the various disciplines and skills they learn in business school is likewise not an insurmountable problem. It is hardly sufficient to assume—as some business schools have done—that students can study several separate disciplines and then figure out by themselves how to knit them together to resolve "real-world" problems. Students need guidance in recognizing the limitations of individual disciplines and learning how to draw upon several modes of thought in analyzing business problems. Although there is no ready-made body of rules for thinking in this way, professors can devise cases for discussion and teach them alone or with colleagues in other fields to demonstrate how one can use different disciplines, along with common sense, to arrive at convincing solutions. In fact, some schools are already moving in this direction by supplementing cases with materials showing how economic models can be improved if one takes account of cognitive biases, mass psychology, and political analysis.

The recent history of executive compensation provides an excellent illustration of how other disciplines and scholarly traditions, such as ethics and the behavioral sciences, can supplement economic analysis to provide a more thoughtful view of how best to reward CEOs. Such exercises may not give students a single all-purpose method with which to combine different disciplines to solve a variety of problems. Yet class materials that provide opportunities to practice interdisciplinary thinking can at least convey an awareness that all disciplines have limitations and that effective leaders need to use a variety of methods to reach sound solutions to most of the important problems they encounter.

The remaining complaints about management training present greater challenges. Obviously, it would be valuable if faculties could help their students learn to approach problems more creatively, observe high ethical standards in practice, and exercise greater leadership ability. Yet neither management professors nor anyone else can claim a great deal of knowledge about how to nurture these behaviors. Psychologists have made some headway in using collaborative brainstorming and other exercises to enhance creativity, but much about this subject is still unknown or controversial. Professors of applied ethics know a great deal about identifying moral issues and thinking about them carefully but understandably know far less about how to help students develop the strength of character to live up to ethical principles when they are pressured by colleagues and superiors to make moral compromises. Leadership has been the subject of many popular books that may contain helpful insights, but it is doubtful that anyone fully understands the intangible qualities that give some individuals a special capacity to lead and command support. In short, while one can look askance at business schools that advertise their ability to train "effective leaders who make a difference in the world" or "executives who know how to think outside the box," one can hardly criticize faculties for not having accomplished what may simply be impossible given our current state of knowledge.

THE ULTIMATE CHALLENGE

Beyond the specific criticisms currently leveled at business schools lie two additional problems of an even more fundamental nature. Neither one is new. On the contrary, both issues have troubled management education since its very beginning, and both remain unresolved to this day.

The first problem has to do with the scope of management's responsibilities. To what constituencies do top executives owe a duty—to investors only or to all groups that are affected by the way the company does business? This question is central, not just because it bears on whether business schools are truly engaged in professional education, but also because it defines the managers the faculty is seeking to produce and the standards by which they should judge themselves and be held accountable by others.

One school of thought, expressed most forcefully by the economist Milton Friedman, maintains that the sole responsibility of a corporate leader is to maximize profits and increase shareholder value.[32] As Friedman saw it, the use of corporate funds and executive time for reasons other than helping the bottom line—whether to protect the environment, support worthy causes, or help employees suffering exceptional hardships—is akin to stealing from investors. Attending to such interests, he claimed, should be the responsibility of the government or of charitable and public interest organizations and was not a proper activity for company officials, who are neither trained nor authorized to use corporate resources for such purposes.

The opposing school of thought takes a more expansive view of corporate responsibility.[33] Companies and their executives should feel a responsibility toward all those whose lives they touch—investors, certainly, but also customers, employees, suppliers, and the local communities in which they do business. In recent years, some commentators (and more than a few CEOs) have even argued that leaders of large, multinational companies should feel some obligation to try to protect capitalism itself by working to overcome problems that threaten the long-term viability of the free market system, such as growing social inequality, environmental degradation, and widespread corruption in other countries.[34]

On closer scrutiny, the disagreement between these two camps is not as great as it might seem. Those who favor an expansive view of corporate responsibility presumably recognize the need to set *some* limit on the extent to which executives can use corporate resources to serve social, ethical, and humanitarian ends. Conversely, those who take the narrow view would presumably agree that acting ethically, even when it costs money to do so, or responding to the legitimate needs of those affected by corporate actions can often be valuable for business by helping to attract better employees, maintain the trust of customers, or obtain favorable treatment by public officials. Milton Friedman himself explicitly endorsed such activities so long as they were deliberately undertaken to promote the corporation's business interests.

Now that the debate has persisted for so many years without having been resolved, the critical task is surely to work at finding larger areas of agreement instead of merely trying to refute the opposing arguments. In seeking common ground, both sides to the debate need to take account of the serious arguments from the opposing camp. Those who define corporate responsibility broadly should think about how to hold chief executives accountable if they are free to address the disparate needs of all the groups affected by the company's actions. They might also give thought to whether executives in the highly competitive global marketplace can attend to many different interests and groups and still pay enough attention to producing goods and services at a price and quality to succeed or even to survive.[35] Conversely, those who favor a narrow view of corporate responsibility should consider whether executives who are focused so heavily on the bottom line can avoid ethical lapses and other irresponsible actions that lead to the kinds of problems encountered by Enron or by British Petroleum in the Gulf of Mexico. They should likewise ask themselves whether it will be possible to avoid irreversible environmental damage, financial crises, and other long-term risks to capitalism and free markets if companies do not take some initiative to help combat the underlying problems that could eventually bring about these harmful results.

The argument over the responsibilities of the corporation shows little sign of being resolved anytime soon. Strong differences of opinion often exist within the same faculty. Under these conditions, business schools would be wise to refrain from taking an official position on the question and try instead to devote more thought and further research to narrowing the differences between the two sides. They should also encourage discussion of the issue in their classes. A faculty of management can hardly claim to prepare its students adequately for positions of leadership without requiring them to think deeply about the appropriate responsibilities of corporations and those who direct them.

Some readers may respond that this conclusion does not go far enough. After all, they will argue, the dispute over the nature of management responsibility is a struggle for the very soul of the corporation. The answer helps define the purpose of management education and could have far-reaching consequences for society. In view of these arguments, one can appreciate the temptation to take an official stand on the issue. Nevertheless, the proper role of an educational institution in dealing with hotly disputed issues is not to risk indoctrinating its students or inhibiting its faculty by proclaiming some sort of official orthodoxy on such a controversial subject. Rather, the best way to prepare students for the real world is to acquaint them with the arguments on both sides of contested questions, engage them in vigorous discussion of the issues, and encourage them to think carefully for themselves and develop their own convictions.

The other fundamental problem facing business schools today is the most difficult of all, more difficult, certainly, than any of the educational challenges currently facing schools of medicine or law. It has to do with the basic rationale and justification for all professional education. As in other professional schools, faculties of management must try to give their students an education that will have a lasting value not readily obtainable in any other way. Ideally, the training should be *essential* to a successful career, just as a legal education is for graduates entering most forms of legal practice and as medical school is for future physicians. At the least, business schools should offer an education that will arm their students with a body of knowledge and skills that gives them a substantial and discernible advantage over those who lack such training in filling positions of responsibility in business enterprises of reasonable size and complexity.

This challenge was clearly not met in the course of the first half century of management education. The weaknesses of these early efforts were exposed all too clearly in the Ford and Carnegie reports, forcing business schools to adopt an entirely different approach. The new model they chose was in large part a response to the stinging criticism in the reports accusing them of failing to achieve the standards of rigor required of respectable universities. Their answer was to strengthen their research by assembling faculties made up predominantly of social science PhDs.

In retrospect, the new model was only partially successful. It did produce a body of research of sufficient quality to satisfy the concerns of the foundations and win the respect of social science faculties. It also proved highly successful in attracting students and gaining financial support from private donors. Yet it suffered, and still suffers, from several weaknesses that hamper business schools in trying to develop an educational program of lasting value to future corporate leaders.

To begin with, most new faculty members recruited from arts and sciences faculties not only lack practical experience in management; they have not even attended a business school. They are often well-trained in analyzing problems and in developing theories that suggest possible solutions. But they tend to be much less successful at teaching students to identify problems in the first place or to implement the strategies adopted in response. And even their theories and solutions can sometimes suffer from excessive abstraction and oversimplification in analyzing business problems.

A second handicap of business school faculties is that so many of their members have been trained in a system of teaching that emphasizes lecturing rather than methods of active learning. As a result, while professors may still assign business cases for their students to read, they often use them as examples in their lectures to explain how social science theories and models can be applied to business situations, instead of employing them to stimulate an active discussion that will help students learn how to analyze problems and arrive at solutions by themselves.

A third basic difficulty with the prevailing model of business education is that it lacks a means of teaching practical management skills equivalent to the clinical experience that medical students undergo on the hospital wards and that law students gain by working on actual cases with real clients under the supervision of experienced attorneys. This deficiency is not primarily the fault of business schools. Corporations do not lend themselves to supervised practice of the kind that exists in teaching hospitals and law school clinics. Corporate problems are not like surgical procedures or legal cases. They do not involve a small number of people in a finite location, such as an operating room or a courtroom, but arise in large organizations. They normally take much longer to get resolved, and the full consequences often do not occur quickly enough for students to learn from experience how to make sound decisions and implement them effectively.

Lacking both a faculty with business experience and a clinical program offering supervised practice, the current model of business education has understandably had difficulty devising a core of knowledge and skills that will have clear and lasting value in managing a company. One way out of this dilemma might be to build the teaching program around training students to analyze business problems rigorously and systematically, much as law schools have done by using the Socratic method to teach students how to reason about legal problems in a more careful, orderly way. This approach, however, requires agreement on a systematic method of analysis applicable to a wide enough array of business situations to enable a majority of their students, once they have embarked on their careers, to identify problems, analyze them carefully, devise a strategy for solving them, and develop a viable plan for implementing their solution. Such a process must be interdisciplinary. Mastering it requires repeated drill through a pedagogy based on active learning and problem-based discussion. Such teaching will not come easily to a faculty trained in separate academic disciplines using methods of instruction that rely heavily on lecturing. And even if these hurdles can be overcome, there will still be a need to find some functional equivalent to the teaching hospital and the legal clinic that will help students acquire the more specific, hands-on skills of effective management.

These problems are substantial, especially for business schools accustomed to valuing research above teaching. In the face of such challenges, one can only ask that faculties acknowledge their problems honestly and try vigorously and imaginatively to find solutions. On this score, fortunately, there are grounds for guarded optimism. Conscious of the widespread criticism of business schools and the declining applications to several well-known institutions, management faculties are hard at work seeking to improve their product. Some schools are actively recruiting experienced business executives to join their faculties in the hope that they can supply some practical knowledge of how to get things done in corporate settings. A few schools are making serious efforts to prepare new faculty members for the special pedagogical demands that professional education requires.

A number of faculties are also responding to their critics by trying imaginative new methods of teaching.[36] Stanford's business school, among others, has collaborated with its faculty of design to develop a course to help its students learn how to think more creatively and collaboratively. Yale's School of Management is experimenting with efforts to integrate the insights of different disciplines. Harvard has made a major commitment to the teaching of ethics and professional responsibility. Many schools are introducing fieldwork in an effort to bridge the gap between the classroom and the real world. For example, Michigan and Chicago, among other schools, are attempting to instill a keener awareness of the problems of doing business abroad by sending students to spend short periods working intensively overseas on specific projects. Several schools have students act as consultants by studying an actual corporate problem and hearing their solution critiqued by company executives. A number of professors are making imaginative efforts to use computer games to develop leadership skills.[37] Experiments of these kinds are welcome. If they are sustained and validated through careful assessment of the results, management faculties may eventually overcome at least some of the deficiencies noted by their critics.

How successful business schools will ultimately be in improving their educational programs remains uncertain. It will not be easy for faculties to agree on a form of systematic analysis that will be truly valuable in addressing a wide variety of real-world business problems and not just useful for a few specialized careers. Nor is it a simple matter to induce a faculty trained in one tradition to excel at different methods of teaching and learning. As for teaching practical skills, even if management faculties develop adequate substitutes for a teaching hospital or a legal clinic, they will not be able to use these methods with lasting effect without a deeper understanding of the skills that go into successful leadership and the capacity to mobilize people and resources to execute corporate plans and policies.

The continued presence of such basic problems could easily lead readers to fault business schools for lagging behind their sister faculties of law and medicine. Yet such a verdict would be unfair. Much of the difficulty in management education is that the subject is less amenable than medicine or law to the development of a body of teachable principles and tools that students need to master in order to succeed in their careers.

In medicine, for all its complexity, human illness occurs within a bounded arena—the human body—in which the genetic, behavioral, and environmental influences tend to operate through more or less regular, discoverable processes of cause and effect. With the help of massive research support, much knowledge of this kind is now understood and can be used to cure many illnesses with the help of skills that can be learned on the wards and through the use of technologically created simulated environments. Law is a construct of man-made rules and precedents that can be applied to new situations by using a process of logic and disciplined common sense that can be mastered through constant practice and put to use with the aid of skills that can be taught in the legal clinic or through various types of simulations and role-playing.

Business education, on the other hand, involves the analysis of individual firms in specific situations—a field of action in which reliable principles of cause and effect are much harder to establish. Moreover, as previously mentioned, it is no easy matter to find a serviceable equivalent of the teaching hospital or the legal clinic in which to practice basic skills under competent supervision. These difficulties may be surmountable; who can foresee what human ingenuity may eventually discover? Yet they are surely harder to overcome than the problems involved in teaching medicine and law. As a result, one should not be surprised if it takes longer to develop a form of management education that has substantial, lasting value for the large majority of graduates. The encouraging fact is that serious efforts to improve are currently underway. With their demonstrated capacity to attract both students and resources, business schools should have ample time, notwithstanding the current criticisms, to try to bring their quest to a successful conclusion.

AFTERWORD (III)

||||||||||||||||||||||||||||||||||||||||||||||||||||||||||||||||||||||||||||||||||||||||||||||||||||||||||

There is much to praise about the condition of the professional schools described in the preceding chapters. Our medical schools came to be widely regarded as the finest in the world as early as the 1930s, and have kept their enviable reputation with the help of generous NIH research support.[1] In recognition of their quality, students come from all over the world to America's academic health centers for advanced training in research or in one of the medical specialties. American business schools have been the model for a remarkable surge in management education around the world. Half or more of the twenty most highly rated business schools in the world are located in the United States.[2] Many schools of management overseas have had their professors trained in American universities, while more than one-third of the students in our leading business schools are attracted here from other nations.[3] It is harder to compare American law schools with their counterparts abroad because of the marked differences in national legal systems. Even so, professors who have taught both in the United States and in countries overseas claim that American legal education has no rival anywhere in the world.[4]

At the same time, schools for all three professions, despite their obvious differences, continue to grapple with the same four basic challenges. As pointed out in the foreword to these chapters, the first of these issues involves the balance to be struck between the values of the academy and the practical needs of the profession. The second common problem is how to cope with the continuous increase in the amount of information and knowledge that practitioners ought to possess. The third has to do with how to help students acquire the lengthening list of skills and competencies that doctors, lawyers, and corporate executives need to master in order to function effectively, some of which are very difficult to teach. The fourth and final challenge is to define and nurture the ethical and social responsibilities that are needed to earn the public's trust and keep each profession appropriately sensitive to the interests of others and of society as a whole.

SATISFYING THE ACADEMY
AND THE PROFESSION

The problem of balancing the claims of the academy and those of the profession will never be fully and permanently solved, but some faculties have achieved a more stable and satisfactory accommodation than their counterparts serving other callings. Medical schools have probably been the most successful, aided by their great size and ample resources. With their impressive cadres of basic scientists and their large clinical faculties based in teaching hospitals, they can provide first-rate research and instruction in basic science while also teaching students to use scientific knowledge in diagnosing and treating illness and helping them master the skills of their profession. Although basic scientists and their clinician colleagues may not always work in perfect harmony or even communicate much with one another, each is considered essential by the other, and both command the respect of students and the profession.

Compared with other faculties of the university, law professors have traditionally been among the least preoccupied with living up to the prevailing academic standards of the academy, perhaps because they receive their professional training in law schools, not in arts and sciences departments. At the same time, they have long been subjected to complaints from the bar that their graduates are insufficiently prepared in the practical skills of the profession. In recent decades, they have responded to these criticisms by building clinical programs of their own. The experienced attorneys who staff these programs teach a variety of skills to complement the doctrinal analysis taught by the traditional faculty. Through their teaching and the opportunities given to students to work on real cases, they offer new ways of learning and fresh challenges to sustain student interest beyond the first year. Moreover, in their effort to develop a suitable pedagogy for the settings in which they teach, they have produced much of the new thought about legal education and the recent experimentation with different methods of instruction.[5] While these contributions are promising, clinical education has not yet acquired the status and importance of its counterpart in medical schools. It neither receives as much space in the curriculum, reaches all the students, nor commands the full respect of the regular faculty. Only time will tell whether its programs will continue to grow and eventually gain the place within the law school that they need to realize their full potential.

Leading business schools have succeeded in winning the respect of the academy for the quality of their research. However, they have the least developed practical training. They have no clinical program, nor is there any obvious way for them to create the equivalent of the teaching hospital or the legal clinic.

Unlike their sister schools of medicine and law, few of their professors have ever worked in the corporate world or even been educated in a business school. Their lack of practical experience has contributed to a chorus of complaints from corporate executives and even from some prominent faculty members questioning whether business schools have much to teach managers with line responsibilities.[6]

Further light can be shed on the accommodation reached between the standards of the academy and the needs of the profession by examining the research carried on within the three professional schools. Once again, with their huge faculties and abundant resources, medical schools have found it easiest to satisfy both audiences. Their basic science departments include investigators who do work of the highest quality and enjoy reputations that often equal or exceed those of biology-based scientists elsewhere in the university. At the same time, medical schools also employ large numbers of clinical professors, many of whom engage in inquiry that results in applications of great practical value to physicians.

Law schools have had a somewhat different history of research. Unlike the basic scientists and clinical investigators in medical schools, law professors—at least until recently—have rarely had much formal training in the methods of inquiry used in academic disciplines. Throughout most of their history, they produced a body of scholarship that consisted mainly of careful analyses of legal opinions to critique their reasoning, evaluate their likely consequences, and suggest how internal conflicts and other deficiencies could be resolved to produce a more consistent and appropriate body of legal doctrine. Works of this kind, from early classics such as *Wigmore on Evidence* and *Prosser on Torts* to more recent examples such as Lawrence Tribe's treatise on constitutional law or Philip Areeda's volumes on antitrust law, have long been useful to the profession. They have suggested arguments for lawyers to make to judges and ways for judges to resolve conflicts and inconsistencies in the law and supply more thoughtful rationales for legal rules. At the same time, apart from the work of a few exceptional scholars, such research has rarely been of much interest to professors in the rest of the university.

In recent years, more and more faculty members, especially in the leading schools, have either received a PhD or had substantial training in an academic discipline. As a result, many articles appearing in leading law journals have become theoretical in nature, applying models and concepts from other disciplines to different bodies of law. Much of the resulting scholarship has been abstract and difficult to follow. Although some of it has had an impact on the law, it has generally received a cool reception from judges and practitioners.[7] Some investigators have found that law review articles are cited less frequently by judges today than in the past, though other studies disagree.[8] Several critics have even claimed that legal scholarship has become irrelevant to the profession, a questionable charge since the majority of articles appearing in legal journals continue to be of the traditional doctrinal variety.[9]

The theoretical interests and broader training of many younger legal scholars have resulted in closer ties with social scientists, especially with economists, who find that a law professor conversant with their discipline can help them build bridges between economics and interesting real-world problems. What knowledge of the disciplines has not yet done, however, is to stimulate a large body of rigorous empirical work either to trace the practical consequences of various laws and legal procedures or to test the assumptions that often underlie judicial opinions.[10] This deficiency not only leaves the field of law without a solid foundation of fact; it limits the interest in law school research among professors in other parts of the university.

The development of scholarship in business schools illustrates yet another response to the differing requirements of corporate executives and colleagues in other parts of the university. Not only are most faculty members, especially in the leading schools, recruited from the ranks of arts and sciences departments; their subsequent promotions and salaries depend in large part on the amount of scholarship they publish in peer-reviewed academic journals. As a result, business school scholars often seem driven by a desire to satisfy colleagues in their discipline more than by a concern to contribute knowledge of immediate value to managers.

These priorities have enabled business schools to win the respect of their colleagues in arts and sciences faculties, and properly so. But the achievement has come at a price. Increasingly, corporate executives and even some business school professors dismiss most of the research in leading schools as irrelevant to the practice of management.[11] One such critic, Jeffrey Pfeffer of the Stanford Business School, has pointed out that few of the books rated "best" by *Business Week* have been written by business school professors, and that fewer than one-third of the most important new ideas for managers have come from business school faculty members.[12] Others add that business school research is seldom interdisciplinary, although most problems managers face cannot be fully understood or properly resolved by using the techniques of a single discipline.[13] It would be wrong, of course, to dismiss all business school research as irrelevant. In certain fields, notably finance, where economic models have their greatest practical utility, academic theories, such as capital asset pricing, have been put to widespread professional use. For managers in most industries, however, it is probably true that much of the scholarship from leading business schools is of little practical value.[14]

Some critics of business school research have not merely claimed that much of it is irrelevant. Professors such as the late Sumantra Ghoshal argue that social science model building of the kind so popular in business schools has relied on simplifying assumptions about human nature that have resulted in conclusions that are ethically questionable and destructive of social responsibility.[15] The agency and efficient markets theories discussed in the preceding chapter are often cited as a case in point.[16] While most leading schools have added ethicists to their faculties, there is little indication as yet that these scholars have had much influence on the work of their economist colleagues.

THE OVERLOAD OF INFORMATION

In addition to trying to balance the claims of the academy and the needs of practice, faculties in all three professions have had to cope with the constant growth of relevant information and knowledge. At some point in the evolution of each of the three schools, it has become impractical to try to teach students all the information they need to know. The critical moment arrived for law schools late in the nineteenth century when the laws of different states began to diverge, making it impossible simply to teach "the rules" to classes made up of students who would eventually practice in different parts of the country. This problem was solved by law dean Christopher Columbus Langdell, who concluded in the 1870s that faculty members should stop lecturing about legal rules and concentrate instead on teaching students the basic substantive and procedural principles of law while training them through Socratic discussion to apply these principles to varying fact situations. Although slow to catch hold, this method eventually spread through virtually every school and still dominates law teaching to this day.

Business schools were next to recognize that teaching students "all the important facts" was not really possible or even very useful, since the field of business was both vast and constantly changing. In the 1920s and 1930s, many faculties responded by emphasizing decision making through the use of cases consisting of detailed descriptions of actual problems facing corporations. Like their colleagues in law schools, business professors grew less concerned with conveying large quantities of information than with using these real-life problems to teach students how to analyze relevant facts and weigh plausible arguments in order to decide how to act. After 1960, however, as business schools hired more PhDs from the social sciences, many of the new recruits chose to spend their class time lecturing in the manner customary in arts and sciences classrooms. Although professors continued to assign cases, they used them less as problems to be resolved through class discussion and more as examples to illustrate the application of social science theories and analytic methods to business situations.

Medical schools were the last to retreat from a curriculum heavily based on transmitting information. Students complained for decades about the endless series of tedious lectures they had to attend in the first two years and the vast quantity of facts they were supposed to remember. Eventually, with the discovery of DNA and the subsequent explosion of medical knowledge, faculty leaders recognized that there was simply too much information, and that knowledge was accumulating and changing too rapidly to make the old methods sustainable. As a result, a number of medical schools followed in the footsteps of business and law and began in the 1980s to limit the number of lectures. Instead, they taught students how to find the necessary knowledge for themselves. Instruction could then take place in small discussion groups using case histories to train students to figure out for themselves what they needed to know and, once they had found the necessary information, how to analyze it to diagnose an illness and prescribe appropriate treatment.

In teaching students to use information to solve the characteristic problems of their calling, professors in all three schools have come to base more of their teaching on active discussion and problem solving. In this respect, they have changed their methods of instruction more than most of their colleagues in arts and sciences departments. At the same time, active learning is still not fully accepted by all members of the faculty. Some medical school professors believe that the new problem-based curricula do not teach enough basic science and that students ought to know more before they start trying to diagnose illnesses.[17] As previously mentioned, many business school teachers still make heavy use of lectures, encouraged, no doubt, by the methods widely used in arts and sciences departments where they earned their graduate degree. Even law professors have begun to lecture more in reaction to the apathy of second- and third-year students resulting from the constant use of the Socratic method.

Progress has also been uneven in adopting other teaching methods that could sustain interest and improve learning. Individual faculty members in all three professions have experimented with faster, better feedback, collaborative learning, simulations, fieldwork, and other promising advances. All of these innovations embody features that reflect what is currently known about student learning. Even so, none of the schools has yet made full use of these methods, let alone launched a serious effort to acquaint its professors with the growing body of knowledge about learning and its implications for effective teaching. Assessment is also underdeveloped in all three schools. Faculties of medicine are furthest along in making systematic efforts to measure the effectiveness of new curricula and innovations in pedagogy. But none of the schools has yet embraced a continuous process of defining learning objectives, evaluating student progress toward these goals in order to identify weaknesses, and experimenting with new ways to remedy the deficiencies.

ACQUIRING ALL THE NECESSARY SKILLS

In recent years, faculties in all three professions have been called upon to teach a wider range of competencies. In responding to this challenge, medical schools have had considerable success, thanks to their long tradition of teaching students to care for patients on the wards of hospitals. Law schools now offer similar learning experiences through the development of clinical programs, although such programs do not yet play as important a role as clinical education in medical schools. Business schools face the greatest problem of all, since there are no obvious venues in which students can gain practical experience under the supervision of seasoned practitioners.

The most daunting pedagogic challenge facing schools in all three professions is how to help students develop important skills and values that are insufficiently understood to be taught effectively. While practitioners in all three fields need to communicate persuasively and empathetically with increasingly diverse audiences, it is not entirely clear how to teach students to acquire such facility. Leadership is another highly prized attribute, especially in business, and many books and courses have appeared on the subject. Even so, few would assert that a great deal is known about why some individuals are effective leaders and what it is they do that makes them successful. Creativity and judgment are still other talents that are highly prized but insufficiently understood to be readily taught to others.

Under these circumstances, it would be unfair to condemn professional schools for failing to help their students acquire all the competencies they need. One can only ask that faculties recognize the challenge and work to overcome it by trying to discover the knowledge and teaching methods needed to nurture the desired qualities. Efforts of this kind are being made in all three schools. To succeed fully, however, faculties will have to go beyond experimentation and find reliable ways to evaluate the results. As previously mentioned, such assessment already occurs in a number of medical schools but is still not widely used in business and law.

TEACHING ETHICS AND
SOCIAL RESPONSIBILITY

A persistent complaint leveled at schools in all three professions is that they have failed to imbue their students with a firm commitment to ethical principles and a strong sense of social responsibility. The need for higher ethical standards has become more evident in all three professions, as public trust in professionals has declined, and conditions have changed to intensify pressures to behave in morally questionable ways. Doctors are tempted to practice "creative billing" to increase their Medicare payments or to engage in conflicts of interest by accepting payments from pharmaceutical companies to promote new drugs. Members of law firms feel pressured to do whatever it takes to win a lawsuit while devoting less time to worthy pro bono causes in order to concentrate on maximizing the firm's revenues. In business, the practice of tying substantial amounts of compensation to corporate performance has increased the temptation for executives to engage in questionable practices in order to earn a larger paycheck.

Schools in each of the professions have responded by appointing professors to teach students about the moral dilemmas and ethical responsibilities common to their calling. All too often, however, these courses exist on the margins of the curriculum and fail to capture student interest and respect. Some faculties could doubtless do a better job of recruiting gifted instructors. With greater effort, they might also find a way to reinforce the subject and emphasize its importance by persuading professors in other courses to discuss ethical problems arising in the subjects that they teach. As yet, however, few faculties in any of the three professions have been notably successful in achieving these results. In fact, investigators in all three schools have found that the sentiment underlying all moral behavior—a sympathetic concern for the needs of others—tends to diminish rather than grow stronger during the course of training.[18]

The effort to nurture professional responsibility has likewise become both more pressing and more complicated in recent decades. In medicine, more than competent, dedicated patient care is required in a health-care system where costs are straining the society's capacity to pay. Should a responsible physician join a boutique practice catering exclusively to the well-to-do? What is the meaning of responsibility when a patient pleads for a medicine the doctor knows is not needed? Should one insert a pacemaker in the chest of a patient nearing the end of a long life? Is a doctor justified in ordering a battery of expensive tests of limited diagnostic value in order to guard against the possibility of a malpractice suit?

The law presents plenty of problems of its own in seeking to define the contemporary meaning of professional responsibility. What does a responsible lawyer do when a major client wishes to hire a professional firm that specializes in breaking union-organizing drives through thinly disguised threats or even flagrant dismissals of key employee leaders in the campaign? Should a lawyer help a client bring suit or make excessive discovery demands in an effort to force the opposing party to settle the case or abandon a lawful course of action? How can a law firm do enough to provide legal services to poor clients or nonprofit organizations when competitors are pressing their members to log extremely high numbers of billable hours in order to maximize profits per partner?

In business schools, the very definition of responsibility has been questioned by faculty members who believe that maximizing shareholder value is the only legitimate aim of corporate managers. This point of view has come under increasing fire from critics in the wake of repeated corporate scandals and excesses over the past twenty-five years. Yet the proper scope of executive responsibility is by no means easy to define. On the one hand, what duties should the term include now that the risks resulting from a single-minded concern for the bottom line have been so vividly revealed? On the other, if increased share values are no longer a sufficient measure of managerial performance, and notions of "balancing the interests of all the stakeholders" seem too vague for practical use, what yardstick can one use to guide executives and hold them accountable?

If students are to think intelligently about such questions, they need, first of all, to be conversant with the principal problems facing their profession. Medical students should be aware of the debates over how to contain medical costs while providing appropriate care to the entire population. Law students need to understand the failure of the legal system to provide adequate and affordable legal services to the poor and middle-class, the issues arising from changes in the size and operation of large law firms, and the difficulties resulting from the high cost and slow pace of litigation, among other issues. Would-be business executives need not only to learn about the long-standing debate over the responsibility of corporate leaders, but to know something of the recurring problems of competitive markets that have led to such misfortunes as the recent crisis in the financial system.

It may well be that professors in each faculty will fail to agree on the reasons or the remedies for these problems. Even so, students should at least be exposed to a lively debate on the issues and encouraged to think more deeply about them before plunging into the pressures of a career. Aspiring practitioners can hardly be expected to develop a strong sense of social responsibility if they do not have a reasonable grasp of the principal deficiencies and unmet needs of their profession.[19]

Important as it is, however, merely teaching students to recognize issues of moral and social responsibility and think about them carefully will not be enough to satisfy critics. What the public seeks from professional schools is an education that develops the students' strength of character to *act* according to enlightened principles amid all the pressures and temptations of the real world. Such expectations are high-minded and wholly understandable. Yet they ask professors to accomplish a task that is not yet understood. There are many who doubt that it is even possible.*

If professional schools ever manage to improve the character of their students, it is unlikely to be through classes alone. As an ancient adage has it, "if you would know virtue, observe the virtuous man." To develop a strong sense of ethical and social responsibility, students need to come in contact with senior practitioners of exemplary character with whom they can identify and try to emulate.

Role models of this kind are most likely to exist within the teaching hospitals where there are large numbers of experienced physicians from whom to choose especially dedicated and exemplary mentors. That is the special promise of the coordinated clerkship described in chapter 12 in which a group of carefully chosen physicians work for a year with a cohort of students who are studying patient care in a series of clinical specialties. Something similar could occur in law schools by having students serve in a legal clinic under the supervision of a dedicated older lawyer. Once again, it is the business schools that are likely to have the greatest difficulty providing suitable role models, since so many members of their faculty are PhDs who have never lived the corporate life their students hope to lead. One possible solution is for deans to persuade exemplary alumni who have retired from active management to join the faculty and spend enough time with students to convey a sense of how one can combine a successful management career with a strong commitment

---

*In view of the problems of building character in students who have already reached their twenties, some might suggest that professional schools concentrate instead on choosing applicants who demonstrate high standards of honesty and concern for others instead of relying so heavily on grades and standardized test scores. On reflection, however, it is not at all clear that even the most character-conscious admissions staff could raise the ethical standards of entering classes. It is all but impossible for a committee to assess the character of thousands of applicants for admission and do so in ways that will withstand the efforts of bright college seniors to game the system and present themselves as upright, ethically spotless candidates. Were such a thing to be tried, many injustices might be inflicted on decent young people whose application forms had somehow raised suspicion in the minds of admissions officers. Besides, one must ask what would happen to the students rejected on grounds of questionable character. Where would they end up, and would they do less damage than if they enrolled in a professional school that made a concerted effort to encourage them to behave ethically? These concerns seem serious enough to rule out efforts to improve the moral standards of the professions by tinkering with the admissions process.

to ethical principles and the social responsibilities of business.[20] Some schools are already moving in this direction.

SEEKING A FRUITFUL LIFE
IN ONE'S PROFESSION

In the last analysis, developing a strong sense of moral and professional responsibility is not merely a matter of learning to think about the issues involved; it is an integral part of figuring out what sort of a person one wants to be and what sort of a life one will be able to look back upon with pride and satisfaction. This is an even greater challenge than teaching about ethics and social responsibility, and few professional schools have considered it within the proper scope of their activities. However, there are reasons why introspection of this kind may have become too important to ignore and why it may come to represent the ultimate challenge for professional schools to meet.

In recent decades, many callings, including the three discussed in these chapters, have evolved in ways that complicate the task of deciding what type of career or practice to pursue. All three professions have become much more competitive, with consequences that could make them more appealing to some students but less so for others. Medical practice has changed significantly with the advent of large organizations (HMOs) that compete with one another in delivering care. Law firms have fewer long-term relationships with large corporate clients and must constantly vie with other firms to handle individual cases or lawsuits. Companies face more intense competition from global rivals, along with heightened demands for short-term profits to satisfy shareholders and greater risks of being overrun by new technologies or hostile takeovers. In all three callings, competition has tended to narrow the autonomy of professionals by subjecting them to growing pressures, whether from the market, the government, or the tendency toward larger, more bureaucratic forms of organization.

In many ways, the new environment for professionals has tended to make their work less satisfying. Levels of stress have increased. Time pressures have restricted the opportunities for careful craftsmanship. Opportunities to engage in charitable activities and public service have often diminished under the pressure of working harder to maximize incomes. The public's trust in all professions has eroded in the wake of well-publicized scandals and a growing sense that practitioners and the organizations in which they work are more concerned with making money than with serving the public wisely and well.

At the same time, changing conditions in the professions have also brought added rewards to many practitioners. Compensation for top corporate executives, leading medical specialists, and senior partners in large law firms have risen to unprecedented levels. In all three professions, successful members are well represented in the highest 1 percent of American earners. At the same time, new career opportunities have emerged in all three fields. In medicine, for example, boutique practices allow participating doctors to have more time per patient and less paperwork, while new nonprofit organizations have arisen to bring medical services to needy communities here and overseas. In law, corporations have expanded their in-house legal staffs (where attorneys are free from having to attract new clients), large nonprofits are hiring their own lawyers, and public interest firms have emerged to litigate on behalf of immigrants, environmental needs, human rights, and other worthy purposes. In business, start-up ventures have been formed at unprecedented rates in biotechnology and other emerging fields, while new opportunities have arisen in the form of social enterprise ventures that attempt to combine profit making with products and services to meet public needs.

In this increasingly complicated professional environment, students need to learn much more than how much money they can make in order to decide what type of career will bring them the greatest satisfaction and fulfillment. Depending on their individual preferences, they may wish to know the average hours of work required, the levels of satisfaction practitioners experience in different specialties and settings, the availability of child care and other family-friendly practices, the rates of turnover and migration to other fields, the opportunities to do public service or charitable work, and much more.

Almost all professional schools operate placement offices to help students find jobs, and many of them collect much of the information students seek. But more than information is needed. Students weighing the growing array of career alternatives need occasions to think more fruitfully about their lives and consider what goals and values will matter most to their personal fulfillment and well-being. This is an educational challenge that few professional schools have grappled with seriously, a challenge unlike anything faculty members face in giving an ordinary class. There are rarely settled facts or established principles to convey. None of the three professional schools has a single vision of the ideal practitioner, and even if they did, it would be wrong to suggest to students that there is only one way for them to live an exemplary life. Instead, the instructor's task must be to give the students the information and the opportunity to think about the issues and arrive at their own conclusions. For those who take this inquiry seriously, enlightenment may come from many sources—not just from acquiring more information or observing appropriate role models but from studying the work of philosophers, or reading biographies, memoirs, or even novels and short stories and discussing them with classmates.

Although courses that provide such opportunities have cropped up here and there, they are still uncommon. Understandably, many faculty members will be reluctant even to consider such an assignment. Given the difficulty of the task, one cannot assume that professional schools that accept the challenge will succeed, nor should one condemn them if they fail. Yet it is not unreasonable to ask them to try. After all, what greater contribution can a professional school give its students than helping them arrive at more enlightened choices in their search for a truly satisfying career?

PART (IV)

||||||||||||||||||||||||||||||||||||||||||||||||||||||||||||||||||||||||||||||||||||||||||||||||||||||||||||||||||||||||||||||||||

RESEARCH

FOREWORD (IV)

||||||||||||||||||||||||||||||||||||||||||||||||||||||||||||||||||||||||||||||||||||||||||||||||||||||

Research has not always been an important part of higher education's mission. No research to speak of took place in American colleges during the eighteenth century. Although scientists and scholars began to appear on campuses prior to the Civil War, publications were not a prerequisite for a faculty appointment, and science existed on the margins of the college, often confined to affiliated schools that granted their own degrees. Not until 1880 did universities begin to offer graduate programs to train students for careers of scholarship and scientific inquiry. Even then, there was opposition on many campuses from those who feared that research would detract from teaching.

The nation was even slower to encourage research. As late as the 1920s and 1930s, academic scientists depended almost entirely on modest grants from corporations and foundations with little help from government sources. On the eve of World War II, Washington appropriated less than $100 million per year to universities for research and development (R&D), much of it for improving agriculture and public health.

THE RISE TO PROMINENCE

World War II marked the start of a new era in which research came to play an increasingly important role in national policy. Inventions such as radar, penicillin, and, of course, the atomic bomb demonstrated the power of discovery and led to the creation of the National Science Foundation (NSF) in 1950. For the next forty years, the Cold War and the imperatives of national security provided much of the impetus for a rapid growth of federal funding. Increases thereafter proved to be more modest and erratic. Overall, however, the NSF budget grew from a mere $3.5 million in 1952 to almost $7 billion in 2010.

The desire to vanquish illness was a second potent source of research support. Discoveries such as antibiotics and polio vaccine dramatized the role of biomedical advances in the conquest of disease and the relief of suffering. Created in 1947, the National Institutes of Health began modestly, disbursing an annual sum for research of only $74 million as late as 1954. By 2010, its budget had risen manyfold to more than $30 billion.

Economists helped to bring about the third great driving force behind research. For centuries, they had debated the causes of economic growth and prosperity. An abundance of raw materials was long thought to play a critical role. Ample supplies of capital for investment were also deemed essential. Only much later did new discoveries, technical advances, and, more generally, additions to knowledge gain prominence as vital stimuli to economic expansion.[1] By the closing decades of the twentieth century, the explosive growth of new industry near Boston and in Silicon Valley fueled by major new science-based products, such as computers, transistors, cell phones, and robots, clearly showed the importance of scientific discovery to a dynamic economy.

While corporations and wealthy donors give large sums for science research, almost 60 percent of the funding for such inquiry comes from the federal government.[2] Over 80 percent of this support goes to just one hundred academic institutions.[3] The growth of funding over the past sixty years has transformed these universities. Massive transfusions of money from the National Institutes of Health have vastly increased the budgets and payrolls of medical schools and their affiliated hospitals. Science departments in faculties of arts and sciences have likewise prospered through the addition of elaborately equipped laboratories, professorships, and cadres of postdocs and technicians to support the work of the faculty.

The increased importance of research has had widely uneven effects on other parts of the university. Schools and departments whose mandate includes subjects of national concern have fared quite well. Schools of public health have prospered. Area centers that produce research on different regions of the world have benefited from America's new role as a dominant superpower with military, diplomatic, and commercial interests throughout the globe. Economics departments have done well as a result of their contributions to the understanding of business, finance, and global trade. Even schools of education have attracted increasing research support since the early 1980s because of the evident need to improve the nation's schools.

At the same time, many parts of the university have gained very little from the growth of research funding. Literature, the arts, history, philosophy, theology, and classics have had to make do with meager support compared with the riches lavished on other faculties and departments. Efforts by humanities scholars and their allies to link their subjects to issues of national well-being have met with scant success. As research funding has boomed in other parts of the campus, humanists have seen their salaries lag behind and their students dwindle in numbers, causing them to feel neglected by a society preoccupied with money and material goods.

Teaching too is widely thought to have been a casualty of the flowering of research. Whether this complaint is justified is a question taken up in the following chapter. What is certainly true is that the summer salaries, consultancies, and public visibility that accrue to prominent researchers can easily leave those who quietly toil in classrooms feeling underappreciated. In short, the growing demand for research may have brought unprecedented riches to many universities, but it has also given rise to problems of overall balance and equitable treatment.

WILL AMERICA'S PREEMINENCE IN RESEARCH CONTINUE?

For several decades, the United States, led by its major universities, has been preeminent in the world in scientific research (and probably in most other fields of scholarship as well).[4] In 2005, the number of scientific papers in refereed journals authored by American researchers far exceeded the total in any other country. America claimed the greatest number of PhDs in science and engineering, the highest percentage of total worldwide R&D funding, and the largest share of the world's high-tech exports.[5] The majority of all Nobel Prizes in science and economics since World War II were won by researchers working in this country. More than half of the world's leading mathematicians, physicists, and microbiologists belonged to faculties in US universities, and American scientists were producing a higher percentage of the most frequently cited articles than all the other countries in the world combined.[6]

In recent years, however, the United States has been losing some of its preeminence in science. From 1981 to 2009, the share of all articles in scientific and social science journals with at least one American author dropped from 40 percent to 29 percent.[7] America's share of the most cited articles in science and engineering fell from 64.6 percent in 1992 to 56.6 percent in 2003.[8]

Two other developments have given further indication of the ebbing dominance of American science and raised doubts about how long our leadership will last. One is the integration of more than twenty European countries into a single European Union (EU). The other is the rapid rise of scientific research in Asia, especially China.

If one counts the EU as a single entity, America's preeminence seems noticeably less imposing. By 2005, the United States was still investing a larger share of its GDP in R&D, accounting for a higher percentage of high-tech exports, receiving a greater number of patents, and producing more highly cited articles and patents than the EU. But Europe enjoyed a big lead in the number of science and engineering PhDs and produced a larger number of scientific papers in refereed journals.[9]

The most remarkable new development, however, is the emergence of China as a rising powerhouse in science and engineering research. In 2006, Chinese authorities announced a plan to double the share of GDP invested in R&D to 2.5 percent by 2020.[10] In an economy expanding at a rate that has often reached 10 percent per year, the absolute growth of investments in science is extremely impressive. Rates of increase in other science indicators have likewise attracted attention. Although China ranks well below the United States and the EU in the number of PhDs produced annually, the growth rate in recent years has exceeded 15 percent.[11] The quantity of papers in refereed journals has been rising by 17 percent per year compared to an annual growth of only 1.5 percent in the United States and 1.3 percent in the EU.[12] China's share of high-tech exports still lags America and the EU but has recently increased at a rate of 30 percent per year, having risen from a mere 3 percent of global exports in 1999 to 15 percent just six years later.[13] In sharp contrast, America's share of global high-tech exports has been declining by 3 percent annually while the EU's share is holding steady but not growing.

Careful extrapolations suggest that by 2020, China may have surpassed the United States in the number of PhDs graduating each year in science and engineering, the share of worldwide investments in R&D, the percentage of all papers published in refereed journals, and the share of global exports of high-tech products. Rapid gains are also being made in South Korea, India, and other Asian countries.[14] In short, a massive shift is gradually taking place in the relative positions in science and technology from the United States and Europe toward Asia. This trend seems likely to persist at least as long as the economic growth rates of these Asian countries continue to exceed those of Western nations, including the United States.

The effect of this shift on the position of university research in the United States relative to other advanced nations is more difficult to predict. While the rapid growth of science funding in Asia is bound to improve the quality of its research, increasing creativity and imagination is a slower, less predictable process than expanding R&D investments or the numbers of new PhDs and published research papers. Political conditions in China and other Asian countries could hamper the progress of universities and their research. Over the longer time span needed to transform the quality of academic institutions, economic growth rates could moderate, perhaps even drastically, as was the case in Japan during the last quarter of the twentieth century.

Equally uncertain is how many of the ablest Chinese, Korean, and Indian scientists now working in the United States will decide to go back to their home countries as conditions for research in those nations improve. Since 1960, the proportion of immigrants among active scientists in the United States has grown from 7.2 percent to almost 30 percent. Still, the percentage of foreign graduate students in science who express a desire to remain and work in America, at least for a few years, seems to be increasing. At least for the next generation, then, there appears to be little danger of a drastic outflow of foreign-born scientists.

The global shift just summarized could bolster rates of economic growth in Asia and add to China's military prowess. As such, it may pose a challenge for Washington policy-makers. As far as academic researchers are concerned, however, the growth of science research in Asia is not a matter of grave urgency, and even if it were, there is relatively little that American universities can do about it. For scientists in this country and elsewhere, the rise of China and other Asian countries promises to have a beneficial effect by quickening the pace of discovery, expanding the available stock of knowledge on which others can build, and increasing the number of able colleagues with whom to interact. Eventually, fewer Asian scientists may remain in this country, and fewer of the best Asian students may apply to do their graduate training in the United States. But overall, science research is not a zero-sum game. Progress in one country tends to benefit research in others.

QUESTIONS TO CONSIDER

In discussing the current condition of research in American higher education, one can proceed in several ways. A frequent topic in much of the writing on the subject has to do with federal policy. Under this heading, one could consider the pros and cons of the trend toward increasing support for biomedical research accompanied by little or no growth in the funding for the physical sciences and engineering. Another important question involves the persistent tendency on the part of funding agencies to give far more money to older, well-established investigators than to younger scientists, despite the fact that many of the most important discoveries have been made by researchers at a comparatively early age. This practice has caused some observers to worry that brilliant students will be discouraged from pursuing careers in science and that important discoveries will be lost because it is now so difficult for younger investigators to obtain support, let alone find a faculty position. Still another persistent problem is the complexity of procedures for obtaining research grants and gaining approvals from the various official bodies responsible for safety and the protection of human subjects. One recent survey has revealed that university scientists have to spend more than 40 percent of their research time getting the funds and approvals to do their work, hiring personnel, and reporting on their administration of the grants they receive.[15]

These issues are all important and can have significant effects on the accomplishments of America's research effort. The principal focus of this study, however, is the performance of universities themselves rather than the policies of the agencies that fund them and regulate their behavior. University practices are complicated enough without attempting to cover these additional topics within the space of a single volume.

Another way to discuss academic research would be to consider the intellectual issues and controversies that have arisen in the various disciplines and fields of inquiry. In economics, for example, one could debate the respective virtues and shortcomings of neoclassical model building, behavioral economics, and more traditional institutional studies. In law, one could examine the relative merits of law and economics, critical legal studies, and conventional doctrinal analysis. In literature, the several schools of thought on literary theory and textual analysis could be evaluated and compared.

Interesting as such discussions might be, they are hardly feasible in a study such as this. There are far too many fields of knowledge to be treated adequately, and the amount of reading and reflection required for such a task would exceed the grasp of the ablest author. It is more sensible, then, to concentrate on questions common to a number of different fields of inquiry. I have chosen three such issues for discussion in the chapters to follow.

The first involves the frequent complaint that too many colleges and universities are pressing their faculties to "publish or perish." It is often said that professors are writing vast quantities of books and articles that no one reads, and that the time taken up by such research has led to a widespread neglect of teaching. Is this assertion correct, and, if so, what can be done about it?

The second topic has to do with the government's efforts to encourage universities to promote economic growth by collaborating more with industry, patenting potentially valuable discoveries, licensing them to corporations, and assisting professors seeking to start new companies based on their discoveries. When universities responded to the wishes of policy-makers after 1980 and began to work more closely with industry, critics warned that campus efforts to promote technology transfer would divert academic scientists from the kind of research they do best and jeopardize the reputation of professors for disinterested, trustworthy work.[16] Now that more time has elapsed, it is possible to examine the record and consider whether these dire consequences have actually come to pass.

The third and final inquiry in this sequence has to do with the campus environment in which scientists and scholars do their work. The classic issue here has been the struggle for academic freedom, including the contentious question of tenure. The subject, however, extends well beyond this familiar topic. Are there biases or imperfections in the processes for judging the quality of scholarship that threaten the nature or originality of the views faculty members can express without risk to their professional advancement? Has an orthodoxy of "political correctness" descended on the campus with stultifying effects on researchers exploring sensitive topics, such as race, class, and gender? Have faculties become so left-liberal in their political views as to narrow the diversity of opinion on campus and threaten the quality of scholarly inquiry? Opinions on these questions differ sharply, giving all the more reason for a careful review of the evidence.

CHAPTER FIFTEEN

"PUBLISH OR PERISH"

||||||||||||||||||||||||||||||||||||||||||||||||||||||||||||||||||||||||||||||||||||||||||||||||||||||||||

OVER THE PAST FORTY YEARS, many voices have been raised expressing concern over inadequate funding for research. Humanists have complained about the miserly sums that Congress appropriates to the National Endowment for the Humanities. Scientists grumble that the federal government has so little money to offer investigators in many fields of inquiry that creative young researchers have difficulty getting grants, and even senior professors have to spend twice as much time submitting multiple proposals to get the same amount of money as they received in times past. Meanwhile, articles appear periodically warning that declining revenues and diminished university subsidies are threatening to destroy academic presses and choke off opportunities for able scholars to publish their work.

With all the hue and cry, one would suppose that the volume of published research must be shrinking. Yet the facts hardly bear this out. From 1980 to 2000, according to Lindsay Waters of the Harvard University Press, the number of new titles published by academic presses grew rapidly.[1] Since then, growth has leveled off, but university presses in North America have continued to publish more than 10,000 titles per year, not to mention all the books authored by professors and published by commercial houses.[2] Some observers claim that the advent of e-books will provide an outlet for even more scholarly monographs.[3] Meanwhile, the number of academic periodicals continues to grow at a rate of approximately 3 percent each year, to the point that there are now said to be more than 100,000 learned journals worldwide.[4]

EXPLAINING THE PARADOX

How can one explain this contrast between the growing volume of printed scholarship and the repeated cries of alarm about inadequate research support and shrinking opportunities to publish? Part of the answer, surely, is that the numbers of scientists and scholars have increased even faster than the supply of funds for research or the outlets for getting scholarly writings published. But another contributing cause is the growth in the number of universities and colleges that require their professors to produce a substantial body of published work in order to be hired or promoted. From 1969 to 1997, the share of faculty members reporting that "it is hard to get appointed or promoted in my university without a strong record of research" rose from 40 to 65 percent.[5] According to a survey published in 2008 by the Modern Language Association Task Force on Evaluating Scholarship for Tenure and Promotion, publication had become more important to promotion in 62 percent of all language and literature departments, while the percentage of department chairs reporting that research counted more than teaching had more than doubled, from 35.4 percent in 1968 to 75.7 percent in 2005.[6]

With the growing emphasis on research, the share of tenure-track faculty members with more than five publications to their credit rose from 11.1 percent in 1969 to 22.5 percent in 1998, while the percentage reporting no publications in the preceding two years fell from 49.5 in 1969 to 28.1 in 2010.[7] Reinforcing the pressure to publish, faculty salaries have been increasingly linked to publications at all types of four-year colleges.[8] The more books and articles professors produce, the higher their salaries. The more hours per week they spend in the classroom, the smaller their paycheck.

The pressure to publish has intensified even further because of the tendency in many universities to emphasize quantity over quality in evaluating the publication records of candidates for appointment and promotion. Even twenty years ago, 45 percent of all professors in a 1992 Carnegie Foundation survey reported that in their institution "publications used for promotion decisions are just counted, not qualitatively evaluated."[9] In almost one-third of all the departments surveyed by the Modern Language Association Task Force in 2008, publishing a second book had become a prerequisite for tenure. Meanwhile, PhD candidates everywhere are told that it is important that they produce several published articles before receiving their degree and starting to look for an academic position. With the number of PhDs seeking academic careers continuing to exceed the number of tenure-track openings, more and more graduate students either delay their degree or seek a postdoctoral appointment for a period of years. While waiting for job opportunities to appear, they concentrate on publishing as much as they can to boost their chances of being chosen from an increasingly crowded field of competitors.

The mounting volume of research manuscripts has made it harder to get articles published in a peer-reviewed journal. The chances of having a manuscript accepted have dwindled further because of a growing number of submissions from scholars overseas seeking to improve their prospects for appointment or promotion. In choosing among candidates, many foreign universities consider not only the number of articles published but the reputation of the journal in which they appear. Since most of the highly regarded scholarly periodicals are located in the United States or Britain, the volume of manuscripts these journals receive has become a deluge. In the highly esteemed *Nature*, for example, fewer than 5 percent of all the articles submitted are accepted for publication, while rejection rates reportedly range between 80 and 90 percent at other leading journals in the sciences and social sciences.

The swelling tide of manuscripts has provoked a contrapuntal question to the laments over inadequate research support. Is all this scholarship necessary? Lindsay Waters has publicly complained about the "mountains of unloved and unread publications" piling up in editors' offices.[10] According to Page Smith, a longtime professor at UCLA, "the vast majority of the so-called research turned out in the modern university is essentially worthless. It does not result in any measurable benefit to anything or anybody. It is . . . busywork on a vast, almost incomprehensible scale."[11] Ironically, now that so many institutions are requiring their professors to publish, almost half of the faculty in surveys of their working conditions complain that they can no longer find the time to keep up with their field.[12] Such reactions presumably stem in part from the mounting number of books and articles that appear each year in most academic subjects.

Those who side with Professor Smith can cite some impressive statistics to support their argument. A staggering 98 percent of all published articles in the arts and humanities are never cited, and the corresponding figure for articles in the social sciences is 75 percent, a figure only slightly less dismaying.[13] Writings in scientific journals fare better; only 25 percent are reportedly never cited.[14] Nevertheless, the average number of citations per article is only between one and two. According to sociologists Jonathan and Stephen Cole, almost all of the scientific papers that are cited most frequently and considered most significant are written by members of a handful of leading departments, while the vast accumulation of other published articles have little or no influence on the progress of the field.[15]

If quantities of published research were simply unread, one might deplore the needless destruction of trees but not worry much otherwise. The growing emphasis on research, however, may present additional risks. The principal concern is a diversion of faculty time from teaching. If more and more professors in more and more colleges and universities feel impelled to turn out articles and books in order to be promoted and earn higher salaries, the hours they take to prepare their manuscripts and conduct their experiments will arguably steal time from preparing for class, seeing students, and commenting on term papers. Over the years, one commentator after another has criticized university policies of "publish or perish" for their tendency to sacrifice teaching and attention to students for an expensive and usually fruitless attempt to acquire the money and prestige that accompany a top-notch research program.[16]

As one would expect, the preceding arguments have not gone unchallenged. Those who take the opposite view declare that any serious effort to produce first-rate research is bound to result in a large number of modest, even trivial publications.[17] Since it is impossible, they argue, to know in advance which projects will make an important contribution, discouraging research runs the risk of doing away with work that will turn out to have lasting value. That is especially likely today when many able young PhDs have accepted appointments in little-known institutions for want of tenure-track jobs at the leading research universities.

Defenders of the status quo also take issue with the assertion that research conflicts with good teaching.[18] On the contrary, they say, professors who are active in research are more motivated than their unproductive colleagues to keep up-to-date with their field. They are less likely to "burn out" in midcareer, since they have their scholarship as well as their teaching to sustain their interest. Not least, they exhibit to their students the special enthusiasm and excitement that come from active engagement in the quest for discovery at the frontiers of knowledge.

Those who look askance at the growing emphasis on research have ready answers to these arguments. They concede that it is often hard to know in advance which projects will make an important contribution. Still, they argue, there is surely a point at which insisting on research is extremely unlikely to yield work of lasting significance. If 98 percent of the publications in the arts and humanities are never cited even once, there can be little risk that much of importance will be lost if departments other than those in research universities and a few topflight liberal arts colleges stop requiring their professors to publish. As for research improving teaching, most of the academic writing today is very highly specialized and bears little relation to the subject matter of undergraduate courses. It is far from clear, therefore, that the hours spent researching these arcane topics will enrich the author's teaching.

Those who defend the spread of publication requirements have one final point to make. Even if research turns out to have little or no impact, they claim, it offers the best possible evidence of a young faculty member's quality of mind and thus helps an institution make sounder appointments and promotion decisions.[19] Yet even this argument can be challenged. If a university emphasizes good teaching rather than research, the best evidence for promotion should presumably come from work relating to the classroom. Examining course syllabi and innovations in instruction, visiting classes, and reading student evaluations should provide a better indication of the candidate's future value to the institution than counting the number of uncited articles listed in a curriculum vitae.

A LOOK AT THE EVIDENCE

Most of the arguments just mentioned have been repeated many times. Oddly, however, the authors who express them rarely support their claims with empirical research even though dozens of inquiries have been conducted over the years on the impact of research on teaching. Most of these studies have compared the teaching of professors who publish a lot with that of their colleagues who do not. The findings tell a good deal about the effects on teaching of emphasizing research as the key to tenure and promotion.

Kenneth Feldman has authored the most comprehensive treatment of this subject.[20] In his article, he analyzed thirty empirical studies comparing student teaching evaluations of professors active in research with those of professors who published little or nothing. He discovered that only one of the thirty studies found that research had a negative effect on teaching, and even there the effect was only modest. Eleven studies showed that research had a moderately positive influence; the rest found no effect either way. Taking all the studies together, the net impact of research on teaching was positive, although the correlation was only barely significant statistically.

Examining the evidence more carefully, Feldman found that the strongest positive relationships between research and teaching involved the professor's knowledge of the subject, organization of the course material, and clarity of the course requirements. Only two aspects of teaching were negatively correlated with an ongoing commitment to research—encouragement of questions and class discussion as well as availability and friendliness to students. In both cases, the correlations were extremely small and not statistically significant.

Later studies have thrown further light on the relationship between teaching and research. Deborah Olsen and Ada Simmons discovered that highly productive scholars held as many office hours as their colleagues who published less but tended to be visited by fewer students.[21] They also reported that active scholars showed no tendency to avoid teaching lower-level undergraduate courses and did not rely more on lecturing or give more multiple-choice exams than their less productive colleagues. Anne Sullivan reported that prolific scholars were just as likely as unproductive faculty members to respect norms of good teaching such as regard for student feelings, meritocratic grading, and scrupulousness in providing course syllabi, ordering textbooks on time, and attending to other details of course planning.[22] On the other hand,

Robert Johnson found that more productive researchers had a slight tendency to ask more "knowledge questions" on exams than colleagues who published less, while asking fewer questions that required critical thinking.[23] Finally, Robert McCaughey, in a separate study, analyzed the student evaluations of a large sample of professors in research universities and highly selective liberal arts colleges.[24] He concluded that the ratings given to well-published scholars were no better and no worse than those given to their less productive colleagues.

All in all, the studies just summarized give little comfort to those who claim that engaging in research undermines undergraduate teaching. Granted, the findings do not *prove* that research has no ill effects. It is conceivable that those who publish a lot are abler than their less productive colleagues and thus might be even better teachers if they did no research. There is no evidence, however, to support this possibility.

Of course, these studies also suggest that research does not have the positive effects on undergraduate teaching that many supporters have claimed. Prolific authors do appear to be somewhat more knowledgeable and better organized in their presentations than less productive faculty members.[25] Yet these tendencies are modest, and it would be unwise to try to make much of them. Instead, the soundest conclusion to draw from the existing studies is that engaging in research has no significant, demonstrable effect, either positive or negative, on the quality of undergraduate teaching.

Further light on the impact of research may be gleaned from periodic surveys of full-time faculty members in four-year colleges that reveal how instructors divide their time between teaching and research when classes are in session. An initial set of surveys begin in 1972 and conclude in 1992, a period in which the percentage of professors reporting that research was essential to promotion virtually doubled.[26] If research takes time away from teaching, one would suspect that such a major increase in the emphasis on publication would reduce the hours devoted to preparing for class. However, nothing much of this kind seems to have occurred. As one would have expected, the average weekly hours devoted to research rose, especially in comprehensive institutions where the emphasis on publishing had increased the most. Interestingly, however, the average number of weekly hours devoted to teaching during term-time did not decline. Instead, the time spent advising students seems to have diminished, while the average length of the workweek increased.

The trends were somewhat different during the subsequent twenty years, from 1992 to 2012.[27] During this period, the average amount of time spent on teaching does seem to have diminished. Nevertheless, the decline appears to have resulted from a reduction in the number of classroom hours required of professors. The figures show no shrinkage in the amount of time per classroom hour that tenure-track faculty spent preparing to teach. In other words, an emphasis on research does not necessarily affect the quality of teaching but may have a delayed effect on the quantity of instruction demanded of professors.

Lower teaching loads are not the only effect that "publish or perish" can have on undergraduate education. The emergence of research as a basic function of the university has resulted in a form of scholarship and graduate (PhD) training that demands specialized knowledge and advanced research skills. Having devoted many years as graduate students and faculty members to mastering their chosen specialty, professors naturally prefer to give courses based on their area of expertise. While universities usually have some intellectually venturesome professors who enjoy teaching new subjects that stretch their intellectual boundaries, and others who enjoy giving introductory courses to freshmen and sophomores, most faculty members prefer to teach the kinds of specialized courses and seminars that are closely aligned with their scholarly interests. Not surprisingly, teaching what professors know best does not always coincide with what undergraduates most need to learn.

Since curricula are devised by professors, it is no accident that the undergraduate requirements in the vast majority of four-year colleges are structured in a way that accommodates the faculty's preferences. Most colleges do include a few requirements that call for courses created to serve particular purposes, such as understanding diversity, learning to write, mastering a foreign language, or—in a minority of colleges—reading the Great Books. More often than not, however, either the courses that emerge are shaped to fit the special scholarly interests of the professor or, if that is impossible, some or all of the teaching is placed in the hands of instructors who are not members of the regular faculty but lecturers, part-time adjuncts, or even graduate students recruited specially for the purpose. The latter practice is now typical for universities in most of the required basic courses in writing, mathematics, and foreign languages and is often employed to help staff sections of broad foundational courses such as those devoted to the Great Books or Western civilization.

The result is a curriculum designed to suit the interests and intellectual strengths of a faculty organized and trained in accordance with established fields of specialized inquiry and scholarship. This is natural enough; professors are best equipped to teach courses within their area of scholarly expertise. Yet the resulting requirements may be less than ideal for educating undergraduates (for reasons set forth in chapter 8). They are also extremely hard to change in any fundamental way, especially in research-oriented colleges and universities where faculties are most powerful and the emphasis on the advancement of specialized knowledge most pronounced.

The implication of all this is not that departments should be eliminated or that the specialization of knowledge should be condemned. Both specialization and the organizational forms that support it serve important purposes. But there is a price to be paid, and that price is usually exacted from the residual portion of the curriculum commonly referred to as general education, where there are simply too few willing professors and too few class hours available to give adequate attention to all the ambitious purposes that are supposedly being served and that the faculty itself considers important.

The growing emphasis on research may also have affected the willingness of faculty members to entertain proposals for fundamental changes in curriculum and teaching methods. Recent surveys have found that more than 60 percent of professors claim to feel stress over the demands of research and committee work, while 74 percent feel concerned over the lack of personal time.[28] Faculty members who feel such pressure will presumably tend to be less enthusiastic about suggestions that they master a new technology for classroom use, attend weeklong faculty workshops on innovations in pedagogy, or reorganize their courses and instructional methods to introduce more active learning. As Bruce Alberts, then president of the National Academy of Sciences, remarked in 2004: "It's just hard to change a system when everybody in it is sort of running at full speed and has got no time. The faculty I see at universities are busier than I am."[29]

The increasing demands on professors may have their greatest effect on the months of the year once identified by Daniel Bell as "the three principal reasons for choosing an academic career—June, July, and August."[30] Faculty members who are expected to publish usually find that the summer months are almost the only times available for serious research and writing. Surveys confirm that in this period, the average professor spends much more time on research than on matters related to teaching and coursework, just the reverse of the pattern during the semester.[31] As more and more colleges have come to emphasize research, it is likely that the time available in the summer for revising old courses, creating new ones, and developing improved methods of instruction has suffered accordingly.

If the growing emphasis on research and administration leaves the faculty less open to making substantial reforms in undergraduate education, the public is indeed being disserved. It is in teaching undergraduates and helping them to learn that the vast majority of colleges can make their most important contributions. Advances in cognitive science, new technologies, and a growing corpus of research on the effectiveness of various methods of instruction have combined to produce a bumper crop of promising possibilities for improving student learning. At the same time, as brought out in chapters 9 and 10, the growing diversity of students, the dwindling hours undergraduates spend on coursework, and the limited progress that many of them seem to be making toward the goals of a college education all point to a need to devote more effort and thought to finding ways to do a better job of engaging students' interest and helping them to learn.

Faculty members would not necessarily be averse to having more time to improve undergraduate education. Surveys reveal that over 70 percent of college professors claim to be oriented more toward teaching than research.[32] Eighty-two percent claim to be interested in undergraduate education, and the percentage declaring a strong interest actually rose by 20 points from 1969 to 1997 (the last available survey).[33] These findings suggest that many faculty members might be receptive to joining an effort to improve the curriculum or experiment with new methods of instruction if they had time to do so. Thus, the demands brought about by the growing insistence on research may have come at a particularly inopportune time.

With these possible consequences in mind, why have so many more colleges and universities decided to require their faculties to publish in order to win promotions and gain tenure? One contributing cause may be the shortage of academic positions that has forced many new PhDs to take positions in institutions without a strong reputation for research. Trained in doctoral programs where research is highly valued, these young recruits may have persuaded their departments to introduce the same standards and priorities they observed during their graduate years.

Even if this explanation is valid, it still leaves open the question why the institutions that hired these young PhDs decided to make published research a *prerequisite* for tenure. They could certainly be supportive of new recruits who wished to do research. But encouraging publication is one thing and requiring it quite another. Even less justifiable is the now-prevalent practice of basing promotion and tenure on the *quantity* of books and articles published. Professors from all kinds of institutions may conceivably write a valuable book or article. But it is most unlikely that they will produce truly distinguished work because they are *required* to publish, especially if they feel impelled to produce a lot of articles rather than concentrate on preparing one or two works of real quality. Forcing faculty members in more and more institutions to churn out more and more research only threatens to create greater stress and added busywork without contributing anything of real value to the corpus of scholarship.

In many, perhaps most of the institutions that have begun to emphasize publications, the impetus has probably come from the administration rather than the faculty. In comprehensive universities, new presidents recruited from research institutions have instinctively tried to impose the standards for hiring and promotion to which they have long been accustomed.[34] Some academic leaders may have felt that a vigorous research effort would attract outside funding with overhead payments that could strengthen their financial position. Even more may have emphasized research in an effort to gain prestige and a higher ranking that could eventually result in more donations, abler students, and greater pride on the part of alumni in their alma mater.

Strategies of this kind are unlikely to be successful and even less likely to serve the public interest. Starting a vigorous research program is a risky and expensive way to try to improve the bottom line. It requires investing a lot of money in higher faculty salaries, lower teaching loads, larger library holdings, graduate student fellowships, and proper laboratory facilities and equipment. Even if research grants materialize, they rarely include enough overhead funding to cover all the costs. It is no accident, then, that almost all experienced observers agree that in institutions lacking a long and successful record of scholarship, mounting a vigorous research program is very likely to drain money from education rather than the reverse.[35]

Efforts to gain a significantly higher place in the published university rankings occasionally succeed, most often in institutions situated in a growing area of the country where there is untapped private wealth but few, if any, strong, existing universities. Most of the time, however, the attempt fails; the price is too high and the advantage of well-established competitors too great to overcome. At best, efforts to advance succeed merely in luring some able students and faculty away from other universities without any net addition to the overall quality of higher education.

From several points of view, the prospects for seeking distinction through improved education are more promising. The cost is far smaller. The competition is less intense and the barriers to success far less formidable. Most important, genuine progress in improving the quality of education does not merely consist of moving faculty "stars" and students with high SAT scores from one institution to another; it adds to the effectiveness of undergraduate education as a whole and increases the number of students who benefit.

Emphasizing improvement in the quality of education need not imply any lowering of academic standards. Every university should insist that candidates for tenure or promotion demonstrate a high level of proficiency in contributing to the mission of the institution. The error lies in insisting that the contribution take the form of published research, the more books and articles the better. All too often, such a policy leads, not to important advances in our knowledge and understanding, but only to larger quantities of "unloved and unread publications" along with missed opportunities to improve the quality of education for undergraduates.

A NEEDED DIGRESSION

A closer look at the lives of faculty members suggests that increased demands for published research are not the only source of added pressure and stress. Hours of work per week have increased. Work-life stress has also intensified over the past twenty years, most noticeably from research and publishing demands but also because of additional time devoted to committee work and coping with institutional procedures and red tape.[36] These trends provoke a further question too rarely considered in writings about the state of higher education. Are there other ways in which faculty time is being needlessly squandered at the expense of more important pursuits?

Throughout the past two centuries, a series of duties previously performed by the faculty have been handed off to others, either entirely or in part—disciplining students and keeping order, which was a major responsibility of instructors in the eighteenth century and much of the nineteenth; and, more recently, in many universities, giving career advice to students and preparing and grading examinations. More often than not, such changes have occurred gradually, almost surreptitiously, without a serious debate, let alone a systematic review of the overall allocation of responsibilities among professors, adjunct instructors, graduate students, and administrators. The result has frequently been reduced teaching loads for professors and less time advising students.

Efforts to review the allocation of faculty time are bound to reach varying conclusions from one institution to another depending on local conditions. Judgments about the results will also differ depending on one's view of faculty priorities. Even so, it is worth pointing briefly to several problems common to enough universities to warrant at least a brief mention.

COMMITTEES

Committees are a necessary part of academic life in order to carry out essential tasks that only professors can perform, such as deciding whom to appoint to the faculty or how to revise the curriculum. On many campuses, however, there is a tendency to create new committees to deal with much more minor matters, such as deciding whom to invite for a named lecture, who should receive this year's teaching prize, or which notables should be given honorary degrees. Although none of these committees may take a great deal of time, the number of them grows and the cumulative demands can be substantial. Many of the tasks involved could be given to a single faculty member rather than a committee (or even to an administrative staff member in some cases) subject to final faculty approval.

Another common practice is to make committees larger than they need to be. This tendency has also grown in recent decades out of a sense that every committee must include representatives from various faculty groups—minorities, women, and junior faculty, in particular. While such representation serves a useful purpose when the committee performs a function directly relevant to the groups in question, the practice often extends to committees whose work has no such connection. Committees end up much larger than they need to be, creating unnecessary burdens for the faculty—especially for minorities and women—and causing meetings to become longer and harder to schedule.

LETTERS OF RECOMMENDATION

The practice of requiring letters of recommendation for applications to every kind of academic program has placed a further burden on the faculty out of all proportion to any real value served. The problems with such letters are well-known. Those who write them often accentuate the positive and eliminate the negative, either through fear that the evaluation will not remain confidential or because, in a world of inflated recommendations, they may do the applicant an injustice if they give a completely honest appraisal. In many cases, the writer has very little knowledge of the applicants apart from the grades they received, which are already available to those requesting the letter. Because members of the committee seldom know the authors of the letters, they cannot be sure how much weight to give to them. Nevertheless, since asking for letters costs them nothing save the time to skim the contents, committees continue to require written recommendations, even though they rarely make a difference save in the rare case when the writer reveals some startling fact—often involving serious misbehavior of some kind—that has not been disclosed in the rest of the applicant's dossier.

Reforming such a system will require some sort of collective action, perhaps by associations of universities or professional schools. At the least, these groups could agree among themselves to ask for a single uniform letter, as some professional schools have already done, so that faculty members do not have to write separate evaluations for each school to which a student has applied. Better yet, they could agree on a form similar to that used by bar associations in which the recommender need only check a box affirming the applicant's suitability and good character with optional space provided for any special information that the recommender may wish to include.

THE BURDEN OF BUREAUCRACY

As universities have grown larger and more complicated, the amount of supervision, coordination, and general administration has grown along with it. In most institutions, the rate of growth in the size of the administrative staff has far exceeded that of the student body or the faculty. This trend is not necessarily ill-advised. Some of the added staff have been needed to respond to increased student demands for services or to new regulations imposed by the government. Others, such as the growth in technical support personnel, are necessary to enable professors to take full advantage of new opportunities in teaching and research made possible by advances in instrumentation, computers, and other kinds of new technology. Still others help to raise the money to fund more fellowships, additional colleagues, and better facilities in which to work.

Whether or not the growth of administration is justified, it contributes in small, incremental ways to the burdens on the faculty. New staff members see new needs for data and institute more surveys and reports for professors and departments to complete. Meetings are called more frequently. New layers of authority must be petitioned and solicited in the process of gaining approval for actions previously taken unilaterally or approved with a single phone call. More administrative offices mean that more coordination is required to ensure that decisions do not conflict with other policies elsewhere in the hierarchy.

Some of these added burdens are required by law, and others serve valuable purposes. Still, it is usually the case that in deciding whether to conduct a survey, call a meeting, or require additional coordination, officials consider the advantages but pay little heed to the extra time and trouble required for faculty members to comply. In the individual case, the burden may seem too small to take seriously. In the aggregate, however, the extra demands accumulate to create a noticeable distraction for professors intent upon their teaching and research. It is worth noting that over the past twenty years, the category of "institutional procedures and red tape" has been second only to "lack of personal time" as a source of faculty stress. As a result, there is much to recommend a periodic review of existing procedures and administrative demands to determine whether some selective pruning is in order.

The message of this chapter contradicts the usual explanation for the conflict between teaching and research. The critical problem is not that emphasizing research leads to the appointment of indifferent teachers who neglect their students in order to spend more time on their scholarly work. Well-published scientists and scholars appear to teach as effectively as colleagues who avoid research to concentrate on their classes. The greatest problem lies in the effect that graduate (PhD) training and a pronounced research orientation have on the curriculum and on the time available for professors to undertake major improvements and innovations in their courses and methods of instruction.

This problem has been aggravated by the failure of many institutions to pay sufficient attention to conserving professors' time for their essential work by preventing a gradual accumulation of unnecessary chores. As a result, recent surveys have found that approximately one-third of professors are dissatisfied with their workload.[37] Almost half report that "my job is the source of considerable personal strain," and only one-third believe that they have "established a healthy balance in their lives personally and professionally."[38] Not surprisingly, faculty members who experience such pressure can often feel reluctant to spend much time mastering new methods of instruction or to support changes in educational policy and practice that would require more effort than they are already devoting to their teaching.

CHAPTER SIXTEEN

THE CHANGING NATURE
OF SCIENTIFIC RESEARCH

||||||||||||||||||||||||||||||||||||||||||||||||||||||||||||||||||||||||||||||||||||||||||||||||||||

DURING THE PAST THIRTY or forty years, the manner in which scientific research is done in universities has changed in fundamental respects. Not all fields of inquiry have been affected, nor are the changes wholly unprecedented. Nevertheless, the differences have become sufficiently widespread and deep to constitute at least a minor transformation.[1]

THE "NEW SCIENCE"

In the 1950s and 1960s, much of the writing about academic science made a sharp distinction between "pure" and "applied" research. Pure research took place primarily in universities and was said to be inspired by the desire of investigators to find new knowledge without regard for its practical use. However, the fruits of this research provided a storehouse of discoveries that applied scientists could draw upon in trying to solve practical problems. These solutions in turn would be used to develop new cures for disease, improved goods and services, entirely new products, and even new industries.

Today, this account no longer seems as satisfactory as it once did. The sharp division previously made between basic and applied research is now more blurred. The notion of a linear progression from fundamental inquiry to applied research and then to the development of new products does not accurately describe the process that currently takes place in science. Many ideas for academic research do not come to university researchers through independent study and reflection but from problems suggested by government sources or industry labs where much good science is currently carried on. Many scientists doing fundamental work are no longer interested solely in discovery for its own sake; they are moved, at least in part, by a desire to solve an important problem in society or help meet some pressing human need. As the distinguished chemist Stuart Schreiber remarked, describing his work with fellow researchers at the Harvard-MIT Broad Institute, "We like to get together and think about the greatest opportunities for improving science and society."[2] Stanford University now defines its mission as helping to solve the major problems of the world. The government has encouraged this approach by steering more of its funds for university research toward areas of science that are related to national needs. The "War on Cancer" and the Human Genome Project are prominent examples.

The research of academic scientists has also become more collaborative and interdisciplinary by comparison with earlier periods. Investigators addressing important human problems or attracted by exciting opportunities in fields such as stem cell research, nanotechnology, or environmental studies are likely to find that progress requires the help of colleagues in several disciplines. Scientists seeking to capitalize on the huge databases now available need the help of computer specialists. Biologists doing research on malaria want to collaborate with epidemiologists or biostatisticians. The Internet facilitates such cooperation by enabling investigators to join forces with colleagues in other parts of the country or even distant areas of the globe.

As the problems to solve grow larger and more complicated, the number of collaborators rises accordingly. Certain forms of research, such as gene sequencing, proteomics, and bioinformatics, require substantial teams of scientists, while experiments in high energy physics using the CERN linear accelerator in Switzerland attract small armies of investigators from many different institutions to join in carrying out experiments. Because of these developments, the number of scientific articles with twenty or more authors has grown steadily since 1980. By now, scores of papers with more than one hundred contributors have appeared in scientific journals, with a few of them boasting more than four hundred authors.[3]

Collaborations in research extend well beyond the academy. Highly talented investigators today are more inclined than they once were to work for a corporation, at least for part of their careers, because of the interesting research being done in many start-up companies, the state-of-the-art facilities that some firms provide, and the relative ease of getting needed funding for projects of interest to the enterprise. As a result, academic scientists are more likely to find researchers in corporate laboratories with whom they want to collaborate.

Many scientists who choose academic careers consult regularly with industry, especially with biomedical companies. Interaction of this kind has multiple benefits. For faculty members, such collaborations can result not only in extra income but in new ideas to pursue along with access to valuable databases and research materials. For companies, closer contact with professors can provide up-to-date knowledge of promising research along with valuable advice on how best to explore complex scientific problems. Students can gain from opportunities to work on real-world problems and learn of possible career opportunities.[4] For universities, cooperation with business may result in additional funds from research grants, patent license royalties, or commercial partners for new ventures to exploit discoveries by faculty members. Government agencies have provided funds and taken other steps to encourage closer collaboration between businesses and universities, because such interaction promises to bring about innovation, economic growth, and ultimately new jobs.

In an effort to harvest the fruits of scientific research and turn them into innovative products and processes, Congress passed the Bayh-Dole Act in 1980 allowing universities to patent discoveries made through government-funded research and keep any royalties that resulted. Following this legislation, research universities quickly established technology transfer offices to scour their labs for patentable discoveries and carry out the task of obtaining patents and licensing them to companies. In addition, universities helped members of their faculty start new companies by putting them in contact with venture capitalists, investing their own funds in enterprises started by their professors, and even providing "incubators" to develop promising inventions to a point at which outside investors would supply the capital to create a viable company.

Now that academic scientists have become more involved with business and their work has such direct, observable consequences for society, they are held accountable by more groups outside the academy. If human beings are the subjects for research, projects must be approved in advance by institutional review boards. Safety rules have become more numerous and detailed. Some types of research are even deemed too harmful or their consequences too dangerous to be allowed. Thus, federal funding for stem cell research was severely restricted under an order approved by President George W. Bush, while efforts to clone human beings have been prohibited entirely. Increasingly, then, academic research is not judged solely on its intellectual merits but on its practical consequences as well. As Piotr Sztompka observes, "The scientific community has been penetrated by politicians, administrators, marketing experts, lobbyists, all of whom are moved by different interests and different values than the disinterested pursuit of knowledge."[5] With closer scrutiny comes more regulation, more red tape, and more delay.

Few of the developments described above are entirely new. Nevertheless, they have now proceeded to such an extent that the nature of academic science seems fundamentally altered. The "ivory tower" has been breached at so many points and the connections with the outside world have grown so numerous and close that the term no longer has descriptive value. The very mission of research universities has expanded to include making contributions to economic development and other national needs, with consequences for science that are not yet fully understood.

ACCOMMODATING INTERDISCIPLINARY RESEARCH

Along with all the benefits, the trends just described have created several problems for research universities. One difficulty is organizational. The collaborative, interdisciplinary nature of much current scientific research fits awkwardly in universities divided into separate discipline-based departments. Departments still exist because they continue to serve important purposes. They provide appropriate units where clusters of similarly trained specialists can train new generations of professors and researchers. They are the most qualified groups within the university to make the critical judgments of intellectual quality in deciding whom to appoint and promote. Together with similar departments nationwide, they offer a common career structure that enables graduate students to prepare themselves in ways that qualify them for faculty positions in a wide variety of other colleges and universities.

Despite the useful functions they perform, departments create obstacles that inhibit interdisciplinary work of the kind increasingly pursued by academic scientists. Departments are often reluctant to hire a new faculty member whose research is interdisciplinary, since they are naturally disposed to prefer work that fits squarely within their traditional subjects and methods of inquiry. They may discourage their members from teaching interdisciplinary subjects, because their first concern is to staff the classes for their undergraduate majors and graduate students. Junior faculty members are particularly sensitive to these pressures and restraints, since teaching interdisciplinary courses or participating in interdisciplinary research may not count in their favor when they try to obtain a tenure appointment either in their current department or in a similar department elsewhere. Even graduate students may be inhibited from pursuing subjects outside their department if such courses are not counted toward their PhD.

Fortunately, the walls that surround departments are not impregnable. Senior faculty members from two or more departments who wish to create an interdisciplinary undergraduate major can usually do so. In rare instances, they may get permission from their university to found a new department; biochemistry and biophysics are two familiar examples. A simpler and more frequent way for members of different departments to come together around a common interest is to form a research center or a joint committee to pursue interdisciplinary topics such as environmental studies or bioengineering.

These solutions, however, while helpful, do not remove all of the obstacles hampering interdisciplinary research. In particular, they do not completely solve the problem of making interdisciplinary appointments, since an established department must typically give its approval. Thus, an environmental research center may badly need to hire an economist, but such an appointment must ordinarily be supported by the economics department, which may not give its consent even if money is available to assume the cost. In theory, this problem could be overcome through the creation of a new interdisciplinary department. In practice, however, universities are reluctant to approve such a step unless the subject matter seems destined to remain important for the indefinite future, since it is usually very hard to dismantle a department even after its subject is no longer intellectually exciting.

In recent years, the pull of interdisciplinary research has become so strong that senior faculty are literally demanding that ways be found to facilitate such work even if it costs a lot of money to do so. In response to these pressures, departments have taken steps to make it easier for graduate students to take courses in other fields. Interdisciplinary programs and even new departments have been created on a university-wide basis to allow professors to teach and collaborate with interested colleagues across the campus to work on subjects such as stem cell research or environmental studies.

The most intriguing of these efforts has been the creation of new structures that allow scientists from different parts of the university to collaborate for a few years on a common research project and receive various forms of technical support and needed funding for their work.[6] One large and successful example of such a structure is the Broad Institute, founded with the aid of a large private gift and jointly directed by Harvard and the Massachusetts Institute of Technology. "The Broad" provides the facilities and equipment to support (mostly health-related) research drawing on the vast pool of researchers working in Boston-area universities and hospitals. A small group of senior professors form a steering committee to guide the organization, choose worthy problems and projects, and select investigators to become affiliated for a period of years. Approved projects are undertaken by temporary research groups drawn primarily from the two universities and the Harvard-affiliated teaching hospitals. When the project is finished, the collaborators return to their respective faculties and departments.

In other universities, the initiative in encouraging interdisciplinary research has come from the central administration. At the University of Wisconsin, for example, interdisciplinary groups of faculty are invited to submit proposals for initial funding. The provost then selects the most promising collaborations and gives them money to get underway. On some campuses, large sums have been raised from industry or state governments to fund and house an interdisciplinary effort devoted to a subject with the potential to spur economic growth. For example, with the aid of a multimillion-dollar investment from the state legislature, Arizona State University developed a new interdisciplinary program in biodesign to bring together researchers from several disciplines "to improve human health and quality of life through use-inspired biosystems research and effective multi-disciplinary partnerships."[7]

At times, new buildings are constructed to facilitate interdisciplinary collaborations. One of the most successful has been the Bio-X facility at Stanford, constructed at a location adjacent to several collaborating schools and departments. A steering committee arranges talks, symposia, and faculty seminars. The focal point is the cafeteria, which is designed to encourage impromptu gatherings of professors from different disciplines around a luncheon table. The building offers space to carry on collaborative projects, and participants resume their normal duties in their respective faculties when the project ends. Several hundred professors have now participated in endeavors of this kind.

These efforts to accommodate interdisciplinary research are commendable and go a long way toward overcoming the obstacles created by the traditional departmental structure. Nevertheless, even well-financed research initiatives such as the Broad Institute cannot fully resolve all the problems of undertaking interdisciplinary, problem-oriented projects. They do not entirely remove the risk for junior faculty who want to participate in research outside the mainstream of their discipline, nor do they avoid the strained relations that can develop when scientists in traditional departments see highly valued members joining interdisciplinary groups and ceasing to participate fully in the work of their former colleagues.

Witnessing these difficulties, some might argue that traditional departments are now an impediment to progress and should simply be disbanded. Yet departments would be hard to do without, for they still perform valuable functions. In particular, they play such an important role in creating viable academic job markets that no single university could abandon them without putting the careers of its graduate students and junior faculty at risk. For this reason, the kinds of arrangement exemplified by interdisciplinary centers or the Bio-X building probably represent the best available compromise to reconcile the needs of the new research with the traditional departmental structure.

COMMERCIALIZATION

The organizational difficulties just described are not the only problems created by the new environment of scientific research. Challenges of a different kind have arisen from efforts to increase the commercialization of scientific discoveries, whether in health-related fields or in such disparate subjects as computer science, polymers, materials science, and even economics and linguistics.

In many ways, the government has succeeded in encouraging technology transfer and other efforts to help academic research to stimulate economic growth. The number of patents for university discoveries has risen sharply since Congress enacted the Bayh-Dole Act in 1980.[8] While universities receive only 2 percent of all patents, they obtain 16 percent of the patents issued in the field of biotechnology and 9 percent of all new drug patents. The number of "spin-off" firms resulting from university-based research grew from 241 in 1994 to 555 in 2007. Various forms of collaboration with industry have blossomed with the aid of government support.

A major stimulus for such activity has been the prospect of making money through closer cooperation with commercial companies. Professors can earn substantial sums from consulting, receiving patent royalties, or founding new companies growing out of their research. A handful of universities have profited handsomely from closer ties with industry through royalties from patent licensing, corporate research support, and even equity holdings in new businesses started by members of their faculty. Although the National Research Council has declared that universities should manage these activities primarily to advance the public interest by promoting a wider, faster use of scientific knowledge, most technology transfer officials admit that their principal goal has been to maximize income.[9]

The Hazards of Commercialization

There are risks for the university from encouraging closer ties with industry, and they are not trivial. It is possible that professors will neglect their academic duties by spending much of their time starting new companies or choosing research projects more for their commercial value than their scientific importance. Faculty entrepreneurs may divert the energies of their graduate students by using them to help start a new firm or work on commercial projects rather than devote their time to activities more directly related to their future careers. Universities may approve the appointment and promotion of professors based on their success in acquiring patents and launching companies rather than their accomplishments in the laboratory and the classroom.[10]

In addition, the commercialization of research threatens to undermine other values that have long been considered fundamental to the optimum progress of science, values best described in the writings of the distinguished sociologist

Robert Merton. In particular, Merton wrote, scientific inquiry must be carried on *openly* in the sense of making the results public and allowing free access to findings and materials that can help other scientists make further progress. Researchers should be *disinterested*, as free as possible from pressures and temptations other than the desire to discover the truth. In addition, research findings should be subject to *verification* by independent testing to ensure their validity.[11]

In the new, more commercial environment of much contemporary academic science, each of Merton's values is potentially at risk.[12] University scientists who are funded by business may undermine openness by agreeing to keep their findings confidential, either indefinitely as trade secrets or for a period of time until their company sponsor can decide whether to file for patent protection. Discoveries may be patented, which can prevent other scientists from using them if university officials or their corporate licensees restrict access by refusing to share materials or data in order to protect their commercial interests. Finally, professors can acquire financial ties that impair their disinterestedness in carrying out research. They may undertake experiments to test new drugs produced by firms for which they consult or whose stock they own. Or they may advise government agencies or write articles on the safety and efficacy of products made by companies in which they have a significant financial interest. In all these ways, commercialization provides a test of how universities and their professors will behave when they must choose between financial gain and traditional academic values.

THE RESPONSE BY UNIVERSITIES

Despite the temptations, there is nothing inherently wrong with a university allowing or even encouraging the translation of discoveries made in its laboratories into useful products and processes. On the contrary, the government has signaled in many different ways its desire to have universities work with industry. In doing so, politicians are surely reflecting a strong public interest in using research to promote health and spur economic growth. Since universities eagerly accept many billions of dollars each year in federal research funds, they have a duty to honor the government's desire to obtain the practical benefits that prompt the use of taxpayers' money to support research. At the same time, universities also have a duty to both themselves and the public to manage their relations with industry in a way that preserves the basic values that have long been deemed essential to the long-term health and vitality of academic research. If they neglect this obligation, they could eventually kill the goose that lays the golden eggs.

In recognition of the risks involved in collaborating with industry, academic officials have erected safeguards to keep their faculty focused on their academic work. Almost all universities have long had a rule forbidding professors to spend more than one day per week on outside activities (which include consulting and establishing and overseeing a for-profit company). Nevertheless, academic leaders have seldom done much to clarify the obvious ambiguities in such rules. Does "one day" include weekends or only Monday through Friday? Does the rule apply during vacations? Are conferences and speeches at other universities counted as "outside activities?" How about consulting with government officials on important national issues? In practice, whatever the terms may mean, few academic leaders make much effort to ensure compliance or to monitor the outside activities of their professors. Many universities ask faculty members to file periodic accounts of their outside activities, but it is difficult to check the accuracy of these reports, and universities rarely do so.

Despite the need to avoid excessive secrecy in science, it is generally agreed that company sponsors deserve a reasonable opportunity to evaluate the results of research they have funded to decide whether to seek a patent. Most observers believe that a period of approximately sixty days should suffice for such purposes. Nevertheless, the latest available comprehensive study of the problem found that fewer than half of the research agreements with companies prohibited funders from keeping research results secret longer than necessary to file for patent protection.[13] Another study revealed that only 12 percent of universities had imposed a specific limit on the length of time that corporate funders can insist on keeping research findings confidential.[14]

Many universities have also been lax in insisting on rules to protect the freedom of professors in conducting research funded by industry. In a 2003 survey of technology transfer officials, 28 percent acknowledged that they had no clear rules forbidding corporate sponsors to demand the right to veto or censor the publication of a professor's findings.[15] At least half of the universities allowed companies to review the grantee's findings prior to publication. Moreover, some universities have approved funding from industry for tests of new products even though the company has insisted on the right to veto publication of results and/or control the release of the data underlying the study.[16]

Campus rules regarding financial conflicts of interest also leave a lot to be desired. Most institutions do have rules requiring researchers to report such conflicts to the university, and most biomedical journals also insist that authors disclose these conflicts to their readers. Nevertheless, few universities and journals specify penalties for failing to comply or make serious efforts to enforce their disclosure rules, and many observers suspect that there is widespread noncompliance.[17] Congressional committees have publicly identified several prominent academic scientists who received much larger payments from industry for delivering lectures or conducting research than they disclosed to their own universities.[18] However, the precise extent of noncompliance is still unknown.

Conflicts of interest can also arise for universities. If a medical school signs a contract with a pharmaceutical company to test its new drugs on a for-profit basis, it has a financial interest in satisfying the client by arriving at positive results in close or ambiguous cases. Once a university takes a large block of stock in a start-up company founded by one of its professors (as many universities have done in the hope of discovering a new Google or Microsoft), it acquires a financial incentive to favor the professor in matters of promotion, leaves of absence, use of graduate students for company purposes, and other personnel decisions.

Such conflicts may raise suspicions of favoritism even when nothing of the kind has occurred, thus casting doubt on the integrity of the university's administrative processes.* Nevertheless, universities have rarely enacted policies to deal with such situations.[19] In fact, they have stoutly resisted efforts by federal officials to regulate institutional conflicts, a stance that can hardly enhance their credibility when they seek to tighten rules concerning the conflicts of their faculty members.[20]

It is only fair to note that at least a few institutions have done much more to protect academic values than the foregoing summary would suggest. It is also likely that tougher rules and safeguards are gradually becoming more common. Still, many university officials appear to have been more lax than they should be in framing and enforcing conflict-of-interest rules. Presumably, they have been fearful that stricter rules might either persuade corporate funders to take their money elsewhere or cause prominent members of the faculty to defect to another institution rather than curtail their consulting and other lucrative activities. Whatever the reason, where conflicts of interest are concerned, money seems to triumph over principle with disturbing frequency.

THE EFFECTS OF COMMERCIALIZATION

The fact that many universities have not been as zealous as they might be in protecting academic values does not prove that harm has occurred. Scientists and

---

*Institutional conflicts of interest have been increasing in areas apart from research. As indicated in chapter 7, the efforts by universities to undertake for-profit ventures in online courses, extension programs, and branch campuses overseas all create institutional conflicts and give rise to risks of compromising standards of educational quality in order to increase profits. Intercollegiate athletics, of course, represent a much older, more flagrant example of what can happen when universities allow conflicts to arise between making money and upholding academic standards.

scholars have reasons of their own to uphold many of the values that are important to academic research. Hence, those seeking to assess the effects of technology transfer need to determine how academic researchers have actually behaved and not merely examine the preventive measures that universities have taken.

In one important respect, fortunately, no adverse effects seem to have occurred. When universities first became active in marketing the discoveries of their professors, critics expressed a fear that basic research would suffer since scientists would be tempted to devote more and more of their energies to the kinds of applied work that could result in lucrative stock holdings or patent royalties.[21] Enough time has now elapsed that the results can be evaluated, and, fortunately, empirical studies reveal little sign of such a shift.[22] Although a substantial fraction of biomedical researchers interact with industry in one way or another, those who are heavily involved seem no less productive, no less engaged and successful in their teaching, and no less active in the work of their departments than colleagues who have few commercial ties. According to one study of more than three thousand academic life scientists, 52 percent acknowledged having some relationship with industry, but the average amount of time devoted to such activities was only 5.8 hours per week, comfortably below the one-day-per-week maximum long allowed to faculty members for such purposes.[23]

Early fears about the effects of patenting on the choice of research topics also seem to have been groundless. In one study of biomedical scientists, only seven among more than five hundred respondents mentioned the prospect of acquiring patents as a significant factor in their choice of research projects.[24] Other studies find that academic scientists who have obtained numerous patents continue to publish as many articles with just as impressive citation counts as colleagues who have no patents, and their productivity seems as strong as it was before they began acquiring patents.[25] One survey (limited to engineering faculty) even found that professors who started companies based on their research continued to produce more papers and compile more impressive citation counts than their colleagues.[26] In short, as one student of commercialization put it, "the evidence appears to reject the assertion that the increase in patenting in academe has come at the cost of diverting researchers' time, interest, and attention from their traditional focus on standard scientific research."[27] A report from a committee of the National Research Council issued in 2010 reached the same conclusion.[28]

Aggressive efforts by universities to patent the discoveries of their professors have also interfered less with access to research materials than some critics feared. This appears to be true although courts have upheld granting patents even to genes and other basic facts of nature and have also made it clear that patents can be infringed not just by corporations but by professors using patented ideas and materials in their research.[29] It is true that some universities have not only sought patents on basic discoveries but made aggressive efforts to protect their rights in order to maximize their royalties.[30] According to a recent study, however, none of the biomedical researchers surveyed who needed information or material covered by a patent had been denied access.[31] In almost all instances where formal requests for material were made to another university, permission was granted, and in only 10 percent of the cases did negotiations last for more than one month.[32] Almost invariably, no fee was charged for the material.

Apparently, most academic researchers feel unhindered by patents simply because they are not even aware of their existence. Patent-holders rarely protest, either because they do not know of the infringement or because it is not worth the effort and expense of pursuing the matter in court. If protests do occur, investigators can often find ways to work around a denial of access without having to abandon their project. Having reviewed the evidence carefully, therefore, one team of researchers concluded that the results "suggest that patents rarely interfere with research, and even material transfers [in response to requests for information or research material from another party] are largely processed without incident."[33] After reviewing this study along with others, the same 2010 report from the National Research Council concurred with this conclusion.[34]

The record is less encouraging in cases involving other risks arising from relationships with industry. With respect to secrecy, 58 percent of corporate funders in one survey admitted that they regularly insisted that their grantees delay publication of research results for more than six months, well beyond the time normally required to decide whether to file for a patent.[35] More than 13 percent of the academic scientists with industry funding admitted in another study that they had delayed publication of their findings beyond six months for commercial reasons.[36] Still another inquiry found that 14 percent of academic researchers with industry funding acknowledged keeping findings confidential as trade secrets.[37] For generations, of course, scientists have sometimes failed to disclose their findings in order to preserve their advantage over rival investigators.* Even so, professors receiving company support were three times more likely to keep their discoveries secret than investigators who received no corporate funding.

---

* At least one recent study seems to indicate that competition among scientists is a more important cause of withholding information than commercial restrictions. David Blumenthal et al., "Data Withholding in Genetics and the Other Life Sciences: Prevalence and Predictors," 81 *Academic Medicine* (2006), p. 137.

Overall, the average delays stipulated in agreements with industry funders may exceed what is necessary, but they still tend to be quite modest, in part because university scientists have strong motives of their own to insist on reasonably prompt publication of their discoveries. Thus, a study of corporate funding in 2007 found that the median time for delaying publication was four months, a period that is probably too brief to have a significant impact on the progress of research.[38]

The most serious problems have arisen from conflicts of interest involving academic scientists who receive research support, consulting fees, or other funding of some sort from companies with an obvious stake in the results of their research. Such conflicts appear to be quite common, especially in the testing of new drugs or other health-related products. Many of the academic researchers involved seem unconcerned, however, confident that their financial ties to a company whose products they are evaluating could not possibly affect their scientific judgment.

Unfortunately, the record does not justify such complacency. Psychologists have found that even small gifts and favors tend to influence the behavior of recipients toward the donor.[39] Studies of research on the efficacy of new drugs or the health effects of consumer products tend to bear out this conclusion. One study of clinical trials that were either paid for by industry or conducted by an investigator who had financial ties to the firm found that such trials were 3.6 *times* more likely to reach findings favorable to the company than trials that were independently funded with no financial conflict involved.[40] Another inquiry showed that 94 percent of studies testing the effects of secondhand smoke that were funded by the tobacco industry found no harmful health effects, while only 13 percent of independently funded studies reached the same conclusion.[41] Studies reporting similar results abound. While the differences may be partially explained by the companies' effort to choose investigators who seem more likely to make favorable findings, it is doubtful that this explanation can fully account for the large discrepancies involved.

In cases that do not involve research on human subjects, the usual remedy for conflicts of interest on the part of researchers is simply a requirement that the investigator disclose the conflict to the university and, if the results are published, to the readers. Unfortunately, it is not at all clear how much disclosure of this kind can accomplish. It may provide a warning, but it does not enable readers to judge whether bias has in fact affected the results and, if so, how seriously. Instead, disclosure may simply create suspicions that further undermine confidence in the work of academic scientists.

There is even some research suggesting that disclosure, far from putting readers on guard, may actually enhance the author's stature in their eyes, while also causing authors to feel less scrupulous, having warned their readers, in presenting their ideas objectively.[42] If these findings are correct, it is hard to know what good can come of requiring authors to reveal their financial ties. To be sure, if all professors with such conflicts could be counted upon to reveal them, disclosure would at least let readers know which published material might be financially biased and which is not. Nevertheless, since compliance with existing university rules seems to leave much to be desired, disclosure may not even provide this benefit.[43]

Because public disclosure is not a complete answer to conflicts of interest, campus officials often use other means to guard against bias where conflicts exist. When notified of financial conflicts, universities can insist on monitoring the research to avoid bias, although there are so many ways by which bias can influence a study that truly effective monitoring will often require more intensive scrutiny than is practical.[44] Alternatively, campus officials may require that the investigator carry out the study in collaboration with other investigators who have no conflicts (assuming that willing collaborators can be found). If these alternative safeguards are not feasible, universities may forbid the research altogether.

Most of the studies and publicity regarding conflicts of interest have involved medical research, which is hardly surprising since so much corporate funding comes from health-related companies. There are other fields of inquiry, however, in which financial conflicts of interest are common yet the efforts of universities to uphold important research values appear to be lax or nonexistent. Social scientists have been paid well by interested parties to write articles on important policy issues without disclosing the payments. In energy research, where the federal government has partnered with oil companies to provide hundreds of millions of dollars for university research, conflicts of interest are common, time limits for keeping results secret are much less stringent than NIH recommends, and projects are funded without undergoing independent peer review.[45] In the field of nutrition, professors often carry out research funded by industry to test the positive effects of new products, and some of them have reportedly been discouraged by their corporate donors from publishing adverse findings.[46]

Even more disturbing cases have come to light involving blatant attempts by corporations to influence the results of academic studies they have sponsored to test the safety and efficacy of their products. Some academic health centers enter into research agreements with industry although provisions of the contract permit company sponsors to revise manuscripts and even decide whether the results should be published.[47] One study revealed that 11 percent of a sample of 809 published reports on drugs and health products ostensibly

authored by academic researchers had actually been ghostwritten by representatives of the company sponsoring the research. The role of the authors named
in the published version amounted to no more than editing a company draft.[48]
In some cases, the faculty investigators did not even have control of the data
but were simply given summaries or edited versions supplied by the sponsoring company. It is hard to imagine behavior much more plainly unprofessional
than allowing a company to exert such influence over research involving its
products. Yet a survey completed in 2007–8 revealed that 70 percent of academic medical centers had no explicit rules prohibiting such practices.[49]

A FINAL ACCOUNTING

Summing up the overall impact of commercialization on the quality and integrity of academic research, one can take comfort from the fact that opportunities to make money from commercially valuable discoveries seem to have had
little or no ascertainable effect on the productivity of university investigators.
There has been no demonstrable shift from basic research to applied and potentially lucrative inquiry, nor have commercial and consulting activities led to
any apparent loss of quality or significance in the subsequent publications of
the scientists involved. Of course, these results do not rule out the possibility
that the lure of making money will eventually have a malign influence. Still,
the fact that a few universities such as MIT and Stanford have encouraged entrepreneurial activity on the part of their faculties over many decades without
apparent harm to their research reputation suggests that a vigilant institution
can manage technology transfer effectively if it tries conscientiously to do so.

On the other hand, the continued lack of strict conflict-of-interest rules in
a number of universities and the absence of vigorous enforcement of existing
rules by many other institutions threaten to place a cloud of suspicion over the
published work of academic researchers, whether it be reports on their research
or commentary on other questions of scientific or general interest. As more and
more studies and articles appear documenting the financial entanglements of
academic authors, the public may come to doubt the objectivity of the research
and lose confidence in the public pronouncements of professors on a wide variety of subjects ranging from new drugs and medical treatments to dietary
advice, global warming, occupational safety, and much else. How can anyone
know whether the statements of scientists and scholars on such subjects are
unbiased or influenced by some undisclosed financial interest in a company
with a stake in the outcome? A democratic society badly needs credible, unbiased information from highly knowledgeable people in order to enlighten

decision-makers and inform public debate. Thus, the country has much to lose if the objectivity of academic researchers can no longer be taken for granted.

All in all, then, the results of commercialization seem decidedly mixed. The net effects have been summarized most succinctly by Professor Roger Geiger in his *Knowledge and Money*. According to Geiger, "the marketplace has, on balance, brought universities greater resources [and] a far larger capacity for advancing knowledge, and a more productive role in the U.S. economy. At the same time, it has diminished the sovereignty of universities over their own activities, weakened their mission of serving the public, and created through growing commercial entanglements at least the potential for undermining their privileged role as disinterested arbiters of knowledge."[50]

In short, if the effects of technology transfer and closer collaboration with business have not been as dire as several early critics predicted, neither have they been wholly positive. To the extent that academic values remain intact, much of the credit must be ascribed either to the strength of traditional norms within the scientific community itself or to intervention from external sources. Too often absent are continuing efforts by university officials to work with their faculties to build effective safeguards and educate professors on the need for strict compliance. While there are notable exceptions, academic leaders as a whole have tended to resist efforts by the government to provide closer over-sight, while often failing to create effective ways of their own to monitor the behavior of their scientists or take appropriate measures to deal with violations of the rules when they occur. In supporting the process of technology trans-fer, therefore, universities may be contributing to innovation and economic growth, but they have yet to do all they should to protect the values essential to the continued integrity of academic research.

CHAPTER SEVENTEEN

THE ENVIRONMENT
FOR RESEARCH

IIIIIIIIIIIIIIIIIIIIIIIIIIIIIIIIIIIIIIIIIIIIIIIIIIIIIIIIIIIIIIIIIIIIIIIIIIIIIIIIIIIIIIIIIIIIIIIIIIIIII

ONE QUESTION THAT IS repeatedly asked of university presidents is what they regard as the hardest part of their job. Fund-raising, some might say. Juggling the endless demands on one's time, others might reply. To me, however, the ultimate challenge was trying to figure out why some intellectual environments have been so much more successful than others in helping to inspire genuinely creative thought. To put it more concretely, what was it about Athens in the fifth century BC, or Florence in the fifteenth century AD, or, for that matter, Budapest around the turn of the twentieth century that produced so many people of such exceptional creativity and talent? If presidents could only understand that, they might be able to bring about something really remarkable in their own university.

Although I was never able to arrive at a fully satisfactory answer to my question, I could easily think of *some* of the ingredients of success. Assembling the most talented faculty one can find was surely one part of the answer. Attracting a collection of people widely diverse in interests, background, and outlook would appear to be another. Guaranteeing the freedom of faculty members to speak and write as they choose must presumably be a third. Granted, the historical evidence for this last proposition is not unequivocal; the most creative periods in human history have hardly been wholly free. Athens in its golden age may have been a model of tolerance for its time, but it was far from guaranteeing all its citizens the right to express ideas freely. Socrates, after all, was put to death for allegedly miseducating the young. Eighteenth-century France was scarcely better. Voltaire and his Enlightenment colleagues were frequently forced to publish their books elsewhere or even to flee the country entirely to avoid being punished for their writings. Still, although some brave souls always seem to find the courage to express controversial thoughts despite real risk to their life and liberty (consider China or Russia, for example), one must assume that restrictions on speech and thought will inhibit other creative minds from contributing all they might to human knowledge and understanding. As a result, freedom of expression is properly thought to be indispensable to academic life in America and has been respected as such for almost a century.

Today, professors are protected in their teaching and writing both by the doctrine of academic freedom and by the First Amendment of the Constitution. As Justice Brennan declared in *Keyishian v. Board of Regents*, "academic freedom is of transcendent value to all of us and not merely to the teachers concerned. . . . That freedom is therefore a special concern of the First Amendment, which does not tolerate laws that cast a pall of orthodoxy over the classroom."[1]

Though academic freedom and the First Amendment overlap, as Brennan observed, they differ in several respects.[2] The Constitution gives protection only against acts of government and thus may not help professors in private universities, while academic freedom applies to private and public institutions alike. On the other hand, in contrast to the First Amendment, which protects every citizen, only the senior faculty enjoy the security of tenure; assistant professors, instructors, and part-time lecturers cannot feel certain that they will be protected. Moreover, freedom of speech is legally guaranteed under the Constitution, while academic freedom is merely a doctrine adopted by the American Association of University Professors (AAUP) and enforced through censure by that organization. As a practical matter, however, the principle of academic freedom is now so widely accepted throughout higher education that few colleges or universities would dare to brazenly fire a professor for expressing unpopular thoughts, if only from fear of the protests that would ensue and the harm that could be done to their reputation.

While faculty members enjoy broad freedom of expression, their liberty is not and cannot be absolute. Academic freedom does not protect professors who insult students in their classes or engage in long harangues about controversial matters unrelated to the subject of their course. Universities regularly deny faculty appointments or promotions on the basis of the candidates' writings and are clearly entitled to do so as long as the judgments are rendered by intellectual peers based on the quality of the scholarly work and not on extraneous matters such as a candidate's political or religious views.

By now, the AAUP rarely has occasion to condemn a college or university for violations of academic freedom. From 1995 to 2004, only 19 out of the more than 4,000 colleges and universities were placed on the censure list (while 16 were removed as no longer deserving condemnation).[3] Nevertheless, surveys reveal a worrisome trend in faculty attitudes about freedom of speech on campus. From 1969 to 1997, the percentage of all professors in America who agreed ("somewhat" or "strongly") that "the administration at your institution supports academic freedom" fell from 76.1 percent to 55.3

percent.[4] The decline in confidence was most severe at research universities, where it dropped from 78 percent to 53.3 percent.[5] A survey in 2007 of faculty from 19 countries found that only 41.1 percent of American professors agreed that "the administration supports academic freedom"—virtually the lowest level of confidence of any of the nations polled.[6] In 2007, when asked how much they felt their own academic freedom had been threatened during the past few years, 28 percent of professors replied "some" or "a lot," a degree of concern even greater than the level recorded in the McCarthy era when members of Congress held hearings to expose professors with Communist ties and the University of California Board of Regents insisted that all professors sign a loyalty oath.[7]

What accounts for this drop in confidence? It is not a product of Al-Qaeda's attack on the World Trade Center. Although a tiny number of professors were dismissed by their universities after 9/11 for expressing sympathy toward terrorists or allegedly having ties to terrorist organizations, faculty confidence about the right to speak freely fell precipitously well before 2001. Nor can the decline be attributed to the steady increase in the number of adjunct or part-time instructors, since confidence plummeted among tenured professors.

A more likely contributing cause was the introduction of official codes on many campuses in the 1980s prohibiting speech or conduct that demeaned individuals because of their race, religion, gender, or sexual orientation. Speech codes were enacted for the most part through a well-meaning effort by campus officials to stop students from uttering threats, derogatory epithets, or engaging in other behavior hostile to women, minorities, and gays that tended to intimidate and interfere with the ability of members of the threatened groups to study and learn. A number of the codes, however, were vaguely written and some were truly ridiculous, condemning such behavior as "leering," "ogling," "sexually derogatory jokes," and "inappropriately directed laughter." Although these prohibitions were chiefly directed at students, professors in some colleges were subjected to secret investigations following allegations by students that they gave racist lectures or made demeaning comments about women.[8] In the wake of such codes and the widespread publicity that accompanied them, the percentage of professors agreeing that "faculty are free to express relevant ideas in class" fell from 83.9 percent to 62.8 percent.[9]

Eventually, speech codes were struck down as unconstitutional by federal judges.[10] Nevertheless, the confidence of professors that their right to speak would be guaranteed by colleagues and administration was shaken on many campuses. Speech codes remain on the books in many universities even though they are rarely enforced.[11] Professors are still not entirely sure how much protection academic freedom provides; in particular, its application to what instructors say in the classroom remains a murky area with few clear precedents. If anything, the extent of the freedom given to professors has become even more uncertain owing to the vague language used by the Supreme Court in upholding the constitutionality of legislation outlawing sexual harassment in the workplace.[12] Even without speech codes, reading about the widely publicized controversies that have arisen on several campuses, many professors presumably wonder how much support they will receive from their own administration if they are condemned and verbally abused for statements students consider to be racist, sexist, anti-Semitic, or homophobic.

Whatever the explanation, it is no small matter that more than half of the faculty in research universities do not now believe that "the administration at your institution supports academic freedom."[13] Deans, provosts, and especially presidents are supposed to nurture and protect basic academic values in their institutions and to clarify doubts about the scope of a professor's right to speak and write freely. The figures just cited suggest that leaders on many campuses are failing to fulfill this responsibility.

THE QUESTION OF TENURE

By now, the idea of academic freedom is widely accepted within colleges and universities, whatever doubts may exist about how stoutly it will be defended. The question that remains controversial is the usefulness of the traditional means of guaranteeing this freedom—lifetime tenure. Debates about this practice continue almost a century after its inception. Few subjects in higher education have aroused such division of opinion or given rise to such dubious arguments on both sides of the issue.

Advocates of tenure have long insisted that job security is essential to the preservation of academic freedom. The validity of this claim, however, is not immediately obvious. It is surely not beyond human ingenuity to devise procedures that afford the necessary protection to free speech without having to guarantee lifetime employment. The First Amendment already provides such safeguards for faculty members employed by public universities—and does so for untenured as well as tenured instructors. One could argue that going to court is a long and costly way to vindicate one's rights, but it may not be more time consuming than working through the censure proceedings of the American Association of University Professors or more expensive than suing for breach of contract.

A cheaper, more expeditious alternative would be to guarantee academic freedom for all faculty members and have it enforced by private arbitration.* A similar process has long been successfully used in collective bargaining agreements to enforce the usual provisions barring termination without just cause. Such a procedure could be established by legislation, by collective bargaining where a faculty union exists, or else by voluntary action on the part of universities, as many institutions have already accomplished by guaranteeing fair treatment for their employees, including the right not to be fired without just cause. Regardless of the method used, the point remains that lifetime tenure is not the only way to protect professors from being penalized for their opinions. Nor does tenure offer comprehensive safeguards to all, or even a majority of instructors.† Arbitration could protect every member of the faculty, not just those with tenure, while covering all forms of retaliation or intimidation that interfere with free speech and not merely termination of employment.[14]

At the same time, the fact that tenure is not essential to the preservation of academic freedom does not necessarily mean that it should be abandoned. Those who advocate such reform contend that guaranteeing lifetime job security interferes with a university's ability to respond easily to changes in educational needs and priorities. Yet this is surely a misleading argument. It is true that without tenure professors can be removed and replaced more easily, thus giving institutions greater flexibility to respond to changing instructional priorities. The decisive rebuttal, however, is that colleges have already hired massive numbers of part-time instructors who clearly have no tenure. Research universities typically use term-limited or part-time nontenured instructors to teach writing and foreign languages. Comprehensive universities make even more extensive use of such appointments. Some community colleges hire almost all of their teachers on this basis. Overall, far more than half of all new instructors hired by colleges and universities today are not eligible for tenure but serve on temporary contracts.[15] This practice gives plenty of flexibility to most institutions to respond to changes affecting their operations.

---

*The American Association of University Professors, longtime guardian of academic tenure, has insisted that proceedings to deny or revoke tenure be made by academic peers. In accordance with this tradition, provision could be made to have arbitrations over academic freedom heard by a panel that included professors. There are a number of other matters not considered here that would need to be addressed in creating a suitable arbitration process, such as the proper burden of proof and the mechanisms for selecting arbitrators.

†According to figures published recently in the *Chronicle of Higher Education*, as many as 70 percent of four-year college instructors (excluding graduate student teaching assistants) are not on a tenure track, and another 10 percent or so are tenure-track but not yet tenured. *Chronicle of Higher Education* (November 9, 2012), p. A6.

Opponents of tenure also assert that universities could save money if they were able to terminate tenured professors who are no longer needed or able to perform capably. Yet this argument too is dubious at best. Many of the professors removed for these reasons would presumably have to be replaced by other salaried faculty. Moreover, it is unlikely that doing away with tenure would be costless. Lifetime job security is presumably worth something to those who hold it. Tenure is also a valued source of personal status for the recipient. As a result, if universities abolished tenure, they would probably find that they would have to pay a price for doing so. They might even discover that they could not compete successfully for first-rate professors without paying a substantial premium.* Under these circumstances, the financial consequences of abandoning tenure are quite unpredictable and could quite possibly be adverse.

The final argument often used for doing away with tenure is that such a step would improve quality by allowing colleges and universities to weed out weaker members of the faculty. Although the security of tenure does not in itself diminish research productivity, it is hard to deny the existence of "deadwood" on every campus. Most faculty members agree that tenure protects some ineffective professors.[16]

This problem has become much more serious now that Congress has outlawed the practice of mandatory retirement. Because of the age discrimination law, the practical effect has been to extend tenure virtually to the end of life. While faculty members in most institutions are inclined to retire voluntarily by the time they reach age seventy, large numbers of professors in leading research universities, especially in the sciences, often have sufficiently low teaching loads and enjoy their work enough to remain well into their seventies or even eighties, especially if they can continue to obtain funding for their research. By so doing, they remove opportunities for recent PhDs and untenured faculty who might bring greater vitality and add more value than the aging colleagues who are blocking their paths.

The continuing presence of many professors over seventy years of age is one more obstacle in a series of handicaps that dim the prospects of students considering a life of research in higher education. An oversupply of PhDs and a shrinking number of tenure-track positions make academic careers more

---

*Opponents of tenure dismiss this argument by pointing to particular institutions that rejected tenure yet managed to attract plenty of applicants willing to work without job protection. The fact that individual colleges could function well without tenure, however, does not mean that large numbers of institutions could do away with this job security and still hire replacements of equivalent quality without paying a premium. Similarly, the fact that candidates will accept jobs without tenure during a period like the present, when tenure-track positions are scarce, does not mean that they will do so when the market changes and qualified faculty candidates are harder to find.

hazardous than in the past. The persistent difficulty experienced by young investigators in obtaining government research grants adds another element of risk. And now, the tendency of many aging professors to remain in their jobs past the traditional retirement age narrows the opportunities for budding scientists and scholars even further. The cumulative effect of all these difficulties could well discourage many talented young people from embarking on careers in research and teaching.

Doing away with tenure, however, is not an ideal solution to this problem. Any effort by the university administration to take such a step for professors over a certain age would almost certainly meet with fierce resistance by the faculty. Morale would suffer, and some professors might leave and take appointments elsewhere.

In addition, the age discrimination law requires that any repeal of tenure for elderly members of the faculty must be applied with equal rigor to professors of all ages. The obvious way to accomplish this result would be to institute a procedure for reviewing all members of the faculty at stated intervals to determine whether they should be retained. Such a procedure, however, would be difficult to implement effectively, especially in research universities.* To determine whether a physicist, say, should be kept or let go, universities would need to solicit expert testimony, since deans and presidents would rarely possess the competence to judge the quality of the professor's research. Members of the scientist's own department would probably not be suitable sources of advice, since they would be colleagues, often friends, and in any event might feel reluctant to offer a negative appraisal of someone who could conceivably sit in judgment on them a few years hence. Professors from other institutions could be solicited, but they too might be reluctant to send a letter, the more so since preparing evaluations conscientiously could become extremely burdensome if all research universities adopted such a procedure. For these reasons, universities could find it difficult to conduct the necessary reviews properly.

Reviewing all professors periodically could also have undesirable effects on the quality of the faculty. As pointed out in chapter 9, instructors without tenure are likely to be especially anxious to obtain high student teaching evaluations and hence may assign less homework and give easier grades. They may also be reluctant to support the hiring of an outstanding young scholar in their own field whose presence might make them seem expendable. Abandoning tenure could even deter talented students from pursuing academic careers in

---

* It is true that many universities have instituted periodic post-tenure reviews for all their permanent faculty. Even so, conducting a review to help professors improve is one thing and doing so to determine which professors to let go is quite another.

fields in which professors terminated in midcareer would have difficulty finding a suitable job in some other line of work.

Doing away with tenure might also weaken the standards for hiring and promoting faculty. Appointing a professor for life is such a consequential matter for a department that even softhearted faculty members will insist on a high standard of work before voting in favor. If the prevailing system were replaced, say, by a practice of making appointments for only five years, faculties might well be less inclined to be tough-minded and more prepared to give younger candidates the benefit of any reasonable doubts. Once such a person had been reappointed for two or three terms, tenured colleagues and other senior professors called on for an opinion might hesitate for compassionate reasons to recommend against reappointment, especially in fields where rejected scholars in their forties or fifties would be hard put to find alternative employment.

In short, while it is doubtful that tenure is essential to academic freedom, the arguments for abolishing it seem equally problematic. The effect on university budgets is unclear at best and could actually prove to be adverse. Similar uncertainties dog any effort to predict the impact of abandoning tenure on the quality of teaching and research. Under these conditions, lifetime job security may not be necessary to secure academic freedom, but it is impossible to know whether abolishing it would improve the status quo or make matters worse. A better way of improving the work of universities would be to create an expeditious procedure that guaranteed freedom of expression to all instructors, coupled with limited relief from the age-discrimination law to allow a simpler means of retiring professors after the age of seventy if their teaching and research were no longer satisfactory.

OTHER PRESSURES ON FREEDOM OF INQUIRY

Attacks on academic freedom are not the only threats to scholarly inquiry. There are many subtler restraints that can inhibit the unfettered search for knowledge and understanding. As Francis Bacon observed in the sixteenth century, "numberless in short are the ways . . . in which the affections color and infect the understanding."[17]

A variety of obvious inhibitions limit the freedom of faculty members to pursue any subject of their choosing. Researchers must take the preferences and predilections of funders into account if they need money to carry out a project. Investigators whose careers depend on getting grants for their research may feel constrained to choose safe problems to pursue in order not to risk being turned down by funding agencies. Young faculty members can have difficulty finding grants for their own research and thus be forced to work with senior investigators whose research is well funded. Fear of intense public disapproval doubtless discourages some professors from writing about highly controversial subjects.

The appointments process is another source of constraint. Faculty members who have not yet received tenure are naturally anxious to gain a secure academic post, if not in their current institution, then in some comparable college or university. As a result, they presumably feel at least some pressure in their research to conform to the conventional wisdom of their field and to its accepted priorities and methods and to avoid bolder, more original lines of inquiry.

The appointments process can have an especially narrowing effect when a department is wedded to a particular ideology or way of approaching the subject matter in its field. A literature department may be dominated by advocates of feminist theory or a political science department by devotees of rational choice analysis. Assistant professors who hope to gain tenure in such a department are likely to feel under some constraint to write according to the prevailing orthodoxy.

It is impossible for an administration to remove all pressures of this kind. The line between originality and wrongheadedness is not an easy one to draw, and reasonable people will sometimes differ in the attempt. Fortunately, once faculty members achieve tenure, they are likely to feel less inhibited by the views of their colleagues. Even prior to tenure, young instructors in doctrinaire departments are not entirely constrained by their elders, since they can always seek employment in other institutions that are free of such orthodoxies.*

Apart from the pressures of gaining tenure, a host of other influences can affect the choices scholars make about what questions to pursue and what research methods to employ. Faculty members with ambitions for a post in some future government may avoid publishing a bold or controversial idea that could

---

* In some cases, conventional modes of thought can have a pronounced effect on the nature of scholarship in an entire field. In business schools, for example, most young faculty are trained in a particular discipline and often harbor thoughts of returning some day to an appropriate arts and sciences department if they find the professional school environment uncongenial. As a result, young economists in schools of management will often look for research topics that connect with business in some way but also lend themselves to work attractive to mainstream economists. Colleagues trained in other disciplines will do the same. Even after such scholars receive tenure, they are likely to continue to do research that is acceptable to their discipline, since their training has conditioned them to seek professional recognition and distinction this way. Not surprisingly, then, business schools have tended to produce a body of scholarly work that is distinguished for its rigor and its contributions to theory but is often criticized for having little practical value for corporate executives. Such influences, however, are not an infringement on academic freedom but simply the result of a decision on the part of business schools regarding the type of faculty to recruit.

cause influential public figures to consider the author unsound or unreliable. Scientists eager for fame and recognition may be more inclined to interpret their data to support a positive and striking conclusion. Conversely, even the most distinguished scholars may shrink from writing about topics that are highly sensitive or likely to expose them to vilification. Charles Darwin reportedly refrained from stating the extent of his reservations about the existence of God for fear of upsetting his deeply religious wife.[18] All manner of inhibitions of this kind can occur, and there is little anyone can do about them.

Occasionally, however, universities try to remove a particular source of pressure on the objectivity of faculty. As pointed out in the preceding chapter, some institutions have adopted strict conflict-of-interest rules to prevent professors with financial ties to a particular company from putting themselves in a position where they may be influenced, at least unconsciously, by a reluctance to publish findings inimical to the firm's interests. Rules of this kind are worth having, even though they deal with only one of the myriad forces that can influence a professor's writings.

On occasion, groups outside the university have exceeded the usual bounds of spirited debate by making determined efforts to mobilize hostile pressure to discourage certain authors or points of view. Pro-Israel groups have often been accused of acting in this manner. One such organization, Campus Watch, is said to have communicated with prospective donors to advise them against contributing to particular professors or research centers that were thought to be pro-Arab and unfairly critical of Israel.[19] In another instance, the Association of Concerned Trustees and Alumni (ACTA) compiled a list of scholars who were thought to be hostile to America, although the list was withdrawn after news of its existence provoked widespread criticism.[20] More recently, a few conservative politicians have ordered public universities to hand over the e-mails of faculty members who have argued publicly for positions the officials dislike, such as the existence of global warming. These demands are said to have been designed to dig up embarrassing facts with which to harass and silence the professors involved.

If all groups that felt strongly about a subject routinely launched such attempts to bring financial or political pressure to bear against professors with whom they disagreed, the effects on scholarly inquiry could be severe. As yet, public opinion seems sufficiently hostile to efforts of this sort that the examples to date have been infrequent. Nevertheless, academic leaders need to resist such attacks by any lawful means at their disposal. If organized harassment should spread, the effects could be as serious as those resulting from the firing of controversial professors almost a century ago that led John Dewey and others to fight for academic freedom. The informed opinion that professors can bring to public debates about important national issues is vital to a healthy democracy. It would be a grave setback if determined public officials and private groups could silence the expression of legitimate points of view with which they happened to disagree strongly.

Social pressure of a similar kind has also arisen within universities in recent decades. In particular, student groups have sought to impose orthodoxies of their own on controversial subjects that not only inhibit discussions among their classmates but can discourage faculty discourse and scholarship as well. Few professors, after all, want to become pariahs on their own campus or be pilloried in student publications.

In 1972, following several years of student unrest, a widely respected political scientist, the late James Q. Wilson, asserted that "the list of subjects that cannot be publicly discussed [on campus] in a free and open forum has grown steadily, and now includes the war in Vietnam, public policy toward urban ghettos, the relationship between intelligence and heredity, and the role of corporations in certain overseas regimes."[21] Fortunately, campuses today are quieter, and most of the subjects Wilson mentioned (with the possible exception of intelligence and heredity) are now open to debate. Nevertheless, controversies arise from time to time that can require a university administration to draw a line between spirited argument and harassment or intimidation.

The most recent publicized examples of this problem have involved expressions of opinion regarding women, minorities, or gay people. Many critics have charged that a new orthodoxy of "political correctness" has emerged on campus which activist students enforce by reacting angrily against those expressing a view that seems critical, disrespectful, or intolerant of anyone belonging to these groups. This state of affairs has provoked much concern from conservatives and civil libertarians, resulting in the appearance of several books and other published commentary on the subject.[22]

It may seem odd that political correctness has aroused such controversy. After all, students have embraced a succession of orthodoxies and prejudices over the years that have inhibited free expression and led to widespread conformity.* In the late 1940s and early 1950s, for example, many women on coed campuses felt constrained to hide any evidence of scholarly interests or academic accomplishment for fear of becoming less attractive to men, who were thought to prefer homemakers to intellectuals as mates. Undergraduates of both sexes

---

*Leon Botstein, longtime president of Bard College, has put it best: "The patterns of group thinking today termed 'political correctness' are no different than they were decades ago. Only the fads, fashion, ideology, and politics change, not the patterns of ostracization and defamation of those who speak with a different voice. *Jefferson's Children: Education and the Promise of American Culure* (1997), p. 191.

excluded African Americans and Jews from their sororities, fraternities, and parties. Now that these attitudes have given way to widespread hostility toward intolerance of many kinds, why should critics choose this moment to protest?

Part of the reason may be that political correctness on many campuses spread beyond the student body to affect a number of departments in the humanities and social sciences, and even became the subject of official policy at several institutions that adopted speech codes in the 1980s and 1990s. It is one thing for students to express disapproval of classmates for criticizing abortion or making lewd or condescending remarks about women, but quite another matter when universities themselves announce prohibitions on "sexually derogatory jokes" or "inappropriately directed laughter" and make violations a punishable offense. There are even greater grounds for concern if universities apply these orthodoxies to faculty members to deter them from expressing views in their teaching and writing that threaten to arouse anger and controversy.

THE LIBERAL BIAS OF THE FACULTY

In all likelihood, an even deeper grievance has contributed to the attack on political correctness, at least that part of the attack emanating from right-wing critics. To conservatives, political correctness and its embrace by professors and university officials may well seem to be one more manifestation of a pervasive liberal consensus within the faculties of most colleges and universities. This tendency is often said to reflect a political orthodoxy that extends well beyond questions of race, gender, and sexual orientation.[23]

In recent years, conservative critics have become more vocal in their complaints about liberal bias and have even sought legislation requiring universities to seek a fairer balance of political and social views within their faculties.[24] The controversy over political correctness, therefore, involves far more than student behavior and touches on issues of fundamental importance to research and scholarship. If faculty opinion on a variety of issues has become sufficiently one-sided, the climate for independent and creative thought may well have taken a turn for the worse.

What is the evidence for the conservative complaint that professors today are much too liberal in their political views? Surveys of faculty opinion do not always reach the same result, and some are more carefully done than others. A recent study by Neil Gross and Solon Simmons, however, conveys as accurate a picture as any of the current situation.[25] According to this account, 9.4 percent of faculty respondents describe themselves as "Extremely Liberal"; 34.7 percent as "Liberal"; 18.1 percent as "Slightly Liberal"; 18.0 percent as "Middle of the

Road"; 10.5 percent as "Slightly Conservative"; 8.0 as "Conservative"; and 1.2 percent as "Very Conservative."

Although other authors have arrived at somewhat different findings, it does seem clear beyond dispute that faculty members whose political orientation inclines to the liberal side of the political spectrum far outnumber those whose views lie to the right or conservative side. The differences vary in strength from one part of the university to another. They tend to be more modest among faculty members in business schools or in science and engineering departments and more pronounced in the humanities and social sciences, especially in history and sociology where the ratio of liberals to conservatives often exceeds 10 or 15 to 1.

Despite the preponderance of professors with various shades of liberal orientation, faculty opinions on matters of government and economic policy are far from radical. According to Gross and Simmons, 60 percent feel "that government should do more to help needy Americans even if it means going deeper into debt."[26] On the other hand, 55 percent feel that government "wastes a lot of money we pay in taxes"; professors are almost evenly split on whether "business corporations make too much profit"; and only 21.4 percent agree that "Washington should see to it that every person has a job and a good standard of living."[27] On social issues, perhaps professors diverge more widely from opinions of Americans as a whole. Thus, 75 percent of professors believe that "it should be possible for a pregnant woman to obtain a legal abortion if the woman wants it for any reason." Sixty-nine percent believe that sexual relations between two adults of the same sex are "not wrong at all."[28] Still, even these opinions can hardly be called extreme.

Some critics have charged that faculties are continuing to grow more liberal. It is difficult to verify or discredit this assertion, however, and those who have examined the evidence are divided on the issue.[29] Different authors have construed the statistics to reveal a trend toward more liberal, more conservative, or even more centrist views. Such disagreements are particularly hard to resolve, since the meanings of "liberal" and "conservative," "Republican" and "Democrat," have changed markedly over the years. As Elliott Richardson once remarked, "If one simply looks at the record, Richard Nixon was actually well to the left of Bill Clinton."[30]

Whatever the actual trends may be, the prevalence of left-liberal political views is not a recent phenomenon caused by some particular event such as an invasion of "tenured radicals" from the rebellious student generation of the 1960s. While evidence from earlier eras is sparse, the sociologist Arthur Kornhauser, who surveyed faculty opinion in 1937, found professors to be more liberal or radical in their socioeconomic views than members of any other occupation.[31] According to Kornhauser, a remarkable 84 percent of social science faculty favored the New Deal, compared with 56 percent of manual workers and only 15 percent of lawyers, doctors, dentists, and engineers. Various authors writing decades ago, such as Richard Hofstadter, Joseph Schumpeter, and Thorstein Veblen, also remarked on the tendency of academics and intellectuals to embrace liberal social and political views.[32] While survey data on the question is rather sparse prior to the late 1960s, it is at least clear that in each of the presidential elections from 1948 to 1956, professors were less inclined to vote for Republican presidential candidates than were members of any other professional or middle-class group.[33]

What accounts for such a persistent preponderance of liberal sentiment among academics? Everett Ladd and Seymour Martin Lipset have made the most extensive study of this question.[34] While they are cautious in espousing any single answer, their preferred explanation seems to be that members of the academic profession are trained to question the status quo and the conventional wisdom and so are naturally inclined to have reform-minded, political views.* George Stigler, a Nobel Prize–winning economist, made much the same point:

> The university is by design and effect the institution in society which creates discontent with the existing moral, social, and political institutions and proposes new institutions to replace them. . . . Invited to be learned in the institutions of other times and places, incited to new understandings of the social and physical world, the university is inherently a disruptive force.[35]

Another reason sometimes given for the preponderance of liberals is that most university faculties have included increasing numbers of Jews, and more recently women and minorities, who are consistently more likely to vote for Democrats than the population as a whole. While this theory may be part of the explanation, it cannot be the whole story, since American professors exhibited liberal tendencies long before Jews or women became so numerous on university faculties. Moreover, the Democratic proclivities of these two groups do not seem pronounced enough to account for the full extent of political imbalance found in most university faculties today.

A more disturbing explanation for the predominance of liberals is that professors are politically biased in deciding whom to appoint as professors and hence tend to exclude conservatives from their ranks. Martin Trow, a well-known scholar of higher education, has reportedly said that "professors have

---

*Curiously, however, when neoconservatives gained prominence in the 1970s by challenging the conventional liberal orthodoxy, there was no marked shift to the right among the professoriate.

so surrounded themselves with comfortably like-minded colleagues; they don't even realize their warped perspectives are causing them to discriminate against people with different views."[36] Trow is not the only academic who shares this opinion. In response to a recent survey asking faculty members whether "colleges and universities tend to favor professors who hold liberal political and social views," 43.4 percent agreed, including 81 percent of professors who identified themselves as conservatives and almost one-third of liberal faculty members.[37]

This theory does not explain how liberals became so dominant in the first place. Moreover, there are telling indications that bias in the appointment process cannot be a major factor accounting for the disproportionate number of liberal professors. No informed observer would claim that political orientation plays a significant role in decisions about whom to appoint in science departments. Yet members of science departments consider themselves almost as liberal (45.2 percent) as their colleagues in the humanities (52.2 percent) or the social sciences (58.2 percent).[38] Similarly, surveys find that conservatives make up only 7.8 percent of the faculty in science departments, and hence are almost as scarce as conservative professors in the humanities (3.6 percent) or the social sciences (4.9 percent).[39]

Two other scholars have argued that the roots of the liberal imbalance lie much deeper than political bias in the appointments process. Matthew Woessner and April Kelly-Woessner studied the political attitudes of students interested in academic careers.[40] Among all seniors in colleges across the country, 19 percent of those identifying themselves as liberals and 24 percent of those claiming to be "far left" expressed an intention to earn a PhD degree, compared with only 9 percent of self-styled conservatives. This imbalance does not seem to result from experience on campus. Conservative students received higher grades and enjoyed college more than their average classmates and claim to have had equally good relations with the faculty. Moreover, even before starting their undergraduate careers, only 15 percent of right-leaning freshmen expressed an intention to earn a doctorate compared with 33 percent of their left-leaning classmates. According to the authors, the principal reason for this early difference in political orientation is that conservative freshmen are much more interested in making a good living and raising a family than their liberal classmates.

Two other scholars, Stanley Rothman and Robert Lichter, sought to explain the predominance of liberals by trying to determine whether academic ability or political bias was most responsible for the degree of career success enjoyed by liberal and conservative professors.[41] Their conclusion was that achievement was far and away the most important factor contributing to advancement. Nevertheless, they also claimed that political bias seemed to have some effect, since comparisons between professors with the same level of scholarly achievement indicated that those holding liberal-left opinions were somewhat more likely to be appointed to prestigious institutions than those with more conservative views. While these conclusions are suggestive, the authors, in commenting on their methodology, acknowledged that "this mode of inquiry, by its nature, cannot prove that ideology accounts for this difference in professional standing. There may be some other factor at work for which we failed to account, or we may have failed to eliminate some source of measurement error."[42]

All in all, the charge that faculties are biased against conservatives remains unproven. Political orientation clearly seems far less important to career advancement than academic ability and achievement. Yet there are signs that bias may play a minor but perceptible role. Such a conclusion, at any rate, seems consistent with findings that the preponderance of liberals is somewhat greater in the humanities and social sciences than in engineering or the sciences, that liberal professors appear to be somewhat more likely to be appointed to more prestigious universities than conservative scholars with comparable intellectual accomplishments, and that a substantial minority of the faculty (including almost one-third of liberal professors) believe that liberals on the faculty *are* treated more favorably than conservatives.

Does it matter that very high percentages of professors are liberal in their political views? Many people seem to think so. According to pollster John Immerwahr, 45.7 percent of the public in 2007 felt that political bias was either "a very serious" or "the most serious" problem facing higher education.[43] What is it, then, that causes such concern?

The most likely explanation is a fear that a predominantly liberal faculty will indoctrinate students by giving them a one-sided view of social and political questions. Student surveys offer some support for such worries. According to a national poll in 2006 commissioned by the American Council of Trustees and Alumni (ACTA) and conducted by the Center for Survey Research and Analysis at the University of Connecticut, 46 percent of undergraduates agreed either "somewhat" or "strongly" that "on my campus, some professors use the classroom to present their personal political views."[44] Forty-two percent agreed "somewhat" or "strongly" (12 percent) that "some courses have readings which present only one side of a controversial issue" (although 26 percent disagreed somewhat and 28 percent disagreed strongly).[45] More troubling was the finding that 22 percent of liberal students and 52 percent of their conservative classmates felt that in some courses they had to agree with the instructor's political or social views in order to get a good grade.[46]

Of course, these impressions may be exaggerated. Nevertheless, they suggest that there may be teachers on many campuses who are not well informed about the proper way to conduct their classes. Academic freedom does not give license to instructors to impose their own political views on students or to present only one side of controversial issues. As the American Association of University Professors made clear in their seminal 1915 report defining academic freedom, "the teacher must also be especially on his guard against taking unfair advantage of the student's immaturity by indoctrinating him with the teacher's own opinions before the student has had an opportunity fairly to examine other opinions upon the matter in question, and before he has sufficient knowledge and ripeness of judgment to form any definitive opinion of his own."[47] The Association of American Colleges and Universities elaborated on this theme in 2006, declaring that students "have a right to be graded on the intellectual merit of their arguments, uninfluenced by the personal views of professors."[48]

It is the responsibility of academic leaders to make sure that faculty members understand the role of the teacher and appreciate not only the freedom of professors to speak and write as they choose but their corresponding obligation to avoid any trace of indoctrination in the classroom. The point is not to try to enact detailed rules for classroom teaching. Such a code would be extremely hard to draft and might well inhibit vigorous class discussions about controversial issues and exacerbate faculty doubts about their freedom to express ideas. Rather, the situation calls for a patient effort to build within the faculty a stronger and clearer understanding of the need to avoid indoctrination and to be conscientious in presenting all sides of controversial issues. There is not much indication that serious efforts of this kind are being made on many campuses.

Whatever professors say or don't say in the classroom, however, it is far from clear that they are having much effect on the political attitudes of students. For a long time, surveys did show that undergraduates tended to become somewhat more liberal in their political orientation during their college career, although there is no proof that their professors were responsible. In 1993, however, after surveying the attitudes of students nationwide over their full four years of college, Alexander Astin concluded that undergraduates were no longer becoming more liberal and that students who did shift somewhat to the left were now balanced by roughly equal numbers who moved to the right.[49] More recent studies tend to confirm this finding.[50]

There is one further reason, however, to be concerned over the heavy preponderance of liberal-left professors, especially in humanities and social science departments where the imbalance is the greatest. Although the point cannot be proved definitively, it is intuitively plausible that scholarship and creativity will flourish best in intellectual environments marked by a diversity of opinion. In such an atmosphere, scholars are more likely to be aware of a wider range of views, to find their assumptions challenged by colleagues, to have to rethink points they might otherwise take for granted. The dominant presence of liberals also affects the civic role of universities as a source of impartial expertise and a constructive critic of government and society. The more faculties are perceived as politically biased, the less inclined the public will be to trust what individual professors have to say, even on factual matters within their special field of competence.

The point is not that the political orientation of departments and faculties must mirror that of the general population or that every possible shade of political opinion must be represented. Moreover, it is likely that most professors are aware of conservative arguments and views from reading newspapers and other sources of opinion about public affairs. But when departments of sociology or political science or history have virtually no conservatives among their members, one cannot help but feel that the immediate intellectual environment in which professors live and work has too little variety of opinion for the good of its members. In addition to the influence that political imbalance may have on the views and arguments of professors, it is possible that the dominance of liberals affects the choice of research topics in certain fields, causing some to be neglected and others studied to excess. For example, the heavy emphasis on issues of race, class, and gender in the research within several fields of the humanities and social sciences may possibly reflect such a tendency, although there is no evidence available to prove or disprove this supposition.

Faculties themselves recognize that the scarcity of conservative opinion constitutes a problem. Almost 70 percent of professors nationwide affirm that "the goal of campus diversity should include fostering diversity of views among faculty members."[51] The difficulty lies in finding an effective remedy. No sensible person would advocate establishing quotas for the appointment of conservatives (or any other group) to college faculties or choosing less qualified candidates for professorships simply because they are known to have right-wing views. Besides, if the root difficulty is the paucity of conservatives who harbor ambitions to become professors, preferential hiring of right-leaning scholars will not correct the problem but will merely shift it from one campus to another.

Is there anything universities can do if they wish to counteract the effects of ideological imbalance? Deans and other influential figures might begin by discussing the subject with departments in the social sciences and humanities, where the imbalance is especially marked, and explore such measures as bringing a more politically diverse range of speakers to the campus and making greater efforts to identify and consider conservative scholars as potential candidates for visiting appointments. In some cases, it might be possible to establish one or more professorships in subjects, such as military history and international relations, that are interesting and important in their own right and are more likely to attract conservative scholars. Departments with PhD programs could be asked to take particular care to identify and discuss applicants to their graduate programs who appear to have conservative views. Measures such as these will hardly establish a healthy diversity of opinion, at least for many years, but they might at least help to mitigate the effects of the current imbalance.

THE CLIMATE FOR RESEARCH

By emphasizing problems and criticisms, the discussion in this chapter may have suggested to some readers that freedom of thought in colleges and universities is in worse shape than is actually the case. In fact, most campuses are lively places that contain much variety of opinion, far more so, in this author's opinion, than was true in the late 1960s and early 1970s. By and large, moreover, faculties in most institutions, and in virtually all research universities, work diligently to appoint the best-qualified candidates they can without conscious regard to their political, religious, or social views.

What the preceding pages have tried to make clear is simply that the environment for creative thought on most campuses today, while generally positive, is still not ideal. In contrast to the situation a century ago, the principal problem no longer involves the heavy-handed intervention of opinionated presidents and trustees, nor is there as great a threat from witch-hunting legislators as there was in the late 1940s and early 1950s. These familiar dangers have not disappeared entirely and still require eternal vigilance. Yet today, the principal threats are subtler and come primarily from within. They are particularly likely to emanate from students and faculty with strong personal views on subjects ranging from women's rights, sexual orientation, and race to the tensions between Israelis and Palestinians, or from the subtler influences resulting from marked political imbalances and methodological orthodoxies within entire departments.

Not all these problems can be solved. There is no such thing as a perfect environment for creative thinkers. Individuals in every social setting experience inhibitions and subtle pressures that can obstruct or distort independent thought in ways no institution can remove. Nevertheless, faculty surveys give reason to believe that more could be done on many campuses both to make scholars feel confident of their right to express their opinions freely and to create as intellectually diverse an environment as imperfect human beings can provide. It is the essential duty of academic leaders to try to maintain such an atmosphere and to make clear to the faculty that the administration will do everything possible to protect them from any and all attempts to invade their right to express their ideas freely.

AFTERWORD (IV)

||||||||||||||||||||||||||||||||||||||||||||||||||||||||||||||||||||||||||||||||||||||||||||||||||||||||||

In order to understand how and why research universities function as they do, it is useful to compare the image of professors as it appears in many critical writings about academe with the picture that emerges from more careful, empirical studies of campus life. The familiar portrait is not a pleasing one. It frequently describes members of the faculty as a set of highly intelligent, driven individuals preoccupied with their reputation in their chosen field of research, endlessly traveling to conferences, and displaying little loyalty to their university or concern for their students.[1] More recently, the picture has sometimes been modified to depict professors as scientific entrepreneurs, no longer as interested in inquiring after truth as in consulting with industry, turning their discoveries into lucrative patents, and starting biotech companies based on their research that can be sold later on for large sums of money.

The external world certainly does a lot to encourage a focus on research. Government agencies reward faculty investigators by awarding them stipends that add 20 percent or more to their salaries for spending the summer months in the laboratory or the library. An ever-increasing array of external prizes and other forms of recognition—with or without accompanying emoluments—go to scientists and scholars who achieve notable success in their research. Invitations to attend conferences, often funded by foundations and located in exotic places, arrive with frequency to those who acquire visibility through their published work or their public commentary. Intriguing opportunities to advise public officials, along with lucrative offers to consult with industry, await prolific scholars in many fields, along with job offers, television appearances, and ample advances from publishing houses. With all the benefits that reward successful inquiry, one can understand why professors might neglect their students in order to concentrate on research.

Universities often contribute encouragement of their own to well-published scholars. Small wonder. Research reputations bear heavily on an institution's position in the highly publicized college rankings and its success in securing government grants with their hefty overhead payments. As a result, many universities have sought to build their "research profile" by making publications the key consideration in hiring and promoting professors. Salaries are consistently higher for successful researchers than for successful teachers. The modest recognition given by many colleges to the "teacher of the year" cannot compare with the rewards provided to well-published professors.

Efforts by governments to transform universities into instruments of economic growth have further skewed the incentives of professors in the direction of research. Public officials look with favor on institutions that promote economic development by urging their faculties to collaborate with industry and helping professors to start companies and obtain patents on their discoveries. A growing number of universities have responded by counting success in starting companies and patenting discoveries as positive factors in setting the salaries of professors and deciding on their promotions.

With such encouragement, it is little wonder that one can discover individual professors on every campus who fit the stereotype of academic entrepreneurs, spending much of their time consulting, attending conferences, giving speeches, and starting companies even at the cost of slighting their students, ignoring their colleagues, and avoiding administrative chores in their departments. What is truly remarkable is not that such faculty members exist but that there are so few of them notwithstanding all the money and attention that the outside world and their own university shower upon them. On average, professors in research universities still devote far more time during the academic year to teaching classes and preparing for them than they spend on their research.[2] Overall, those most active in writing books and articles continue to teach as much and as well as colleagues who publish little.[3] Faculty members who frequently consult likewise publish more, teach as much, and serve on as many committees as those who consult only seldom or not at all.[4] The average amount that professors earn through paid consulting even in research universities remains quite small.*

In recent decades, moreover, for all the attention paid to patenting discoveries and commercializing science, there is no convincing evidence that a substantial number of academic scientists have shifted their research to highly applied, potentially profitable work or that those who have received numerous patents have become any less productive in publishing highly cited work of a

---

*According to the latest major survey of the faculty, less than 3 percent of professors in either public or private universities spent more than eight hours (one day) per week in consulting activities during 2010–11, and over 90 percent spent only four hours or less. Sylvia Hurtado, Kevin Eagan, John H. Pryor, Hannah Whang, and Serge Tran, *Undergraduate Teaching Faculty: The 2010 HERI Faculty Survey* (2012), p. 28.

fundamental nature.[5] As educators, they may be slow to change accustomed methods of instruction or to question the basic curricular structure. Yet their commitment to teaching undergraduates remains intact and has, if anything, increased in recent decades, even in research universities.[6] Only in failing to disclose their conflicts of interest have significant numbers of professors failed to live up to the standards of their profession.

Why is it, then, that professors have not responded more eagerly to the incentives offered by the larger society and reinforced by their own universities? Much of the explanation must surely be that extrinsic, material rewards matter less and the intrinsic rewards of teaching and research matter more than most critics seem to imagine. Individuals do not choose the scholarly life out of a desire to make a lot of money, so it is not so surprising that financial incentives have but a limited effect on faculty behavior. Professors embark on academic careers because they derive a special satisfaction from teaching young people, exploring new subjects, developing ideas, and discussing them with colleagues. They are usually loath to sacrifice these pursuits by spending inordinate amounts of time starting companies or consulting with industry. After all, for many who choose the professor's life, no other occupation can compare. As a colleague once remarked, "Where else would someone pay me to read?" Where else, moreover, could one have as much freedom to pursue whatever intellectual interests seem most intriguing?

Essential to the intrinsic satisfactions of academic life are the shared restraints and obligations embodied in the traditional academic values. These values represent the collective sense of mutual responsibility needed to preserve the advantages that academic life provides—the freedom to write and think as one chooses, to prepare one's courses as one thinks best, to organize one's life and schedule one's time with minimal oversight and direction by superior authority. Such exceptional autonomy can exist only if professors are willing to exercise a certain amount of self-discipline and self-restraint.

Academic values have proved to be remarkably durable in the face of the mounting temptations and distractions of the outside world. In part, their persistence reflects an instinctive, unspoken recognition by professors that such limits are essential to the continued existence of the very features of academic life that make it so attractive. In part, academic values also owe their survival to recognition of the fact that those who ignore their professional responsibilities place additional burdens on their colleagues and hence strain the bonds of collegiality that are also an important part of faculty life.

Ironically, however, the very strength of academic values could eventually turn out to be the cause of their undoing. Since they can often endure for a considerable time in spite of competing temptations and inducements, those who guide academic institutions may be lulled into a false complacency, imagining that the values will remain forever without much conscious effort to preserve them. Such neglect comes easily in an age when presidents and deans are more and more preoccupied with fund-raising and administration, increasingly separated from their faculties by layers of staff, and often reluctant to raise sensitive subjects that could lead to controversy and unwanted publicity.

Neglecting academic values, however, is dangerous. Once erosion has begun, it can easily gain strength as more and more faculty members, seeing nothing being done about colleagues who abuse their freedom, feel less obliged to behave responsibly themselves. Should this process proceed beyond a certain point, it will be more and more difficult to reverse. The consequences will be extremely serious, for there is no good substitute for voluntary self-restraint in an academic institution. Requiring professors to fill out time sheets, maintain a fixed quota of office hours, follow detailed regulations prescribing the meaning of "one day per week" for external activities, and fulfill elaborately defined mandatory teaching loads can quickly sully the quiet joys of academic life. Strenuous efforts to enforce such rules will destroy these satisfactions even faster. Something precious will disappear from universities, causing losses that are beyond precise calculation.

There are worrisome signs that important values may be beginning to fray. Maintaining an appropriate balance between research and teaching is not the only responsibility at risk. Various other academic values and obligations may also be weakening. Many university officials seem unwilling to do very much about the dwindling confidence of the faculty that their administration will stoutly defend their academic freedom. Respected observers such as Clark Kerr and Henry Rosovsky have commented on a growing reluctance on the part of their colleagues to participate in the necessary committee work of the university.[7] The traditional consensus about the duty of teachers to refrain from any form of indoctrination appears to have blurred with little sign of an administrative response.[8] Although the meaning of "cheating" and "plagiarism" has become confused in the minds of many students in this age of Google, Wikipedia, and collaborative learning, both academic leaders and professors often fail to see to it that these vital prohibitions are clearly understood.

Such neglect is a serious matter. There is no good substitute for strong academic values and shared responsibilities. They are the foundation on which much that is important depends—not only in research but in all aspects of academic life. Those in positions of authority who make little effort to clarify and uphold these tacit obligations do so at considerable peril to the academic enterprise.

PART V

A FINAL RECKONING

FOREWORD (V)

||||||||||||||||||||||||||||||||||||||||||||||||||||||||||||||||||||||||||||||||||||||||||||||||||||||||||

Forming conclusions about American colleges and universities can easily become confusing because of the sheer number of criticisms—some valid and important, some highly exaggerated, and some possessing little or no substance whatsoever. The latter complaints are not merely insubstantial; they divert the reader's attention from more important problems that need all the attention they can get. Before trying to identify the genuine weaknesses, then, I will try to separate out some of the fallacious, unproven, and highly exaggerated criticisms that frequently appear in discussions of the subject.

A few complaints crop up repeatedly even though they are contradicted by a large body of evidence. For example, one often reads that professors, especially in the best-known universities, continually neglect their teaching in order to concentrate on their research. Yet according to several comparative studies, faculty members in the United States express greater interest in teaching than their counterparts in virtually any other advanced nation.[1] Moreover, surveys have consistently found that professors in America, on average, spend more time on their classes during term-time than they do on their research, even in the more prominent universities.[2] The related charge that research detracts from teaching is likewise contradicted by the available evidence. Numerous studies comparing prolific researchers with colleagues who rarely publish have found no significant difference between the two groups in the quality of their instruction.[3]

Another unsubstantiated claim alleges that the practice of shared governance is in serious disrepair. Trustees and former academic leaders have condemned it for causing costly delays. Disgruntled professors have written books deploring the lack of meaningful faculty consultation. Yet such empirical evidence as one can find on the subject suggests that neither of these criticisms is valid on a large majority of campuses.

Still another complaint that ignores much evidence to the contrary is that universities are unusually conservative and slow to react to new needs and opportunities.[4] The late Irving Kristol once remarked that "the university has been—with the possible exception of the post office—the least inventive (or even adaptive) of our social institutions since the end of World War II."[5] Yet even a cursory look at the progress of higher education over the past sixty years reveals that colleges and universities have adjusted in timely fashion to a series of major challenges—from the sudden influx of veterans after World War II, and the massive enrollment growth that followed, to the rapid response to government efforts after 1980 to speed the commercialization of scientific discoveries and the recent surge in online education and massive open online courses (MOOCs). Professors have been quick to add new courses on emerging subjects and to adapt their research to incorporate new methods and technologies. In light of this record, statements about the inherent conservatism of universities and their faculties are too broad to be of help in defining an appropriate agenda for reform. Rather than make such sweeping claims, critics need to specify particular needs and opportunities that universities have been slow to address.

Some other discussions have become so muddled that writers on all sides seem to talk past one another endlessly without coming to grips with the important issues. Arguments over tenure are illustrative.[6] After many years of debate, proponents of tenure have yet to present a convincing argument that lifetime job security is an essential, or even the most effective, way to protect academic freedom. It is especially hard to make such a case now that a large and growing majority of faculty members do not enjoy tenure and hence are without the protection it affords to write and speak freely. At the same time, arguments by those who oppose tenure are likewise open to question. The common complaint that the practice wastes money by keeping unproductive professors on the payroll overlooks the higher salaries that universities might have to pay if they no longer gave professors job security. Assertions that tenure deprives universities of the flexibility to adjust to new opportunities or sudden changes in student interests ignore the fact that most faculty members today do not have tenure but serve on short-term contracts. Moreover, critics rarely acknowledge the risk that instructors who lack tenure may give easier grades and less homework in order to gain better student evaluations of their teaching that will help to assure their reappointment. All things considered, then, it is not at all clear that tenure causes inefficiency and waste. In fact, it is quite possible that abandoning the practice would actually cost universities money and lower the quality of education.

Other familiar criticisms identify genuine problems but fail to recognize that it is virtually impossible for universities to do much about them. For example, it is true that liberals outnumber conservatives by a very wide margin on most campuses and that this imbalance may diminish the quality of scholarly debate.[7] Even so, no one has yet figured out a way to ensure a diversity of political opinion within university faculties that wouldn't do more harm than good. Similarly, though many unscrupulous lawyers and corporate executives have graduated from elite professional schools, it would be wrong to hold faculties responsible, since neither educators nor anyone else knows how to improve the character of young adults. It is likewise unfortunate that the competition to enter selective colleges has become so intense and that colleges spend such large sums vying with one another to attract the most talented students. Nevertheless, it is unfair to blame colleges for this state of affairs, since no single institution can risk putting itself at a competitive disadvantage by unilaterally abandoning the effort to recruit able students, while the occasional proposals urging some sort of collective action have been either impractical or illegal under existing antitrust laws.[8]

Still other familiar complaints have a kernel of truth but are often discussed in such a way as to be misleading or impossible to verify or disprove. Chief among these is the blanket charge that colleges cost too much. High tuitions are undoubtedly a problem. Yet there are such huge variations in the amounts charged by the several thousand colleges in America that sweeping assertions about excessive costs are almost certain to be misleading. For example, several media accounts bearing titles such as "Those Scary College Costs" have turned out to talk only about the tuitions charged by the most selective colleges, an argument akin to citing the price of Cadillacs and Bentleys to prove that automobiles have become too expensive.[9] Other popular treatments of college costs have focused on tuitions without taking account of financial aid, even though only a minority of students on most campuses are actually charged the full "sticker price."

The principal problem with many of the criticisms just described is not that they are wrong but that their sweeping nature diverts attention from significant weaknesses that can and should be remedied. Universities and their professors are not always resistant to reform or consistently neglectful of their teaching, but they have frequently been very slow to make needed changes in the prevailing structure of the undergraduate curriculum or to introduce new and better methods of instruction. Arguments about tenure are often unconvincing, but in combination with the prohibition against age discrimination, the practice does create a genuine problem in many research universities by inhibiting the timely retirement of elderly faculty members and thereby shrinking opportunities for promising young scholars. Professional schools may not be able to improve students' character by strengthening their will to do what they know is right, but many faculties could at least do a better job of teaching students to recognize ethical issues when they arise and to think more clearly about how to resolve them. Finally, although broad generalizations about excessive college tuitions and inflated costs are hard to prove (or disprove), there are undoubtedly specific expenditures that do waste money and ought to be eliminated.[10]

In short, real progress is hard enough to achieve without muddying the waters with complaints that are either unfounded, excessively broad, or impossible to do much about. If we are ever to reach an agreement on an agenda to improve American higher education, we must try hard to identify the weaknesses that are both genuine and susceptible to significant reform, with an emphasis on those that are most important and in greatest need of attention.

CHAPTER EIGHTEEN

MATTERS OF GENUINE CONCERN

||||||||||||||||||||||||||||||||||||||||||||||||||||||||||||||||||||||||||||||||||||||||||||||||||||||||

EARLIER CHAPTERS HAVE TOUCHED upon many strengths and accomplishments of our colleges and universities, but they have also identified an ample list of problems and unrealized opportunities. At this point, one could simply list the shortcomings as an agenda for reform and improvement. Such a summary, however, would not have much to say about the underlying causes of our current difficulties or the deeper tendencies at work that could lead to further trouble in the future. Instead, it seems more useful to recall the vulnerabilities in our system of higher education that were described at the end of chapter 1 and ask what they have contributed to our present shortcomings and how their effects might be minimized in the future.

EXTERNAL RISKS

As in every country, the performance of higher education in the United States is strongly affected by outside forces over which colleges and universities have little or no control. Throughout the eighteenth and nineteenth centuries and continuing through the first half of the twentieth, the external environment was unusually supportive. Governments, religious denominations, and local communities encouraged the founding of colleges and universities and supported them, if not lavishly, at least adequately. Legislators interfered very little in campus affairs and academic policies. Meanwhile, a strong public school system, backed by the early initiation of compulsory primary and secondary education, supplied an ample stream of qualified students to attend the nation's colleges.

World War II ushered in an era of even more remarkable growth for higher education aided by strong public support. Throughout the 1950s and 1960s, the federal government appropriated increasing sums of money to build the strongest program of basic research in the world. State legislatures financed a huge expansion of colleges and universities to accommodate the transition from an elite to a mass and, ultimately, to a well-nigh universal system of postsecondary education. Through this partnership between campus and government, American higher education became a model for the world.

Ironically, these successes gave rise to a variety of new tensions and difficulties. The mounting cost of a mass higher education system coupled with the competing demands of other expensive social programs eventually brought an end to the postwar period of continuous growth and prosperity. In recent decades, financial support from both state and federal governments has become more erratic, with periods of generous increases alternating with stagnating, or even reduced, appropriations. At the same time, the growing importance of higher education to a host of interested groups has led to increased regulation and demands for greater accountability. Although the new rules and restrictions have rarely sought to control academic policies, the burden of compliance has grown heavier and the points of friction have multiplied.

Meanwhile, with larger and larger segments of young people seeking a college education, the well-known difficulties of the public school system have caused increasing problems for community colleges and comprehensive universities as faculties struggle to cope with larger numbers of students who arrive on campus unprepared for college-level work. While there are steps that colleges can and should take to alleviate the resulting burden, major increases in the numbers of young people earning college degrees are unlikely to occur without enough government investment to increase financial aid and strengthen the community colleges and comprehensive universities that will bear the brunt of accommodating further growth in the undergraduate population.

Midway in the second decade of a new century, therefore, higher education depends more than ever on government policies for its continued success, while governments increasingly look to universities as a vital source of innovation and prosperity. Even so, the relationship has gradually become more difficult for both sides. On the one hand, public officials are impatient with academic representatives who constantly seek more money while resisting efforts to hold themselves more accountable to the society that sustains them. On the other, academic leaders no longer look upon government as a benevolent partner in progress but eye it warily as an all-powerful force whose support is essential but whose effects on higher education seem increasingly problematic.

INTRINSIC VULNERABILITIES

More germane to this book than external threats are the stress points in the system of higher education itself and the kinds of problems and shortcomings to which they have contributed. By examining the record with these weaknesses in mind, we may not only review the problems that have actually occurred but gain some insight into which of them are remediable and which are so embedded in the way our colleges and universities have evolved that they cannot be overcome without threatening to do more harm than good.

THE MIXED RESULTS OF COMPETITION

Paradoxically, the spirit of competition that so often pervades the activity of colleges and universities and has contributed such energy and dynamism to the system has also been at the root of many of its problems. The effort and initiative that rivalry inspires are all to the good when directed toward goals that are clearly worthwhile. They are not so advantageous, however, when universities compete with one another in pursuing aims of a more questionable nature.

A persistent source of difficulty in the choice of ends is the natural tendency of academic leaders to emphasize objectives that are tangible rather than those that are subtler and harder to measure. This tendency is strongly reinforced by the surrounding environment. Magazines such as *U.S. News & World Report* issue influential rankings based on precise quantitative indicators that bear little proven relationship to the quality of education. Many states demand that universities submit regular reports on the progress they have made toward objective goals, such as enrollment targets and increased graduation rates, that rarely have much to do with how much students are learning. Federal funding is concentrated heavily on scientific research, which can be measured by discoveries and evaluated by experts, while providing far smaller amounts to efforts aimed at improving the methods of instruction, initiatives that are more difficult to assess.

The effects of this process have become noticeable in recent decades. Goals such as raising the SAT scores and high school rank of entering students, boosting fund-raising totals, creating new programs, adding new buildings, and other visible signs of progress have taken precedence over the intangible but pressing need to improve the quality of education. Surpluses that could have been usefully employed to improve online teaching or experiment with innovative forms of instruction have been routinely siphoned off from executive programs, continuing education courses, and overseas campuses to bolster activities that contribute directly to the national rankings. Colleges have devoted increasing fractions of their financial aid budget to raising the average test scores of their entering classes by awarding merit scholarships instead of aiding those who really need the money. The emphasis on research has spread far beyond major universities, causing scores of institutions to spend large sums to establish PhD programs in the hope of attracting research-oriented professors who will bring additional grants and prestige along with them. Many universities with no tradition of scholarship have made "publish or perish" a condition for faculty appointments and promotions, producing a flood of books and articles that are never cited even once.

While many academic leaders have been trying to improve their reputation through the pursuit of tangible goals, most professors go on teaching much as they always have. Graduate programs still concentrate on training students for research while doing far less to acquaint them with the growing body of knowledge about teaching and learning. Selective colleges spend more on recruiting students and upgrading residence halls than they do on experimenting with new methods of instruction. Meanwhile, evidence is accumulating that students are learning less than most people had previously assumed and devoting less time and effort to their coursework.[1]

It is easy to understand how the fixation on tangible goals has diverted money and effort away from teaching and learning. But why has so little been done to raise the percentage of college students who earn a degree? Increases in graduation rates can be measured quite precisely. They are even included as a significant component of the widely publicized college rankings. Yet graduation rates have grown quite slowly in recent decades, while enrollments in other developed countries have risen to a point that America no longer leads the world in levels of educational attainment.

One reason for this disappointing record is that many of the factors that keep students from graduating from college or even enrolling in the first place—the poor quality of public schools coupled with the effects of crime-ridden neighborhoods, broken families, and other familiar handicaps of low-income students—are largely beyond the reach of even the most dedicated colleges. To add to these problems, funding for the kinds of institutions that enroll most of the high-risk, underprepared students has typically been far lower per undergraduate than the resources available to universities with more affluent student bodies, resulting in insufficient support services and personal attention for students at risk of dropping out.

While this explanation is accurate as far as it goes, studies comparing colleges with similar types of student bodies and resource levels have found that some have much higher graduation rates than others.[2] Such differences suggest that there is a lot that colleges with heavy dropout rates could do to improve their record despite their limited resources. Why, then, have so many of them continued to suffer such high attrition?

This question has not received enough study to permit a definitive answer. But part of the explanation probably has to do with the lack of attention paid to the problem by the outside world, at least until recently. Even the controversial college rankings that have influenced the priorities of many institutions do not evaluate most of the community colleges and comprehensive four-year universities that educate large numbers of high-risk students and have the highest dropout rates. In addition, most community colleges and some of the comprehensive universities as well have little competition and do not vie with one another for greater prestige. As a result, few of these institutions have suffered any adverse consequences from their low completion rates, giving them little incentive to work harder at helping their students graduate.

Under these conditions, the effort devoted to raising graduation rates in the colleges with the largest number of high-risk students has depended very largely on the personal commitment and concern of academic leaders and their faculties. In some institutions, the dedication has been very great. Instructors and college officials alike have considered it their mission to make their institution a stepping-stone to opportunity for students who have had few advantages in life. Without the reinforcement of competition and recognition from the outside world, however, this level of commitment has not been universally shared, thus contributing to the wide variations among colleges in their graduation rates.

Competition in higher education can also lead to questionable results by causing colleges to be too accommodating to the desires of those they serve. At first glance, this statement may seem puzzling. In most commercial markets, a signal virtue of competition is the effort it inspires to satisfy the needs and preferences of clients and customers as effectively as possible. In higher education, however, students frequently have preferences that do not serve their own best interests, let alone those of the larger public. It is possible, then, for competition to make universities *too* responsive to those who patronize them.

When students consider college either as applicants or as undergraduates, they often have mistaken ideas about their own self-interest. Because they cannot know in advance which institution will help them learn the most, they may choose a college for questionable reasons, such as which campus has the most appealing appearance, the liveliest social life, the most attractive living accommodations, or even the best athletic teams. Once enrolled, students may be so preoccupied with getting a good job that they regard vocational courses as the only subjects that really matter and neglect other aims such as developing new intellectual interests, improving their ability to think about ethical issues, or preparing themselves for citizenship in a democratic nation. Being easily tempted and distracted, they are also inclined to spend too little time on their coursework to acquire much of the knowledge that a college education should convey. If competition causes universities to cater to preferences such as these, the value of the education they provide will suffer.

To their credit, most academic leaders, college faculties, and accrediting agencies have resisted the tendency of students, as well as government officials, to emphasize vocational preparation and the economic advantages of a college degree to the point of excluding other worthwhile ends of a well-rounded college education. In some cases, however, competition has led campus leaders to yield ground. Many colleges have acquiesced, at least partially, to the widespread impulse to concentrate too much on vocational preparation. Most of them have also succumbed to the quiet pressure from undergraduates who wish to devote less effort to their studies. Almost everywhere, as the time students spend on homework has shrunk, their grades have continued to rise.

There are limits to what we can expect of universities in resisting the temptation to cater excessively to student desires. If we enjoy the advantages of a higher education system that emphasizes institutional autonomy and competition, we must anticipate that individual colleges will do what it takes to attract the best students they can, whether by providing upscale dorm rooms or by overemphasizing vocational courses at the expense of less popular general education offerings. Yet universities are not powerless. They can try to resist the decline in studying by doing a better job of explaining the goals of undergraduate education to their incoming students and persuading them of the multiple contributions that college can make to their future lives. They can also try harder to introduce more engaging methods of instruction that will increase student interest in their studies. They can find better ways of reviewing their part-time and term-limited faculty than relying so heavily on student evaluations, a practice that can easily lead instructors to seek higher ratings by giving better grades and shorter homework assignments.

There is also much that other interested constituencies can do to help colleges and universities resist the student pressures just described. If top corporate executives really mean what they say about wanting college graduates with better communication and analytical skills, heightened understanding of ethical issues, and greater appreciation of global affairs and other cultures, they could do more to convey their desires to undergraduates and make sure that the company's recruiters share their priorities. They could also pay more attention to college grades in deciding whom to hire instead of giving tacit support to the misguided impression of many students that earning a degree is all that matters.* Otherwise, the qualities they claim to seek will be undervalued by both colleges and students, and the results will continue to be less than they might be.

Government officials could also help by ceasing to speak about education as if the only purpose it served was to contribute to economic growth and global competitiveness. If presidents, governors, and prominent lawmakers all talk exclusively in economic terms, why should one expect young people to take a broader view of the benefits they can derive from a well-rounded college education?

Last but not least, the tendency to cater excessively to student desires provides another reason for government agencies and foundations, as well as academic leaders, to support efforts to develop better ways of assessing student learning. At bottom, most of the problems just described are the result of ignorance about what matters most in a college education. If students knew how much (or how little) they were learning, they might work harder in their courses. If faculty members understood the varying effects of different methods of instruction on the amount that students learn, they would be more inclined to adapt their teaching accordingly. If academic leaders realized how little intellectual progress many of their students are making, they might try harder to improve the quality of education instead of attaching such importance to college rankings and other dubious indicia of success.

THE INFLUENCE OF MONEY

Students are not the only constituency that can be catered to excessively by university officials. Since academic leaders are under constant pressure to raise increasing amounts of money, they may also be tempted to accede too readily to the desires of those on whom they depend for support. To their credit, they have generally resisted blatant attempts by donors to exert improper influence by choosing the professor to fill a new chair they have endowed or shaping the

---

*Apparently, grades do matter. One careful study has shown that even though companies pay little attention to academic records in hiring high school graduates, those with higher grades end up after several months earning more than other high school graduates. James E. Rosenbaum, *Beyond College for All: Career Paths for the Bottom Half* (2001). Moreover, in their study of alumni of selective colleges up to fifteen years after their graduation, William Bowen and Derek Bok found that those who received higher grades in college were consistently likely to earn significantly more than those with poorer records. *The Shape of the River: Long-Term Consequences of Considering Race in College and University Admissions* (1998), pp. 140–41.

content of the academic programs they support. Here and there, one encounters a contrary example, such as the willingness of many medical schools to allow pharmaceutical firms to fund continuing education programs despite the risk that company sponsors will influence the menu of programs, the choice of speakers, and the content of the presentations.[3] Examples of this kind are rare, however, and even medical schools may be beginning to tighten their rules for accepting corporate support for continuing education.

While direct donor influence over academic decisions has been quite well contained, donors as a group undoubtedly have a pronounced effect on the nature and shape of universities. Faculties and departments with wealthy alumni, such as leading business schools and elite colleges, attract a lot of support. Those that prepare students for modestly paid professions and occupations do much less well.

Academic leaders can try to offset these tendencies in a number of ways—by "taxing" more prosperous faculties to subsidize less fortunate programs or by making extra efforts to help raise money for parts of the university that lack wealthy patrons. Still, measures of this kind will seldom come close to offsetting the effects of donor preferences. To appreciate the results, one need only visit the campus of a leading university and compare the facilities of the business school with those of the schools of education, divinity, architecture, or social work.

The preferences and priorities of wealthy donors may not be ideal for shaping the priorities of a university. Nevertheless, it is difficult to conceive of any other way of allocating resources that would be clearly preferable. One can imagine a system in which the vast bulk of financial support took the form of block grants from the state that universities could allocate as they chose. The British government followed this practice for many years. Yet it is not self-evident that academic leaders will be better or wiser in choosing appropriate priorities than the mix of government agencies, foundations, corporations, and individual donors that share this function with universities in the United States. Academic institutions have their own internal politics and preferences that do not always reflect the legitimate needs of the various stakeholders with an interest in the work of higher education. As a practical matter, therefore, a system offering multiple sources of support may be the best that one can hope for, even though it does not always produce ideal results.

Relying heavily on private donations not only produces large differences in funding among different faculties in the same institution; it also gives rise to great disparities between institutions. That is certainly true of the United States, where research universities with multibillion-dollar endowments coexist with small liberal arts colleges that can barely continue to operate, not to mention all of the struggling community colleges with expenditures per student far below those of Ivy League institutions.

Is this a desirable state of affairs? That is not a question one can put to a former president of Harvard and be confident of a wholly objective answer. It does seem clear that community colleges and many comprehensive universities have not received the funding they will need to raise their graduation rates while providing an education of appropriate quality. However, Europe has hardly achieved better results by relying almost entirely on government support. By encouraging multiple sources of funding, America has been able to provide greater aggregate support for higher education as a whole than other advanced countries.

At the same time, the colleges that have gained the most from this system need to recognize certain obligations, if only to acknowledge the benefit they derive from tax deductions and other forms of official encouragement for private giving. Among these obligations is a responsibility to do their best to give students of limited means a chance to enroll and earn a degree if their academic qualifications are sufficient to make them reasonably competitive with the rest of the entering class. In this way, the best-endowed universities can try to temper the effects of great disparities of wealth by helping to create opportunities for all talented students instead of becoming a means for perpetuating hereditary patterns of affluence and privilege. By doing so, they can move America closer toward achieving one of its noblest, most fundamental ideals.

At the end of the twentieth century, it was apparent that elite institutions were not doing enough to satisfy this responsibility. Thousands of low-income students with high academic ability were not even applying to selective colleges.[4] Since then, a number of prominent institutions have recognized the problem and revised their financial aid policies accordingly. Many others, however, divert too much of their financial aid to merit scholarships and strategic tuition discounts that do not help the neediest students. What is also lacking is a determined effort by every well-endowed selective college to recruit lower-income students, since only a small fraction of the very ablest among them even think to submit an application, presumably because they cannot imagine that attending such a school is even conceivable. By doing more to reach out to these young people, selective colleges could enrich the diversity of their student bodies while helping to serve the public interest.

In addition to the distributive effects of philanthropy, the very process of seeking private donations can affect the behavior of universities in questionable ways. Their insatiable need for money, coupled with the existence of multiple funding sources, has led to a consuming effort on the part of academic leaders to gain financial support, a quest intensified by the struggle for preeminence throughout large segments of American higher education. These efforts have contributed much to the success of our universities, but they have also given rise to a host of troubling side effects.

The constant search for money affects almost every aspect of university behavior. Academic leaders are frequently chosen in part on the basis of evidence of their fund-raising abilities. Once in office, they frequently spend more time raising money than they give to academic affairs, and assemble larger and larger staffs to assist them. Only a few decades ago, a leading university might have had a mere handful of professional development officers. Today, such staffs often number in the hundreds, especially if one includes alumni affairs personnel and others whose work is intended in large part to assist the development effort.

The influence of fund-raising extends far beyond academic leaders and their assistants. Trustees are often appointed, especially in private universities, because of their ability to make a large donation. Professors are frequently hired or promoted in part because of their capacity to bring in research grants and corporate support. Students applying to selective colleges will generally have an advantage in admissions if their parents are wealthy enough to make a substantial gift or they are talented enough in football or basketball to strengthen a profitable team that helps support the college's athletic program.

It is difficult for campus authorities to resist the tendencies just described. The advantages gained by successful fund-raising are clear and measurable—more scholarships, added professorships, new buildings, and the like. The costs—apart from the salaries paid to the development office—are largely invisible and impossible to measure. How many promising candidates have refused positions of academic leadership because of the fund-raising burdens involved? What intellectual contributions might academic leaders make to their institution if such large fractions of their time were not taken up by soliciting gifts? With questions as speculative as these, is it surprising that the tangible benefits of fund-raising have a greater and greater influence over the life of universities? What else can one expect when each institution sees its competitors raising ever-larger sums with which to strengthen their faculties and improve their research and teaching programs?

In view of these multiple influences, one may again ask whether having to raise so much money from multiple sources, with all its attendant temptations and costs, is the best way to finance higher education. Yet what other system can one suggest? For all its disadvantages, the current modus operandi seems much like democracy—the worst possible system . . . except for all the known alternatives. After all, American universities, especially selective colleges and research universities, are much more amply supported than their counterparts abroad. They are better protected from disruptive fluctuations in government funding, as well as from the vagaries of politics that can affect how public funds are distributed. It is doubtful that higher education as a whole would do better by having all its funds provided by a federal government that is subject to the pressure of powerful interest groups and prone to earmarking appropriations for projects of questionable value that are dear to the hearts of individual lawmakers.

Could American higher education have achieved the level of financial support it has enjoyed under any other system? Could it have produced so many world-class research universities? Policy-makers in other advanced nations do not seem to think so. Instead, they are trying to wean their universities from an exclusive dependence on government support and encouraging them to follow our example by seeking funding from a variety of sources.

That said, it is still important that there be *some* limits to the influence of money, especially when important academic values are at stake. Almost anyone connected with a university would agree that donors should be rebuffed if they seek to dictate the choice of the professor to fill a chair they have funded. No sensible dean or president would agree to auction off places in the entering class to the highest bidder. Such agreements strike at essential academic values. To disregard these values threatens to erode the respect of the faculty and all those associated with the institution.

With this caution in mind, one has to question a number of current practices of universities, such as the advantages in admission many private colleges give to children of wealthy parents and the lowering of admissions standards, along with the creation of easier courses and majors, for recruited athletes by colleges engaged in big-time intercollegiate athletics.[5] Troubling signs also exist of a willingness on the part of many universities to compromise academic values in the course of working with industry to convert scientific discoveries into useful products. Campus officials have been accused of an excessive use of exclusive licensing and an overly zealous defense of lucrative patents in order to maximize their royalties. Anxious to preserve existing opportunities to make money, academic leaders have staunchly resisted government efforts to regulate institutional conflicts of interest.[6] In their effort to attract support from companies, many universities have been reluctant to set clear limits on the length of time that industry funders can embargo the findings of academic scientists. Some have even been notably lax in preventing corporate donors from keeping control of the data used in the experiments they fund or ghostwriting the published reports of the professors they support.

Once again, therefore, the role of competition turns out to be two-edged. The struggle for financial advantage creates a potent incentive to emulate the successful practices of rival institutions. This process improves performance when the practices involved enhance the quality or lower the cost of education. But it can also cause universities to adopt inappropriate methods of their rivals if they appear to be effective. Thus, a number of dubious practices have spread widely under the pressure of competition, such as compromising academic standards either to admit the children of wealthy parents or to achieve athletic success. No one can predict how much effect such behavior has on the reputation of universities and the respect they command from faculty, students, and the public. But it is surely unwise and unworthy to test the limits, for trust, reputation, and self-respect are assets of great value that are hard to restore once they have been lost.*

THE LEADERSHIP QUESTION

Still another potential weakness in our system of higher education is the problem of finding academic leaders equal to the challenge of presiding over a modern university. In choosing individuals to lead these institutions, trustees will usually select a candidate with prior experience as a professor, a calling not noted for attracting large numbers of people with either the talent or the ambition to lead and administer large institutions. The individuals selected from this limited pool preside over organizations that are frequently very difficult to manage. Many universities have huge budgets that often run into billions of dollars. The teaching and research that occur within their walls are too varied and technical for presidents to understand much of what is being done. The professors who carry on this work are independent by nature and inclined to resist the efforts of academic leaders to regulate their behavior.

Given the difficulties of the job, the results have been considerably better than one might have expected. American universities continue to be widely admired around the world, especially for their research and their graduate and professional schools. Although many people have contributed to these

---

*Where basic academic values are not at stake, the proper emphasis on raising funds becomes a matter of judgment, and it is difficult to draw appropriate lines. How many fund-raisers should a university employ? How much of a president's time can a university afford to have spent on courting donors? How many activities, alumni committees, and elaborate dinners should one conjure up to induce prospective givers to get more involved with the university? There are no certain answers to such questions. In recent decades, the guiding principle has been to raise as much money as possible, and the only limit on the number of fund-raising events has been the ingenuity of those whose job it is to think up new ways to elicit gifts. At some point, universities will have to devote more thought to setting limits on this process.

accomplishments, it is hard to imagine how such success could have been achieved without the benefit of reasonably capable leaders.

The system of governance in the United States has also helped to make effective leadership possible. In comparison with most other countries, the greater powers given to American university presidents, the longer periods many of them serve, and the fact that they are chosen by independent boards and not by faculty vote have allowed able leaders to accomplish more in the United States than their foreign counterparts could achieve. As a former president of the University of Geneva has remarked, "perhaps the biggest weakness of the European system compared with the U.S. lies with the governance/leadership of European universities."[7] It is not surprising, then, that other countries seeking to improve their universities have altered their methods of selecting and empowering presidents to resemble more closely the American model.

On the other hand, the current record of academic leadership is not without flaws. A recent survey of nineteen countries found that faculty members in the United States were among the least inclined to feel that "top level administrators are providing competent leadership."[8] One possible reason for this reaction is the gradual withdrawal of university presidents from involvement in academic matters in order to devote more attention to fund-raising, external affairs, and administrative responsibilities.* For leaders of any organization to detach themselves from the principal functions of the institution must surely be counted as a problem. Presidents who are not perceived to be participating actively in the promotion of education and research are less likely to acquire the moral authority and respect of the faculty that academic leaders need in order to guide an institution composed of independent professors. Delegating these responsibilities to provosts and deans is not a wholly satisfactory solution. First mates may keep a ship afloat and even steer it with consummate skill, but they are unlikely to chart a bold new course when the opportunity arises or to initiate those imaginative innovations that distinguish first-rate leadership from competent management.

The likelihood of distinguished leadership is also threatened by the growing preoccupation with the image of universities, a tendency encouraged by the absence of reliable information about their actual performance. Such concerns can easily lead presidents and deans to avoid raising questions about the quality of education that could anger their faculty or provoke adverse publicity that

---

*A survey of university presidents to determine how they allocate their time has found that academic affairs receive the least attention of any of the six possibilities offered. American Council on Education, "College Presidents Say Planning, Fundraising, Budgeting, and Personnel Issues Occupy Much of Their Time," *Higher Education and National Affairs* (October 9, 2000), p. 2.

might raise doubts in the minds of donors and alumni. Thus, it is not entirely surprising that so many university leaders have been unwilling to make a determined effort to improve the quality of teaching or reform the nature of graduate education.

Another example of the same cautious tendency is the uneven record of academic leaders in upholding basic academic values. Values are essential to the progress, the internal cohesion, and the successful governance of institutions populated by independent-minded professors whose conduct and cooperation cannot be controlled by hierarchical means. As a result, one has to worry when roughly half of America's faculty members, especially in research universities, are no longer confident that their right to express ideas freely will be firmly protected by their campus administration. Whether or not these fears are warranted, academic leaders are responsible for making sure that their professors feel secure about their right to speak and write freely. There are also indications that traditional guidelines against indoctrinating students in the classroom have been allowed to become blurred. (It is surely a matter of concern that a substantial fraction of undergraduates report having taken classes in which they felt obliged in writing papers and exams not to take issue with their professor's political views in order to be sure of receiving a good grade.)[9] Still further signs of eroding values are the examples previously noted of laxity on the part of many universities in enforcing appropriate restrictions on corporate influence over research or financial conflicts of interest on the part either of faculty researchers or of the university itself.

The failings just described are by no means universal. There are certainly presidents who have been vocal and resolute in defending free speech, resisting the excesses of commercialization, and maintaining appropriate policies governing fund-raising, admissions, athletics, and other activities where essential standards are at risk of being compromised for immediate gain. Yet these examples appear to be more the exception than the rule. Fortunately, most basic faculty values have held up fairly well despite the lack of attention. Still, they are so essential to the university's well-being and so difficult to restore once they have eroded that any evidence of neglect by the leadership is a matter of serious concern.

There is also reason to be concerned about the role of presidents and trustees in choosing goals for their university. The central responsibility of academic leaders (and trustees) is to set the directions and priorities for their institution. They must therefore be held accountable for the widespread tendency to place excessive emphasis on climbing to a higher level in the conventional academic hierarchy.[10] Occasionally, such efforts are appropriate. More often than not, however, they result in spending too much money and effort on encouraging research of little quality, creating advanced degree programs that are arguably unnecessary, and allocating excessive amounts of scholarship money to applicants with high SAT scores instead of aiding students who actually need help.

There are different grounds for concern about the quality of leadership in community colleges and comprehensive universities. The critical challenge facing these institutions is to raise graduation rates (without lowering academic standards) and increase the growth in national levels of educational attainment that has lagged during the past thirty-five years. To their credit, some comprehensives and community colleges have done an excellent job of adapting their programs to lift completion rates while meeting the needs of students, many of whom are over twenty-five, employed at least part-time, and handicapped by having attended mediocre public schools. As previously mentioned, however, many other institutions have not done nearly as well. In comparing community colleges and comprehensive universities possessing student bodies of similar socioeconomic background and academic ability, one cannot help but be struck by the large differences in graduation rates and job placement records between the least successful half of these institutions and their most successful peers.[11] It is possible, of course, that there are subtle differences beyond the control of the most capable leaders that account for the large disparities. Such research as has been done, however, suggests that the successful institutions have employed a number of practices that could be adopted by colleges with lower graduation and placement records if their leaders displayed greater determination and initiative.[12]

All in all, therefore, the quality of leadership in American higher education is a classic case of the proverbial half-filled glass. It is true that some presidents have wasted money in the pursuit of dubious goals, allowed academic values to erode from neglect, failed to challenge curricular requirements and methods of instruction that are less than ideal, and tolerated dropout rates that are higher than necessary. At the same time, it is equally true that other academic leaders have performed remarkably well, despite the difficulties of the job and the limited supply of promising candidates for leadership positions.

In short, one can find much to praise and much to criticize about the current state of university leadership. Although room for improvement undoubtedly exists, there are no plausible proposals for sweeping structural changes in the presidency of American universities or major procedural reforms in the way presidents are selected that promise to lift performance significantly. Choosing leaders is always a difficult undertaking, and an element of luck is forever present to some degree. As a result, it is likely that commentators will continue indefinitely arguing whether the glass of university leadership is half-full or half-empty.

ENFORCING MINIMUM STANDARDS OF QUALITY

The last chink in the armor of American higher education is the danger that institutions of very low quality will be allowed to remain in operation. Such a risk is virtually inevitable under a large system like ours in which it is easy to create new colleges that then enjoy broad discretion to determine the content and standards of their educational programs. The problem could well become more serious in the future as the number of students seeking a college education expands to include more and more young people with weak academic backgrounds and limited access to reliable advice in choosing which institutions to attend.

The traditional mechanism in the United States for guarding against such hazards is a system of accreditation backed by the necessity of gaining approval in order to qualify for federal financial aid. While accreditors have done a reasonable job of encouraging colleges to pay more attention to educational reform, they have not been as successful in enforcing appropriate minimum standards of quality.[13] Many colleges have managed to remain in operation despite graduation rates that are egregiously low and records of employment for their graduates that fall well short of reasonable expectations.

There are two known ways to cope with the problem of substandard educational institutions. They are not mutually exclusive. One way, exemplified by the accreditation system, is for the government or some designated entity to evaluate colleges and universities and force those of unacceptable quality to cease operating. The other method is to require all educational institutions to reveal enough accurate information about their operations and their record of performance that prospective students can make an informed decision about whether to enroll. Unfortunately, both methods have serious weaknesses.[14]

The first approach runs into trouble because of the difficulty of deciding when an institution is of such poor quality and has so little prospect of improvement that it must be made ineligible for public funds. Such a question has no obvious objective answer; it is inescapably a matter of judgment. Nevertheless, any agency charged with making such decisions is bound to decide that it must try to set minimum requirements, both to provide some demonstrable consistency in its judgments and to give adequate notice to institutions of what they must do to remain accredited.

Since the institutions being evaluated vary so widely in size and nature, even the most conscientious accreditors soon discover that suitable rules of general application are hard to find. For example, accreditors have sometimes sought to require a minimum number of books in the college library, but what minimum will be suitable for an array of educational institutions broad enough to include large research universities, small liberal arts colleges, and specialized schools such as music conservatories and academies of the arts and design?

Standards can also be overtaken by events and become unintended barriers to progress. A rule requiring a minimum number of books may seem reasonable enough when first adopted. Yet it can eventually inhibit innovation when applied mechanically to a new online university that has no books but simply provides access to readings via the Internet.

Occasionally, by dint of political pressure or skillful maneuvering, the institutions that are accredited can "capture" the process by getting their supporters appointed to staff the oversight body. Thus, law professors allegedly gained control of the law school accreditation process by dominating accreditation teams and using the process to introduce self-serving requirements. As a result, observers have criticized accreditors for driving up the cost of a legal education by insisting on the equivalent of three years of study, ample libraries, and restrictions on the use of part-time faculty.* Accreditors have responded that they are simply trying to ensure that students receive a proper education. Such controversies illustrate the difficulty of distinguishing between rules to ensure appropriate quality and rules that protect vested interests against the threat of low-cost competition.

Since it is so difficult to measure student learning, even the most cleverly designed accreditation rules can rarely be applied mechanically to assess the adequacy of educational programs. Some measure of judgment will still be required. In such a process, marginal colleges have the advantage. They have an intense interest in resisting efforts to deny accreditation and shut them down, while those who stand to benefit from proper standards tend to be diffuse and disorganized. Under these circumstances, the chances are great that when broad standards are applied to specific cases, exceptions will be made, temporary reprieves granted, and death sentences long delayed if not avoided altogether.[15]

Requiring universities to publish pertinent information about their programs—including costs, course offerings, financial aid, employment records of recent graduates, and the like—is also a useful but imperfect method for protecting students from poorly run institutions and exploitative tactics. It is easy enough to specify helpful types of information and demand that they be made public. But as law schools have demonstrated in striving to improve their rankings, there are many ways to manipulate data in order to disguise weaknesses. Colleges faced with the threat of having to shut down can be endlessly inventive. The meaning of "students" can be defined to exclude categories of high-risk individuals; the term "dropouts" can be manipulated through the classification of groups of departed students as "on leave"; and employment

---

*As a result, the Justice Department sued the American Bar Association over these practices and obtained a settlement designed to halt the abuses. Achieving compliance with the terms of the settlement, however, has proved to be difficult. See Brian Z. Tamanaha, *Failing Law Schools* (2012).

records of recent graduates can be compiled to include types of jobs very different from those for which students were ostensibly trained. Even if the published information is accurate, it can be presented in confusing ways that make it difficult for prospective students to understand. Investigating the claims of hundreds of different schools and digging deeply enough to expose the flaws in the data can be a vast and expensive undertaking for government officials.

For these reasons, disclosure requirements can be useful, but they will almost certainly be less than perfect. Moreover, even with the most complete information, students may keep on coming to marginal institutions. As P. T. Barnum famously remarked, "A sucker is born every minute." To the extent that the gullible enroll and receive federal grants and loans, they may continue to drop out and default on their loans, leaving the government to pick up the tab.

For all these reasons, the outlook for imposing more effective methods of quality control is not especially bright. Neither the past experience of accrediting agencies nor the record of efforts to uphold minimum standards for charter schools and other institutions in society gives much reason for optimism. Recently, the Department of Education launched a new initiative to protect students by issuing precise minimum standards that colleges must meet to remain eligible for federal student aid.[16] Only time will tell how successful this effort will be. The difficulty of the task, however, creates high odds that the United States will continue tolerating a substantial number of colleges and universities that would not be allowed to exist in many other advanced nations.

A tightly controlled regulatory system of higher education with strict conditions for founding new institutions might well have resulted in fewer defaulted loans, wasted years, and disappointed hopes. But it is far too late to install such a process in the United States. It is also unlikely that a closely regulated procedure of this kind would have yielded as much variety and innovation as our own loosely administered system. In particular, it might have been much slower to produce the more convenient, student-oriented programs of education for working adults or the recent surge of online classes that our competitive, decentralized system has helped to bring about.

PROSPECTS FOR REFORM

As the preceding discussion has revealed, not all of the problems intrinsic to higher education are within the power of colleges and universities to resolve. In a few cases, improvements are blocked by intractable forces in the larger society. A small but highly visible example is big-time athletics. Despite the endless parade of shabby compromises and petty scandals, the high-profile sports, such as football and basketball, have gained such a large and avid public following that academic leaders are powerless to do much more than punish violations of existing rules and try to prevent the current situation from getting worse.

More often, higher education's problems are the predictable by-products of essential features of the system itself and thus cannot be removed without threatening to do more harm than good. As we have seen, in a system marked by large numbers of colleges and universities that rightly possess broad discretion over their academic affairs, the quality of leadership is bound to be uneven and institutions of dubious quality are all but certain to exist and survive. Similarly, the tradition of funding higher education from a variety of sources (rather than entirely from the state) has produced more money but has also led to great differences in resources between the wealthiest and poorest institutions. As a result, while many of the richest universities are numbered among the best in the world, community colleges and comprehensives must make do with funds that are insufficient to cope with the growing cohorts of poorly prepared students who come to them in search of a degree. Even so, as previously pointed out, it is hard to imagine any other method of financing higher education that wouldn't create more problems than it solved.

The aspect of our system that seems to produce the most mixed results is the keen competition among member institutions for funds, students, and stature. This rivalry is the source of much of the energy and innovation that characterize our universities at their best. At the same time, it also intensifies many troubling tendencies—the wasteful pursuit of conventional prestige, the temptation to cater to the questionable desires of constituent groups, and the pressure on universities to adopt the successful tactics of competitors even when they are unsavory and inappropriate.

Examining the various sins and excesses in the struggle to compete, one can easily think longingly of a less rivalrous system in which institutions would try to excel for the sheer love of acquiring new knowledge and educating the young. Yet musings of this kind are unrealistic. It is simply not possible to banish competition from the hearts and minds of those responsible for the work of universities, whether they be professors, trustees, or deans and presidents. For better or worse, the struggle to finish first is a way of life in America, an essential motive for improvement and innovation that cannot be exorcized by Congress, the Supreme Court, or any other temporal authority. Rather than indulge in such fantasies, the better course for those who shape our system of higher education is to do what they can with the carrots and sticks at their disposal to channel the energies unleashed by competition toward constructive ends, while discouraging the use of improper methods for getting ahead of one's peers.

This discussion may suggest to some readers that there is little prospect of making much headway against the flaws and failings of our colleges and universities. Such an interpretation is surely not intended. While the progress of each institution is limited by the nature of the system to which it belongs (as well as by larger forces in the society over which it has little or no control), colleges and universities can almost always do something constructive to lift their performance and strengthen areas of weakness. Take almost any problem and one will find some institutions doing a great deal better than others in similar circumstances. Perfection may be forever out of reach. Yet enough opportunity for improvement remains to keep academic leaders and their faculties usefully occupied for the foreseeable future and beyond.

Fortunately, the prospects for improvement seem brightest for some of the most pressing areas in need of improvement. For example, there are clear indications now that government leaders and philanthropic organizations are concerned about the high rates of attrition from college. President Obama has called attention to the effects of stagnating graduation rates on the economy and has set ambitious goals for improvement. Federal funding for low-income student (Pell) grants has increased massively. Several large foundations have also begun to take an active interest in improving graduation rates by funding research and experimentation to lower attrition, especially in the frequently overlooked community colleges where dropout rates are highest. Better yet, a recent survey has found that almost 90 percent of the chief academic officers of comprehensive universities and almost 94 percent of their counterparts at community colleges now agree that improving retention and graduation rates is "very important."[17] In pursuing this goal, these academic leaders should benefit greatly from the increased knowledge about why some colleges have much less attrition than others with similar student bodies, and what steps college officials can take to keep their students from dropping out.

At this early stage, the prospects for increasing graduation rates are still uncertain. Success will probably take considerably longer than policy-makers like to assume, and it is unclear in today's forbidding fiscal climate whether the current federal efforts will be sustained long enough to make a major difference. Nevertheless, at long last, there are at least grounds for hope.

The outlook is also promising for improving the quality of undergraduate education. State officials have become more concerned about the issue. Recent research reports revealing the modest intellectual gains of college students have been widely publicized.[18] The realization that many students are not learning as much as most people expected, coupled with the relentless increase in college tuitions, creates a toxic brew that academic leaders and their faculties can ignore only at their peril. Already, only 35 percent of the public feel that "colleges today care mainly about education and making sure students have a good educational experience," while 60 percent believe that "colleges today . . . care mainly about the bottom line."[19] As these sentiments build, there are growing signs that colleges are getting the message.

After years of patient effort, the much-maligned accrediting organizations have begun to achieve some success in persuading campus officials to define what they intend their students to learn and to evaluate the progress undergraduates make during their college years. Surveys also show a slow but perceptible increase in the use of more effective methods of instruction.[20] Ultimate success will depend crucially on whether colleges, especially those in the great research universities, recognize the full scope of the task before them. The effort required extends all the way from changing how large introductory freshman courses are taught to revamping PhD programs to help future generations of faculty improve their classroom skills by drawing on the growing store of knowledge about teaching and learning.

These needs provide further evidence of the importance of developing reliable measures of student learning. Without them, it will be difficult to sustain the momentum for reform, since academic leaders and their faculties will often have no way of knowing whether their efforts are succeeding. Even competition cannot bring about improvement under such conditions. After all, how much effort would be expended on scientific research and how much progress would scientists make if they could devise their elegant experiments and conduct them with state-of-the-art equipment but had no way of ascertaining the results? For much the same reason, policy-makers are unlikely to know which reforms to encourage if they are unable to determine the effects on student learning of such trends as the increased use of part-time instructors, the growth of online degree programs, and the rapid rise of for-profit institutions. As a result, efforts to devise better ways of evaluating student progress deserve a high priority from government agencies and foundations. So do experiments to test the results of the many efforts currently underway to experiment with technology and other innovative methods to improve college teaching.

In the end, the key ingredients of progress will be a determination on the part of academic leaders to concentrate on raising graduation rates *and* improving the quality of education coupled with a willingness on the part of public officials, foundations, and other donors to support the research and experimentation required before embarking on expensive reforms of unproven value. Fortunately, unlike programs to address many other domestic problems, successful efforts to improve the quality of teaching and learning do not have to cost massive amounts of money. The same is true of many of the steps required to increase graduation rates. Even in this era of limited resources, then, significant progress is not beyond our reach.

THE LAST WORD

||||||||||||||||||||||||||||||||||||||||||||||||||||||||||||||||||||||||||||||||||||||||||||||||||||||||||||||

The preceding catalog of problems may have left some readers with a gloomy feeling that our colleges and universities are in worse condition than is actually the case. Books like this one that try to define an agenda for improvement are bound to concentrate on flaws and weaknesses and thus create just such an impression. Yet that can hardly give an accurate picture of a system widely regarded here and abroad as the best of its kind in the world. To obtain a complete and balanced accounting of the state of American higher education, one must consider its performance from a variety of perspectives rather than dwell so heavily on its shortcomings. How does the current record of our colleges and universities compare with their accomplishments in earlier periods? How well have they performed relative to the results in other nations? Which of their weaknesses are serious enough to be of grave and immediate importance to the nation and which are merely problems that, though real and deserving of attention, are neither so pressing nor so vital to the public as to constitute a major cause for concern?

THE URGENT PRIORITIES

Of all the problems previously discussed, only two are serious enough to be in urgent need of reform. The first priority is to raise the percentage of young Americans who earn a college degree. Unless current levels can be increased substantially, most experts believe that the inequality of income will continue rising, the nation's economy will grow more slowly, and many deserving students will be denied opportunities to succeed according to their abilities and aspirations. Most of the additional students needed to raise our educational attainment levels will not arrive as freshmen fully prepared to succeed at college-level work. Even so, with the aid of what is now known about teaching and learning and in light of the successes already achieved in some of our community colleges and comprehensive universities, something can surely be done to reduce drop-out rates and increase the number of college graduates.

The second urgent priority is to increase not only the quantity of students graduating from college but the amount they learn while they are there. In recent years, a growing body of evidence has accumulated indicating that many professors are still using methods of instruction that are demonstrably less than optimal, that undergraduates are not working as hard at their studies as they once did, and that a substantial percentage are making dismayingly little progress toward the goals that most professors consider essential to a successful college education. These findings suggest that many young people may be graduating lacking the knowledge and skills to succeed in their careers, become engaged and enlightened citizens, or gain the insights and interests that will help them live fuller and more rewarding lives.

Increasing the quality of undergraduate education and eliciting greater student effort will require substantial improvement in the methods of instruction. Sustaining such progress will entail a long overdue effort to reform PhD programs so as to prepare aspiring college professors, not just as researchers, but as teachers and educators as well.

Improving the quality of education while simultaneously increasing the number of college graduates would be a difficult test for higher education under any circumstances. Accomplishing this task at a time when funds for the purpose are in short supply will be an especially daunting challenge. College costs must somehow be kept within reasonable limits. Yet unless academic leaders and public officials act with great skill, the likely result will be a decline in the quality of education, since slippage of this kind is much more difficult to detect, and hence much easier to tolerate, than growing budget deficits and stagnant graduation rates.

Other flaws in the performance of American higher education are of a lesser magnitude than the two challenges just mentioned. Our professional schools continue to be unsurpassed and widely admired throughout the world. They have shortcomings, but most of them are not major problems, and those that are tend to be chiefly the product of outside forces over which the faculties involved do not have much control.

For example, medical schools have some unresolved issues in their MD programs, but they are issues of the sort that educators regularly encounter, and will presumably be dealt with satisfactorily in the course of time. Many of the graduate medical programs are believed to have more serious shortcomings. Nevertheless, these programs are largely under the control of the teaching hospitals and the specialty boards, and medical schools have only limited power to improve them.

Law schools likewise suffer from several long-standing weaknesses that are being addressed, albeit gradually. More recent and more serious are problems caused by the high cost of legal education and the tendency for the number of graduating law students to exceed the supply of legal jobs available. Bringing the number of new lawyers into alignment with the existing employment opportunities promises to be a painful process for all concerned. Yet law schools cannot solve this problem satisfactorily by themselves. The best remedies will require reforms initiated by the organized bar that relax some unnecessarily rigid requirements for accreditation or better yet, allow individuals with briefer, less expensive training to perform various simple legal services that must now be performed by law school graduates and hence are too expensive for most low- and middle-income people to afford.

Management faculties may be facing a more basic educational challenge than their colleagues in medicine and law. Although American business schools stand high in international rankings, it is not clear that even the best of them have succeeded in devising a program of study that gives their graduates a lasting advantage as a corporate executive, save in a few specialized careers. The standard curricula, drawn heavily from the more quantitative social sciences, seem insufficient for the practical demands of running a business. Overcoming this problem will be hard. Still, the better American business schools continue to attract a host of applicants. They can easily survive and even prosper while their faculties continue their active search for ways to address the criticisms leveled against them.

Apart from the familiar complaints about federal funding levels, the current state of research in our universities seems free of serious weaknesses, at least for the time being. The achievements of our scientists and scholars continue to be unsurpassed. Our methods of training aspiring researchers remain a model for the rest of the world. Notwithstanding the well-publicized uncertainties of an academic career, most department chairs still believe that they are attracting very able candidates to their graduate programs.

One possible source of concern is our heavy reliance on students and scholars from abroad to fill our graduate schools and maintain the excellence of our research faculty. Of course, America has never been able to rely entirely on native talent. Our universities only became the envy of the world following the influx of eminent scientists and scholars from Europe in the wake of Hitler's rise to power. For the time being, fortunately, America is still the country of choice for highly talented young researchers seeking advanced training, and many of these young people remain in this country after they have completed their education. Nevertheless, nations such as China, India, and South Korea are making determined efforts to increase their numbers of scientists and engineers and produce a growing supply of published papers. In time, these countries may be able to offer facilities and colleagues of sufficient quality to lure back many of their investigators who have migrated to America. Should such an exodus occur, the United States will need to take vigorous steps to increase the limited number of American students who currently seek careers in scientific research. That day, however, still seems far enough in the future not to pose an immediate threat to the preeminence of American science.

THE TRAJECTORY OF AMERICAN HIGHER EDUCATION

To arrive at a full and fair assessment of our higher education system, it is also important to note that today's colleges and universities, whatever their shortcomings, are superior in many respects to their antecedents fifty years ago. The scope and variety of the courses they offer have increased enormously. Their faculties are open to women and minorities to a far greater degree than they were in the early 1960s. Their student bodies are more diverse, and they are educating a much larger fraction of the population. By capitalizing on the Internet and creating innovative ways to meet the mounting demands for education, their professors are reaching new audiences here and abroad in ways inconceivable in earlier generations.

Of course, the fact that our colleges and universities have made progress in the past half-century gives no guarantee of future success. The deficiencies of undergraduate education will be hard to overcome; the funds provided for improvement may be grossly inadequate; and the government may enact poorly conceived and burdensome regulations in their eagerness to bring about reform. Yet these risks could also be the spur that inspires our colleges and universities to question traditional practices and experiment with novel ways to improve their performance.

The possibilities for progress are unusually abundant. The potential learners within the reach of our campuses have now grown to include adults of every age in all parts of the world. This fact alone creates exciting prospects for rethinking and redefining the role of higher education—the relative importance universities assign to the many different audiences they can serve, the appropriate form and substance of the education they give to each, and the terms on which they offer their instruction, whether free of charge, at cost, or for a profit.

Meanwhile, advances in technology and cognitive psychology offer fresh opportunities for universities to improve upon their traditional ways of teaching. In response, promising new methods of instruction are being developed that could enhance learning and make instruction more interesting. As these innovations spread, they may elicit greater effort from existing students and provide more effective ways of educating the larger, more diverse cohorts that will enter college over the next generation.

Finally, the growing importance of new knowledge and new discoveries has led public officials and other funding sources to direct more of their support towards efforts to find solutions to important national problems. While this shift runs a risk of neglecting the subtler values of pure research, it increases opportunities to break down long-standing intellectual barriers and engage in more of the interdisciplinary inquiry that professors have long been criticized for neglecting. In exploring these possibilities, investigators can now utilize computers to assemble and analyze databases of a hitherto unimaginable size and use advances in communication to work with colleagues anywhere in the world.

Faced with all these opportunities, faculties are showing ample evidence of entrepreneurial vigor and innovation. Though the pace of progress may seem slow, the rapid spread of online courses, the birth of new ventures offering MOOCs with massive enrollments, the building of campuses in Asia and the Middle East, and the emergence of a flock of experimental efforts to devise cheaper yet effective models of undergraduate education testify to the willingness to try new things. Indeed, a catalog of all the changes underway in American colleges and universities would reveal an astonishing amount of invention and experimentation. How far these initiatives will take us cannot now be foretold. Yet the energy with which they are currently being pursued gives reason to hope that the next twenty-five years will eventually take their place along with the several decades around the end of the nineteenth century and the generation that followed World War II as another of the great creative periods in the history of American higher education.

NOTES

INTRODUCTION

1. Ben Wildavsky, *The Great Brain Race: How Global Universities Are Reshaping the World* (2010), pp. 70–99.

2. R. D. Sheldon and P. Foland, "The Race for World Leadership of Science and Technology: Status and Forecasts" (paper presented at the 12th International Conference on Scientometrics and Informetrics, Rio de Janeiro, Brazil, July14–17, 2009).

3. Ibid., p. 22; "The Almanac, 2012–13," *Chronicle of Higher Education* (August 31, 2012), p. 59.

FOREWORD (I)

1. Christopher Jencks and David Riesman, *The Academic Revolution* (1968).

CHAPTER ONE
THE AMERICAN SYSTEM OF HIGHER EDUCATION

1. Samuel E. Morison, *Three Centuries of Harvard, 1636–1936* (1964), pp. 7–10.

2. Clark Kerr, *The Uses of the University* (1963), is the seminal descriptive analysis of the modern research university. See also Roger L. Geiger, *Knowledge and Money: Research Universities and the Paradox of the Marketplace* (2004), and Hugh D. Graham and Nancy Diamond, *The Rise of American Research Universities* (1997).

3. On metropolitan universities, see Daniel M. Johnson and David A. Bell (eds.), *Metropolitan Universities: An Emerging Model of American Higher Education* (1995).

4. On liberal arts colleges in general, see David Breneman, *Liberal Arts Colleges: Thriving, Surviving, or Endangered* (1994); Samuel Schuman, *Old Main: Small Colleges in Twenty-First Century America* (2005).

5. See Alice W. Brown et al., *Cautionary Tales: Strategy Lessons from Struggling Colleges* (2012), and Alice W. Brown and Sandra L. Ballard, *Changing Course: Reinventing Colleges, Avoiding Closures* (2011).

6. On community colleges, see Kevin Dougherty, *The Contradictory College: The Conflicting Origins, Impacts and Futures of the Community College* (1994); W. Norton Grubb and Associates, *Honored but Invisible: An Inside Look at Teaching in Community Colleges* (1999); Arthur M. Cohen and Florence B. Brawer, *The American Community College* (5th ed., 2008); Paul Osterman, "The Promise, Performance, and Politics of Community Colleges," in Ben Wildavsky, Andrew P. Kelly, and Kevin Carey (eds.), *Reinventing Higher Education: The Promise of Higher Education* (2011), p. 129.

7. Paul Osterman, note 6, pp. 120, 140–41.

8. Compare, e.g., Cecilia E. Rouse, "Democratization or Diversion: The Effect of Community Colleges on Educational Attainment," 13 *Journal of Business and Economic Statistics* (1995), p. 217, with Steven Brint and Jerome Karabel, *The Diverted Dream: Community Colleges and the Promise of Economic Opportunity, 1900–1985* (1989), and Mariana Alfonso, "The Impact of Community College Attendance on Baccalaureate Attainment," 47 *Research in Higher Education* (2006), p. 873.

9. National Center for Education Statistics, *Digest of Education Statistics* (2010), table 275 (2011). For studies of for-profit universities, see David W. Breneman, Brian Pusser, and Sarah E. Turner (eds.), *Earnings from Learnings: The Rise of For-Profit Universities* (2006); David J. Deming, Claudia Goldin, and Lawrence F. Katz, *The For-Profit Postsecondary School Sector: Nimble Critters or Agile Predators?* National Bureau of Economic Research, Working Paper No. 17710 (December 2011); Guilbert C. Hentschke, "For-Profit Sector Innovations in Business Models and Organizational Cultures," in Ben Wildavsky, Andrew P. Kelly, and Kevin Carey (eds.), note 6, p. 159; Guilbert C. Hentschke, Vincent M. Lechuga, and William G. Tierney (eds.), *For Profit Universities: Their Markets, Regulation, Performance, and Place in Higher Education* (2010).

10. Tamar Lewin, "University of Phoenix to Shutter 115 Locations," *New York Times* (October 17, 2012), p. A22; "Almanac, 2012–13," *Chronicle of Higher Education* (August 31, 2012), p. 46.

11. David J. Deming, Claudia Goldin, and Lawrence F. Katz, note 9, p. 10. Guilbert C. Hentschke, note 9, p. 165.

12. General Accounting Office, Statement of Gregory D. Katz, "For Profit Colleges: Undercover Testing Finds Colleges Encouraged Fraud and Engaged in Deceptive and Questionable Marketing Practices" (August 4, 2010).

13. David J. Deming, Claudia Goldin, and Lawrence F. Katz, note 9, p. 15.

14. See pp. 63–69.

15. OECD, *Education at a Glance* (2011), table B2.1.

16. James Monks and Ronald G. Ehrenberg, *The Impact of "U.S. News & World Report" Rankings on Admissions Outcomes and Pricing Policies at Selective Private Institutions*, National Bureau of Economic Research, Working Paper 7227 (1999).

17. Clifford Adelman, *The Bologna Club: What U.S. Higher Education Can Learn from a Decade of European Reconstruction* (May 2008), pp. 12, 13.

18. Ben Wildavsky, *The Great Brain Race: How Global Universities Are Reshaping the World* (2010), pp. 70–99.

19. On the shift in Europe toward the US model, see David Palfreyman and Ted Tapper (eds.), *Structuring Mass Higher Education: The Role of Elite Institutions* (2009).

20. Barbara M. Kehm and Ute Lazendorf (eds.), *Reforming University Governance: Changing Conditions for Research in Four European Universities* (2006); Frans A. Van Vught (ed.), *Mapping the Higher Education Landscape: Toward a European Classification of Higher Education* (2009).

CHAPTER TWO
PURPOSES, GOALS, AND LIMITS TO GROWTH

1. Bill Readings, *The University in Ruins* (1996).

2. For an account of the classical curriculum and the prevailing attitude toward the purpose of the college prior to the Civil War, see Laurence R. Veysey, *The Emergence of the American University* (1965), chapter 1.

3. Clark Kerr, *The Uses of the University* (1963).

4. For a detailed study of college mission statements, see Barrett J. Taylor and Christopher C. Morphew, *An Analysis of Baccalaureate College Mission Statements* (2010).

5. Gary C. Fethke and Andrew J. Policano, *Public No More: A New Path to Excellence for America's Public Universities* (2012), pp. 26–27.

6. David A. Longanecker, *Mission Differentiation vs. Mission Creep: Higher Education's Battle between Creationism and Evolution* (November 2008), p. 5.

7. Peter D. Eckel, "Mission Diversity and the Tension between Prestige and Effectiveness: An Overview of U.S. Higher Education," 21 *Higher Education Policy* (2008), pp. 175, 185.

8. The conventional hierarchy of colleges and universities is well described by David Riesman, *Constraint and Variety in American Education* (1956).

9. Ellen Hazelkorn, "Rankings and the Battle for World Class Excellence: Institutional Strategies and Policy Choices" (paper presented at OECD Institute for Higher Education Management, General Conference, September 2008), cited by Peter D. Eckel and Adrianna Kezar, "Presidents Leading: The Dynamics and Complexities of Campus Leadership, " in Philip Altbach, Patricia Gumport, and Robert O. Berdahl (eds.), *American Higher Education in the Twenty-First Century* (3rd ed., 2011), pp. 279, 292.

10. See, e.g., Malcolm Gladwell, "The Order of Things," *New Yorker* (February 14, 2011), p. 68.

11. James Monks and Ronald G. Ehrenberg, *The Impact of "U.S. News & World Report" Rankings on Admissions Outcomes and Pricing Policies at Selective Private Institutions*, National Bureau of Economic Research, Working Paper 7227 (1999).

12. Ellen Hazelkorn, *Rankings and the Reshaping of Higher Education: The Battle for World-Class Status* (2011), pp. 106, 159.

13. Quoted by David L. Kirp, *Shakespeare, Einstein and the Bottom Line: The Marketing of Higher Education* (2002), p. 111.

14. See, generally, James L. Shulman and William G. Bowen, *The Game of Life: College Sports and Educational Values* (2001).

15. Rory P. O'Shea, Thomas J. Allen, Arnand Chevalier, and Frank Roche, "Entrepreneurial Orientation, Technology Transfer, and Spinoff Performance of U.S. Universities," 34 *Research Policy* (2003), p. 994; Djordje Djokovic and Vangelis Souitaris, "Spinouts from Academic Institutions: A Literature Review with Suggestions for Further Research," 33 *Journal of Technology Transfer* (2008), p. 225.

16. Derek Bok, *Universities in the Marketplace: The Commercialization of Higher Education* (2003), pp. 38–39 and sources cited therein.

17. Josh Lerner, "Venture Capital and the Commercialization of Academic Technology: Symbiosis and Paradox," in Lewis Branscomb, Fumio Kodama, and Richard Florida (eds.), *Industrializing Knowledge: University-Industry Linkages in Japan and the United States* ((1999).

18. Gabriel E. Kaplan, "How Academic Ships Actually Navigate," in Ronald G. Ehrenberg (ed.), *Governing Academia: Who Is in Charge at the Modern University?* (2004), pp. 165, 196.

CHAPTER THREE
THE GOVERNANCE OF NONPROFIT UNIVERSITIES

1. National Commission on the Academic Presidency, *Renewing the Academic Presidency: Stronger Leadership for Tougher Times* (1996), p. 118.

2. Werner Z. Hirsch and Luc E. Weber (eds.), *Governance in Higher Education: The University in a State of Flux* (2001), p. 86.

3. Michael D. Cohen and James G. March, *Leadership and Ambiguity* (1986), p. 151.

4. American Council on Education, "College Presidents Say Planning, Fundraising, Budgeting and Personnel Issues Occupy Much of Their Time," *Higher Education and National Affairs* (October 9, 2000), p. 2.

5. In a 2005 survey, 83.8 percent of presidents had earned a PhD or EdD degree. "What Presidents Think about Higher Education, Their Jobs, and Their Lives," *Chronicle of Higher Education* (November 24, 2005), pp. A-25, 39.

6. James J. Duderstadt, "Governing the Twenty-First Century University: A View from the Bridge," in William G. Tierney (ed.), *Competing Conceptions of Academic Governance: Negotiating the Perfect Storm* (2004), pp. 137, 138.

7. Robert M. Rosenzweig, *The Political University: Policy, Politics, and Presidential Leadership in the American Research University* (1998), p. 121.

8. See, e.g., Jerry A. Jacobs and Sarah E. Winslow, "Overworked Faculty: Job Stresses and Family Demands," 596 *Annals* (November 2004), p. 104.

9. Philip S. Babcock and Mindy Marks, *The Falling Time Cost of College: Evidence from Half a Century of Time Use Data*, National Bureau of Economic Research, Working Paper 15954 (April 2010).

10. For a more detailed account of this review, see Phyllis Keller, *Getting at the Core: Curriculum Reform at Harvard* (1982).

11. Quoted by Senator Christopher Dodd in Committee on Banking, Housing, and Urban Affairs, United States Senate, *Federal Reserve's First Monetary Policy Report for 2005*, p. 9.

12. E.g., Thomas J. Tighe, *Who's in Charge of America's Research Universities?* (2003).

13. E.g., James J. Duderstadt, *A University for the 21st Century* (2000), pp. 246–49.

14. Jack H. Schuster and Martin J. Finkelstein, *The American Faculty: The Restructuring of Academic Work and Careers* (2006), p. 358.

15. Stanley Rothman, April Kelly-Woessner, and Matthew Woessner, *The Still Divided Academy: How Competing Visions of Power, Politics, and Diversity Complicate the Mission of Higher Education* (2011), p. 45.

16. Gabriel Kaplan, "How Academic Ships Actually Navigate," in Ronald G. Ehrenberg (ed.), *Governing Academia: Who Is in Charge at the Modern University?* (2004), pp. 165, 184.

17. Ibid.

18. Stanley Rothman, April Kelly-Woessner, and Matthew Woessner, note 15, p. 45.

19. Gabriel Kaplan, note 16, pp. 176, 178, 183.

20. Stanley Rothman, April Kelly-Woessner, and Matthew Woessner, note 15, p. 47.

21. Jack H. Schuster and Martin J. Finkelstein, note 14, pp. 105, 485.

22. Gabriel Kaplan, note 16, p. 200.

23. Ibid., p. 177.

24. Ibid.

25. Ibid.

26. Ibid.

27. Linda De Angelo, Sylvia Hurtado, et al., *The American College Teacher: National Norms for the 2007–2008 HERI Faculty Survey* (2009), p. 38.

28. Stanley Rothman, April Kelly-Woessner, and Matthew Woessner, note 15, p. 51.

29. Gabriel Kaplan, note 16, pp. 165, 204.

30. Donald E. Heller, "State Oversight of Academia," in Ronald G. Ehrenberg (ed.), note 16, p. 49.

31. Donald E. Heller, *The State and Higher Education Policy: Affordability Access and Accountability* (2001). Aims C. McGuinness, "The States and Higher Education," in Philip G. Altbach, Robert O. Berdahl, and Patricia J. Gumport (eds.), *American Higher Education in the Twenty-First Century* (2005), p. 198.

32. Clark Kerr and Marian Gade, *The Guardians. Boards of Trustees of American Colleges and Universities: What They Do and How Well They Do It* (1989), p. 107.

33. Katherine C. Lyall and Kathleen R. Sell, *The True Genius of America at Risk: Are We Losing Our Public Universities to De Facto Privatization?* (2006), pp. 12, 13.

34. David L. Kirp, *Shakespeare, Einstein, and the Bottom Line* (2003), p. 130.

35. James C. Garland, *Saving Alma Mater: A Rescue Plan for America's Public Universities* (2009).

36. The problems resulting from competition among universities are summarized on pp. 389–93.

37. For an account of this approach in Virginia, together with brief descriptions of similar efforts in other states, see the chapter by William Zumeta and Alicia Kinne, "Accountability Policies: Directions Old and New," in Donald E. Heller (ed.), *The States and Public Higher Education Policy: Affordability, Access, and Accountability* (2nd ed., 2011), p. 173.

38. J. Fredericks Volkwein and David A. Tamberg, 49 *Research in Higher Education* (2008), p. 180.

AFTERWORD (I)

1. See Michael D. Cohen and James G. March, *Leadership and Ambiguity* (1986).

CHAPTER FOUR
GOING TO COLLEGE AND EARNING A DEGREE

1. *New York Times*, "Education Life" (July 24, 2011), p. 19.

2. Deborah Wadsworth, "Ready or Not? Where the Public Stands on Higher Education Reform," in Richard H. Hersh and John Merrow (eds.), *Declining by Degrees: Higher Education at Risk* (2005), p. 23; Public Agenda figures are given in John Immerwahr and Jean Johnson, "Squeeze Play 2010: Continued Public Anxiety on Cost, Harsher Judgments on How Colleges Are Run," *Public Agenda* (February 2010), p. 4.

3. William G. Bowen, Matthew M. Chingos, and Michael S. McPherson, *Crossing the Finish Line: Completing College at America's Public Universities* (2009), p. 6.

4. The figures that follow appear in US Department of Education, *College Completion Toolkit* (2011), p. 8.

5. Andrew Hacker, "Can We Make America Smarter?" 56 *New York Review of Books* (April 30, 2009), p. 37.

6. T. Alan Lacey and Benjamin Wright, "Occupational Employment Projections to 2018," 132 *Monthly Labor Review* (2009), p. 82. For a more extended discussion of the debate over education requirements for future jobs, see William Zumeta, David W. Breneman, Patrick M. Callan, and Joni E. Finney, *Financing American Higher Education in the Era of Globalization* (2012), pp. 33–58.

7. Anthony Carnevale, Nicole Smith, and Jeff Strohl, *Help Wanted—Projections of Jobs and Education Requirements through 2018* (2010), p. 6.

8. David Boesel and Eric Fredkind, *College for All? Is There Too Much Emphasis on Getting a Four-Year Degree?*, National Library of Education, US Department of Education (1999).

9. Anthony P. Carnevale and Donna M. Desrochers, *Help Wanted . . . Credentials Required: Community Colleges in the Knowledge Economy* (2001), p. 69. For a more extended analysis concluding that employer requirements for college education are based on genuine needs, see James Rosenbaum, *Beyond College for All: Career Paths for the Bottom Half* (2001), pp. 108–31.

10. William G. Bowen, Matthew M. Chingos, and Michael S. McPherson, note 3, p. 5.

11. Claudia Goldin and Lawrence F. Katz, *The Race between Education and Technology* (2008).

12. Paul Osterman, *College for All? The Labor Market for Educated Workers*, Center for American Progress (2008).

13. Robert D. Putnam, *Bowling Alone: The Collapse and Revival of American Community* (2000), p. 213.

14. Walter M. McMahon, *Higher Learning, Greater Good: The Private and Social Benefits of Higher Education* (2009), p. 119.

15. Ibid.

16. Charles Murray, *Real Education: Four Simple Truths for Bringing America's Schools Back to Reality* (2008).

17. Jay P. Greene and Greg Forster, *Public High School Graduation and College Readiness Rates in the United States*, Education Working Paper, Manhattan Institute (2003).

18. Anthony Carnevale and Donna M. Desrochers, note 9, p. 54.

19. James Rosenbaum, note 9, p. 57.

20. Thomas Bailey, "Challenge and Opportunity: Rethinking the Role and Function of Developmental Education in Community College," *New Directions for Community Colleges*, no. 145 (2009), p. 11. Estimates of the percentages of students taking remedial courses vary widely. Thus the Department of Education indicates that only 42 percent of all students entering community colleges in 2007–8 and 36 percent of entering students in all colleges had taken one or more remedial courses. Department of Education, *Digest of Educational Statistics* (2011), table 243.

21. Thomas Bailey, note 20, p. 13.

22. See, e.g., Eric P. Bettinger and Bridget Terry Long, "Remediation at the Community College: Student Participation and Outcomes," 129 *New Directions for Community Colleges* (2005), p. 13; Thomas Bailey, note 20, p. 11.

23. Ellen C. Lagemann and Harry Lewis (eds.), *What Is College For? The Public Purpose of Higher Education*, (2012), p. 105.

24. Susan Choy, *College Access and Affordability*, National Center for Education Statistics (1999), p. 5.

25. Ibid.

26. Ibid.

27. Rethinking Student Aid Study Groups, *Fulfilling the Commitment: Recommendations for Reforming Federal Student Aid* (2008), p. 5.

28. Anthony P. Carnevale and Jeff Strohl, "How Increasing College Access Is Increasing Inequality, and What to Do about It," in Richard T. Kahlenberg (ed.), *Rewarding Strivers: Helping Low-Income Students Succeed in College* (2010), pp. 71, 155.

29. Ernest T. Pascarella and Patrick Terenzini, *How College Affects Students, Vol. 2, A Third Decade of Research* (2005), pp. 375–82. As these authors explain, it is by no means easy to determine just how much enrolling in a community college lowers the chances of earning a BA. Although there is general agreement that the odds of earning a BA decline, analysts differ in their estimates of how great the decline will be.

30. Melissa Roderick, Jenny Nagaoka, Vanessa Coca, and Eliza Moeller, *From High School to the Future: Making Hard Work Pay Off*, Consortium on Chicago School Research (April 2009).

31. See e.g., Andrew S. Belasco, "Creating College Opportunity: School Counselors and their Influence on Postsecondary Enrollment," 54 *Research in Higher Education* (2013), p. 781. For a vivid example of what a college counselor can accomplish for lower income students in an inner city high school, see Beth Zasloff and Joshua Steckel, *Hold Fast to Dreams: A College Guidance Counselor, His Students, and the Vision of a Life Beyond Poverty* (2014).

32. Katherine Mangan, "Despite Push for College Completion, Graduation Rates Haven't Budged," *Chronicle of Higher Education* (December 10, 2013), p. A3.

33. Ibid.

34. Katherine Mangan, "New Tally Counts All Graduates, Even Transfers," *Chronicle of Higher Education* (November 23, 2012), pp. A-1, A-10.

35. Ibid.

36. Arthur M. Hauptman, *Increasing Higher Education Attainment in the United States: Challenges and Opportunities*, Andrew P. Kelly and Mark Schneider (eds.) *Getting to Graduation: The Completion Agenda in Higher Education* (2012), pp. 17, 23.

37. Bridget Terry Long, *Grading Higher Education: Giving Consumers the Information They Need* (paper jointly released by the Center for American Progress and the Hamilton Project, December 2010), p. 6.

38. Address to Joint Session of Congress, February 24, 2009.

39. Melissa Roderick et al., note 29, p. 4.

40. James E. Rosenbaum, Regina Deil-Amen, and Kevin Carey, *After Admission: From College Access to College Success* (2006), p. 69.

41. Ibid.

42. David Spence, "State College Initiatives and Community Colleges," in Andrea C. Bueschel and Andrea Venezia (eds.), *Policies and Practices to Improve Student Preparation and Success* (2009), p. 98.

43. See James Rosenbaum, note 9, p. 276.

44. John M. Braxton, Willis A. Jones, Amy S. Hirschy, and Harold Hartley, III, "The Role of Active Learning in College Student Persistence," in John M. Braxton (ed.), *The Role of the Classroom in College Student Performance* (2008), p. 70.

45. For a comprehensive recent review of these measures, see Vincent Tinto, *Completing College: Rethinking Institutional Action* (2012).

46. E.g., Vincent Tinto, "Research and Practice of Student Retention," 8 *Journal of College Student Retention* (2006), p. 1.

47. Douglas A. Webster and Ronald G. Ehrenberg, *Do Expenditures other than Instructional Expenditures Affect Graduation and Persistence Rates in American Higher Education?* National Bureau of Economic Research, Working Paper 15216 (2009).

48. See, e.g., Stephen V. Cameron and James J. Heckman, "The Dynamics of Educational Attainment for Black, Hispanic, and White Males," 109 *Journal of Political Economy* (2001), p. 455. However, college costs have a pronounced effect on which type of college students attend.

49. Tamar Lewin, "College Dropouts Cite Low Money and High Stress," *New York Times* (December 10, 2009), p. A23.

50. *New York Times* (December 3, 2008), p. A19.

51. "Survey: Secrets of Success," 376 *Economist* (September 10, 2005), p. 6.

52. See, e.g., Dan Angel and Terry Connelly, *Riptide: The New Normal for Higher Education* (2011), p. 51, pointing out that from 1990 to 2008 average tuition and fees rose by 248 percent while the cost of living increased by only 66 percent.

53. US Department of Education, note 4, p. 15.

54. College Board, *Trends in College Pricing 2011* (2011), p. 15.

55. College Board, *Trends in Student Aid 2011* (2011), p. 11.

56. College Board, *Trends in College Pricing 2011* (2011), p. 15.

57. Ibid.

58. Ibid.

59. Sandy Baum and Jennifer Ma, *Trends in College Pricing 2013* (2013), p. 23.

60. Id., p. 21.

61. College Board, *Trends in Student Aid, 2011* (2011), p. 11.

62. Sandy Baum and Kathleen Payea, *Trends in Student Aid 2013* (2013), p. 21.

63. Beth Akers and Matthew M. Chingos, *Is a Student Loan Crisis on the Horizon?* Brookings Institution (2014). It should be noted, however, that one reason why the burden has not increased is that the average term of years for repayment has increased.

64. See, generally, Robert B. Archibald and David H. Feldman, *Why Does College Cost So Much* (2011).

65. College Board, *Trends in College Pricing, 2009* (2009), p. 16.

66. See, e.g., William Zumeta et al., note 6, p. 22.

CHAPTER FIVE
PAYING FOR COLLEGE: THE CHALLENGE
FOR POLICY-MAKERS AND ACADEMIC LEADERS

1. Byron G. Auguste, Adam Cota, Kartik Jayaram, and Martha C. Laboissiere, *Winning by Degrees: The Strategies of Highly Productive Higher-Education Institutions* (2010), pp. 7–8.

2. Ibid.

3. Michael S. McPherson and Morton O. Schapiro, *The Student Aid Game: Meeting Need and Rewarding Talent in American Higher Education* (1998), p. 39.

4. Scott Carlson and Goldie Blumenstyk, "The False Promise of the Education Revolution," *Chronicle of Higher Education* (December 17, 2012), p. A1.

5. The College Board, *Trends in College Pricing 2011* (2011), pp. 13, 18.

6. Anthony Carnevale and Jeff Strohl, "How Increasing College Access Is Increasing Inequality, and What to Do about It," in Richard D. Kahlenberg (ed.), *Rewarding Strivers: Helping Low-Income Students Succeed in College* (2010), pp. 131–32.

7. See, e.g., William Zumeta, David W. Breneman, Patrick M. Callan, and Joni E. Finney, *Financing Higher Education in the Era of Globalization* (2012), p. 21; Frank Newman, Laura Couturier, and Jamie Scurry, *The Future of Higher Education: Rhetoric, Reality, and the Risks of the Market* (2004), p. 10, pointing out that state spending on merit scholarships rose 18.3 percent from 1991 to 2001 compared to an increase of only 3.7 percent in need-based aid.

8. William G. Bowen, Matthew M. Chingos, and Michael S. McPherson, *Crossing the Finish Line: Completing College at America's Public Universities* (2009), p. 110.

9. Delta Cost Project, *Trends in College Spending: Where Does the Money Come From? Where Does It Go?* (2009), p. 33.

10. Katherine Mangan, "National Tally Counts All Graduates, Even Transfers," *Chronicle of Higher Education* (November 23, 2012), pp. A-1, A-10.

11. See Byron G. Auguste et al., note 1.

12. For a detailed description of how such reforms were introduced at one of the model institutions, see Clayton M. Christensen and Henry J. Eyring, *The Innovative University: Changing the DNA of Higher Education from the Inside Out* (2011).

13. There is evidence that cost cutting by comprehensive universities in the 1990s led to *lower* graduation rates. John Bound, Michael Lovenheim, and Sarah Turner, *Why Have College Completion Rates Declined? An Analysis of Changing Student Preparation and Collegiate Resources*, National Bureau of Economic Research, Working Paper 15566 (2009), pp. 13, 25.

14. E.g., John Braxton, Willis Jones, Amy S. Hirschy, Harold Hartley, III, "The Role of Active Learning in College Student Persistence," in John Braxton (ed.), *The Role of the Classroom in College Student Performance* (2008), p. 70.

15. Barbara Means, Yukie Toyama, Robert Murphy, Marianne Bakia, and Karla Jones, *Evaluation of Evidence-Based Practices in Online Learning: A Meta-Analysis and Review of Online Learning Studies*, US Department of Education (2009).

16. James E. Rosenbaum, Regina Deil-Amen, and Kevin Carey, *After Admission: From College Access to College Success* (2006), p. 147.

17. Tamar Lewin, "Report Finds Low Graduation Rates at For-Profit Colleges," *New York Times* (November 23, 2010), p. A18.

18. Mamie Lynch, Jennifer Engle, and Jose L. Cruz., *Subprime Opportunity: The Unfulfilled Promise of For-Profit Colleges and Universities*, The Education Trust (November 2010), p. 3.

19. See Paul Osterman, "The Promise, Performance, and Policies of Community Colleges," in Ben Wildavsky, Andrew P. Kelley, and Kevin Carey (eds.), *Reinventing Higher Education: The Promise of Innovation* (2011), p. 129.

20. Dan Angel and Terry Connelly, *Riptide: The New Normal for Higher Education* (2011), p. 94.

21. Paul Osterman, note 19, pp. 129, 148.

22. See Byron G. Auguste et al., note 1.

23. For a more detailed, thoughtful analysis of government policies, see William Zumeta et al., note 7, especially pp. 155–91.

24. Public Agenda Study, March 3, 2010, HigherEdMorning.com (only 40 percent believe that the quality of education would suffer if colleges cut their budgets). See also John Immewahr, Jean Johnson, and Paul Gasbarra, *The Iron Triangle: College Presidents Talk about Cost, Access, and Quality*, National Center for Public Policy and Higher Education and Public Agenda (October 2008), detailing the gap between public perceptions and the views of college presidents.

25. Richard Vedder, *Going Broke by Degree: Why College Costs Too Much* (2004).

26. Ibid.

27. Ibid., p. 44.

28. See, e.g., Kevin Kiley, "Where Universities Can Be Cut," *Inside Higher Ed*, http://www.insidehighered.com; Jeff Denneen and Tom Dretler, *The Financially Sustainable University* (2012).

29. See William K. Balzer, *Lean Higher Education: Increasing the Value and Performance of University Processes* (2010).

30. See Clayton M. Christensen and Henry J. Eyring, note 12, p. 214. See also Daniel L. Sullivan, "The Hidden Costs of Low Four-Year Graduation Rates," *Liberal Education* (Summer 2010), p. 24.

31. William G. Bowen and Kelly A. Lack, "Current Status of Research on Online Learning in Postsecondary Education" (unpublished paper, April 27, 2012).

32. William G. Bowen, Matthew M. Chingos, and Michael S. McPherson, note 8, p. 231.

33. See Byron G. Auguste et al., note 1.

34. See William G. Bowen and Derek Bok, *The Shape of the River: Long-Term Consequences of Considering Race in College and University Admissions* (1998), pp. 72–90; Douglas S. Massey, Camille Z. Charles, Garvey F. Lundy, and Mary J. Fischer, *The Social Origins of Freshmen at America's Selective Colleges and Universities* (2003); Camille Z. Charles, Mary J. Fischer, Margaret A. Mooney, and Douglas S. Massey, *Taming the River: Negotiating the Academic, Financial, and Social Currents in Selective Colleges and Universities* (2009).

35. Eric P. Bettinger and Rachel Baker, "The Effects of Student Coaching: An Evaluation of a Randomized Experiment in Student Mentoring" (unpublished paper, March 7, 2011).

36. College Board, *Trends in College Pricing* (2009), p. 16.

CHAPTER SIX
ENTERING THE RIGHT COLLEGE

1. Anthony P. Carnevale and Jeff Strohl, "How Increasing College Access Is Increasing Inequality, and What To Do about It," in Richard D. Kahlenberg (ed.), *Rewarding Strivers: Helping Low-Income Students Succeed in College* (2010), p. 146.

2. See, e.g., Jerome Karabel, *The Chosen: The Hidden History of Exclusion at Harvard, Yale, and Princeton* (2005); Daniel Golden, *The Price of Admission: How America's Ruling Class Buys Its Way into Elite Colleges—and Who Gets Left outside the Gates* (2006); Peter Sacks, *Tearing Down the Gates: Confronting the Class Divide in American Education* (2007).

3. See, e.g., William G. Bowen, Matthew M. Chingos, and Michael S. McPherson, *Crossing the Finish Line: Completing College at America's Public Universities* (2009), pp. 228–29, 233–35.

4. Ernest T. Pascarella and Patrick T. Terenzini, *How College Affects Students*, vol. 2, *A Third Decade of Research* (2005), pp. 267–76. Among the more recent studies, Stacy B. Dale and Alan B. Krueger, "Estimating the Returns to College Selectivity over the Career Using Administrative Earnings Data," National Bureau of Economic Research, Working Paper 17159 (June 2011), compared the later earnings of students attending highly selective colleges with those of students who were admitted to one of these colleges but chose to attend a less selective institution instead. They found no significant difference between the two groups except that Blacks, Hispanics, and students from less educated families earned more if they attended a more selective school. In contrast, two additional studies found substantial earnings advantages from attending more selective schools. Mark Hoekstra, "The Effect of Attending the Flagship State University on Earnings: A Discontinuity-Based Approach," 91 *Review of Economics and Statistics* (2009), p. 717, and Dan A. Black and Jeffrey A. Smith, "Estimating the Returns to College Quality with Multiple Proxies for Quality," 24 *Journal of Labor Economics* (2006), p. 701.

5. Ernest T. Pascarella and Patrick T. Terenzini, note 4, p. 473.

6. Ibid., p. 469

7. Ibid.

8. See Caroline M. Hoxby, "The Changing Selectivity of American Colleges," 23 *Journal of Economic Perspectives* (2009), pp. 95, 111–14.

9. Elizabeth A. Duffy and Idana Goldberg, *Crafting a Class: College Admissions and Financial Aid, 1955–1994* (1998).

10. Quoted by William G. Bowen, Martin A. Kurzweil, and Eugene M. Tobin, *Equity and Excellence in American Higher Education* (2005), p. 169.

11. Daniel Golden, note 2; Peter Sacks, note 2.

12. "Public Views on Higher Education: A Sampling," *Chronicle of Higher Education* (May 7, 2004).

13. William G. Bowen, Martin A. Kurzweil, and Eugene M. Tobin, note 10, p. 71.

14. Thomas J. Espenshade, Chang Y. Chung, and Joan L. Walling, "Admissions Preferences for Minority Students, Athletes, and Legacies at Elite Universities," 85 *Social Science Quarterly* (2004), pp. 1426, 1431.

15. Richard D. Kahlenberg (ed.), *Affirmative Action for the Rich* (2010), pp. 8–9.

16. James L. Shulman and William G. Bowen, *The Game of Life: College Sports and Educational Values* (2001), pp. 40–50.

17. Ibid., pp. 261–62.

18. Ibid.; Andrew Zimbalist, *Unpaid Professionals: Commercialism and Conflict in Big-Time College Sports* (1999).

19. James L. Shulman and William G. Bowen, note 16, pp. 199–204.

20. See, e.g., Paul M. Sniderman and Thomas Piazza, *The Scar of Race* (1995).

21. *Grutter v. Bollinger et al.*, 539 US. 306 (2003).

22. Ibid.

23. See William G. Bowen and Derek Bok, *The Shape of the River: Long-Term Consequences of Considering Race in College and University Admissions* (1998), pp. 218–55.

24. Ibid., p. 225.

25. Ibid., p. 281.

26. Ibid., pp. 256–74.

27. Ibid., pp. 72–90.

28. Sandy Baum and Jennifer Ma, *Education Pays: The Benefits of Higher Education for Individuals and Society* (2007), p. 35. (Children from families in the upper third of the income scale who have high math scores and finished high school in 1992 graduated at a rate of 74 percent by 2000. Children from the lowest third of the income scale with high math scores graduated at a rate of 29 percent.) See also Susan P. Choy, *The Condition of Education, 1998: College Access and Affordability* (1999), p. 10. (The percentage of high school seniors in 1992 from families in the highest-income and highest-achievement quartile enrolled in a four-year college within two years at a rate of 86 percent. High school seniors from the highest-ability quartile but the lowest-income quartile enrolled in a four-year college within two years at a rate of only 58 percent.)

29. Christopher Avery and Caroline Hoxby, *The Missing "One-Offs": The Hidden Supply of Low-Income, High Achieving Students for Selective Colleges* (2009).

30. William G. Bowen, Matthew M. Chingos, and Michael S. McPherson, note 3, pp. 228–29, 233–35.

31. For an account of ConnectEDU's progress, see Kevin Carey, "The End of College Admissions As We Know It: Everything You've Heard about Getting in Is About to Go Out the Window, 43 *Washington Monthly* (September/October 2011), p. 22.

32. This suggestion was made convincingly by William G. Bowen, Martin A. Kurzweil, and Eugene M. Tobin, note 10.

33. William G. Bowen, Matthew M. Chingos, and Michael S. McPherson, note 3, p. 226.

34. Ibid.

35. Marian Wang, "The Quest by Public Colleges for Revenue and Prestige Squeezes Already Needy Students," *Chronicle of Higher Education* (Sept. 20, 2013), p. A-16. Despite efforts by some private colleges to reduce the cost for low-income students, the number of such students entering highly selective private colleges has continued to decline. Richard D. Kahlenberg (ed.), note 1, p. 3.

36. See Michael S. McPherson and Morton O. Schapiro, *The Student Aid Game: Meeting Need and Rewarding Talent in American Higher Education* (1998).

37. Marian Wang, note 35, p. A-16.

38. Jerry Sheehan Davis, *Unintended Consequences of Tuition Discounting*, Lumina Foundation (2003). In a similar vein, Michael S. McPherson reported as follows on the results of a bidding war among four colleges using merit-aid scholarships. "At the end, the schools have lost a total of $1.6 million that might have been used to improve teaching and learning and instead have improved their average SAT scores by one point—from 597 to 598." *Washington Post* (May 7, 2005), p. A08.

CHAPTER SEVEN
THE EXPANDING AUDIENCE FOR HIGHER EDUCATION

1. See, e.g., Elaine Allen and Jeff Seaman, *Online Nation: Five Years of Growth in Online Learning* (2007).

2. See, e.g., Amanda Ripley, "College Is Dead. Long Live College! Can a New Breed of Online Megacourses Finally Offer a College Education to More People for Less Money?" *Time* (October 29, 2012), p. 33.

3. Peter Drucker, quoted in Robert Lenzner and Stephen S. Johnson, "Seeing Things as They Really Are," *Forbes* (March 10, 1997), p. 127.

4. Edward Glaeser, *Triumph of the City: How Our Greatest Invention Makes Us Richer, Smarter, Greener, Healthier, and Happier* (2011).

5. For a description of the growth of WGU, see John Gravois, "The College For-Profits Should Fear," *Washington Monthly* (September–October 2011), p. 38.

6. William G. Bowen and Kelly A. Lack, *Current Status of Research on Online Learning in Postsecondary Education* (April 10, 2012).

7. See, e.g., Jeffrey R. Young, "Dozens of Plagiarism Incidents Are Reported in Coursera's Free Online Courses," *Chronicle of Higher Education* (August 16, 2012), http://chronicle.com/article/Dozens-of-Plagiarism-Incidents/133697/.

8. James J. Duderstadt, *Current Global Trends in Higher Education and Research: Their Impact on Europe*, Dies Amiens Address, University of Vienna (March 12, 2009).

9. Charles M. Vest, *The American Research University from World War II to World Wide Web* (2007), pp. 91–109; Taylor Walsh, *Unlocking the Gates: How and Why Leading Universities Are Opening Up Access to Their Courses* (2011).

10. General Accounting Office, Statement of Gregory D. Katz, *For-Profit Colleges Undercover Testing Finds Colleges Encouraged Fraud and Engaged in Deceptive and Questionable Marketing Practices* (August 4, 2010).

11. David Noble, *Digital Diploma Mills: The Automation of Higher Education* (2001).

12. There are already scattered reports of campuses abroad offering programs of highly questionable quality. E.g., D. D. Guttenplan, "An Albanian College, Relying on U.S. Cachet," *New York Times* (March 20, 2012), p. A8.

CHAPTER EIGHT
WHAT TO LEARN

1. For a more detailed account of the classical curriculum, see Laurence R. Veysey, *The Emergence of the American University* (Phoenix ed., 1970), pp. 22–50.

2. Noah Porter, *The American Colleges and the American Public* (2nd ed., 1878), p. 36.

3. William F. Allen, *Essays and Monographs* (1890), p. 141.

4. Sylvia Hurtado, Kevin Eagan, John H. Pryor, Hannah Whang, and Serge Tran, *Undergraduate Teaching Faculty: The 2010–2011 HERI Faculty Survey* (2012), p. 26.

5. Time-Carnegie survey, *Time* (October 29, 2012), p. 40.

6. Louis Menand, "Live and Learn: Why We Have Colleges," *New Yorker* (June 6, 2011).

7. Anthony P. Carnevale and Donna M. Desrochers, *Help Wanted . . . Credentials Required: Community Colleges in the Knowledge Economy* (2001).

8. Association of American Colleges and Universities, *The LEAP Vision for Learning: Outcomes, Practices, Impact, and Employers' Views* (2009), pp. 23–27; see also Diana G. Oblinger and Anne-Lee Verville, *What Business Wants from Higher Education* (1998); Michael Useem, *Liberal Education and the Corporation: The Hiring and Advancement of College Graduates* (1989).

9. Ernest T. Pascarella and Patrick T. Terenzini, *How College Affects Students*, vol. 2, *A Third Decade of Research* (2005), pp. 282–83.

10. For a more extended discussion on the pros and cons of requiring foreign language instruction, see Derek Bok, *Our Underachieving Colleges: A Look at How Much Students Learn and Why They Should Be Learning More* (2006), pp. 233–35.

11. Alexander Astin, *What Matters in College: Four Critical Years Revisited* (1993), pp. 236–41, 302–10, 370–72.

12. Ernest T. Pascarella and Patrick T. Terenzini, *How College Affects Students: Findings and Insights from Twenty Years of Research* (1991), pp. 65–66, 614.

13. National Survey of Student Engagement, *Examining Engagement by Field of Study: Annual Results, 2010* (2010), p. 34.

14. Derek Bok, note 10, pp. 257–72.

15. E.g., *Report on Yale College Education, College of Arts and Sciences Curriculum Initiative as Amended by the FAS Faculty* (April 11, 2005), p. 14.

16. See, e.g., William J. Bennett, *To Reclaim a Legacy: A Report on the Humanities in Higher Education* (1984); Lynne V. Cheney, *50 Hours: A Core Curriculum for College Students* (1989).

17. Richard J. Light, *Making the Most of College: Students Speak Their Minds* (2001), p. 8.

18. Rebekah Nathan, *My Freshman Year: What a Professor Learned by Becoming a Student* (2005), p. 101.

19. Ashley Finley (Association of American Colleges and Universities), *Making Progress? What We Know about the Achievement of Liberal Education Outcomes* (2012), p. 6.

20. Ibid. Most experts consider self-reports as worthless. E.g. Stephen R. Porter, "Using Student Learning as a Measure of Quality of Higher Education," http://www.hcmstrategists.com/contextforsuccess/, (2012).

21. Patricia M. King and Karen S. Kitchener, *Developing Reflective Judgment: Understanding and Promoting Intellectual Growth and Critical Thinking in Adolescents and Adults* (1994), pp. 224–25.

22. Ernest T. Pascarella and Patrick T. Terenzini, , note 9, p. 580.

23. Ashley Finley, note 19, p. 14. Another study found that over half of college seniors and 75 percent of students in their last year at community college could not understand the arguments of newspaper editorials or to summarize the results of a poll about parental involvement in schools. Justin Baer, Andrea L. Cook, and Stephanie Baldi, *The Literacy of America's College Students*, American Institutes for Research (2006).

24. P. Barton and A. La Pointe, *Learning by Degrees: Indicators of Performance in Higher Education* (1995).

25. The Conference Board, *Are They Really Ready to Work? Employers Perspectives on the Basic Knowledge and Applied Skills of New Entrants to the 21st Century Work Force* (2006).

26. Association of American Colleges and Universities, *How Should Colleges Assess and Improve Student Learning?* (2008), p. 4.

27. See, e.g., Mary Grigsby, *College Life through the Eyes of Students* (2009); Rebekah Nathan, note 18.

CHAPTER NINE
HOW TO TEACH

1. Rebekah Nathan, *My Freshman Year: What a Professor Learned by Becoming a Student* (2005), p. 100.

2. Another recent study of undergraduate life has come to similar conclusions. Mary Grigsby, *College Life through the Eyes of Students* (2009).

3. Rebekah Nathan, note 1, p. 102.

4. Frederick Rudolph, *Curriculum: A History of the American Course of Study since 1636* (1977), p. 12.

5. Quoted in Page Smith, *Killing the Spirit: Higher Education in America* (1990), p. 73.

6. Philip S. Babcock and Mindy Marks, *The Falling Time Cost of College: Evidence from Half a Century of Time Use Data*, National Bureau of Economic Research, Working Paper 15954 (April 2010).

7. Ofer Malamud, "The Structure of European Higher Education in the Wake of the Bologna Reforms," in Charles T. Clotfelter (ed.), *American Universities in a Global Market* (2010), pp. 205, 212.

8. Steven Brint and Allison M. Cantwell, "Undergraduate Time Use and Academic Outcomes: Results from the University of California Undergraduate Experience Survey," 112 *Teachers College Record* (2010), p. 2441; Josipa Roksa and Richard Arum, "The State of Undergraduate Learning," *Change* (March/April 2011), pp. 35, 36.

9. Frank Newman, Lara Couturier, and Jamie Scurrie, *The Future of Higher Education: Rhetoric, Reality, and the Rise of the Market* (2004), pp. 100–101. From 1985 to 2000, the proportion of freshmen claiming to be bored in class reportedly rose from 26 percent to 40 percent. According to Amy Liu, Jessica Sharkness, and John H. Pryor, *HERI Findings from the 2007 Administration of Your First College Year (YFCY) National Aggregates* (2008), p. 9, the percentage of freshmen reporting that they were "frequently" bored in class stood at 37.1 percent.

10. Steven Brint and Allison M. Cantwell, note 8, pp. 2442, 2445. (Study time had more than twice the effect on academic success as any other variable.)

11. Philip S. Babcock and Mindy Marks, note 6, pp. 1, 3.

12. Kenneth C. Green, *The 2011–12 Inside Higher Ed Survey of College and University Chief Academic Officers* (2012), p. 12.

13. National Survey of Student Engagement, *Assessment for Improvement: Tracking Student Engagement over Time* (2009), p. 34.

14. Ibid.

15. Kenneth C. Green, note 12, p. 12.

16. Ibid.

17. Jack H. Schuster and Martin J. Finkelstein, *The American Faculty: The Restructuring of Academic Work and Careers* (2006), p. 89.

18. Peter J. Bentley and Svein Kyvila, "Academic Work from a Comparative Perspective: A Survey of Faculty Work-Time across 13 Countries," 69 *Higher Education* (2012), pp. 529, 537 (American faculty were least likely to report that they were more interested in research than in teaching); Martin Finkelstein and William Cummings, "The Global View: American Faculty and Their Institutions," *Change* (May–June 2012), pp. 48, 51. See also Ernest L. Boyer, Philip G. Altbach, and Mary Jen Whitelaw, *The Academic Profession: International Perspective* (1994), p. 81.

19. *Chronicle of Higher Education* (November 9, 2012), p. A6; Jack H. Schuster and Martin J. Finkelstein, note 17, pp. 194, 356.

20. Linda De Angelo, Sylvia Hurtado, et al., *The American College Teacher: National Norms for the 2007–2008 HERI Faculty Survey* (2009), p. 1.

21. Lion F. Gardiner, *Redesigning Higher Education: Producing Dramatic Gains in Student Learning* (1994), p. 2. A more recent survey of professors found that 99.9 percent considered critical thinking to be either "very important" or "essential," the highest level of support for any purpose. Linda De Angelo, Sylvia Hurtado, et al., note 20, p. 1.

22. National Survey of Student Engagement, note 13.

23. Ernest T. Pascarella and Patrick T. Terenzini, *How College Affects Students*, vol. 2, *A Third Decade of Research* (2005), p. 101.

24. See, e.g., Lion F. Gardiner, note 21, pp. 46–50.

25. John Biggs and Catherine Tang, *Teaching for Quality Learning at University* (3rd ed., 2007), p. 109.

26. Bob Boice, "Classroom Incivilities," 37 *Research in Higher Education* (1996), pp. 453, 462.

27. Donald A. Bligh, *What's the Use of Lectures?* (2000), p. 20.

28. Ibrahim A. Halloun and David Hestenes, "The Initial Knowledge State of College Physics Students" and "Common Sense Concepts about Motion," both published in 53 *American Journal of Physics* (1985), pp. 1043 and 1056.

29. See, e.g., John Biggs and Catherine Tang, note 25; Carl Wieman, "A Scientific Approach to Science Education—Reducing Cognitive Load" (March 23, 2009), http://www.science20.com/carl_wieman/scientific_approach_science_education_reducing_cognitive_load.

30. Linda J. Sax, Alexander W. Astin, William S. Korn, and Shannon K. Gilmartin, *The American College Teacher: National Norms for the 1989–1999 HERI Faculty Survey* (1999), p. 36. More recent surveys suggest that faculty members are gradually moving away from extensive lecturing to more active forms of learning. Sylvia Hurtado, Kevin Eagan, John H. Pryor, Hannah Whang, and Serge Tran, *Undergraduate Teaching Faculty: the 2010–2011 HERI Faculty Survey* (2012), p. 25 (showing that the percentage of faculty who lectured extensively in all or most of their courses had dropped from 54.2 percent to 47.4 percent since a previous survey twenty years earlier, Eric L. Dey, Claudia E. Ramirez, William S. Korn, and Alexander W. Astin, *The American College Teacher: National Norms for the 1992–93 HERI Faculty Survey* (1993), p. 36).

31. Richard J. Light, "Ask the Students: A Good Way to Enhance Their Success," in Michael S. McPherson and Morton O. Schapiro (eds.), *College Success: What It Means and How to Make It Happen* (2008), pp. 173, 176–77.

32. Much of this description is taken from reports submitted to the Spencer Foundation on the progress made in a project to improve teaching methods funded by Spencer and the Teagle Foundation. For a published account of the Indiana approach to teaching history, see Arlene Diaz, Joan Middendorf, David Pace, and Leah Shopkow, "The History Learning Project: A Department 'Decodes' Its Students," *Journal of American History* (March 2008), p. 1211.

33. Eric Mazur, *Peer Instruction: A User's Manual* (1997); and Catherine H. Crouch and Eric Mazur, "Peer Instruction: Ten Years of Experience and Results," 69 *American Journal of Physics* (2001), p. 970.

34. Heather Kannke and Charmaine Brooks, "Distance Education in a Post-Fordist Time," in M. F. Cleveland-Innes and D. R. Garrison (eds.), *Understanding Teaching and Learning in a New Era* (2010), p. 69.

35. Barbara Means, Yukie Toyama, Robert Murphy, Marianne Bakia, and Karla Jones, *Evaluation of Evidence-Based Practices in Online Learning: A Meta-Analysis and Review of Online Learning Studies*, US Department of Education (2009).

36. Robert M. Bernard, Philip C. Abram, et al., "How Does Distance Education Compare with Classroom Instruction? A Meta-Analysis of the Empirical Literature," 74 *Review of Educational Research* (2004), pp. 397, 406.

37. Marsha Lovett, Oded Meyer, and Candace Thille, *The Open Learning Initiative: Measuring the Effectiveness of the OLI Statistics Course in Accelerating Student Learning*, jime.open.ac.uk/jime/article/download/2008-14/352 (2008); Candace Thille, "Building Open Learning as a Community-Based Research Activity," in Toru Iiyoshi and M. S. Vijay Kumar (eds.), *Opening Up Education: The Collective Advancement of Education through Open Technology, Open Content, and Open Knowledge* (2008), p. 165.

38. William G. Bowen, Matthew M. Chingos, Kelly A. Lack, and Thomas I. Nygren, *Interactive Learning Online at Public Universities: Evidence from Randomized Trials* (May 2012).

39. Carol A. Twigg, "New Models for Online Learning: Improving Learning and Reducing Costs," *Educause* (September–October 2003), p. 28.

40. Ibid.

41. William G. Bowen and Kelly A. Lack, *Current Status of Research on Online Learning in Postsecondary Education* (April 10, 2012).

42. For a more detailed account of the CLA test, see Richard J. Shavelson, *Measuring College Learning Responsibly: Accountability in a New Era* (2010), pp. 44–70.

43. John M. Braxton, "Selectivity and Rigor in Research Universities," 64 *Journal of Higher Education* (1993), p. 657; John M. Braxton and Robert C. Nordvall, "Selective Liberal Arts Colleges: Higher Quality as Well as Higher Prestige?" 56 *Journal of Higher Education* (1985), p. 538.

44. Leon Neyfakh, "What to Test Instead: A New Wave of Test Designers Believe They Can Measure Creativity, Problem Solving, and Collaboration—That a Smarter Exam Could Change Education," *Boston Globe*, Ideas (September 16, 2012), p. 4.

45. Uri Treisman, "Studying Students Studying Calculus: A Look at the Lives of Minority Mathematics Students in College," *College Mathematics Journal* (1992), p. 362.

CHAPTER TEN
PROSPECTS FOR REFORM

1. I am indebted for this remark to Nannerl Keohane, former president of Duke, and her book *Higher Ground: Ethics and Leadership in the Modern University* (2005), p. 118.

2. Francis M. Cornford, *Microcosmographia Academica* (1908), reprinted in Gordon Johnson, *University Politics: F. M. Cornford's Cambridge and His Advice to the Young Academic Politician* (1994), p. 105.

3. Martin Finkelstein and William Cummings, "The Global View: American Faculty and Their Institutions," *Change* (May–June 2012), pp. 48, 51; Ernest L. Boyer, Philip G. Altbach, and Mary Jen Whitelaw, *The Academic Profession: International Perspective* (1994), p. 81.

4. Ernest T. Pascarella and Patrick T. Terenzini, *How College Affects Students*, vol. 2, *A Third Decade of Research* (2005), p. 580.

5. Richard Arum and Josipa Roksa, *Academically Adrift: Limited Learning on College Campuses* (2011), p. 81.

6. Ibid., pp. 79–80.

7. Alexander Astin, *What Matters in College: Four Critical Years Revisited* (1993), pp. 236–41, 302–10, 370–72.

8. See Association of American Colleges and Universities, *The LEAP Vision for Learning: Outcomes, Practices, and Employers' Views* (2011), pp. 23–27.

9. See National Governors Association, *A Time for Results* (1986).

10. See the account of state efforts to use the budget and performance indicators to bring about reform in Donald E. Heller (ed.), *The States and Public Education: Affordability, Access, and Accountability* (2000); Joseph C. Burke and Associates, *Achieving Accountability in Higher Education: Balancing Public, Academic, and Market Demands* (2003).

11. Joseph C. Burke and Associates, note 10, p. 236. One recent study of performance funding and performance reporting covering 467 colleges (to measure the impact on graduation rates) and 166 research universities (to measure effects on research funding) found that these programs had no significant effect. Jung Cheol Sing, "Impacts of Performance-Based Accountability on Institutional Performance in the U.S.," 60 *Higher Education* (2010), p. 47.

12. See, e.g., Vickie Schray, *Assuring Quality in Higher Education: Recommendations for Improving Accreditation*, Issue Paper released at the request of Charles Miller, Chairman of the Secretary of Education's Commission on the Future of Higher Education (2006).

13. See, e.g., Philip I. Kramer, "Assessment and the Fear of Punishment: How the Protection of Anonymity Positively Influenced the Design and Outcomes of Postsecondary Assessment," 31 *Assessment and Evaluation in Higher Education* (2006), p. 597.

14. Center on Educational Policy, *Instructional Time in Elementary Schools: A Closer Look at Changes for Specific Subjects* (February 2008).

15. See, generally, Peter T. Ewell, *Assessment, Accountability, and Improvement, National Institute for Learning Outcomes Assessment*, Occasional Paper No. 1 (2009).

16. Staci Provezis, National Institute for Learning Outcomes Assessment, *Regional Accreditation and Student Learning Outcomes: Mapping the Territory* (2010), p. 13: "Despite calling for faculty involvement, all regional accreditation standards are weak in respect to means of assuring such involvement." See also George Kuh and Stanley Ikenberry, *More Than You Think, Less Than We Need: Learning Outcomes Assessment in American Higher Education* (2009). (Having surveyed 1,518 colleges, the authors found a nearly universal use of assessment measures of one kind or another but far less use of the results to bring about reform. Faculty resistance proved to be the chief barrier to progress.)

17. Charles Blaich and Kathleen Wise, *From Gathering to Using Assessment Results: Lessons from the Wabash National Study*, National Institute for Learning Outcomes Assessment, Occasional Paper No. 8 (2011), p. 11.

18. In its first year, NSSE surveys were administered in 270 colleges. By 2010, a decade later, the number had grown to more than 600 institutions each year.

19. See, e.g., Peggy L. Maki (ed.), *Coming to Terms with Student Outcomes' Assessment: Faculty and Administrators' Journeys to Integrating Assessment in Their Work and Institutional Culture* (2010).

20. See, e.g., Thayer E. Reed, Jason Levin, and Geri Malandra, "Closing the Assessment Loop by Design," *Change* (September/October 2011), p. 44.

21. Candace Thille, "Building Open Learning as a Community-Based Research Activity," in Toru Iiyoshi and M. S. Vijay Kumar (eds.), *Opening Up Education: The Collective Advancement of Education through Open Technology, Open Content, and Open Knowledge* (2008), p. 165; William G. Bowen, Matthew M. Chingos, Kelly A. Lack, and Thomas I. Nygren, *Interactive Learning Online at Public Universities: Evidence from*

Randomized Trials (2012); see also Carol A. Twigg, *Increasing Success for Underserved Students: Redesigning Introductory Courses*, National Center for Academic Transformation (2009), especially pp. 11–13.

22. Katherine Mangan, "MOOC Mania: It's Raising Big Questions about the Future of Higher Education," *Chronicle of Higher Education: Online Learning* (October 5, 2012), p. B4. See also Marc Parry, "5 Ways that edX Could Change Education," *Chronicle of Higher Education: Online Learning* (October 5, 2012), p. B6.

23. National Survey of Student Engagement, *Major Differences: Examining Student Engagement by Field of Study, Annual Results* (2010), p. 7.

24. Richard J. Shavelson, *Measuring College Learning Responsibly: Accountability in a New Era* (2010), pp. 44–70.

25. Richard Arum and Josipa Roksa, note 5.

26. See, e.g., Trudy W. Banta and Charles Blaich, "Closing the Assessment Loop," *Change* (January–February 2011), pp. 22, 25. (Resistance to assessment by faculty and students is more intense when efforts are made to impose standards of measurement from outside.)

AFTERWORD (II)

1. Ray Uhalde and Jeff Strohl, *America in the Global Economy: A Background Paper for the New Commission on the Skills of the American Workforce* (2006).

2. For firsthand accounts of the attitudes of students about what matters in college, see Mary Grigsby, *College Life through the Eyes of Students* (2009); and Rebekah Nathan, *My Freshman Year: What a Professor Learned by Becoming a Student* (2005).

3. See, generally, John M. Braxton (ed.), *The Role of the Classroom in College Student Persistence* (2008).

4. National Survey of Student Engagement, *Promoting Student Learning and Institutional Improvement: Lessons from NSSE at 13* (2012), p. 10.

CHAPTER ELEVEN
GRADUATE EDUCATION

1. See Michael Nettles and Catherine M. Millett, *Three Magic Letters: Getting to PhD* (2006), p. 14.

2. National Science Foundation, *Doctorate Recipients from U.S. Universities, 2011* (2012). See also Stacey Patton, "Doctoral Degrees Rose in 2011, but Career Options Weren't So Rosy," *Chronicle of Higher Education* (December 14, 2012), p. A17.

3. See, e.g., Maresi Nerad and Joseph Carny, "From Rumors to Facts: Career Outcomes of English PhDs, Council of Graduate Schools," 32 *Communication* (1999).

4. Ibid.

5. Jack H. Schuster and Martin J. Finkelstein, *The American Faculty: The Restructuring of Academic Work and Careers* (2006), pp. 287–319.

6. Ibid., p. 293.

7. OECD, *Education at a Glance* (2009), OECD Indicators, table A-35.

8. E.g., *Rising above the Gathering Storm: Energizing and Employing America for a Brighter Economic Future*, report prepared for the National Academy of Science, the National Academy of Engineering, and the Institute of Medicine (2007).

9. Elaine Seymour and Nancy M. Hewitt, *Talking about Leaving: Why Undergraduates Leave the Sciences* (1997), p. 33.

10. Richard B. Freeman and Daniel L. Goroff (eds.), *Science and Engineering Careers in the United States: An Analysis of Markets and Employment* (2010); David Cyranoski, Natasha Gilbert, Heidi Ledford, Anjali Nayar, and Mohammed Yahia, "The PhD Faculty: The World Is Producing More PhDs Than Ever Before: Is It Time to Stop?" 472 *Nature* (2011), pp. 276, 277–78; Daniel Teitelbaum, "Do We Need More Scientists?" *The Public Interest* (Fall 2003). p. 40.

11. Homer Neal, Tobin L. Smith, and Jennifer B. McCormick, *Beyond Sputnik: U.S. Science Policy in the Twenty-First Century* (2008), p. 288.

12. Quoted by Daniel Teitelbaum, note 10, p. 49.

13. David Dill and Frans van Vught (eds.), *National Innovation and the Academic Research Perspective: Public Policy in a Global Perspective* (2010), p. 428.

14. Charles T. Clotfelter (ed.), *American Universities in a Global Market* (2010), p. 11.

15. Ibid., p. 95.

16. Yu Xie and Alexandra A. Killewald, *Is American Science in Decline?* (2012), p. 96.

17. Ibid., pp. 56–57.

18. Dongbin Kim, Charles A. S. Blankart, and Laura Isdell, "International Doctorates: Trends Analysis on Their Decision to Stay in US," 62 *Higher Education* (2011), p. 141.

19. Ronald G. Ehrenberg, Harriet Zuckerman, Jeffrey A. Groen, and Sharon M. Brucker, *Educating Scholars: Doctoral Education in the Humanities* (2010), pp. 194–96.

20. Ibid.

21. Council on Graduate Schools, *PhD Completion and Attrition: Findings from Exit Surveys of PhD Completers* (2009).

22. Barbara E. Lovitts, *Leaving the Ivory Tower: The Causes and Consequences of Departure from Doctoral Study* (2001).

23. William G. Bowen and Neil L. Rudenstine, *In Pursuit of the PhD* (1992), p. 144.

24. Barbara E. Lovitts, note 22, p. 6.

25. Ibid., p. 26.

26. Ibid., p. 6.

27. Ibid., p. 270.

28. Jeffrey A. Groen, George H. Jakubson, Ronald G. Ehrenberg, Scott Condie, and Albert B. Liu, "Program Design and Student Outcomes in Graduate Education," 27 *Economics of Education Review* (2008), p. 211.

29. "Students reported that they decided to enter a doctoral program without having a good idea of the time, money, clarity of purpose and perseverance that doctoral study entails." Chris M. Golde and Timothy M. Dore, *At Cross Purposes: What the Experiences of Today's Graduate Students Reveal about Doctoral Education* (2001), pp. 29, 31.

30. Ibid., p. 41.

31. Michael T. Nettles and Catherine M. Millett, note 1, p. 95.

32. Barbara E. Lovitts, note 22.

33. On the weak predictive value of the Graduate Record Examination, see, e.g., Robert J. Sternberg and Wendy M. Williams, "Does the Graduate Record Examination Predict Meaningful Success in the Graduate Training of Psychologists?" 52 *American Psychologist* (1997), p. 630.

34. Barbara E. Lovitts, note 22, p. 6.

35. Debra W. Stewart (president of the Council of Graduate Schools), "'Important If True': Graduate Education Will Drive America's Future Prosperity," *Change* (January–February 2010), pp. 36, 40.

36. Jack H. Schuster and Martin J. Finkelstein, note 5, pp. 89–92.

37. Chris M. Golde and Timothy M. Dore, note 29, p. 9.

38. Melissa S. Anderson (ed.), *The Experience of Being in Graduate School: An Exploration* (1998), p. 6.

39. Chris M. Golde and Timothy M. Dore, note 29.

40. Ibid., p. 22.

41. Ibid., p. 27.

42. For a helpful summary of what teachers can learn from developments in neurobiology, see Michael J. Friedlander et al., "What Can Medical Education Learn from the Neurobiology of Learning," 86 *Academic Medicine* (2011), p. 415.

43. Chris M. Golde and Timothy M. Dore, note 29, p. 24. There is little research as yet on the effect on student learning of training prospective college teachers. One study of a British training program published in 2004 found that teachers who took a year-long course improved student learning and led the participants to adapt their teaching methods from teacher-centered to student-centered. Graham Gibbs and Martin Coffey, "The Impact of Training of University Teachers in Their Teaching Skills, Their Approach to Teaching, and the Approach to Learning of Their Students," 5 *Active Learning in Higher Education* (2004), p. 87. Another European study, by Ann Stes, Liesje Coertjens, and Peter Van Petegem, discovered a change in teacher orientation following training toward student-centered instruction, but found that students detected no change in teaching methods. This study did not attempt to measure the effects on student learning. "Instructional Development for Teachers in Higher Education: Impact on Teaching Approach," 60 *Higher Education* (2010), p. 187.

44. George E. Walker, Chris M. Golde, Laura Jones, Andrea Bueschle, and Pat Hutchings, *The Formation of Scholars: Rethinking Graduate Education for the Twenty-First Century* (2008), p. 69.

45. Philip S. Babcock and Mindy Marks, *The Falling Time Cost of College: Evidence from Half a Century of Time Use Data*, National Bureau of Economic Research, Working Paper 15954 (April 2010).

46. Teagle Foundation: Teagle Foundation Grants in Higher Education (March/May 2010), announcing grants for innovative pilot programs at Columbia, Cornell, Harvard, Northwestern, Princeton, Stanford, and U.C. Berkeley.

FOREWORD (III)

1. Graduate Management Admissions Council, 2011, *Women and Graduate Management Education* (2011).

2. First Year and Total J.D. Enrollment by Gender (2011), http://www.americanbar .org/content/dam/aba/administrative/legal_education_and_admissions_to_the_bar/ statistics/jd_enrollment_1yr_total_gender.authcheckdam.pdf.

3. Graduate Management Admissions Council, 2011, note 1; First Year and Total J.D. Enrollment by Gender, note 2; Association of American Medical Colleges, *U.S. Medical School Applications and Students 1982–83 to 2010–2011* (2012).

4. Association of American Medical Colleges, *Diversity in Medical Education: Facts and Figures* (2008), p. 72.

5. Tamar Lewin, "Law School Admissions Lag among Minorities," *New York Times* (January 6, 2010), p. A22.

6. Alison Go, "Business Schools Look for Different Kinds of Students: Admissions Offices Are Pursuing More Women and Minority Candidates," *U.S. News & World Report* (April 22, 2009), p. 62.

7. Eli Y. Adashi and Philip A. Gruppuso, "The Unsustainable Cost of Undergraduate Medical Education: An Overlooked Element in U.S. Health Care Reform," 85 *Academic Medicine* (2010), p. 763.

8. The soaring cost of legal education and the mounting debt loads and repayment problems experienced by law school graduates are discussed in detail by Brian Z. Tamanaha, *Failing Law Schools* (2012), pp. 126–59.

9. Scott Turow, *One L: The Turbulent True Story of a First Year at Harvard Law School* (1977); Charles LeBaron, *Gentle Vengeance: An Account of the First Year at Harvard Medical School* (1981).

CHAPTER TWELVE
MEDICAL SCHOOLS

1. See, e.g., Perri Klass, *A Not Entirely Benign Procedure* (1987); Melvin Konner, *Becoming a Doctor: A Journal of Initiation in Medical School* (1987).

2. Robert D. Richardson, *William James: In the Maelstrom of American Modernism* (2006), p. 61.

3. Charles M. Wiener, Patrick A. Thomas, Elizabeth Goodspeed, David Valle, and David G. Nicols, "'Genes to Society'—the Logic and Process of the New Curriculum for the Johns Hopkins University School of Medicine," 85 *Academic Medicine* (2010), pp. 498–506.

4. Ibid,, p. 505.

5. Ibid., p. 498.

6. See e.g., Derek Bok, *The Politics of Happiness: What Governments Can Learn from the New Research on Well-Being* (2010), pp. 127–28.

7. Philip S. Wang, Gregory Simon, and Ronald C. Kessler, "The Economic Burden of Depression and the Cost-Effectiveness of Treatment," 12 *International Journal of Methods in Psychiatric Research* (2003), p. 22; David Mechanic, *Mental Health and Social Policy* (3rd ed., 1989), p. 147.

8. E.g., American Medical Association, *Initiative to Transform Medical Education, Phase 3: Program Implementation; Recommendations for Optimizing the Medical Education Learning Environment* (2007), p. 14.

9. J. R. Agrawal, J. Huebner, J. Hedgecock, J. Sehgal, P. Jung, and S. R. Simon, "Medical Students' Knowledge of the U.S. Health Care System and Their Preference for Curricular Change," 80 *Academic Medicine* (2005), p. 484.

10. Ibid.

11. For an arresting account of human error among doctors, see Marty Makary, "How to Stop Hospitals from Killing Us," *Wall Street Journal* (September 22–23, 2012), pp. C1, C2. (The author is a surgeon at the Johns Hopkins Hospital in Baltimore. As Dr. Makary points out, part of the responsibility for medical errors lies with the lack of

accountability and transparency on the part of hospitals and not simply shortcomings in the training of doctors.)

12. For an excellent, concise account of the long-standing criticisms of graduate medical education and the reasons why the problems are hard to remedy, see Kenneth Ludmerer, "The History of Calls for Reform in Graduate Medical Education and Why We Are Still Waiting for the Right Kind of Change," 87 *Academic Medicine* (2012), p. 34. Surveys based on self-reports by graduating residents in academic health centers indicate that current training, though hardly perfect, may be better than the published reports might suggest. See, e.g., David Blumenthal, Manjusha Ghokale, Eric G. Campbell, and Joel S. Weissman, "Preparedness for Clinical Practice: Reports of Graduating Residents at Academic Health Centers," 286 *Journal of the American Medical Association* (September 5, 2001), p. 1027.

13. DeWitt C. Baldwin, Steven R. Daugherty, and Beverley D. Rowley, "Unethical and Unprofessional Conduct Observed by Residents during Their First Year of Training," 73 *Academic Medicine* (1998), p. 1195.

14. Chris Feudtner, Dmitri A. Christakis, and Nicholas A. Christakis, "Do Clinical Clerks Suffer Ethical Erosion? Student Perceptions of Their Ethical Environment and Personal Development," 69 *Academic Medicine* (1994), p. 670.

15. Delise Wear and Janet Bickel, *Educating for Professionalism: Creating a Culture of Humanism in Medical Education* (2000), p. 185.

16. Eric G. Campbell et al., "Professionalism in Medicine: Results of a National Survey of Physicians," 147 *Annals of Internal Medicine* (2007), pp. 795, 799.

17. Ibid.

18. Ibid., p. 800.

19. See, e.g., Grace Huang, Bobby Reynolds, and Chris Candler, "Virtual Patient Simulations at U.S. and Canadian Medical Schools," 82 *Academic Medicine* (2007), p. 446.

20. Vimla L. Patel and David R. Kaufman, "Medical Education Isn't Just about Solving Problems," 47 *Chronicle of Higher Education* (February 2, 2001), p. B-12.

21. Vimla L. Patel, Guy J. Groen, and Geoffrey R. Norman, "Effects of Conventional and Problem-Based Medical Curricula on Problem Solving," 66 *Academic Medicine* (1991), p. 380.

22. See, e.g., Linda Distlehorst, Randall S. Robbs, and Howard S. Barrows, "Problem-Based Learning Outcomes: The Glass Half Full," 80 *Academic Medicine* (2005), p. 294. See also Geoffrey R. Norman and Henk G. Schmidt, "The Psychological Basis of Problem-Based Learning: A Review of the Evidence," 67 *Academic Medicine* (1992), p. 557.

23. See, e.g., Jerome Groopman, *How Doctors Think* (2007); "Diagnosis: What Doctors Are Missing," *New York Review of Books* (November 5, 2009), p. 26.

24. E.g., Eric S. Holmboe et al., "Faculty Development in Assessment: The Missing Link in Competency-Based Medical Education," 86 *Academic Medicine* (2011), p. 460; David R. Lambert et al., "Standardizing and Personalizing Science in Medical Education," 85 *Academic Medicine* (2010), p. 181.

25. This summary description of the teaching hospital prior to World War II and much of the discussion of the changes thereafter owe much to Kenneth M. Ludmerer's excellent book *Time to Heal: American Medical Education from the Turn of the Century to the Era of Managed Care* (1999).

26. Jane Gross, "A Fast Growing Specialty Helps Patients and Cuts Cost," *New York Times* (May 27, 2010), pp. A-13, 16.

27. Robert Steinbrook, "Medical Student Debt: Is There a Limit?" *New England Journal of Medicine* (2008), p. 2629.

28. E.g., American Medical Association, note 8, p. 14; Mohammadreza Hojat et al., "The Devil Is in the Third Year: A Longitudinal Study of Erosion of Empathy in Medical School," 84 *Academic Medicine* (2009), p. 1182.

29. See, e.g., The Blue Ridge Academic Health Group, *Reforming Medical Education: Urgent Priority for the Academic Health Center in the New Century* (2003); Report of the Ad Hoc Committee of Deans, *Educating Doctors to Provide High Quality Medical Care: A Vision for Medical Education in the United States* (July 2004).

30. Judy Shea, Arlene Weissman, Sean McKinney, Jeffrey S. Silver, and Kevin G. Volpp, "Internal Medicine Trainees' Views of Training Adequacy and Duty Hours Restrictions in 2009," 87 *Academic Medicine* (2012), p. 889.

31. See Kenneth Ludmerer, note 12, pp. 36–37.

32. The Harvard clerkships are described in Sigall K. Bell, Edward Krupat, Sara Fazio, David H. Roberts, and Richard M. Schwartzstein, "Longitudinal Pedagogy: A Successful Response to the Fragmentation of the Third-Year Medical Student Clerkship," 83 *Academic Medicine* (2005), p. 467; Barbara Ogur and David Hirsh, "Learning through Longitudinal Patient Care—Narratives from the Harvard Medical School-Cambridge Integrated Clerkship," 84 *Academic Medicine* (2009), p. 844; David Hirsh et al., "Educational Outcomes of the Harvard Medical School-Cambridge Integrated Clerkships: A Way Forward for Medical Education," 87 *Academic Medicine* (2012), p. 643.

33. The many reports by deans and faculty members on reforming and improving medical education suggest that medical schools are not complacent about the status quo. See, e.g., The Blue Ridge Academic Health Group, note 29; Report of the Ad Hoc Committee of Deans, note 29.

CHAPTER THIRTEEN
LAW SCHOOLS

1. For an interesting comparison of legal and medical education, see Roger C. Crampton, "Professional Education in Medicine and Law: Structural Differences, Common Failings, Possible Opportunities," 34 *Cleveland State Law Review* (1986), p. 349.

2. Robert Granfield, *Making Elite Lawyers: Visions of Law at Harvard* (1992).

3. John P. Heinz, Robert R. Nelson, Rebecca L. Sandefur, and Edward R. Laumann, *Urban Lawyers: The New Social Structure of the Bar* (2005), pp. 57–60.

4. Bureau of Labor Statistics, *Employment by Occupation, 2008–2018, Employment Projections* (2010), table 1.2.

5. Brian Z. Tamanaha, *Failing Law Schools* (2012), p. 114.

6. Bureau of Labor Statistics, note 4, table 1.2.

7. Mitu Gulati, Richard Sander, and Robert Sockloskie, "The Happy Charade: An Empirical Examination of the Third Year of Law School," 51 *Journal of Legal Education* (2001), pp. 235, 244–45.

8. Ibid., p. 246.

9. Stefan H. Krieger, "The Development of Legal Reasoning Skills in Law Students: An Empirical Study," 56 *Journal of Legal Education* (2006), p. 332.

10. E.g., the so-called Carrington Report, Association of American Law Schools, *Training for the Public Professions of the Law* (1971).

11. American Bar Association Task Force on Law Schools and the Profession, *Narrowing the Gap: Legal Education and Professional Development—an Educational Continuum* (1992) (MacCrate Report). See also, David E. Van Zandt, *Foundational Competencies: Innovation in Legal Education*, Faculty Working Paper, Northwestern Law School (2009).

12. American Bar Association Task Force on Law Schools and the Profession, note 11.

13. Margaret M. Barry, Jon C. Dunn, and Peter A. Joy, "Clinical Education for the Millennium: The Third Wave," 7 *Clinical Law Review* (2000), p. 1.

14. James R. P. Ogloff, David R. Lyon, Kevin S. Douglas, and V. Gordon Rose, "More Than 'Learning to Think Like a Lawyer': The Empirical Research on Legal Education," 34 *Creighton Law Review* (2000–2001), pp. 73, 218–28.

15. E.g., William M. Sullivan, Ann Colby, Judith W. Wegner, Lloyd Bond, and Lee S. Shulman, *Educating Lawyers: Preparation for the Profession of Law* (2007), p. 30.

16. Greg Winter, "Legal Firms Cutting Back on Free Services to Poor," *New York Times* (August 17, 2000), p. A1.

17. Professionalism Committee, American Bar Association, Section of Legal Education and Admission to the Bar, note 11.

18. Deborah Rhode, "Ethics by the Pervasive Method," 42 *Journal of Legal Education* (1996), p. 32.

19. E.g., Maury Landsman and Steven P. McNeel, "Moral Judgment of Law Students across Three Years: Influences of Gender, Political Ideology, and Interest in Altruistic Law Practice," 45 *South Texas Law Review* (2004), p. 801. See, generally, William M. Sullivan et al. note 15, p. 133.

20. Lawrence S. Krieger, "Human Nature as a New Guiding Philosophy of Legal Education and the Profession," 47 *Washburn Law Review* (2007–8), p. 247.

21. Ibid., p. 248.

22. Gerald F. Hess, "Heads and Hearts: The Teaching and Learning Environment in Law Schools," 52 *Journal of Legal Education* (2002), p. 75; Lawrence S. Krieger, "The Inseparability of Professionalism and Personal Satisfaction: Perspectives on Values, Integrity, and Happiness," 11 *Clinical Law Review* (2005), p. 425.

23. Roy Stuckey, *Best Practices for Legal Education* (2007), pp. 72–73; Susan S. Daicoff, *Lawyer, Know Thyself: A Psychological Analysis of Personality Strengths and Weaknesses* (2004).

24. See, e.g., Ron Aiken, "Four Ways to Better 1L Assessment," 54 *Duke Law Journal* (2004), p. 765.

25. See, generally, Roy Stuckey, note 23; Michael H. Schwartz, "Teaching Law by Design: How Learning Theory and Instructional Design Can Inform and Reform Law Teaching," 38 *San Diego Law Review* (2001), p. 349; Linda S. Anderson, "Incorporating Adult Learning Theory into Law School Classrooms: Small Steps Leading to Large Results," 5 *Appalachian Journal of Law* (2006), p. 127.

26. In a survey of one major law school, barely more than one-third of third-year students agreed that "the faculty at this law school wants to help every student do well." Mitu Gulati, Richard Sander, and Robert Sockloskie, note 7, pp. 235, 249.

27. See. e.g., John A. Lynch, Jr., "The New Legal Writing Pedagogy: Is Our Pride and Joy a Hobble?" 61 *Journal of Legal Education* (2011), p. 231.

28. Deborah Zalesne and David Nadvorney, "Why Don't They Get It? Academic Intelligence and the Under-Prepared Student as 'Other,'" 61 *Journal of Legal Education* (2011), p. 264.

29. Law schools seem little touched by the assessment efforts being made in undergraduate education. Roy Stuckey, note 23, pp. 236–39; Anthony S. Niedwiecki, "Lawyers and Learning: A Metacognitive Approach to Legal Education," *Widener Law Review* (2006), p. 33.

30. Mitu Gulati, Richard Sander, and Robert Sockloskie, note 7, pp. 235, 248.

31. See, e.g., Michael H. Schwarz, note 25, p. 349.

32. American Bar Association, Section on Legal Education and Admissions to the Bar, *Standards for Approval of Law Schools and Interpretations* (1996).

33. Legal Services Corporation, *Documenting the Justice Gap in America: The Current Unmet Civil Legal Needs of Low-Income Americans* (2009). "According to most estimates, about four-fifths of the legal needs of low-income individuals, and two- to three-fifths of the needs of middle-income individuals remain unmet." Greg Winter, "Legal Firms Cutting Back on Free Services to Poor," *New York Times* (August 17, 2000), p. A-17.

34. William M. Sullivan et al., note 15, p. 192.

35. See, e.g., Elaine McArdle, "Bridging Theory and Practice in Corporate Law," *Harvard Law Bulletin* (Winter 2012), p. 32.

36. Margaret M. Barry, Jon C. Dunn, and Peter A. Joy, note 13, pp. 1, 32.

CHAPTER FOURTEEN
BUSINESS SCHOOLS

1. For an excellent, informative history of management education in the United States, see Rakesh Khurana, *From Higher Aims to Hired Hands: The Social Transformation of American Business Schools and the Unfulfilled Promise of Management as a Profession* (2007). Much of the historical summary that follows owes a debt to this volume.

2. Edward D. Jones, "Some Propositions concerning University Instruction in Business Administration," 21 *Journal of Political Economy* (1913), pp. 190, 195.

3. Quoted in Rakesh Khurana, note 1, p. 130.

4. Melvin T. Copeland, *And Mark an Era: The Story of the Harvard Business School* (1958), p. 17.

5. Abraham Flexner, *Universities: American, English, German* (reprint, 1994), p. 166.

6. Frederick Lewis Allen, "The Big Change: America Transforms Itself, 1900–1950 (1952)," quoted in Rakesh Khurana, note 1, p. 127.

7. American Association of Collegiate Schools of Business, *Proceedings of the Tenth Annual Meeting* (1928), p. 1.

8. American Association of Collegiate Schools of Business, *Proceedings of the Sixteenth Annual Meeting* (1934), p. 37.

9. Fritz Roethlisberger and W. J. Dickson, *Management and the Worker* (1939); Elton Mayo, The *Human Problems of an Industrial Civilization* (1933).

10. Robert A. Gordon and James E. Howell, *Higher Education for Business* (1959); Frank C. Pierson, *The Education of American Businessmen: A Study of University-College Programs in Business Administration* (1959).

11. Robert A. Gordon and James E. Howell, note 10, p. 6. Gordon and Howell couched their critique in measured words: "well documented is the failure of most business schools to develop in their students the qualities of mind and character and the kinds of professional-type skills for which business and society have the most need," ibid., pp. 70–71. Pierson was more blunt. Business school programs "should be represented for what they are—vocational training in trade techniques to prepare students for specific job openings." Quoted by Rakesh Khurana, note 1, p. 269.

12. Earl F. Cheit, "Business Schools and Their Critics," 27 *California Management Review* (1985), p. 49.

13. Jean-Jacques Servan-Schreiber, *The American Challenge* (1st English ed., 1968).

14. Robert H. Hayes and William J. Abernathy, "Managing Our Way to Economic Decline," *Harvard Business Review* (July–August 1980), p. 66.

15. Thomas J. Peters and Robert H. Waterman, *In Search of Excellence: Lessons from America's Best-Run Companies* (1982).

16. Peter Navarro, "The MBA Core Curricula of Top-Ranked U.S. Business Schools: A Study in Failure?" 7 *Academy of Management Learning and Education* (2008), p. 108.

17. See Philip D. Broughton, *Ahead of the Curve: Two Years of Harvard Business School* (2008), for a student's perspective on the first and second years by a British journalist who decided to go to business school.

18. See, e.g., Frederick G. Crane, "The Teaching of Ethics: An Imperative of Business Schools," 79 *Journal of Education for Business* (2004), p. 149.

19. Srikant M. Datar, David A. Garvin, and Patrick G. Cullen, *Rethinking the MBA: Business Education at a Crossroads* (2010), pp. 75–107.

20. Graduate Admissions Council, *Women and Graduate Education* (2011), p. 7. Over 90 percent of business school graduates surveyed in 2006 also indicated that they would enroll in business school if they had to choose again. Graduate Management Admission Council, *MBA Alumni Perspective Survey: Comprehensive Data Report* (2006).

21. Carter A. Daniel, *MBA: The First Century* (1998), p. 286. (The poll in question was conducted in 1986.)

22. Jeffrey Pfeffer and Christine Fong, "The End of Business Schools? Less Success Than Meets the Eye," *Academy of Management Learning and Education* (2002), pp. 78, 81.

23. Srikant M. Datar, David A. Garvin, and Patrick G. Cullen, note 19, pp. 30–34.

24. Peter Navarro note 16, pp. 108, 112.

25. Henry Mintzberg, *Managers Not MBAs: A Hard Look at the Soft Practice of Managing and Management Development* (2004).

26. See, e.g., Michael C. Jensen and William H. Meckling, "Theory of the Firm: Managerial Behavior, Agency Costs, and Ownership Structure," 3 *Journal of Financial Economics* (1976), p. 303.

27. See, e.g., Michael C. Jensen and Kevin J. Murphy, "CEO Incentives—It's Not How Much You Pay, but How," *Harvard Business Review* (May–June 1990), p. 138.

28. See Sumantra Ghoshal, "Good Management Theories Are Destroying Good Management Practices," 4 *Academy of Management Learning and Education* (2005), p. 75.

29. Christine Quinn Trank and Sara L. Rynes, "Who Moved Our Cheese? Reclaiming Professionalism in Business Education," 2 *Academy of Management Learning and Education* (2003), pp. 189, 190. See also, Andreas Rasche, Dirk U. Gilbert, and Ingo Schedel, "Cross-Disciplinary Ethics Education in MBA Programs: Rhetoric or Reality?" 12 *Academy of Management Learning and Education* (2013), p. 71.

30. "Global MBA Rankings 2009," *Financial Times*, http://rankings.ft.com/business schoolrankings/global-mba-rankings.

31. Ibid.

32. Milton Friedman, "The Social Responsibility of Business Is to Increase Profits," *New York Times Magazine* (September 13, 1970), p. 32. For a more rigorous statement of this position, see Elaine Sternberg, "The Defects of Stakeholder Theory," 5 *Corporate Governance* (1997), p. 3.

33. See, e.g., Lynn S. Paine, *Value Shift: Why Corporations Must Merge Social and Financial Imperatives to Achieve Superior Performance* (2003).

34. Joseph L. Bower, Herman B. Leonard, and Lynn S. Paine, *Capitalism at Risk: Rethinking the Role of Business* (2011).

35. Robert Simons, "The Business of Business Schools: Restoring the Focus on Competing to Win," 8 *Capitalism and Society* (2013), http://ssrn.com/link/Capitalism -Society.html.

36. See Srikant M. Datar, David A. Garvin, and Patrick G. Cullen, note 19, pp. 167–319.

37. See, e.g., Byron Reeves, Thomas W. Malone, and Tony O'Driscoll, "Leadership Online Labs," *Harvard Business Review* (May 2008), p. 59.

AFTERWORD (III)

1. Kenneth M. Ludmerer, *Time to Heal: American Medical Education from the Turn of the Century to the Era of Managed Care* (1999), p. 122.

2. "Global MBA Rankings 2011," *Financial Times* (2011), http://rankings.ft.com/ exportranking/global-mba-rankings-2011/pdf.

3. Srikant M. Datar, David A. Garvin, Patrick G. Cullen, *Rethinking the MBA: Business Education at a Crossroads* (2010), p. 109

4. For example, Joseph Weiler, director of the Global Law School Program at New York University Law School, remarked at a panel discussion of the American Society of International Law meetings in 2007, "I taught for many years in Europe. I have taught and teach in Asia, Australia, South America and elsewhere. There is, in my view, nothing quite like the American law school in its seriousness, its profundity, and the diverse way it teaches and engages its students in the richness of its intellectual endeavor, and its professionalism." *American Society of International Law Proceedings* (2007), pp. 189, 190.

5. See, e.g., Michael H. Schwarz, "Teaching Law by Design: How Learning Theory and Instructional Design Can Inform and Reform Law Teaching," 38 *San Diego Law Review* (2001), p. 349.

6. Srikant M. Datar, David A. Garvin, and Patrick G. Cullen, note 3, p. 92.

7. E.g., Richard Posner, "The State of Legal Scholarship Today: A Comment on Schley," 97 *Georgetown Law Journal* (2009), p. 845; Harry T. Edwards, "The Growing Disjunction between Legal Education and the Legal Profession," 91 *University of Michigan Law Review* (1992), p. 34.

8. Compare Max Stier, Kelly M. Klaus, Dan L. Bagatell, and Jeffrey J. Rachlinski, "Law Review Usage and Suggestions for Improvement: A Survey of Attorneys, Professors, and Judges," 44 *Stanford Law Review* (1992), p. 1467, with David L. Schwartz and

Lee Petherbridge, "The Use of Legal Scholarship by the Federal Courts of Appeals: An Empirical Study,'" 96 *Cornell Law Review* (2011), p. 96.

9. E.g., Chief Justice Roberts is said to have remarked, "What the academy is doing, so far as I can tell, is largely of no use or interest to people who actually practice law." Quoted in Brian Z. Tamanaha, *Failing Law Schools* (2012), p. 55. However, one tabulation of articles in three law reviews at ten-year intervals from 1900 to the 1990s has revealed that the vast majority of articles have continued to be about legal doctrine and that only a modest percentage of current articles deal with nondoctrinal theory. Robert W. Gordon, "Lawyers, Scholars, and the 'Middle Ground,'" 91 *Michigan Law Review* (1993), pp. 2075, 2099–2100.

10. E.g., Peter H. Schuck, "Why Don't Law Professors Do More Empirical Research?" 39 *Journal of Legal Education* (1989), p. 323.

11. Srikant M. Datar, David A. Garvin, and Patrick G. Cullen, note 3, pp. 77–78.

12. Jeffrey Pfeffer and Christina T. Fong, "The End of Business Schools? Less Success Than Meets the Eye," 1 *Academy of Management Learning and Education* (2002), pp. 78, 86–88.

13. Paul J. H. Schoemaker, "The Future Challenges of Business: Rethinking Management Education," 50 *California Management Review* (2008), p. 119.

14. Two authors have recently claimed that progressively fewer articles in management journals provide "actionable conclusions," i.e., conclusions that could lead management to change its behavior. Jone L. Pearce and Laura Huang, "The Decreasing Value of Our Research to Management Behavior," 11 *Academy of Management Learning and Education* (2012), p. 24.

15. Sumantra Ghoshal, "Bad Management Theories Are Driving Out Good Management Practices," 4 *Academy of Management Learning and Education* (2005), p. 75.

16. See pp. 295–97.

17. Critics point to the decline in student performance on basic science questions on the medical licensing exams and the failure of medical schools to integrate basic science and clinical practice throughout the entire four-year program. See "Symposium," 85 *Academic Medicine* (2010), pp. 181, 352–54.

18. See, e.g., Melanie Neumann et al., "Empathy Decline and Its Reasons: A Systematic Review of Studies with Medical Students and Residents," 86 *Academic Medicine* (2011), p. 996; Lawrence S. Krieger, "The Inseparability of Professionalism and Personal Satisfaction: Perspectives on Values, Integrity and Happiness," 11 *Clinical Law Review* (2005), pp. 425, 434 ("All indications are that when students graduate and enter the [legal] profession, they are significantly different people from those who arrived to begin law school: they are more depressed, less service-oriented, and more inclined toward undesirable, superficial goals and values."); Aspen Institute, *Where Will They Lead: MBA Student Attitudes about Business and Society* (2008), p. 10.

19. Thoughtful books that explore this theme include Kenneth M. Ludmerer, note 1; Rakesh Khurana, *From Higher Aims to Hired Hands: The Social Transformation of American Business Schools and the Unfulfilled Promise of Management as a Profession* (2007).

20. Chief executive officers who come to talk at business schools are not always role models who inspire students. For example, one recent business school graduate reflecting on his experience concluded that a disturbing number of the CEOs who came to

speak to students seemed to have disastrous family lives. Philip Broughton, *Ahead of the Curve: Two Years of Harvard Business School* (2008), p. 270.

FOREWORD (IV)

1. This development is ably described by David Warsh, *Knowledge and the Wealth of Nations: The Story of Economic Discovery* (2006).

2. Christine Matthews, *Federal Support for Academic Research*, Congressional Research Service (June 17, 2011), p. 9.

3. Ibid.

4. See, generally, Jonathan R. Cole, *The Great American University: Its Rise to Preeminence, Its Indispensable Role, Why It Must Be Protected* (2009).

5. Loet Leydesdorff and Caroline Wagner, "Is the United States Losing Ground in Science? A Global Perspective on the World Science System," 78 *Scientometrics* (2009), p. 23. The estimates of the percentages of American faculty members among leading mathematicians, physicists, and microbiologists are given by James Duderstadt and Luc Weber (eds.), *The Globalization of Higher Education* (2008), p. 68.

6. Loet Leydesdorff and Caroline Wagner, note 5, p. 29.

7. Yu Xie and Alexandra Killewald, *Is American Science in Decline?* (2012), p. 35.

8. Derek Hill, Alan I. Rapoport, Rolf F. Lehming, and Robert K. Bell, *Changing U.S. Output of Scientific Articles: 1998–2003*, National Science Foundation (2007), http://www.nsf.gov/statistics/nsf07320/.

9. R. D. Shelton and Geoffrey M. Holdridge, "The US-EU Race for Leadership of Science and Technology: Qualitative and Quantitative Indicators," 60 *Scientometrics* (2004), p. 353.

10. R. D. Shelton and P. Foland, "The Race for World Leadership of Science and Technology: Status and Forecasts" (paper presented at the 12th International Conference on Scientometrics and Informetrics, Rio de Janeiro, Brazil July 14–17, 2009).

11. Ibid.

12. Ibid.

13. Ibid.

14. Ibid.

15. Sara Rockwell, "The FDP Faculty Burden Survey," 16 *Research Management Review* (2009), p. 29.

16. E.g., Martin Kenney, *Biotechnology: The University-Industrial Complex* (1986).

CHAPTER FIFTEEN
"PUBLISH OR PERISH"

1. Lindsay Waters, *Enemies of Promise: Publishing, Perishing, and the Eclipse of Scholarship* (2004), p. 7.

2. Figures received from the Association of American University Presses, October 24, 2011.

3. See, e.g., Colin Steele, "Scholarly Monograph Publishing in the 21st Century: The Future More Than Ever Should Be an Open Book," 11 *Journal of Electronic Publishing*, http://quod.lib.umich.edu/j/jep/3336451.0011.201?rgn=main;view=fulltext.

4. Michael Mabe, Research Information, http://www.researchinformation.info/ridecjan06profile.html; Deborah L. Rhode, *In Pursuit of Knowledge: Scholars, Status, and Academic Culture* (2006), p. 29. A recent tabulation finds that the number of academic articles rose from 258,284 in 1950 to 1,132,291 in 2000, and 1,477,383 in 2009. Michael Barber, Katelyn Donnelly and Saad Rizvi, *An Avalance Is Coming*, Institute for Public Policy Research (2013), p. 7.

5. Jack H. Schuster and Martin J. Finkelstein, *The American Faculty: The Restructuring of Academic Work and Careers* (2006). p. 490.

6. *Report of the MLA Task Force on Evaluating Scholarship for Tenure and Promotion* (2007), p. 10.

7. Jack H. Schuster and Martin J. Finkelstein, note 5, p. 476. The figure from 2010 comes from Sylvia Hurtado, Kevin Eagan, John H. Pryor, Hannah Whang, and Serge Tran, *Undergraduate Teaching Faculty: The 2010–2011 HERI Faculty Survey* (2012), p. 24.

8. James S. Fairweather, "Beyond the Rhetoric: Trends in the Relative Value of Teaching and Research in Faculty Salaries," 76 *Journal of Higher Education* (2005), p. 401.

9. Carnegie Foundation for the Advancement of Teaching, *International Survey of the Academic Profession* (1992).

10. Lindsay Waters, note 1, p. 7.

11. Page Smith, *Killing the Spirit: Higher Education in America* (1990), p. 7.

12. Martin J. Finkelstein, Robert K. Seal, and Jack H. Schuster, *The New Academic Generation: A Profession in Transformation* (1998), p. 60. According to these authors, only 48.5 percent of the respondents to their extensive survey felt either somewhat or very satisfied with the time available to keep current with their field.

13. Lynne V. Cheney, "Melange: Foolish and Insignificant Research in the Humanities," *Chronicle of Higher Education* (July 17, 1991), p. B2.

14. David P. Hamilton, "Who's Uncited Now?" 251 *Science* (1991), p. 25.

15. Jonathan R. Cole and Stephen Cole, "The Ortega Hypothesis: Citation Analysis Suggests That Only a Few Scientists Contribute to Scientific Progress," 178 *Science* (October 1972), p. 308. To much the same effect, just two hundred institutions receive more than 95 percent of all patents awarded to US universities. Christine M. Matthews, *Federal Support for Academic Research*, Congressional Research Service (June 17, 2011).

16. E.g., Henry H. Crimmel, "The Myth of the Teacher-Scholar," 70 *Liberal Education* (1984), p. 183.

17. See, e.g., Richard A. Posner, "The Deprofessionalization of Legal Teaching and Scholarship," 91 *Michigan Law Review* (1993), p. 1921.

18. See, e.g., James Axtell, *The Pleasures of Academe: A Celebration and Defense of Higher Education* (1998).

19. See, e.g., J. H. Hexter, "Publish or Perish—a Defense," *The Public Interest* (Fall 1968), p. 60.

20. Kenneth A. Feldman, "Research Productivity and Scholarly Accomplishment of College Teachers as Related to Their Instructional Effectiveness," 26 *Research in Higher Education* (1987), p. 227.

21. Deborah Olsen and Ada Simmons, "The Research versus Teaching Debate: Untangling the Relationships," in John M. Braxton (ed.), *Faculty Teaching and Research: Is There a Conflict?* (1996), p. 31.

22. Anne V. S. Sullivan, "Teaching Norms and Publication Productivity," in John M. Braxton (ed.), note 21, p. 18.

23. Robert M. Johnson, "Faculty Productivity and the Complexity of Student Exam Questions," in John M. Braxton (ed.), note 21, p. 76.

24. Robert McCaughey, *Scholars and Teachers: The Faculties of Select Liberal Arts Colleges and Their Place in American Higher Learning* (1994).

25. Kenneth A. Feldman, note 20, pp. 242, 244.

26. Jeffrey F. Milem, Joseph B. Berger, and Eric L. Dey, "Faculty Time Allocation: A Study of Change over Twenty Years," 71 *Journal of Higher Education* (2000), p. 454.

27. Compare Sylvia Hurtado et al., note 7, pp. 26–27, with Eric L. Dey, Claudia E. Ramirez, William S. Korn, and Alexander W. Astin, *The American College Teacher: National Norms for the 1992–1993 HERI Faculty Survey* (1993), p. 31.

28. Linda De Angelo, Sylvia Hurtado, et al., *The American College Teacher: National Norms for the 2007–2008 HERI Faculty Survey* (2009), p. 133. In Jerry A. Jacobs and Sarah E. Winslow, "Overworked Faculty: Job Stresses and Family Demands," 596 *Annals* (November 2004), p. 104, the authors concluded their survey by noting, "The data presented here suggest that the demands of academic life are becoming excessive and are making it difficult for individuals to succeed at work while having the time to be caring and responsible parents," p. 127.

29. Quoted in Daniel S. Greenberg, *Science for Sale: The Perils, Rewards, and Delusions of Campus Capitalism* (2007), p. 148.

30. The quotation comes from private conversations with Daniel Bell.

31. Peter J. Bentley and Svein Kyvik, "Academic Work from a Comparative Perspective: A Survey of Faculty Working Time across 13 Countries," 63 *Higher Education* (2012), pp. 529, 536.

32. Jack H. Schuster and Martin J. Finkelstein, note 5, p. 466.

33. Ibid., p. 488.

34. See, e.g., Ted I. K. Youn and Tanya M. Price, "Learning from the Experience of Others: The Evolution of Tenure and Promotion Rules in Comprehensive Institutions," 80 *Journal of Higher Education* (2009), p. 220.

35. See, e.g., Gordon C. Winston, "The Decline in Undergraduate Teaching," 26 *Change* (September–October 1994), p. 8.

36. Jack H. Schuster and Martin J. Finkelstein, note 5, pp. 484–85.

37. E.g., Jerry A. Jacobs and Sarah E. Winslow, note 28, p. 104.

38. See, e.g., Linda De Angelo, Sylvia Hurtado, et al., note 28, p. 133; Carnegie Foundation for the Advancement of Teaching, *The Condition of the Professoriate: Attitudes and Trends* (1989), p. 82; Jack H. Schuster and Martin J. Finkelstein, note 5, p. 152.

CHAPTER SIXTEEN
THE CHANGING NATURE OF SCIENTIFIC RESEARCH

1. Michael Gibbons, Camille Limoges, Helga Nowotny, Simon Schwartzman, Peter Scott, and Martin Trow, *The New Production of Knowledge: The Dynamics of Science and Research in Contemporary Societies* (1994); Helga Nowotny, Peter Scott, and Michael Gibbons, *Re-Thinking Science: Knowledge, and the Public in an Age of Uncertainty* (2001); see also John Ziman, *Real Science: What It Is and What It Means* (2000).

2. Joanne Kotz, "Chemical Biology at the Broad Institute," 3 *Nature Chemical Biology* (2007), p. 199.

3. Kim A. McDonald, "Too Many Co-Authors? Proliferation of Papers Written by 100 or More Researchers Tests Limits of Scholarship," *Chronicle of Higher Education* (April 28, 1995), p. A35.

4. Roger L. Geiger and Creso M. Sá, *Tapping the Riches of Science: Universities and the Promise of Economic Growth* (2008), p. 210.

5. Piotr Sztompka, "Trust in Science: Robert K. Merton's Inspiration," 7 *Journal of Classical Sociology* (2007), pp. 211, 219.

6. On efforts by research universities to facilitate interdisciplinary research, see Holden Thorp and Buck Goldstein, *Engines of Innovation: The Entrepreneurial University in the Twenty-First Century* (2010); Association of American Universities, *Report of the Interdisciplinary Task Force* (2005).

7. Roger L. Geiger and Creso M. Sá, note 4, pp. 172–73.

8. There is dispute about whether the Bayh-Dole legislation actually brought about an increase in university patenting. E.g., Bhaven Sampat, "Patenting and US Academic Research in the 20th Century: The World before and after Bayh-Dole," 35 *Research Policy* (2006), p. 772.

9. See, e.g., Jerry G. Thursby and Marie C. Thursby, "University Licensing," 23 *Oxford Review of Economic Policy* (2007), pp. 620, 630–31.

10. Derek Bok, *Universities in the Marketplace: The Commercialization of Higher Education* (2003).

11. Robert Merton, *The Sociology of Science: Theoretical and Empirical Investigations* (1973).

12. Piotr Sztompka, note 5, p. 211; Mark P. Jones, "Entrepreneurial Science: The Rules of the Game," 39 *Social Studies of Science* (2009), p. 821.

13. Eric G. Campbell and Eran Bendavid, "Data-Sharing and Data-Withholding in Genetics and the Life Sciences: Results of a National Survey of Technology Transfer Officers," 6 *Journal of Health Care Law and Policy* (2002–3), pp. 241, 254.

14. Mildred K. Cho, Ryo Shohara, Anna Schissel, and Drummond Rennie, "Policies on Faculty Conflicts of Interest at US Universities," 284 *Journal of the American Medical Association* (November 1, 2000), pp. 2203, 2206.

15. Eric G. Campbell and Eran Bendavid, note 13, p. 241.

16. See, e.g., Kevin C. Elliott, "Scientific Judgment and the Limit of Conflict-of-Interest," 15 *Accountability in Research* (2008), pp. 1, 8; Justin E. Bekelman, Yan Li, and Cary P. Gross, "Scope and Impact of Financial Conflicts of Interest in Biomedical Research: A Systematic Review," 289 *Journal of the American Medical Association* (January 29, 2003), pp. 454, 464.

17. E.g., Kevin C. Elliott, note 16, pp. 1, 8. Neetika P. Cox, Christopher Heaney, and Robert M. Cook-Deegan, "Conflict between Commercial and Scientific Roles in Academic Health Research," in Thomas H. Murray and Josephine Johnston (eds.), *Trust and Integrity in Biomedical Research: The Case of Financial Conflicts of Interest* (2010), p. 331.

18. See, e.g., Gardiner Harris and Benedict Carey, "Researchers Fail to Reveal Full Drug Pay," *New York Times* (June 8, 2008), p. 1; Gardiner Harris, "Top Psychiatrist Didn't Report Drug Makers' Pay," *New York Times* (October 4, 2008), p. A1; Gardiner Harris and Janet Roberts, "Doctors' Ties to Drug Makers Are Put on Close View," *New York Times* (March 21, 2007), p. A1.

19. See, generally, Sheila Slaughter, Maryann P. Feldman, and Scott L. Thomas, "U.S. Research Universities' Institutional Conflict of Interest Policies," 4 *Journal of Empirical Research on Human Research Ethics: An International Journal* (2009), p. 3.

20. David Korn, "Financial Conflicts of Interest in Medicine: Whence They Came, Where They Went," 8 *Indiana University Health Law Review* (2011), pp. 3, 17–18.

21. E.g., Martin Kenney, *Biotechnology: The University-Industrial Complex* (1986), p. 246.

22. E.g., Jerry G. Thursby and Marie Thursby, "Has the Bayh-Dole Act Compromised Basic Research?" 40 *Research Policy* (2011), p. 1077; Marie Thursby, Jerry Thursby, and Swasti Gupta-Mukherjee, "Are There Real Effects of Licensing on Academic Research: A Life-Cycle View," 63 *Journal of Economic Behavior and Organization* (2007), p. 577.

23. Darren E. Zinner, Dragana Bolcic-Jankovic, Brian Clarridge, David Blumenthal, and Eric G. Campbell, "Participation of Academic Scientists in Relationships with Industry," 28 *Health Affairs* (2009), pp. 1814, 1820.

24. John P. Walsh, Wesley M. Cohen, and Charlene Cho, "Where Excludability Matters: Material versus Intellectual Property in Academic Biochemical Research," 36 *Research Policy* (2007), pp. 1184, 1188.

25. Robert A. Lowe and Claudia Gonzalez-Brambila, "Faculty Entrepreneurs and Research Productivity," 32 *Technology Transfer* (2007), p. 173; Guido Buenstorf, "Is Commercialization Good or Bad for Science? Individual-Level Evidence from the Max-Planck Society," 38 *Research Policy* (2009), p. 281; Sanjay Jain, Gerard George, and Mark Maltarich, "Academics or Entrepreneurs? Investigating Role Identity Modification of University Scientists Involved in Commercialization Activity," 38 *Research Policy* (2009), p. 922. Two other researchers, however, have found that citation counts for publications by authors who repeatedly patent their research do appear to decline modestly after a significant interval of time. Kira P. Fabrizio and Alberto Di Minim, "Commercializing the Laboratory: Faculty Patenting and the Open Science Environment," 37 *Research Policy* (2008), p. 914.

26. Robert A. Lowe and Claudia Gonzalez-Brambila, note 25, p. 173.

27. Pierre Azoulay, Waverly Ding, and Toby Stuart, *The Impact of Academic Patenting on the Rate, Quality, and Direction of (Public) Research*, National Bureau of Economic Research, Working Paper 11917 (2006), p. 30.

28. National Research Council, *Managing University Intellectual Property in the Public Interest* (2010), p. 47.

29. *Madey v. Duke University*, 307 F.3d 1351 (2003).

30. Roger L. Geiger and Creso M. Sá, note 4, pp. 146–49.

31. See, e.g., David Blumenthal et al., "Data Withholding in Genetics and the Other Life Sciences: Prevalences and Predictors," 81 *Academic Medicine* (2006), pp. 137, 142.

32. John P. Walsh, Wesley M. Cohen, and Charlene Cho, note 24, pp. 1184, 1189.

33. Ibid., p. 1197.

34. National Research Council, note 28, p. 70.

35. David Blumenthal, Eric G. Campbell, et al., "Withholding Research Results in Academic Life Science," 30 *Journal of the American Medical Association* (April 16, 1997), p. 1224.

36. Darren E. Zinner et al., note 23, p. 1820.

37. Ibid.

38. National Research Council, note 28, p. 38.

39. Statement of Read Montague, "The Perspective from Neuroscience, Association of American Medical Colleges," *The Scientific Basis of Influence and Reciprocity: A Symposium* (June 12, 2007), p. 12; George Loewenstein, "The Behavioral Economics Perspective," ibid., p. 23.

40. Bernard Lo and Marilyn J. Field, *Conflict of Interest in Medical Research, Education, and Practice* (2009), p. 104.

41. Deborah A. Barnes and Lisa A. Bero, "Why Review Articles on the Health Effects of Passive Smoking Research Reach Different Conclusions," 279 *Journal of the American Medical Association* (May 20, 1998), p. 1566.

42. See, e.g., George Loewenstein, Daylian M. Cain, and Sunita Sah, "The Limits of Transparency: Pitfalls and Potential of Disclosing Conflicts of Interest," 10 *American Economic Review: Papers and Proceedings* (2011), p. 423.

43. Neetika P. Cox, Christopher Heaney, and Robert M. Cook-Deegan, "Conflicts between Commercial and Scientific Roles in Academic Health Research," in Thomas H. Murray and Josephine Johnston (eds.), *Trust and Integrity in Biomedical Research: The Case of Financial Conflicts of Interest* (2010), p. 33.

44. Kevin C. Elliott, "Scientific Judgment and the Limit of Conflict-of-Interest Policies," 15 *Accountability in Research* (2008), p. 1.

45. Jennifer Washburn, *Big Oil Goes to College: An Analysis of 20 Research Collaboration Contracts between Leading Energy Companies and Major U.S. Universities* (2010).

46. See, e.g., Marion Nestle, *Food Politics: How the Food Industry Influences Nutrition and Health* (2002); Cat Warren, "Big Food, Big Agra, and the Research University," *Academe Online* (November–December 2010).

47. Leemon B. McHenry and Jon N. Jureidini, "Industry-Sponsored Ghost-Writing in Clinical Trial Reporting: A Case Study," 15 *Accountability in Research* (2008), p. 152. For a more extended treatment of the way companies "manage" research appearing in medical journals under the authorship of faculty members, see Sergio Sismondo, "Ghosts in the Machine: Publication Planning in the Medical Sciences," 39 *Social Studies in Science* (2009), p. 171.

48. Susan Chimonas, Lisa Patterson, Victoria H. Raveis, and David J. Rothman, "Managing Conflicts of Interest in Clinical Care: A National Survey of Policies at U.S. Medical Schools," 86 *Academic Medicine* (2011), p. 293. For additional findings of the influence of corporate funders on researchers in medical schools, see Patricia M. Terskerz, Ann B. Henric, Thomas M. Guterbock, and Jonathan D. Moreno, "Prevalence of Industry Support and Its Relation to Research Integrity," 16 *Accountability in Research* (2009), p. 78.

49. Susan Chimonas et al., note 48, pp. 293, 297.

50. Roger L. Geiger, *Knowledge and Money: Research Universities and the Paradox of the Marketplace* (2007), p. 265.

CHAPTER SEVENTEEN
THE ENVIRONMENT FOR RESEARCH

1. *Keyishian v. Board of Regents*, 385 U.S. 589, 603 (1967).

2. See Robert Post, "The Structure of Academic Freedom," in Beshara Doumani (ed.), *Academic Freedom after September 11* (2006), p. 61.

3. Matthew W. Finkin and Robert C. Post, *For the Common Good: Principles of American Academic Freedom* (2009), p. 51.

4. Jack H. Schuster and Martin J. Finkelstein, *The American Faculty: The Restructuring of Work and Careers* (2006), p. 498.

5. Ibid.

6. Martin Finkelstein and William Cummings, "The Global View: American Faculty and Their Institutions," *Change* (May–June 2012), pp. 48, 53.

7. Neil Gross and Solon Simmons, *The Social and Political Views of American Professors*, National Bureau of Economic Research, Working Paper 15954 (2007), p. 70.

8. Donald A. Downs, *Restoring Free Speech and Liberty on Campus* (2005), pp. 213–14. See, generally, Alan C. Kors and Harvey A. Silverglate, *The Shadow University: The Betrayal of Liberty on America's Campuses* (1998).

9. Jack H. Schuster and Martin J. Finkelstein, note 4, p. 497.

10. E.g., *Doe v. University of Michigan*, 721 F.Supp. 852 (1989); *The VWM Post v. Board of Regents of the University of Wisconsin System*, 774 F.Supp. 1163 (1991), In a contemporaneous Supreme Court case, *R.A.V. v. St. Paul*, 505 U.S. 377(1992), the Court held that a city could not impose "special prohibitions on those speakers who express views on the disfavored subjects of 'race, color, creed, religion, or gender.'" On the current status of speech codes, see J. B. Gould, *Speak No Evil: The Triumph of Hate Speech Regulation* (2005).

11. J. B. Gould, note 10.

12. See Robert M. O'Neil, "Academic Freedom: Past, Present, and Future," in Robert O. Berdahl, Philip G. Altbach, and Patricia J. Gumport (eds.), *American Higher Education in the Twenty-First Century: Social, Political, and Economic Challenges* (3rd ed., 2011), pp. 88, 96–99. Further doubts about the scope of protection afforded to free speech in universities has arisen from the Supreme Court decision in *Garcetti v. Ceballos*, 547 U.S. 410 (2006) in which a majority of the Court ruled against a police official who was demoted for criticizing his superiors. According to the majority opinion, the First Amendment did not include such speech by an employee uttered "pursuant to . . . official duties." The majority opinion expressly reserved judgment on whether the ruling would or would not extend to "speech related to scholarship or teaching." See, generally, Lawrence White, "Free Speech Ruling's Impact on Colleges," *Chronicle of Higher Education* (April 27, 2010).

13. Jack H. Schuster and Martin J. Finkelstein, note 4, p. 498.

14. For a contrary view, see Matthew W. Finkin, *The Case for Tenure* (1996); Erwin Chemerinsky, "Is Tenure Necessary to Protect Academic Freedom?" 41 *American Behavioral Scientist* (1998), p. 638.

15. Jack H. Schuster and Martin J. Finkelstein, note 4, p. 356.

16. Richard P. Chait (ed.), *The Questions of Tenure* (2002), p. 11.

17. Francis Bacon, *Novum Organum: With Other Parts of the Great Instauration* (Peter Urbach and John Gibson, eds., 1994), p. 44.

18. Janet Browne, *Charles Darwin: The Power of Place* (2002), pp. 67–68.

19. Joel Beinin, "The New McCarthyism: Policy Thought about the Middle East," in Beshara Doumani (ed.), note 2, pp. 237, 252.

20. Ibid., p. 245.

21. Quoted by Fred Siegel, "Anti-Rationalism," in Edith Kurzweil and William Phillips (eds.), *Our Country, Our Culture: The Politics of Political Correctness* (1994), pp. 258, 259.

22. Hilton Kramer, "Confronting the Monolith," in Edith Kurzweil and William Phillips (eds.), note 21, p. 72; Marilyn Friedman and Jan Narveson, *Political Correctness: For and Against* (1995); Paul Berman (ed.), *Debating P.C.: The Controversy over Political Correctness on College Campuses* (1992).

23. E.g., David Horowitz, *Indoctrination U: The Left's War against Academic Freedom* (2007); Dinesh D'Souza, *Illiberal Education: The Politics of Race and Sex on Campus* (1991); Roger Kimball, *Tenured Radicals: How Politics Have Corrupted Our Higher Education* (1990).

24. See Stanley Rothman, April Kelly-Woessner, and Matthew Woessner, *The Still Divided Academy: How Competing Visions of Power, Politics, and Diversity Complicate the Mission of Higher Education* (2011), pp. 65–66; Michael Berubé, *What's Liberal about the Liberal Arts? Classroom Politics and Bias in Liberal Education* (2006), p. 26.

25. Neil Gross and Solon Simmons, note 7, p. 26.

26. Ibid., p, 43

27. Ibid., p. 47.

28. Ibid.

29. Compare Daniel Klein and Charlotta Stern, "Professors and Their Politics: The Policy Views of Social Scientists," 17 *Critical Review* (2005), p. 257, with John H. Zipp and Rudy Fenwick, "Is the Academy a Liberal Hegemony? The Political Orientations and Educational Values of Professors," 70 *Public Opinion Quarterly* (2006), p. 304–26.

30. Private conversation between the author and Secretary Richardson.

31. Arthur Kornhauser, "Attitudes of Economic Groups," 2 *Public Opinion Quarterly* (1938), p. 260.

32. Richard Hofststadter, *Anti-Intellectualism in American Life* (1963), p. 39; Joseph Schumpeter, *Capitalism, Socialism, and Democracy* (1962), p. 148; Thorstein Veblen, *Essays on Our Changing Social Order* (1934), pp. 226–27.

33. Everett C. Ladd and Seymour M. Lipset, *The Divided Academy: Professors and Politics* (1975).

34. Ibid., p. 22.

35. Quoted in William G. Bowen, *Ever the Teacher* (1988), p. 326.

36. Quoted in Karl Zinsmeister, "Case Closed: There's No Politically Undiverse Place in America," *The American Enterprise* (January–February 2005), pp. 42, 45.

37. Neil Gross and Solon Simmons, note 7, p. 68.

38. Ibid., p. 46.

39. Ibid.

40. Matthew Woessner and April Kelly-Woessner, "Left Pipeline: Why Conservatives Don't Get Doctorates," in Robert Maranto, Richard E. Redding, and Frederick M. Hess (eds.), *The Politically Correct University: Problems, Scope, and Reforms* (2009), p. 38.

41. Stanley Rothman and S. Robert Lichter, "The Vanishing Conservative—Is There a Glass Ceiling?" in Robert Maranto, Richard E. Redding, and Frederick M. Hess (eds.), note 40, p. 60.

42. Ibid., p. 75. Interestingly, in a book written by Stanley Rothman, April Kelly-Woessner, and Matthew Woessner, the authors found that only 2 percent of faculty members felt they had been discriminated against for political reasons and that the percentage was the same for Democrats and Republicans, note 24, p. 102.

43. John Immerwahr and Jean Johnson, *Squeeze Play: How Parents and the Public Look at Higher Education Today* (May 2007), http://www.highereducation.org/reports/squeeze_play/squeeze_play.pdf.

44. *Politics in the Classroom: A Survey of Students at the Top Colleges and Universities*, Center for Survey Research and Analysis, conducted for American Council of Trustees and Alumni (October–November 2004). For a summary of the findings, see Anne Neal, "Professors Who Preach," *The American Enterprise* (June 2, 2005), p. 30.

45. Anne Neal, note 44, p. 30.

46. Ibid.

47. American Association of University Professors, "Declaration of Principles: General Report of the Committee on Academic Freedom and Academic Tenure," 1 *AAUP Bulletin* (December 1915), p. 117.

48. "Statement of Board of Directors," Association of American Colleges and Universities, 92 *Liberal Education* (2006), p. 8.

49. Alexander Astin, *What Matters in College? Four Critical Years Revisited* (1993); Eric L. Dey, "Undergraduate Political Attitudes: An Examination of Peer, Faculty, and Social Influences," 37 *Research in Higher Education* (1996), p. 535; Ernest T. Pascarella and Patrick T. Terenzini, *How College Affects Students*, vol. 2, *A Third Decade of Research* (2005), pp. 286–88.

50. The studies are discussed by Professor Neil Gross in "The Indoctrination Myth," *New York Times*, Sunday Review (March 4, 2012), p. 12.

51. Neil Gross and Solon Simmons, note 7, pp. 69–70.

AFTERWORD (IV)

1. E.g., Martin Anderson, *Imposters in the Temple: American Intellectuals Are Destroying Our Universities and Cheating Our Students of Their Future* (1992); Charles J. Sykes, *Profscam: Professors and the Demise of Higher Education* (1988).

2. Jack H. Schuster and Martin J. Finkelstein, *The American Faculty: The Restructuring of Academic Work and Careers* (2006), p. 489.

3. Kenneth Feldman, "Research Productivity and Scholarly Accomplishment of College Teachers as Related to Their Instructional Effectiveness," 26 *Research in Higher Education* (1987), p. 227.

4. David Blumenthal and Eric G. Campbell, "Academic Industry Relationships in Biotechnology, Overview," in Thomas J. Murray and Maxwell J. Mehlman (eds.), *Encyclopedia of Ethical, Legal and Policy Issues in Biotechnology* (2000), pp. 1, 6; Darren E. Zinner, Dragana Bolcic-Jankovic, Brian Clarridge, David Blumenthal, and Eric G. Campbell, "Participation of Academic Scientists in Relationships with Industry," 28 *Health Affairs* (2009), p. 1814; Carl V. Patton, "Consulting by Faculty Members," 66 *Academe* (1980), pp. 181–85.

5. See studies cited in chapter 16, note 25.

6. Jack H. Schuster and Martin J. Finkelstein, note 2, p. 488.

7. Henry Rosovsky, "No Ivory Tower," in Werner Z. Hirsch and Luc E. Weber (eds.), *As the Walls of Academia Are Tumbling Down* (2002), p. 13. Clark Kerr made the same point in conversations with the author in the late 1980s; see also Philip G. Altbach, Robert O. Berdahl, and Patricia J. Gumport, *American Higher Education in the Twenty-First Century* (1999), p. 142.

8. See *Politics in the Classroom: A Survey of Students in the Top Colleges and Universities*, Center for Survey Research and Analysis, conducted for the American Council of Trustees and Alumni (October–November 2004).

FOREWORD (V)

1. Peter J. Bentley and Svein Kyvik, "Academic Work from a Comparative Perspective: A Survey of Faculty Working Time across 13 Countries," 63 *Higher Education* (2012), pp. 529, 537; Ernest L. Boyer, Philip G. Altbach, and Mary J. Whitelaw, *The Academic Profession: International Perspective* (1994), p. 81.

2. Jack H. Schuster and Martin J. Finkelstein, *The American Faculty: The Restructuring of Academic Work and Careers* (2006), p. 469.

3. Kenneth A. Feldman, "Research Productivity and Scholarly Accomplishment of College Teachers as Related to Their Instructional Effectiveness," 26 *Research in Higher Education* (1987), p. 227.

4. E.g, Yehuda Elkana and Hannes Klöpper, *The University in the 21st Century: Teaching the New Enlightenment at the Dawn of the Digital Age* (2012), p. 4: "The university is arguably one of the—if not the—most conservative institutions we know."

5. Irving Kristol, "A Different Way to Restructure the University," *New York Times Magazine* (December 8, 1968), p. 50.

6. See pp. 361–65.

7. See pp. 369–76.

8. See pp. 140–42.

9. E.g., Tom Morgenthau and Seema Nayyar, "Those Scary College Costs," *Newsweek* (April 29, 1996), p. 208.

10. See pp. 109–15.

CHAPTER EIGHTEEN
MATTERS OF GENUINE CONCERN

1. Philip S. Babcock and Mindy Marks, *The Falling Time Cost of College: Evidence from Half a Century of Time Use Data*, National Bureau of Economic Research, Working Paper 15954 (April 2010).

2. Frederick M. Hess, Mark Schneider, Kevin Carey and Andrew P. Kelley, *Diplomas and Dropouts: Which Colleges Actually Graduate Their Students (and Which Don't)*, American Enterprise Institute (2009).

3. Derek Bok, *Universities in the Marketplace: The Commercialization of Higher Education* (2003), pp. 173–76.

4. Richard D. Kahlenberg (ed.), *Rewarding Strivers: Helping Low-Income Students Succeed in College* (2010), pp. 1–2.

5. See, generally, James L. Shulman and William G. Bowen, *The Game of Life: College Sports and Educational Values* (2001); Derek Bok, note 3, pp. 35–56.

6. See, e.g., David Korn, "Financial Conflicts of Interest in Medicine: Whence They Came, Where They Went," 8 *Indiana University Health Law Review* (2011), pp. 3, 16–18; Derek Bok, note 3, pp. 66, 70–71.

7. Luc E. Weber, "European Strategy to Promote the Knowledge Society as a Source of Renewed Economic Dynamism and of Social Cohesion, " in Luc E. Weber and James J. Duderstadt (eds.), *Universities and Business: Partnering for the Knowledge Society* (2006), p. 15.

8. Martin Finkelstein and William Cummings, "The Global View: American Faculty and Their Institutions," *Change* (May–June 2012), pp. 48, 53. It is conceivable that

this result is affected by the fact that heads of universities overseas, at least until recently, have tended to be chosen by their faculties and not by trustees, as is the practice in the United States.

9. *Politics in the Classroom: A Survey of Students at the Top Colleges and Universities*, Center for Survey Research and Analysis, conducted for the American Council of Trustees and Alumni (October–November 2004).

10. See pp. 35–39.

11. Frederick M. Hess et al., note 2.

12. Byron G. Auguste, Adam Cota, Kartik Jayaram, and Martha Laboissiere, *Winning by Degrees: The Strategies of Highly Productive Higher Education Institutions* (2010).

13. Neil Gross and Solon Simmons, *The Social and Political Views of American Professors*, National Bureau of Economic Research, Working Paper 15954 (2007), p. 70.

14. Andrew Gillen, Daniel L. Bennett, and Richard Vedder, *The Inmates Running the Asylum? An Analysis of Higher Education Accreditation*, a Policy Paper from The Center for College Affordability and Productivity (October 2010).

15. Ibid.

16. See pp. 38–39.

17. Kenneth C. Green, *The 2011–12 Inside Higher Ed Survey of College and University Chief Academic Officers* (2012), p. 16.

18. Richard Arum and Josipa Roksa, *Academically Adrift: Limited Learning on College Campuses* (2010).

19. John Immerwahr and Jean Johnson, "Squeeze Play 2010: Continued Anxiety on Cost, Harsher Judgments on How Colleges Are Run," *Public Agenda* (February 2010), p. 12.

20. Linda De Angelo, Sylvia Hurtado, et al., *The American College Teacher: National Norms for the 2007–2008 HERI Faculty Survey* (2009), p. 2.

INDEX

||||||||||||||||||||||||||||||||||||||||||||||||||||||||||||||||||||||||||||||||||||||||||||||||||||||||